Resource Guide for Oregon and SW Washington

Bravo!
wedding

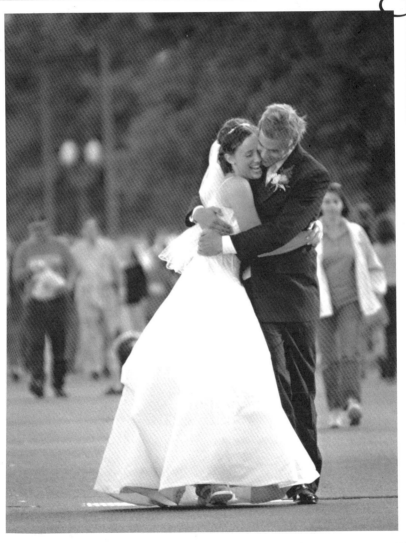

2 0 0 4

Bravo!® Publications, Inc.
P.O. Box 1647
Lake Oswego, Oregon 97035
503.675.1380, 800.988.9887; Fax 503.675.1204
E-mail: info@bravoportland.com

Visit our Web site:
www.bravowportland.com

This resource guide is comprised of paid advertisements. Although advertisers must meet a quality level of standards to be featured in this guide, Bravo! Publications, Inc. cannot and does not guarantee or take responsibility for services provided by said advertisers. No affiliation exists between Bravo! Publications, Inc. and any advertiser featured. Every reasonable effort has been made to provide the most accurate and up-to-date information.

ISBN 1-884471-33-1

ENTERTAINMENT — MUSICIANS...................387–404

FLORISTS & FLOWER PRESERVATION...............405–438

ACKNOWLEDGEMENTS

This Guide would not have been possible without the hard work, dedication, and endless hours from the following people:

Publisher
Mary Lou Burton

Account Managers
Denise Hall
Tracy Martin
Jennifer Maust
Carinne McCulloch
Heather Willig

Production Manager
Amy Drews

Production Assistant
Katalin Linder

Web Design & Production
Amy Drews

Contributing Writers
Katalin Linder
Dian Lindsay, *EWE-ME & CO.*

Public Relations
Terri Wheeler

Special Projects
Helen Kern

Prepress & Printing
NuWay Printing, *Portland*

COVER

Cover Design
Amy Drews

Photos
Bride at Sunset:
©*AJ's*
See page 495

Beach Lanterns:
©*Holland Studios*
See page 511

Mt. Hood:
©*Stewart Harvey & Associates*
See page 545

Chinatown Carriage Ride:
©*AJ's*
See page 495

Chocolate Cake:
©*Artful Images*
See page 498

SPINE

Wedding Day Rain:
Anne Ryan Florist
See page 411
©*KubotaPhotoDesign.com*

BACK COVER

Photos listed from top to bottom
Violinist:
©*Misty Bay Photography*
See page 530

Wine Glasses:
©*Mount Burns Photography*
See page 531

Bride and Groom on Steps:
©*Valls Photographic*
See page 550

Church Lights:
©*Holland Studios*
See page 511

Bravo! Team *(page 18)*
photo by Christine Linder

TITLE PAGE

Happy Couple:
©*Patrick Prothe Studio*
See page 533

photo by Christine Linder

Front row: Katalin Linder, Amy Drews, Tracy Martin **Back row:** Denise Hall, Heather Willig, Mary Lou Burton, Jennifer Maust, Carinne McCulloch; Not Pictured: Helen Kern, Erin Mussallem

Mary Lou Burton

All great things begin with only a single thought. On her honeymoon, with the planning of her huge Italian wedding still fresh in mind, she and husband John relished in the thought of having a single resource to use when planning such an important event. Turning that into reality, Mary Lou and friend Marion Clifton crafted the first Bravo! Publications Wedding Resource Guide in 1990 with an Apple IIe and a single-sheet bubble-jet printer. By 1994, the idea was taken a step further into publishing the first Event Resource Guide to hit the Oregon and Southwest Washington market. Mary Lou is proud to announce the birth of yet a third resource aimed at another unanswered market starving for attention. The Family Resource Guide marked its debut in April 2002.

Life is never quiet at the Burton household. Graced with husband and best friend, John, for over 15 years, and four wonderful children: Alex, Nick, Will and Greta, Mary Lou is no stranger to the need for an organized, simple way to entertain, educate, and care for her family. She dedicates her life to acting with intention: if it is going to bring a smile upon a sad face, light the fire within a soul, or illuminate a cloudy path, she will find the time and energy to accomplish it. Admired and respected within the event industry, Mary Lou finds her ability to persevere both personally and professionally in the inspiration and support of her husband. "It would all still be just an idea without his positive 'can do' attitude," says Mary Lou.

Carinne McCulloch

After several years in the recreation industry and a previous client of Bravo! herself, Carinne now is the company's veteran at eight years and counting! A graduate of Oregon State University, she takes her Beaver football seriously, while experiencing the many ups and downs of "game day." She and her husband Derek are enjoying life from a child's perspective as their 4-year old daughter, Hailey, continues to paint the perfect picture of independence, not to mention the walls, her bed and her dolls as well! They are currently celebrating the newest addition to their family, daughter Aiden, who celebrated her first birthday this October.

Amy Drews

Production Design, Web Development, Publications Specialist....what more can this girl do? With a degree in Communications from Valparaiso University in Indiana, Amy has spent the better part of her professional life wearing many hats here at Bravo! When not working on house projects or trying to train their dog, Madi, she and husband Jason can be found running, hiking, skiing, cooking, and spending time with family and friends.

Tracy Martin

Tracy joined Bravo! five years ago as an Account and Show Manager, planning and managing the Bravo! Meeting and Event Planners' Show. She and husband Darin are enjoying their sons Grayson and Austin, along with the newest addition to their family, Bartles, a black lab. Tracy expects the coming years to be filled with soccer games, muddy pawprints, pet snakes and all kinds of surprises stored as keepsakes in those jean pockets!

Helen Kern

In charge of Bravo! Human Relations for the past five years, Helen is not only Mary Lou's mother but a mother to all of us as well. There isn't a day that goes by where the grapefruit, fresh flowers or tasty treats aren't topped with a beautiful smile and a lot of love. Her inspiration, parenting advice (as a mother of nine herself), and charisma are all integral to the morale here at the office.

Jennifer Maust

Jen joined the Bravo! team four years ago as a Marketing Manager. She obtained her Bachelor of Science degree from Portland State University in 1997. Jen added home owner to her resume this past summer, and when not busy designing, decorating or landscaping, most would expect to find her biking, traveling and in the company of good friends.

Heather Willig

Heather joined Bravo! three years ago as an Account Manager. She draws on her experience in PR/Promotions, Event Planning and Marketing. Sewing, Central Oregon and traveling are the best ways Heather spends quality time with her husband Mike and son, Jackson. As true Beaver-believers, the fall and winter months she and her boys can be found cheering on her alma mater, Oregon State University. Go Beavs!

Denise Hall

Denise joined Bravo! in June 2002 during her summer vacation. She has spent the past eight years as an elementary teacher. In August she made the transition to a sales and marketing position at Bravo! During her free time she and her husband, Tom, enjoy reading, running, biking and playing with their Boston Terrier, Abby. They have recently purchased a new home and are looking forward to taking on many house projects.

Katalin Linder

Katalin, a recent graduate from the University of Oregon with a degree in Magazine Journalism and Public Relations, joined Bravo! as a production assistant in June 2003. When she's not speeding cross-country destined for Montana to visit her boyfriend, Kyle, at grad school, she can be found attempting to play golf and tennis and reading the latest *People Magazine*. Katalin will move to Missoula in December where she will continue to pursue a career in journalism, publishing and photography.

SPREAD THE WORD!

We need your help. To continue to supply this Guide we rely on you, the reader, to let the businesses and services in this book know that you heard about them through the *Bravo! Wedding Resource Guide*. Our featured businesses will recognize the Bravo! name.

Pass it on to a friend. Before they walk away with *your* copy, let them know they can fill out the order form on page 25 to receive their own copy.

The Bravo! Difference

- ### Location... Location... Location!
  This Guide will help you find the perfect spot for your ceremony or reception, whether at an intimate garden setting or a downtown glamorous ballroom—it's all right at your fingertips.

- ### All the important details about the sites
  From cost and terms to what's included and what's extra, the *Bravo! Wedding Resource Guide* includes descriptions of each facility for easier selection based on what you need. By the time you call a facility, you're thoroughly informed.

- ### The ultimate tool for brides and grooms
  From listings of over 500 ceremony and banquet sites to exceptional caterers, decorators, rental equipment, and entertainment. You'll find everything for your upcoming wedding in this one resource guide.

- ### This is a book you will rely on
  Everything has been thoroughly researched to ensure that you have the most current information, updated annually. Everyone we've included is outstanding!

Visit our Web sites:
www.bravoevent.com
www.bravowedding.com
www.bravofamily.com

Take A Look At Our Web Site

www.bravoportland.com

If you like our guide… you'll love our Web site!

- The Guide is online
  Every client in the book is linked on our Web site with location, phone number, contact and type of business or service.

- Links to event services and facilities
  Many of our client pages have direct links to their home pages with more details and photos of their facility or service. You can get more detailed information or communicate with many of these services easily online or through e-mail.

- Guest book and order form
  We'd love to hear from you. Sign-in to our guest book and let us know what you like about the Bravo! products or services. We love suggestions of what we could do better. You can order any of our products online.

- Calendar of Events
  Our Web site has a comprehensive Calendar of Events that will let you know when and where the next bridal shows will be taking place.

www.bravoportland.com

BRAVO!® RESOURCE GUIDES

When you want information, not glossy ads—you want Bravo!

Bravo! Publications is proud to offer five regional *Resource Guides* for planning meetings, events, weddings and family activities. Each of the Guides featured on this and the following page is filled with important information and details about the area's finest businesses and services providers, and is presented in easy-to-read, resumé style formats, alphabetically, by category. Designed to be user-friendly, each of these Guides truly are your planning *Resource!*

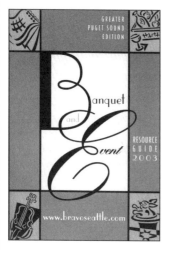

Greater Puget Sound
Event Resource Guide

Venues, Attractions & Activities, Audience Participation, Ad Specialties, Corporate Gifts & Awards, Food & Beverage Services, Accommodations, and more...

The 2004 Edition features 704 pages of easy-to-read, resumé-style write-ups on area businesses and service providers, listings of area Banquet and Event Sites, how-to's, check lists, and all the helpful hints you've come to expect from Bravo!

Suggested Retail: $11.95

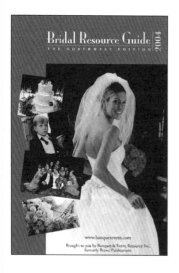

Greater Puget Sound
Bridal Resource Guide

Churches, Chapels, Banquet & Reception Sites, Caterers, Florists, Photographers, Videographers, Invitations, Bridal Attire, Tuxedo Rentals, Bridal Registry, Favors, Accessories, Consultants and more...

The 2004 Edition features 672 pages of easy-to-read, resumé-style write-ups on area businesses and service providers, listings of area Banquet and Reception Sites, how-to's, check lists, and all the helpful hints you've come to expect from Bravo! Available January 9, 2004

Suggested Retail: $9.95

TO ORDER CALL 888.832.7286

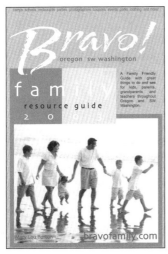

Bravo!® Family Resource Guide
Oregon and Southwest Washington

Activities and Attractions, Camps, Clothing Stores, Family Activities, Music and Arts, Toy and Learning Stores and more...

352 pages of easy-to-read, resumé-style write-ups on area businesses and service providers, how-to's, helpful hints and valuable coupons make this an indispensable guide for moms, dads, grandparents and teachers alike.

Available throughout the Portland/Vancouver metro area.

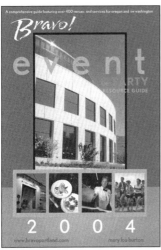

Bravo!® Event & Party Resource Guide
Oregon and Southwest Washington

Venues, Accommodations, Audience Participation, Gifts & Promotional Items, Food & Beverage, Rental Services and more...

The 2004 Edition features 560 pages of easy-to-read, resumé-style write-ups on area businesses and service providers, listings of Banquet and Event Sites, how-to's, checklists and all the helpful hints.

Complimentary to pre-qualified Meeting and Event Planners.

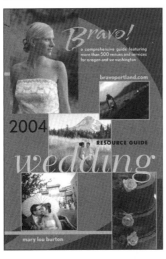

Bravo!® Wedding Resource Guide
Oregon and Southwest Washington

Churches, Chapels, Banquet & Reception Sites, Caterers, Florists, Photographers, Videographers, Invitations, Bridal Attire, Tuxedo Rentals, Bridal Registry and more...

The 2004 Edition features 640 pages of easy-to-read, resumé-style write-ups on area businesses and service providers, listings of banquet and reception sites, how-to's, check lists and all the helpful hints!

Suggested Retail: $9.95

TO ORDER CALL 503.675.1380

The Bravo!® Wedding Organizer

What Every Bride Needs to Plan a Perfect Wedding . . .

Wedding Organizer Features

- Sturdy three-ring binder — it's easy to customize
- 14 easy-to-find tabbed sections
- Directs brides to ask all the right questions
- Contracts included to formalize agreements
- Worksheets to record details
- Pockets for swatches, samples and brochures
- Business Card Holder

For more information or to place an order: 800.988.9887

bravowedding.com

The Bravo!® Wedding Worry Candle

Bravo! Publications, Inc. has created a **Wedding Worry Candle.** The package includes a fragrant bag of Gardenia candle crystals in a reusable silver tin, which merge together when the wick is lit. Wrapped in a natural-fiber box and tied with a tulle bow, the box is conveniently ready for gift giving.

A poem, attached to both the can and outside of the box reads: *Planning a wedding has many a concern, So light this candle and let it burn, Your worries will rise up into the air, And your wedding is sure to be a most splendid affair.*
$16.95

**For more information or to place an order
800.988.9887
E-mail: jen@bravoportland.com**

If you are planning a wedding,
getting married or know someone who is, order
what every bride needs to plan a perfect wedding!

The Bravo! Wedding Organizer

&

Wedding Resource Guide

☐ *Bravo! Wedding Organizer* $24.95
☐ *Bravo! Wedding Resource Guide* $9.95

Please select Bridal Guide edition:

☐ *Portland • Vancouver • Salem '04 Edition*
☐ *Puget Sound '04 Edition*

Shipping and handling additional—$5 per item $ _____
TOTAL: $ _____

METHOD OF PAYMENT:

☐ Check or money order enclosed ☐ Charge to: Visa or MasterCard

Name of card holder: _____

Account No: _____

Exp. Date: _____ Signature: _____

Please allow 7 to 10 days for delivery

Name: _____ _____

Address: _____ Mail Stop: _____

City: _____ State: _____ Zip: _____

Phone: _____ Fax: _____ E-mail: _____

Wedding date: _____

Send order to: Bravo! Publications, Inc.
P.O. Box 1647 • Lake Oswego, OR 97035
503.675.1380, 800.988.9887; Fax 503.675.1204; E-mail: jen@bravoportland.com
Web site: www.bravoportland.com

From the rehearsal to the wedding, reception and honeymoon, these special events should be fun, memorable and perfect. In other words, the events that people remember for years to come are the events that have been planned down to the last detail. That's exactly what this book is about.

It comes from a real-life need—and a real-life situation. In 1988 Mary Lou Burton had a wedding and reception for 500 Italian relatives. In the months leading up to the wedding, she learned enough through her experiences to write a book. So the week after the honeymoon, she sat down with her friend, Marion Clifton, and planned the first *Portland–Vancouver Bridal Guide*. Now in its 13th year, this book has become a best seller—the largest, most complete bridal, event, and party resource guide in the Pacific Northwest.

The goal of the *Bravo!® Wedding Resource Guide* is to help brides and event planners like yourself find the facilities, caterers, florists, bakers, photographers, musicians, and other specialty services best able to fit their precise needs. Before any business is listed in this guide, it's screened to make sure the information is reliable, descriptive and factual. It's then organized in clear and detailed descriptions and easy-to-read formats that allow you to quickly and easily make apple-to-apple comparisons of similar services.

This edition has grown to include over 500 ceremony, reception, and event sites in the Portland, Vancouver and Salem areas, by location and capacity. Hundreds of additional business and service listings are at your fingertips, saving you countless hours of research time. Unlike other guides that simply compile advertisements and photographs, we have tried to create a bridal and event resource guide that's filled with truly useful information. We've even included pages of helpful hints that help you check references, protect deposits, secure dates, decorate inexpensively and much more.

The Bravo!® Wedding Resource Guide is designed to fit in most handbags. It's easy to carry with you and includes spaces for notes. That's why so many brides call it their "Bridal Bible." And the free gifts and discounts offered by many of the companies will more than pay for the cost of the book as you use it in planning your big event!

HOW TO USE THIS BOOK

Congratulations! You've just purchased the most complete wedding, party, and event planning resource in the Pacific Northwest. Before you start, here are some tips on how to use it to your best advantage.

DISCOVER YOUR OPTIONS

Over 500 businesses, services and resources are listed in this book. It provides detailed information about companies that can help you plan everything from engagement to the honeymoon. Within these pages you'll find a variety of resources with descriptions, services and policies listed in detail. You'll appreciate the wealth of knowledge and be amazed by the talents and services our area supports, including outstanding caterers and exquisite florists as well as special services like talented seamstresses and unique gift shops.

IT'S EASY TO FIND THE SERVICES YOU NEED

Each page is designed to read like the resumé of a company. It's up to you to select the services that meet your needs and requirements.

As you explore your options, be sure to view samples, ask questions, get written estimates and take notes. Make sure you feel absolutely comfortable that the companies you select will be able to provide the services or deliver the merchandise you're requesting. If you have any doubts, go to the next business on your list.

Remember, you're the customer. Use this book to help you create exactly the kind of wedding, party or special event you've always dreamed of having!

IT'S EASY TO COMPARE THE SERVICES YOU FIND

As you start working your way through this book, you'll find it's filled with key information organized in a consistent format that allows you to compare and reference the various services easily.

For example, if you've invited 500 guests to your reception, you'll find only a few facilities that can accommodate that large of a group. That quickly narrows down the number of phone calls you'll need to make. In the *Bravo!® Wedding Resource Guide*'s "Banquet & Reception Sites" on pages 57-194, you'll find capacity listed first.

All the basic facts are listed at the top of each page, including company name, address, phone number, business hours and contact person. The rest of the page describes the company's services, costs, deposits, reservation requirements, etc., and a special note. The Portland, Vancouver and Salem edition contains information on over 450 churches, chapels, parks and reception sites. This puts the key facts you need right at your fingertips.

USE THE HELPFUL HINTS

Most sections start with a Helpful Hints page. They're there to save you time, money and headaches!

Professional planners with years of knowledge and experience in wedding planning and event coordination share their secrets on how to avoid the pitfalls and offer ways to make everything run smoothly. At one time or another, they've seen or tried it all! Some of the tips have come from brides who told us, "If only I had it to do over again, I would..." All the tips are worth reading. Some will apply, some won't. But by reading through the pages, you'll find creative and inspiring ideas that you can incorporate into your event—whatever the size or style!

USE IT AND ABUSE IT. THIS IS *YOUR* WORKBOOK!

This book is designed to fit in your purse or briefcase. Keep it handy so you can make phone calls on your coffee breaks, or book appointments during lunch. It lies flat for easy note-taking. Use Post-it notes as bookmarks. Tear pages out, doodle on it or scream into it! (Its special muffle-guard paper spares you any embarrassment.)

We know this book will make planning easier, leaving you more time to enter into the festivities surrounding your special event. So relax, and let the *Bravo!® Wedding Resource Guide* work for you!

The *Bravo!® Wedding Organizer* offers a more detailed workbook for organizing all the details of your wedding. More detailed information can be found on page 31.

The order form is located on page 25 of this guide.

Notes

photo by Coughlin-Glaser Photography • See page 506

Organizational Tools

•

Budgeting Tips

•

Schedules and Checklists

•

Etiquette

•

Blank Calendars

•

Start a Wedding Tradition

•

Wedding Day Survival Kit

www.bravoportland.com

SO NOW I'M ENGAGED—WHAT DO I DO NEXT?

He proposed—the day you've been waiting for has finally arrived! You have to tell your parents, his parents, call all your friends, call the church, get time off for the honeymoon, buy a wedding dress, find a caterer.... STOP!

First things first! Before all the hustle begins, do yourself a favor and **sit down with your fiancé and ask yourselves the following questions:**

• Are your families large or small?
• What is your budget?
• What style of wedding would you prefer to have—do you like intimate gatherings, large parties, or impromptu, unique events?
• Do you want a romantic theme or a formal affair?

Work together so that you both agree on the same things, and then commit your thoughts to paper so that you will have a plan.

ONCE YOU MAKE YOUR PLAN, STICK TO IT!

Everyone seems to become an expert on wedding planning when they find out you're engaged. You'll receive loads of unsolicited advice, and everyone will try to sway your thinking. Don't let anyone steer you away from what's important to you and your fiancé. If you do, your wedding will be a combination of everyone else's dreams but your own!

A CONSULTANT CAN EASE THE STRESS

Hiring a consultant is a wise idea, especially if there is arguing between mother and daughter, between families, divorced parents and even attendants. This is an emotional time and if you can have an objective opinion of a consultant buffering between the two, it can sometimes ease the pressure. Money can be one of the biggest problems and obstacles. If a third party is involved, such as a consultant, they can collect the money without it being embarrassing. Many times these arguments result from lack of communication, emotional overload and misconceptions. The two parties just need to communicate; sometimes writing it down and having someone calm present to the other half is a good way to deal with it. They say you hurt the ones you love the most, the stresses of a wedding can truly test your relationships with family, friends and even your fiancé, remember to keep focused on what's important that day!

DELEGATE DUTIES

Every bride thinks, "If I don't do it, it won't get done the way I want it!" This may be true, but you'll soon realize you can't do it all and keep your sanity. You and your fiancé have figured out the plan, now delegate duties to family and friends. Everything can and will be done the way you want it if you give a clear description of what you need accomplished and when. Family and friends will enjoy knowing they helped contribute to making your special day a success!

RELAX AND ENJOY YOUR WEDDING DAY!

We suggest you get someone to coordinate all the details on the day of your wedding. Hire a professional or ask a trustworthy friend or family member who is not directly involved in the wedding party to oversee and coordinate delivery and setup of flowers, rental equipment, decorations, etc. Provide this person with a comprehensive list of everything he or she will need to keep an eye on, including the arrival of musicians and where they need to set up, where and when the formal photographs will be taken, phone numbers with a contact name for all the businesses providing services, etc. Your months of planning and coordination will pay off! You and your groom should be concerned and consumed only with the joy of the day and your love for each other!

The Bravo!® Wedding Organizer

Get Organized!

Every event planner has his or her own way of getting organized. Over the years of publishing this book, we've encountered a lot of systems, both personally and professionally. From that experience and exposure, we have developed a special Bravo!® Wedding Organizer that incorporates the best of all the plans – along with some specially designed forms of our own. Everything you need is included:

- 40 detailed worksheets designed to double as contracts for reception site, caterer, photographer, florist, musicians, and more
- Time schedules and checklists
- "To Do" lists and forms
- Financial responsibilities guidelines

- "Delegating Duties" lists
- Guest and gift lists
- Business card holders
- Helpful Hints
- Pockets for swatches, samples, coupons, and receipts

In short, everything you need to keep you organized, on budget, and on schedule has been thought of and incorporated into the 14 tabbed sections of the Bravo!® Wedding Organizer. The tab headings serve as a reminder and makes it convenient to organize and store information. When it's time to deal with each element of the event, the information is there at your fingertips. Just three-hole punch and slip everything into your three-ring binder, and you're as organized as you can get.

To order your Bravo!® Wedding Organizer

Complete order form on page 25 and
send $24.95 plus $5.00 for postage and handling to:

Bravo! Publications, Inc.
The Bravo!® Wedding Organizer
P.O. Box 1647
Lake Oswego, Oregon 97035

If you don't read any other page from top to bottom, make sure to read this one. The following suggestions will ensure that your wedding turns out the way you want it while keeping your budget in line.

The most important advice we can offer both you AND your parents is **DO NOT GO INTO DEBT!** Weddings come in a variety of types and sizes; one is not necessarily better than the other, based on the size or how much money you spend. Whatever you do, don't start your married life in debt.

BE REALISTIC WITH YOUR BUDGET

Your wedding budget should be handled like a business budget. If your boss said, "The budget for the Christmas party is $5,000," you would use only those services that would keep you within budget. The same is true for your wedding. Find the services that can accomplish what you want within the budget you've designated. Be realistic about your budget. If you have only $2,000 for your reception, it's unlikely you're going to be able to afford a full sit-down dinner for 300 guests, but a buffet with hot and cold hors d'oeuvres may work very well. Follow your budget allocations as closely as possible. This will eliminate financial stress.

SAMPLE BUDGET SHEET

Service	Budget	Actual	Deposit	Due	Balance	Due
Caterer	$2,500	$2,750	$500	5/5	$2,250	8/6
Florist						
Photos						

SETTING UP A BUDGET

It is recommended you keep a spreadsheet of all your wedding costs. Create one ahead of time that shows what you are spending on which wedding categories. This will help you keep within your budget. If you have to go over on one category then you know you need to cut back on another. A wedding coordinator can help analyze your budget and give you helpful hints on how to cut back on a specific category. Always pay businesses or services with a check or credit card for better records and tracking of expenses. Allocation of your budget depends on what is most important to the bride, groom and family contributing. Some spend more on music and entertainment or photography than others. The following is a percentage break-out of what the average dollar spent is:

- Ceremony site rental—3%
- Reception site rental, food and beverage—37%
- Photography—10%
- Florist—10%
- Music—10%
- Bride's and groom's attire—10%
- Invitations, programs, calligraphy—5%
- Wedding Coordinator—10%
- Miscellaneous (clergy fees, guest favors, attendants gifts, transportation)—5%

WAYS TO SAVE MONEY

It's amazing how fast wedding costs can exceed the planned budget. If you find yourself in the position of needing to trim back to make everything fit within your budget, consider the following:

- **Avoid peak wedding days and seasons.** You can save money by having your wedding during the months considered to be "off-season" (October through May) and on a Thursday or Friday evening or Sunday during the day. Because these times are in less demand, many businesses and services provide what you are looking for at reduced prices. You're also more likely to get your first choices!

- **Consider a daytime versus evening wedding.** Considering a Friday, Saturday or Sunday daytime wedding gives additional options for your wedding date. Food and alcohol costs are considerably less for daytime events than evening events. People don't drink as much if at all, and the food itself is far simpler and therefore less expensive.

- **The guest list.** Guest lists can be the first thing to get out of control. Begin by deciding what size you would like your wedding to be and be firm with your figures of how many guests each family can invite. Generally, if you have not been in contact with someone in the past year, you should not invite them to your wedding. Stick to family and close friends, adding other guests only if your budget allows. Remember that caterers charge per person, so consider having a buffet instead of a sit-down dinner as a way to cut costs.

- **Determine what is most important to you** and put your money into that, but trim back on other areas. If fabulous flowers have always meant the most to you, spend a little less on your entertainment. If you've always wanted the most incredible dress in the world, cut back on the flower budget and have a DJ instead of a band.

- **Don't be afraid to shop around.** A little time on the phone could save you a lot of money. There can be a considerable difference in prices between different businesses for the same items or services. Just make sure that you are going to receive exactly the same item or level of service from the less-expensive company and that no short cuts are being taken at your expense.

If you're very clear about what budget you have to work with from the beginning, you'll find that the people in the wedding industry can be very helpful with all kinds of clever ideas on how to save money. Don't be afraid to ask for suggestions or ideas.

CONTRACTS

Contracts can be the most confusing and difficult part of planning a wedding. Keep in mind that this is a business arrangement. You're the customer and you are contracting with certain businesses to provide the services you request on a certain date, at a certain time, and within a certain budget. Contracts are a **MUST** when doing business with the many types of wedding-related services. Your wedding is an emotional experience, but remember—money is changing hands. A contract will spell out everything in black and white, as well as clarify any grey areas. If the business doesn't have a formal contract, write up your own and have them sign it. Estimates are a good first step, but they aren't final. Many brides have been shocked a week before their wedding when a supplier has said, "We had a price increase in the last six months; now it will cost this much for what you want." Remember, you're holding a book filled with other options. **BEWARE** of contracts you feel pressured to sign! Make sure you don't sign something that you haven't thoroughly read or don't understand. Never sign a contract that makes you feel uncomfortable or that you can't afford. A contract is a legally binding document that commits you to the service or provider. Be well informed about what you are signing; ask questions, or take a copy of it home to look over if you have any hesitation at all.

CHECK OUT REFERENCES

The best way to research a business is to ask for references and then take the time to call them. This way you will rapidly discover if the services or merchandise were provided or delivered as promised. **Getting recommendations from vendors you already trust is also a good place to start.**

DEPOSITS

In most cases a deposit is required to place an order formally or to reserve a certain date. Brides and grooms make the common mistake of assuming that the reception site is reserved based on a verbal commitment for date and time. **The agreement is not always valid, let alone recorded, until after the deposit has been received.**

YOU'RE THE CUSTOMER!

Always remember that you're the customer! Even though this can be an emotional time, **don't settle for less than what was contracted for.** Insist on the best service and accept nothing less. You may be spending more money on this one day than most people spend in a year! Clarify your expectations and never make assumptions.

WEDDING EXPENSES

The division of expenses depends on the financial ability of the bride, groom and their respective families. Sit down and discuss the type of wedding you want to have and use the following list of items so each participant can choose what he or she would like to pay for. Remember that the reception can sometimes amount to 50% or more of your total expenses. If your costs need to be reduced, you may want to change to a less formal reception.

The bride and her family's expenses traditionally include:
* the wedding gown and accessories
* invitations and personal stationery
* flowers for the church, reception, and wedding attendants
* photographs, videography
* reception, including room charge, food, servers, refreshments and wedding cake
* music
* transportation for wedding attendants to church and reception
* gifts for bridesmaids
* accommodations for bridesmaids, if necessary

The groom and his family's expenses traditionally include:
* groom's wedding attire
* the clergy or judge's fees
* the marriage license
* all honeymoon expenses
* rehearsal dinner
* bride's bouquet and both mothers' corsages
* boutonnieres for groomsmen
* groomsmen gifts
* accommodations for attendants, if necessary

The wedding attendants' expenses are:
* wedding attire
* traveling expenses
* wedding gift

The lists mentioned above are used as traditional guidelines, however, you don't have to follow tradition and can have those wanting to contribute pay for whatever they can afford.

YOU'VE WAITED A LONG TIME TO GET MARRIED.

Many reception facilities are reserved as far as a year in advance during the summer months and December. The size and formality of your wedding will play an important part in determining your date and schedule. Even if your wedding is small and less formal, allow yourself a minimum of three months. The more time you have to plan, the better your chances of reserving your first choices. With all you have to do, time will fly quicker than you think!

The following schedule and checklist provide you with the basis for organizing your planning time and ensure that all the details will be handled. These are strictly recommendations; we encourage you to look on the following pages to see when the businesses themselves say they need to be reserved.

AFTER ENGAGEMENT—SIX MONTHS AND BEFORE

❒ Select a wedding date and time — be flexible.

❒ Buy a wedding notebook. *See the Bravo!® Wedding Organizer* info on page 31.

❒ Figure out your budget and write it down.

❒ Determine type of wedding and reception: formality, size, colors and theme.

❒ Decide on the ceremony site and make an appointment with the clergy.

❒ Reserve a reception facility; if there's no in-house catering, you will need to find a caterer.

❒ Start compiling names and addresses of guests.

❒ Decide on wedding attendants — bridesmaids and groomsmen.

❒ Shop for your wedding gown and headpiece.

❒ Select a professional photographer and videographer.

❒ Start collecting favorite photographs from both of your childhoods through present that you'll want to use in your wedding video or multi-image slide program.

❒ Select dresses for your bridesmaids.

❒ Find a florist.

❒ Mail out engagement announcements.

❒ Send an announcement to your local paper.

❒ Register at the bridal registry stores of your choice.

❒ Reserve a band, DJ, or orchestra for your reception.

❒ Decide on honeymoon destination; if it's a popular area, make reservations now.

FOUR TO FIVE MONTHS BEFORE

- ❐ Compile the final guest list; delete or correct as needed.

- ❐ Make sure all deposits are paid for services reserved.

- ❐ Finish planning the honeymoon.

- ❐ Order bridal attire; some manufacturers require up to six months for delivery.

- ❐ Order the wedding cake.

- ❐ Have groom, groomsmen and ushers fitted for formal wear.

- ❐ Purchase your wedding rings.

- ❐ Order invitations, thank-you notes, imprinted napkins and wedding programs.

- ❐ Ask people to handle certain duties like candle lighting, guest book, cake serving.

- ❐ Select musicians for ceremony

TWO TO THREE MONTHS BEFORE

- ❐ Plan ceremony rehearsal and rehearsal dinner.

- ❐ Address invitations (mail six to eight weeks prior to wedding).

- ❐ Organize details with service providers: reception facility, photographer, etc.

- ❐ Check accommodations for out-of-town guests; send them information.

- ❐ Make beauty appointments: hair, nails, massage, facial and makeup.

- ❐ Arrange for final fittings for your gown and bridesmaids dresses.

- ❐ Make your transportation arrangements for the wedding day.

- ❐ Purchase gifts for your attendants.

- ❐ Shop for your lingerie and going-away outfit.

- ❐ Give a bridesmaids' luncheon or bachelor/bachelorette party (optional).

- ❐ Send thank-yous for gifts received early.

- ❐ Get accessories: garter, unity candle, toasting goblets, ring-bearer pillow, etc.

ONE WEEK TO A MONTH BEFORE

☐ Change your name (if you choose) on your driver's license and Social Security card; organize which credit cards and bank accounts will be used.

☐ Decide where you'll be living and send change-of-address cards to post office.

☐ Confirm accommodations arranged for out-of-town guests.

☐ Get your final count of guests to caterer.

☐ Delegate last-minute errands and details.

☐ Make any necessary lists for photographer, videographer and musicians.

☐ If you haven't hired a wedding coordinator, ask a responsible person to coordinate services and people on the wedding day; give them a list of who and what is supposed to be where and when.

☐ Meet with your wedding coordinator to go over final details.

☐ Pack for honeymoon.

☐ Get your marriage license. *Note: if you were married before, you'll need to know the date and place of the divorce or annulment. You may also need to have paperwork proof of divorce or annulment.

☐ Pick up your wedding rings; make sure they are the correct sizes.

☐ Pick up wedding attire; try it all on one last time to make sure it fits.

☐ Make sure bridesmaids have their dresses and they all fit.

☐ Keep up on writing thank-yous; don't let them pile up.

☐ Pamper yourself and make sure you eat right and get enough sleep.

THE WEDDING DAY

☐ Eat a good breakfast.

☐ Relax and enjoy getting ready for your big day.

☐ Go to hairdresser or start fixing your hair a few hours prior to the wedding.

☐ Put all the accessories you will need for dressing in one place.

☐ If pictures are being taken before ceremony, begin at least two hours prior.

☐ Just enjoy the day! All your months of planning will make your day perfect!

MONTH:

MONDAY	TUESDAY	WEDNESDAY	THURSDAY	FRIDAY	SATURDAY	SUNDAY

Today, wedding etiquette consists of good manners and a blending of traditional customs with contemporary ones. The following tips show you how to incorporate proper etiquette into every aspect of your wedding, giving you greater confidence in every situation.

ANNOUNCING YOUR ENGAGEMENT

Share your good news with your families as soon as possible—it's only right that they hear it from you first. If you'd also like to announce your engagement formally in both your and your fiancé's hometown papers, contact the lifestyles editor to learn the appropriate way to prepare your information. Ask if photos are also accepted.

ORDERING INVITATIONS

Order your invitations at least four months in advance to give you plenty of time for printing, addressing and mailing. There are many different styles of wedding invitations. Make sure you shop around for the supplier who is going to give you the style, quality and price you are looking for. You should choose your invitation based on both your and your fiance's tastes and what you want the invitation to represent to your guests. Invitations can be the starting point of the entire feel of your wedding. Also ask about deadlines to get your programs ordered so that they coordinate with the look of your invitation.

ADDRESSING INVITATIONS

Create a master list of names in order to avoid duplications. Make sure all names and titles are spelled correctly and addresses are accurate. Below are some typical examples of different addressing styles.

When addressing invitations to married couples, use the following format:

Mr. and Mrs. John Smith
1022 Robins Court
City, California 12345

Keep in mind that some women have retained their maiden names or prefer to be called by their titles or professional names. In these cases, you may send one invitation to both husband and wife, putting her name above his on the envelope. Follow the same rule for couples with different last names or unmarried couples living together.

Ms. Jane Smith
Mr. Joseph Thomas
122 Maple Street, Apartment R-10
Dayton, Ohio 12345

Be sure to write out in full the names of streets, cities, and states as well. Don't send an invitation to a couple and "family." Instead, on the inner envelope, include the name of each child invited as:

Mr. and Mrs. Smith
Kevin, Brian, and Amy

Adult members of a family who are over age 18 should always receive separate invitations. You may, however, send one invitation to two sisters or brothers living together at one address.

MAILING INVITATIONS

Invitations are usually mailed six to eight weeks before the wedding. Do send invitations to your wedding official, your fiancé's immediate family, all members of the wedding party, and a guest list made up of both your friends and his, as well as other relatives and coworkers with whom you want to share your day. Keep in mind your budget limitations and refrain from letting your list get out of control. Selection may sometimes be difficult, but it is best to stick as closely as possible to your list. If you haven't received an RSVP by two weeks before the wedding, have a family member call and check. When each invitation is accounted for, tell your caterer how many guests to expect.

POSTAGE FOR INVITATIONS

Remember before purchasing stamps for your invitations to go to the post office and have the invitation weighed. Normally the postage will be 37 cents, but if the invitation has many inserts or is a larger size it might require more postage. You can also have your invitations hand cancelled so that they still look beautiful after being mailed.

SAVE-THE-DATE LETTERS:

Inform out-of-town guests about the upcoming wedding date far enough in advance, so if they need to take time off work or save for the trip they will have time. This letter can also give details about hotel accommodations in different budgets, special wedding rates and who to contact at the destination and the toll-free number. Send six months in advance or in January of the year you are getting married. January is a great time because the holidays are over and people start looking forward to the new year and planning their vacations.

BANQUET AND RECEPTION SITES

Rehearsal Dinner: The rehearsal dinner is traditionally hosted by the groom's parents. This is either formal or casual and follows the ceremony rehearsal the night before the wedding, although many brides and grooms are choosing to have the rehearsal two days before the wedding. It is the beginning of the festivities and an opportunity for all wedding party attendants and family to get to know each other. Invitations should be sent or telephoned at least three weeks prior and should be extended to all those participating in the wedding: attendants and groomsmen and their spouses, the clergy, parents of any children, immediate family and out-of-town guests who have arrived. The best man begins the toasts following dessert and then the gifts are presented to the wedding party and any other special helpers. This evening usually ends early so everyone can get a good night's sleep. See "Rehearsal Dinner Sites" section on pages 181–194.

Outdoor weddings: Always play it safe with an outdoor site—make sure you either have a back-up location or rent and set up tents. In the wonderful Pacific Northwest you can never be too sure of the weather. These tents or canopies can be expensive; don't forget to figure this into your budget.

Non-traditional sites and times: Saturdays are the most popular day to get married, and most businesses and services will charge top dollar for this prime time. Consider Friday nights or Sunday weddings as an option; some services will give a discount for booking this off-day. Also, sites such as restaurants, parks, historical sites and beaches can be non-traditional, but also very fun and exciting with atmosphere and unique cuisine.

ROLES MEMBERS OF THE WEDDING PARTY PLAY

Maid of Honor: Although she has no prewedding responsibilities, she is expected to assist the bride whenever she can. She lends moral support and plays a big role in making sure the other bridesmaids are dressed to perfection and they all make it to the church on time. She is responsible for her own wedding outfit and pays for everything except the flowers. She also attends all prewedding parties and may even give one herself. The maid of honor is usually one of the witnesses required by law to sign the marriage certificate. Walking down the aisle, she precedes you and your father, arranges your train and veil, carries the groom's ring if there is no ringbearer, and holds your bouquet during the ceremony. She also stands next to the groom in the receiving line and sits on his left at the bride's table.

Best Man: His duties are many and varied and carry a lot of responsibility to ensure the wedding runs smoothly. The best man serves as the personal aide and advisor to the groom, supervises the ushers, carries the bride's ring and the marriage certificate, which he also signs, tips the altar boys in a Catholic ceremony, and acts as a right-hand man to the groom on his special day. The best man sits at the right of the bride and, as official toastmaster of the reception, proposes the first toast to the new couple, usually wishing them health, happiness, and prosperity. His final duties are to ensure the new couple takes off for the honeymoon without a hitch and that all the ushers return their rented formal wear on time.

Bridesmaids: Although they don't have any prewedding responsibilities either, they often will volunteer to help with any errands or duties that need to be accomplished. They are invited to all prewedding parties and may also give one if they wish. Traditionally they purchase their own attire.

Groomsmen/Ushers: Their responsibility is to seat guests at the wedding ceremony and act as escorts for the bridesmaids. To avoid seating delays, there should be at least one usher for every 50 guests. They also attend all prewedding parties the groom goes to and are required to provide their own wedding clothes, renting the proper formal attire if they do not own it. As guests arrive, each usher should offer his right arm to each woman and escort her to her seat on the left or right of the aisle, depending on whether she is a friend of the bride or groom.

The Bride's Mother: Your mother usually helps compile the guest list and helps with any other details you desire assistance with as well. It is her responsibility to keep the bride's father and future in-laws informed about wedding plans. She should also inform the groom's mother of her wedding attire so that their dresses are similar in length and style. The mother of the bride is privileged to sit in the very first pew on the bride's side. She is the last to be seated and the first to be escorted out of the church after the ceremony. She can also greet all guests in the receiving line and sits in a place of honor at the bride's parents' table at the reception.

The Bride's Father: Your father escorts you down the aisle. He is also seated in the first pew behind the bride during the ceremony and later stands in the receiving line greeting and thanking guests. At the reception, he should dance the second dance with the bride and will usually make a short toast or welcoming speech to all the guests.

The Groom's Parents: Your fiancé's mother should be invited to all showers and both his parents should be included in the rehearsal dinner, if they don't host it themselves. They should also contribute to the guest list for the wedding and reception and may or may not offer to share expenses. The groom's parents are honored guests at the ceremony and are seated, just before your mother, in the first pew on the groom's side of the aisle.

WHEN PARENTS ARE DIVORCED

Dealing with divorced parents may add a complication to your wedding plans, but if handled well, everything can still work out just the way you planned. The key is to provide separate places of distinction at the ceremony, in the receiving line, and at the reception to ensure their happiness and enjoyment of the day.

GUIDELINES FOR DIVORCED PARENTS

- **Invitations:** Invitations are usually issued by the parent you have currently lived with. If both parents have contributed, then both names and stepparents can be mentioned.
- **Ceremony seating:** For seating at the ceremony there are two options: if parents are friends and they are not remarried, they can sit side by side in the front pew. Otherwise the parent you have lived with would sit in the front pew with his or her spouse, and the other parent sits in the second or third pew with his or her spouse.
- **Photographs:** Each set of parents will most likely want to have a photo taken with the bride and groom; it is important to spell this out to the photographers earlier. This can take longer for photographs so appropriate time needs to be allocated.
- **Down the Aisle:** Walking down the aisle can be more than just a scary walk when trying to decide whether your father or stepfather should escort you. Consider whether you have remained close to your father and if you want him to fulfill this traditional role; or if your stepfather has filled the role of your father you may decide this is more appropriate. If your father and stepfather get along, you may ask both. If the decision is impossible, choose neither and ask your mother to walk you down.

- **Receiving Line:** For the receiving line and reception, customarily the parent who is paying for the wedding greets the guests with you. The other parent can be mingling. At the reception a good solution to feuding families is to have two different parent tables.

RECEIVING LINE

Usually held at the beginning of the reception, this event allows parents and the wedding party members to greet guests and receive their good wishes. The line traditionally begins with your mother, followed by the groom's mother, the bride and groom, your maid of honor and the rest of the bridesmaids. The fathers can join in and, if so, should stand to the left of their wives. **If your parents are divorced**, your mother stands alone or with your stepfather, while your father circulates among the guests. Or, to avoid confusion, decide not to include fathers in the line. The important thing is to avoid hurt feelings or misunderstandings. Another alternative is to have your father and his new wife stand on the other side of the groom. If you feel it becomes too difficult to orchestrate, it is **perfectly acceptable to mingle and greet your guests during the reception rather than have a receiving line**. Whatever works well for your situation is fine.

SEATING ARRANGEMENTS AT THE RECEPTION

The bride's table, which should be the focus of the reception, can be of any shape and is sometimes elevated so everyone can see the wedding party. The groom usually sits to the bride's left with the maid of honor on his left. To the right of the bride is the best man, and the rest of the bridesmaids and ushers sit at the table male, female, male, female. If it's a small wedding party, the officiant and husbands and wives of the wedding party may also sit at the bride's table. Otherwise, a separate table for parents is set where your mother heads the table and the groom's father sits at her right and the wedding officiant sits at her left. The groom's mother sits on your father's right. However, if your parents are divorced, consider arranging a separate table for each set of parents.

DON'T FORGET THANK-YOU NOTES!

You and your groom must send personal, handwritten notes of appreciation thanking everyone who gave you and your new husband a gift. It is suggested you begin sending thank-you notes immediately upon receiving your gifts. Try to acknowledge each gift within two weeks of its arrival.

If you need more information or advice, several excellent books by the editors of popular bridal magazines and by etiquette experts are available at libraries and book stores. Bridal consultants and bridal-shop personnel are also sources of lots of useful tips and information.

Weddings make us all sentimental. By including a special item or tradition in your ceremony and reception that has been used by other family members, or that you yourself may wish to pass on to future generations, you allow family and friends to share in your joy as well as the traditions of your family.

Here are some ideas that you may wish to incorporate into your wedding:

- Select a Bible that you can comfortably carry down the aisle with you. At the completion of the ceremony, you and your groom can sign your names and your wedding date in the front of the Bible as well as the location and time of your marriage. As each future bride and groom uses it, their names will be added.

- The kneeling cushions and ring-bearer's pillow used during the ceremony can be made from the wedding gown of one of the bridal couple's mothers or grandmothers or from fabric selected for the occasion, then passed on to future generations of family brides and grooms.

- If you decide not to use your mother's wedding dress, you could carry the same kind of flowers your mother did or replicate other details of her wedding.

- Many brides choose to carry a family memento during their wedding. A handkerchief made from the lace of a family member's gown or veil can be easily carried with your bridal bouquet.

- Your wedding garter can be made from satin and lace used by other family members in their wedding attire. Just make sure you have a backup garter for the groom to throw at the end of the reception.

- Instruct your florist to design your bridal bouquet with two detachable flowers that you can give to your mother and mother-in-law as you return down the aisle.

- Since the first toast at the reception signifies the celebration and coming together of two families as well as the beginning of a new one, silver or pewter toasting goblets make wonderful gifts to be passed on to future family brides.

- Your cake knife and server are something you will want to save and pass on.

- The day of your wedding, plant a tree or a rose bush that you can watch grow throughout the years of your marriage.

- A perfect gift from the groom can be a charm bracelet. With each year, in celebration of your wedding anniversary, a new charm can be added.

When you've returned from your honeymoon and have packed away your dress, you'll want to get a special box in which you can carefully pack all of your wedding treasures. Someday you can share them with your daughter(s) and future daughters-in-law.

You will want to put some things together a few days before your wedding to take to the church. We call it the "Wedding Day Survival Kit." It includes all those little odds and ends that you'll need for quick repairs and to cover the things others may have forgotten.

- ☐ Scissors
- ☐ Needles and thread (in the colors of your bridal and attendant gowns)
- ☐ Safety pins
- ☐ Iron and ironing board (if none are available at church or ceremony site)
- ☐ Makeup kit (for light touchups)
- ☐ Hand mirror and makeup mirrors
- ☐ Kleenex
- ☐ Smock or towels to protect dresses from last-minute makeup touchups
- ☐ Electric curlers and curling iron
- ☐ Bobbie pins and combs to anchor veils and headpieces
- ☐ Hair spray
- ☐ Deodorant or antiperspirant
- ☐ Dress shields
- ☐ Extra nylons in the appropriate colors
- ☐ Extra socks for groomsmen and ushers (someone is bound to forget)
- ☐ Toys to keep flower girls and ring bearers busy in a quiet way
- ☐ Smocks for flower girls and ring bearers to wear over their wedding attire until it's time for the photos or ceremony (kids will get dirty!)
- ☐ Masking tape (for last-minute fix-up jobs on decorations)
- ☐ Scotch tape for taping cards to gifts so they don't fall off
- ☐ Lightweight wire (for last-minute repairs on decorations)
- ☐ Super glue
- ☐ Breath freshener and perfume
- ☐ Aspirin
- ☐ Refreshments (pop, ice tea, juice....everyone is bound to get thirsty)
- ☐ Straws (never drink directly from a glass or can; you will undoubtedly spill)
- ☐ A hand-held fan for those hot summer months

Put all your supplies for your "Wedding Day Survival Kit" into a carryall bag and put it next to the things that are going to the church. You'll be glad you have it!

One final tip. Find out whether your church has a stool that you can use in the dressing room. If not, bring one with you. You'll get tired of standing after you've dressed in your gown. If you sit in a chair, you'll wrinkle your gown. This is where the stool comes in handy! Drape your gown skirt and train over the stool, then sit; no wrinkles!

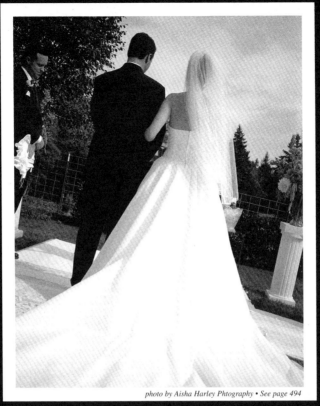

photo by Aisha Harley Phtography • See page 494

Giving Away The Bride

The custom of the bride being

given away by her father has its origins in

ancient times when women were considered

to be owned by and slaves to men.

The marriage was treated as

a property transaction, with the

right of ownership being passed from

one man to another.

www.bravoportland.com

- **You will have the opportunity to attend several excellent bridal shows throughout the year.** The advantage to these shows is that it is a perfect time to meet and talk with area businesses and services and see what they have to offer all in one place.

- **Be prepared!** It's very helpful if you have a **target list** of items and services you will need to have to make your wedding day complete. Don't wander. Have a **plan of action** and go and find the booths that have the services you are looking for.

- **Take notes.** You will receive a lot of information as you are touring the booths, and it can get confusing. Be sure to write down the names of the companies that impress you the most, so that you can contact them later. If you are collecting information as you go, **fold down the corners of the brochures or hand-outs** of the companies you like so that you can go directly to their material when you need it.

- **Keep information organized!** *The Bravo!® Wedding Organizer* is the perfect place to store all the valuable information you gather. After the show, pull out the important information and discounts and put into appropriate categories in *The Bravo!® Wedding Organizer*...it's the perfect system. For more information see page 31.

- **Dress comfortably.** Make sure you wear comfortable shoes and clothing. You'll be on your feet for a long time.

- **Take your mother or a friend to help you.** If you have an assistant, they can carry all the information you are gathering so that you can **keep your hands free** to take notes and review information.
   (**Note:** Don't take too many people with you. You'll end up spending all your time trying to find them as they wander off or start talking with other people and you won't accomplish what you set out to do.)

- **Have sticky labels or mail labels with your name and address.** You'll be signing up for a lot of door prizes. It's very quick and easy if you have a label to put on the entry forms.

- **Fashion shows.** This is always one of the biggest features of Bridal Shows. You'll see all the latest fashions for the entire wedding party, in addition to resort wear, attire for mothers of the bride and groom, and more. Most shows will provide you with a program. Keep it in-hand so that if you see something you fall in love with, you'll know where to go to find it after the fashion show is over.

For more assistance with staying organized during the wedding planning process, check out the Bravo! Wedding Organizer. Detailed question worksheets double as contracts. This step-by-step system will keep every detail of your wedding organized. To order, refer to the order form on page 25 in this Guide.

MEIER & FRANK

Upcoming Bridal Event

Sunday, January 25 • 12pm
Downtown Portland Store, 10th Floor Auditorium
621 S.W. Fifth Avenue, Portland

The day will provide an exceptional opportunity for the bride to hear
nationally renowned speakers discuss how to choose the gifts for her registry.

- **Opportunity to meet with vendors to discuss individual registry needs**
- **Enter to win fabulous prizes**
- **Register to win a romantic honeymoon**

For more information
please call (503) 223-0512 ext. 5158
or look on our events page at
www.MeierAndFrankWeddings.com

Don't miss our Making Memories gown sale.
Thousands of wedding gowns sale priced from $49-$599.
Friday 1/23, Saturday 1/24 and Sunday 1/25

Making Memories Breast Cancer Foundation is a non-profit organization
that sells donated wedding gowns and utilizes 100% of the funds to grant "wishes" to women
*and men with breast cancer. For more information, visit **www.makingmemories.org**.*

Four Great Wedding Shows!

Mid-Willamette Valley
Bridal Show

Oregon State Fairgrounds
2330 17th St NE – Salem, Oregon

January 10 & 11, 2004...................Admission: $7
September 11 & 12, 2004..............Admission: $5

	Show Hours	**Fashion Show**
Saturday	10:00 a.m. to 5 p.m.	11:00 a.m. & 2:30 p.m.
Sunday	11:00 a.m. to 5 p.m.	12:30 p.m. & 3:00 p.m.

Emerald City
Bridal Show

Lane Event Center
796 W 13th Ave – Eugene, Oregon

January 17 & 18, 2004...................Admission: $7
October 16 & 17, 2004.................. Admission: $5

	Show Hours	**Fashion Show**
Saturday	10:00 a.m. to 5 p.m.	11:00 a.m. & 2:30 p.m.
Sunday	11:00 a.m. to 5 p.m.	12:30 p.m. & 3:00 p.m.

Produced by: Oregon Wedding Shows   www.oregonweddingshows.com

Mix107.5 sponsors

The Original
Portland
Bridal Show

Don't Miss ... Portland's *BIG* Bridal Shows!

Plan your wedding with over 150 "Wedding Related" exhibitors

Two Great Shows in 2004!
Original Winter Show - January 17 & 18
and
New "Summer Edition" Show
May 15 & 16

Oregon Convention Center

Exquisite Bridal Fashion Shows each day
Honeymoon Get-Aways from the Columbia Gorge Hotel
given away at <u>each show!</u>

Pre-Registration Bonuses!
Pre-register online for our Grand Door Prizes
and receive valuable bonus gifts
www.portlandbridalshow.com

$1 off discount coupons for the show are available
at all exhibitor locations in advance
Hurry! Shows Sell Out Early!
Advance tickets guarantee admission - Limited Tickets at the Door
Advance Tickets at: **TicketsWest**
For Additional Info: See our Website or call 503-274-6027

Please let this business know that you heard about them from the Bravo! Wedding Resource Guide.　**49**

Notes

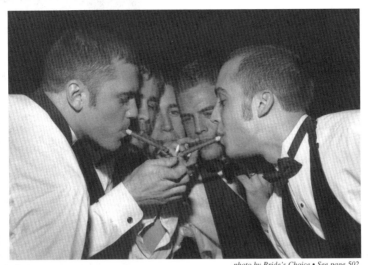

photo by Bride's Choice • See page 502

The Bachelor Party

The traditional purpose of the bachelor party

was to raise a special fund so that the

groom could continue to go drinking with his

buddies after the responsibility of the household

budget had been taken over by the bride.

www.bravoportland.com

53 N.W. 1st Avenue
Portland, Oregon 97209
On the corner of 1st & Couch
in Portland's Old Town

Call: 503-241-3840
Fax: 503-241-3841
E-mail: voodooloungepdx@aol.com
Or log onto: www.voodoopdx.com

Open: Tuesday through Sunday 5pm to 2am
VIP rooms available by reservation only

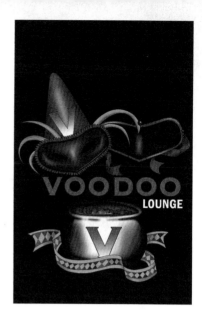

LET VOODOO LOUNGE LEAD THE WAY TO A FLAWLESS BACHELORETTE CELEBRATION!

It is customary to give the bride-to-be the proper send off into marital bliss. Voodoo Lounge provides a festive setting conducive to creating an entertaining and memorable bachelorette party.

Voodoo Lounge is Portland's exclusive themed lounge. With a Mardi Gras feel, New Orleans inspired cuisine, outrageous cocktails and unique accommodations, Voodoo Lounge is a destination like no other.

Cajun Inspired Cuisine & Outrageous Cocktails:

Voodoo Lounge offers cocktail and dinner seating and serves a superbly concocted, culinary-driven Cajun infused menu that is available until 2am. Voodoo boasts the most inventive drink menu in Portland. Cocktails are taken to an elevated level with the advent of herbal infused potion drinks. These medicinal drinks are spiked with herbs, served in cast iron cauldrons and exude a mystical fog. The house drinks are also spectacular. Popular selections include the Mesmerize Martini, Flaming Lemon Drop, Hypnotic Cocktail, and the famous New Orleans Hurricane. Voodoo also features a variety of bowl drinks perfect for sharing.

Bachelorette VIP Rooms:

Voodoo Lounge offers two VIP rooms that are ideal for throwing that perfect bachelorette celebration, whether your party is for 5 or 55. Each room is unique in style and amenities. Voodoo's Red Room is a spacious fire-inspired spot that is decorated with soft velvet couches, beanbag chairs and a fireplace. Voodoo's Blue Room offers a cozier locale. The star and mirror laced walls of this rectangular shaped room are lined with an oversized couch that is draped in blue velvet and covered with stuffed pillows. Tropical fish can be found meandering in the 200-gallon pristine, blue-tinted fish tank. Each room, although private, offers a great viewing spot of the entire lounge. VIP rooms are available by reservation only, so call ahead to book your room.

photo by Holland Studios • See page 511

"*Grow old along with me!*

The best is yet to be.

The first of life

For which the last was made."

– Robert Browning

www.bravoportland.com

Portland Spirit   Willamette Star   Crystal Dolphin

110 SE Caruthers Portland, OR 97214
503-224-3900 • 800-224-3901
E-mail: sales@portlandspirit.com • www.portlandspirit.com

The fleet of the Portland Spirit will provide a unique, memorable experience for your next event. Portland Spirit cruises are ideal for entertaining guests for corporate events, reunions, conventions, weddings and more. Cruise with us for a breakfast or luncheon meeting, anniversary party, or gala holiday event. Our knowledgeable sales staff and professional event planners will handle all the details, making your planning process easy and stress-free!
Price Range: prices vary – please inquire
Catering: in-house, food minimums apply

Portland Spirit

Our flagship yacht combines a classic nautical experience with a fine-dining atmosphere. One-deck rentals, private charters of the entire vessel and public group reservations are available. Two levels are fully enclosed and climate controlled, each with a baby grand piano. The Columbia Deck has a built-in marble dance floor and open air viewing deck.
Capacity: up to 540 guests
Seating: tables and chairs for 340 plus outside seating

Willamette Star

Elegance and style has been custom built into the Willamette Star, from its solid cherry wood interior to brass accents and plush carpeting. The Willamette Star has two enclosed, temperature-controlled levels, two outdoor viewing decks, piano and a sound system.
Capacity: up to 144 guests
Seating: tables and chairs for 100 plus outside and bar seating

Crystal Dolphin

This sleek and luxurious vessel provides a bright, contemporary setting for any event. The Crystal Dolphin features three fully enclosed and climate controlled levels, a baby grand piano, outdoor viewing decks and sound system
Capacity: up to 120 guests
Seating: tables and chairs for 50 plus outside and lounge seating

Description of Vessel Services and Facilities

Linens: linen tablecloths and napkins provided
China: house china and glassware provided
Servers: included with food and bar service
Bar facilities: full service bar, liquor, bartenders and liability insurance
Cleanup: provided; **Parking:** commercial and street parking available
ADA: limited with assistance; please call for more information

STERNWHEELER "COLUMBIA GORGE" & MARINE PARK

Sales Office: P.O. Box 307
Cascade Locks, Oregon 97014
(541) 374-8427; (800) 643-1354
Web site: www.sternwheeler.com; E-mail: sales@sternwheeler.com

Owned & operated by the Port of Cascade Locks

Capacity: 200 sit-down, 350 reception
Price Range: varies depending on number of guests and length of cruise; minimum of two hours; please call
Catering: full range of catering services provided including menu selections from champagne toasts, to complete dinners and hors d'oeuvres packages
Types of Events: weddings, receptions, party cruises, casino cruises—hors d'oeuvre or dinner-style

Availability and Terms

We offer a variety of accommodations for wedding parties up to 350 aboard the Sternwheeler "Columbia Gorge." Two fully enclosed heated decks provide a comfortable setting for any time of year. Marine Park and Thunder Island can accommodate up to 1,000 guests. A 25% nonrefundable deposit is required upon booking; final payment is due 30–60 days prior to scheduled event depending upon the season.

Description of Facility and Services

Seating: tables, chairs and standard linens provided
Servers: provided
Bar facilities: two to three full-service bars with bartenders available
Dance floor: dance area available; full electrical hookup
Linens and napkins: vinyl linens and cloth napkins; color coordination available–inquire
China and glassware: house china available with our catering service
Decorations: elegant turn-of-the-century motif requires little decoration
Cleanup: provided courtesy of the Sternwheeler crew
Parking: *Cascade Locks Marine Park:* free parking; *Portland:* City Center and off-street parking available for a fee
ADA: disabled accessible

Special Services

With two rivers and an abundance of breathtaking views to choose from, the Sternwheeler "Columbia Gorge" and Marine Park continue to provide a unique venue for your wedding/ceremony and reception.

As a unique wedding site, we can provide catering and menu selection, music and entertainment. We can also coordinate a performance of your ceremony by one of our credited Captains. Please call our sales office to arrange a tour of either of the Sternwheeler "Columbia Gorge" or our 23-acre Marine Park and Thunder Island.

THE STERNWHEELER
ROSE

6412 SW Vermont St.
Portland, Oregon 97219
(503) 286-ROSE (7673)
Business Hours: Mon–Fri 8am–5pm

ROMANTIC RIVER SETTING

Cruising aboard *The Sternwheeler Rose* is a unique way to make your wedding special. It's also a festive place for a rehearsal dinner, bachelor party or a bridal shower. We offer a standard wedding package that includes boat charter, ceremony by Captain, elegant hors d'oeuvre buffet, champagne, flowers, invitations, napkins and wedding cake. Of course, you are welcome to create your own package. Our experienced caterer can provide you with suggestions or create the specific menu of your choice—you're limited only by your imagination and budget! Additionally, our staff, crew and captains are available to help you plan every step and execute every detail to make your wedding a wonderful and memorable event.

Capacity: up to 130 people; you may reserve the entire boat for your private cruise
Price Range: customized wedding packages available; prices vary; please inquire
Catering: licensed, in-house catering available; flexible menus
Types of Events: wedding ceremonies, receptions, dinners, dances, rehearsal dinners, parties

Availability and Terms

The Sternwheeler Rose is Portland's finest year-round charter boat. It cruises on the Willamette river. A deposit of 50% is required. Terms are available.

Description of Facility and Services

Boarding location: OMSI; other boarding sites can be scheduled
Seating: tables and chairs provided
Servers: provided
Bar facilities: beer, wine, champagne, soft drinks and bartender standard; full-service bar available
Dance floor: floor for up to 80 people; electrical hookups available
Linens and napkins: all colors of linen tablecloths and cloth napkins available
China and glassware: glass plates, glasses and barware available
Decorations: No candles, confetti or propane allowed
Cleanup: complete cleanup courtesy of The Sternwheeler Rose with catering
Parking: free at OMSI

Special Services

Be sure to ask about decorations both for ideas and logistics

Please call if you have any questions or would like more information.
(503) 286-7673

Visit us at www.sternwheelerrose.com

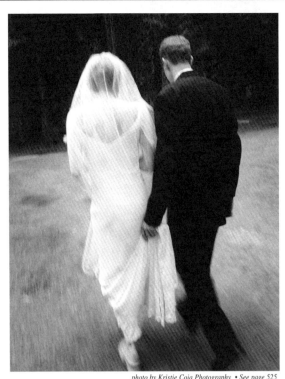

photo by Kristie Coia Photography • See page 525

The Toast

The touching or clinking of glasses was meant as an

unspoken, audible message from the guests to

produce a bell-like sound that would banish the

devil, who is repelled by bells, from the festivities.

After the wedding toast, guests would break the wine

glasses or other objects to scare off evil spirits.

www.bravoportland.com

Banquet & Reception Sites

- **Begin looking for your reception, banquet, or meeting site immediately:**
  The first decision to be made is where to hold the event. Popular venues fill up quickly, so it is important to narrow down your search early.

- **Selecting your location:**
  - Make sure the venue you choose is large enough for your expected attendance and situated in a way that is conducive to the activities you will have.

  - There should be ample room for a bar area, dance floor and dining tables as well as areas where guests can mingle and talk without feeling cramped with other entertainment.

  - Choose a location that has the level of privacy you desire; a crowded hotel will not be a private as a venue that only has one event at a time.

  - Pay attention to color, architecture and landscape to insure they won't clash with the color and theme you have selected.

  - Plenty of outlets and good acoustic conditions are necessary for a band or DJ.

- **Visit the location:** When you narrow down the options of sites available, view the room in person before you reserve it or send a deposit. Often the look and feel of a room or location will sway a decision one way or another. Try to visit the location at the same time of day as your event; lighting can alter the mood and look of a room or space and you want to make sure you know what your guests will be seeing. It is also easier to plan an event by keeping the room's layout and size in mind.

- **Be flexible:** If you are insistent about a certain date and time, you may spend weeks searching all over town for a place to accommodate your needs. By the time you finally discover that no options are available on your first choice, your alternate dates may also be booked.

- **Be honest about your budget:** Do not be afraid to tell the facility coordinator or event planner what your budget is. This very important information can be used as a guideline and can save time and effort. Trust the person in charge to help create a successful event. They can offer time- and budget-saving recommendations based on experience.

- **Deposits are important:** Remember that when you reserve a facility, a deposit is usually required. Even though you thought your date was secure, the site is not formally reserved until a deposit is received. Many brides have lost their reception site by overlooking this fact.

- **Gift table:** Assign a reliable person to be in charge of gifts at the ceremony and reception. He or she should have scotch tape handy to tape loose cards to packages. It is a good idea to have a basket or box for cards that are given without a gift. If the gift table is displayed at the ceremony site, the person in charge of it needs to make sure it is transferred the reception site. Gifts should be taken to a safe, designated place after the reception is underway.

For more assistance with staying organized during the wedding planning process, check out the Bravo! Wedding Organizer. Detailed question worksheets double as contracts. This step-by-step system will keep every detail of your wedding organized. To order, refer to the order form on page 25 in this Guide.

Abernethy Center

EVENTS ◆ GARDENS

606 15th Street • Oregon City, Oregon 97045
(503) 722-9400; Fax (503) 722-5377; Web site: www.abernethycenter.com
Business Hours: Mon–Fri 9am–5pm; appointments recommended

Capacity: indoors up to 300; outdoors 300+
Price Range: varies according to event; please call for information
Catering: full service, in-house catering only
Types of Events: We have complete indoor and outdoor facilities for all of your events, including but by no means limited to: weddings, receptions, corporate meetings and banquets, fundraisers, sit-down dinners, trade shows, retreats, seminars, reunions and auctions.

Availability and Terms
Every attempt will be made to accommodate your event no matter when it is booked; however, we do recommend early reservations. A deposit is required at the time of booking.

Description of Facility and Services
Seating: table and chair setup for up to 300 is included in the site rental
Servers: provided with catering service
Bar facilities: available through Abernethy Center
Dance floor: included in the site rental
Linens: available through Abernethy Center
China: provided with catering service
A/V: Bose® surround sound system, 9x12 ft. screen and projector, DVD, VCR and CD players, wireless microphones available (indoor only)
Equipment: podium and staging available
Cleanup: included in the site rental
Parking: 125 free parking spaces; additional street parking
ADA: fully accessible

INDOOR OR OUTDOOR, WE HAVE IT ALL!
Abernethy Center is the perfect location for any event. Built in 1960 as an Oregon City Post Office and completely remodeled and renovated in 2001, the Center has character and charm that are not often seen in venues of similar size. From the granite, tile and marble entry leading to over 5,000 square feet of beautifully appointed event space, to the spacious rooms with 13 to 15-foot high ceilings displaying chandeliers and wall sconces that add elegance and ambience, the Abernethy Center has everything you need to create a memorable event. The outdoor patio hosts a babbling brook, gorgeous flower baskets and a quiet escape. Adjacent to the Center, over 3.5 acres of outdoor garden area are nestled along Abernethy Creek. Its gradual slope will accommodate groups of 100 to 1,000. Clients my choose from one of two gazebo gardens for the ceremony; a full-size tent with closeable sidewalls is included for the reception.

Just three blocks from I-205 in Oregon City, the Abernethy Center is conveniently located for the Portland area. The Center offers over 125 free parking spaces, with plenty of street parking as well.

Indoors or out, we can accommodate your needs and look forward to meeting with you soon.

THE ACADEMY CHAPEL & BALLROOM

400 E. Evergreen Boulevard
Vancouver, Washington 98660
Windsor Wedding Consultants, Suite 216
(360) 696-4884
Web site: www.the-academy.net
Business Hours: Tues–Fri 10am–5pm;
evenings by appointment

Capacity: up to 225 guests, ceremony; up to 300 guests, reception
Price Range: beginning at $350 and up for chapel, and $900 and up for ballroom
Catering: no in-house catering; full kitchen facility available
Types of Events: sit-down, buffet, hors d'oeuvres, cake and punch

Availability and Terms

The Academy has a ballroom and a chapel. The ballroom's maximum capacity is 300 people; prices start at $900 for weekday rental. The chapel will hold a maximum of 225 people; $350 fee for weekdays. A deposit is required, and advance reservation of two to six months is recommended.

Description of Facility and Services

Seating: tables and chairs provided
Servers: provided by your caterer or yourself
Bar facilities: portable bar available in ballroom; you provide bartenders, liquor and liability
Dance floor: 17'x26' dance floor in ballroom
Linens and napkins: can be rented on location
China and glassware: not available from the Academy
Cleanup: included in price
Decorations: inquire about our table decorations
Parking: free parking for 400 cars
ADA: yes

BREATHTAKINGLY BEAUTIFUL

Located in the historic Academy building in Vancouver, Washington, the Academy Chapel features a breathtaking, three-story-high carved altar, beautiful stained-glass windows, and a lovely balcony at the rear of the chapel—perfect for a soloist. The grand ballroom is decorated with elegant wallpaper, chandeliers, and blue-gray carpet. The Academy is only 15 minutes from downtown Portland and is easy to find, with ample free parking. Give Windsor Weddings a call today to tour our facility.

The ACADIAN *Ballroom*

1829 N.E. Alberta Street, Portland, Oregon 97211
503.546.6800, 360.258.7533; Fax 503.231.7728
E-mail: events@theacadianballroom.com; Web site: www.theacadianballroom.com

Capacity: luxury, butlered dining for up to 400; stand-up receptions for up to 600
Price Range: our complete wedding packages start at $23 per guest and the room rental
fee can be waived with a minimum food and beverage purchase
Catering: full service, in-house catering provided
Types of Events: we specialize in formal wedding buffets, butlered dinners and elegant
evening cocktail receptions

Availability and Terms
Reception dates are booked and prices are secured with a 30% deposit. Proposals are valid for
30 days.

Description of Facility and Services
Seating: all of your furniture requirements are included with the ballroom booking
Servers: professionally trained butlers, bartenders and doormen included with receptions
Bar facilities: full service club-style bar with star-like halogen lighting, stainless steel accents
and velvety midnight blue walls and ceiling
Dance floor: our hardwood polished mahogany ballroom floor is perfect for dancing
Linens: fine starched linens included with all packages
China and glassware: bone china, luxury stemware and goldware included
Decorations: candles, marble centerpieces and coordinated color accents are featured with
every package; the buffet island created with large palms, Brazilian granite and tapestry is
fashioned to your special colors and theme; your personal Event Manager will help you
coordinate all of your decorating needs.
Parking: on-site, free parking
ADA: fully accessible

HISTORIC PALLADIAN BALLROOM
In the heart of the Alberta Art District, The ACADIAN Ballroom is a beautifully restored
1925 formal ballroom with a modern club twist. With hand finished mahogany floors, 18-ft.
barrel vaulted ceilings, starlight bar and Carrara marble pillars, The ACADIAN Ballroom is
specially designed for your elegant wedding reception.

The Adrianna Hill Grand Ballroom

An Enchanting Place of Celebration

918 S.W. Yamhill • Second Floor • Portland, Oregon 97205
Philip Sword (503) 227-6285, (503) 227-4061 • Shown by appointment only
E-mail: accentevnt@aol.com; Web site: www.adriannaballroom.com

Capacity: up to 300 guests
Price Range: fully inclusive wedding and reception packages, charges vary
Catering: in-house catering and beverage service only
Types of Events: wedding ceremonies and receptions, corporate and private celebrations, concerts, dances, fundraisers, reunions, holiday parties, proms, auctions, movie and commercial shoots and more

Availability and Terms
A deposit is required to confirm your date at one of the most unique and sought-after facilities in the Pacific Northwest. Early reservations suggested.

Description of Facility and Services
Packages include Victorian ballroom decor, all tables and chairs, dressing room for bride and bridesmaids, Roman columns, gold candleabras, ambient lighting, gift and guest book tables and coat racks.
Coordination: all packages include bridal consultation and wedding planning
Event staff: included in costs
Bar facilities: full bar services provided in-house (host, no-host or combination)
Dance floor: hardwood floors perfect for dancing; bands and DJs welcome
Silverware, china, glassware and linens: included in costs
Cleanup: included in costs
Parking: across the street at 10th Avenue and Yamhill Street—City Center Smart Park

VICTORIAN GRAND BALLROOM
The Adrianna Hill Grand Ballroom is an elegant 8,000-square-foot Victorian ballroom with a beautiful restored hardwood floor, suspended "U" shaped balcony, 55 foot-long stage backed by a high cathedral-style wall, large ornate brass chandeliers and 35-foot high beamed and vaulted ceiling. Built in 1901, this storybook setting with distinctive architecture has been recently refurbished. Elaborate Old World designs along the sculpted balcony are highlighted by white lights and tulle. Large gold framed mirrors, elegant artwork, antique-style foyer furniture, statuary, specialty lighting and decorative floral further enhance this unique setting. No additional decoration needed. We are proud to offer you a treasured and unforgettable experience in this nonsmoking environment.

"So Cinderella, Are You Going To The Ball?"

9901 N.E. Seventh Avenue, Building C
Vancouver, Washington 98685
Contact: Cheryl Taylor (360) 574-7124; Fax (360) 574-2936
Business Hours: 8:30am–4:30pm

Capacity: Aero Club Banquet Room: 1,900 sq. ft.; 100 with tables
Catering: available through three on-site restaurants or you may provide your own caterer
Price Range: Friday–Saturday, $425; Sunday–Thursday, $250
Types of Events: wedding receptions, anniversaries, reunions, birthdays, parties, business meetings and other group events

Availability and Terms
A $125 rental deposit and signed rental agreement reserves your date. Full payment is due three weeks prior to your reservation date.

Description of Facility and Services
Seating: 100 with tables and chairs
Servers: not provided, self serve coffee is provided to clients
Bar facilities: user provides liquor license; $10 fee
Dance floor: 1,200 sq.ft. hardwood dance floor; electrical available
Decoration limitations: little or no decoration needed; the Aero Club is tastefully decorated in nostalgic/romantic 1940s aviation theme; please discuss decoration with our staff; early decoration is usually available.
Audiovisual: overhead projector, TV/VCR, CD player and speakers
Cleanup: caterer or client to provide; must be left clean to receive deposit refund
ADA: limited; must ascend one flight of stairs to access the Aero Club
Parking: ample free parking available, one block west of I-5

Special Services
We have three on-site restaurants that cater directly to the Aero Club. Bortolami's Pizzeria offers gourmet and traditional homemade, hand-tossed pizza, soups, salads and a variety of soft drinks (360) 574-2598. Clancy's Family Restaurant offers a full service menu including burgers, fish and chips, soups, Mexican food, desserts and more (360) 573-3474. Primo's offers a variety of sub sandwiches, party platters, salads and desserts (360) 574-0501.

WE'VE GOT THE "WRIGHT" STUFF
Conveniently located one block west of I-5 at the 99th street exit in Vancouver, the Aero Club is Vancouver's best kept secret for your wedding reception or other group event. Affordable, flexible, cozy and tastefully decorated in a nostalgic/romantic 1940s aviation theme. The Aero Club includes tables, chairs, serving counter, a hardwood dance floor, kitchenette and coffee. You can bring your own caterer, do it yourself or have one of our three on-site restaurants cater your event. We're only 10–15 minutes from downtown Portland. Call Cheryl for a tour or for more information (360) 574-7124.

Albertina's

The Shops at Albertina Kerr

424 N.E. 22nd Avenue
Portland, Oregon 97232
503.231.3909
www.albertinakerr.org

Capacity: up to 200 for receptions; 90 for formal dinners
Price Range: varies according to event and menu; please call for information
Catering: full service, in-house catering
Types of Events: weddings and receptions, anniversaries, retirement parties, birthdays, family reunions, holiday functions, rehearsal dinners, business meetings, showers, brunches, luncheons, hors d'oeuvres and formal dinners.

Availability and Terms
Albertina's offers four beautifully appointed rooms and two garden patios that can accommodate up to 200 guests in the summer and 150 guests in the winter. We suggest you reserve early to ensure availability. A $500 deposit will secure your date. Let our catering coordinator help plan your special day. Call 503-231-3909 for an appointment.

Description of Facility and Services
Servers: all servers, hostess/host are provided by Albertina's
Bar facilities: champagne, wine, beer service; bartenders and servers provided
Dance floor: dance floor available upon request; ample electrical hookups
Linens: cloth tablecloths and skirting for service tables and paper napkins included for receptions; individual tablecloths and cloth napkins included with formal sit down events
China, glassware and silver service: provided by Albertina's
Decorations: beautiful fresh floral arrangements, including service tables, fireplace mantels and more, in colors of your choice, are provided; please discuss your decorating ideas with Albertina's catering coordinator
Cleanup: provided
Parking: on-site parking as well as free street parking
ADA: fully accessible

CHARMING HISTORIC SETTING FOR ALL SPECIAL OCCASIONS
Listed on the National Register of Historic Places and a Portland landmark, the stately, three story Georgian-style Old Kerr Nursery, is conveniently located barely a mile from downtown Portland. Renovated in 1981and refurbished in 2001, the Nursery is equally beautiful inside and out. The charming, home-like building and garden patios are the perfect setting for your special occasion. Experience the history of the Nursery building and the gracious attention to detail provided by Albertina's dedicated volunteer staff. Albertina's, one of The Shops at Albertina Kerr, is operated as a nonprofit business with all proceeds donated to Albertina Kerr Centers, whose programs provide services for children and youth at risk, families in need and individuals with disabilities.

Romantic Mansion located on
two wooded acres overlooking the Willamette River

Amadeus
at the FERNWOOD
2122 S.E. Sparrow (Off N. River Road Exit)
Milwaukie, Oregon 97222
Contact: Kristina (503) 659-1735, (503) 636-6154
Business Hours: Tue–Sun; Open at 5pm for dinner
Sunday Brunch 10am–2pm
cpoppmeier@msn.com • amadeus.citysearch.com

Capacity: 300 people

Price Range: full course sit-down dinners or buffet style $40 Friday or Sunday, $40 Saturday during the day, $50 Saturday evening; plus 18% gratuity all days. Weddings are also available at the Lake Oswego location, same prices!
Business lunches: $20 plus 18% gratuity; business dinners: $30 plus 18% gratuity.

Catering: full-service in-house and off location catering

Types of Events: individual rooms for conferences, seminars, private meetings, large group luncheons, holiday parties, celebration dinners; from small intimate events up to 300, weddings and rehearsal dinners

Availability and Terms

Reservations should be made as soon as possible to ensure availability. A deposit is required at the time of booking. Half the deposit is refundable if cancellations are made at least nine months prior to your event. **No** cost for using the facility, bartending services, linens, flowers, and candles, valet parking and classic piano.

Description of Facility and Services

Seating: table and chairs provided for up to 300
Servers: provided with catering services
Bar facilities: full-service bar with bartender provided; host/no host; liquor provided according to OLCC regulations
Dance floor: available
Linens: cloth tablecloths and napkins provided in cream color
China and glassware: fine china and glassware
Cleanup: provided by Amadeus at the Fernwood
Decorations: early decorating available; fresh flowers for guest tables provided by Amadeus; please discuss ideas with Kristina
Parking: ample free parking; valet service; **ADA:** disabled access available

ROMANCE OVERLOOKING THE WILLAMETTE RIVER

Amadeus at the Fernwood is the perfect setting for an annual, monthly or quarterly function; or dinner for two. You and your guests will enjoy fine continental dining in a wonderful old mansion on two wooded acres, filled with antiques, fireplaces, crystal chandeliers, candlelight and fresh flowers, overlooking the Willamette River. We offer a full bar with a wide variety of Oregon and international wines, outdoor dining and wedding ceremonies on our patio is available. Three hours of piano music is also included. **SUNSET DINNER SPECIAL:** Tue–Sun • 5–6:30pm • $9.95

Please let this business know that you heard about them from the Bravo! Wedding Resource Guide. **65**

Ambridge Event Center

formerly the Portland Conference Cener
300 N.E. Multnomah Street
Portland, Oregon 97232
Web site: www.portlandcc.com
Contact: Event Coordinator (503) 239-9921
Business Hours: Mon–Fri 8am–5pm

"Celebrate Your Special Occasion With Us!"

Capacity: Twelve private rooms including our Ambridge Rose Ballroom; we can accommodate group sizes from seven guests conference-style, to 1,000 guests in a standing reception.

Price Range: Various packages available; please call for specific information.

Location: We are conveniently located in the Lloyd District, just north of the Oregon Convention Center and east of the Rose Quarter.

Catering: Full in-house service; off-site catering available.

Types of Events: Ceremonies, wedding receptions, rehearsal dinners, bridal showers and bachelor parties.

Availability and Terms

To ensure your special date in our Ambridge Ballroom, or smaller Morrison and Marquam Rooms, we recommend making your reservation as early as possible; one year is suggested. Use our on-line reservation system to inquire about available space. You may confirm an afternoon or evening reception with a $500 deposit.

Description of Facility and Services

Seating: tables and chairs provided

Servers: provided in formal attire

Bar facilities: full-service professional bar

Dance floor: original hardwood dance floor in our Abridge Rose Ballroom and portable parquet dance floor available; electrical hook-ups for a band or DJ

Linens and napkins: full array of tablecloths and napkins ranging from linen, cloth or paper

China and glassware: white china and glassware provided with catering

Cleanup: included in catering

Decorations: we provide decorations, table décor and centerpieces, handcrafted bows in your wedding colors, fresh flowers and ice sculptures available

Special services: we provide extensive decorating, wedding consulting, in-house catering, custom designed wedding cake and above all we offer you personalized service to help you through your special day

Parking: ample parking for clients, plus MAX lightrail stops at our door

ADA: main and mall-levels fully comply

"Your Event is as Important to Us as it is to You."

Whether you are planning a small simple gathering or a large elegant affair, you can rest assured that you will receive all the attention you deserve.

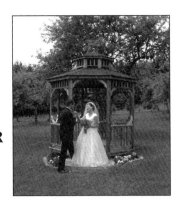

ANDERSON LODGE RETREAT CENTER

Home Office: 18410 N.E. 399th Street
Amboy, Washington 98601
(360) 247-6660; www.andersonlodge.com

Capacity: 100 indoors, 200+ outdoors
Price Range: starting at $530; rates vary with size and time use
Catering: receptions with country charm, buffets, barbecues, sit-down meals; in-house catering encouraged; a 20% fee will be charged for outside caterers for receptions
Types of Events: weddings, receptions, anniversaries, reunions, celebrations of all kinds

Availability and Terms

Reservations required as soon as possible for summer events. Deposit is due upon booking, with final deposit due 60 days in advance. Deposits are nonrefundable. Visitations by appointment only.

Description of Facility and Services

Seating: number of chairs and tables provided vary with facility
Servers: arranged through our catering service
Bar facilities: Washington state liquor permit required
Dance floor: conference rooms are fully carpeted; electrical outlets available
Linens and china: limited numbers of dinnerware and glassware available; tablecloths must be rented from an outside source
Decorations: please inquire; no tape, tacks or nails
Cleanup: renter is responsible to remove all decorations and supplies; renter may choose to completely clean the facility or a fee will be charged if renter wishes our staff to clean
Parking: ample parking available on site
ADA: limited access

SCANDINAVIAN LODGE IN FOREST SETTING

Weddings and wedding receptions that take place at Anderson Lodge truly are unique and unforgettable. The usual concept of a wedding and reception is limited to an afternoon. Family and friends stay at local motels and gather only for the ceremony and reception. However, weddings at Anderson Lodge take place over a day or several days. Anderson Lodge offers lodging and a wedding/reception site all in one, allowing your family and friends to be more a part of this wonderful event.

Guests appreciate the homey atmosphere complete with hot tubs, saunas and recreation. Nestled in the heart of luxurious forest land, just one hour from Portland, is a charming lodge offering a perfect site for an indoor or outdoor wedding and reception. We rent to one group at a time, providing the entire facility for your celebration. Our spacious covered picnic area, picturesque gazebo and scenic view of the valley provide a memorable setting for outdoor celebrations. In the event of chilly weather, the grand conference rooms are available for your use. Our quaint Swedish cottage with hot tub is perfect for the happy couple. You owe it to yourself to make your wedding a truly momentous occasion. Check us out on the Web at www.andersonlodge.com.

Please let this business know that you heard about them from the Bravo! Wedding Resource Guide.   **67**

Arnegards

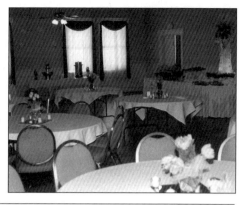

Ninth and Hawthorne
1510 S.E. Ninth • Portland, Oregon 97214
Contact: Event Coordinator
(503) 236-2759; Fax (503) 231-8837
After-hour and weekend
appointments available

Capacity: our entire facility can accommodate up to 450 people; we have two ballrooms and a meeting room available

Price Range: Ballroom rental rates $900 to $1,500; discounts available Monday–Thursday

Catering: catering is supplied by renter, or you may choose from our list of caterers

Types of Events: wedding ceremonies and receptions, rehearsal dinners, private parties, cocktail parties, luncheons, dinners, banquets, dances, holiday parties, retirement parties, meetings, all-day seminars, corporate parties, and any other event imaginable

Availability and Terms

Please reserve rooms as early as possible. Short notice reservations depend on availability. A 50% deposit is due at time of booking with the balance and security deposit due one month prior to event.

Description of Facility and Services

Seating: round tables and chairs; provided up to 240; banquet tables, guest book table, and cake table included

Servers: provided by caterer

Bar facilities: provided by caterer or renter; bar located off The Winnington Ballroom

Dance floor: large dance floor available; capacity: 300+, electrical: supplied

Linens: provided by caterer or client

China: provided by caterer or client

Decoration limitations: establishment is well decorated; we are flexible to your needs; no tape, tacks, or nails on walls; no rice, birdseed or plastic confetti; please consult Event Coordinator prior to decorating

Cleanup: renter or caterer is responsible for cleanup; security deposit required

Parking: some off-street parking available; plenty of street parking

Special Services

We have a large stage available.

NEWLY RESTORED
1920s BALLROOM AND CONFERENCE ROOM

Our newly renovated 1920s ballroom has been open and available to rent since December 1998. We are located conveniently in Southeast Portland. Have your next event in any of our three rooms: *The Winnington Ballroom:* This maple hardwood-floored ballroom has a stage, 14-foot high ceilings, chandeliers, lighted ceiling fans and great acoustics. It can accommodate up to 320 people. *The Grace Ballroom:* This oak hardwood-floored ballroom is perfect for wedding ceremonies, company functions, holiday parties, banquets or receptions and can accommodate up to 100 people. *The Meeting Room:* Can accommodate up to 20.

THE ATRIUM

100 S.W. Market Street
Portland, Oregon 97201
Contact: Catering Director
(503) 220-3928
www.theatriumcafe.net
Business Hours: please call
for an appointment

Capacity: up to 300
Price Range: $20-$30 per person
Catering: The Atrium provides all catering services tailored to your special day.
Types of Events: hors d'oeuvres, dinner buffet, sit-down service

Availability and Terms

Our magnificent two-story glass building and convenient location one block from Naito Parkway in the heart of downtown Portland make The Atrium a popular facility for wedding receptions and other special events. To ensure reserving the date you want, plan to make your reservations six months to a year in advance. The $600 room-rental fee is required at the time of booking and is also considered the deposit for your event.

The $600 Rental Fee Includes:

Seating: tables and chairs for 300
Servers: full wait staff (four per 100 people)
Bar facilities: all bartenders, servers
Dance floor: 100-person
Linens and napkins: linen, cloth napkins and tablecloths in assorted colors; included in room rental
China and glassware: provided
Setup and cleanup: included
Decorations: bring your own and we can help decorate free of charge
Parking: ample **free** parking
ADA: yes

GET THE FEELING OF BEING OUTDOORS
YEAR-AROUND IN OUR MAGNIFICENT
TWO-STORY GLASS STRUCTURE

The Atrium's unique structure offers a beautiful setting. Its two-story windows and lush greenery as well as the glass-covered roof along with the back patio in a beautiful parklike setting will have a profound impact on all its guests. The Atrium is easily accessible on the corner of First and Market, one block from the Marriott Hotel and Front Street, and only three blocks from the RiverPlace Hotel. Please call our Catering Director at (503) 220-3928 for information or reservations.

Please let this business know that you heard about them from the Bravo! Wedding Resource Guide. **69**

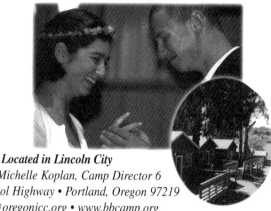

Located in Lincoln City
Contact: Michelle Koplan, Camp Director 6
651 SW Capitol Highway • Portland, Oregon 97219
bbcamp@oregonjcc.org • www.bbcamp.org
Phone: 503.452.3444 • Fax: 503.245.4233

Capacity: Up to 250 indoors; 500+ outdoors

Price Range: Various packages available; starting at $500 for entire day or starting at $20 per person overnight fee; please call for information

Catering: In-house catering available or fully equipped kitchen available to rent for your own caterer; Kosher cooking facilities also available upon request

Types of Events: Weddings and receptions, rehearsal dinners, engagement parties, showers, picnics, reunions, anniversaries, retreats, meetings, conferences, and more

Availability and Terms:

Available for rental mid-August through mid-June for day, overnight, weekend, or weeklong events. We recommend making your reservation early; however, we welcome short notice events depending on availability. A non-refundable deposit, certificate of liability, and signed rental agreement are required to secure your date.

Description of Facility and Services:

Seating: Tables and chairs are provided; seating indoors up to 250

Servers: Staff available for additional fee or provided by client

Bar facilities: Available for additional fee or provided by client

Dance floor: Hardwood floors perfect for dancing; Bands and DJ's welcome

Linens: Available for additional fee or provided by client

China and glassware: Available for additional fee or provided by client

Cleanup: Client to provide; must be left clean and damage-free to receive deposit refund

Decorations: Provided by client

Parking: Free parking on-site, up to 50 cars

ADA: Accessibility to most buildings and program areas

A Beautiful Place to Gather on our Lakeside Campus

B'nai B'rith Camp offers a uniquely beautiful setting for your wedding and reception. Nestled on beautiful Devil's Lake near Lincoln City, B.B. Camp is only 2 hours from Portland and only minutes from the untamed beauty of the Oregon coast. Our buildings and scenic grounds provide for the perfect spot to make your special day the most romantic and memorable day of your lives. Overnight accommodations are available in our beautiful lakefront Executive House, which is ideal for enjoying the coziness with family and friends. This elegant four bedroom, three bath home sleeps up to 10 people, with a private kitchen and dock. Also available are our many heated cabins. *Facilities include:* Reception Hall, Outdoor Amphitheater, Library, Indoor Stage, Meeting Rooms, Ropes Challenge Courses, Tennis Courts, Softball Field, Sand Volleyball Court, Gym, Game Room, Heated Swimming Pool & Hot-tub, and Canoeing. Whatever your vision, at B'nai B'rith Camp: It's possible! We look forward to working with you to make your special day the most memorable and amazing day of your life!

Ballroom *Parkrose*

4848 N.E. 105th Avenue • Portland, Oregon
503-254-1920

Capacity: 150 guests
Price Range: $750 - $1,200
Catering: Your choice of caterer; or we have several we can recommend
Types of Events: Wedding receptions, dances, reunions, parties

Availability and Terms
Weekend rental, reservations recommended as early as possible. Deposit required.

Description of Facilities and Services
Dance Floor: 2,500 square foot dance floor
Seating: chairs provided for 100 guests; serving tables, side tables; we can recommend rental service companies for a more extensive selection
Servers: provided by caterer
Bar Facilities: provided by caterer or client to provide bartender, liquor, and liability
Linens/Tableware: We have a limited selection of linens, china and glassware
Cleanup: Deposit required; fully refundable with cleanup
Parking: Ample free street parking available, and a nearby lot.
ADA: No

Our Big, Beautiful, historic ballroom was originally built in 1941 as a USO hall for the army. Since then, it has served time as a church, a gym, and a hardware store. Now, it has been lovingly restored, and is open again for dancing as it was always meant to be. The facility encompasses over 4,000 square feet, and includes a Ballroom of over 2500 square feet, Men's and Ladies' lounges/dressing rooms, and a food prep area for the caterers.
WE'RE VERY EASY TO GET TO FROM JUST ABOUT ANYWHERE! Right off of I-205 - JUST ONE EXIT SOUTH OF THE AIRPORT. From I-205, take the Sandy Blvd. EAST exit, and go four blocks to 105th Ave. The big tan building fronts onto Sandy Blvd., but our entrance is on 105th.

Please contact Dave Watson or Jo Ellen Jarvis at 503-318-7048 or 360-750-9366 or email jojarvis@pacifier.com.

300 Reuben Boise Road • Dallas, Oregon 97338
(503) 831-3652
Web site: www.beckenridge.com
Call for an appointment

Capacity: indoor table seating for up to 150, and up to 250 if patios or grounds are used; ceremony seating for 120 indoors or on patios, and 250+ on lawn

Price Range: various prices available starting at $1,600; rental is for entire day and includes many extras

Catering: fully equipped kitchen available to your caterer of choice

Types of Events: weddings, receptions, reunions, business meetings and training sessions

Availability and Terms

Open year round; call for appointment to visit. Reservations held with a 50% deposit; balance due 60 days prior to event.

Description of Facility and Services

Seating: five-foot round tables and comfortable, attractive chairs to accommodate 150; accessory tables of various sizes are also included in rental fee

Servers: provided by caterer

Bar facilities: nice selection of wines from Airlie Winery, beer, champagne, and non-alcoholic beverages available; setup and glassware included

Dance floor: hardwood floor throughout great for dancing; built-in stereo sound system

Linens: ivory and white tablecloths available on site for rent

China and glassware: provided by caterer or client

Decorations: stone platform and hand crafted metal arch on lawn, trellised arch for patio or indoors – all available at no extra charge

Cleanup: we provide setup and cleanup of our furnishings; client to setup and remove rental equipment; caterer responsible for cleanup of kitchen and food-related items

Parking: ample parking available on site

ADA: fully equipped and accessible to accommodate ADA requirements

Special Services

BeckenRidge Vineyard is designed for private events and includes a stone fireplace, grand piano, a private dressing room for the bride, and a large covered patio.

CELEBRATE YOUR SPECIAL OCCASION
NESTLED IN THE BEAUTY OF THE VINEYARD

Combine the serene country setting of an outdoor ceremony and the comfort of an indoor reception with our facility specifically designed for weddings, receptions and special occasions. BeckenRidge has a warm, friendly atmosphere with a commanding view of the Willamette Valley. Special features include a lawn area with platform and arch, and a vineyard patio. Since there is no public access to the property, you are assured your event will be private. Our personal attention will help you create a memorable event for you and your special guests.

309 S.W. Broadway at Oak Street
Portland, Oregon 97205
(503) 295-4140; Fax (503) 471-3921
Office Hours: Mon–Fri 8am–6pm
Available other times by appointment
E-mail: sales@bensonhotel.com
Web site: www.bensonhotel.com

Capacity: seated dining for up to 400 guests; stand-up reception for up to 600 guests
Price Range: brunch and luncheon receptions starting at $25 per person; evening receptions starting at $30 per person
Catering: full-service in-house catering; preferred caterer for the Portland Art Museum
Types of Events: sit-down, buffet, hors d'oeuvre receptions, rehearsal dinners, brunch and luncheons

Availability and Terms

We are able to book your wedding date one year in advance. A nonrefundable deposit of 20% is required to make your booking definite. Full payment is due one week prior to your event. We encourage you to call as soon as possible to secure your desired date.

Description of Facility and Services

Seating: chairs provided; round tables seating 4 to 10 guests are provided
Servers: all servers and support staff included at no charge
Bar facilities: full-service bar; we provide all bartenders, servers and beverages
Dance floor: provided in a variety of sizes at no additional charge
Linens and napkins: fine linens and napkins provided at no additional charge
China and glassware: fine china, glassware and silver provided
Parking: ample parking available, rates vary; valet available upon request
ADA: handicap accessibility and facilities in all areas

PORTLAND'S GRAND HOTEL

Begin your reception with cocktails in front of the fireplace and experience the old-world charm of our grand lobby. Then move into the Crystal Ballroom to celebrate your first dance under crystal chandeliers. The Mayfair Ballroom is found at the top of our grand staircase, on the mezzanine, and is the perfect setting for larger wedding groups with a built-in stage showcasing a baby grand piano. The mirror on the staircase landing was made in Paris in 1883 and was designed for the ballroom of the Castle Mansion on the slopes of Diamond Head in Honolulu; it has been with The Benson since 1958 and remains a photography favorite. For more intimate weddings and a view of Broadway, enjoy the classic Cambridge Room. Complete your event with a romantic night with our Honeymoon package.

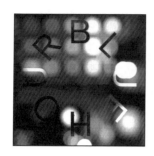

bluehour
250 Northwest Thirteenth Avenue at Everett Street

l'heure bleue
1220 Northwest Everett Street
Portland, Oregon 97209
Contact: Kari Giambalvo or Bruce Carey
503-226-3394   fax 503-221-3005
kari@bluehouronline.com   bluehouronline.com

Capacity:	**L'Heure Bleue:** 60 seated, 100 cocktail
	Bluehour Dining Room: 160 seated, 200 cocktail
Catering:	Exclusively Bluehour
Price Range:	**L'Heure Bleue:**
	$1,500 room minimum food and beverage
	Bluehour Dining Room:
	$10,000 room minimum food and beverage Sunday and Monday only

Description of Facility and Services

Seating:	Tables and chairs provided; custom layout as requested
Servers:	Professional dining room staff
Bar facilities:	Custom bar menu, specialty house cocktails
Linens and napkins:	Bluehour dining room settings
China and glassware:	Bluehour dining room settings
Music:	In-house staff of DJs or outside DJ
Floral:	Customized floral on request or outside florist
Parking:	Complimentary valet parking, street parking available
ADA:	Yes

Availability and Terms

L'Heure Bleue is available seven days a week for both day and evening events. The Bluehour dining room is available Sunday and Monday only. Payment is due the day or evening of your event.

BLUEHOUR EVENTS

For private dinners and events, Bluehour and L'Heure Bleue offer guests unmatched service and style in a unique, urban setting. Specially designed by owner Bruce Carey, both rooms function as the perfect venue for a sit-down dinner or a festive cocktail gathering. Every event is treated with great detail and can be customized as much as a guest needs.

Simple, delicious and classic describes the Mediterranean cuisine executive chef Kenny Giambalvo creates for the restaurant. Items are subject to seasonal availability and the chef's preferences. This focus on food ensures that each dish is intrinsically flavorful. The chef is happy to design the ideal menu for any party.

Shown by appointment.

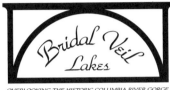

OVERLOOKING THE HISTORIC COLUMBIA RIVER GORGE

P.O. Box 5
Bridal Veil, Oregon 97010
Contact: Jennifer Miller (503) 981-3695
Web site: www.bridalveillakes.com
Shown by Appointment

Capacity: 400 outdoor
Price Range: price varies according to event
Catering: renter may select caterer of choice
Types of Events: picnics, reunions, anniversaries, weddings and receptions

Availability and Terms

Reservations are recommended one year in advance, and are confirmed with a $500 deposit. We only schedule one event per day. Months of operation are May through October; please inquire for off-season pricing.

Description of Facility and Services

Seating: tables and chairs provided for 200
Servers: provided by caterer
Bar facilities: caterer or renter provides licensed bartender, liquor, and liability insurance
Linens: provided by caterer
China and glassware: provided by caterer
Dance floor: 800 sq. ft. available in pavilion, or 800 sq. ft. covered outdoor patio available for dancing
Decorations: no rice, paper or metallic confetti
Cleanup: renter/caterer is responsible for leaving grounds as found
Other services: arch for ceremony is provided; four canoes and a number of RV spaces available
Parking: ample parking available; parking attendants strongly suggested
ADA: accessible

NATURAL BEAUTY IN ITS MOST SPECTACULAR FORM

Nestled in the heart of the historic Columbia River Gorge, just 30 minutes east of Portland, natural beauty is in its' most spectacular form at Bridal Veil Lakes. Beautiful wildflowers and lush forest are the perfect backdrop for your lakeside wedding. The view of the Columbia River Gorge and the serene lakeside setting add just the hint of romance that will make your wedding memories last a lifetime. The photo opportunities are endless! Bridal Veil Lakes recreational area is protected from the Columbia Gorge east wind and our Lakeside Pavilion is wonderful for weather protection. Please call and make an appointment to visit our exclusive and private setting for the wedding of your dreams.

BRIDGEPORT BREWING COMPANY

1313 N.W. Marshall Street • Portland, Oregon 97209
Contact: Manager of Special Events (503) 241-7179 ext. 210; Fax (503) 241-0625
Hours: Mon–Thurs 11:30am–11pm; Fri–Sat 11:30am–midnight; Sun 1pm–9pm
Web site: www.bridgeportbrew.com

Capacity: Heritage Room up to 220; Blue Heron Room up to 30
Price Range: varies depending on group size, time and day of event
Catering: casual menu including assorted appetizers, hand-crafted pizzas and fresh salads
Types of Events: wedding ceremonies and receptions, rehearsals, showers, and engagement celebrations; great for both daytime and evening events

Availability and Terms

BridgePort Brew Pub has two unique rooms available every day of the week for private functions. Our Blue Heron conference room accommodates up to 30 people; our Heritage banquet room accommodates up to 220 people. We suggest that you reserve early to ensure availability. An advance deposit is required to hold your reservation, and is applied toward your room rental. The balance for an event is due at the conclusion of the function.

Description of Facility and Services

Seating: tables and chairs provided for your group; arranged as requested
Servers: friendly, professional staff included
Bar facilities: serving up to six handcrafted ales ranging from our bright and hoppy India Pale Ale to our Heritage Blue Heron Ale; local wines, juice, sodas, fine coffee and teas are also available
Dance floor: accommodates DJ or band setup; electrical outlets available
Linens and napkins: napkins provided; linen can be arranged upon guest request
China and glassware: china provided by client; glassware provided by BridgePort
Decorations: please discuss decorating ideas with the Manager of Special Events; early access available with prior arrangement
Cleanup: included in room rental
Parking: limited street parking; complimentary evening parking offered in lot across street; daytime parking can be arranged upon request
ADA: yes, within the limitations of a historic building; elevator accessible

HISTORIC LOCATION—RELAXED ATMOSPHERE

BridgePort is Oregon's oldest Craft Brewery, located in Portland's historic Pearl District. Exposed brick and timber beams, combined with the fresh aroma of microbrewed ales and homemade pizza, create a cozy pub atmosphere. All of our ales are handcrafted; our kitchen adheres to the same standard of quality that made our beers regionally famous. Uniquely Northwest, BridgePort (an entirely nonsmoking brewpub) is comfortable for meetings, social gatherings, and weddings. View or tour the brewery to see how the famous BridgePort Ales are made.

The Historic
𝔅𝔯𝔬𝔢𝔱𝔧𝔢 𝔥𝔬𝔲𝔰𝔢

3101 S.E. Courtney
Milwaukie, Oregon 97222
Contact: Lorraine or Lois
(503) 659-8860
Web site: www.broetjehouse.citysearch.com
www.sayIdo.com
Business Hours: Mon–Fri 10am–4pm;
weekends by appointment

Capacity: 150 inside or outside
Price Range: $150 to $7,500; please call for specific price information
Catering: in-house catering only
Types of Events: sit-down, buffet, garden, cocktails and hors d'oeuvres, cake and punch

Availability and Terms
Rental hours are: Sunday through Friday, 8am to 9pm; Saturday, 9am to 2:30pm with 11am ceremony, or 3:30pm to 9pm with a 5pm ceremony. A one-third deposit is required on booking.

Description of Facility and Services
Seating: tables and chairs for 150
Servers: provided as needed during the event
Bar facilities: we provide beer, wine, champagne, bartender and liquor liability
Dance floor: yes
Linens and napkins: linen or cloth in many colors for an added charge
China and glassware: variety of china and wine/champagne glassware
Cleanup: included in package price
Decorations: special arrangements must be made for early decorating
Parking: plenty of free parking space; valet parking also available
ADA: yes

Special Services
Our in-house catering, use of our serviceware, china, glass stemware, coffee pots, punch bowls and ladles, serving dishes, chafing dishes and silverware are provided with the package price. You'll also find lovely honeymoon suites and rooms available for changing or an overnight stay.

ENJOY TURN-OF-THE-CENTURY ROMANTIC AMBIANCE
Enjoy the romantic ambiance offered by this magnificent, turn-of-the-century, Queen Anne–style bed and breakfast. Built in 1890 by John F. Broetje, the house features a unique four-story, 50-foot-high water tower. Over an acre of picturesque grounds with a gazebo grace this elegant estate, making it an ideal setting for your wedding and reception! Each event is specially designed to meet the needs of the bride and groom.

Camp Colton

The Chapel at Camp Colton

30000 S. Camp Colton Drive
Colton, Oregon 97017
Contact: Mary, Jarred or Kathy Lundstrom
(503) 824-2267; Fax (503) 824-5779
www.campcolton.com
Business Hours: Please call for an appointment

Capacity: up to 250 guests for ceremony or reception; 200 guests for seated indoor reception

Price Range: varies according to package; $1,500 to $8,200

Catering: renter chooses caterer from our preferred list

Types of Events: weddings, receptions, retreats, seminars and meetings

Availability and Terms

The Chapel at Camp Colton is available year round. Reserve as early as possible; we recommend six months to a year in advance. An $800 non-refundable deposit will hold your date, with the remainder due one month prior to your event.

Description of Facility and Services

Seating: tables and chairs provided for your group, arranged to make your event most attractive

Servers: provided by caterer

Bar facilities: antique bars in reception area; beer, wine and champagne are permitted; caterer or renter provides alcohol; we provide OLCC bartender(s)

Dance floor: indoor or outdoor 16'x16' dance floor with electrical hook-ups for DJs and bands

Linens, china and glassware: provided

Cleanup: set up and break down included

Decorations: this delightfully rustic chapel requires little decoration; reception centerpiece decorations available for rent

Parking: ample, convenient parking available

ADA: disabled facilities available, with limitations of historic building

Special Services

Event day coordination provided for wedding and reception.

SIMPLE ELEGANCE IN A BEAUTIFUL COUNTRY SETTING

The Chapel at Camp Colton offers rustic charm and simple elegance for your special day. This unique facility offers year round use, an historic rustic chapel, separate reception site(s) and overnight accommodations. Nestled among tall firs and cedars, lush greenery, beautiful gardens and rushing creeks, the camp is located only 30 miles outside of Portland. The buildings and grounds provide the perfect location for the most romantic and memorable day of your lives. We look forward to making your wedding dreams come true!

See page 313 under Ceremony Sites.

12353 S.E. Lusted Road • Sandy, Oregon 97055
Contact: Keri (503) 663-0772; Fax (503) 668-8371
Web site: www.cedarspringscountryestate.com
Park is available for viewing by appointment only

Capacity: up to 250 guests
Price range: please inquire
Catering: in-house catering and bar service
Types of Events: day or evening weddings, elegant Victorian or casual country; or with dancing under the stars

Availability and Terms

Cedar Springs Country Estate is available from July 1 through September 30. A $500 nonrefundable deposit reserves your special day. We host only one wedding per day. Saturday noon–6pm or 4–10pm; Sunday 2–8pm.

Description of Facility and Services

Bridal consultant: Keri Baird is on staff to assist you in planning and coordinating all your wedding needs
Seating: tables, linens, and chairs provided for up to 250 guests; amphitheater seating is used for ceremony seating
Servers: provided by caterer
Dance floor: softly lit Victorian gazebo provides a large 350-square-foot dance floor
Linens: white linens provided for guest and banquet tables
China and glassware: disposable products included by caterer; china and glassware available to rent
Cleanup: the staff at Cedar Springs will set up and clean up
Decorations: hanging baskets, pedestals and urns for flowers, plus many other unique items
ADA: limited accessibility

A ROMANTIC COUNTRY WEDDING PARK

As if somewhere in time... At the edge of the forest, this unforgettable place is five miles north of Sandy. If you've been wanting an exciting and different outdoor wedding, this may be just the setting you've dreamed of! A picturesque white Victorian gazebo is the perfect backdrop for the wedding ceremony. A spring-fed trout lake rests placidly at the foot of towering alders and fringed cedars. With seating on the terraced hillside, your guests can view a very intimate and private ceremony. In the evening, the subdued lights, water, trees, and gardens become an enchanted setting.

© Strong Photography

Cherry Hill

located in the Columbia River Gorge National Scenic Area
1550 Carroll Road • Mosier, Oregon 97040
Contact: Elizabeth Toscano (541) 478-4455; cherryhill@gorge.net
Business Hours: By Appointment

Capacity: 200 in the garden; 150 in the barn
Price Range: varies according to type of event
Catering: full-service in-house catering
Types of Events: sit-down, buffets, cocktails and hors d'oeuvres

Availability and Terms
Cherry Hill is available for your private use from June 15 through September 30. A $500 deposit holds your day and is refundable if we can rebook.

Description of Facility and Services
Seating: tables and chairs for up to 200
Servers: service staff provided
Bar facilities: licensed bartender required; beer, wine and liquor permitted
Dance floor: available with electrical outlets
Linens and napkins: included
China and glassware: included
Cleanup: provided by Cherry Hill
Parking: on and off-street parking; **ADA:** limited

Special Services
Cherry Hill looks forward to helping you plan every aspect of your wedding and reception. Our caterer, florist and pastry chef work closely together to ensure that no detail is overlooked and that all is in the best of taste.

COUNTRY GARDEN SETTING
Whether you imagine an intimate wedding or a grand reception, Cherry Hill is the premiere outdoor event site in the Columbia Gorge. Our turn-of-the-century farmhouse is perched on an orchard-covered hillside with panoramic views. Ceremonies take place on the shaded lawn under the spreading limbs of towering Oregon oaks. Receptions are held beneath starry skies or in our classic American red barn. Brides and grooms often choose our Wedding Weekend, including rehearsal and dinner, lodging for bridal party, ceremony and reception, with every detail thoughtfully arranged by the staff at Cherry Hill.

"Toscano's matter-of-factness, combined with an impeccable sense of taste and organization, has helped her to become the Martha Stewart of Gorge weddings."
—*Hood River News*, August 20, 1997

CELEBRATE IN GRAND STYLE!
CLARA'S OWN GRAND OREGON LODGE

Visit our Web site: www.claraswedding.com

You and your guests will be surprised and delighted to step from the sidewalk of today's Oregon City into the grandeur of the early 20th Century.

Capacity: up to 299 indoors

Price Range: call for price schedule

Catering: open to licensed caterers

Types of Events: wedding ceremonies, receptions, banquets, anniversaries, birthdays, school events, seminars, concerts, meetings, holiday parties, and corporate events

Availability and Terms
Available daytime or evenings, Monday through Sunday. A 50% deposit holds your date.

Descriptions of Facility and Services
Seating: all tables and chairs provided

Bar facilities: allowed; call for details

Dance floor: fully restored wood floor vintage ballroom

Billiard room: two 9-ft. antique Brunswick slate pool tables

Linens: available at extra charge

Decorations: available at no additional cost: candelabras, centerpieces, mirror tiles, ring bearer pillow, cake knife and server.

Audiovisual: choose from our DJ list; upright piano and Hammond organ available

Parking: adjacent free city lot and ample street parking

ADA: Stair Glide chairlift and ADA bathrooms

HISTORIC WEDDING AND RECEPTION VENUE
Clara's Own Grand Oregon Lodge, located in the charming Historic District of Oregon CIty, was designed, built, and operated as a private club from 1922 until 1997. Now open to the public, this grand facility has been renovated for elegant weddings, receptions, events and celebrations. Your guests will delight in the palatial room proportions, hotel height ceilings, and architectural details. Dance the night away in the Vintage Ballroom, or play one of the oak-and-leather pool tables in the antique Billiard Room. Our beautiful banquet room makes an excellent food and beverage room with a convenient caterer's kitchen adjoining. These grand rooms flow openly into each other, keeping your party active and lively. Brides often rave that, "My friends and relatives loved having places to go, things to do, and easy ways to meet and mingle with each other…they say it is the best wedding they've ever been to!" Come see what they're talking about.

See page 226 under Bridal Salons and page 381 under Disc Jockeys.

Please let this business know that you heard about them from the Bravo! Wedding Resource Guide. **81**

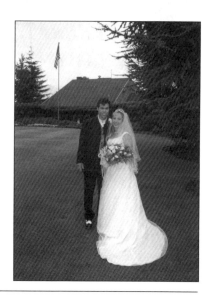

2220 N.E. Marine Drive
Portland, Oregon 97211
Contact: Stephanie Akin (503) 285-3676
Fax (503) 285-3977

Capacity: main dining room 250 to 300 people; other rooms available for smaller events: **Library** 20 to 30 people; **Vista Room** up 50 people

Catering: in-house

Types of Events: anniversaries, cocktail parties, luncheons, holiday parties, dinners, dances, receptions, seminars, buffets, weddings, proms, corporate functions and meetings

Availability and Terms

Please make your reservation as early as possible as dates fill up quickly. A nonrefundable deposit is required.

Description of Facility and Services

Seating: tables and chairs provided
Servers: provided
Bar facilities: full-service bar and bartenders available
Dance floor: provided
Linens: variety of colors; no extra charge
China: china and glassware provided
Audiovisual: provided
Equipment: podiums, risers and staging provided
Cleanup: provided
Parking: free in large lot; easy access from freeway to CECC
ADA: yes

CECC is a unique setting for your event due to the close proximity to the Columbia River and the exceptional view of one of the finest golf courses in Oregon.

COOPER SPUR MOUNTAIN RESORT

10755 Cooper Spur Road • Mt. Hood, Oregon 97041
(541) 352-6692, (800) ski-hood
www.cooperspur.com

Capacity: groups of up to 70, or take your event outdoors
Price Range: moderate to customized events; please inquire
Catering: in-house catering only; cabins include kitchenettes; log home has full kitchen
Types of Events: business meetings, team building, conferences, seminars, retreats, weddings, social gatherings, buffet, sit-down, cocktails, overnight lodging, skiing, hiking, snowshoeing

Availability and Terms

Advanced bookings are encouraged. Deposits required with payment due in full upon arrival.

Description of Facility and Services

Seating: provided to accommodate group size
Servers: provided
Bar facilities: full-service bar available
Audiovisual: full selection of audiovisual services available; please inquire for pricing
Parking: ample complimentary parking available
ADA: fully applies

Social Services:

Cooper Spur Mountain Resort is a mountain lodge and meeting center on the north side of Mt. Hood, featuring log cabins, lodge condo suites, hotel rooms, a log home, restaurant and lounge, Alpine ski area, Nordic Center with cross country trails, tennis court, spa facility with a deck, four hot tubs and two massage therapy rooms. Cooper Spur Mountain Resort facilitates business meetings, team building sessions and recreational pursuits, as well as family vacations. It is located on 775 acres of private forest land, a 1,400 acre US Forest Service permit area, all surrounded by the Mt. Hood National Forest. The cabins and lodge structures portray a simple elegance and invite you to come and stay. Our cabins and log home provide the perfect place to meet and retreat. Intimate and private yet fully supported by the Cooper Spur meeting planner and restaurant staff.

MT. HOOD MEADOWS SKI RESORT

Cooper Spur Mountain Resort is located just 12 miles from Mt. Hood Meadows Ski Resort. Guests of Cooper Spur ski for just $25. Group rates are also available for lessons and rental equipment.

McMenamins
Cornelius Pass Roadhouse

40045 N.W. Cornelius Pass Road
Hillsboro, Oregon 97124
Contact: Group Sales (503) 693-8452
Fax (503) 681-9799
Web site: www.mcmenamins.com
E-mail: cpr@mcmenamins.com
Business Hours: Mon-Fri 9am-5pm,
tours by appointment

Capacity: 20 to 600 people
Price Range: food and beverage minimum varies based on room size and time of day
Catering: in-house catering only; family style, buffet, and hors d'oeuvres; prices vary
Types of Events: This mid-19th-century property resting on a farmstead suits a variety of events, including meetings, weddings and receptions, banquets, reunions and holiday parties.

Availability and Terms

Cornelius Pass Roadhouse's English chestnut and black walnut trees, and buildings of rustic elegance date back to Oregon's youth and offer a variety of striking spaces, indoors and out. For the best availability, we suggest booking events as early as possible to ensure availability. Deposit required. Please contact our sales staff for details.

Description of Facility and Services

Seating: tables and chairs arranged to fit your needs
Servers: staff included in price; 17% gratuity added to bill
Bar facilities: full-service bar featuring McMenamins ales, wines and spirits
Dance floor: the Octagonal Barn's wood floor provides a natural dance floor
Linens: assorted tablecloth and napkin colors; no charge
China and glassware: available for additional cost
Audiovisual: available upon request
Equipment: available upon request
Cleanup: included in price
Parking: ample parking available
ADA: the estate's two barns and farmhouse (lower level only) are accessible

GLORIOUS REMNANT OF AGRARIAN PAST

Cornelius Pass Roadhouse is a glorious remnant of the area's agrarian past and offers several meeting spaces: a two story historic farmhouse, Imbrie Hall Restaurant, The Octagonal Barn, The Granary, and the cozy little White Shed. Grounds also feature the Roadhouse Brewery surrounded by established evergreens.

COURTYARD BY MARRIOTT—PORTLAND NORTH HARBOUR

on the Columbia River

1231 N. Anchor Way • Portland, Oregon 97217
Business Hours: Mon–Fri 8am–5pm, or by appointment
Contact: Charlotte Corvi (503) 735-1818; Fax (503) 735-0888; www.courtyard.com/pdxnh

Capacity: *Indoor:* **Columbia Room:** 1,100 square feet, ideal for receptions of up to 100 people; *Outdoor:* our patio offers seating for up to 300 people, or up to 500 reception

Price Range: price will vary depending on the type of event and menu selections

Catering: full-service in-house catering

Types of Events: smaller, more intimate family weddings, rehearsal dinners and bridal showers; patio is available for larger gatherings, weather permitting; tenting available at an additional charge

Availability and Terms

To secure preferred date, reservations must be made six months to one year in advance. There is a $500 nonrefundable deposit to hold the date, with a minimum deposit of 50% of total charges due 90 days prior to the function, and the balance due three days from the date of the event.

Description of Facility and Services

Seating: tables and chairs for up to 300

Servers: staff included; a 20% service charge will be added to your bill

Bar facilities: full beverage service available; an additional charge is required for bartenders if minimum is not met

Dance floor: available at an additional charge

Linens and napkins: all colors available

China and glassware: bone china and glassware provided

Decorations: hotel provides center mirror and three votive candles; additional decorations are renter's responsibility

Cleanup: included in site charge

Parking: complimentary parking

ADA: fully accessible

Special Services

The Portland North Harbour Courtyard by Marriott on the Columbia River has 131 guestrooms decorated in a palette of colors adopted from those typically found in the French and Italian Riviera. Guestrooms feature amenities including in-room coffee and tea service, 25″ television, hair dryer, iron and ironing board. King Suite and Spa King available. Honeymoon Suite with in-room spa and parlor room is available.

MEDITERRANEAN STYLE ON THE COLUMBIA RIVER

The North Harbour Courtyard has an ambiance of casual elegance and sophistication both inside and out. A resort-like atmosphere is apparent throughout, but especially on our large seasonally landscaped plaza. Complete with gazebo, fountain, and peaceful scenic views, the plaza is the ideal location for summer and fall wedding receptions, rehearsal dinners, cocktail parties and celebrations.

THE CROWN BALLROOM
& GARDEN COURT

918 S.W. Yamhill, Fifth Floor • Portland, Oregon 97205
Contact: Raven David (503) 227-8440; Fax (503) 227-2654
Business Hours: shown by appointment only
www.thecrownballroom.com or email: party@thecrownballroom.com

Capacity: private rooms located on the Penthouse level; capacity: 50 to 400
Price Range: from $700 to $3,500, depending on room, date and size of party
Catering: full-service in-house catering, complimentary buffet and wine tasting for all
signed clients, full-service menu planning and sample menus available
Types of Events: weddings and elegant receptions, masquerade balls, film and
commercial shoots, proms, holiday parties and corporate events

Availability and Terms

Early reservations suggested. A nonrefundable deposit is required to reserve The Crown
Ballroom. We welcome short notice events depending on availability.

Description of Facility and Services

Banquet seating: from 50 to 300, tables and double-padded dining chairs are provided
Servers: all servers, bartenders and support staff are included at no charge
Bar facilities: full bar services, including liquor liability, are provided in-house
Linens and napkins: fine linens and napkins are provided at no additional charge
China and glassware: fine china, glassware and silver are included in menu prices
Dance floors: large upper dance floor, lower dance floor available on request; bands are
showcased on the Ballroom stage; mirror balls, spot light, fog and dance lights included
Convenient parking: seven-level parking structure adjacent to building with economy rates

"WELCOME TO THE FINE ART OF CELEBRATION!"

Consider The Crown Ballroom's Italian Renaissance elegance in concert with the 1st Class
Resort inspired ambiance of The Garden Court, add designer decorated VIP rooms for the
Bride and Groom and you will appreciate The Crown as being uniquely qualified to host our
city's most beautiful weddings and photographed receptions. We invite you to experience the
charm of a Tuscan Villa, the elegance of a luxury hotel and the artfulness of a fine art gallery.

The Crown Ballroom
Artful. Elegant. Exciting.

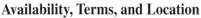

CROWNE PLAZA®

HOTELS · RESORTS

14811 Kruse Oaks Drive
Lake Oswego, Oregon 97035
For banquet reservations:
Director of Catering (503) 624-8400 ext. 6253
Sleeping room rates:
Director of Sales (503) 624-8400 ext. 6151

Capacity: groups up to 300+
Price Range: inquire about prices
Catering: incredible full-service custom catering
Types of Events: sit-down dinner, buffet, cocktails and hors d'oeuvres, luncheons, any custom party

Availability, Terms, and Location

One ballroom and one boardroom are available for banquets and receptions. We recommend making reservations as early as possible. The Crowne Plaza is conveniently located at the intersection of Interstate 5 and Highway 217. Its accessibility to Portland, Beaverton, Tigard, and Lake Oswego makes it ideally situated for your wedding and reception, rehearsal dinner or brunch!

Description of Facility and Services

Seating: tables and chairs for up to 250 people
Servers: included
Cleanup: handled by The Crowne Plaza
Bar facilities: full-service bar facilities; bartenders available for private reception
Dance floor: space available for band; large dance floor
Linens and napkins: all colors available (custom orders may have additional charge)
China and glassware: classic styles (no plastic)
Decorations: elegant mirror tiles, votive candles and ficus trees with twinkle lights throughout the room at no additional charge; inquire about decorations we can provide for an extra cost
Parking: plenty of free parking; valet parking available
ADA: fully accessible

Special Services

• **Weddings:** Our six-story atrium with cascading waterfalls makes a beautiful setting for your wedding ceremony. **When booking your reception, a complimentary suite will be provided for the bride and groom.** Special rates are available for your out-of-town guests.

LUXURIOUS AND ELEGANT

The luxurious and elegant Crowne Plaza features a six-story waterfall in the atrium and 161 tastefully decorated rooms. Other amenities include an indoor-outdoor pool, spa, sauna, exercise facility, gift shop, free local shuttle, tastings and local shopping discounts. This hotel is ideal for rehearsal dinners, bridesmaid luncheons, and wedding receptions.

www.crowneplaza.com/lakeoswegoor

CRYSTAL BALLROOM

1332 W. Burnside
Portland, Oregon 97209
Contact: Group Sales (503) 288-3286
Web site: www.mcmenamins.com
E-mail: sales@mcmenamins.com
Business Hours: Mon–Fri 9am–5pm;
tours weekends and by appointment

Capacity: 1,000 persons reception-style; 300 seated
Price Range: please contact an event coordinator for price ranges; food and beverage
minimum required to waive rental; based on day of week and time of day
Types of Events: the Crystal provides a unique setting for weddings, receptions, reunions,
meetings, seminars, exhibits, banquets, concerts, dances, holiday parties and beyond

Availability and Terms

We suggest that you book your event six months to one year in advance for a weekend date
and three to nine months in advance for weekday functions. Deposit required. Please contact
our sales staff for details.

Description of Facility and Services

Seating: thirty rounds of 10 max with banquet chairs; additional tables and chairs may be
rented; fixed seating in the ballroom, including theater seats in the mezzanine and benches
surrounding the ballroom, totals 180
Servers: staff included in price; 17% gratuity added to the bill
Bar facilities: full-service bar featuring McMenamins ales, wines and spirits
Dance floor: the Crystal's most remarkable feature is its maple "floating" dance floor; one of
the last of its kind, it is said to have the ability to make a good dancer out of anyone
Live music: live music is welcome to complement your event; the cost is the responsibility of
the renter, but recommendations will gladly be made
Linens and napkins: assorted linens included in rental fee
China and glassware: silverware and plates included; due to the nature of the "floating"
dance floor, some glassware is discouraged
Decorations: responsibility of renter
Cleanup: included in price
Parking: covered parking structure across street and several paid parking structures are in
close walking distance

BEAUTIFULLY RENOVATED HISTORIC BALLROOM

The historic Crystal Ballroom boasts 7,000 square feet of floating dance floor. Its eclectic and
festive decor make it an ideal setting for events ranging from an award banquet to a wedding
reception. Available for more intimate gatherings, our recently renovated Lola's Room
features a "floating" dance floor and full bar. The Crystal has been a forum for music,
dancing, and personalities that have helped define several eras. Extracting inspiration from
more than 80 years of history, a team of artists have added dimension to the Crystal's walls by
painting murals throughout the building and on-site brewery.

The Best Value Under The Sun.™

DAYS INN CITY CENTER

1414 S.W. Sixth Avenue • Portland, Oregon 97201
Contact: Sales Department
(503) 221-1611 or (800) 899-0248; Fax (503) 274-7325
E-mail: jeannine.geist@starwoodhotels.com; judy.kaski@starwoodhotels.com
Web site: www.the.daysinn.com/portland05313

Capacity: we offer three rooms and one suite to accommodate up to 200 people; seasonal outdoor space up to 400 people

Catering: in-house catering available

Price Range: varies depending on menu and type of event

Types of Events: breakfast meetings, brunches, lunches, business meetings, seminars, dinners, banquets, weddings, wedding receptions, any social or business gathering

Availability and Terms

Days Inn City Center recommends that you make your reservation for space as early as possible, particularly for our outdoor pool and pavilion area

Description of Facility and Services

Seating: tables and chairs provided; banquet, round and classroom tables available

Servers: staff included in catering cost

Bar facilities: full beverage service available

Linens and napkins: an extensive array of colors available at no extra charge

China and glassware: white china and stemmed glassware

Decorations: mirrored tiles, votive candles, bud vases, silk plants, themed decor available

Audiovisual: available upon request

Equipment: podiums, risers and staging available

Cleanup: provided by hotel staff

Parking: on-site, subject to availability

ADA: accessible

Special Services

Days Inn City Center features 173 newly renovated guest rooms, including one suite. Your guests will enjoy our "heart of downtown" location and other amenities including on-site parking, complimentary daily newspaper delivered to your door, data ports, and pay-per-view movies and games in each room. Our heated outdoor pool is available seasonally, and an adjacent Health Club is available complimentary to all guests. Group rates are available for 10 or more rooms.

IN THE HEART OF DOWNTOWN PORTLAND

Plan your event in our flexible meeting space and banquet facilities. We will cater to the needs of your guests while you focus on the business at hand. *We are truly at your service!*

DOUBLETREE
HOTEL™
PORTLAND • DOWNTOWN

310 S.W. Lincoln • Portland, Oregon 97201
Contact: Sales Office (503) 221-0450; Fax (503) 225-4303
Business Hours: Mon–Fri 8am–5pm; Evenings and Weekends by Appointment

Capacity: Seating from 25 to 250 in our four private banquet rooms and seasonal outdoor courtyard

Price Range: evening packages beginning at $20; customized packages available

Catering: full in-house catering exclusively

Types of Events: ceremonies, receptions, rehearsal dinners, bridal showers, luncheons, cocktail and dinner affairs as well as meetings and corporate events

Availability and Terms

Experience the DoubleTree Hotel • Portland Downtown's elegant new Willamette Falls Ballroom, accommodating up to 125 guests. Plan your more intimate event at our poolside courtyard or for larger events of up to 250 guests, the Columbia Falls Ballroom offers private space for dining and dancing. We recommend that you make your reservation at least six months in advance to ensure your preferred date. A $500 non-refundable deposit is required.

Description of Facility and Services

Seating: tables and chairs provided, banquet rounds

Servers: included in catering costs

Bar facilities: host or no-host; portable bars, themed bars, domestic, microbrew and non alcoholic beer, wine, mixed drinks, champagne and soft drinks

Dance floor: appropriately sized dance floor provided complimentary

Linens and napkins: white and ivory linens provided complimentary, additional colors available, prices vary

China and glassware: included

Clean-up: provided by hotel staff

Decorations: wide variety of theme or floral decorations — cost varies, no glitter or confetti

Parking: complimentary on-site parking, based on availability; **ADA:** yes

A MEMORABLE OCCASION .....

Awaits you at the DoubleTree Hotel • Portland Downtown! Allow our experienced wedding coordinator to work hand-in-hand with you in all of your planning, choosing and questions in the months to come! Feel comfortable and confident as you visit with family and friends who have come to share in your special day. Our Ballrooms combine simple elegance and versatility to reflect a variety of wedding themes. From simple to extravagant, you need a hotel that can accommodate and foresee your wedding reception needs. We offer creative menus to tantalize all taste buds.

DoubleTree Hotel • Portland Downtown is conveniently located on the Southwest side of downtown, directly off major interstate access. We are pleased to extend a complimentary guestroom accommodation for the Bride and Groom on their wedding night as well as special guestroom rates for your loved ones.

Sweet Dreams abound at the DoubleTree Hotel • Portland Downtown. Come see how memorable your wedding reception can be! **www.portlanddowntown.doubletree.com**

DOUBLETREE
HOTEL™
HAYDEN ISLAND COMPLEX

©Adams & Faith

Jantzen Beach	*Columbia River*
909 N. Hayden Island Drive	*1401 N. Hayden Island Drive*
Portland, OR 97217	*Portland, OR 97217*
(503) 283-4466	*(503) 283-2111*

Contact: Sales and Catering Office
Office Hours: Mon-Fri 8am-5pm

Capacity: up to 1,400 guests
Price Range: price will vary depending on type of event and menu selection; average $30 per person for receptions
Catering: full service in-house catering provided by the hotel exclusively
Types of Events: from light hors d'oeuvre receptions to elegant luncheon and dinner affairs; rehearsal dinners, bridal showers, post wedding brunches, ceremonies, etc.

Availability and Terms

Our hotels feature many spacious ballrooms to accommodate weddings of all sizes, several of which have gorgeous floor to ceiling windows to allow for dramatic views of the beautiful Columbia River. It is suggested that reservations be made as soon as possible. A 30% deposit is required at the time of booking. Please call the Catering Office for details.

Description of Facility and Services

Seating: your choice of banquet rounds or informal cabaret style
Servers: staff included in catering costs
Bar facilities: full beverage service; hotel provides all beer, wine and liquor
Dance floor: ample size available at no additional charge
Linens and napkins: an extensive array to select from at no additional charge
China and glassware: white china; stemmed glassware included
Cleanup: provided by hotel staff
Decorations: arched trellis, silk plants, mirror tiles, candle votives, silk trees, access for early decoration by prior arrangement.
Parking: ample, complimentary parking; **ADA:** accessible

Special Services

The Doubletree Hotels Jantzen Beach and Columbia River provide complimentary deluxe accommodations (based on availability) for the bride and groom on the night of your wedding reception, along with a complimentary bottle of champagne. In addition, we offer special group rates for your guests' sleeping needs.

BEAUTIFUL RIVERFRONT SETTING – UNPARALLELED SERVICE

Watch the water sparkle as you celebrate your truly special occasion in the best riverfront rooms around! From menu planning to room décor and design, our experienced and professional wedding team is specially trained to ensure a memorable and worry-free event. Just north of downtown, our convenient location and ample parking make attending your event enjoyable for your guests, and our reputation for exquisite food with unparalleled service make us the ideal location to host your wedding reception. Come see the beauty for yourself!

DOUBLETREE HOTEL™

PORTLAND • LLOYD CENTER

1000 N.E. Multnomah • Portland, Oregon 97232
Contact: Catering Office (503) 249-3121
Business Hours: Mon–Fri 8am–5pm

Capacity: four ballrooms seating up to 1,100
Price Range: price will vary depending on type of event and menu selection
Catering: full-service in-house catering provided by the hotel exclusively
Types of Events: hors d'oeuvre receptions, elegant luncheons and dinners, wedding receptions, meetings, seminars and conventions

Availability and Terms
The DoubleTree Hotel Portland • Lloyd Center offers four ballrooms to accommodate up to 700 guests. Recently renovated, our ballrooms provide flexibility and elegance.

Description of Facility and Services
Seating: your choice of banquet seating styles
Servers: staff included in catering costs
Bar facilities: full beverage service available; DoubleTree Hotel Portland • Lloyd Center to provide all beer, wine, and liquor
Dance floor: available at no additional charge
Linens and napkins: an extensive array of linen colors at no additional charge, based on availability
China and glassware: white china; stemmed glassware
Cleanup: included in price
Audiovisual and meeting equipment: in-house audiovisual company; podium, risers and staging available
Parking: parking for more than 550 cars
ADA: hotel meets ADA requirements

Special Services
The DoubleTree Hotel Portland • Lloyd Center offers concierge services as well as a business center to meet all your business and meeting needs. We offer special group rates on our 476 beautifully appointed guest rooms.

RELAX AND ENJOY YOUR DAY!
The DoubleTree Hotel Portland • Lloyd Center is a full-service hotel dedicated to making your event a success! Our professional catering coordinators can accommodate all your planning needs. From menu planning to room decor and design, our experienced and friendly staff are trained to take the stress and pressure out of planning your event. Our convenient location and ample parking make attending your special event easy for you and your guests. Beautiful ballrooms, a great location and service beyond your expectations make the DoubleTree Lloyd Center the perfect choice.

East Fork
Country Estate

9957 S.E. 222nd
Gresham, Oregon 97080
Contact: Tami Kay Galvin, owner
(503) 667-7069
(503) 319-3531 cell
www.eastforkestate.com
(3.9 miles south of Gresham
on Regner Road)

Capacity: up to 250 seated ceremony and reception
Price Range: please call for specific prices on wedding packages
Catering: in-house catering
Types of Events: full-service wedding receptions with sit-down buffet dinners; traditional cake, coffee, and punch receptions

Availability and Terms
Friday evening weddings are from 5 to 11pm; Saturday bookings are from 9am to 3pm; (11:30am ceremony, followed by a reception from noon to 3pm) and from 4:30 to 10:30pm (6pm ceremony, followed by a reception from 6:30 to 10:30pm). Sunday weddings are any six-hour period until 9pm.

Description of Facility and Services
Assistance: your personal, professional wedding consultant is included in our package price
Bar facilities: beer, wine, and champagne available
Dance floor: yes, with electrical hookups
Linens and napkins: many colors to choose from
China and glassware: clear glass china with a pattern; glass coffee cups and stemware
Cleanup: included in our wedding packages
Decorations: included in our wedding package price; the gardens include hundreds of bedding plants, roses, and willow and fir trees
Parking: ample free parking is available
ADA: yes

Special Services
You may wish to reserve our horse and vis-à-vis carriage as part of your wedding processional. Each event is given special, thoughtful, caring attention. We specialize in "stress free" weddings.

THE ESTATE FACES MOUNT HOOD
AND OVERLOOKS A SERENE FARM VALLEY
Your guests will be seated under white canopies on lawn areas in front of the gazebo. The Estate includes a large, beautifully decorated indoor reception area with hardwood floors and oriental carpeting, several covered patios, four canopies on the lawn areas, and spacious bride and groom changing rooms.

Your guests will arrive to find terraced lawns and flowering gardens facing Mount Hood, horses grazing on the Estate's pastures, and a view overlooking a farm valley, the Cascade foothills, and Mount Hood. The result is a warm, relaxed country setting.

Eastmoreland Grill

at the Eastmoreland Golf Course

2425 S.E. Bybee Boulevard
Portland, Oregon 97202
Contact: Jerilyn Walker, Events Coordinator
(503) 775-5910; Fax (503) 775-6349
Web site: www.eastmorelandgrill.com
Office Hours: 9am–5pm

Capacity: 125 for a sit-down dinner; 175 for a reception; 250 including outside area
Price Range: price varies according to season and time of day
Catering: full-service catering available in-house
Types of Events: cocktails, hors d'oeuvres, cake and champagne, buffet, sit-down

Availability and Terms

The Eastmoreland Grill encourages your reservations up to one year in advance. A deposit is required and is nonrefundable. Half-payment is required 30 days in advance, with the remaining half payable on the day of the event.

Description of Facility and Services

Seating: tables and chairs provided for up to 125 sit-down guests
Servers: full staff available; a gratuity will be added to food and beverage purchases
Bar facilities: full-service bar and staff bartender provided upon request; host/no-host; liquor, beer, and wine
Dance floor: we can provide a dance floor; rental fee varies according to size
Linens and napkins: cloth tablecloths and napkins available in some colors
China and glassware: white china; glassware available in plastic or glass, as required
Cleanup: cleanup provided
Decorations: our catering manager will discuss with you and help develop your decoration plans
Parking: large parking lot with overflow area
ADA: full facilities

GRACIOUS STYLE OVERLOOKING LUSH GREENS

The lush, beautiful greens of the Eastmoreland Golf Course are the setting for our gorgeous Tudor-style clubhouse. The banquet room overlooks the tenth tee and has a large, gracious veranda for outdoor entertaining. Winter events are equally blessed with a handsome fireplace where guests love to gather. Our staff has extensive experience in wedding receptions, rehearsal dinners, corporate events, anniversaries, birthdays, and reunions, and we will create a personal menu exactly to your specifications.

EMBASSY SUITES
HOTELS®

EMBASSY SUITES PORTLAND DOWNTOWN

319 S.W. Pine Street • Portland, Oregon 97204
Catering Office (503) 279-9000; Fax (503) 220-0206

Capacity: 180 sit down; 300 reception
Price Range: from $15 for luncheons, from $26 for dinners and average of $45 for receptions
Catering: complete in-house catering only
Types of Events: wedding receptions, rehearsal dinners, bridal brunches and luncheons

Availability and Terms

Two large ballrooms plus a ceremonial room and six smaller rooms, great for rehearsal dinners. Most rooms have large windows and are decorated with the elegance and style of the historic Multnomah Hotel, including all of the amenities in an Embassy Suites. Once an event is confirmed, a deposit is required.

Description of Facility and Services

Seating: all tables and chairs provided
Servers: professional service staff provided
Bar facilities: hotel provides bar facilities and professional alcoholic beverage servers
Dance floor: 15' x 15' floor available with electrical hookups
Linens, napkins, china and glassware: provided by hotel
Decorations: please check with catering representative
Cleanup: provided by hotel
Parking: valet and parking garage
ADA: all facilities handicapped accessible

Special Services

Let our catering representative help make your occasion one to remember. Experience the elegance and style of our restored historic hotel. You will find table decorations included with rooms and a professional staff that is flexible in helping you set up your function with confidence. Enjoy a complimentary suite for the bride and groom.

WHERE HISTORY MEETS HOSPITALITY

Come discover Portland's premier historic hotel where you will find contemporary amenities in a classic setting. Along with nine meeting rooms, the hotel has 276 guest suites all designed and furnished to complement the hotel's early 20th century architecture. First opened in 1912 as the Multnomah, the hotel was the hub of Portland society. The same holds true today. Plan your event at the new Embassy Suites Portland Downtown and be a part of history.

EMBASSY SUITES ®

PORTLAND—WASHINGTON SQUARE

9000 S.W. Washington Square Road
Tigard, OR 97223
Contact: Kim McCandlish
503-644-4000

Capacity: up to 800 people
Price Range: price to be determined by event and menu selections
Catering: full service catering
Types of receptions: elegant served dinners or buffets, hors d'oeuvres receptions, special private parties, wedding receptions, rehearsal dinners, bar/bat mitzvahs

Availability and Terms

The Embassy Suites Hotel has a wide variety of banquet facilities for your special event. Our function rooms can accommodate from 10–800 guests.

Description of Facility and Services

Seating: provided for up to 800 guests
Servers: included in catering cost
Bar facilities: full service hosted or no host bar; beer, wine and champagne service; we provide all beverages, bartenders and servers
Dance floor: available
Linens and napkins: fine linens available in colors to coordinate with banquet room decor
China and glassware: fine china, silver and glassware provided
Cleanup: included in catering charges
Decorations: limited decorations available at no additional charge
Parking: complimentary parking
ADA: fully equipped to accommodate ADA requirements

Special Services

The Embassy Suites Hotel provides a complimentary Suite for that special bride and groom on the night of the wedding. Special rates are available for your out-of-town guests in our luxurious suites. Contact our Catering Professionals to see why Embassy Suites is the perfect setting for your memorable occasion.

The Fairgate Inn

2213 NW 23rd Avenue   Camas, Washington 98607
(360) 834-0861
www.FairgateInn.com   TheFairgate@aol.com

"The Northwest Premier Wedding Facility…Where All Your Wedding Dreams Come True!"

Capacity: Up to 100 seated indoors, 150 standing indoors; 400 outdoors
Price Range: Charges vary, please call for specific information
Catering: We are proud to offer full service, in-house catering
Types of Events: Wedding ceremonies & receptions, corporate & private celebrations, business meetings, seminars, training sessions, reunions, bridal showers, high teas, murder mystery dinners, and more.

Availability & Terms
A deposit holds your date. Early reservations are suggested.

Description of Facility and Services
Seating: Tables & chairs provided for up to 200 guests; set up & clean up is included in the rental price
Event Staff: Included in costs
Bar Facilities: All bar services are provided in-house
China & glassware: China, silver, & glassware is provided for up to 250 guests
Dance Floor: Dance areas are in the Georgian Ballroom and under the Gazebo
Decorations: Table linens are provided. We also have a variety of decorations available for your use. See event manager for details and/or restrictions
Parking: Ample, free parking available
ADA: Fully accessible; please inform us of any special needs

Special Services:
The Fairgate Inn is conveniently located just 15 minutes from the Portland International Airport. Our staff works to make sure your event is one of a kind and spectacular. We offer only one event per day to insure your day is special. We have eight guest suites that are complete with their own individual style as well as a fireplace & private bath. Full breakfast is included with the nights lodging.

ELEGANT GEORGIAN ESTATE
The Fairgate Inn possesses many special features found only in this Georgian Colonial style home. We are open for year-round events.

Garden Vineyards

Helvetia, Oregon
Contact: Melinda 503-647-5192

Capacity: Small intimate parties to grand events of 500 or more
Price Range: Varies based on size and style of celebration, call for details
Catering: In-house
Types of Events: High-style social events including weddings and associated pre-wedding parties; executive level multi-course luncheons and dinners; corporate parties and events.

Availability and Terms
Call for current availability, a deposit is required to reserve your date.

Description of Facilities and Services
Seating: Entire estate including interior of villa and gardens are designed and appointed for grand entertaining, including small intimate talking circles and large open areas for groups. Abundant outdoor and garden furniture as well as comfortable height walls and steps for sitting. Very large sit-down dining events are accommodated through rental.
Servers: All types of service presentations are available.
Bar facilities: Full bar available. Garden Vineyards wine is served at all events.
Floral arrangements: Our gardens provide the flowers and foliage for some of Portland's premier event floral designers. We can work with your floral designer to provide material for display or you can simply allow the gardens to provide the floral design themselves.
Music: We can accommodate a wide variety of music options, ranging from a selection of your favorite CD's playing throughout the villa, terraces and gardens to live band performances.
Dance floor: Portable dance floor can be set-up in a variety of locations.
Tenting: Large flat lawn adjacent to gardens and villa for tent set-up
Linens and napkins: Many options available
China and glassware: Many options available
Cleanup: Completed by staff
Parking: Valet service is provided for all large events.
ADA: Accessible

Special Amenities and Services
Garden Vineyards wines, Pinot Noir and Pinot Gris. Private hotel style suite quarters for wedding party preparations. Permanent gazeboes and other garden seating and structures. Permanent outdoor sound system and landscape lighting.

A Grand Celebration Venue
Just 15 miles from downtown Portland or in the heart of Tuscany? A Grand Italian Villa perched atop a hillside vineyard. Gardens showcasing the most beautiful flower, the garden rose. Wine grown on-site and produced by one of Oregon's premier wine makers, Peter Rosback.

The gated entry, the vineyard, the acres of lawn, the expansive view of the valley, the gourmet cuisine and the villa itself, create a grandness of scale your guests will never forget. The intimate details like an ancient birdbath hidden amongst lavender and foxglove, the carefulness of a staff member or the beauty of a single perfect rose are the small things that you will always remember.

JAKE'S CATERING
A T   T H E
GOVERNOR
H O T E L

611 S.W. 10th Avenue
Portland, Oregon 97205
(503) 241-2125; Fax (503) 220-1849
Web site: www.JakesCatering.com

Capacity: 600 reception; 450 sit-down dinner
Price Range: $32 to $50 per person
Catering: Jake's Catering is the exclusive caterer for The Governor Hotel; off-premise catering available
Types of Events: from stand-up cocktail/appetizer receptions to fabulous buffet presentations to complete sit-down dinners for groups and gatherings of all sizes

Availability and Terms
Our Italian Renaissance-style rooms offer variety and flexibility for groups of 20 to 600. The majestic Ballroom, Renaissance Room, Fireside Room, Library, and eight additional rooms gracefully complement the charm of The Governor Hotel. We require a 50% deposit to confirm your event and payment in full 72 hours prior to event for estimated charges.

Description of Facility and Services
Seating: tables and chairs for up to 450
Servers: all servers included as hotel service
Bar facilities: full-service bar and bartender
Linens and napkins: cloth napkins and linens provided in a variety of colors
China and glassware: fine china and glassware provided
Decorations: please inquire about specific decoration ideas and needs
Parking: ample parking available near hotel
ADA: committed to full service for guests with disabilities

Jake's Catering... A Tradition
Jake's Catering at The Governor Hotel is a part of the McCormick & Schmick Restaurant Group and "Jake's Famous Crawfish." Jake's is one of the most respected dining institutions in the Portland area, and Jake's Catering at The Governor Hotel upholds this prestigious reputation.

Known for offering extensive Pacific Northwest menu selection, including fresh seafood, pasta, poultry and prime cut steaks, Jake's Catering at The Governor Hotel has the flexibility and talent to cater to your needs.

CLASSIC ELEGANCE AND SERVICE
Listed on the National Register of Historic Places, The Governor Hotel is an architectural beauty. Built in 1909 and renovated in 1992, the hotel has been completely restored to its original grandeur. The original design and ornate craftsmanship of the grand banquet space area were preserved in the original Italian Renaissance styling. The room's chandeliers, high vaulted ceilings, marble floors, and black-walnut woodwork and walls are truly unique.
See page 292 under Catering Services.

Please let this business know that you heard about them from the Bravo! Wedding Resource Guide.   **99**

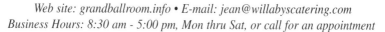

THE GRAND BALLROOM
DOWNTOWN SALEM

187 High Street N.E. • Salem, Oregon 97301
Phone: (503) 362-9185
Web site: grandballroom.info • E-mail: jean@willabyscatering.com
Business Hours: 8:30 am - 5:00 pm, Mon thru Sat, or call for an appointment

Capacity: Lodge Room: 270 seated in chairs/ 170 seated at tables/chairs
Ballroom: 200 guests dancing/ 100 guests seated at tables/chairs
Dining Room: 160 guests seated in chairs/80 guests seated at tables/chairs
Price Range: Varies according to day of week- $600 to $1,550
Catering: Willaby's Catering is our in-house caterer
Type of Events: Weddings, receptions, banquets, bar mitzvah/ bat mitzvah, proms, corporate meetings, trade shows, retreats, seminars and reunions.

Availability and Terms:
A 50% deposit is required to hold a reservation, with the balance due 30 days prior to event. Cleaning deposit required, partially refundable.

Description of Facility and Services
Facility Rental: Included in rental fee: 350 upholstered chairs, 25 five foot round tables, 15 six-foot rectangular tables. Art Deco Ballroom with fireplace. Lodge Room has raised a platform, PA system w/ 3 mics, hand carved podium. Dining Room/Kitchen has commercial refrigerator, proofer, dishwasher, garbage disposal, double sink.
Servers: OLCC licensed server supplied by caterer.
Dance floor: Ballroom with pecan wood dance floor, mirror ball, electrical for DJ or live music.
Decorations: We will try to accommodate your needs, no tape, nails or tacks in walls or woodwork, no birdseed, bubbles (inside), rice, or confetti please.
Set-up: Free set-up.
ADA: Elevator access to event space, ADA restroom
Security: Willaby's Catering will supply on-site staff during each event.
Parking: Free on-street parking, large public parking structure nearby; adjacent private parking for wedding party.

Special services
Dedicated bride's dressing room, and separate groom's dressing room.
Event Coordination and Design.

1900 HISTORIC BUILDING NEWLY RENOVATED
The new Grand Ballroom opened September 2002 in the Historic Grand Theater building in the heart of downtown Salem. The 9,500 square foot space is divided into three large rooms, which allows your guests the option to visit in quiet spaces, or dance to their hearts content. The facility has all new restrooms, air conditioning, carpet, chairs and tables.

McMENAMINS GRAND LODGE

3505 Pacific Avenue • Forest Grove, Oregon 97116
Web site: www.thegrandlodge.com; E-mail: sales@thegrandlodge.com
Contact: Group Sales (503) 992-9530; Business Hours: Mon–Fri 9am–5pm

Capacity: 150 people indoors; 1,000+ people outdoors
Price Range: $300 to $2,600
Catering: in-house catering only
Types of Events: This former Masonic Lodge turned historic hotel is ideal for meetings, seminars, weddings, receptions, retreats, banquets and holiday parties.

Availability and Terms

Expressive gathering spaces are numerous among the property's buildings and grounds. The Grand Lodge can accommodate groups from eight to 1,000 outdoors. Reserve your space as early as possible to ensure availability. Deposit required. Please contact our sales staff for details.

Description of Facility and Services

Seating: tables and chairs arranged to fit your needs
Servers: staff included in price; 17% gratuity added to the bill
Bar facilities: full-service bar featuring Edgefield ales, wines and spirits
Dance floor: wood floor in Compass Room
Linens and napkins: linens include a wide variety of colors; no charge
China and glassware: all china and glassware included
Decorations: please discuss with our event coordinators
Cleanup: included in price
Parking: plenty of free parking
ADA: specific banquet facilities and guest rooms are accessible

Special Services

The historic Grand Lodge has 77 overnight rooms, the Ironwork Grill and the Yardhouse pub, soaking pool, game room, gardens, massage, salon, specialty bars, wine tasting room, artwork and history.

HISTORIC COLONIAL IDEAL GETAWAY

This brick-and-columned wonder rests majestically on 13 acres just east of Forest Grove. Accommodations are of the European style with private marble bathrooms located down the hall. A congenial atmosphere is encouraged by the lodge's common spaces: overstuffed couches, artwork, music, roaring fires and full bars can be found around every corner. The airy first-floor pub serves delicious and hearty breakfasts, lunches and dinners daily. Call the Group Sales Office for a complete catering packet.

Gray Gables Estate

Westervelt Hall
Indoor and Out Year-round Wedding Gardens
3009 S.E. Chestnut • Milwaukie, Oregon 97267
(503) 654-0470, (877) 500-GRAY (4729)
Fax (503) 654-3929
Business Hours: 7 days a week
Web Site: www.graygables.com

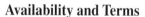

Capacity: up to 290; seating indoor and outdoor
Price Range: various wedding and reception packages
Catering: in-house catering
Types of Events: weddings and receptions, meetings, trade shows, corporate events, business parties

Availability and Terms
Gray Gables takes bookings for its facility up to one year in advance, but shorter notice can be accommodated. You and your guests will have exclusive use of the estate. A $1,500 reservation fee is required to hold your date.

Description of Facility and Services
Consultation: every package includes bridal consultation and event coordination
Seating: tables and chairs provided for up to 290 people indoors or outdoors
Servers: all parking and service attendants included
Bar facilities: full bar; extensive selection of beer, wine and champagne
Dance floor: outdoors and indoors
Linens and napkins: elegant linen tablecloths and skirting; quality paper napkins; specialty linens available at additional cost
China and glassware: clear crystal china, appropriate glassware; silver service available at an additional cost
Decorations: we are proud to offer a variety of decorating options
Cleanup: provided by Gray Gables staff
Parking: ample FREE parking; **ADA:** accessible

Special Services
We can assist with invitations, cakes, ministers, photographers, videographers, florists, disc jockeys and live musicians. Our consultants understand the significance of your special day. We assist you in planning and executing all details, to make your event a unique and wonderful occasion. We are the Northwest's premier full-service wedding and reception center.

HISTORIC, COLONIAL ESTATE: MANOR HOUSE AND NEW 6,000 SQ. FT. WESTERVELT HALL A WEDDING AND RECEPTION CENTER
We invite you to share the joy of having your wedding and reception at our two-acre historic estate. Enjoy the rich, old-world elegance of the manor house and Westervelt Hall and discover the beauty of the English-style gardens accented with ponds, waterfalls and garden statuary. Gray Gables is conveniently located just a few minutes south of downtown Portland. Please call for a guided tour of our lovely facility.

404 S.W. Washington
Portland, Oregon 97204
Contact: Ted (503) 224-2288
Business Hours: Mon–Thurs 7am–midnight;
Fri and Sat 7am–2:30am

Capacity: up to 200
Price Range: varies by number of persons and menu selection
Catering: in-house catering only; off-premise catering always available
Types of Events: wedding ceremonies and receptions, rehearsal dinners, banquets, holiday parties; you may choose from sit-down dinners, buffets, cocktails and hors d'oeuvres

Availability and Terms
Please make reservations as soon as possible. Short-notice reservations gladly accepted upon space availability.

Description of Facility and Services
Seating: up to 200
Servers: provided
Bar facilities: provided by Greek Cusina
Dance floor: with electrical hookups
Linens: included
China: china available at no extra charge
Decorations: we can decorate or client can
Cleanup: provided by Greek Cusina
Parking: available on street or in adjacent parking structure
ADA: accessible

Special Services
Music—come see what's making the Greek Cusina *the* place for entertainment. Live Greek performances!
Off-premise catering—let us cater your next event, whatever the occasion, whatever the location.

A TOUCH OF GREECE IN THE HEART OF PORTLAND
Our new Minoan Room is now open and awaiting you. Decorated in warm hues of gold and stunning architecture, The Minoan Room is inviting as well as elegant and romantic—the ideal place for your special day.

Let us dazzle you with our exceptional food as you enter a world of Mediterranean charm and flavor.

The Minoan Room
"A Must See Event Facility"
No Room Charge with Food and Beverage Minimum

8187 S.W. Tualatin-Sherwood Road
Tualatin, Oregon 97062
Contact: Jennie Bernard (503) 691-9111; Fax (503) 691-9112
E-mail: Catering@Haydensgrill.com
Business Hours: Mon–Fri 8am–5pm

Capacity: Boardroom up to 18; Small Lakefront Room: up to 40; Hayden Room: up to 65; Century Room: up to 65; Large Lakefront Room: up to 150; outdoors up to 500; **Off-premise:** unlimited

Price Range: rooms from $25-$600; pricing is negotiable with qualified food purchase; a $10 discount applies to each room booked at the Century Hotel. Breakfast starts at $5.50, lunch at $12.95 and dinner at $18.95

Catering: extensive catering services; both in-house and off-premise catering available; fun menus and decorative décor will accompany both our in-house and off-premise catering

Types of Events: perfect for rehearsal dinners and receptions

Availability and Terms

Hayden's Lakefront Grill has four rooms from 320 sq. ft. up to 1,400 sq. ft. Rooms require a deposit prior to events and we are flexible with date changes.

Description of Facility and Services

Seating: provided; all types of seating arrangements available
Servers: provided by Hayden's
Bar facilities: provided; fully licensed
Dance floor: available to rent
Linens and napkins: choose your own colors at no extra charge
Decorations: simple table decor provided at no charge; decorating may take place two hours prior to your event
China and glassware: bone china provided
Cleanup: provided by Hayden's
Parking: available
ADA: yes

Special Services

We can assist you in all of your party needs. We offer groups rates for $89 at the Century Hotel, located next to Hayden's Lakefront Grill.

Off-Premise Catering

We offer off-premise catering as well as in-house catering. We can handle any group size from 20 on up to 5,000. Not the average catering company, known locally for our great reputation, our off-premise catering will "wow" any guests that you may be trying to impress. Give us a call at (503) 691-9111.

CHARMING LAKEFRONT SETTING

Hayden's Grill and the Century Hotel are unique to Tualatin. Locally owned, we are located in the heart of Tualatin on the Lake of the Commons, right off I-5. Hayden's Grill is the place to take your date to the prom as well as the place to take your kids for our fun environment. We offer many options for meetings, receptions, weddings, rehearsal dinners and more. For more information, check us out at Haydensgrill.com and take a virtual tour!

HEATHMAN PRIVATE DINING

1001 S.W. Broadway at Salmon Street • Portland, Oregon 97205
Contact: Catering (503) 790-7126; Web site: www.Heathmanhotel.com

Capacity: 300 people reception; 200 people seated
Price Range: varies depending on type of event and menu selection
Catering: full-service in-house and off-premise catering available
Types of Events: sit-down meals, buffets, receptions

Availability and Terms

You may reserve one of our eight private rooms, or the entire mezzanine for larger receptions. Please contact the catering office for details.

Description of Facility and Services

Seating: tables and chairs provided
Servers: provided, with 19% service charge
Bar facilities: full-service bar with bartenders available for your event; The Heathman supplies the liquor, beer and wine
Dance floor: available
Linens and napkins: variety of linen selections available
China and glassware: fine china, silver and crystal supplied
Decorations: assorted decorative items available at no charge; additional decorations can be arranged
Cleanup: included in price
Parking: parking available; price varies
ADA: fully accessible

OUR GOAL IS TO INDULGE YOU

Walk through the doors into the most elegant and romantic atmosphere in Portland. Located in the heart of the arts and culture district of downtown Portland, the historic Heathman Hotel will exceed your highest expectations. Enjoy the stylish, warm ambiance of one of our eight private dining rooms. Adorned with silk wall coverings, classic wood shutters, topiary plants or even a fire-lit room , each room has its own distinct character. The ambiance is perfectly matched by our staff. Dedicated personally to your event, our goal is to indulge you! Enjoy the cuisine of Chef Philippe Boulout, winner of the James Beard Award as the Best Chef in the Northwest. Chef Boulout maintains his reputation as a culinary star. For a rehearsal dinner, wedding reception, or special event—relax and let The Heathman worry about the details.

Heritage House Farm & Gardens

Aurora, Oregon
Contact: Bill and Derolyn Johnston
(503) 678-5704 or (888) 479-3500
Shown by appointment

Capacity: up to 250 in a lovely garden setting; small, intimate settings also available
Price Range: varies depending on function and size of group; please call for information
Catering: full-service catering—from casual barbeques to specialty buffets to elegant banquet dinners; Heritage House can also arrange for rehearsal dinners or Sunday brunch following the event
Types of Events: lovely spring, summer and fall garden events including, but not limited to, weddings, receptions, family parties and events, business meetings and parties

Availability and Terms

Make reservations as soon as possible, up to a year in advance. We can accommodate on shorter notice if the facility is not booked. Site is reserved with a one-third deposit. Liability insurance required. Only one event per day is scheduled.

Description of Facility and Services

Heritage House Farm and Gardens is a hazelnut farm nestled halfway between Portland and Salem in the beautiful Willamette Valley. The house is a 1934 Colonial-style home decorated in country elegance and the grounds are lovely gardens and lawns surrounded by giant trees and nut orchards. The historic Aurora Colony is nearby for sightseeing and antique shopping, or take time to golf, view the beautiful Willamette River, or visit the Oregon Gardens.

Seating: tables and chairs provided
Bar facilities: alcohol served by arrangement
Dance floor: dance area available
Linens and napkins: provided by caterer
China and glassware: provided by caterer
Decorations: beautiful floral setting; please inquire about specific decorating ideas
Cleanup: provided by staff
Parking: ample parking is available

**Experience Country Elegance
on Your Special Day**

Holiday Inn

Portland Airport
Hotel and Trade Center
8439 N.E. Columbia Boulevard
Portland, Oregon 97220
(503) 256-5000; Fax (503) 256-5631
E-mail: karen.chaney@jqh.com
www.holidayinnportlandairport.com

Capacity: maximum of 1,000 guests
Price Range: customized to meet your needs
Catering: full-service catering; wedding packages available
Types of Events: we offer a large number of rooms to accommodate your rehearsal dinner, ceremony and/or reception and will cater everything from a simple cocktail party to an elaborate, multicourse sit-down dinner

Availability and Terms

We offer a wide selection of rooms to fit your needs. Advance reservations are strongly encouraged. Deposits are required and are non-refundable.

Description of Facility and Services

Seating: various setup styles available
Servers: accommodating, friendly staff included in catering cost
Bar facilities: full beverage service available; Holiday Inn Portland Airport to provide all beer, wine and liquor
Dance floor: cost varies per size of dance floor
China and glassware: white china and stemmed glassware
Decorations: silk plants, mirror tiles, votive candles and ficus trees
Cleanup: included in price
Equipment: podium, risers and specialty props
Sleeping accommodations: 286 modern guest rooms with 16 suites; we offer special rates for your out-of-town guests
Parking: complimentary parking for 900 vehicles
ADA: accessible

Special Services

Our professional sales and catering staff are ready to assist you with all your needs. Allow the Holiday Inn Portland Airport to take the stress out of your next event. The success of your event is our ultimate goal.

YOUR EVERY EXPECTATION WILL BE EXCEEDED!

The Holiday Inn Portland Airport is part of the John Q. Hammons Hotel Corp., one of the nation's largest. It has 286 guest rooms with the largest meeting facility within five minutes of the airport. In addition to the 12 meeting and banquet rooms totaling 33,607 square feet of flexible meeting space, we have the ability to fulfill any client's needs. The staff at the Holiday Inn Portland Airport is well versed at accommodating your personal needs on the most special day of your life; you can rest assured that your every expectation for your wedding will be exceeded. We welcome the opportunity to give you 100% guest satisfaction.

PORTLAND DOWNTOWN
1441 N.E. Second Avenue
Portland, Oregon 97232
Contact: Kellie Ohlfs, Director of Catering
(503) 233-2401
Business Hours: Mon–Fri 8am–5pm

E-mail: kellie.ohlfs@mindspring.com; Web site: www.Holiday-Inn.com/hiprtldwtn

Capacity: the Horizon Ballroom can accommodate up to 200 guests

Price Range: many options available; please check with our catering department

Catering: the Holiday Inn offers full-service in-house catering; we specialize in creative menu design to make your reception a beautiful experience

Types of Events: elegantly served luncheons and dinners, and hors d'oeuvre buffets

Availability and Terms

Early reservations are strongly recommended. A deposit is due within 14 days of reserving banquet space. Remaining balance is due seven days prior to the reception. Guaranteed number of guests is required to be called in seven days prior to event.

Description of Facility and Services

The Horizon Ballroom features over 2,600 sq. ft. of beautiful banquet space and includes a large foyer area that is perfect for your receiving line, buffet or guest bars. The ballroom is located on the main level of the hotel and features private entrances.

Servers: professional service staff is included with reception package

Bar facilities: the Holiday Inn can arrange for a hosted or no-host bar for your reception; our portable bars include full setup, mixed drinks, beer, wine, champagne and soft drinks

Dance floor: portable dance floor available; please check with our catering department

Linens and napkins: available in a variety of colors—please check with our catering department

China and glassware: ivory china, stemmed glassware

Decorations: early access for setup prior to your event; banquet staff will set up tables and chairs according to your specifications

Cleanup: included at no extra charge

Parking: ample, validated parking is available for your guests; **ADA:** fully accessible

Bridal suite: with the selection of a full wedding package, the Holiday Inn will extend a complimentary guestroom for the bride and groom on the evening of the reception; the guestroom includes a bottle of champagne/sparkling cider.

BACKED WITH EXPERIENCED
RECEPTION AND MEETING COORDINATORS

The Holiday Inn Downtown has a warm traditional atmosphere with a convenient location for you, your family and guests. We are near the Rose Quarter arena, Oregon Convention Center and shopping at Lloyd Center. The 10-story hotel has 235 guest rooms, each featuring a view of the city, Willamette River, West Hills or Mount Hood. We also offer a full-service restaurant and lounge. We look forward to making this a memorable day for you and your guests!

Hostess House, Inc.

10017 N.E. Sixth Avenue
Vancouver, Washington 98685
(360) 574-3284
www.thehostesshouse.com

Featured in *Modern Bride Magazine*
as the place to have your wedding
in the Pacific Northwest!

Open seven days a week;
please call for an appointment

Capacity: chapel holds 200; reception area with enclosed decks can accommodate 300
Price Range: wedding and reception packages starting at $1,595 to $2,995; price depends
on the day of the week, time of day and number of guests
Catering: full in-house catering and bakery
Types of Events: all types from cake and punch to sit-down dinners

Availability and Terms

A $700 deposit reserves your date and applies toward purchases. Reservations are taken as far
as a year in advance; however, we can occasionally accommodate reservations on short notice.

Description of Facility and Services

Seating: as many chairs and tables as needed; plus patio
Servers: we provide all serving attendants and any additional personnel needed
Bar facilities: full-service bar and bartenders; we provide all alcoholic and nonalcoholic
beverages and liquor liability
Dance floor: oak dance floor for 75 to 100 people; house DJ available for $100 for the first
hour and $50 each additional hour
Linens and napkins: lace tablecloths and engraved napkins
Serviceware: fine china; long-stem crystal; silver serving pieces
Cleanup: Hostess House provides at no extra charge
Decorations: chapel and reception facility will be decorated throughout with floral
arrangements in your colors. A 15 unit candelabra with flower arrangement, two sprays of
flowers, and six pew arrangements decorate the chapel. A fresh flower arrangement will be
at the guest book and fresh bud vases on every dining room table.
Parking: ample free parking provided; **ADA:** completely disabled accessible

INTRODUCING THE HOSTESS HOUSE...THE FIRST
FULL-SERVICE WEDDING CENTER IN THE NORTHWEST

The candle-lit chapel seats 200 guests and looks out onto a beautiful garden with a waterfall.
Now you can have the excitement and joy of a perfectly planned wedding with none of the
work or worry. Our bridal consultants will assist you with every detail. The reception center is
absolutely gorgeous! It has an indoor fountain, oak dance floor, and a fireplace. The covered
decks open onto a lovely landscaped yard with a beautiful gazebo. The Hostess House—
where the bride's wedding dreams come true! DIRECTIONS: We are located 10 minutes
North of Portland. From I-5 North or South, take the 99th Street exit (#5) and go West two
blocks. Turn right onto Sixth Avenue.

See page 222 under Bridal Attire and page 315 under Ceremony Sites.

HOTEL
ELLIOTT

357 12th Street
Astoria, Oregon 97103
(503) 325-2222
or 1-877-EST-1924
Fax (503) 325-2002
E-mail: info@hotelelliott.com
Web site: www.hotelelliott.com

Capacity: up to 75 in conference room; 20 in Presidential Suite
Pricing: please call for current pricing
Catering: several options available
Types of Events: meetings, social events, conferences, presentations, parties, weddings, receptions

Availability and Terms
Reservations based on availability. Cancellation up to seven days in advance. Deposit required to hold date.

Description of Services and Facility
Banquet services
- **Seating:** tables and chairs provided
- **Servers:** included in price
- **Bar facilities:** host and no host available
- **Dance floor:** no
- **Linens and napkins:** hotel can provide white or ecru
- **China and glassware:** provided by hotel
- **Decorations:** no restrictions
- **Cleanup:** hotel responsible

Meeting and event services
- **Audio visual and equipment:** request at reservation—available for a fee; entire hotel wired for free high speed internet access

Parking: available
ADA: compliant

Special Services
Rooftop garden available for use with presidential suite (seasonal, holds up to 15).

HISTORIC CHARM WITH MODERN AMENITIES.
This newly renovated historic hotel offers the charms of yesterday with the amenities and conveniences of today. A unique and beautiful location for your next event. Accommodations also available.

McMENAMINS HOTEL OREGON

310 N.E. Evans Street • McMinnville, Oregon 97128
Web site: www.hoteloregon.com; E-mail: sales@hoto.com
(503) 472-8427, (888) 472-8427

Capacity: meeting and banquet facilities ranging from eight to 120 person capacity
Catering: full-service in-house catering
Price Range: $200 to $2,000
Types of Events: The historic hotel is ideal for banquets, retreats, receptions, conferences, holiday parties, anniversaries and beyond.

Availability and Terms
Reservations are recommended at least three months in advance. Deposit required. Please contact our sales staff for details.

Description of Facility and Services
Seating: tables and chairs are arranged to fit your needs
Servers: staff included in price; 17% gratuity added to the bill
Bar facilities: full-service bar featuring McMenamins ales, wines and spirits
Linens and napkins: assorted linens included in room minimum
China and glassware: all china and glassware included
Audiovisual: A/V equipment available
Cleanup: provided by Hotel Oregon
Parking: on-street parking available; free parking lot located two blocks away
ADA: banquet facilities are accessible as well as some guestrooms

Special Services
Hotel Oregon features 42 antique-filled guest rooms, a cozy Cellar Bar, Rooftop Bar, and a McMenamins Pub serving breakfast, lunch and dinner.

RICH IN HISTORY
Hotel Oregon offers 42 guestrooms and surroundings rich in history spanning back to its opening in 1905. Enjoy breakfast, lunch or dinner in the spacious McMenamins Pub. Sip regional wines in the Cellar Bar after perusing the hotel's own "gallery" of artwork and historical photographs covering every wall. Or take a short elevator ride to the Rooftop Bar and sample craft ales and wines while drinking in the spectacular sights of Yamhill County's orchards and the coastal range.

John Palmer House

4314 N. Mississippi Ave.
Portland OR 97217
Contact: Roger Goldingay, (503) 493 1903
Website: www.JohnPalmerHouse.com

Capacity: Maximum 49 indoor, 100 outdoors.
Price Range: Call for pricing.
Catering: From our preferred list of caterers.
Types of Events: Weddings, receptions, rehearsal dinners, parties, banquets, business meetings, photo shoots, fundraisers. Guest lodging with reservations only.

Availability and Terms:

The John Palmer House is available 365 days a year. Early reservations are recommended, but we may be able to accommodate last minute bookings. A deposit is required at the time of your reservation and is non-refundable unless a replacement is found. Remaining balance is due at least one week prior to your event.

Description of Facility and Services:

The John Palmer House is a sophisticated and elegant Eastlake Victorian mansion built in 1890. The house is a work of art, with subtle light changes throughout the day that constantly vibrate through the original Povey stained glass windows. The colors, designs and sheen on the Bradbury & Bradbury wallpapers are an ever-changing dynamic, reflecting a glowing, golden light that follows you through the rooms. We welcome you to call us and make an appointment to tour the house, which is listed on the National Register of Historic Places.

While maintaining the elegance and beauty of traditional Victorian architecture, the John Palmer House has been updated with modern conveniences, including high-speed wireless Internet access and a hot tub. The beautifully landscaped gardens and front porch are a wonderful location for outdoor events. The interior is an exquisite site for intimate gatherings of under 50 people. Several configurations can be arranged to suit your needs. Arrangements can also be made to provide overnight lodging for some of your special guests. The John Palmer House is best suited for smaller groups. Keep your guest list exclusive for the best experience.

Seating: Limited tables and chairs are available. Special requirements are renter's responsibility.
Servers: Provided by caterer.
Bar Facilities: A licensed, bonded and insured bartender must serve liquor.
Linens, China, and Glassware: Provided by caterer
Dance Floor: Outdoors on front porch or lawn
Cleanup: Client or caterer to provide.
Decorations: All decorations must be approved in advance
Audiovisual and equipment: Must be rented.
Parking: On-site for 10 cars, plenty of free street parking.
ADA: Limited due to historic nature of building.

PORTLAND'S IRISH RESTAURANT & PUB

112 S.W. Second Avenue Portland, Oregon 97204
Contact: Brad Yoast (503) 227-4057; Fax (503) 227-5931
E-mail: portland@kellsirish.com • Web site: www.kellsirish.com

Capacity: private banquet facilities located on second floor; capacities range from 15–150 and up to 300 reception-style

Price Range: varies according to room and services

Catering: full-service in-house and off-premise catering

Types of Events: we provide buffet and formal sit-down service for receptions, rehearsal dinners, business luncheons, cocktail and hors d' oeuvre parties, holiday and surprise parties, fund raisers and gala events

Availability and Terms

Located on the second floor of the historic Kells building near the waterfront in downtown Portland. With the Irish ambiance, excellent service and outstanding food you've come to expect, Kells invites your guests to celebrate in the stately ballroom and mingle in the intimate Ulster and Cigar Rooms.

Description of Facility and Services

Seating: variety of seating customized to meet your needs from 15–150

Menus: visit our Web site at www.kellsirish.com to view our menu options

Servers: included in service

Bar facilities: host/no host bar; largest single malt selection in the northwest, full range of micro beers, extensive wine list; fine cigars also available

Dance floor: we offer two separate locations for bands, a long list of our most popular local acts, electrical hook-ups available

Linens and napkins: included in service; inquire about our color selection

China and glassware: white china with glassware to complement

Cleanup: included with full-service catering

Decorations: discussion of your ideas and needs welcomed

Parking: parking for events may be made in advance, garages within close proximity

ADA: yes; elevator to second floor

PORTLAND'S FAVORITE IRISH RESTAURANT & PUB

Kells has become a Portland landmark since its opening in 1990. One of Portland's favorite nightspots, Kells offers a great menu of New World Irish cuisine mixing traditional favorites with fresh, Northwest seafoods, produce, and all-natural ingredients. Kells also features live Irish music seven nights a week, a grand stone fireplace and comfortable cigar room. All this and the warm, friendly service and atmosphere of a genuine Irish Pub.

McMENAMINS KENNEDY SCHOOL

5736 N.E. 33rd Avenue
Portland, Oregon 97211
Contact: Group Sales Office (503) 288-3286
Web site: www.kennedyschool.com
E-mail: sales@kennedyschool.com
Business Hours: Mon–Fri 9am–5pm;
Tours by appointment

Capacity: meeting and banquet facilities ranging from 10 to 112-person capacity
Price Range: food and beverage minimum varies based on size of room and time of day
Catering: in-house catering only
Types of Events: This 1915 schoolhouse suits a variety of events, including ceremonies, receptions, rehearsal dinners, meetings, retreats, banquets, reunions and holiday parties.

Availability and Terms

Kennedy School has several small rooms that seat 10 to 100 people. The theater accommodates up to 200. Reserve your date as early as possible to ensure availability. Deposit required. Please contact our sales staff for details.

Description of Facility and Services

Seating: tables and chairs are arranged to fit your needs
Servers: staff included in price; 17% gratuity added to food and beverage bill
Bar facilities: full-service bar featuring McMenamins wines, ales and spirits
Dance floor: our gymnasium's hardwood floor provides a fun dance location
Linens: linens include a wide variety of colors; no charge
China and glassware: all china and glassware included
Decorations: please discuss your decorating ideas with our event coordinator
Audiovisual: a full line of A/V available and most rooms have chalkboards
Cleanup: included in price
Parking: plenty of free parking
ADA: all banquet facilities are accessible as well as some guest rooms

Special Services

Kennedy School has 35 overnight rooms to accommodate your out-of-town guests. Movies shown nightly in the theater. A soaking pool is available to guests.

HISTORIC BUILDING, GREAT GATHERING SPOT

McMenamins Kennedy School is a unique gathering spot for your group. This historic grade school has been transformed into a wonderful guest facility offering art-filled rooms with original chalkboards, restaurant, movie theater, gymnasium, wine tasting, bar, brewery and soaking pool. It is conveniently located minutes from downtown and the Portland Airport. Call the Group Sales Office for a complete catering packet.

for Meetings and Events

15450 S.W. Millikan Way in Beaverton
(503) 626-MEET (6338); Web site: www.kingstad.com

Capacity: largest room accommodates up to 300 people; 14 event spaces; 24,000 net square feet total

Price Range: varies according to event size and menu selection; Complete Event Packages available

Catering: full-service catering

Types of Events: weddings, receptions, rehearsal dinners, luncheons, dinners, meetings, conferences

Availability and Terms

Reservations should be made as early as possible to ensure availability. A nonrefundable deposit of 25% of expected expenditures is required to confirm your date. Payment in full is due the day of your function. All major credit cards accepted.

Description of Facility and Services

Seating: various seating arrangements offered
Servers: appropriate service staff provided with catering service
Bar facilities: alcoholic beverages allowed; coffee, tea, and beverage service
Linens and napkins: cloth tablecloths and napkins
China and glassware: off-white china; variety of glassware
Dance floor: slate tile and wood floors ideal for dancing
Cleanup: provided by Kingstad Meeting Centers
Technology equipment: video projectors, VCR and monitor, DVD players, built-in sound systems, computer projection equipment, ISDN lines, video conferencing
Parking: free
ADA: yes

Special Services

Kingstad Center for Meetings and Events can custom-design your event to meet a wide range of tastes and budgets.

Kingstad Center for Meetings and Events offers full-service facilities that specialize in providing event space for groups of 300 or less. Every aspect of our service and facilities have been designed to help make your event memorable and easy to plan.

21160 N.E. Blue Lake Road • Fairview, Oregon 97024
(503) 667-3483 • Email: lakehouse@salvadormollys.com

Capacity:
Indoors: sit-down seating for 80-120, standing reception for 150
Outdoor garden: 250

Price Range: varies according to time of year and day of week

Catering: outside catering provided by Salvador Molly's, or bring-your-own (pot luck)

Type of Events: including, but not limited to, weddings, receptions, corporate functions, private parties and meetings.

Availability and terms
Early reservations are recommended, particularly for summer months. Deposits are required.

Description of Facility and Services
Seating: tables and chairs available
China, linens, glassware and bar service: provided by caterer
Parking: on-site
ADA accessible and pleny of handicapped parking

Newly Updated at Blue Lake Park
The picturesque, private setting features the newly updated Lake House at Blue Lake Park. Perfect for weddings and receptions, the Lake House offers a tranquil setting with natural beauty just 20 minutes from downtown Portland. Large picture windows offer a view of the lake and the gorgeous surrounding gardens. Our professional on-site event coordinator will work with you to help create your dream event.

LAKESIDE GARDENS

16211 S.E. Foster Road
Portland, Oregon 97236
(3.4 miles east of I-205 on Foster Road)
(503) 760-6044; Fax (503) 760-9311
Business Hours: Mon–Fri 10am–2pm;
evenings and weekends by appointment
Web site: www.lakesidegardens.citysearch.com

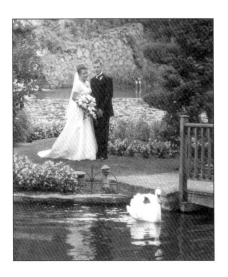

Capacity: 225 people—sit-down wedding at gazebo; 180 people—sit-down wedding inside; 300 people—buffet reception; 120 people—sit-down buffet

Price Range: price is determined by the event and menu selection

Catering: full-service in-house catering only

Types of Events: elegant wedding receptions all year-round, birthdays, anniversaries, barbecues, corporate parties, Christmas parties, business meetings, or seminars

Availability and Terms

Please make your reservations as early as possible; we recommend one year to six months in advance. A $1,000 booking fee will hold the date and time frame scheduled for your event.

Description of Facility and Services

Seating: tables and chairs are provided; terrace and garden seating available

Servers: we provide all serving attendants

Bar facilities: beer, wine, and champagne; we provide beverages and bartenders

Dance floor: hardwood dance floor with electrical hookups for DJs and bands

Linens and napkins: linen tablecloths; linen and paper napkins available

Serviceware: fine china, glassware, and silver serving pieces available for your use

Cleanup: provided by Lakeside Gardens

Decorations: elegant building requires little decoration

Parking: plenty of convenient free parking

ADA: completely disabled accessible

THE IDEAL PLACE RIGHT IN YOUR OWN BACKYARD

Lakeside Gardens is a private event facility situated on approximately seven acres. We schedule events year-round. Outside, Lakeside Gardens blends tall cedars, weeping willows, mute swans, and lakes surrounded by a garden paradise. During cooler weather Lakeside Gardens also offers a complete inside facility. Inside amenities consist of beautiful chandeliers, brass railing, an elegant oak and marble fireplace, a black ebony baby grand piano, and mirrored wall that reflects an inspiring panoramic view of the lake and surrounding gardens. We are conveniently located only minutes from downtown Portland and Portland International Airport. Lakeside Gardens offers superb catering. We are able to provide ice sculptures and other decorations to create the setting of your choice. A knowledgeable wedding consultant or program coordinator will work with you to plan and execute everything. Please call us for more details and personal assistance as you plan your next event.

LAKEWOOD CENTER FOR THE ARTS
368 S. State Street
Lake Oswego, Oregon 97034
(503) 635-6338
Business Hours: Mon–Fri 9am–5pm
Web site: http://www.lakewood-center.org

Capacity: 150 for sit-down dinner, 225 for cocktail party
Price Range: $500 for the room
Catering: provided by renter; kitchen available
Types of Events: banquets, receptions, reunions, office parties, business meetings.

Description of Facility
Lakewood Center is conveniently located on State Street (Highway 43) at the south end of Lake Oswego. The Community Meeting Room, on the lower level at the Center, has windows on two sides and is decorated with a forest green and cream color scheme. A full-catering kitchen is attached to the space. The room comes with tables, chairs and place settings for up to 150.

Availability and Terms
Reservations should be made as soon as possible, six months to a year in advance. A security deposit is required to reserve your date. This fee is nonrefundable if you cancel your date. Your room fee balance of $500 is due one week before your event. The security deposit will be refunded, 2–3 weeks after your event, if there is no damage and the room is clean.

Description of Reception Services
The Lakewood Center is the perfect facility for those who wish to coordinate the details for themselves or bring in their own consultant or catering company. The room is ideal for banquets, receptions, reunions, office parties and business meetings.
Seating: up to 150
China: place settings of plate, salad plate, coffee cup, water glass and silverware for up to 150 are included
Dance floor: room is carpeted; many groups dance on the carpet or rent a dance floor from outside sources
Decorations: please inquire; no tape, tacks, or nails please
Cleanup: done by the renter
Parking: paved lot behind facility
ADA: full handicap accessibility
Special note: the Center rents only the room, tables and chairs, and place settings for up to 150; items such as linens, silver, crystal, serving utensils, coffee urns, and dance floor need to be arranged with other vendors

24377 N.E. Airport Road
Aurora, Oregon 97002

503-678-GOLF (4653)
E-mail: info@langdonfarms.com
www.langdonfarms.com

Langdon Farms Golf Course is conveniently located 20 minutes south of Portland off I-5. The course is situated on several acres of pristine greens designed from the former farmland of the Langdon Family. This tranquil setting is ideal for the elegant dinner or casual reception. The staff at Langdon is relentless to please and will go the extra mile to make your event a success. Whether your event is outside or in, your guests will delight in the serenity and splendor of the surroundings.

Capacity: Space for up to 250 people; inside and outside facilities available

Price Range: Room charge waived if minimum food/beverage purchases are met

Catering: Available in-house

Types of Events: Wedding reception, rehearsal dinner, bridal shower, groomsmen golf and lunch

Availability and Terms

Reservations can be made anytime, but it is recommended that they be made at least six months in advance. A deposit is required to hold reservation date.

Description of Facility and Services:

Seating: All table and chairs provided

Servers: Fully trained and licensed professional servers

Bar facilities: Full-service bar and licensed bartender(s) provided; full selections of liquor, beer, wine and champagne

Dance floor: Available to rent

Linens and napkins: Provided

China and glassware: Provided

Cleanup: Included

Decorations: Please check with catering representative

Parking: Ample FREE parking

ADA: Fully accessible

LEWIS RIVER GOLF COURSE

3209 Lewis River Road
Woodland, Washington 98674
360-225-8254 or 800-341-9426
Visit us on the web at www.lewisrivergolf.com

Capacity: North Fork Great Room-160; Great Room Deck-90; Bar and Grill-70; Riverside Patio-400.
Price Range: varies depending on event
Catering: full service in-house
Types of Events: indoor/outdoor weddings, receptions, rehearsal dinners, conferences, banquets, fund raising dinners and auctions

Availability and Terms
A $500 deposit is required to reserve your date.

Description of Facility and Services
Seating: tables and chairs provided
Servers: full staff included in catering cost
Bar facilities: full service, portable bar available
Dance floor: hardwood floor with electrical hook-ups
Linen and napkins: included in set-up fee; many colors to choose from
China and glassware: white china and stemware
Clean up: included in set-up charge
Equipment: sound system, cordless mic, projection screen
Parking: on-site
ADA: fully accessible
Additional services: changing room for bride

SERENE SETTING FOR YOUR SPECIAL DAY
Lewis River Golf Course is tucked away along one of the most scenic stretches on the Lewis River. The Northwest Lodge Clubhouse featuring log and river rock accents and hand forged iron, combined with a serene setting makes Lewis River Golf Course the perfect choice for your special event.

www.lewisrivergolf.com

MALLORY HOTEL

729 S.W. 15th Avenue • Portland, Oregon 97205
Contact: Marianne Donaldson-Bradley, Banquet Coordinator
E-mail: marianned@malloryhotel.com
503-223-6311, 800-228-8657
Fax 503-827-0453
www.malloryhotel.com

Classic...Charming...Elegant...Affordable
Built in 1912, the **Mallory** is Portland's premier uptown Hotel. This classic and architecturally significant boutique hotel offers traditional decor and ambiance. Located on the corner of S.W. 15th and Yamhill, adjacent to the MAX light rail, the Mallory is ideally situated within walking distance of downtown and the trendy Northwest and Pearl districts.

Capacity: 3,400 square feet of meeting and banquet space. **The Mallory Dining Room** accommodates up to 105 for plated meal service; available with a minimum guest room reservation. **The Crystal Room** accommodates up to 90 for plated meal service or 120 for receptions and meetings. **The Garden Room** accommodates up to 26 for plated meal service or 35 for receptions. **The Executive Room** accommodates up to 16 for plated meal service or 24 for meetings.

Price Range: Room fees may apply depending upon food and beverage purchase.

Catering: $9.95 to $35.95 per person plus 17% gratuity.

Types of Events: weddings, receptions, rehearsal dinners, anniversary parties, reunions, fundraisers, corporate events, holiday parties, theme parties and awards banquets

Availability and Terms
Call for availability information. Signed contract and 25% deposit are required to secure a reservation.

Description of Facility and Services
Included: licensed servers and bartenders; set up/clean up, tables, chairs, linens, cloth napkins, skirting, glassware, silverware, dinnerware, chafing dishes, mirror and votive center pieces

Liquor: provided in-house; served by in-house licensed bartenders; corkage available with fee.

Dance floor: available for an additional fee; please inquire for availability and fees.

Decorations: clients may decorate prior to their event if availability allows. Our staff may secure other arrangements such as risers, staging, etc., through outside venders.

Audiovisual: equipment and services available; fees vary, please inquire.

Internet: Complimentary high-speed wireless Internet access available.

ADA: compliant

Guest Rooms and Suites
130 deluxe guest rooms, including 13 suites. Overnight guests enjoy complimentary continental breakfast, free parking, daily newspaper, HBO, pay-per-view movies and free local calls. Check-out is always at 1 pm. Other amenities include in-room refrigerators, safes, iron and ironing board. Group and corporate rates are available. High-speed wireless Internet access.

Parking and Ground Transportation: Mallory Park Garage is across the street and is complimentary for overnight guests and guests attending functions at the hotel. MAX light rail is adjacent to the hotel on Yamhill Street.

PORTLAND Marriott.
DOWNTOWN

1401 S.W. Naito Parkway
Portland, Oregon 97201
Contact: Sales and Catering Department
(503) 499-6360; Fax (503) 226-1209
Business Hours: Mon–Fri 7am–5pm

Capacity: up to 1,000 people
Price Range: price will be determined by event and specific menu
Catering: provided by the hotel exclusively
Types of Events: from intimate champagne receptions to elegant multi-course dinners, including rehearsal dinners and bridal showers; the addition of the beautiful Mount Hood Room offers a spectacular view of Portland; overlooking the Willamette River and Mount Hood, the perfect room with the perfect view will enhance your special day

Availability and Terms
The Portland Marriott Hotel offers a wide selection of rooms to fit your specific wedding needs. Since most weddings occur on Saturdays, we suggest reserving your reception site as soon as possible.

Description of Facility and Services
Seating: tables, chairs, and head tables provided
Servers: included in price
Bar facilities: full beverage service available; Portland Marriott Downtown to provide all beer, wine, liquor, and bartenders
Dance floor: available at no charge
Linens and napkins: extensive linen selections at no charge
China and glassware: Portland Marriott Downtown uses only fine china, crystal, and silver-plated flatware
Cleanup: included in price
Parking: limited valet parking available in hotel; plenty of public parking adjacent to hotel
ADA: yes

Special Services
The Portland Marriott Downtown provides **a complimentary deluxe upgraded king room the night of the wedding** for that special bride and groom.

WEDDING CELEBRATIONS
At Marriott, we bring something extra to the wedding party—a tradition of care, concern, and service that assures peace of mind for the bridal couple and a memorable reception for everyone. After playing host to hundreds of bridal couples and their families, Marriott has the art of reception planning down to a science. Let us assist you in planning the wedding celebration of your dreams.

2126 S.W. Halsey • Troutdale, Oregon 97060; Contact: Sales Office (503) 492-2777
Web site: www.mcmenamins.com; E-mail: edgesales@mcmenamins.com
Business Hours: Mon–Fri 9am–5pm; Sat–Sun 10am–5pm, tours by appointment

Capacity: 200 people seated; 250 people reception-style
Price Range: $100 to $4,000 food and beverage minimum required; based on size of room and day of week
Catering: in-house catering only; plated, buffet, and hors d'oeuvres; prices vary
Types of Events: Edgefield is the perfect getaway for practically any occasion, including wedding ceremonies and receptions, rehearsal dinners, bridal showers and parties, meetings, conferences and retreats.

Availability and Terms

Edgefield has several beautiful and unique locations for wedding ceremonies and receptions, accommodating both small and large parties. Large banquet rooms are available for receptions, seating between 100 and 200 people each. The movie theater makes an ideal room for ceremonies, or try a natural setting outdoors. Additional set-up fees for outdoor receptions and ceremonies. For the best availability, we suggest booking summer or holiday weekend events at least one year prior. Our dedicated wedding coordinators can assist you in booking and planning your event. Deposit equals 25% of estimated food and beverage total and is due 30 days after booking. An additional 75% is due 60 days before your event.

Description of Facility and Services

Seating: round and rectangular tables for assorted seating; cushioned banquet chairs
Servers: staff included in price; 17% gratuity added to bill
Bar facilities: full-service bar featuring Edgefield ales, wines and spirits
Dance floor: available in two banquet rooms
Linens and napkins: assorted tablecloth and napkin colors; no charge
China and glassware: china, glassware, and flatware; no charge
Cleanup: included in price
Decorations: client responsibility
Parking: free parking and lots of it!**; ADA:** 11 out of 12 banquet rooms are accessible

Special Services

More than 100 quaint guestrooms with both private and shared bathrooms; built-in stereo systems in most even spaces, two on-site restaurants (three in summer); 18-hole golf course; small bars; massage.

EUROPEAN-STYLE VILLAGE

McMenamins Edgefield is the classic gathering place for weddings. The historical Main Lodge is surrounded by specialty buildings with spectacular gardens and landscaping, making the 38-acre property a virtual paradise and providing beautiful backdrops for photographs. Included on-site is a winery, brewery, distillery, movie theater, gift shop, sports bar, golf course, artisans, special events and daily tours. Edgefield is 20 minutes from downtown Portland and only 15 minutes from the airport. Call the Group Sales Office for a complete banquet packet.

THE MELODY BALLROOM

615 S.E. Alder • Portland, Oregon 97214
Contact: Kathleen Kaad (503) 232-2759; Fax (503) 232-0702
E-mail: mballroom@Qwest.net
www.themelodyballroom.com
Business Hours: Tue–Sat 10am–4pm or by appointment

Capacity: two rooms, up to 1,100 people; used separately, 300 and 800 people
Price Range: varies, please call
Catering: in-house catering and beverage services only
Types of Events: sit-down, buffet, theme, cocktails and hors d'oeuvres

Availability and Terms
The Melody Ballroom requires a room rental fee as a deposit to reserve your date. Reservations are accepted one year or more in advance. Catering cost must be paid one week prior to the event.

Description of Facility and Services
Seating: tables and chairs provided as needed
Servers: staff included in catering costs; gratuity on food and beverage
Bar facilities: full-service bar provided; host/no-host; liquor, beer, and wine
Dance floor: 30'x30'; 300 capacity; two large stages; can accommodate full touring bands
Linens and napkins: cloth and linen tablecloths and napkins; limited colors
China and glassware: china and glassware
Cleanup: included in catering cost
Decorations: few limitations; we can provide fresh flowers and limited decorating accessories
Parking: free street parking

Special Services
The Melody Ballroom rents on a per day basis, giving our clients the flexibility for decorating and music set up at your convenience. Our event coordinators will be happy to help you plan and execute your event to perfection… just ask.

EXTRAORDINARY FOOD AND FRIENDLY SERVICE WILL MAKE YOUR EVENT A SUCCESS!
The Melody Ballroom is a unique, historic facility, owned and operated by a professional chef. Our philosophy is to say "Yes!" and to make your event truly individual. We work with diverse menus and styles—even your favorite recipes! Our caring staff provides friendly service that will make your guests feel as if they were in your own home.

©Powers Studio

MILL CREEK GARDENS

Sheridan, Oregon
www.millcreekgardensbb.com • 503-843-4218, 877-792-4737

Capacity: 25 to 200 guests
Price Range: please call for specific prices on complete packages
Catering: full service in-house catering provided (**www.countryside-catering.com**)
Types of Events: weddings, receptions, rehearsal dinners, corporate meetings and retreats, reunions, anniversary parties and any special occasion

Availability and Terms
We are open daily from 9am-9pm. We are able to book your event up to one year in advance. A nonrefundable $500 deposit is required to reserve your booking date.

Description of Facility and Services
Seating: chairs and tables **provided**
Servers: friendly, professional staff **provided**
Bar facilities: provided
Dance floor: accommodates DJs and bands with electrical outlets **provided**
Linens and napkins: provided upon request
China and glassware: provided upon request
Decorations: basic decorations **provided**; additional decorations are responsibility of the renter
Consultation: event coordinator **provided**
Dressing rooms: provided
Cake and flowers: provided in some packages
Honeymoon: domestic and international accommodations **provided** in some packages
Setup and cleanup: provided
Parking: ample parking is **provided**
ADA: partially accessible

Special Services
Also Available from Mill Creek Gardens… Weddings Cabo Style! We make all your wedding arrangements, leaving you to enjoy a worry-free WEDDING and HONEYMOON vacation in PARADISE. For a two to 200 person event, we will use the best locations in the area and provide professional photographers, videographers, caterers and musicians. **www.weddingscabostyle.com.** We can make any event in Cabo San Lucas a memorable occasion. * *Our weddings are recognized as legal worldwide.*

IT'S YOUR SPECIAL DAY, LET US DO ALL THE WORK!
From the planning, to the set-up, through the reception onto the honeymoon travel and accommodations, we arrange it all. Our wonderful Event Coordinator and great staff will make your event a memorable, stress free occasion.

Mill Creek Gardens blends majestic fir and oak trees, beautiful flowers and lush lawns with the peaceful sounds of the rippling creek and the quiet rustle of the trees. If you are planning a fairytale ceremony or a less formal event this is the perfect setting to make your WEDDING DAY DREAMS COME TRUE.

Please let this business know that you heard about them from the Bravo! Wedding Resource Guide.   **125**

MILWAUKIE CENTER/
SARA HITE MEMORIAL ROSE GARDEN

5440 S.E. Kellogg Creek Drive • Milwaukie, Oregon 97222
Contact: Lin Dahl (503) 653-8100; Please contact us for an appointment
Fax (503) 794-8016; Email: lind@co.clackamas.or.us
Web site: www.co.clackamas.or.us/ncprd

Milwaukie Center and the Sara Hite Memorial Rose Garden are located in beautiful North Clackamas Park. The new outdoor Rose Garden is available for weddings, receptions and photo opportunities. The Center is an air conditioned, nonsmoking facility; perfect for any size group up to 400 for a sit-down dinner. The Facility Use Coordinator will help to make your event a pleasant experience whether your event is out in the Rose Garden or inside the Milwaukie Center. We provide you with lots of choices.

ROSE GARDEN:
Capacity: to 150 people
Price Range: call for prices
Seating: chairs for 100; eight 6' tables; 20' x 20' canopies available at an additional fee
Availability and Terms: call for schedule availability; a 50% deposit is required to hold your date

MILWAUKIE CENTER:
Capacity: North Wing: 200 standing, 125 seated; South Wing: 600 standing, 400 seated
Price Range: call for specific price information
Catering: use your own catering arrangements or use the Center's caterer with no additional cost for the use of the commercial kitchen
Alcohol: allowed with specific regulations; proof of liability insurance required; additional fee of $100
Availability and Terms: make your reservation as soon as your date is established; a 25% deposit is required to hold your date

Description of Facility and Services
Seating: chairs for 500; tables for 400; equipment request (number of tables and chairs) required at time of application
Servers: renter or caterer provides
Bar facilities: renter or caterer to provide bar, liquor, licensed server, and liability insurance
Dance floor: available; PA system also available
Linens and napkins: renter or caterer provides
China and glassware: Melamine china and silverware for 250; no glassware
Cleanup: renter responsible for removing all decorations and cleanup
Decorations: please discuss your decoration ideas with the Facility Use Coordinator
Candles: tapered and birthday candles are not allowed due to fire safety; limited votive candle use
ADA: yes

Special Services
The Milwaukie Center will have a Building Coordinator on duty during your event to assist with necessary details.

2236 S.E. Belmont • Portland, Oregon 97214 • (503) 297-9635 ext. 111

Capacity: up to 80 people for sit-down dinner; up to 120 for reception
Price Range: negotiable rate varies according to day of week and size of event
Catering: exclusively by Salvador Molly's Catering
Types of Events: including, but not limited to, weddings, receptions and rehearsal dinners

Availability and Terms
Space available for lunch and dinner events any day of the week. Deposits are required.

Description of Facility and Services
Seating: limited quantity of tables and chairs available
Servers: available through caterer
Linens: available through caterer
Bar facilities: available through caterer
Decorations: our on-site staff can assist with decor needs
Clean-up: handled by caterer
ADA: accessible

MOLLY'S LOFT ON BELMONT
If you're looking for a new space for your wedding, rehearsal dinner or private celebration, check out Molly's Loft on Belmont. Located at 2236 S.E. Belmont, this one-of-a-kind contemporary event space offers unique spaces, surfaces and lighting that can easily adapt to many distinctive decor options. The newly remodeled loft-like environment features large windows allowing for lots of natural light. Our experienced event and catering staff can assist you with all of your wedding planning needs.

MONTGOMERY PARK

2701 N.W. Vaughn Street
Portland, Oregon 97210
Contact: Bonnie August, Event Coordinator (503) 224-6958
Office Hours: Mon–Fri 8am–5pm

Capacity: 15 to 800 people (up to 400 seated, 800 standing); 12,100 square feet
Price Range: $95 to $3,400
Catering: inside catering contracted to Food in Bloom; approved caterers: Premiere Catering, Salvador Molly's, DeAngelo's Catering and Gina's Catering
Types of Events: weddings, receptions, buffets, meetings, trade shows, corporate events, business parties

Availability and Terms

Montgomery Park has a large banquet facility, a beautiful atrium and two meeting rooms. Deposits are required. Book up to one year in advance. Available hours are 7am to midnight.

Description of Facility and Services

Seating: tables and chairs provided (one setup included in room cost)
Servers: provided by caterer
Bar facilities: bar services and liquor provided by caterer
Dance floor: dance floor in the Atrium accommodates 500+ people with electrical hookup for bands or disc jockeys available
Linens, china and glassware: provided by caterer
Decorations: *no helium balloons* or tape; table decorations must be obtained from caterer, florist, or other source
Cleanup: you must remove all materials you bring in; some or all of your deposit may be kept for damage or extra labor for cleanup
Equipment: podium, easel, flip chart, whiteboard, overhead projector
Parking: 2,200 free spaces available on weekends and evenings

Special Services

An event coordinator, security or maintenance personnel may be available depending on the time of the event.

SOARING ATRIUM AND MODERN DECOR

Montgomery Park, a beautifully renovated historic building, features a 135-foot soaring atrium, a light airy atmosphere, and a contemporary black-and-white decor. It is an impressive site for your function. Montgomery Park is located in Northwest Portland at the bottom of the Northwest hills, providing a beautiful setting for your special event.

MT. HOOD BED & BREAKFAST

8885 Cooper Spur Road • Parkdale, Oregon 97041
Contact: Jackie Rice (541) 352-6885
Office Hours: Mon–Fri 8am–7pm

Capacity: up to 200⁺ (indoors or outdoors)
Price Range: available upon request
Catering: local catering
Types of Events: receptions with country elegance, buffets, barbecues, weddings, wedding receptions

Availability and Terms

Four guest rooms and outdoor gardens are available for weddings and receptions. Deposit is 50% of total with balance due 30 days prior to event.

Description of Facility and Services

Seating: for up to 200⁺
Servers: service staff included with catering
Dance floor: available with electrical outlets
Linens: provided by caterer
China and glassware: provided by caterer
Decorations: early decorating possible; cleanup to be immediately after event
Cleanup: client and caterer responsible
Parking: off-street
ADA: limited accessibility

ENCHANTING COUNTRY SETTING WITH SPECTACULAR MOUNTAIN VIEWS

Mount Hood Bed & Breakfast has everything you need for your wedding or event. Situated on the north shoulder of Mount Hood just out of the Columbia Gorge, the facility offers spectacular views of Mount Hood, Adams and Rainier. Our 7,200-square-foot facility can be used to move to the indoors in case of inclement weather. Come see us on the sunny side of Mount Hood. A little more than one hour from Portland.

Visit our Web site at www.mthoodbnb.com

See page 316 under Ceremony Sites.

211 Tumwater Drive
Oregon City, Oregon 97045
Contact: Judi Isbell
(503) 655-5574; Fax (503) 655-0035
Web site: www.orcity.com/museum

Capacity: up to 299
Price Range: please call for current prices
Catering: choose from our list of caterers or by special arrangement of your preferred
caterer
Types of Events: weddings, receptions, seminars, banquets, dances

Availability and Terms
Deposit required.

Description of Facility and Services
Seating: round tables, banquet tables, and chairs provided
Servers: provided by caterer
Bar facilities: provided caterer, additional insurance needed
Dance floor: hardwoods throughout
Linen and napkins: provided by caterer
China and glassware: provided by caterer
Parking: 48 spaces on site, additional on street
ADA: meets all ADA requirements

OVERLOOKING HISTORIC WILLAMETTE FALLS
The Museum of the Oregon Territory is an impressive building perched on a basalt cliff overlooking historic Willamette Falls. Among our many cherished heritage treasurers is the plat map of San Francisco, filed here in 1850 because Oregon City was the site of the only federal courthouse in the Northwest.

The Museum's third floor features a unique new meeting facility with dramatic 360-degree views, plenty of easy parking, and a capacity of up to 299. Tumwater, the Indian word for waterfall, commemorates this historic location which for centuries has been the crossroads of communication, trading, commerce and travel.

NORTH STAR BALLROOM

635 N. Killingsworth Court
Portland, Oregon 97217
Contact: Claire (503) 240-6088
www.northstarballroom.com

Capacity: from 20-300
Price Range: competitive and affordable, varies with event
Catering: on site caterers Flaming Carrot Catering, outside caterers welcome
Types of Events: weddings, receptions, rehearsal dinners, fundraisers, reunions, workshops, concerts, corporate and private celebrations

Availability and Terms
The North Star Ballroom has a classic two-story ballroom space, adjoining salon and bar, dining room, private parlor, and meeting rooms. A deposit is required to book the space. We welcome you on short notice, but encourage clients to book early.

Description of Facility and Services
Seating: tables and chairs provided for up to 150 in ballroom, 250 entire building
Servers: caterer to provide
Dance floor: maple floors, flexible dancing area depending on how much seating is required
Linens and Napkins: caterer to provide
China and glassware: caterer to provide
Cleanup: responsibility of caterer or client
Parking: free on street parking
ADA: yes

Special Services:
The rooms are accessible for early decorating. Built-in sound system, lighting equipment, micro-phone and piano are available. We are flexible, patient, and will do everything to make your experience a distinctly positive celebration.

HIP OASIS IN URBAN NORTH PORTLAND
In the heart of revitalized North Portland, conveniently located just ten minutes from downtown, the North Star Ballroom is an urban oasis; a palette for the offbeat Oregonion who longs for an alternative to the traditional wedding and a model of simple elegance for the more conventional. Celebrate with 2,100 square feet of maple floors, dramatic windows, and theater quality sound and lighting, plus an intimate bar and dining room setting, in a building whose history is as rich and remarkable as yours.

Nottinghams of Sherwood

Small Town Charm with Downtown Elegance

198 N. Pine Street • Sherwood, Oregon 97140
Phone 503-925-8779; Fax 503-925-1790
Contact: Lorrie or Carrie
E-mail: LBIDGOOD@aol.com; Web site: www.nottinghams.org

Capacity: indoor ceremony seating up to 120; indoor table seating up to 100; indoor cocktail reception up to 135; outdoor ceremony seating up to 150; outdoor/indoor table seating up to 165; outdoor/indoor cocktail reception up to 200.

Price Range: wedding and reception packages starting at $1,250

Catering: provided exclusively by Nottinghams' experienced chefs and staff

Types of Events: Weddings, receptions, rehearsal dinners, reunions, holiday parties, bridal showers, corporate and private celebrations, cooking classes and seminars.

Availability & Terms:

Nottinghams accepts reservations up to 13 months in advance. Early reservations are recommended but short notice can be accommodated. A $500 non-refundable deposit secures your date.

Description of facility and Services

Facility rental: all wedding and reception packages include tables and chairs, table linens, linen napkins, glassware, flatware, dinnerware, set up and clean up, beautiful bridal quarters, rustic grooms room, black ebony baby grand piano, sound system and event coordinator. Additional services are available.

Event Staff: the experienced owners of Nottinghams will be there for you every step of the way and will be guiding you on your journey. Our experienced staff will ensure a beautiful, professional and memorable event.

Bar facilities: All bar service provided by Nottinghams; full bar services are available; your option of hosted or no-host is available.

Dance floor: large raised dance floor inside

Parking: free on-street parking

Small Town Charm Meets Downtown Elegance

Located in Old Town Sherwood's historic district, your first impression is a classic old church but as soon as you enter the building your breath is taken away. You are transported from a quaint church to stunning chandeliers, a room adorned in black and white, rich wood floors and elegance surrounding you. You in vision yourself greeting your guests, as a newly married couple, from the mezzanine area. As you descend the staircase you enter the beautiful English garden. During the evening, enjoy the twinkling of hundreds of lights. Every detail is watched over personally by ourselves and our staff—from making sure grandma is comfortable to making sure every detail has been handled. Your catering selection will be made fresh for you on your day and presented beautifully. With many complements such as "your food is better than anything I've had at any wedding" and "your food and facility is simply the best" you are assured a wonderful event. Our goal at Nottinghams is to provide the most memorable and enjoyable day from the first moment we meet with you.

OAKS PARK
HISTORIC DANCE PAVILION
at Oaks Park

Portland, Oregon 97202
Contact: Catering (503) 238-6622; Fax (503) 236-9143
Web site: www.oakspark.com
Business Hours: Mon–Fri 8am–5pm

Capacity: dance pavilion with formal seating for 350; festival setup with dancing for 450; outdoor gazebo area for 700

Price Range: will be determined by event, specific menu choices and services

Catering: our in-house catering menus are individually designed to suit your own taste, personality, and style. Our goal is to give you exactly what you want. If you are using an outside caterer, we will charge you a fee of 20% of their final bill

Types of Events: reunions, bar/bat mitzvahs, bachelor/bachelorette parties, proms, corporate meetings and seminars, private parties, formal sit-down, retirement, anniversary, birthday and office parties, weddings, receptions, rehearsal dinners, bridal luncheons, buffets, and hors d'oeuvres

Availability and Terms

Our indoor facility is available for bookings on any day or evening. Our outdoor gazebo and grounds are extremely popular; please don't hesitate to call and inquire. A deposit of 10% is required on the day of booking with event paid in full 10 days prior to the event.

Description of Facility and Services

Seating: we can formally seat 350 people

Servers: we can provide any equipment necessary and the personnel to guarantee your event will run smoothly and at a level of service you expect

Bar facilities: Oaks Park Association provides liquor at the liability of the renter; it is Oaks Park's policy to provide a staff bartender

Dance floor: 99'x54' dance floor with a capacity for 400 people

Linens and napkins: all colors of linen and cloth napkins and tablecloths available for an additional cost

Decorations: creative catering staff to help you—and offer the bonus of fanciful historic carousel horses

Parking: ample free parking

ADA: yes

A LOVELY, ROMANTIC, AND HISTORIC SETTING

Join us in our historic riverside park on the Willamette River and let us create the perfect memory for you and your guests. Our beautiful lighted gazebo is framed by a forested setting and mystic city skyline backdrop. The gazebo offers a lovely, romantic setting for your wedding or reception. In case of chilly weather, our historic, multiwindowed dance pavilion is just steps away. Our facility is ideal for weddings, reunions, receptions, birthdays, and anniversaries. It is our policy to work with you and offer exemplary step-by-step service all during the celebration, allowing you to enjoy the day.

Oregon City Golf Club
at Lone Oak

20124 S. Beavercreek Road
Oregon City, Oregon 97045
Contact: Rose Holden (503) 518-1038
Business Hours: Mon–Sun 8am–6pm
E-mail: rose@ocgolfclub.com

Capacity: 125 seated; 160 standing; can accommodate additional guests depending on season; up to 300 during summer season.

Price Range: $250 to $2,500

Catering: we work with an approved list of caterers or your caterer

Types of Events: wedding receptions, bridal showers, private parties, baby showers, graduations, retirements, birthdays, tournaments, meetings, seminars

Availability and Terms

We suggest that you reserve as early as possible but we are sometimes able to accommodate parties on short notice. A deposit is required to secure your date.

Description of Facility and Services

Seating: round or adjustable tables with double padded white chairs for 125+ guests

Bar facilities: host or no-host; beer, wine, champagne available; bartenders provided; compliance with all local and state liquor laws; liquor liability provided

Dance floor: available; CD player provided; electrical available

Linens: white linens provided; a variety of colors available from caterer for an additional cost

China and glassware: available through caterer

Cleanup: provided by Oregon City Golf Club

Decorations: no staples, nails, tacks or tape; artist's putty may be used

Parking: free parking

ADA: yes

Special Services

Our event coordinator will work with you in planning and executing all details, to make your event a total success.

SOCIAL EVENTS TO TOURNAMENTS

Oregon City Golf Club was built in 1922 and is the third oldest public golf course in the State of Oregon still in operation. With our newly remodeled clubhouse and banquet facility, we can handle all of your social events and tournament needs.

OREGON COAST AQUARIUM

2820 S.E. Ferry Slip Road
Newport, Oregon 97365
Contact: Events Office (541) 867-3474 ext. 5224
Fax (541) 867-6846
Business Hours: summer 9am–6pm; winter 10am–5pm
E-mail: hughd@aquarium.org; Web site: www.aquarium.org

Capacity: 15-120 seated, 30-1,000+ reception/dinner throughout exhibit galleries
Price Range: please call for specific price and catering information
Catering: exclusive full-service, in-house catering available
Types of Events: elegant sit-down dinners, progressive dinners throughout the galleries, barbecues, buffets, wedding receptions, holiday parties, corporate functions, etc.

Availability and Terms

The lobby, overlooking an estuary (2,140 square feet) with vaulted ceilings and bay windows, is perfect for elegant sit-down dinners and receptions. Four indoor galleries provide opportunities for strolling buffets and cocktail parties. The Sandy Shores gallery (1,360 square feet) features exhibits including leopard sharks, skates and sea pens. A touch pool in the Rocky Shores gallery (1,051 square feet) permits guests to gently handle tide pool animals. The Coastal Waters gallery (1,125 square feet) features our largest indoor exhibit, a wall-to-wall salmon and sturgeon display. Moon jellies and sea nettles are also focal points in the Coastal Waters gallery. The Wetlands and New Currents gallery features Enchanted Seas including a rainbow of tropical fish, sea horses and sea dragons. Slide presentations or lectures can be held in the US West Theater (1,037 square feet).

The Oregon Coast Aquarium is available for booking year-round. All exhibits are open for after-hours events. A 20% deposit is required upon booking, with balance due within two weeks of event.

Description of Facility and Services

Seating: tables and chairs provided
Servers: provided by in-house caterer
Bar facilities: full-service bar available/OLCC regulated
Dance floor: provided upon request; 110-volt hookups available
Linens: linen tablecloths and napkins available in assorted colors at no cost
China and glassware: white china and stemmed glassware provided
Decorations: all decorations must be approved in advance
Audiovisual and equipment: available upon request
Cleanup: provided
Parking: ample free parking; **ADA:** yes

IMMERSE YOURSELF AT OREGON COAST AQUARIUM

The Oregon Coast Aquarium offers the perfect setting for your special event. Experience Passages of the Deep, an underwater adventure leading you on a journey through shark filled waters—all in the safety of a 200-foot acrylic walkway nestled deep beneath our Oregon sea. Adjacent to the exhibit is an elegant banquet space (1,175 sq.ft.) with a large viewing window that looks back into the spectacular exhibit, and a viewing deck overlooking the picturesque Yaquina Bay.

25700 S.W. Pete's Mountain Road
West Linn, Oregon 97068
Contact: Catering Department (503) 650-6900
Business Hours: 8:30am–5pm
Web site: www.oregongolfclub.com

Capacity: up to 500 people sit-down dinner
Price Range: customized reception package
Catering: full-service, in-house catering
Types of Events: sit-down, buffet, cocktail and hors d'oeuvres, outdoor garden setting for receptions and ceremonies

Availability and Terms

Please make reservations as early as possible. Four rooms are available to meet your special needs. An advance deposit is required; payment is due seven days in advance.

Description of Facility and Services

Seating: tables and chairs provided for up to 500 guests
Servers: provided
Bar facilities: full-bar service provided
Dance floor: 18' X 18' floor; electrical available
Linens and napkins: provided; in all colors
China: fine white china provided
Decorations: we will be happy to discuss your specific needs
Cleanup: provided by The Oregon Golf Club
Parking: free parking
ADA: yes

Our private country club setting, the natural beauty and charm, the exceptional service and attention to detail will allow you to have a first-class event that you and your guests will thoroughly enjoy.

Nestled in the Willamette Valley against a backdrop of the majestic Cascade Mountain Range, The Oregon Golf Club boasts an exceptional reputation. Inspired by the Scottish traditions of golf's birthplace and enlivened by the beauty of the Pacific Northwest, our spectacular facility is an ideal location for your wedding and reception.

4001 S.W. Canyon Road
Portland, Oregon 97221
(503) 220-2789
Fax (503) 220-3689
E-mail: zoocatering@metro.dst.or.us
Business Hours: Mon–Fri 8:30am–5pm

The Oregon Zoo offers a unique location for your wedding reception.

Our goal is to provide you and your guests with a memorable and stress-free occasion. The Oregon Zoo is situated in an ideal location right on the Max light rail line and only five minutes from downtown Portland. All proceeds go towards the funding of daily operations for the Oregon Zoo.

Capacity: up to 400 people for a wedding reception
Price Range: inclusive, tiered wedding reception packages available
Catering: in-house catering
Types of Events: wedding receptions, company picnics, award banquets, holiday parties, auctions and theme parties…anything is possible!

Availability and Terms

An initial non-refundable deposit is required to confirm any reservation. A second non-refundable deposit is due 14 days prior to the event.

Description of Facility and Services

Seating: tables and chairs included in cost
Servers: uniformed catering staff and cake-cutting service included in package
Bar facilities: host or no-host bar available
Dance floor: 18' x 21' dance floor included (Skyline Room: 15' x 15' only)
Linens and napkins: house linen and paper cocktail napkins available
China and glassware: china, silverware and serviceware
Cleanup: included in catering costs, as well as setup.
Decorations: no balloons allowed for the safety of the animals
Parking: large lot adjacent to entrance
ADA: yes

Also included is a basic reception floor plan and a buffet including self-serve coffee and punch. Cake, gift and guest-book tables are also included. All menu selections can be customized to your specific needs. Beverage service beyond coffee and punch is not included in the package but can be added. All hosted food and beverages added to your package are subject to a 17% service fee.

Please contact our friendly catering office for more information.

OVERLOOK HOUSE

3839 N. Melrose Drive
Portland, Oregon 97227
(503) 823-4524; fax (503) 285-7843
Tours: Tuesdays 5pm–7pm

Capacity: winter (November-April) up to 75; spring, summer, and early fall months (May–October) up to 150
Price Range: call for current information
Catering: select your favorite caterer; we provide complete kitchen facilities
Types of Events: bridal showers, rehearsal dinners, weddings and receptions

Availability and Terms

The home and grounds are included in the rental period. Reservations may be made as soon as the date of your event is determined, up to a year in advance. A deposit is required, with a portion refundable if we have a minimum of 30 days notice. Rental fees are due 30 days in advance of the event. Tours are offered Tuesdays from 5 to 7pm.

Description of Facility and Services

Seating: tables and 90 chairs provided
Servers: provided by your caterer or yourself
Bar facilities: you provide your own beverages and liquor liability; no kegs allowed
Cleanup: setup and cleanup are your responsibility
Decorations: please inquire about restrictions
Parking: on-street parking available
ADA: facilities available

THE ROMANCE AND ELEGANCE
OF A MANSION AND GARDENS

The Overlook House is a 1927 brick, English Tudor home on more than an acre of beautifully landscaped grounds overlooking the Willamette River and Portland's West Hills. The grounds are graced by a rose garden and trellis, making it an ideal setting for an outside wedding and reception during the spring, summer, and early fall months. Inside, the beveled glass, original woodwork and fireplace make the living room a lovely site for an intimate wedding or gathering. The Overlook House is also an ideal setting for rehearsal dinners, memorials, retreats, reunions, meetings and more.

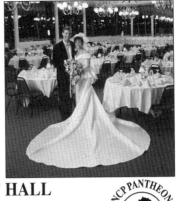

NCP PANTHEON BANQUET HALL

5942 S.E. 92nd Avenue • Portland, Oregon 97266
Contact: Effy Stephanopoulos (503) 775-7431, Fax (503) 775-3068
Business Hours: Mon–Fri 11:30am–6pm; or by appointment
E-mail: effystephanopaulos@hotmail.com • Web site: www.pantheonbanquethall.com

Capacity: up to 450
Price Range: various packages available; call for details
Catering: in-house catering
Types of Events: weddings, rehearsal dinners, bridal showers, birthdays, anniversaries, retirement, proms and holiday parties; corporate functions and business meetings

Availability and Terms

Our two banquet rooms are available any day of the week. Please make reservations as soon as possible, but we always try to accommodate receptions on shorter notice. Pantheon Banquet Hall accommodates up to 450 people and our smaller banquet room accommodates up to 80 people.

Description of Facility and Services

Seating: tables and chairs provided for up to 400
Servers: professional serving staff
Bar facilities: full-service bar; bartender
Dance floor: 18'x18' up to 24'x60'; electrical outlets available
Linens and napkins: tablecloths and napkins in an assortment of colors
China and glassware: china and crystal glassware provided
Cleanup: provided by Pantheon Banquet Hall
Parking: ample parking available

WE MAKE WEDDINGS SPECIAL

Every wedding is special and exciting as we focus on each bride—attending to every detail of the most perfect day of her life. Enjoy our finest cuisine prepared by our chef of 35 years experience. Also a private bridal room, complete with a bottle of champagne or nonalcoholic champagne awaits you. Enjoy a complimentary limo service to and from the Pantheon, along with a seven day honeymoon at a luxurious condo with a breathtaking view of the Puerto Vallarta Marina in Mexico— Effy, Bridal Consultant.

Fairytale Experience

"Anyone that employs your service can expect, after arriving in your MAGICAL COACH, to walk through your doors into a WONDERLAND of special treatment. The PRINCE AND PRINCESS are introduced with a spotlight entrance into the PANTHEON HALL, which is nothing less than CINDERELLA'S BALLROOM. I have many friends who still are discussing how this FAIRYTALE atmosphere was hidden in a structure centrally located in the middle of the Rose City." ~Mrs. Judy Stowell

P A R A G O N

Restaurant & Bar

1309 N.W. Hoyt Street
Portland, Oregon 97209
Contact: Joseph Moreau (503) 833-5060
Charles Flint, Chef
Web site: www.paragonrestaurant.com
Office Hours: Tues–Sat 11am-6pm

Capacity: 20 to 150 guests
Catering: full-service in-house; off-site events
Types of Events: receptions, rehearsals, lunch and dinner parties; you may select full
sit-down service, buffet or cocktail party

Availability and Terms
Two separate, private rooms and the semi-private upper dining room are available for private functions. Outside seating is available. Ask about a restaurant buyout for groups over 100. A deposit of $250 is required to secure the date. Final payment is due upon completion of the event.

Description of Facility and Services
Seating: Gallery Room: 25-90; Banquet Room: 10-20; Restaurant: up to 140;
Outdoor: up to 50
Servers: provided by Paragon
Bar facilities: full bar or limited bar
Dance floor: 20 person capacity; stage and electrical available for musicians
Linens: white linen; other colors available for minimal charge
China and glassware: white china; clear glassware
Decorations: candles provided; schedule early decorating; no nails, tacks, tape or confetti
Cleanup: provided by Paragon
Parking: ample street and pay lot parking; valet service available for minimal charge
ADA: fully accessible

Special Services
We are happy to assist you in all aspects of your special day including menu selection, decorations, music and any other details to make your event especially memorable. We are pleased to recommend photographers, florists and bakeries.

"A DIAMOND IN THE PEARL" – *WILLAMETTE WEEK*
Located in the heart of the Pearl District, Paragon is within easy walking distance of galleries and retail shops. The Portland Streetcar allows for easy access from the Pearl District to downtown area hotels. Paragon's design mixes the timeless elements of a traditional grill-style restaurant with modern artistry in a converted warehouse. The unique private banquet room features a slide-up wall to adapt to your privacy needs. The Gallery Room, separate from the restaurant with its own private entrance, showcases artwork from area galleries. The Gallery Room also features a slide-up wall, which opens to a raised outdoor patio. This covered patio will accommodate an additional 50 guests for cocktails and outside seating. Starting at only $6000 in food and beverage sales, the entire restaurant is available for an evening buyout. For a cocktail reception or sit-down meal, the Paragon is the perfect venue for a memorable event.

500 S.E. Butler Road
Gresham, Oregon 97080
Contact: Catering Department (503) 674-3259
Business Hours: Mon–Sat 9am–6pm
Web site: www.persimmongolf.com

Capacity: 300 people
Price Range: varies
Catering: in-house by Persimmon Grille
Types of Events: weddings, receptions, rehearsal dinners, bridal luncheons, bachelor golf parties

Availability and Terms

Persimmon features elegant and scenic event sites for entertaining up to 300 guests. Reserve space up to one year in advance. A deposit is required to reserve your event site.

Description of Facility and Services

Seating: tables and chairs provided for up to 300
Servers: professional service staff is provided
Bar facilities: full-service, professional bar service is available
Dance floor: beautiful parquet dance floor; electrical outlets available
China and glassware: white china; glass beverage ware
Linens and napkins: white or ivory tablecloths and your choice of napkin color
Decorations: please inquire with events coordinator
Cleanup: courtesy of Persimmon
Parking: free on-site parking
ADA: disabled accessible

Special Services

Persimmon's precise attention to detail will assure your wedding day is flawless. Please inquire regarding decorating assistance. Golf carts provided for access to the many spectacular photo sites Persimmon has to offer.

THE PERFECT SETTING
FOR WEDDINGS AND RECEPTIONS

Persimmon offers a wide variety of services in an elegant relaxed environment set among spectacular scenery overlooking magnificent views of Mount Hood.

Portland Spirit

Willamette Star

Crystal Dolphin

110 SE Caruthers Portland, OR 97214
503-224-3900 • 800-224-3901
E-mail: sales@portlandspirit.com • www.portlandspirit.com

The fleet of the Portland Spirit will provide a unique, memorable experience for your next event. Portland Spirit cruises are ideal for entertaining guests for corporate events, reunions, conventions, weddings and more. Cruise with us for a breakfast or luncheon meeting, anniversary party, or gala holiday event. Our knowledgeable sales staff and professional event planners will handle all the details, making your planning process easy and stress-free!
Price Range: prices vary – please inquire
Catering: in-house, food minimums apply

Portland Spirit

Our flagship yacht combines a classic nautical experience with a fine-dining atmosphere. One-deck rentals, private charters of the entire vessel and public group reservations are available. Two levels are fully enclosed and climate controlled, each with a baby grand piano. The Columbia Deck has a built-in marble dance floor and open air viewing deck.
Capacity: up to 540 guests
Seating: tables and chairs for 340 plus outside seating

Willamette Star

Elegance and style has been custom built into the Willamette Star, from its solid cherry wood interior to brass accents and plush carpeting. The Willamette Star has two enclosed, temperature-controlled levels, two outdoor viewing decks, piano and a sound system.
Capacity: up to 144 guests
Seating: tables and chairs for 100 plus outside and bar seating

Crystal Dolphin

This sleek and luxurious vessel provides a bright, contemporary setting for any event. The Crystal Dolphin features three fully enclosed and climate controlled levels, a baby grand piano, outdoor viewing decks and sound system
Capacity: up to 120 guests
Seating: tables and chairs for 50 plus outside and lounge seating

Description of Vessel Services and Facilities

Linens: linen tablecloths and napkins provided
China: house china and glassware provided
Servers: included with food and bar service
Bar facilities: full service bar, liquor, bartenders and liability insurance
Cleanup: provided; **Parking:** commercial and street parking available
ADA: limited with assistance; please call for more information

12930 Old Pumpkin Ridge Road
North Plains, Oregon 97133
Contact: Catering Department
(503) 647-4747; Fax (503) 647-2002
Business Hours: 8:30am–5pm
Web site: www.pumpkinridge.com

Capacity: accommodates up to 500 guests
Price Range: price varies according to menu selection
Catering: full-service, in-house catering provided
Types of Events: weddings, receptions, rehearsal dinners, bridal showers, formal sit-down, buffet, cocktail and hors d'oeuvres

Availability and Terms
We suggest early reservations but can accommodate events on short notice if space is available. A deposit is required; payment is due seven days before your event.

Descriptions of Facilities and Services
Seating: tables and chairs provided for up to 500 guests
Servers: provided
Bar facilities: full-service bar provided
Dance floor: parquet dance floor available in a variety of sizes
Linens and napkins: provided; available in a variety of colors
China and glassware: provided
Decorations: a variety of centerpieces and room accents available
Cleanup: provided by Pumpkin Ridge Golf Club
Parking: convenient free parking
ADA: wheelchair access to all rooms

WEDDINGS WITH ELEGANCE AND CLASS
At Pumpkin Ridge Golf Club we pride ourselves on creating unforgettable events. Set on the edge of the beautiful Willamette Valley, yet convenient to downtown Portland, our Ghost Creek facility offers a gracious 18,000-sq. ft. clubhouse featuring dramatic architecture and an old Portland flavor. Your guests will delight in views of our two championship courses where golfing legends have made history on numerous occasions. Our Sunset Room is a spacious banquet facility with open beam ceilings, skylights, a generous deck and sweeping golf course views. Our expert catering and event planning staff promise to deliver culinary expertise and an event that far exceeds your expectations. Whether you're planning an intimate gala or a corporate outing, you can relax knowing you and your guests will enjoy nothing less than perfection.

THE DAVID COLE
QUEEN ANNE
VICTORIAN MANSION

1441 NORTH McCLELLAN
PORTLAND, OREGON 97217
PHONE 1-503-283-3224

Capacity: 200 seated at outdoor gazebo (glassed in for winter months); 300 reception
Price Range: weekend, weekday and holiday rates available. Please call for specific price information
Catering: Irresistible house catering, featuring Kati's Catering
Types of Events: weddings, receptions, rehearsal dinners, buffets, cocktail parties, corporate meetings, fund-raisers, class reunions, picnics, birthdays, anniversaries, photo shots, movies, and many other events

Availability and Terms
The mansion is a 6,300-square-foot beautiful Victorian with a 42' round enclosed gazebo. Reserve as early as possible. Reservations have a 90-minute and six-hour time limit per function. Available year-round, the mansion is conveniently located just minutes north of downtown Portland, just off I-5.

Description of Facility and Services
Seating: tables and chairs for up to 300 guests included in rental fee
Servers: provided by caterer
Dance floor: space for 200+ guests in gazebo and a house DJ to entice your guest to the dance floor
Bar facilities: provided by Queen Anne
Cleanup: provided by the Queen Anne staff
Decorations: completely decorated in Victorian era antiques, colorful floral garlands and arrangements throughout the home; meticulously landscaped gardens outdoors
Parking: plenty of free parking

Special Services
Lovely appointed dressing rooms, one for the bride and another for the groom.

A MAGICAL STORYBOOK PLACE
Every bride deserves perfection on her wedding day whether it is formal, informal, or a simple family ceremony. The Queen Anne staff is very detail oriented and will make sure you and your family are at ease knowing everything is taken care of start to finish. Easily accessible and very private sitting on over two acres, the mansion is a beautiful and perfect location to create your special day. Built in 1885 by David Cole as a wedding gift for his wife, the mansion is truly a work of art. It features incredible original woodwork, chandeliers and one of the largest private collections of Povey stained glass windows in the world. Call to set up your appointment and allow our staff to dazzle you with a tour of the grounds and mansion. Appointments are made through the week; the weekends are reserved for us to give our undivided attention to our beautiful brides and grooms just as you would want on our special day!!

RAMADA INN AND SUITES PORTLAND AIRPORT

6221 N.E. 82nd Avenue
Portland, Oregon 97220
Director of Catering: Ann Conger
(503) 255-6511; Fax (503) 255-8417
Web site: www.ramadapdx.com
Business Hours: Mon-Sat 8am to 6pm

Capacity: **Cascade Executive Ballroom:** 4,200 square feet, seats 300; **Columbia Ballroom:** 2,820 square feet, seats 175; **Board Room:** Seats 12

Price Range: Please call for current pricing. Complete meeting room packages are available per your personal requirements.

Catering: Full service catering available on-site and off-site.

Types of Events: weddings, receptions, anniversaries, birthday parties, class reunions and much more!

Availability and Terms
Please make reservations early to get your desired space!

Description of Facility and Services
Seating: Chairs and linens plus decorated accessories provided
Dinnerware: China and glassware provided
Linens: Linen tablecloths and napkins available in a variety of colors
Servers: Provided by The Ramada Inn and Suites Catering Staff
Bar facilities: Full service bar available
Dance floor: Provided upon request
Audiovisual equipment: Available upon request
Parking: Free parking
ADA: Compliant rooms

Hotel Accommodations
202 spacious rooms, 108 are Mini Suites. Less than two miles away from the Portland Airport, 24-Hour complimentary shuttle, remote TV with cable, refrigerators, microwave, coffee and coffee maker, iron and ironing board, hairdryers, room service, outdoor heated pool, jacuzzi, exercise room, sauna, on-site restaurant and sports bar.

- **Jacuzzi suites available!**
- **Boxed breakfast to go for early morning risers!**
- **Special rates for groups and extended stays!**

RED LION HOTEL®

CONVENTION CENTER

1021 N.E. Grand Avenue • Portland, Oregon 97232
Contact: Sales and Catering Office
(503) 235-2100; Fax (503) 235-0396
E-mail: lacy.buswell.gaha.biz;
Web site: www.redlion.com

Capacity: *Ballroom:* up to 300; *Windows Sky Room:* up to 200; *Terrace:* up to 100 people
Price Range: varies with menu selections
Catering: full-service in-house catering
Types of Events: weddings, receptions, themed events, meetings and conventions, breakfasts, luncheons, dinners, retirement and anniversary parties, and any special event.

Availability and Terms

The recently redecorated Grand Ballroom can accommodate up to 300 guests. However, the Ballroom can also be separated into four rooms or combinations to comfortably seat smaller events. Windows Sky Room with floor-to-ceiling windows offers a spectacular view of downtown Portland. Adjacent to Windows, we offer our open-air Terrace, perfect for a ceremony or reception. All banquet facilities are located on the top floor of the Red Lion Hotel. A deposit is required to reserve space.

Description of Facility and Services

Seating: tables and chairs provided
Bar facilities: full beverage services are available; hotel provides all alcoholic beverages
Dance floor: dance floor, electrical hookups and staging are available at an additional charge
China and glassware: white china and stemmed glassware
Linens: table cloths, cloth napkins, and skirting are available complimentary with all catered events at the hotel
Entertainment, props and decorations: mirrored table tiles and lush silk plants are provided by the hotel. Other entertainment, props or decorations can be available for additional charges.
Cleanup: provided by banquet staff
Parking: the hotel provides a parking garage, subject to availability, at a minimal charge
ADA: yes

Special Services

The Red Lion Hotel Portland—Convention Center offers 174 renovated guest rooms, including in-room coffee, refrigerators, iron/board, hairdryers, data ports, voicemail, cable television with premium channels, Pay Per View and Nintendo. The Red Lion is a full-service hotel with a restaurant, lounge, room service, fitness center and business center. The Red Lion is also adjacent to the MAX light rail with free transportation to downtown and to Portland International Airport at a minimal charge.

ELEGANCE AND SPECTACULAR CITY VIEW

Our flexible 6,000 square feet of space will provide your group with an ideal setting for receptions. Windows Sky Room, located on the sixth floor of the hotel, offers your guests a panoramic view of the Portland area.

Ask our staff about Guest Awards, the Red Lion loyalty program, offering points for every eligible dollar charged to your room.

Red Lion Hotels — known for care, comfort and value for over 40 years.

Red Tail Canyon Event Center

Portland, Oregon
Appointment Only ~ Contact: Norma Hermanson 503.656.6428
Web site: www.countrelanegardens.com   Email: countrelane@adam

Capacity: 85 guests indoors only; 200 guests indoor and outdoor.
Price Range: prices vary; special winter pricing, please inquire.
Catering: off-site catering permitted May thru September. Small service kitchen only. In-house only October thru April; special packages available.
Types of Events: Wedding and receptions, corporate events, private events.

Availabilities and Terms
Available year round, indoor and outdoor gardens.
Saturday events 2:00-10:00pm. Weekday pricing available; $500 deposit required.

Description of Facility and Services
Seating: tables and chairs up to 200 guests
Servers: provided by caterer
Bar facilities: wine, beer and champagne only, provided by bartender
Dance floor: available
Linens: provided
Decorations: Table decor, archway, floral baskets and tiki torches provided
Cleanup: setup and cleanup provided

EXPERIENCE EUROPEAN STYLE AND CHARM
Simply elegant, enjoy the romantic old world charm. Delight in the outdoor water feature with floating candles and surrounded by tiki torches. A backdrop of lush trees is perfect for pictures and relaxation. The perfect place for your special day.

THE RESORT AT THE MOUNTAIN

68010 East Fairway Avenue
Welches, Oregon 97067 (at the western base of Mount Hood)
(503) 622-2220 from the Portland area
(800) 733-0800 from outside the Portland area

Capacity: Up to 400 at our outdoor wedding area, which includes a large tented area; from 20-450 people in our indoor ballrooms and banquet rooms.

Price Range: Call for package prices; customized plans available

Catering: In-house catering only

Types of Events: weddings and receptions; rehearsal dinners; groomsmen's golf tournaments, meetings, retreats and reunions

Availability and Terms

Reservations are accepted up to 18 months in advance. Deposit required.

Description of Facility and Services

Seating: chairs and tables provided

Servers: provided by The Resort

Bar facilities: provided by The Resort

Dance floor: provided with our wedding reception packages

Linens: floor length ivory or white complimentary; other colors available as well.

China: fine china and all glassware included

Decorations: simple centerpieces and buffet décor included in our reception packages; arbor and runner included in our wedding package; customized decorating available

Consultation: event coordinator provided

Audiovisual: well-equipped with in-house audiovisual; equipment and technicians; T-1 high-speed Internet access in all meeting rooms

Parking: ample complimentary parking

ADA: fully complies

Special Services

The Resort at the Mountain offers 160 luxury guest rooms, including suites and golf villas at special rates for your wedding guests. A complimentary Fireside Studio room is provided complimentary for the bride and groom on their wedding night when a reception package for a minimum of 75 guests is ordered.

We specialize in Celtic style weddings.

Visit our Web site: www.theresort.com

River City Promotions

251 St. Helens Street
St. Helens, Oregon 97051
ph: 503.366.1664 • fax: 503.366.3898

Capacity: unlimited up to 260 guests

Price Range: price varies according to menu selection

Catering: select from a closed list of professional caterers for food service (except cake); alcohol must be served by attendant.

Types of Events: buffets, brunches, luncheons, rehearsal dinners, wedding receptions, anniversary, special event celebrations, proms, theme galas, seminars, birthday parties.

Availability and Terms

Two smaller themed conference rooms for up to 35 guests; auditorium with balcony to seat up to 260 guests.

Description of Facilities and Services:

Seating: tables and chairs, balcony booths

Servers: included in catering costs

Bar facilities: beer, wine and champagne

Dance floor: 14 x 25

China and glassware: white china; assorted glassware

Decorations: wide variety of theme decorations and props available; cost varies

Parking: ample parking

ADA: accessible by chairlift off Third Street entrance.

BANQUETS AND RECEPTIONS WITH YOUR THEME AND OUR ATTENTION TO DETAIL

Each bride and groom deserves perfection on their wedding day whether it is formal, informal, a theme gala or a simple family ceremony. Every event is creative and professional at "The Olde School."

River City Promotions is proud to be located in the beautiful Olde School, in historic old town St. Helens. The Olde School in on the National Historic Register. Built in 1919, it served as a school until 1999. Located two blocks from the beautiful St. Helens Marina on the Columbia River, one can view Mt. St. Helens from the front steps.

Come celebrate your special occasion with us!

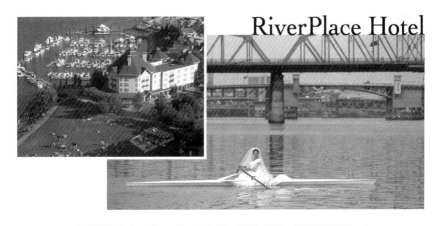

RiverPlace Hotel

1510 SW Harbor Way · Portland, OR 97201-5105 · 503.228.3233 hotel
503.423.3112 sales & catering · sales@riverplacehotel.com
www.riverplacehotel.com

Capacity: 10 to 200 guests
Price Range: customized menus at varying prices
Catering: provided by the hotel exclusively
Types of Events: wedding ceremonies and receptions; sit-down meals and buffets

Availability and Terms
RiverPlace Hotel offers a variety of banquet space to fit your specific social function. The beautiful space RiverPlace Hotel has to offer may be used for rehearsal dinners, special family events or an exquisite wedding reception; the possibilities are endless. Our staff will provide outstanding service and exceed your expectations.

Description of Facility and Services
Seating: tables, chairs and head tables provided
Servers: professional servers and bartenders provided
Bar facilities: full beverage service available
Dance floor: complimentary dance floor
Linens and napkins: white and ivory linens and napkins; inquire about color selection
China and glassware: china and glassware provided
Decorations: please inquire with catering manager
Cleanup: included at no additional charge
Parking: available
ADA: fully accessible
Lodging: complimentary bridal suite; special group rates for your out-of-town guests

Special Services
Specialized menus can be created by our Executive Chef to accommodate your tastes for whatever occasion you may be planning.

A Waterfront Location in Downtown Portland
RiverPlace Hotel overlooks the marina on the Willamette River, a perfect setting for a Northwest wedding. The hotel is an urban getaway, known for providing the ultimate in personalized service, offering banquets, private dining and overnight guest room accommodations.

RIVERS AT AVALON HOTEL & SPA

0470 S.W. Hamilton Court • Portland, Oregon 97239
Contact: Catering
(503) 802-5814; Fax (503) 802-5830
www.riversatavalonhotel.com
Business Hours: 7am–11pm

Rivers
Avalon Hotel & Spa

Capacity: 2,285 square feet
Catering: in-house, full-service
Price Range: call for pricing
Types of Events: weddings, rehearsal dinners, bridal luncheons, bar mitzvahs

Availability and Terms
A 50% deposit is required on social events.

Description of Facility and Services
Seating: up to 180 for standing reception
Servers: provided
Bar facilities: full-service bar and bartender
Dance floor: available for rent
Linens: included
China and glassware: provided
Audiovisual: available to rent
Equipment: available to rent
Cleanup: provided
Parking: complimentary valet parking
ADA: accessible

Special Services
Located adjacent to the Avalon Hotel & Spa offering 99 guestrooms, full-service spa, salon and fitness club in John's Landing on the Willamette River. Event room blocks and group spa appointments are available.

LOCATED ON THE SHORES OF THE WILLAMETTE RIVER
Our banquet space is located on the second floor of Rivers Restaurant. Our 2,285 square foot ballroom offers floor to ceiling windows with an outdoor patio, providing spectacular views of the Willamette River and its surroundings. The Avalon Hotel & Spa offers meeting space for up to 16 persons in our suites and up to 25 persons for small receptions. Contact our catering department to reserve your next event.

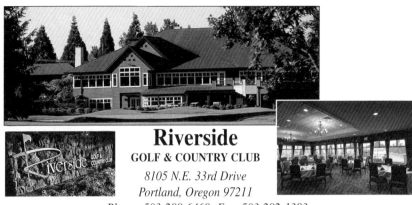

Riverside
GOLF & COUNTRY CLUB
8105 N.E. 33rd Drive
Portland, Oregon 97211
Phone: 503-288-6468; Fax: 503-282-1383
Contact: Bill Price, Clubhouse Manager or Richard Ransome, General Manager
Business Hours: Mon–Sat 9am–6pm; www.riversidegcc.com

Capacity: The ballroom and formal dining room may accommodate up to 300 guests with additional outdoor seasonal seating: smaller more intimate events may be hosted in the Pierre Alarco Board Room.

Price Range: Fees/price varies according to event size and menu selection. Please inquire for more information.

Catering: Creative, customized menus may be designed to make your event truly memorable.

Type of Events: Wedding ceremonies and receptions, bridal showers/luncheons, rehearsal dinners, anniversary celebrations, special events, holiday parties, seminars, meetings, corporate events and tournaments, including bachelor/ bachelorette golf events.

Availability and Terms
Riverside Golf & Country Club, a private club established in 1925, caters to those with excellent taste and style. The ballroom and formal dining room look out onto the 18th green. Reservations are taken up to 18 months in advance with a nominal deposit required to secure the date. Please contact Bill Price to schedule a tour or event.

Description of Facility and Services
Seating: provided for up to 300 guests
Servers: professional staff provided to ensure excellent service
Bar: full service bar with additional porta bars available
Linens: forest green, burgundy and white available at no additional charge
China and glassware: Riverside house china and glassware are provided; silver serving pieces and coffee set are also available
Dance floor: available upon request
Cleanup: courtesy of Riverside
Decorations: please discuss decorating ideas with our staff: early access for decorating is available by prior arrangement
Parking: complimentary gated private lot with porte cochere
ADA: disabled access available

ELEGANCE YOU CAN AFFORD!
Conveniently located between I5 and I205 within 15 minutes of downtown Portland or Vancouver, Riverside Golf & Country Club offers a panoramic view of the 18th green and acres of park like scenery. It is truly inspiring. Following the Riverside tradition of the friendliest hospitality, excellent service and incomparable cuisine – the Formal Dining Room and Terrace, the Ballroom and Fireside Room are available for your special occasion. The Riverside professional staff continues to meet and exceed your expectations.

THE CLUBHOUSE AT ROCK CREEK

5100 N.W. Neakahnie Avenue
Portland, Oregon 97229-1964
Contact: Michelle Edwards
Phone: 503-645-8843 Fax: 503-645-8788

Capacity: banquet room holds up to 250 people; outdoor seating in our picturesque, manicured surroundings holds up to 500 guests.

Price Range: standard menus range from $10 to $40; room charges start at $200; prices subject to change.

Catering: full-service on and off premise catering.

Types of Events: from simple hors d' oeuvre receptions to buffet, sit-down dinners and outdoor barbeques. Wedding receptions, parties, corporate events and meetings.

Availability and Terms

The facilities can accommodate groups ranging from 10 to 500 people. Our main banquet room is a spacious open area that can seat 250 guests. All facilities have access to the surrounding grounds of the golf course, subject to availability. Rooms should be reserved six months in advance. A nonrefundable fee is required to reserve a facility.

Description of Facilities and Services

Seating: variety of table sizes and seating options
Servers: included in your catering cost; 18% additional gratuity charge
Bar facilities: full-service bar in all facilities
Dance floor: 12' x 12' parquet dance floor
Linens and napkins: cloth tablecloths and napkins available in all colors
China and glassware: white china, stemmed glassware
Cleanup: cleanup is provided by The Clubhouse
Parking: ample parking available

Special Services

We offer complete event planning, including catering, beverages, decorations, entertainment, flowers, cake, photographers, video services, plus much more.

WE SPECIALIZE IN WEDDING RECEPTIONS

The Clubhouse at Rock Creek is located at Rock Creek Country Club, conveniently located near downtown Portland. The Clubhouse is set against our picturesque, manicured 18-hole Championship Course, providing a lovely backdrop for your wedding photos. We pride ourselves in making each catering event as unique as the individual planning it. We welcome the opportunity to make special arrangements or work with your individual needs. Our experience and facilities are unmatched in the Washington County area.

Sheraton Portland Airport
H O T E L

8235 N.E. Airport Way
Portland, Oregon 97220-1398
Contact: Julie Bradford
(503) 249-7606
Business Hours: Mon - Fri 9am–6pm
E-mail: jbradford@sheratonpdx.com
Web site: www.sheratonpdx.com

Capacity: 75 to 420 seated; 750 standing reception
Price Range: $20 to $30 per person
Catering: full-service in-house catering
Types of Events: sit-down, buffet, cocktails and hors d'oeuvres, rehearsal dinners

Availability and Terms
The Sheraton features four reception rooms on the lobby level for entertaining. Facilities may be reserved 18 months in advance with a $500 deposit. Cancellations must be made at least six months in advance for a refund of your deposit.

Description of Facility and Services
Seating: tables and chairs provided
Servers: award-winning staff included
Bar facilities: full-service bar with bartenders provided; Sheraton provides liquor, beer, wine, and champagne
Dance floor: complimentary
Linens and napkins: large selection of colors at no additional cost
China and glassware: white china provided; all types of glassware provided
Cleanup: provided by Sheraton staff
Decorations: Sheraton supplies candle centerpieces, silver punch fountain, silver coffee service, white lace skirting on cake and beverage tables, white lights and silk foliage. Extensive decorating at no additional cost.
Parking: convenient, complimentary parking available
ADA: yes

Special Services
A special wedding night package is included with your wedding reception. Enjoy spending this evening in a deluxe guestroom, upgraded to a suite upon availability, enhanced with champagne and chocolates.

Hotel Accommodations
Special rates available for your guests. Located half mile from Portland International Airport, with a 24-hour shuttle service. Ammenities include 213 superior guestrooms, a restaurant, lounges, 24-hour room service, fitness center, swimming pool and therapy pool.

SUITES HOTEL

and Conference Center—
Portland Airport/I-205
11707 N.E. Airport Way
Portland, Oregon 97220-1075
Contact: Sales/Catering Office
(503) 252-7500, ext 270
E-mail: portland205@shiloinns.com
Business Hours:
Mon–Fri 8am–5:30pm;
Sat by appointment

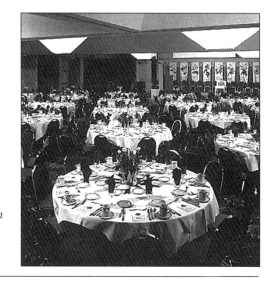

Capacity: 10,402 square feet of flexible banquet space
Price Range: packages to fit most budgets
Catering: full-service at our deluxe hotel
Types of Events: business meetings to formal affairs

Availability and Terms
You are invited to visit our facility to discuss your needs.

Description of Facility and Services
Seating: banquets of up to 400 guests
Servers: professional, full-service staff for all events
Bar facilities: hosted or no-host bars and table service
Entertainment: musician and DJ referrals available
Dance floor: wood floor available for a minimal setup fee
Linens: available to compliment your colors
China and glassware: included; styled to complement formal and informal themes
Cleanup: setup and cleanup by our staff
Decorations: chandeliers, mirrored walls, table and buffet decorations included
Guestroom accommodations: 3-Diamond/AAA rated; 200 Suites; special wedding packages
   and group rates available; two full dressing vanities in every room
Parking: free parking available on site
ADA: fully accessible

CONVENIENT LOCATION AND PROFESSIONAL STAFF
Located conveniently to I-205, Portland Airport, Vancouver and Downtown Portland, this
beautiful property offers spacious accommodations and wonderful family dining. An indoor
heated pool, a spa, steam room and fitness center are open 24 hours a day to delight any guest.
Free shuttle to Portland Airport.

Our professional catering coordinators will assist you in planning your event. We offer the
convenience of a full-service banquet facility, restaurant and deluxe hotel on one property.

Children under 12 stay free at Shilo Inns with a parent. Enjoy free Showtime. All guest
rooms come with microwaves, refrigerators, hair dryers and first run movies and
entertainment. Call toll free 1-800-222-2244 or visit our Web site for online pictures,
information and reservations at www.shiloinns.com.

Please let this business know that you heard about them from the Bravo! Wedding Resource Guide.

"AFFORDABLE EXCELLENCE"

SHILO INNS HOTEL
& CANYON GRILL
RESTAURANT

9900 Canyon Road • Portland, Oregon 97225
Contact: Catering Office 503-297-2551 ext 552
Hours: Monday–Friday 9am–5pm; Saturday by appointment

Capacity: 4,206 sq. ft. of flexible banquet space
Price Range: tailored to fit most budgets
Catering: full service at our newly remodeled location
Types of Events: ceremonies, receptions, rehearsal dinners and business meetings

Availability and Terms:
Come tour the property and discuss your special day. Be sure to reserve your dates as early as possible.

Description of Facility:
Seating: Banquet seating for up to 200 people with a dance floor
Servers: professional, full-service staff provided by us
Entertainment: DJ referral available
Dance floor: available by requested size
Linens: specially ordered to match your color scheme
China and glassware: beautiful place settings provided by us
Cleanup: all done by us with no stress to you
Decorations: newly decorated banquet rooms with chandeliers; table and buffet decorations included
Accommodations: Three-Diamond full-service hotel with 141 guest rooms, full-service restaurant, Martini Lounge and Sports Den Cigar Bar.
Amenities: heated pool and fitness center; complimentary hot breakfast, local phone calls, popcorn, fresh fruit and cookies available in the lobby. All guest rooms are equipped with a refrigerator, microwave oven, coffee maker, data port and an iron and ironing board.
Parking: free parking on site
ADA: disabled access available

Have your wedding in our beautiful courtyard complete with a picturesque gazebo and three beautiful fountains in the background.

See page 182 under Rehearsal Dinner Sites and page 310 under Ceremony Sites.

SILVER FALLS VINEYARDS

4972 Cascade Highway, S.E.
Sublimity, Oregon 97385
Contact: Duane Defrees
(503) 769-5056

Capacity: 150 inside, 300 inside and outside
Price Range: $350 to $850; limited to one event per day
Catering: your choice of caterer; excellent selection of caterers recommended upon request
Types of Events: weddings, receptions for any occasion, reunions, business meetings, company parties, proms, holiday parties

Availability and Terms
Reservations are recommended as early as possible for summer, fall, and holiday events.
Deposit required.

Description of Facility and Services
Seating: tables and chairs provided for 80 guests; list of rental services available
Servers: provided by caterer or client
Bar facilities: bar facilities on premises; licensed caterer or client to provide bartender, liquor, and liability
Dance floor: inside dance floor; capacity: 75
Linens and napkins: ivory tablecloths and coordinating market umbrellas available
China and glassware: provided by caterer or client
Cleanup: deposit required; fully refundable with limited cleanup
Parking: ample free parking available
ADA: yes

Special Services
The facility includes a bridal party lounge with a mirrored wall, oriental rug and daybed. The vaulted and beamed reception area has a piano, built-in CD sound system, wood stove, French doors, faux marble floor and a stained glass entry. A galley kitchen is equipped with a range, refrigerator and microwave. Several charming bed & breakfasts are located within 10 miles of the site; a very nice motel is located just three miles away.

A GREAT PLACE FOR A GREAT TIME
Silver Falls Vineyards is an elegant, old-world rustic facility surrounded by a horse ranch, vineyard, and miles of rolling countryside. Conveniently located 12 miles east of Salem in a private setting, Silver Falls Vineyards is a unique, versatile place to hold your wedding and reception.

STOCKPOT RESTAURANT & CATERING COMPANY

8200 S.W. Scholls Ferry Road
Beaverton, Oregon 97005
Contact: Gary or Murray (503) 643-5451
Business Hours: 9am–2am DAILY

Capacity: **The Club Room:** seating in our clubhouse for groups up to 70 guests; **Stockpot Grille Patio:** outdoor seating for groups up to 100 guests; **The Hawks Nest Tent:** groups up to 350 guests**; The Main Dining Room**: groups up to 250 guests

Price Range: will vary depending on food services required

Catering: in-house only

Types of Events: specialize in custom menus designed to complement your style of reception; a variety of buffets—traditional fare and many ethnic styles are available, as well as full-course sit-down dinners, hors d'oeuvre selections, or even a Southwest barbecue on the patio

Availability and Terms

The entire restaurant is available for private use on Saturday during the day. The patios overlooking the ninth green are available during the spring and summer months. Reservations are taken at your convenience with a $200 nonrefundable deposit at time of booking.

Description of Facility and Services

Seating: all tables and chairs provided

Servers: professional staff included in catering costs

Beverages: full beverage service offered; liquor liability included

Dance floor: available for you and your guests; ample electrical outlets for bands

Linens: provided with catering costs

China and glassware: a full selection of china and disposable available

Decorations: table decorations available; however, you may bring your own; rooms open for early decorating

Parking: free parking space for 600 cars; handicapped parking available

Special Services

Our desire is to give your reception those personal touches that reflect your style and personality. Menu planning, service, and other minute details are all part of the process. We don't forget whose wedding it really is.

PATIO OVERLOOKS THE GOLF COURSE

The Stockpot Restaurant is a unique catering facility with an elegant indoor reception room and spacious patios that overlook the ninth green. Enjoy your rehearsal dinner or wedding reception indoors, outdoors, or a combination of both. The Stockpot Restaurant at the Red Tail Golf Course looks forward to making your event a great success.

STONEHEDGE GARDENS

"Romantic setting and the best meal I had in town."
– The Los Angeles Times

3405 Cascade Avenue • Hood River, Oregon 97031
Contact: Leilani Caldwell (541) 386-3940
www.stonehedgegardens.com; E-mail: stonehedge@gorge.net

Capacity: 10 to 250 outside, six to 100 inside
Price: varies with event; wedding packages available
Catering: full-service, on or off-site
Types of Events: indoor/outdoor weddings, rehearsal dinners, buffets, sit-down dinners,
full service restaurant open daily at 5pm

Availability and Terms
Please make your reservation as early as possible. A deposit is required with refundable terms;
open year round.

Description of Facility and Services
Seating: up to 200
Servers: included
Bar facilities: full bars, hosted and no-host
Dance floor: hardwood floors indoors, patios outside
Linens: provided
Cleanup: provided
Decorations: natural setting, floral available; please no rice or confetti
Special Services: very professional on-site coordination and planning; cakes, flowers,
ministers, tuxedos, etc.
Parking: ample parking on site
ADA: yes

THE MOST BEAUTIFUL TERRACES
IN THE COLUMBIA RIVER GORGE
Owned by a winemaker and a chef, Stonehedge Gardens is Hood River's newest premium
wedding venue. The remodeled home, now a restaurant, was built in 1898. The Italian stone
terraces were constructed in 2001. Carved into five amazing levels and surrounded by a
private six acre forest and restaurant, the new gardens create the perfect setting for your
wedding and reception. We are less than a mile from the Columbia River. Golf courses, hotels,
wineries and downtown Hood River are less than five minutes away. Host site of the 2001
Subaru Gorge Games V.I.P. Dinner (200 people) and the USWA Windsurfing Nationals
awards banquet (145 people).
Featured in N.W. Best Places, Best Places to Kiss, Sunset Magazine and the L.A. Times.
AAA Diamond rated.

Imagine a truly unique setting for your special day, where quality service and attention to detail combine to create great memories. **WE DID.**

Surfsand RESORT
AT CANNON BEACH

1.800.797.4666
cannonbeachmeetings.com

Capacity: The Surfsand Resort Ballroom: 3,000 square foot ballroom with ocean view deck, beautifully appointed with natural coastal décor, open beam ceiling and elegant fireplace. Groups from five to 300 people.

Price Range: Prices vary depending on the time of year.

Catering: Full-service catering provided by The Wayfarer Restaurant and Lounge.

Types of Events: weddings, ceremonies, receptions and rehearsal dinners

Availability and Terms
Please call for availability. A deposit is due at time of booking.

Description of Facility and Services
Seating: five to 300 people
Servers: Provided
Bar facilities: Full beverage service provided by The Wayfarer Restaurant and Lounge
Dance floor: Available
Linens and napkins: Available in a variety of colors
Cleanup: Provided
Guest rooms: 83 oceanfront and ocean view guest rooms ranging from $99 to $399 (additional rooms available nearby)
Amenities: Beautiful views of Haystack Rock, indoor pool and jacuzzi, guest laundry facilities, complimentary use of the athletic club, high-speed wireless Internet, DVD players, gas fireplaces, premium in-room coffee, fully equipped kitchens, complimentary newspaper, bell and summer cabana, Sunday Weenie Roast, Saturday Ice Cream Social, kids crafts, the oceanfront Wayfarer Restaurant and Lounge and spa services available.
Recreation: Hiking, biking, volleyball, golf, shopping, crabbing, horseback riding and art galleries.

THE ULTIMATE BEACH RESORT
Nestled between the Coastal Mountain Range and the Pacific Ocean at the foot of Haystack Rock, is the oceanfront Surfsand Resort in Cannon Beach. Just 70 miles from Portland, this ultimate beach resort, welcomes guests with warmth and hospitality. Over a dozen different room styles are available, with amenities including panoramic ocean views, jacuzzis, fireplaces and fully equipped kitchens. The Surfsand Resort is 100% non-smoking and pet friendly.

6393 N.W. Cornelius Pass Road • Hillsboro, Oregon 97124
503-614-8747 • Fax 503-531-4065
www.sweetoregongrill.com
Hours: Mon–Thurs: 11am–10pm; Fri: 11am–11pm
Sat: 8am–11pm; Sun: 8am–10pm
Summer to Winter Hours May Vary

Capacity: indoors: up to 125; Lawn/Patio area: up to 300 (indoor w/ courtyard: up to 200)

Price Range: varies according to event; please call for more information

Catering: full service, in-house catering

Types of Events: we have complete indoor and outdoor facilities for all your events including: wedding ceremonies, receptions, corporate and private celebrations, concerts, dances, fundraisers, reunions, holiday parties, business meetings, movie and commercial shoots, anniversaries, birthdays, retirement parties and formal dinners.

Availability and Terms

Sweet Oregon Grill offers two rooms, two garden patios, a garden, an indoor music stage and dance floor, and an outdoor dance floor and bandstand. Reservations should be made as early as possible to ensure your desired date and time. **A deposit is required.**

Description of the Facility and Services

Servers: hostess and servers provided

Bar facilities: full-service bar, bartender provided — host or no host

Dance floor: a small dance floor inside and large dance floor and bandstand outdoors

Linens: oil cloth on tables, paper napkins provided *(rental fee for cloth linens)*

China and glassware: provided by Sweet Oregon

Decorations: we can assist you with beautiful floral arrangements *(extra fee item)*

Entertainment: Sweet Oregon can assist in finding a wide variety of live music or DJ *(extra fee item)*

Cleanup: we provide setup and cleanup

Parking: on-site *(valet service can be provided for an extra fee)*

ADA: fully accessible

COUNTRY GARDEN SETTING

Sweet Oregon Grill is located on four acres. Your celebration can take place in our beautiful gardens or in our historic American barn. We have two large patios for receptions or rehearsal dinners. A beautiful bandstand and dance floor joins one of our outdoor patios, with a large lawn and fenced garden.

We can arrange for: a make-up artist, photographer and live music. Our staff can arrange every detail.

Visit our web site for more pictures and information at **www.sweetoregongrill.com.**

Sweetbrier
Inn & Suites

7125 S.W. Nyberg Road (Exit 289 off I-5)
Tualatin, Oregon 97062
Contact: Sales & Catering Office
(503) 692-5800, (800) 551-9167; Fax (503) 404-1950
Web site: www.Sweetbrier.com
Office Hours: Mon–Fri 7:30am–5:30pm; Sat 9am–1pm

Capacity: up to 400 guests
Price Range: creative, customized menus to fit your budget
Catering: full-service in-house catering
Types of Events: cocktails, hors d'oeuvres, buffets, sit-down breakfasts/brunches, luncheons or dinners, rehearsal dinners, wedding receptions, anniversary, special event celebrations, holiday parties

Availability and Terms
Four separate rooms are available; we can seat up to 400 guests. You can reserve for day or night.

Description of Facility and Services
Seating: tables and chairs
Servers: staff included in catering costs
Bar facilities: full-service bar available; $25 service fee
Dance floor: 225 square feet of dance floor; PA systems and risers available for a fee
Linens: white linen tablecloths and colored napkins; white skirting
China and glassware: white china; assorted glassware
Decorations: creative catering staff to assist you
Parking: ample free parking
ADA: all facilities ADA accessible

Hotel Features
The Sweetbrier Inn offers 131 guest rooms including 32 luxury two-room suites, with complimentary continental breakfast. Honeymoon packages are also available.

PARKLIKE SETTING
The Sweetbrier Inn & Suites is conveniently located off Interstate-5, and offers a bistro-style restaurant, a lounge featuring live jazz, meeting and banquet facilities, and 131 guest rooms. The banquet rooms overlook a garden setting which provides the perfect atmosphere for a rehearsal dinner, reception or wedding. The spiral staircase in the lobby, or the garden area by the pool, offer excellent ambiance for those special photographs on your memorable day.

See page 183 under Rehearsal Dinner Sites.

The Dalles Ranch

6289 Upper Five Mile Road ~ The Dalles, Oregon 97058
Contact: Lorraine or Gene Gravel 1-360-892-7352 or 1-541-298-9942
www.thedallesranch.com

Capacity: up to 50 indoors and 100+ outdoors
Price Range: available upon request
Catering: full service catering can be arranged, or you may choose you own caterer
Types of Events: rehearsal dinners, wedding ceremonies, wedding receptions, reunions, corporate retreats and getaways

Availability and Terms
The Dalles Ranch has overnight accommodations for up to 16 guests. Book up to one year in advance. Deposit is required with balance due 30 days prior to the event.

Description of Facility and Services:
Seating: for up to 100+
Servers: service staff to be included in catering
Dance floor: available with electrical outlets
Linens, china and glassware: provided by caterer
Decorations: early decorating possible
Cleanup: client and caterer responsible
Parking: on-site
ADA: limited accessibility

A RUSTIC ELEGANT WILDERNESS RETREAT
The Dalles Ranch is the perfect location for your rehearsal dinner, wedding and reception. Your rehearsal dinner will be served at our beautiful Bubinga dining room table beneath the glow of a one-of-a kind Roc Corbett chandelier. Your wedding ceremony will take place among the ponderosa pines with majestic Mt. Hood as a backdrop. Your guests will view the ceremony from 100 lineal feet of cedar decking with ledgestone walls and green lawns below for a magnificent setting. About two hours from Portland and a beautiful drive for your guests.

Visit our Web site at www.thedallesranch.com

TIFFANY CENTER

1410 S.W. Morrison • Portland, Oregon 97205
(503) 222-0703 or (503) 248-9305
Office Hours: Monday–Friday 9am-5pm
Appointments recommended; after hours and
Saturday appointments available

Capacity: from 10 to 1,200 people; seven rooms and two elegant grand ballrooms ranging from 200 to 6,918 square feet

Price Range: call for price schedule

Catering: exclusively by Rafati's Elegance in Catering, prepared on-site in their commercially licensed kitchen; Rafati's full-service catering can assist you with your selection of the perfect menu for your wedding—from brunch to casual or formal reception services, all events are customized to reflect each bride's individual taste and style; personalized menu planning in all price ranges

Types of Events: wedding ceremonies, receptions, rehearsal dinners, private parties, dances, concerts, theater productions, exhibits, fund-raising events, corporate meetings and seminars

Availability and Terms

The Tiffany Center has three ballrooms with dance floors, stages and dressing rooms. Early reservations are suggested, but short notice reservations will be accommodated with space availability. A refundable deposit is required at the time of booking. Client must provide liability insurance.

Description of Facility and Services

Seating: table and chair setup included in room rental
Servers: provided by Rafati's Elegance in Catering
Bar facilities: provided by Rafati's Elegance in Catering; fully licensed
Dance floor: accommodates up to 700 people
Parking: convenient street and commercial lot parking; located on MAX line
ADA: all event rooms are fully ADA accessible
• Central air conditioning in second floor Ballroom; spot cooling available in fourth floor Ballroom

Special Services

The Tiffany Center's expert staff can provide you with complete event planning services. From candle and floral centerpieces, wedding cakes, decorated ice carvings, place cards and balloons to musicians and limo services and much more.

PORTLAND'S PREMIER WEDDING FACILITY

The Tiffany Center features traditional charm and elegance in a centrally located historic downtown building. Large ballrooms and cozy foyers together with gilded mirrors, gleaming hardwood floors and emerald green accents will provide you with an elegant setting for your wedding ceremony and/or reception. Our experienced, professional staff will provide you with everything you need to ensure that your once-in-a-lifetime event is a treasured memory.

TIMBERLINE LODGE

Timberline, Oregon 97028
Catering Sales Office
(503) 622-0722; Fax (503) 622-0708
Business Hours:
Mon–Sun 9am–5pm
Email: weddings@timberlinelodge.com
www.timberlinelodge.com/groups/wedding.shtm

Capacity: up to 200 seated, four banquet rooms, outdoor patio
Price Range: packages begin at $34 per person
Catering: in-house only
Types of Events: ceremony, reception (buffet or sit-down), cocktails, lodging, rehearsal
dinners, bridal lunches, bachelor parties, engagement dinners

Availability and Terms

The Raven's Nest can accommodate 175 for ceremonies, 75 for receptions, and is a loft-style
room with cathedral ceilings and large picture windows. Two patios with majestic Mount Hood as
a backdrop are also available for outdoor ceremonies. The Ullman Hall banquet room has an
attached patio, picture windows, NEW light fixtures and seating for up to 200 people. The
historic Barlow Room with original carved artwork can accommodate 150 for ceremonies or 80
for receptions. The Market Cafe in the Wy'east Lodge has an attached deck for outside seating
and fantastic views of the Cascade Mountain Range and Mt. Jefferson. Silcox Hut is also
available for up to 45 people. Packages are for a four-hour duration (from start of ceremony to
end of reception) and include food and beverage services and a wedding cake. A deposit is
required upon reservation. Contact the Catering Office for a complete wedding packet.

Description of Facility and Services

Seating: round tables and chairs are available for up to 200
Servers: Timberline has a full staff of professional servers and bartenders
Bar facilities: full-service bar available
Dance floor: 400-square-foot dance floor in Raven's Nest; 300-square-foot dance floor in
Ullman Hall; electrical outlets available
Linens and napkins: white floor length linen; cream or white overlay and napkins
China and glassware: fine china; appropriate glassware available (no disposables used)
Decorations: two-hour setup time for decorating included; complimentary votive candles;
optional centerpieces for minimal fee
Parking: Sno-Park permit required Nov–April
ADA: disabled facilities available with the limitations of a historic building

Special Services

Timberline, a National Historic Landmark, has 70 guest rooms available for your event. Your
guests can enjoy the convenience of the ceremony and reception at one site, plus the unique
overnight experience of this historic lodge.

TIMBERLINE—A CLASSIC FOR OVER 60 YEARS

For over 60 years Timberline has been a favorite destination for millions of visitors from
around the world. Located just 60 miles from Portland on the 6,000-foot level of Mount Hood,
Timberline is the epitome of the classic alpine ski lodge. Unique lodging, gourmet dining,
skiing and panoramic views of the Cascade Mountain Range welcome guests year-round.

www.davidbarssphotographer.com

326 S.W. Broadway Street, Portland, Oregon
(503) 226-1240 • www.treasuryballroom.com
Mailing Address:
P.O. Box 5982, Portland, Oregon 97228

Capacity: Ballroom: up to 300; Board Room: up to 50
Price Range: varies according to room, time of year and day of week; please call for details
Catering: choose from our list of preferred caterers
Type of Events: including but not limited to weddings, receptions, corporate functions, private parties, fundraisers, meetings and conferences

Availability and Terms
Early reservations are recommended; however, we will make every effort to accommodate short-notice reservations. Deposits are required.

Description of Facility and Services
Seating: tables and designer chairs provided
Dance floor: marble floor; stage setup available
China, Linens, Glassware and Bar Service: provided by caterer
Parking: on-site parking garage or in several nearby lots
ADA: accessible

Discover The Treasury Ballroom and Board Room, located in the historic U.S. National Bank Building.

A grand staircase descends into the Ballroom, which features neo-classical architecture, arches with floors and columns of Italian marble. A turn-of-the-century bar, restoration light fixtures, stained glass and rich velvet curtains complete the extraordinary and unique atmosphere. The luxurious lounge is perfect for bridal preparations. There is a catering kitchen and ADA accessible restrooms.

The magnificent Board Room, designed by Pietro Belluschi, is ideal for rehearsal dinners, showers and brunches. Gold cherubs adorn the chandelier and accent the grand marble fireplace. Enhancing the Board Room is elegant woodworking, backlit stained glass windows and a high-end sound. Behind the Board Room is an ADA upgraded restroom and a prep/warming kitchen.

Tuality Health Education Center
Facilities for your special events.
A member of the Tuality Healthcare family.

334 S.E. Eighth Avenue
Hillsboro, Oregon 97123
(503) 681-1700
Business Hours: Mon-Fri 9am-5pm

Capacity: rooms range in size from 270–3,100 square feet and can accommodate up to 400 people or 250 in banquet/seating format
Price Range: price varies according to event
Catering: choose from one of our preferred caterers
Types of Events: receptions, banquets, parties, meetings, seminars

Availability and Terms
A 50% rental deposit and signed license agreement reserves your space up to one year in advance. Day, evening and weekend space is available. Minimal kitchen fee per person.

Description of Facility and Services
Seating: tables and chairs provided and set up to your specification
Servers: provided by caterer
Bar facilities: provided by caterer
Dance floor: dance floor available up to 18' x 18'
Linens: provided by caterer
China and glassware: white Wedgwood china; variety of glassware available
Decorations: no rice, birdseed or confetti; enclosed dripless candles only
Cleanup: handled by caterer
Parking: ample free parking
ADA: building fully accessible

Special Services
Choose from our preferred caterers who have access to our cold kitchen, china, silverware, glassware, and some table decorations. Early decorating may be arranged with the caterer. Equipment such as a CD player, video, slides, data projection, computer screen or satellite broadcast may be rented. An audiovisual technician can be provided.

PERFECT FOR SMALL OR LARGE EVENTS
The Tuality Health Education Center features a beautiful sunlit foyer area that is perfect for cake and buffet service tables. The combination of skylights and foliage in our lobby is a perfect setting for your guests to mingle. Moveable walls allow for creating a space that is just the right size for your event.

OF OREGON

Jeffrey Leal Silva, Farm Manager
8000 N.E. Parrish Road
Newberg, Oregon 97132
Phone (503) 538-9895; Cell (503) 569-6745
Fax (503) 537-0249
Web site: www.willamettefarms.com

Capacity: up to 250 outdoors; up to 25 indoors for bridal party, rehearsal dinner, retreats or other events

Price Range: dependent upon number of guests and client's requirements

Catering: our well-arranged kitchen and ample outdoor space is available for caterer and barbequing

Types of Events: outdoor weddings and receptions, picnics, concerts, retreats, rehearsal dinners and other more intimate indoor functions

Availability and Terms

Large weddings are seasonal, but smaller events are year around. Deposits and partial payments are required and early booking is encouraged.

Description of Facility and Services

Seating: 250 outdoors, 25 indoors; tables and chairs provided by caterer or client

Servers: provided by caterer

Bar facilities: provided by caterer

Linens and glassware: provided by caterer or client

Dance floor: inside and outside dance areas available

Decorations: beautiful natural site is usually complimented with decorations provided by the caterer

Cleanup: provided by caterer

Parking: ample parking for 125 plus automobiles

ADA: facilities accessible in most areas; your special needs are always considered

Special Services

We will assist you in arranging your desired "special effects" — carriage arrival for bride and groom; flooring for outdoor dancing, events (or barn dances); boat landings and departures; hay rides; barbeques. See our web site at www.willamettefarms.com to envision your event.

A BEAUTIFUL SETTING FOR YOUR SPECIAL DAY

Willamette Farms of Oregon is a beautiful farm situated along the Willamette River in Oregon's wine country — a working farm less than 45 minutes south of Portland, Oregon. Willamette Farms of Oregon offers an Oregon most of us just get to hear or read about — and we are so close to Portland and Salem. We invite you to come and enjoy yourself.

The Willamette Farms staff is always ready and willing to assist the caterer and client as needed. Our goal is to make your event memorable.

WILLAMETTE
V A L L E Y

900 Country Club Place • Canby, Oregon, 97013
Phone: 503-266-4066 • Fax: 503-266-7663
Contact: Catering Department
Web Site: www.willamettevalleycc.com
Business Hours: Please call for an appointment

Capacity: Our Ballroom may accommodate up to 250 guests with additional outdoor seasonal seating on our deck overlooking the golf course. Smaller rooms available for more intimate functions. Use of the entire second floor accommodates up to 400 guests.

Price Range: prices varies according to menu selections

Catering: WVCC offers full service in-house catering; we specialize in custom menu design to make your event something to remember for years to come

Types of Events: wedding ceremonies and receptions, rehearsal dinners, holiday parties, anniversaries and birthdays, themed galas, corporate events, and all day seminars.

Availability and Terms:
Willamette Valley Country Club is a private club with its magnificent ballroom on the second floor overlooking the golf course. Reservations are made up to 14 months in advance of your event with a deposit to secure your special date. Please contact the catering department for details.

Descriptions of Facilities and Services:
Seating: tables and chairs provided up to 250
Servers: professional, friendly well-trained service staff
Bar facilities: full service bar with portable bars available upon request
Dance floor: available upon request with no additional charge
Linens and napkins: linen cloth and napkins available in a variety of colors at no additional charge
China and glassware: WVCC china and glassware are provided
Decorations: please inquire with event coordinator
Cleanup: provided by WVCC staff
Parking: ample complimentary parking is available
ADA: yes

Special Services:
Let our talented Catering Staff assist you with your special day when planning your wedding. Secluded, quiet and relaxing away from the hustle and bustle, we are conveniently located off I-5, 20 minutes from downtown Portland. Our elegant Ballroom offers a panoramic view of the golf course and surrounding greens. Have your outdoor wedding ceremony on our beautiful wedding site. WVCC Golf carts are provided for "first looks" with access to the many spectacular photo opportunities Willamette Valley Country Club has to offer. Let us make your unique day one to remember.

WORLD FORESTRY CENTER
FOREST DISCOVERY CENTER
4033 S.W. Canyon Road
Portland, Oregon 97221
Contact: Facilities Coordinator
503-488-2101 ext. 101; Fax 503-228-4608
Office Hours: Mon–Fri 8:30am–4:30pm
www.worldforestry.org

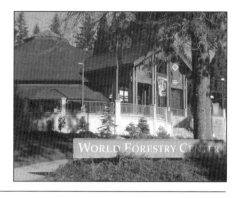

Capacity: banquet, 40-250; classroom, 35-175; conference, 50-300; stand-up reception, inside—200–400, outside plaza—1,000

Price Range: price varies by type of facility and time; please call for specific pricing.

Catering: preferred caterers, full kitchens available; caterer referral list on request

Types of Events: weddings, banquets, receptions, formal dinners and buffets

Availability and Terms
Located in Portland's Washington Park, our three meeting halls and 10,000-sq.-ft. outdoor plaza are available year-round, seven days a week for day and evening events. Our 30,000-sq.-ft. museum is open after-hours for events, such as receptions. A deposit is required for booking; deposit is nonrefundable unless date can be booked in same calendar year.

Description of Facility and Services
Seating: Miller Hall: 300 chairs, 25 eight-foot tables, 30 five-foot round tables; Cheatham Hall: 200 chairs, 25 eight-foot tables; David Douglas Room: 50 chairs

Servers: provided by caterer

Bar facilities: liquor allowed, OLCC regulations apply

Dance floor: Cheatham Hall, 18′ x 18′ dance floor available

Stage: Miller Hall, 12 sections, 3′ x 4′ portable stage, two sets of steps

Linens and napkins: provided by client or caterer

China and glassware: provided by client or caterer

Decorations: buildings are available three hours prior to event for decorating; please no confetti, glitter, mylar, rice or birdseed; candles are allowed only in hurricane shade or water base; no nails, push pins, tacks, staples or tape

Audiovisual: PA system, microphone, screen

Cleanup: client or cater to remove everything brought into facility

Parking: shared lot with Oregon Zoo; on MAX line (easy access from hotels)

ADA: meets most ADA requirements; upgrades planned

A SERENE, SYLVAN SETTING
Escape to Portland's beautiful Washington Park, where the World Forestry Center offers a quiet sylvan setting for your wedding or event. Enjoy the natural warmth of wood tones in Miller and Cheatham Halls, which are inviting spaces with large, open ceilings. Select a preferred caterer to use our full kitchen facilities. When the season permits, gaze into a star-studded evening from our outdoor plaza.

WORLD TRADE CENTER
Two World Trade Center Portland
25 S.W. Salmon Street • Portland, Oregon 97204
Reservations: (503) 464-8688 • Office Hours: Mon–Fri 8am–5pm

Capacity: inside: 400 reception, 300 seated; **outside:** 800 reception, 500 seated; **Flags riverfront space:** 125 reception, 80 seated

Price Range: please call for specific price information

Catering: we can host a rehearsal dinner or reception, or we can package your entire wedding, handling all the details for you!; full-service in-house catering available with creative and helpful event coordinators to assist you

Types of Events: sit-down, buffet, hors d'oeuvres

Availability and Terms
A variety of rooms are available to meet your specific needs. Choose between the glassed-in Mezzanine or our covered Plaza for your outdoor ceremony or reception. Our riverfront banquet space offers a fantastic view of the river and Tom McCall Waterfront Park. There is also a 220-seat auditorium for indoor ceremonies. Reservations are suggested at least six months in advance—particularly during spring and summer months. A 25% deposit of anticipated total expenses is required at the time of booking.

Description of Facility and Services
Seating: seating capacity based on room(s) selected and seating arrangement; table and chair setup included in rental price

Bar facilities: full beverage service provided

Dance floor: dance floor upon request at standard rental rate; electrical hookup for bands or disc jockey available

Decorations: creative theme events may be arranged

Parking: underground daytime and evening parking available in the building

ADA: all rooms are disabled accessible

INVITE YOUR GUESTS TO SEE THE WORLD
Imagine your special day at Portland's showcase—the World Trade Center! Located in the heart of the city between Southwest Salmon and Taylor streets, First Avenue and Naito Parkway, this award-winning facility has a commanding view of the beautiful Tom McCall waterfront and provides the finest in facilities. You'll enjoy our cooperative and helpful staff, prepared to do whatever it takes to make your special time a wonderful experience. Please call for a tour and complete information packet.

Notes

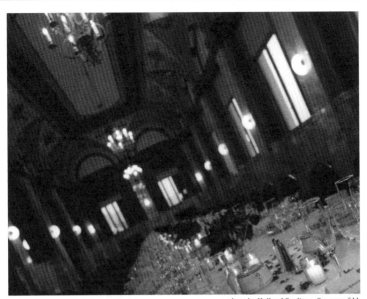

The Noisier The Better

In order to chase away any evil spirits that

may be lurking about, rehearsal dinners were

a melee of broken glass and china,

reaffirming the belief that the more noise made

the better when it came to disposing of evil spirits.

Banquet & Rehearsal Dinner Sites

www.bravoportland.com

Romantic Mansion located on
two wooded acres overlooking the Willamette River

Amadeus
at the FERNWOOD
2122 S.E. Sparrow (Off N. River Road Exit)
Milwaukie, Oregon 97222
Contact: Kristina (503) 659-1735, (503) 636-6154
Business Hours: Tue–Sun; Open at 5pm for dinner
Sunday Brunch 10am–2pm
cpoppmeier@msn.com • amadeus.citysearch.com

Capacity: 300 people

Price Range: full course sit-down dinners or buffet style $40 Friday or Sunday, $40 Saturday during the day, $50 Saturday evening; plus 18% gratuity all days. Weddings are also available at the Lake Oswego location, same prices!
Business lunches: $20 plus 18% gratuity; business dinners: $30 plus 18% gratuity.

Catering: full-service in-house and off location catering

Types of Events: individual rooms for conferences, seminars, private meetings, large group luncheons, holiday parties, celebration dinners; from small intimate events up to 300, weddings and rehearsal dinners

Availability and Terms
Reservations should be made as soon as possible to ensure availability. A deposit is required at the time of booking. Half the deposit is refundable if cancellations are made at least nine months prior to your event. **No** cost for using the facility, bartending services, linens, flowers, and candles, valet parking and classic piano.

Description of Facility and Services
Seating: table and chairs provided for up to 300

Servers: provided with catering services

Bar facilities: full-service bar with bartender provided; host/no host; liquor provided according to OLCC regulations

Dance floor: available

Linens: cloth tablecloths and napkins provided in cream color

China and glassware: fine china and glassware

Cleanup: provided by Amadeus at the Fernwood, no cost

Decorations: early decorating available; fresh flowers for guest tables provided by Amadeus; please discuss ideas with Kristina

Parking: ample free parking; valet service; **ADA:** disabled access available

ROMANCE OVERLOOKING THE WILLAMETTE RIVER
Amadeus at the Fernwood is the perfect setting for an annual, monthly or quarterly function; or dinner for two. You and your guests will enjoy fine continental dining in a wonderful old mansion on two wooded acres, filled with antiques, fireplaces, crystal chandeliers, candlelight and fresh flowers, overlooking the Willamette River. We offer a full bar with a wide variety of Oregon and international wines, outdoor dining and wedding ceremonies on our patio is available. Three hours of piano music is also included. **SUNSET DINNER SPECIAL:** Tue–Sun • 5–6:30pm • $9.95

Restaurant and Catering
1331 SW Washington
Portland, Oregon 97205
Contact: Christine, Bob or Mercedes
503-223-0054 email: christine@cassidysrestaurant.com

A PORTLAND FAVORITE SINCE 1979!

Capacity: 20 to 120 people

Private Banquet Room

Cassidy's private banquet room is warm and inviting, and your guests will enjoy all the privileges of our restaurant service. The room is accented with beveled glass windows, natural woodwork and original art by local artists. The room accommodates receptions of up to 50 people and sit-down dinner parties of up to 30 people. Semi-private areas can accommodate groups of up to 120 people.

Food and Beverages

Cassidy's exceptional menu features regional cuisine of delicious seafood, premium-cut meats, and fresh pasta. A well-chosen wine list, a beer selection including the best microbrews, classic cocktails and a bar that has earned its reputation as one of the finest in town—all in a friendly and comfortable atmosphere.

Experience

We have extensive experience, with more than 20 years in event planning and catering. From formal sit-down dinners or extensive buffets, to casual receptions, Cassidy's staff of experienced professionals will take care of every detail.

Cost

Cost is based on your choice of menu. There is never a room charge for use of the banquet room or restaurant. White tablecloths are available at no additional cost.

Catering

Cassidy's also offers full service catering at the location of your choice.

OPB
BUSINESS
PARTNERS

www.cassidysrestaurant.com

CLARKE'S

455 Second Street between Avenues A & B • Lake Oswego, OR 97034
Contact: Laurie or Jonathan Clarke • Phone: 503-636-2667 • Fax: 503-636-2753
www.clarkes.citysearch.com E-mail: ljclarke@teleport.com

Business Hours: lunch Tuesday-Friday 11:30 am-2 pm, dinner Tuesday-Thursday 5pm-9pm, dinner Fri-Sat 5pm-9:30pm; CLOSED Sunday/Monday except for private functions.

Capacity: CLARKE'S has two dining rooms (400 and 750 square feet) that can be used individually for groups of 10-60, or in combination for up to 90

Price Range: Varies according to selection. No room charge provided certain minimums are met.

Types of Events: Full sit-down dining or stand-up cocktail receptions.

Availability and Terms

Call for availability; A deposit is required at booking to secure the date with the balance due the day of your event. The deposit is refundable if notice is given at least 60 days in advance.

Description of Services

Seating: customized seating arrangements for each event; seating for up to 90 is arranged per your wishes

Servers: experienced and professional servers provided by CLARKE'S

Bar facilities: full service bar including liquor, wine, and beer; host/no-host options available; variety of wines available for every occasion and budget

Linens and napkins: provided by CLARKE'S and included in price

China and glassware: provided by CLARKE'S and included in price

Audiovisual: please ask if available — if we don't have it we can rent it for you

Cleanup: included in price

Parking: ample, free parking outside the door

ADA/disabled access: yes

FABULOUS FOOD IN A WARM & INVITING RESTAURANT

CLARKE'S restaurant features dishes made with local ingredients, freshly and simply prepared with French, Italian, and American influences- all areas of inspiration for the chef, Jonathan Clarke. Cozy and comfortable, the restaurant emphasizes Northwest food and wine and professional service. Jonathan and Laurie Clarke, a hands-on husband and wife team will work with you to customize your event.

"Best American Restaurant"   —2002 Portland Zagat Guide

Our current menus, pictures, reviews and more at: **www.clarkes.citysearch.com**

Dragonfish Asian Café
Located in Downtown's newest boutique hotel

808 S.W. Taylor Portland, Oregon 97205
Contact: Hilary Parish (503) 243-5991 ext. 1668; Fax (503) 243-6731
Email: hparish@portlanddragonfish.com
Office Hours: Tue–Sat 8am–5pm • Restaurant Hours: 6:30am–1am

Capacity: up to 70 people
Price Range: please call for current prices, customized menus available
Catering: full-service in-house catering
Type of Events: rehearsal dinners, bridal luncheons, receptions, social events, business functions, private breakfasts or any other time you want a truly unique event

Availability and Terms
Dragonfish Asian Café has two separate dining rooms that can be used individually for groups of 15 to 70 or in combination to host as many as 150 guests. Dragonfish requires a deposit of $150 in advance to reserve space for your event. Deposits are credited to your final bill. We suggest that you book early to ensure availability but also welcome you on short notice.

Description of Facility and Services
Seating: We can create seating arrangements appropriate for any event.
Services: staff included
Bar facilities: full-service bar available including liquor, beer and wine, no host/host options available. We also have an extensive variety of sake available to make your event unique.
Linens and napkins: white or black linen included; color coordination available
China: included in price
AV: slide projector, screen, TV/VCR and flip charts available for rent
Cleanup: included in price
Parking: plenty of on street parking as well as two adjacent parking lots
ADA: all facilities are ADA accessible

You can find the Drgaonfish Asian café's unique catering facilities on the mezzanine level of the Paramount Hotel. These rooms overlook the European-style lobby and offer French doors that open to a view of Park Avenue. The Paramount Hotel is Portland's newest boutique hotel, which combines traditional elegance with distinctive amenities in the perfect city-center location.

Make your event unique with a collection of eclectic pan-Asian cuisine, mouth-watering sushi and trendy cocktails. We are a dedicated team of professionals devoted to providing a unique, creative and cutting edge dining experience for you and your guests. There is passion, purpose and pride in all that we do.

Il Fornaio

115 N.W. 22nd Avenue
Portland, Oregon 97210
(503) 248-9400; Fax (503) 248-5678

Business Hours: Mon–Thurs 11:30am–10pm, Fri–Sat 11:30am–11pm, Sun 10:30am–10pm
E-mail: info@ilfo.com; Web site: www.ilfornaio.com

Capacity: main dining room: 230 seated, 20-85 private dining rooms,
indoor and outdoor piazza
Price Range: prices vary, please call for details
Catering: in-house catering
Types of Events: business meetings, rehearsal dinners, family gatherings, corporate
presentations, cocktail parties, bar mitzvahs and breakfast programs

Availability and Terms

Il Fornaio offers two distinctive private dining rooms, which can accommodate groups of up
to 80 people. There are no room charges although food and beverage minimums apply. A
confirmation is required to secure reservations. An 18% service charge is applied to all events.

Description of Facilities and Services:

Seating: flexible according to group needs
Servers: provided
Bar facilities: full-service bar is available
Linens: white
Parking: complimentary valet parking
ADA: elevator access

AUTHENTIC ITALIAN CUISINE

Enjoy friendly and professional service in a setting that is comfortable and intimate. Let
Il Fornaio provide your event with authentic Italian cuisine and an award-winning wine list.
Our event coordinator will assist you in customizing a menu and environment that meets all of
your needs.

photo by David Barss

HOTEL VINTAGE PLAZA

627 S.W. Washington • Portland, Oregon 97205
Contact: Private Dining (503) 412-6316
www.pazzoristorante.citysearch.com • www.vintageplaza.com
Business Hours: Mon–Fri 9am–5pm

Capacity: 300 people reception; 150 people seated; 120 people seated with dance floor
Price Range: varies with menu selection, call for details
Catering: full-service in-house and off-premise catering from Pazzo Ristorante
Types of Events: sit-down, buffet, hors d'oeuvres, receptions, wedding ceremonies

Availability and Terms

The Hotel Vintage Plaza has banquet rooms available to accommodate functions of many sizes. These rooms are located on the second floor of the hotel and display the same European ambience seen throughout the hotel lobby, restaurant, and guest rooms. Also available is the Pazzo Cellar, which has the capacity for seating up to 72 guests, 80 for a reception. The Pazzoria bakery can accommodate up to 25 people for an evening event. We encourage you to reserve as soon as possible to secure your desired date. A deposit is required to confirm your space.

Description of Facility and Services

Seating: up to 150; 120 with dance floor
Servers: serving attendants available; 19% gratuity
Bar facilities: full-service bar with liquor, beer, and wine provided
Linens and napkins: linens available in ivory; specialty colors available upon request
China and glassware: white china; sheer-rim wine glasses and flute champagne glasses available
Cleanup: included in catering charges
Decorations: candles; we'll also assist you with any floral arrangements and decorations you may need
Parking: valet parking available
ADA: yes
Guest rooms: Hotel Vintage Plaza has 107 guest rooms and suites; each evening the hotel serves an Oregon Wine Reception in the lobby; call (503) 228-1212 for details

THE PERFECT EUROPEAN FAIRY TALE

From the warm and friendly greetings of the doorman to the pampering from our wait staff, our guests experience personalized service. Pazzo Ristorante offers exquisite food that embraces the warmth of Italian cuisine. You can drink "with the stars" from the panoramic windows in our Starlight Rooms or relax with a glass of wine in a two-person soak tub in an exquisite Townhouse Suite. You will quickly see why this hotel has been rated as one of Portland's most romantic places to stay.

ON THE COLUMBIA

3839 N.E. Marine Drive
Portland, Oregon 97211
Contact: Matthew Carter
(503) 288-4444; Fax (503) 284-7397
Web site: www.saltys.com

Restaurant Hours:
Lunch Mon–Sat 11:15am–3pm; Dinner Mon–Thur 5–10pm, Fri–Sat 5–10:30pm;
Sunday Brunch 9:30am–2pm; Sunday Dinner 4:30–9:30pm; winter hours vary

Capacity: up to 200 guests
Price Range: available online at saltys.com
Catering: full-service catering; in-house or off-premise
Types of Events: rehearsal dinners, wedding receptions, bridal showers, anniversary celebrations and other events; private breakfasts, sit-down dinners and luncheons, seafood and brunch buffets, cocktails and hors d'oeuvres

Availability and Terms

We recommend reserving your space three to six months in advance. But if you need assistance with last minute planning—we can help! A deposit is required to reserve your date. Room fees are waived with a minimum purchase of food and beverage.

Description of Facility and Services

Seating: a variety of table sizes and seating options
Servers: after a specified minimum gratuity or 20%, servers provided at no additional charge
Bar facilities: full-service bar provided courtesy of Salty's; host/no-host; liquor, beer and wine
Linens: house colors available at no additional charge
China and glassware: restaurant silver, china and glassware available at no charge
Audiovisual: overhead and slide projector with screen; TV, VCR, flip charts available for rent
Cleanup: handled by Salty's staff
Parking: plenty of free parking; complimentary valet service available Mon–Sat nights
ADA: first floor accessible for handicapped; Wine Room and North Shore View Room are on second floor

Special Services

Our catering director works closely with you to ensure your event's success. We print a personalized menu for you and your guests. We are happy to refer you to florists, DJs and musicians. At Salty's, we pride ourselves on catering to your every whim.

GIVE YOUR WEDDING A BETTER POINT OF VIEW!

Salty's is located on the riverfront only 15 minutes from downtown Portland. We provide the perfect recipe for memorable occasions; rehearsal dinners, wedding receptions, or bridal showers for up to 200 guests. Salty's exceptional Northwest cuisine, warm hospitality, and spectacular views of the mighty Columbia and majestic Mount Hood will make your event a very special occasion! We're easy to get to, and ready to serve you the very best seafood, steaks, Sunday Brunch, and riverfront view in Portland.

SETTLEMIER HOUSE

355 N. Settlemier Avenue
Woodburn, Oregon 97071
503-982-1897
Business Hours: open by appointment

Capacity: inside the house: 60 to 85; outdoors: 300+
Price Range: starting at $400, facility rental varies; midweek discounts available
Catering: we recommend professional caterers or you may select your own
Types of Events: weddings, receptions, rehearsal dinners, buffets, cocktail parties, meetings, picnics, office parties, family reunions, fund-raisers, class reunions, birthdays, anniversaries, memorials, photo shoots, movies, and many other events

Availability and Terms
A $400 deposit is due at time of booking.

Description of Services and Facility
Seating: some tables and chairs provided
Servers: provided by caterer or client
Bar facilities: client provides bartender, beverages, and liquor liability; beer, wine, and champagne only—no hard liquor allowed
Dance floor: gazebo; capacity: 25+; electrical outlets available
Linens and napkins: provided by caterer or client
China and glassware: available in limited quantity
Cleanup: responsibility of client, unless other arrangements are made
Decorations: please inquire about restrictions and details on early decorating
Parking: free street parking

Special Services
The Settlemier personnel are on site at all times to answer questions and make sure that everything is taken care of and running smoothly.

A LOVELY ROMANTIC SETTING PLEASANTLY SITUATED IN THE HEART OF THE WILLAMETTE VALLEY
The Settlemier House is an 1892 Victorian home located on nearly an acre of beautifully landscaped grounds. The backyard is surrounded by a photinia hedge with a gazebo, offering a romantic and private setting for an outdoor wedding and reception during the spring, summer, and early fall months. It is our policy to provide friendly service—we want you and your guests to feel welcome and to have a truly memorable experience. The Settlemier House is located 30 minutes south of Portland and 20 minutes north of Salem, making it ideally accessible for all your guests.

"AFFORDABLE EXCELLENCE"

CANYON GRILL

9900 Canyon Road
Beaverton, Oregon 97225
(503) 297-2551
Business Hours: Mon–Fri 9am–5pm
Saturday by appointment only

Capacity: we cater to intimate groups of 10 to 200 people or more with ample banquet space
Price Range: tailored to fit within most budgets
Catering: full-service with well-trained and professional staff
Type of Events: wedding receptions, rehearsal dinners, ceremonies and business meetings

Availability and Terms
Come tour the property and discuss your special event. Please schedule your event in advance.

Description of Facility
Seating: 10 to 200 people
Bar facilities: host and no-host bars available by request
Dance floor: available by request in a variety of sizes
Linens, china and glassware: provided
Cleanup and setup: all included
Decorations: you may bring your own or have us do flower arrangements for an extra fee
Parking: ample parking and access to all the banquet rooms and restaurant
ADA: disabled access available

AMBIANCE AND CHARM
The Canyon Grill is located just minutes from downtown Portland inside the historic Shilo Inn Hotel in the beautiful West Hills of Beaverton.

Our newly redecorated hotel has all of the ambiance and charm of one of the oldest hotels in Beaverton with all the modern amenities. We offer a wide range of services for all your hotel and banquet needs. Please contact our Catering Director for an appointment.

**See page 156 under Banquet & Reception Sites
and page 310 under Ceremony Sites.**

Sweetbrier
Inn & Suites

7125 S.W. Nyberg Road (Exit 289 off I-5)
Tualatin, Oregon 97062
Contact: Sales & Catering Office
(503) 692-5800, (800) 551-9167; Fax (503) 404-1950
Web site: www.Sweetbrier.com
Office Hours: Mon–Fri 7:30am–5:30pm; Sat 9am–1pm

Capacity: up to 400 guests
Price Range: creative, customized menus to fit your budget
Catering: full-service in-house catering
Types of Events: cocktails, hors d'oeuvres, buffets, sit-down breakfasts/brunches, luncheons or dinners, rehearsal dinners, wedding receptions, anniversary, special event celebrations, holiday parties

Availability and Terms
Four separate rooms are available; up to 400 guests. You can reserve for day or night.

Description of Facility and Services
Seating: tables and chairs
Servers: staff included in catering costs
Bar facilities: full-service bar available; $25 service fee
Dance floor: 225 square feet of dance floor; PA systems and risers available for a fee
Linens: white linen tablecloths and colored napkins; white skirting
China and glassware: white china; assorted glassware
Decorations: creative catering staff to assist you
Parking: ample free parking
ADA: all facilities ADA accessible

Hotel Features
The Sweetbrier Inn offers 131 guest rooms including 32 luxury two-room suites. Honeymoon packages are also available.

PARKLIKE SETTING
The Sweetbrier Inn & Suites is conveniently located off I-5, and offers a bistro-style restaurant, a lounge featuring live jazz, meeting and banquet facilities, and 131 guest rooms. The banquet rooms overlook a garden setting which provides the perfect atmosphere for a rehearsal dinner, reception or wedding. The spiral staircase in the lobby, or the garden area by the pool, offer excellent ambiance for those special photographs on your memorable day.

See page 162 under Banquet & Reception Sites

WIDMER GASTHAUS

955 N. Russell • Portland, Oregon 97227
Contact: Gasthaus Managers (503) 281-3333; Fax (503) 331-7242
Business Hours: Mon–Thurs 11am–11pm, Fri–Sat 11am–1am, Sun noon–9pm

Capacity: private room, 20-46 guests; parties of 47–75 require special arrangements
Price Range: $10-$20 per person
Catering: in-house only
Types of Events: rehearsal dinners, birthdays, retirements, holiday parties, business dinners, or any other event where great beer and delicious food will make your party complete

Availability and Terms

All parties require a nonrefundable $200 deposit to secure a date and will be considered tentative until receipt of deposit. A food and beverage minimum of $350 is required Sunday through Thursday; $500 minimum on Friday and Saturday. A 17% gratuity is applied to all food and beverage including no host bar.

Description of Facility and Services

Seating: tables and chairs for up to 46; up to 75 requires special arrangements
Servers: provided
Bar facilities: hand-crafted beers brewed on location as well as a variety of wines and soft drinks available
Dance floor: not available
Linens: white linen is provided on food and beverage tables during banquets with an array of colors available for formal dinners at a nominal fee
Decorations: no nails, tacks or confetti please
Audiovisual: large screen TV, video, DMX sound system
Equipment: overhead and slide projectors and other equipment available at a minimal charge
Cleanup: included
Parking: plenty of on-street parking as well as two parking lots
ADA: yes

FRIENDLY SETTING COUPLED WITH FINE BEER AND WINE

Widmer Gasthaus is a friendly place to enjoy fine food and our excellent handcrafted beers. The Gasthaus is housed in a turn-of-the-century brick building, adjacent to the famous Widmer Brewery. Our chef and staff are experienced in all types of events, from formal dining to Super Bowl parties, so let us make your next celebration one to remember! All information regarding the Gasthaus and its menus can be faxed to you and our managers will be happy to answer any questions you may have regarding availability or menu planning. Until then, PROST!

Notes

Notes

photo by Coughlin-Glaser • See page 506

Illusion Of Beauty Law

A law was passed in 1775 stating that a young

woman could not wear makeup at her wedding.

If she did, her marriage would not be

considered legitimate, because the groom

would have been "ensnared" by the

illusion of beauty made by the makeup.

www.bravoportland.com

Beauty, Salons & Spas

- **Eat right and get enough sleep:** It gets very hectic prior to the wedding with all the planning and parties. Be sure to take care of yourself! You'll need every ounce of energy. Eat right and get enough sleep to look your very best on this special day.

- **Pamper yourself:** A couple of weeks before the wedding, take time to pamper yourself. Schedule a massage to relieve tension and stress. A facial is wonderful for your skin, but be sure to allow some time for your face to benefit from it. Avoid using unfamiliar products too close to the wedding in case your skin has an allergic reaction. Prepare your hands and nails with a manicure. A pedicure will do wonders for your feet and toes for the honeymoon.

- **Hair consultation:** When you have selected your headpiece, make an appointment for a consultation with your hairdresser. This allows time to experiment with different hairstyles that complement your face and work well with the headpiece. This way there are no "surprise" hairstyles the morning of your wedding. You and your hairdresser should agree on the style and look well in advance. Also make sure your hairstyle will look nice even when you take off the headpiece.

- **Makeup consultation:** A makeup consultation can help you apply makeup in a natural and flattering way to highlight your features. The photographer may ask for a heavier application for the photos. Ask the consultant how to obtain the best look without overdoing it. There are make-up artists available who will come to you on the day of the wedding to apply your make-up. This service is very convenient when you have so many other things to worry about on the wedding day.

- **Bridesmaid lunch and manicure:** A fun idea is to take your bridesmaids to lunch and then treat them to a manicure. This usually takes place a day or two before, or the morning of the wedding. For parties of three or more it is best to schedule an appointment at least three months in advance.

- **On-site beauty service:** Many salons and beauty consultants offer hairstyling and make-up for you and your bridesmaids at the ceremony site. Fees are based on services, number of people, and travel time.

For more assistance with staying organized during the wedding planning process, check out the Bravo! Wedding Organizer. Detailed question worksheets double as contracts. This step-by-step system will keep every detail of your wedding organized. To order, refer to the order form on page 25 in this Guide.

CHRIS WILDSCHUT
STYLIST

PHONE/FAX   503.647.2688

PAGER   503.301.6486

Would you like a fairy-godmother to pamper you on your wedding day or special event? Relax and let me do my magic! Enjoy the comfort and soothing personal attention which will enable you to feel, look and radiate your most elegant self on this memorable occasion.

Services Include:

- On-site make-up, hair and styling for the bride and entire wedding party, including mothers and kids

- Free consultation at the location of your preference

- Optional make-up and hair trial run (bridal only)

- Styling and touch-ups during candid and professional photo sessions

- Assistance available if needed

I bring with me 24 years of professional experience in national and international film, print and commercial video, providing hair styling and make-up for top models and many celebrities. Whatever your special wishes… I can help them materialize into timeless visuals and the fondest of memories. References provided on request.

Gypsyana

515 Saltzman Road, #721
Portland, Oregon 97229
Contact: Tammy Brant
(503) 810-8035
E-mail: gypsy1makeup@cs.com
Web site: www.gypsyana.com

Your wedding day is your day. You want to look your best, but not like a different person. Let Tammy help to make this a lovely memory that lasts your lifetime. During a free consultation, she will take all your desires into consideration when planning your special day. Feel confident with her 13 years of experience with make-up and hair styling, NYC film, video, print and runway.

Services Include:

Make-up and hair styling on location

Make-up and hair styling available for photo shoots

Free consultation

Assistance available for large groups

Swiss skin care product purchases available/Not required

Make-up and hair trial run available

Reasonable package prices

Available to travel

Photography packages with make-up and hair included

A soothing personality for that big day

Don't run around to several locations the morning of your wedding day! Let Tammy come to you, where you're most comfortable. She can arrange for her team to assist if you have a large group. Please call at least one month in advance, if not sooner. Please visit her web site at: www.gypsyana.com. References available upon request.

"I DO"
Artistic Hair Designs On Site

Creative Styling
By:
Deborah Wright
(503) 250-0871

visit online@
portlandweddinghair.com

Relax, Enjoy your Day

Let me sculpt your hair into

A work of Art

Deborah is a true "Hair Artist"! With her 16 years experience she is exceptional at combining your ideas with her creativity to design a look that is unique to you. With a consultation, you and Deborah can explore different styles, from elegant or classic to contemporary.

- **On-site, at your home, or in the salon hairstyling**
- **Eliminate stress getting to and from the salon**
- **Consultation offered to explore different styles**
- **Make up artist available upon request**
- **Assistants available for large parties**
- **No travelling fee up to 50 miles**
- **Pre-wedding salon services if desired**

Let your Special Day be relaxed and enjoyable. No more stress trying to get yourself and your wedding party to the salon and back, on time. Let Deborah bring her artistic ability and the salon to you.

portlandweddinghair.com

Lucky Girl Make-up Services

Tonya Elizabeth
503.331.0310
Licensed Aesthetician

We specialize in makeup only. At your location, we offer our 10 years experience, including weddings, runway, print and film. We have had extensive training, in addition to working for MAC cosmetics for five years. We are knowledgeable in techniques for enhancing features on all skin tones and our expertise in color theory will enable us to choose the best colors for you and your wedding party. We work quickly and efficiently to eliminate any stress on your special day.

• On-site Services
- We use products specially formulated for film, video and photography
- Engagements, rehearsal dinners and other special events
- Entire wedding parties—including men and mothers, too
- Waterproof mascara and false eyelashes (if desired) at no extra charge
- Lessons available

In Advance
Prior to your wedding, we will meet for a consultation to discuss the details and choose your look. At this time we can schedule any additional appointments that will best suit the needs of you and your wedding party.

Make-Up and Hair Design by

Tonya

Contact: Tonya Powell
(503) 658-4815 or (503) 341-0054

Let Tonya pamper you and the whole wedding party with her professional knowledge of makeup and hairstyling, for perfect portraits and a beautiful walk down the aisle. Tonya has over 17 years of makeup and hair design experience including film, print and runway, and has taught seminars in the United States and overseas.

Services Include

• **On-site** makeovers including beautiful hairstyling

• Consultation at no charge

• Assistant availability for large parties at low additional fee

• Haircut and color done prior to wedding if desired

• A calm nature and a great attitude to put you at ease

Perhaps you prefer a dramatic look for an evening affair or a more subtle touch for a morning ceremony—Tonya can tailor your makeover and hair design to fit your exact needs.
To set up a free consultation, please call at least two months in advance, however, Tonya does welcome last minute calls.

Dosha offers unsurpassed creativity and exceptional quality in salon and spa services. Our professional team, including Aveda trained stylists, specialize in TV, Film, Video and Special Events. We have a full-time wedding and events coordinator to help plan and fulfill all your beauty, styling and relaxation needs. Services are available seven days a week in Northwest, with a new location soon to open on SE Hawthorne. Visit our web site for photos of wedding and other special occasion styles. Gift Certificates are available online at anytime. Email us at **weddings@dosha.org** for more information.

Salon Spa Services

- Full body massage including Swedish, deep tissue, geo-thermal, and hydrotherm
- Facials, waxing, lash and brow tinting
- Photo and corrective makeup
- Plant-derived haircolor and textural services
- Expert haircutting and session styling

Dosha's Grand Bridal Package — $887 and up

The Grand Bridal Package begins four weeks prior to the wedding.

Four weeks prior to the wedding: Body Elixir, Body Glow, Aromatherapy Spa Facial, Aromatherapy Spa Manicure and Pedicure

Two weeks prior to the wedding: Body Glow, Spa Facial, One Hour Body Massage, Practice Wedding Style and Practice Wedding Makeup.

Two days prior to the wedding: Body Glow, Spa Pedicure, Waxing (leg, bikini, brow, lip)

Wedding Day! One Hour Body Massage, Spa Manicure, Wedding Style and Wedding Makeup.

The Bridal Suite — $150 and up

Spa Manicure, Spa Pedicure, Wedding Style and Wedding Makeup

SALON NYLA

THE DAY SPA

327 S.W. Pine Street • Portland, Oregon 97204
(503) 228-0389; Fax (503) 228-1219
www.salonnyla.com • Open 7 days a week • Closed on major holidays

Your wedding day is one of the most important days in your life. In the course of planning your wedding, don't forget one of the most important details…YOU! You deserve to be the most luxurious gift of all. And, you can be. Pampering yourself is not a luxury in your wedding plans. It is a necessity. After all, it is your day. Make sure you enjoy it, stress free.

Salon Services:

- Complete Hair Care
- Hotel Spa Packages
- Bridal Packages
- Spa Manicure
- Spa Pedicure
- Aveda Retail Center
- Body Treatments: Bodywraps, Saltglow, Body Polish, Body Waxing
- Aromatherapy
- Vichy Shower
- Reflexology
- Massage Therapy
- Gift Certificates
- Esthetics: Facial, Skin Care, Make-up, Waxing

Bridal Services:

Special requests such as food, beverage and amenities can be added to any package.

- Customized Packages
  Customize a package to fit your individual needs.
  Create a package for your entire bridal party.
- Bride Package
  Wedding Consultation (Style & Makeup)
  Special Day Style, Makeup & Spa
  Manicure, Spa Pedicure

Groom Services:

- Groom Package: Haircut & Style, Spa Manicure, Sports Facial and Hour Massage

At Salon Nyla The Day Spa we are committed to providing outstanding customer service. Our philosophy is to pursue advanced levels of education, training and teamwork to create a relaxed and serene environment. As an Aveda concept salon we are also dedicated to environmental concerns and community service.

We make any day special and your special occasions unforgettable.

Notes

The Bride's Value

The bride's value was judged by

her beauty, ability to work, produce children,

and by the size of her dowry.

The more household goods, land,

and money the bride had in her dowry,

the higher esteem she was held in.

Bridal Accessories & Specialty Stores

www.bravoportland.com

Bridal Accessories

- **How to make candles burn slower and drip less:** If you plan to use candles at your wedding, put them into a freezer in a foil-wrapped box the night before. This prevents the candles from burning down too far while the photographer is taking formal portraits before the ceremony. An alternative is to bring an extra set of candles. You don't want it to look like the candles were already used before the wedding actually begins.

- **Guest-book pen:** Bring an extra pen for the guest book. Sometimes fancy plume pens run out of ink or don't write well. You want to make sure you have a complete list of who attended your wedding.

- **The unity candle:** Unity candles used during the ceremony are not only symbolic, but can be enjoyed for many years to come to celebrate your anniversaries.

- **Wedding gown slips:** These slips can be very expensive to wear for just one day. Some shops have slips available for rent.

- **Garters:** It is nice to buy two garters, one to throw and the other to keep as a fun memento.

- **Toasting goblets:** You'll find a variety of glass, crystal, pewter, or silver goblets and toasting glasses to choose from. You can have them engraved with your names or initials and your wedding date. Your florist will be able to provide decorations such as ribbons and fresh flowers to place around the stems of your glass or goblet. These are mementos you'll want to keep for years to come, or to pass on to the next generation.

- **Something old:** Ask your mother or grandmother for something she carried at her wedding or a piece of sentimental jewelry you can wear or carry.

For more assistance with staying organized during the wedding planning process, check out the Bravo! Wedding Organizer. Detailed question worksheets double as contracts. This step-by-step system will keep every detail of your wedding organized. To order, refer to the order form on page 25 in this Guide.

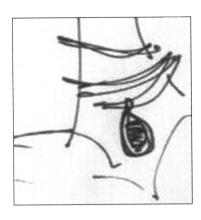

unique semiprecious jewelry

[adorn]

studio 2 : 5 w t f s
www.adornonline.com
twelve fifteen southwest alder portland: 503.224.6465

*you are cordially
invited,
to peruse the
collection of unique
handcrafted semiprecious stone & sterling silver jewelry
created by designer artist loren peters
for the bride and bridal party
to enhance the details
of your
wedding day.*

[adorn]

a small intimate accessory design studio and adornment boutique
emphasizing a uniquely personal and innovative approach
to creating custom and one of a kind jewelry
located downtown at twelve fifteen southwest alder
open two till five wednesday through saturday

please
call ahead regarding
individually designed items and appointments
503.224.6465

BRIDESMAIDS : BRIDES : MOTHERS : SISTERS

Fabric Depot

700 S.E. 122nd • Portland, Oregon 97233
Contact: Bridal Department (503) 252-9530 or (800) 392-3376
Visit our Web site: www.fabricdepot.com

Fabrics and Patterns Available
- **Bridal-gown fabrics:** satin, brocade, shantung, taffeta, chiffon, organza, jacquard, georgette, Swiss batiste, damask, velvet, and linen
- **Wedding party:** satin, taffeta, velvet, lamé, jacquard, silks, faille, crêpe, silk, and shantung
- **Specialty silk:** dupioni, suiting, crêpe de chiné, beaded
- **Patterns:** full line of patterns available at 50% off every day

Lace, Trims and Accessories
Fabric Depot has almost every kind of lace fabrics and trims. Many of our laces are available with beads and sequins, and in a large array of colors.

Laces: Cutwork, Galloon, Florence, Alençon, Venice, Chantilly, embroidered organza and embroidered tulle

Trims: specialty trims include sequins, beaded dangle, satin piping, pearl edging, rhinestone strands, and button loops

Appliques and Motifs: huge variety of bodice motifs, collars, collar appliqués with and without beads and sequins

Buttons: large selection of fabulous special occasion buttons

Headpieces and Veils
We carry a large assortment of tiaras and headpieces. We also have a fabulous selection of tulle and netting in many colors and in 54", 72", and 108" widths. A variety of veiling including illusion, point de esprit, Russian and 116" silk

Special Services
The Palmer Pletsch International School of Sewing Arts, located in our huge classroom, offers many specialized sewing classes to help with your bridal sewing projects, including classes in fit and couture sewing.

Discounts and Ordering
Fabric Depot offers a 40% discount off our already low retail prices when a "full bolt" (10–25 yards) is purchased. Special orders are available on most fabrics and notions.

OFFERING THE LARGEST SELECTION IN THE WEST
Fabric Depot has the largest in-stock quantities of fabrics, trims, and notions in the West. Our 40,000-square-foot retail store is an awesome display of every kind and type of fabric and notion available in the industry. Our fully stocked 30,000-square-foot attached warehouse allows us to provide large quantities of fabrics and notions.

UPTOWN STYLE

Glisan Center
1627 N.W. Glisan • Portland, Oregon 97209
503.223.3400 • fax: 503.223.3456
Joy Walker, Owner
Monday-Friday 10-6, Saturday 10-5:30

Yes!! To Mothers!!

Extensive Selection
We carry an extensive selection of special occasion dresses. If you are a mother-of-the-bride, mother-of-the-groom, or attending a special event, Joy's has the perfect look for you.

Special Orders
We are happy to place special orders for our customers. Some of our special order lines include Daymor, Teri Jon, Cattiva, Jovani, El Ana and Damianou.

Personal Care
Our knowledgable staff will halp make your special occasion memorable. At Joy's our goal is to provide extraordinary service to all of our customers.

Serving Exclusively Size 14 -7x

4240 N.E. Sandy Boulevard
Portland, Oregon 97213
(503) 288-5450
Business Hours Mon–Fri 10am–7pm,
Sat 10am–6pm Sun Noon–5pm
E-mail: MCBI1@aol.com

Location

Located in the heart of the historic Hollywood District, only 10 minutes east of downtown Portland and 15 minutes from Vancouver.

Premier Plus-Size Shop

As the premier plus-size shop in the greater Portland area, we at Magical Creations Boutique have dressed many attendants, rubenesque mothers of the bride and groom, as well as brides who seek the one-of-a-kind or non-traditional look for their special wedding.

We serve exclusively size 14W–7X and provide a warm, supportive environment with comfortable, spacious fitting rooms, each equipped with a fan.

Styles and Price Range

In addition to formal wear, we carry lingerie, jewelry, accessories, active wear, natural fiber casual clothes and ethnic garments for all activities associated with the wedding. A wide variety of designs are featured, representing creations from small local designers to nationally known manufacturers, with prices ranging from $65–$325.

Catering to Your Individual Needs

Each of our customers are special to us. We are dedicated to providing individualized customer service to ensure a satisfying shopping experience. Allow us to assist you with your fashion needs and eliminate some of the special occasion stress!

**We believe that Magical Creations Boutique creates
an environment for plus size goddesses…where magic truly happens.**

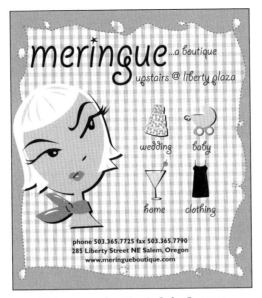

meringue ...a boutique
upstairs @ liberty plaza

wedding   baby

home   clothing

phone 503.365.7725 fax 503.365.7790
285 Liberty Street NE Salem, Oregon
www.meringueboutique.com

Visit our new location in Lake Oswego:
Lakeview Village Mall, 385 First Street, Suite 121

Wedding Invitations:
- Anna Griffin
- Cross-my-Heart
- Roger la Borde
- Fitzgraphics

Wedding Servers

Frames

Tableware
- Silver
- Vietri

Toasting Glasses

Plates and Napkins

Wedding Albums and Guestbooks

Gift Registry

503.365.7725
285 Liberty Street N.E. Salem, Oregon
Lakeview Village Mall, 385 First Street, Suite 121, Lake Oswego, Oregon
www.meringueboutique.com

MINK

hair jewels + veils

twelve fifteen southwest alder portland oregon 97205 503.224.6465

style . a mink design is quickly becoming a must have for the local bride. classic or modern—romantic or whimsical—mink designs appeal to women who appreciate sophisticated, chic fashion while indulging their personal style.

desire . whatever it may be, we can create it.
tiaras, combs, crowns, vines and hairpins in helical arrays of crystals and pearls make up mink's dazzling collection of hair adornments custom designed and exquisitely detailed each cluster and jeweled garland resonates beauty.

experience . you will be comfortable in mink—relaxed and elegant. every bride works with our designer to create the perfect complement to her gown and unique vision. we look forward to your visit...

W T F S noon–5 or gladly by appointment

NORDSTROM

Washington Square 503-620-0555
Downtown Portland 503-224-6666
Lloyd Center 503-287-2444
Salem Center 503-371-7710
Clackamas Town Center 503-652-1810
Vancouver Mall 360-256-8666

AT NORDSTROM, WE HAVE A BEAUTIFUL SELECTION OF FINISHING TOUCHES FOR YOUR SPECIAL DAY

From pearls to the perfect shoe, you'll find surprising selections for the beautiful bride. Plus, we have special occasion attire for the mother-of-the-bride or groom and the entire wedding party.

Hosiery
You'll find a variety of styles and colors to complement you and your attendants' bridal attire from Spanx, Calvin Klein, and Donna Karan.

Fashion Jewelry
You'll enjoy an extensive selection of Austrian Crystal jewelry from Swarovski and Nadri, as well as freshwater pearl designs from Cardee.

Fashion Accessories
Finishing touches for your bridal party are easy with our extensive accessory collection, including decorative hairpieces and satin gloves. We are also happy to place special orders for your individual needs.

Lingerie
Complete your trousseau with selections from our beautiful collection of bridal lingerie, including bustiers, garter belts with matching panties, peignoir sets and garters.

Handbags
Our handbag section features a unique selection of styles including satin, velvet and beaded handbags.

Fine Jewelry
Whether you're shopping for an engagement ring or wedding set, you'll find a breathtaking array of contemporary and traditional rings. Custom jewelry designing is also available in selected stores.

Cosmetics
Our professional makeup artists will assist you in creating the perfect look for your special day and in choosing a memorable fragrance.

Main Store
4775 S.W. Watson Avenue
Beaverton, Oregon 97005
(503) 643-9730
Downtown
421 S.W. Fourth Avenue
Portland, Oregon 97204
(503) 827-4578

www.weddingcottageoregon.com

The most enormous selection of elegant accessories from economical to extravagant.

A trip to The Wedding Cottage is a must for anyone planning a wedding. The variety and beauty of our wedding accessories are like no other in the Pacific Northwest. There is so much to see, that brides return again and again.

The Wedding Cottage carries many lines including Beverly Clark, Marcela, Lillian Rose, Simply Charming and Cathy's Concepts. Many items are custom-made or customized to fit a bride's individual or wedding theme.

An extensive amount of inventory is on hand. However, we take pride in our ability to special order items not in stock in the exact color or style needed.

Every bride receives a Bride's Card that allows her a $10 instant credit every time her cumulative purchases reach $100. Brides who do all their shopping at The Wedding Cottage find they have substantial savings.

- ♥ Bridal books and planners
- ♥ Guest and memory books
- ♥ Unity candles and holders
- ♥ Bridal jewelry
- ♥ Knives and servers
- ♥ Custom cake tops and charms
- ♥ Bubbles (10 varieties)
- ♥ Favor boxes and bags
- ♥ Wedding Candy
- ♥ Personalized napkins and ribbons
- ♥ Toasting goblets
- ♥ Cameras
- ♥ Invitations and announcements in over 60 books

- ♥ Bridesmaid and groomsmen gifts
- ♥ Plume and guest book pens
- ♥ Ring bearer pillows
- ♥ Flower girl baskets
- ♥ Garters, hankies, gloves
- ♥ Photo albums
- ♥ Veils and tiaras
- ♥ Purses and money bags
- ♥ Shower invitations and games
- ♥ Rehearsal dinner invitations
- ♥ Specialty and anniversary gifts
- ♥ Save the date cards
- ♥ CD of wedding music
- ♥ and more

See page 472 under Invitations & Announcements.

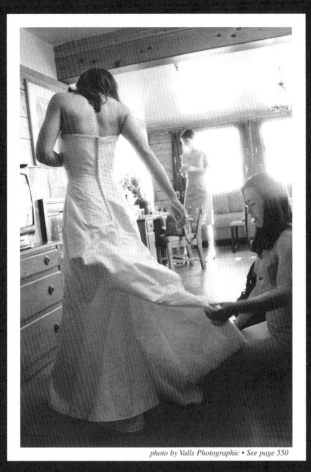

Tradition

By the 14th century, the bride's garter

became so highly valued that guests would rush the

bride at the altar to gain the garter's possession.

Today, things have settle down considerably.

Now the groom throws the bride's garter to

the unmarried men at the reception.

www.bravoportland.com

Dress Design & Alterations

- **Where to begin:** Start by browsing through bridal magazines, web sites and shows to see a variety of dress designs and styles. Then try on as many different types and styles of dresses as you can before you contact a professional seamstress. That way, if you plan to have your dress made, you will know what length of sleeves, skirt and train you prefer as well as which neck and waist designs work best for your body type.

- **Dress design:** If you haven't found the dress of your dreams or if the dress you have in mind doesn't exist, take your ideas, pictures, and dreams to a dress designer. Designers offer a variety of options, taking a sleeve from one dress and a bodice from another to design a gown especially for you. Many expensive original designer dresses with designer prices can be copied, allowing you to stay within your budget.

- **Hemming:** Consult with a seamstress on hemming your dress. Many dresses can be lifted at the waistline to avoid taking lace off the entire hemline, and without distorting the lines and design of the dress. Also ask about ways to bustle up the train so it is comfortable and convenient for you to get around in at the reception.

  NOTE: Make sure you are wearing the shoes you will wear to your wedding when making any decisions about hemming. A slight difference in heel height can change the measurements.

- **Reserving alterations services:** As soon as you have selected your gown, be sure to make an appointment to reserve services for alterations. Many bridal-alterations specialists are booked months in advance. Your bridal shop can recommend a reliable seamstress or may have someone they work with. Brides should be prepared to pay for alterations and include this in their budget. They are seldom included in the price of the gown.

- **Making bridesmaid dresses:** You should buy the fabric all at once, even if each bridesmaid is paying for her own dress. Fabric comes in different dye lots and is difficult to match. Make sure that all the different fabrics you buy come from the same bolts to be sure everything matches. Remember to buy extra fabric, especially if you are working with delicate fabrics such as velvet or chiffon. This is not the time to come up short. Also, have the dresses made by the same seamstress to keep the dresses similar.

  NOTE: Most professional seamstresses will make your pattern out of a cotton muslin. Ask if there is an additional charge for this service or if it is included in the price of the gown.

- **Veils:** While not all brides choose to wear a veil, it is still considered a traditional part of the wedding ensemble. If you choose to wear a veil, decide if you would like to have a blusher (a veil that covers your face), or one that is attached to a headpiece that stays in back. If your dress has a lot of detail, chose a simple veil; if you have a more simple dress design, you may choose a more elaborate veil. Decide before the wedding whether or not you want your veil to be in the photographs at the reception, which includes the first dance and cake cutting. Many brides take off their veil after the ceremony, while some keep it on.

For more assistance with staying organized during the wedding planning process, check out the Bravo! Wedding Organizer. Detailed question worksheets double as contracts. This step-by-step system will keep every detail of your wedding organized. To order, refer to the order form on page 25 in this Guide.

August Veils

Showroom located in: The Bridal Loft
2808 N.E. Martin Luther King Blvd. Suite 3 • Portland, Oregon 97212
(503) 788-5280; Fax (503) 788-5281; Web site: www.augustveils.com

August Veils appreciates the planning and endless attention to detail that contribute to a wedding—the kind of details that make your experience uniquely yours.

Experience and Attention to Detail

Let August Veils help you create the headpiece or veil that is just right for your occasion. We will guide you through creative choices and playful suggestions to make your decisions a reality. Headpieces may be embellished with Austrian crystals, pearls, and sequins. Off-the-rack veils are also available for purchase.

Affordable Elegance

We will work with you to create a design within your budget. August Veils prides itself not only on its craftsmanship, but also in ensuring brides with prompt service. Quick turnarounds are available as time allows.

Gown Alterations and Custom Design Gowns

We also offer services for bridal and special occasion alterations. We have vast experience working on such name brands as Lazaro, Amsale, Christos, Maggie Sottero and Jasmine to name a few. Can't find the gown of your dreams? Call us about our custom design services!

www.augustveils.com

Brenda Boitz

Alterations • Bridal Gowns • Veils • Etc.

Call for an appointment (503) 638-8646 • (503) 939-9858
brenboitz@hotmail.com

Custom Veils • Garters • Ring Bearer Pillows
Choose your color and style

Brides Maids

Prom

Special Occasion

Flower Girl

Tuxedo

♥ 10 years experience in custom sewing and alterations,
   providing comfort on your wedding day

♥ Discount for large parties

♥ References upon request

♥ Free consultations

Let me help you make your special day beautiful

fletcher artworks
A T I L I E R
and custom clothiers

1012 N.E. Birchwood Drive
Hillsboro, Oregon 97124
Contact: Paula Smith-Danell
503-693-7725
E-mail: paula@fletcherartworks.com
Business Hours: by appointment

Services

We can help you create the dress of your dreams if you've been unable to find it or if you've found the gown but it is a costly haute couture original. If you have no idea what you want we can still help create a look for you that is unique.

We can create the perfect dress for you from just a drawing or one or more magazine cuttings; or you may want to peruse the vast fashion library for ideas, both contemporary or historical. If you are planning to wear your mother's or grandmother's dress but find you can't zip it up, we can alter or reconstruct the gown to fit you.

European Couture Experience

Paula has her bachelor's degree in Fashion Design from the American College for Applied Arts in London, England. She graduated summa cum laude and was awarded most outstanding student for her graduating class.

She has been in the fashion industry since 1984. A portfolio is available for viewing by appointment, and references are available upon request.

Ordering your Dress

Please call for an appointment, and bring all your design ideas or plan to spend time looking through the many volumes of dress designs that Paula has spent years acquiring and cataloging. An estimate will be given at the time of the design selection, and a 50% deposit will be required when the dress is ordered. The balance will be due on receipt of the completed dress. Please plan on placing your order at least six months before your wedding date.

A series of measurements will be taken at our first meeting and will be turned into a flat pattern that will fit only you. It is helpful to bring the foundation garments that you are planning to wear as well as a shoe in the heel height that you are considering.

We will make a mock-up of your dress, so you can decide if this is the style you want. Any changes that you desire will happen at this point. Then it's on to the final fabric and final fitting, and you will have the dress of your dreams to wear on your special day. Please see our web site at **www.fletcherartworks.com**.

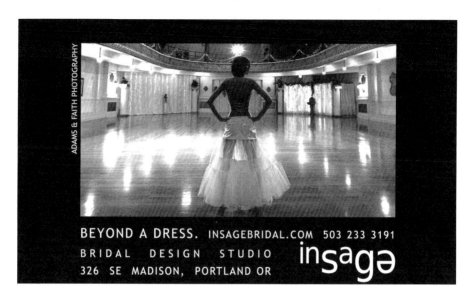

CONCEPT | Personalized Garb

Unlike ordinary bridal salons that solicit generic and inflexible styles, Insage manufactures completely personalized and custom-fit bridal gowns and evening wear. Insage lends over 30 years of experience in bridal and evening wear design, commercial apparel production and fine tailoring, for the highest quality and workmanship.

DESIGN | Infinite Selection

Whether its a traditional ballgown in silk satin, a haute couture original or a red carpet rendition, an Insage gown will satisfy the whims of any bride. Insage offers the industry's finest silk and natural fiber fabrics. Of course, color is abound, with hundreds of silks in a montage of modern shades.

FIT | Individually Tailored

Using computer-aided design ("CAD"), along with personal measurements, each gown is digitally patterned and produced to fit, eliminating the need for most alterations.

EXPERIENCE | Refreshingly Simple

From the first encounter to the last, it's an experience like no other. Whether it's creative guidance she needs, or she knows exactly what she wants, the process is flexible and accommodating. Construction typically takes eight weeks. Most designs fall in the $800 to $1,500 range; some may be higher of course depending on design, fabrication and embellishment. The result - quality and style unmatched by conventional dressmakers or by mass-producers and a truly enjoyable and effortless experience.

Visit insagebridal.com to view a digital portfolio
of select Insage brides.

Lorraine Huey, Seamstress
14854 S.W. Scholls Ferry Road #U-203
Beaverton, Oregon 97007
(503) 521-0469 • (503) 522-1574 cell
lhuey49@hotmail.com

Experience

Lorraine has over 15 years experience working with a major bridal shop doing alterations. She has worked on dresses from many different manufacturers and different styles. She has experience with LDS temple ready dresses and can make yours temple ready if necessary. She is capable of doing design changes on your dress.

Prices

You'll find her prices are very reasonable and will give you an estimate of possible costs.

Environment

Your dresses are professionally altered in a non-smoking and pet-free environment.

She is available to do rush jobs on wedding dresses and bridesmaid dresses. She is by appointment only so don't put off having your dream dress fitted to your satisfaction.

Notes

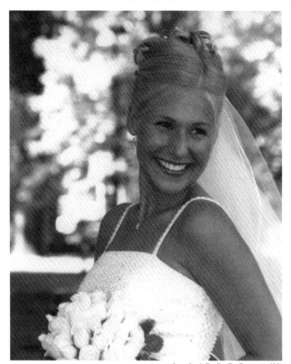

photo by A Studio C • See page 490

Talismans

Talismans a bride may choose to wear or

carry on her wedding day came about from a

mix of tradition and superstition.

Something Old

to bring a sense of continuity

Something New

adds an optimistic note

Something Borrowed

the superstition that happiness rubs off

Something Blue

for purity, fidelity and love

A Penny In Your Shoe

to help ensure a life of fortune

Bridal Attire

- **Selecting your bridal gown:** Take the time to try on the various styles available at different shops. Most importantly, pick the dress you feel the best and most comfortable in. **NOTE:** Allow at least six months to order your wedding gown.

- **Bridesmaid dresses:** There are several factors to keep in mind when selecting bridesmaid dresses. Colors and fabrics vary with the seasons. The style usually complements the bridal gown. The formality is based on whether it is a daytime or evening wedding. Choose a dress color and style that will be flattering on all the bridesmaids, and keep in mind that the main focus will be on the backs of the dresses during the ceremony. You can even have different styles for each bridesmaid, using the same color and fabric. A new trend is to have dresses that the bridesmaids will want to wear again; choose dresses that can be easily altered for post-wedding use.

- **Formal and evening attire:** Many bridal shops carry a nice selection of formal and evening gowns for special occasions and pageants. Bridal salons may carry one-of-a-kind gowns.

- **Guideline for lengths:** The bridesmaid dresses are traditionally shorter than the bride's gown. Bridal gowns now come in a variety of lengths.

- **Headpieces and veils:** Pick a headpiece that enhances your face and hairstyle; it should complement, not overwhelm. If you attempt to press your own veil, be extremely careful. Press the veil between white tissue. Do not put an iron directly on the veiling. Ask about care when you buy the veil.

- **Accessories:** Most bridal shops carry a nice selection of bridal accessories, including garters, slips, gloves, jewelry, shoes, albums and guest books.

- **Looking good all day long:** You may want to consider the fabric for your dress more closely, depending on how long you will be in the dress. There is no way to avoid wrinkling a dress once it is put on; however certain fabrics wrinkle more easily. Here are a few ways to preserve your dress: Get dressed at the ceremony site, eliminate traveling in dress before ceremony, bring a stool to the ceremony site for sitting on, and make sure there is an aisle runner if you have a long train. Detachable trains and veils make it easier to travel about and dance at the reception. Just remember, this is a day to enjoy, don't worry if your dress is tattered and stained at the reception; with a cleaning and preservation service most stains and problems can be fixed.

- **Picking up your dress:** It might be smart to leave the dress at the bridal shop even if the dress is ready far in advance of the wedding day. The bridal shop may be better equipped to store and keep the dress fresh and pressed.

- **IMPORTANT NOTE:** The following recommendations are for your protection: 1) Be careful about where you buy your wedding dress. Ask your friends and family about where they went and what their experiences were; 2) make sure the delivery date of your dress is well in advance of your wedding; 3) get a copy of the order or receipt with a guarantee of delivery date to keep with your wedding records; 4) if a contract is used, **read it carefully** (even the fine print) before signing! If you have any questions or concerns about the company, check it out with organizations that keep track of the reputations of companies.

3970 S.W. Mercantile Drive, Suite #150
Lake Oswego, Oregon 97035
503.636.1474; Fax 503.636.1694
www.annasbridal.com

ANNA'S BRIDAL BOUTIQUE features elegant designer gowns and accessories. We carry dresses to suit any price range, body type and color preference. Displayed in our newly remodeled salon are several exclusive lines including:

Melissa Sweet	Vera Wang	Janell Berte
Marisa	Jim Hjelm	Bellissima
Casablanca	Barbara Allin	St. Patrick
Dessy Creations	After Six	Jovani
Winters & Rain	Salon & Grace Shoes	Many More!

Wedding Party Attire, Accessories, and More

Anna's also offers a large selection of sample dresses and a range of designers for the whole wedding party including bridesmaids, flower girls, junior bridesmaids, mothers and more. In our showroom we showcase exquisite headpieces, tiaras, hairpins, veils, shoes and undergarments. Some of our headpieces feature real pearls and crystals which the bride can have made into a necklace after the wedding. Also available are gown preservation, expert in-house alterations, and of course, you will always be treated with impeccable customer care.

Our happy brides have been showcased on TLC's A Wedding Story and Martha Stewart Weddings and several of our sample gowns have been featured in Portland Bride and Groom Magazine.

Wedding Coordination

Anna's is very proud to present the newest addition to the salon, **BRIDAL BLISS**, an in-house wedding coordination and consultation service. Bridal Bliss will listen to your needs and ideas, offer creative suggestions, and bring your wedding dreams to life.

See Page 244 under Bridal Consultants.

Anne Mauro
designer bridal

1720 NW Lovejoy #106
Portland OR
503.866.4696
www.AnneMauro.com

A unique blend of retail and custom, Anne Mauro Designer Bridal offers an original collection of wedding gowns with the versatility to customize.

Brides can choose directly from the collection or have the option of modifying the silhouette, embellishment, or fabrication to better suit their personal preference or style of wedding.

The designer coordinates each step of the process, ensuring that the gown envisioned by the bride for her wedding day becomes a reality and the experience singular.

Please call for an appointment to view the collection.

921 SW Morrison • Suite 113
Portland, Oregon 97205
(503) 230-9600
www.bellabridalportland.com

Mon-Fri 11-6 • Sat 11-5
Evenings & Sundays by Appointment

Exclusively for the Bride

- Designer Gowns
- Exclusive Couture Gowns
- Custom Designed Veils
- Headpieces & Tiaras
- Jewelry
- Shoes
- Foundations
- Couture & Custom Purses
- Attendant & Guest Gifts

Simply the Best!

Belle & Beau Bridal

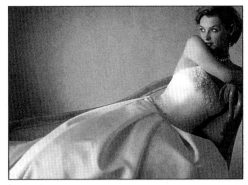

4306 NE HANCOCK, PORTLAND, OREGON 97213
503.284.5969 • www.belleandbeaubridal.com

Having been established as one of Portland's premiere bridal shops, we try to create a personal relationship with each one of our brides. We have discovered a fail proof technique of selling our gowns, honesty. We guarantee that each one of our bridal wear consultants will give a honest and informative opinion on what styles best suit your body type.

Our motto—*"We are here to please."*

Bridal Designers:
- Alfred Angelo
- Maggie Sottero
- Venus
- Casablanca

Hours:
Monday through Friday: 10–7 • Saturday: 10-6 • Sunday: By appointment only
Hours are subject to change during off-season October through January

FREE:
…with a $300 gown purchase is a custom bustle, gown bag, and a slip rental. Everything but the cost of alterations is included with the purchase. Plus every bride gets a 10% discount on all other purchases (bridesmaids dresses, headpiece, shoes, etc…) and 30% off your invitations.

Our in-store seamstress can make any dress a custom fit for the best price in town. We also store your dress in our storage room away from light, children, dirty hands and nosy fiancés.

YOU CAN ALSO FIND…
- Bridesmaids dresses by Dessy Creations, After Six, Alfred Angelo and Venus
- Shoes by Dyeables and Salon
- Headpieces by Erica Koesler, Bel Air and JL Johnson
- Lingerie by Felina
- Jewelry and accessories by Cathy's Concepts
- Flower Girl dresses
- Mother dresses

"We are a salon for today's bride."

Presented by the Hostess House:

THE BRIDAL ARTS BUILDING

10017 N.E. Sixth Avenue
Vancouver, Washington 98685

(360) 574-7758; Web site: www.bridalarts.com
Business Hours: Mon–Sat 10am–6pm; open late Thursday night until 8pm;
Sun noon–5pm; closed most holidays; No appointment necessary

Styles and Selections of Wedding Gowns

Come visit and experience our truly elegant and complete Bridal Salon. We offer nationally advertised designer gowns at affordable prices. Select from over 1,000 gowns in stock. Bridal Arts also offers rental slips.

Ordering Your Gown

Allow two to six months after your gown has been ordered for delivery. A 50% deposit is required when you place your order, with monthly payments on balance available. Ask about our layaway plan. Rush orders are welcome. Don't want to wait? You can buy your gown off the rack.

Description of Wedding Gowns

- **Colors:** white, ivory, blush, pink, blue, rum and café
- **Fabrics:** satin, taffeta, silk, lace, peau de soie, tulle and chiffon
- **Styles:** cathedral, chapel length, sweep train, floor length, and street length
- **Sizes:** 4 to 30 in stock
- **Price range:** starting at $99 to $1,500
- **Sales:** shop our magnificent sale room; discontinued designer gowns, save 25 to 75%

Headpieces

So many ways to crown the bride. Tiaras, bun wraps, combs, hair jewels, traditional headbands, hats and veils. Buy in stock or custom order.

Service

Because you are so special to us, **we pay the sales tax for Washington buyers**. We also include a garment bag to protect your gown; can store your gown until your wedding and professionally steam your gown, so it's perfect for your wedding. We will match any other store's prices and services.

Bridal Attendant and Mothers of the Bride Attire

We feature nationally advertised designer bridesmaid gowns in all the popular styles, fabrics, and colors. A 50% deposit is required for special orders. **Sizes:** 4 to 28. We cater to mothers for informal to formal attire for weddings. We carry a lovely collection of mother's dresses that can be ordered in a variety of fabrics in as many as 40 colors; sizes 4 to 26.

Flower Girl Dresses

We carry a beautiful selection in sizes 2 through 16; some feature trains and many have accent colors to match your bridesmaids. A 50% deposit is required on all special orders or you can purchase out of stock.

Accessories and More

Bridal shoes, dyeable shoes, gloves, jewelry, bras, garters, specialty items and gifts. We also have a large selection of guest books, ring pillows, flower girl baskets and candles.

Special Occasion

Be sure to see our exciting line of holiday and cruise attire.

Alterations and Custom Design Available

Alterations by appointment only.

Exquisite Wedding Cakes

Looking for a baker to copy MARTHA STEWART? We can do it! Our cakes are scrumptious. Always baked fresh—never frozen, and custom decorated to your specifications. Dozens of flavors and fillings to delight your guests. Fondant, French buttercream, white chocolate—our exceptional bakers can do it all. We offer fresh flower decor and fountain set-ups are available. Price: $1.90 per serving and up, depending on your fondest dream. A deposit is required at the time of order. The balance is due in full one week prior to the wedding. Delivery available (fee depending on distance).

Bridal Arts Florist

Our florists truly specialize in gorgeous wedding arrangements at affordable prices. We will even meet with you at your church to design your flowers to your needs. A free toss bouquet with your order. We are "the" experts in this field. We have done thousands of weddings—each one very unique and special.

Special Bonus

When you order both your cake and flowers from us, we will waive the delivery and setup fee and include a fountain setup under the cake at no extra charge.

FULL-SERVICE WEDDING FACILITY

The Hostess House and Bridal Arts Building is the first full-service wedding facility in the Northwest. We have everything for your wedding, including a candle-lit chapel that seats 200 guests and an absolutely gorgeous reception center; invitations and imprinted napkins, party supplies and decorations, custom-designed cake tops, unity candles, gift shop and bridal registry, DJ services, musicians and vocalists, catering and much more.

Directions: located 10 minutes north of Portland. From I-5 north or south, take the 99th Street exit (#5) and go west two blocks, turn right onto Sixth Avenue.

See page 109 under Banquet & Reception Sites.

BRIDAL ATTIRE & FULL SERVICE BRIDAL SALONS

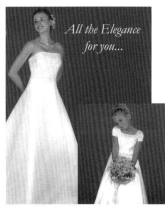

All the Elegance for you...

Celeste's Bridal

Now at the all new Island Station Wedding Emporium

Yes! I Do
Plus Sizes!
Bridal

At Island Station Wedding Emporium

It is great to be a bride at Celeste's Bridal. Allow us to treat you to superior friendly service and a vast selection of gowns to match your tastes. At Celeste's Bridal we are committed to making your gown shopping experience pleasurable. We specialize in one-on-one attention, maintaining a courteous and a warm helpful atmosphere along with a magnificent variety of gown styles.

At Celeste's Bridal you will find the most popular wedding gown styles, including bridesmaids, flower girl, rentals, two-piece, custom fitting, small to large sizes, gown cleaning and preservation, temple-ready and much more.

Celeste's Bridal at the All New Island Station Wedding Emporium
11923 S.E. McLoughlin Blvd. (Two lights North of The Bomber Restaurant on 99E)
Next to Class Act Tuxedo and Yes I Do Plus Size Bridal
(503) 659-2341 • www.CelestesBridal.com

Yes I do Bridal – Specializing in Plus-size Wedding Gowns
You will love the vast selection and warm friendly service at Yes I Do *Plus-Size* Bridal, Portland's largest selection of plus-size wedding gowns! Yes I Do Bridal is located at the new Island Station Wedding Emporium sharing a space with Celeste's Bridal Too, Island Station Wedding Resource Center and the all-new Class Act Mega Tuxedo Center.
(503) 659-2341 • www.YesIDoBridal.com

Island Station Wedding Emporium
11923 S.E. McLoughlin Blvd. (Two lights North of The Bomber Restaurant on 99E)

Don't miss the NEW Class Act Mega Tuxedo Center at Island Station Wedding Emporium. Renting a tuxedo has never been better. Huge selection of tux styles, pool table, big screen TV, Limo pad, excellent service, games and contests for free stuff. It's a bachelor party everyday at Class Act Tuxedo. More details at **ClassActTuxedo.com or call (503) 659-2349.**

8925 S.W. Beaverton-Hillsdale Highway
Portland, Oregon 97225
(503) 297-9622; Fax (503) 297-9061
Web site: www.charlottesweddings.com
call for your personal appointment
Mon–Fri 11am–8pm; Sat 9:30am–5:30pm

We are the "Dream Makers"

In our fairytale setting, a tradition carried on by Charlotte's Weddings, your dreams come true. You will find splendid attire for all types of weddings, no matter if you're planning a Traditional, Informal, or an LDS Temple Wedding, we have them all. We have attire for every member of your bridal party, from the maid of honor to the littlest flower girl, and styles that are appropriate for mothers and guests, too. Not to forget the groom and his attendants, we will fit them in fabulous tuxedos in the most current styles offered today.

Six Critical Characteristics to Look For When Choosing A Bridal Shop…

1. **Great Selection:** Charlotte's carries over 533 different styles, over 28 designers, in sizes from 2 to 48. They can be purchased off the rack or special ordered. We have exclusive gowns that are really exclusive. Charlotte's brides say no shop compares with the selection and prices at Charlotte's Weddings & More.
2. **High Quality Gowns:** Charlotte's uses a "Wedding Gown Quality Checklist" that designers must pass before being featured in the shop. Hidden quality issues like manufacturer reputation, fabrics, stitching, seams, beading, zippers and more are quality issues manufactures must pass.
3. **Low Prices:** Since we work with over 28 designers, and because of our large sales volume, we are able to provide wedding gowns at consistently low prices. Charlotte's prices are one of the lowest in town and we will match the price of any full-service shop if a lower price can be found. You save 15% off invitations, 10% to 15% off Bridesmaids and 20% off Gown Preservation when you purchase your wedding gown at Charlotte's Weddings & More.
4. **Professionally Trained Bridal Consultants:** At Charlotte's each bride has her own professionally trained Bridal Consultant that stays with that bride and only that bride! Each Bridal consultant has successfully completed a 22-point Training and Certification Program and works with their assigned Bride every step of the way.
5. **Private Bridal Rooms:** Each bride has her own large private bridal room. Rooms vary in size from 125 to 216 square feet. The consultant works with the bride in a private atmosphere that makes it fun and easy to find the perfect gown. Family members and friends are welcome to be in the room to share the excitement.
6. **One-Stop Shopping:** Charlotte's carries over 193 styles of bridesmaids dresses, and a fantastic selection of mothers' dresses and flower girl dresses. Also the most current styles of veils, headpieces, tiaras, jewelry, shoes, hosiery, slips, garters, bustiers, gloves, and not to forget the most current styles of tuxedos. Rent six tuxedos and the seventh is free; rent eight and all the basic shoes are free. Also bridal accessories, cake knives, etc.—all with the help of your personal bridal consultant at no extra charge. Your consultant can fit you with the perfect bra for your gown. Find the perfect bridesmaid style, and we'll help you pick out invitations and assist you with the wording.

Visit our Web site at www.charlottesweddings.com

2900 S.E. Belmont • Portland, Oregon 97214 (at the corner of 29th and S.E. Belmont Street)
(503) 234-3484; Fax (503) 234-0404
Business hours: Mon–Fri 11am–8pm; Sat 10am–6pm
E-mail: claraswe@sprynet.com; Web site: www.claraswedding.com

EVERY BRIDE DESERVES A GUARDIAN ANGEL!

Clara's Wedding Establishment Ltd. is Portland's unique bridal shop. At Clara's, we take all of the stress out of your wedding.

Clara's…Your First Stop!

- ♥ **Wedding gowns :** Clara's carries a wide range of the latest designer styles of beautiful wedding gowns in sizes 2-48.
- ♥ **Women's sizes 18-48:** Clara's has a large number of gowns in stock in our women's size department.
- ♥ **Bridesmaids Dresses:** We carry a fantastic line of affordable bridesmaid dresses. Come in and see! Wide range of sizes in every color.
- ♥ We now carry a great line of **tuxedos** for rent.
- ♥ **On-site coordination:** Clara's offers on-site coordination to make your wedding day stress-free. We offer a three or five-hour package including rehearsal, ceremony and reception.
- ♥ **Free vendor coordination:** Clara's is truly the one place to come to plan your wedding. We offer wedding planning and vendor coordination at no cost to you. From start to finish, you can plan your entire wedding without leaving Clara's comfortable surroundings.
- ♥ **Limousine service:** White stretch limousines attended by well groomed, courteous, professional drivers. Check out our classic car for your day—1951 Lincoln Cosmopolitan!
- ♥ **DJ Service:** Clara's own Ultimate Entertainment offers complete music for your ceremony and reception. Packages include music, lighting, bubble machine.
- ♥ **Grand Oregon Lodge :** Clara's historic ballroom in Oregon City…perfect for your wedding and reception!

Visit our shop soon to learn more about our unique services. Brides are always encouraged to drop by Clara's at any time to relax with a cup of tea. Let us handle all of the details while you concentrate on making your dreams come true. We look forward to seeing you soon.

"LET CLARA'S BE YOUR GUARDIAN ANGEL!"

Visit our Web site at www.claraswedding.com

See page 81 under Banquet & Reception Sites and page 381 under Disc Jockeys.

SOPHISTICATION  INDIVIDUALITY  ROMANCE  ELEGANCE

Divine Designs

WHERE DREAMS BEGIN

EXCLUSIVE BRIDAL BOUTIQUE   437 nw twenty third portland oregon 97210
www.divinedesignsbridal.com

FULL SERVICE BRIDAL SALON
DESIGNER BRIDAL GOWNS BY:

Vera Wang

Amsale

Anne Barge

Christos

Elizabeth Fillmore

Lazaro

Monique Lhuillier

Suzanne Ermann

Please call for upcoming Trunk Show date

BRIDAL SALON BY APPOINTMENT
503.827.0667

Here Comes the Bride!

(located inside Here We Go Again Boutique)
9519 SW Barbur Boulevard
Portland, Oregon 97219
Contact: Chris Gauger (503) 546-7692
Business Hours: Mon–Sat 10am–6pm;
Thurs 10am–7pm; Sun Noon–4pm
E-mail: hwga-chris@comcast.net
Web site: www.herecomesthebride.hwga.com

Pronovias USA

Congratulations

on your upcoming wedding! The search for the perfect gown should be fun, exhilarating, affirming, intimate and did we mention *fun*?

The Perfect Gown

At Here Comes the Bride, we enjoy what we do — helping you find the perfect gown. We believe the perfect gown is designed to make YOU look fabulous, not the other way around.

Extensive Selection

Here Comes the Bride is a small store, but this doesn't mean our stock of gowns is limited! We have over 150 gown styles in stock, all specially selected for simplicity, elegance, timelessness, quality and value. Being a small shop, you'll get one-on-one assistance with our expert sales staff. We know our stock and can make recommendations if you're not sure what style will look best. You'll find a range of sizes in stock and all our gowns can be purchased off the rack or time permitting, most can be ordered especially for you.

Personal Service

Shopping for a gown should be enjoyable. You don't have to spend a fortune to be treated like someone special—we love helping you! Regardless of your budget or size, we want to help you find the gown of your dreams. At Here Comes the Bride, you'll find unexpected extras: expert in-house alterations, convenient seven-day-a-week hours, layaway and flexible payment options, and noncommissioned sales people who really care—not about making the sale but about helping you find what you want to make your wedding dreams come true.

Check us out online at www.herecomesthebride.hwga.com

Exquisite Designs & Impeccable Service
Hours: Mon & Tues 11-7 • Wed-Fri 11-5:30 • Sat 10-5

11545 S.W. Durham Road Tigard, Oregon 97224 • Pacific Hwy-99W & Durham Road
503-603-0363; rosewoodbridal.com

Impeccable Service
Our genuine commitment to personal attention and service is the difference you will feel at Rosewood Bridal. You will be welcomed into our boutique and we will work together to find that perfect gown, which will make you look and feel your most beautiful on your wedding day.

Exquisite Designs
◆ Unique Selection of Gowns
◆ Fresh & Elegant Color
◆ Unparalleled Figure Flattering Fit

◆ Maggie Sottero
◆ Essense of Australia
◆ Many Other Top Designers

◆ Impression
◆ Eden

Alteration Services for the Bride
◆ Experienced Alteration Professional
◆ Slip Rental

◆ Gown Pressing

The Bridal Party
◆ Wide Selection of Bridesmaid Styles

◆ Adorable Flowergirl Dresses

Tuxedo Rentals
◆ Modern and Traditional Styles

◆ 10-30% Off Competitor's Prices

Accessories From A-Z
◆ Beautiful Tiaras
◆ Jewelry
◆ Shoes
◆ Ring Pillows

◆ Elegant Veils
◆ Gloves
◆ Guest Books
◆ Toasting Flutes and Much More!

Gown Preservation
◆ Museum Quality Preservation Service; Call for Details.

For the gown you love and the attention you deserve.

503-603-0363
rosewoodbridal.com

Please let this business know that you heard about them from the Bravo! Wedding Resource Guide.   **229**

Helping brides for 13 years

5331 S.W. Macadam, Portland, OR 97239, 503-274-8940
www.towerbridal.com

Free Parking

Designer/Couture Wedding, Bridesmaid Gowns

Barbara Allin	Jim Hjelm
Monique Luo	Dessy
Ian Stuart	B-2
Maggie Sottero	Bella Formals
Diamond Bride	Aimee Monet
Venus	Alfred Angelo
Anjolique	Alfred Sung

Flowergirls
Accessories
Invitations
Tuxedos
Alterations staff on site

Monday - Friday: 10–7, Sat 10–6, Sun 12–5
No appointment necessary

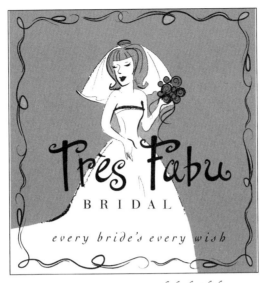

503.233.0004   www.tresfabubridal.com
Mon-Thurs 10-6 Fri 10-9 Sat 9:30-5:30 Sun (Jan-Aug) Noon-5

Quite Simply The Finest Collection

- couture gowns
- custom gowns
- special occasion gowns
- bridesmaids and mothers
- flowergirls
- accessories
- tuxedo rentals and sales
- plus sizes
- alterations on premise
- invitations

Gowns Priced from $300 — $10,000

6910 S.E. Milwaukie Ave. • Portland, Oregon 97202
503.233.0004
www.tresfabubridal.com

Notes

photo by SJ Harmon • See page 602

"When you realize you want to spend the rest of

your life with somebody, you want the rest of

your life to start as soon as possible."

— from "When Harry Met Sally"

www.bravoportland.com

Bridal Concept & Theme Design

- Call an event design firm before you make any plans. A designer will first help you conceptualize the overall look and feel of the event, then put you in touch with specific professionals—caterers, site coordinators, etc—who are best suited to realizing and enhancing your vision.

- Examine the designer's credentials. A terrific sense of style is a vital attribute, but advanced training guarantees an ability to adapt the materials to the methods.

- A good designer exposes your signature style, not his or her own. Check references and confirm that the designer implemented previous clients' visions and did not simply rework earlier versions of his or her favorite event.

- Find someone whose taste you admire and whose personality "clicks" with yours. Celebrations are supposed to be fun—get off on the right foot by working with a designer whose company you enjoy.

- Give the designer latitude to generate creative concepts and the autonomy to implement them for you. Expect the designer's staff to oversee the implementation of every detail. Family and friends often graciously offer to help out, but often wind up overwhelmed or implementing their concept of what you want rather than yours. You are paying for the designer's spectacular ideas and flawless implementation; take advantage of that!

- Rent from the designer whenever possible; you can often get good deals on hard-to-find items. Do make sure the items suit your style and aren't just things that seem to be in stock and used at every event in the designer's portfolio.

- While you should expect to pay a premium price for the exceptional service and impeccable presentation a design professional delivers, a savvy designer will also help you use your money to its greatest advantage by eliminating unnecessary flourishes and focusing funds on those essential items that provide the most dynamic visual impact.

– by Jen Elle Event Design

For more assistance with staying organized during the wedding planning process, check out the Bravo! Wedding Organizer. Detailed question worksheets double as contracts. This step-by-step system will keep every detail of your wedding organized. To order, refer to the order form on page 25 in this Guide.

Tropical Plants

"Everyone, Everyday,
Each Customer "

*11959 S.W. Garden Place
Tigard, Oregon 97223*

*503-684-0570; Fax 503-624-0255
E-mail: bhopkins@rentokil-tps.com; www.rentokil-tps.com*

Add value to your guests experience with the addition of Tropical Plants.

Fresh Tropical Plants enhance your mood and add a bit of luxury to any festive setting. With over 25 years of experience, the professionals at Initial Tropical Plant Services are experts at plantscapes that are exactly right for your space and budget. We want to help you make your special occasions more special. Rent plants for a day, a week or more. Make your surroundings more attractive. Plants bring life and beauty into every environment.

Events:

Special Meetings	Holiday Parties	Graduations	Corporate Events
Trade Shows	Weddings	Grand Openings	

Tropical Plant Rental
Nothing accents your setting more beautifully than lush greenery. We can help you select the appropriate foliage from our elaborate menu of choices to provide a living welcome to your guests. Our plants are uniformly full with healthy deep green foliage.

Exterior Plant Rental
Provide a living welcome to your guests with overflowing containers of exterior trees and flowering plants. Our inventory includes an assortment of plants and seasonal blooming staged in decorative containers. Greet your visitors with a sense of quality, harmony and serenity.

Holiday Decor Rental
Regardless of whether you prefer traditional or contemporary holiday decorations, our designers will create displays to please the most discriminating tastes. We take the headache out of design, installation, removal and storage so that trees, wreaths and garlands appear as if by magic. Plus we do more than Christmas decor. Award winning Spring, Summer and Autumn displays are available to give your space a visual boost throughout the year.

Decorative Containers
Our standard install includes a high grade polyresin container of either "granite " or "terra cotta " finished with a top dressing of spanish moss. Other choices include an extensive palette of colors in gloss or matte, metallic or crackled finishes. All are available in many styles from contemporary cylinders to Mediterranean and Asian designs.

Call or email us for a FREE information pack, color brochure and price list.

Please let this business know that you heard about them from the Bravo! Wedding Resource Guide.

event design & flowers

©Ray Bidegain Photography

©Mount Burns Photography

Incorporating personal meaning into public functions

Jen Elle's owners, Ellen Hiltebrand and Jennifer Greenberg, came together with the vision of producing elegant events instilled with a sense of intimacy. With signature attention to each detail, they attend to every aesthetic element of your wedding, translating your dreams into a cohesive design. Whether helping you focus as you initially begin planning, or transforming challenging spaces, they are an invaluable resource. Along with complete design and implementation services, Jen Elle offers:

- One-time or ongoing consulting services
- Floral design
- Custom rental items
- Access to stylish decor and creative favors
- Inspired pre/post wedding celebrations
- Personal stationary and invitations

New Service Offered: We are pleased to announce the opening of a coordination department to handle any of your practical planning needs. Now with one phone call, Jen Elle can see you through not only the design and implementation, but also each and every logistical detail associated with your wedding day.

Please view our portfolio on our website or contact us for more information.
We look forward to working with you!

www.jen-elle.com   503.789.6978

CRYSTAL LILIES & Soirée
503.230.9311

Concept & Design

Love is wild, spontaneous, impulsive… Weddings are planned! Together Crystal Lilies and Soirée will help you focus your ideas and dreams to create and design a wedding concept that expresses the personal details that are truly special to each couple. We focus our attention on helping to formulate visions by providing fresh ideas and unexpected elements that make weddings truly unique and unforgettable. Let professionals make your wedding a success.

Details

Come explore a wonderful array of flowers, linens, place settings, chairs, etc., to help visualize the overall look of your special day. Whether you choose to transform a ballroom into a romantic Italian villa, line tents with lavish chiffon and fragrant jasmine or even create a dramatic ceremony with an exotic aisle runner and soft candlelight, anything is possible. All details, from reception site, invitations, cake, flowers and decor, among many others, are important elements that present style, whether intimate or grand.

Crystal Lilies

Crystal Lilies specializes in creating weddings that are gorgeous, timeless and elegant. Being an expert in her field, Kimberley has the experience, reputation and relationships to make your wedding an affair to remember. Our custom floral designs are exceptional and define a mood; with textures, fragrances, beautiful flowers, fruits and seasonal botanicals, making you depart from your everyday lives and transport you to a magical place. Visit our studio by appointment and view extensive portfolios of our work. We have an amazing selection of custom unique props; urns, columns, Chuppahs, arches, silver containers, candelabras, chiffon, custom made aisle runners, and much more. Visit Crystal Lilies' additional page in the Floral Section.

Soirée

Soirée is a full service wedding planning company with over 10 years of experience in the Portland metropolitan area. Soirée's dedicated approach ensures a distinctive event, built upon the countless details handled during the wedding planning process. Along with concept and design, these details may include, but are not limited to, vendor research and management, agenda and timeline preparation, legal assistance, budget analysis, contract negations, as well as rehearsal and wedding day facilitation. Soirée's wealth of knowledge, creative touch and extensive vendor relationships allow clients to gain the very best services in our area. Visit Soirée's additional page under Bridal Consultants.

We provide a complimentary consultation. Our concept and design fee is customized for each wedding, based on services provided by both Crystal Lilies and Soirée.

Special Package: Contract both Crystal Lilies (floral and décor) and Soirée (wedding consultant) and you will receive our fabulous concept and design services at a discounted fee
Let us design a vibrant wedding that uniquely represents you!

Please let this business know that you heard about them from the Bravo! Wedding Resource Guide. **237**

West Coast Event Productions

1400 N.W. 15th Avenue
Portland, Oregon 97209
(503) 294-0412; Fax (503) 294-0616
Business Hours: Mon–Sat 8:30m–6pm
Appointments available any hour

Services

West Coast Event Productions is the Northwest's premier idea center for all events and special occasions. We specialize in the custom planning and design of your wedding decorations to mirror your vision. Our many divisions offer you everything you might need: centerpieces, tents and custom canopies, glassware, china, catering supplies, tables and chairs, dance floors, stages, audiovisual equipment, lighting, candleabras in a variety of finishes, carpeting and aisle runners, the Northwest's largest selection of linens, and the list goes on. Our wedding specialists will help you make all of your important planning decisions. Come in to visit our showroom and to tour our warehouses.

Rental Items Available

Table art: West Coast Event Productions features the Northwest's most outstanding selection of specialty linens and tabletop décor. Choose from designer florals, theme print linens, damasks, hand-painted tabletops and unique floral arrangements, along with a complete palette of solid colors with coordinating napkins and runners. Ask about our specialty chair covers and gold ballroom chairs. Choose from fourteen different china patterns.

Custom themes: West Coast designers work in tandem with your project manager to create the perfect environment or individual features, which solve design problems or enhance the mood of your event. Between our Portland, Bend and Las Vegas locations, our collection of sets and props is one of the largest available outside of Hollywood. And what we do not have already, we can build to your specifications. The West Coast reputation is one of total commitment to quality work, creativity and thorough professionalism in everything we do.

Wedding accessories: select from several styles of candelabras, brass and silver table candelabras, brass and contemporary full standing candelabras; wedding aisle and carpet runners; custom chuppahs; gazebos and arches; wood, ceramic, marble finish and Grecian columns; table accessories include urns, vases, hurricanes, votives, cherubs and table lamps.

Table Top: West Coast's unique approach to table top design affords you an unusual selection of ideas. Indoors or out, big or small, with fountains and waterfalls, non-floral theme centerpieces, topiaries, statuary, sculptures, garlands, opulent bouquets and leafy accents, our designers will create a magical focal point for your tables and buffets.

Linens and Skirting: The largest selection of linens in numerous patterns, solid colors and types of material. Various skirting colors and sizes are also available for any type of event or theme.

West Coast Event Productions

We are dedicated in providing you with a service that is unmatched anywhere else. By providing a number of services in one location we are able to handle all your special event needs and requests. It is our personal attention to detail, client devotion and experience in the event rental and production field that has propelled West Coast Event Productions into one of the most celebrated "entertainment" companies in the Northwest.

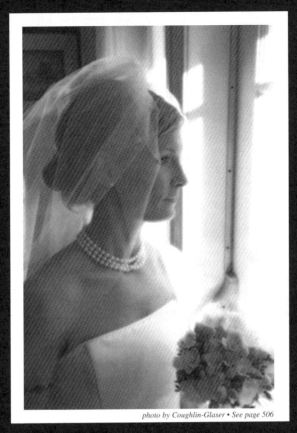

photo by Coughlin-Glaser • See page 506

Bridesmaids Tea

Traditionally, a cake that had a special ring baked

into it was served to all the bridesmaids at a tea. The

bridesmaid who was served the lucky slice was

believed to be the next one to marry.

Bridal Consultants

- **A consultant can help ease the stress:** Remember, this is your big day and hiring a consultant is a wise idea to ease tension between family members, the couple and the bridal party. This is an emotional time and an objective opinion of a consultant can sometimes ease the pressure.

- **A consultant can save money and mistakes:** Brides and grooms sometimes feel a consultant can be an additional expense that they cannot afford. In fact, a consultant can be your best investment, especially if you are on a strict budget. An experienced consultant can help a couple avoid common mistakes. Working with vendors can be costly if the right questions are not asked and a bride and groom, with the help of a consultant, will never feel pressured into booking a service, because the consultant can help find the right vendor for each couple.

- **Services available:** Wedding consultants and event planners can arrange as little or as much of your event or wedding as you want. How they bill for their services varies. Even though you are paying them for their time, in most cases they can save you money in other areas because of their familiarity with different services and discounts that are available to them as frequent customers.

- **Why hire an event planner or consultant?** People are often under the misconception that planning your own event and preparing the food, setup, decorating and cleanup will save money. In fact it can sometimes cost more—not just in money, but in time and headaches as well. A good consultant can work with you and your budget, saving valuable time and money allowing you to enjoy the event.

- **Selecting a consultant:** Talk to several consultants before making your final decision and find out who is familiar with providing the types and level of service you're looking for. Don't be afraid to ask questions or to see portfolios and *ask for references*. The person or company you select should be the one you feel most comfortable with personally and professionally.

- **Finding a banquet, reception, or ceremony site:** Qualified consultants have been to and seen locations that you may never have heard of, but that are perfect for your event. Some consultants have videotapes and photographs of various sites, so you can preview a variety of locations without having to drive all over town. Once you have made your selection, your consultant can make sure your date and time are available, and arrange for you to visit the location.

- **NOTE:** Be specific about the services you want and what your budget is. From this information, a consultant will be able to offer you a variety of suggestions that will work for you and your wedding plans. Be sure to read any and all contracts before signing them so that there is no confusion at a later date about who is responsible for what and how much it will cost.

For more assistance with staying organized during the wedding planning process, check out the Bravo! Wedding Organizer. Detailed question worksheets double as contracts. This step-by-step system will keep every detail of your wedding organized. To order, refer to the order form on page 25 in this Guide.

An Affair To Remember

1121 North Loring Street
Portland, Oregon 97227
503.223.9267 Office
1.888.838.8444
503.223.4746 Facsimile
www.anaffairtoremember.com

About Us

As the Northwest's premiere event planning and design company, we have been participants in some of the areas most creative and compelling wedding events. Whether you prefer an intimate and graceful cocktail party in a private home to and elegant outdoor tented affair with crystal chandeliers and silk chiffon draping; from exquisite cathedral ceremonies to a formal, black-tie hotel ballroom reception, we can make your ideas, your dreams and your vision a reality. We are not merely wedding consultants, but wedding designers! Creating and designing your fantasy wedding is our mission.

Attention To Detail

Attention to detail and impeccable organization is what makes the difference between an ordinary event and a truly extraordinary experience. Let us orchestrate the multitude of details to leave you free to live your dream wedding.

> *"The whole wedding weekend was a glorious success—you did a magnificent job. Everything was just lovely, the couple is married—the families got along—and the mothers are happy!"*
>
> *– Mrs. Ann Gerache*

Fee Schedule

A no cost-no obligation initial consultation is always provided. In the comfort of our new design studio and showroom, we will together pour over our extensive collection of wedding photo portfolios, client references and wedding videotapes, discuss in detail the services we offer and determine your needs. A price will be quoted dependent on the complexity of the event.

Producing a Truly Memorable Event

In this same studio, we later design your wedding day from the rehearsal to the reception send off. Together we create your invitation and announcement package, sample reception menu offerings, conduct cake tastings, listen to local and national musician demo tapes, coordinate floral and fantasy decor, script the ceremony, choose photography ensemble and so on. We are there coordinating every element, every detail to plan and produce a truly remarkable event.

See page 410 under Florists.

Jules Rupae, President

Office: (503) 744-0702, ext. 1
jules@anotherperfectproduction.com
www.anotherperfectproduction.com

YOUR WEDDING DAY
THE ONE DAY IN YOUR LIFE THAT YOU WANT TO BE PERFECT!
Our primary goal is to put the fun back into your wedding day!

Your wedding day should be just as perfect as you've dreamed that it should be; after all it is the biggest day of your life! But is there no price tag too big to take chances on anything less than perfection, and to get the peace of mind when you need it most?

Let your wedding day be an experience you'll never forget, unlike any other...Let the friendly experts at Another Perfect Production take care of all of the intricate details for you; from the inception of your perfect day, all the way through the closing out of the reception site so that you don't have to!

"From Dream up to Clean up," we'll turn your wedding wishes into reality, and at an affordable price that is sure to fit into even the tightest budget.

Services include, but not limited to:
- ❤ Budget Development & Analysis
- ❤ Vendor Research, Specifications & Management
- ❤ Cakes & Catering
- ❤ Site Selection
- ❤ Etiquette
- ❤ Entertainment
- ❤ Theme/Creative Development
- ❤ Travel/Hotel Accomodations
- ❤ Invitations, Programs & Favors
- ❤ Gift Registry
- ❤ Agenda & Timeline Preparation
- ❤ Photography & Videography
- ❤ Specialized Wedding Website
- ❤ Rental Equipment
- ❤ Floral Design & Décor
- ❤ Rehearsal Dinner
- ❤ Bridal Party Attire
- ❤ Transportation Services
- ❤ Beauty Services
- ❤ Pre & Post Wedding Celebrations
- ❤ Guest Activities
- ❤ On-Site Coordination

Call us for a Complimentary 1-Hour Consultation!
Mention that you saw this ad in Bravo! and book a minimum of 15 hours of coordination, and automatically receive a $50 gift certificate to your favorite day spa, in addition to being entered to win a complimentary winery tour of the Oregon Countryside and a gourmet lunch for up to 12 people!

Another You

Simply the BEST~

Celebrating 10 years in Portland~
Experience **DOES** *make the difference.*

Donna Gabrielson
28 Years Experience

503-699-5060
donna@anotheru.com
www.anotheru.com

Excerpts From Client Letters

"When I first started thinking about my wedding, I didn't have the first clue of how to go about it. I was so scared. Thank God I met you!! You truly made my dream come true. Even better than what I imagined."

— Christine and SamJung Choi

"There are not enough words to describe our thanks to you for everything you did to make Melanie and Mike's day all they wanted it to be. And more! It simply wouldn't have happened without you and the countless hours you spent working so that we could play."

— Patti Schmidlin, Mother of the Bride

"We'll always have memories of a lovely, relaxed wedding day."

— Julie and Michael Mace

"My fiancé was skeptical about needing a coordinator but on the day of the wedding he was so thankful to have you. We definitely needed you as we would have gone crazy with all the details. You are extremely professional, calm under pressure, supportive and SO easy to work with. We were able to enjoy OUR day. Not all weddings are like that."

— Leta and Mark Gorman

"I knew I was in the presence of someone who was a capable organizer and who views the whole wedding experience as a positive one. The word 'hassle' isn't in her vocabulary, no matter what the circumstances!"

— Sara Perry, Mother of the Bride

"You were full of beautiful, creative ideas and brought both a sense of calm and confidence to our wedding planning venture."

—Jennifer and Ron Brady

"Your helpful suggestions and simple common sense, coupled with efficiency and organizational skills added up to one fantastic wedding. I couldn't have fine-tuned all the details without your help. Just knowing you were there allowed me to relax and truly enjoy my daughter's special day."

— Lynn Dougherty, Mother of the Bride

© Powers Studios

3970 S.W. Mercantile Drive, Suite #150
Phone: 503.804.4901; Fax: 503.636.1694; www.bridalbliss.com
Contact: Nora Totonchy, Owner

You found the perfect man, now let us help you plan the perfect wedding!

Bridal Bliss is Portland's premiere bridal consultation group and our goal is to put the "fun" back into planning a wedding. We bring a fresh perspective to event design, and work with you and your budget to create innovative events with contemporary style and elegance.

We are unique in that we give our clients our undivided attention. Bridal Bliss will listen to your needs and ideas, offer creative suggestions, and bring your wedding dreams to life. We create events suited to a couple's unique style — a true expression of the bride and groom's relationship and individuality. Very little stress and extremely amazing results are what you should count on from Bridal Bliss.

"Thank you so much for all of your help with Elizabeth and Casey's wedding! It was so nice to not have to worry about a thing. You were wonderful and I will refer as many people as possible."
 – Mrs. Beth Corey, Mother of the Bride

"You were great to work with, very mild-mannered and pleasant! You were on top of everything and made everything run so smoothly. Much thanks and appreciation!"
 – Mrs. Ginean McInthosh, Bride

Vendor Relationships
Through our experience in the industry, we have established extensive professional vendor relationships that enable us to produce a top rate event in every aspect. By continually working with these contacts, special rates are passed on to you, the client.

Customized Services and Fees
Bridal Bliss offers a variety of services to best meet your needs. We can assist you as much, or as little, as you wish. Our services include but are certainly not limited to:

Budget Development & Analysis	Site Selection	Agenda & Timeline Preparation
Vendor Research and Specifications	Cakes & Catering	Photography & Videography
Contract Negotiations	Rental Equipment	Floor Plan Preparations
Floral and Design Décor	Etiquette	Entertainment
Theme/Creative Development	Rehearsal Direction	Invitations, Programs, & Favors
Bridal Party Attire/Accessories	Transportation	Travel, Hotel Accommodations

Planning a wedding should be a blissful time in your life, not one full of anxiety and exhaustion. Whether you are planning the wedding yourself, looking for a little guidance, or are in need of someone to take charge of the entire event so that you can relax and enjoy a worry-free day, Bridal Bliss is here to assist you.

Contact Bridal Bliss today to schedule your complimentary consultation and prepare to have all of your wedding day expectations surpassed.

CLASS ACT
EVENT COORDINATORS, INC.

Ring: **Portland** 503.295.7890
 Salem 503.371.8904
 Corvallis 541.766.2961

Fax: 503.589.9166 • **E-mail:** weddings@classactevents.net • **Web site:** www.classactevents.net

Because planning your wedding should be as enjoyable and memorable as the wedding day itself...

Because you will remember this day for the rest of your life...

You need Class Act...

Specialists in Wedding Planning

Founded in 1987, Class Act, Event Coordinators' many years of wedding consulting and coordinating experience give us the skills necessary to attend thoroughly to all wedding planning details. We have coordinated weddings for as few as 50 guests and as many as 650. Our innovative style, calm approach and professional attention to detail combine to give you the highest quality of wedding planning and coordination services including, but not limited to:

-Budget preparation
-Assistance with site selection
-Vendor research & specifications
-Personalized time line
-Preparation of floor plans & agendas

-Rehearsal direction
-Complete set-up & decorating
-Coordination of wedding & reception
-Complete teardown
-Many other services available

The coordinators at Class Act are committed to personalized service. Your event should match your style, your vision, and your budget. We will spend time listening to you describe your preferences, your goals and your expectations regarding your wedding. After an initial consultation, we will submit a service proposal to you based on your needs and expectations.

"Thank you for all the time you spent making our day truly fabulous. We had so much fun with all our family and friends and it was nice not having to worry about anything that day and just enjoy it all. It would have been a nightmare without you. We appreciate your tact and professionalism in dealing with hassles. We will miss the check-ins and meetings as you became part of our lives. We appreciated your advice for decisions but also allowing us to make it 'our day'. We can't recommend you enough. Looking back at pictures and sharing memories, we have nothing but positive things to remember thanks to you."

—Sandi and Michael Cox, Portland, Oregon

Additional Services

Class Act offers unique tabletop décor and other decorative elements available for rent to enhance your wedding.

We would love to help you create a most memorable event while relieving you of the responsibility of the details. Please contact us for your complimentary consultation.

Please be sure to visit us at our fabulous new showroom located at 910 Commercial Street S.E. in Salem to view the latest in wedding trends and distinctive rentals.

Do Me A Favor

favors · wedding consulting · stationery

7400 SW Florence Lane
Portland, Oregon 97223
503.970.9876
By Appointment Only
www.favorflare.com   info@favorflare.com

Wedding Consulting by Do Me A Favor

Every bride dreams and desires an exquisite wedding. She wants every detail perfected. Every bride wants a wedding that she, her groom, and her family and friends will remember and cherish forever. Do Me A Favor can help you reach these aspirations. We specialize in planning unforgettable, unique, and stylish weddings in any budget range. We want you to enjoy the entire wedding experience and not worry about anything! We plan each wedding as if it were our own. Because of this, each client receives personalized, one-on-one attention and planning, in-depth research and negotiations with vendors, and unlimited meetings with our packages. We love weddings! We love meeting new brides and creating a spectacular event together. Some of our consulting services include:

- All-Inclusive Package—for everything from your bridal shower, rehearsal dinner, wedding day, and wedding brunch.

- Wedding Day Package—complete planning and coverage of your special day.

- Individual Services—let us help you plan and coordinate individual services for your wedding and related wedding events.

- Wedding Day Coordination—oversight and supervision on your wedding day (this service is included with our two packages above).

- Individual Consulting—on an hourly basis, you can browse our books and resources and meet to discuss ideas for your wedding.

Please visit the Do Me A Favor website for more extensive information: **www.favorflare.com**. Please email or call to receive more extensive information and to schedule an appointment. In the Portland area, you can visit our office not only for your wedding consultation, but to see our line of **customized favors and exquisite stationery** as well. I look forward to working with you! Happy wedding!

ejp events

Wedding Consulting · Event Planning

Conveniently located at The Bridal Loft
2808 NE MLK Boulevard, Suite 3, First Floor • 97212
(503) 284-6756 • info@ejpevents.com
www.ejpevents.com • www.thebridalloft.net

©*David Barss 2002*

Q: Aren't wedding consultants really expensive?
A: It is a common misconception that only the very wealthy use wedding consultants. The fact is, we have helped many couples of all budgets create quality weddings that reflect their tastes and personalities.

A good consultant will work within your budget to gather all of the vendors who will meet your needs — so you don't overspend, yet still get quality service providers, plus the organizational assistance and peace of mind that a consultant provides.

Q: I don't want a full-on wedding consultant. I just need advice on a few things.
A: One-time or occasional consulting is what you're looking for, where you meet with a consultant for a fixed number of meetings to accomplish specific tasks. The consultant does not go to the wedding. Some examples are: a bride had her consultant produce and assemble the wedding favors and programs...or, a couple had their consultant research pricing and availability on all downtown reception sites that could accommodate 350 guests.
Most local one-time or occasional consulting projects carry a flat fee in the $50—$500 range.

Q: I will be doing (or have already done) all the planning. Do I need a consultant?
A: Congratulations on doing all that work! But don't work on your wedding day! Day-of or "wrap up" wedding consulting is appropriate for you, where you go over outstanding planning concerns and tie up your loose ends. We reconfirm with all of your vendors, create an event itinerary, then carefully oversee the details on site.

"Where do you want me to put these linens? Is this the table for the cake/guest book/favors? Where should the band set up?" — these questions and more are invariably asked on the day of the wedding. A wedding coordinator will have your event plan in hand and handle these details for you, giving you and your family more time to enjoy the day.
Most local day-of wedding coordination projects carry a flat fee in the $500—$1,500 range.

Q: I have limited time and resources and need help with many aspects of the wedding.
A: Relax. You're looking for a full-service wedding consultant. We help you set a budget and create a theme, brainstorm unique ideas with you, then research and book the vendors who make it happen. You're reminded of important planning and payment deadlines. From time to time, you'll meet with us and take care of planning and etiquette concerns.

As the wedding approaches, we reconfirm your arrangements, troubleshoot logistics and crystallize your vision into a final plan. At the rehearsal and on the wedding day, we ensure that your instructions are followed. Finally, we supervise the cleanup and closing of the site. We even return your tuxedos! All you do is enjoy.
Most local full-service wedding consulting projects carry a flat fee in the $1,500—$3,000 range.

Please call EJP Events today to find out how easy it can be to get the wedding you really want.
The initial consultation to create your customized proposal is free of charge.

event design & flowers

©Ray Bidegain Photography

©Mount Burns Photography

Incorporating personal meaning into public functions

Jen Elle's owners, Ellen Hiltebrand and Jennifer Greenberg, came together with the vision of producing elegant events instilled with a sense of intimacy. With signature attention to each detail, they attend to every aesthetic element of your wedding, translating your dreams into a cohesive design. Whether helping you focus as you initially begin planning, or transforming challenging spaces, they are an invaluable resource. Along with complete design and implementation services, Jen Elle offers:

- One-time or ongoing consulting services
- Floral design
- Custom rental items
- Access to stylish decor and creative favors
- Inspired pre/post wedding celebrations
- Personal stationary and invitations

New Service Offered: We are pleased to announce the opening of a coordination department to handle any of your practical planning needs. Now with one phone call, Jen Elle can see you through not only the design and implementation, but also each and every logistical detail associated with your wedding day.

Please view our portfolio on our website or contact us for more information.
We look forward to working with you!

www.jen-elle.com   503.789.6978

portland wedding planner

Marilyn Storch
(503) 520-9667
E-mail: mstorch@teleport.com
Web site: portlandweddingplanner.com

You're engaged! Now what do you do?

You and your fiancé should look forward to the big day with the least amount of stress possible. After all, this "business" of planning a wedding is quite an undertaking! It involves your closest friends, your loving families, months of planning, legal documents, decisions and deadlines, the hiring of many professionals, emotional overload...and YOU...the star!

A wedding is a complex event to orchestrate. Even the most efficient bride and groom can be overwhelmed by the endless details involved in pulling together a successful wedding. And, anyone who has ever attended a memorable wedding and reception knows that the difference is in the details. You can be assured that with Marilyn, every detail will be attended to so you can relax and blissfully enjoy your wedding day. Allow yourself the luxury of experiencing your extraordinary day the way you should—the way you've always dreamed it to be.

Sometimes the well meant help from family and friends can end up causing stress or hard feelings as the planning process takes on a life of its own. A wedding planner's unbiased point of view can be of great help during this time. As your consultant and/or coordinator, Marilyn works toward helping you plan your event smoothly so it will come together "effortlessly" on the day you exchange your vows.

In times gone by, the hiring of a wedding consultant was a luxury afforded by a select few. Today, you don't have to be a society matron with a debutante daughter to have need and access to such professional help. Today, with our lives so filled with schedules, and our time and energy sapped, it just makes good sense.

Marilyn has excellent working relationships with a vast variety of vendors and suppliers in the wedding business. Although it may seem like an indulgence at first, the professional advice, access and expertise that a consultant offers can actually help save money in the end.

With her very specialized knowledge and experience, her goal is to help you plan an affair that is true to your personality and is original in spirit. With her calm nature and professional demeanor, Marilyn will lift the load off of your shoulders and into her hands. Her behind-the-scenes guidance and attention to detail will put that extra special polish on your wedding day and allow YOU...the star!...to shine.

careful • professional • calm

"I relaxed the day we met" ...   – Gail Y.

"I feel like you are my own personal wedding consultant and you have no other weddings you're working on. You're always there when I need you. I love that you are so excited about my wedding. I'm having so much fun!" ...   – Francesca S.

"What would my mom and I have done without you?!" ...   – Erin S.

"I've so appreciated all your hard work, persistent follow-through, attention to every detail. Most of all, I will remember your listening ear and caring attitude. Thank you for making this wedding a memorable occasion for us all." ...   – Mary R.

Serendipity

Heather Houck
503.635.8868 • 503.407.4993 • Fax 503.210.0231
16902 Lower Meadows Drive • Lake Oswego, Oregon 97035
www.serendipity-events.com • heather@serendipity-events.com

Dear Future Bride and Groom,

Your wedding is a very special day, one that should be smooth, stress-free, fun, reflects your personal style, and provides a lifetime of beautiful memories.

Whether you want it to be small and intimate, or grand and elegant, let Serendipity help. Serendipity will provide the organization, creativity and style to bring the day off perfectly. We begin by taking the time to learn what you want, from the engagement party to your honeymoon send-off. Then we plan every detail with the care and attention your special day deserves. We find and work with the best and most professional wedding resources available.

Our goal is to make this, the most special of days, yours and yours alone, one that fulfills your dreams and exceeds your every expectation.

SERVICES OFFERED:

- Weddings
  - ~ Budget planning, vendor negotiations, progress reports and contract review
  - ~ Timetables and agenda for the bride and groom, family, and wedding party
  - ~ Event planning, bridal shower, bachelorette/bachelor party planning, and food and beverage for day of wedding preparation
  - ~ Lodging and travel arrangements for out of town guests at Oregon's premiere locations
- Resource research and booking such as…
  - ~ Facility coordination for your function
  - ~ Resource recommendations and booking including and not limited to photographers, florists, clergy, DJs, bands, caterers, transportation, unique handmade invitations, calligraphers, and cake artistry
  - ~ Creative Services, ideas that will add special details to your event or for your guests, from in-room massage, manicure and pedicure to personalized gift baskets, tours, extraordinary wedding favors to fit the bride and groom's personalities, and many others
  - ~ Coordination of all details and communication for rehearsal and day of the wedding between wedding party and vendors

How do you put us to work for you? Just call — we offer a free consultation to learn what you have in mind for your special day.

Our goal is to make your wedding day uniquely yours in every way and making your wedding day dreams come true.

Serendipity's services are also available for special event and corporate event planning

soirée
special event planning

By appointment only
2236 S.E. Belmont, Portland, Oregon

Mailing address
P.O. Box 5982, Portland, Oregon 97228

503.230.9311
503.230.9312 fax

www.bonsoiree.com

**With over 10 years experience in the Portland area,
Soirée has many contacts and resources to draw from to make your
Wedding Day perfect and stress-free.**

**Let us help make your special day one to remember by handling all the details
so you and your family don't have to worry about a thing. We work closely with our
clients and take their thoughts and vision to help create the wedding of their dreams.**

**We focus on coordinating weddings with style and quality. Effectively managing all
aspects is essential for making sure your wedding is amazing and flawless.
Whether you are planning a small intimate gathering or a grand celebration,
we give you our full attention so you feel like you are our only client.**

**We offer a complimentary consultation to access the needs of our future clients. We ask
precise questions to determine the goals and expectations of the client and their
wedding. A custom proposal is prepared based on the planning assistance needed.**

- View our wedding showcase and read letters from past clients at www.bonsoiree.com
- Visit Soirée's additional page under Bridal Concepts and Theme Design.
- Please give us a call if you have any questions or would like to set up your complimentary consultation.

ÜNÌ Ø ÜE

Contact: Meghan M Morgan—Owner
Office 503.286.2153 • Cell 503.975.3600
Email: mmmuniqueevents@comcast.net • Web site: www.be-u.biz

From an intimate affair to an outrageous celebration
UNIQUE will make your wildest dreams come true...

We'll start by talking about you...who you are, what you love and how you imagine your Wedding Day. Your personal taste and style will be reflected in each decision we make along the way.

Once you've decided on a Wedding date, that day will be exclusively yours. You will have the undivided attention you need to make each moment, from your breathless walk down the aisle to your fabulous farewell, effortless. Every detail will be accounted for; all you have to do is glow.

UNIQUE will handle every aspect of the planning process

- Budget Planning & Management
- Design Conception
- Vendor Recommendation
- Site Selection

- Pre & Post Wedding Parties
- Guest Accommodations
- Rehearsal
- Complete Wedding Day Coordination

UNIQUE is also available for one-time or occasional consulting as well as Wedding Day Only coordination.

Please contact UNIQUE for a complimentary consultation & custom proposal.

Be UNIQUE...Be U.

photo by Patrick Prothe • See page 533

Wedding Showers

The custom of giving wedding showers

began in Holland, when friends or even entire

communities gathered together to "stake" a young

bride of modest means for all her household goods.

The lack of dowry was considered to be

an impediment to marriage.

www.bravoportland.com

Bridal Registry

- **Unique shops for registry:** There are many wonderful stores where you can register. The china, glassware, flatware, and special accessories you select will be with you the rest of your lives. Look at the registry stores in this book and remember, you can register at more than one.

- **Why you should register:** By registering, you let your family and friends know the gifts you would most like to have, and will ensure that what you receive will suit both your tastes and styles. Even if you and your fiancé can't imagine using fine china, stemware, and flatware in the near future, you'll appreciate them in years to come. It is very expensive to invest in formal china down the road. Family and guests enjoy giving gifts knowing they will be treasured and eventually passed on to future generations.

- **Mixing and matching:** Many shops allow you to mix and match your patterns to design your own dishware theme. Ask about ideas they may have. Most important, have fun selecting items that you and your fiancé will enjoy using.

- **When to register:** Soon after you become engaged is the best time to register. If your friends want to send engagement gifts, you can tell them where you are registered. Or for showers, your guests can select from a variety of items that you have on your "wish list."

- **Check with your registry:** It is a good idea to check your registry list periodically and keep it up to date with items you have received. Some gift givers will be making purchases in your behalf from other stores or will forget to let the store you are registered at know whom they are buying the gift for. It's nice for your guests to know what items you have or haven't received so they may plan their purchases accordingly.

- **Damaged items:** No business can be responsible for gifts that get broken after they leave their store. If gifts are damaged or broken, it usually happens in shipping. Packages that are carefully packed will reach you intact. However, if you find breakage upon unpacking, please call your delivery carrier (Postal Service or U.P.S.) for an inspection and claim. **NOTE:** Most shippers require that all packing, boxes, and wrappings be retained for inspection, so be sure to keep everything!

- **Thank-you notes:** It is important and proper etiquette to send thank-you notes immediately after receiving a gift. This way you let the gift giver know that the gift was received. Keep up with the many thank-you notes you will need to write, rather than waiting until after the honeymoon.

For more assistance with staying organized during the wedding planning process, check out the Bravo! Wedding Organizer. Detailed question worksheets double as contracts. This step-by-step system will keep every detail of your wedding organized. To order, refer to the order form on page 25 in this Guide.

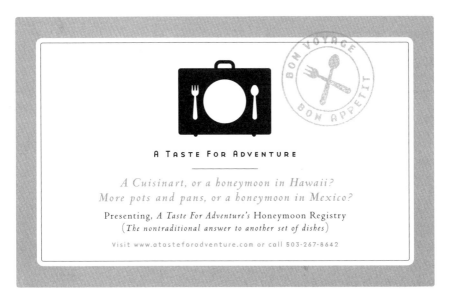

Why is a honeymoon registry such a great idea? The traditional wedding gifts are something you might not need. You love to travel and gather experiences rather than more things for the house. With A Taste For Adventure's honeymoon specialist, Lisa Hetzler, you will be able to create the perfect registry full of exciting items for your guests to purchase like wine tastings in Tuscany, elephant trekking in Thailand, or picnicking in Provence (just to name a few). Each registry is custom made for you and the possibilities are endless.

How do we get the word out about our registry? Your registry will be posted on the A Taste For Adventure website. Your guests will be able to click on the items they would like to purchase. A return receipt of the purchase will be given to them and a gift certificate will be given to you.

Of course we realize that not everyone wants to use a computer, so Lisa will be just a phone call away, local and toll-free. You will also be provided with A Taste For Adventure postcards to let your friends and family know about your registry if you wish.

*To learn more, please visit our website at **www.atasteforadventure.com**, or give Lisa Hetzler a call at **503-267-8642**.*

A Taste for Adventure is proudly affiliated with Focus On Travel, the honeymoon specialists (www.focusontravel.com or 503-646-3700).

(800) 366-0161

www.kitchenkaboodle.com

DOWNTOWN
SW 6th & Alder, second floor (503) 464-9545

BROADWAY
NE 16th & Broadway (503) 288-1500

CLACKAMAS TOWN CENTER
Upper Level (503) 652-2567

NORTHWEST
NW 23rd & Flanders (503) 241-4040

PROGRESS SQUARE
SW Hall Blvd. & Scholls Ferry Rd. (503) 643-5491

ORENCO STATION, HILLSBORO
Cornell Rd. at N.E. 61st (503) 846-1515

EVERY WEDDING IS SPECIAL. SHOULDN'T YOUR GIFTS BE, TOO?

Kitchen Kaboodle's Bridal Registry — like each of our convenient Portland area stores — is brimming with a dazzling array of the kinds of things that give your house its special character. The kinds of things that make your house a home.

We carry just about everything you'll need as you begin your lives together. From high-quality cookware to decorative accessories, gorgeous dinnerware to finely-crafted furniture, Kitchen Kaboodle carries a wide variety of:

- Dinnerware
- Barware
- Stemware
- Cookware
- Bakeware
- Kitchen Appliances
- Gadgets & Utensils
- Cutlery
- Cook Books
- Table & Kitchen Linens
- Candles & Candlesticks
- Decorative Accessories
- Lamps & Rugs
- Furniture
- Much, much more

UNIQUELY YOU

Looking for something out of the ordinary? Kitchen Kaboodle's the place. We're the exclusive Oregon retailer for many exciting items, and our buyers always work hard to uncover the kinds of unique items you won't find at the chain stores.

WE'VE DONE THE WORK SO YOU DON'T HAVE TO.

We know this is a busy time for you, so we burned the midnight oil to make sure our Bridal Registry is convenient and easy to use. Each store updates your registry daily with items purchased at other locations, so your registry is always current. We'll even keep your registry list on file for one year following your wedding date.

WE'RE AT YOUR DISPOSAL

We're ready and willing to help. In addition to the registries available in each of our stores, our Bridal Consultant is available for free consultation. Call (503) 243-5043 ext. 208 in Portland or toll free (800) 366-0161 ext. 208. We'll be happy to sit down, discuss your wants and needs, and recommend the products that will best meet those needs.

(503) 243-5043 ext. 208 or (800) 366-0161 ext. 208

MEIER & FRANK

Downtown	*Washington Square*
(503) 241-5158	*(503) 620-3311, ext. 2086*
Lloyd Center	*Clackamas Town Center*
(503) 281-4797, ext. 2086	*(503) 653-8811, ext. 2086*
Vancouver	*Salem*
(360) 256-4411, ext. 2086	*(503) 363-2211, ext. 2086*
Eugene	*Rogue Valley*
(541) 342-6611, ext. 2086	*(541) 772-3700, ext. 2086*

WEDDING NETWORK
MeierAndFrankWeddings.com
1-800-445-9959

VISIT US AT ONE OF OUR 14 STORES (in Oregon, Washington and Utah.)

WELCOME TO THE WEDDING REGISTRY NATIONAL NETWORK

REGISTER AT OVER 350 PREMIER DEPARTMENT STORES BY VISITING ONE.

Easy on Planning
Visit our web address **MeierAndFrankWeddings.com** for all the free tips and tools you'll
need to plan your wedding. You'll find a Budgeter, Task Scheduler, Guest List Manager and
more.

Guest Convenience
Your guests can purchase and send gifts from any of our department stores, by phone at
1-800-445-9959 or on-line at **MeierAndFrankWeddings.com.**

Schedule Your Registry
Use the Make an Appointment feature on-line to set up a meeting with one of our bridal
consultants that fits your busy schedule.

Completion Program
After your wedding, enjoy a 15% discount on most items you purchase to complete your
registry. This should ensure that you have the things you need and want for the home you'll
share together.

Free Gift Wrap
For their convenience, we will provide complimentary gift wrap when your guests make a
single registry purchase of $50 or more.

Tabletop Club Plan
This interest-free charge account makes purchases more affordable through convenient
monthly payments.

One Year Registry File
Your registry list remains on-line for 13 months after your wedding date. This serves as a
helpful reference for additional gift-giving occasions, like birthdays, holidays and your first
anniversary.

David's Bridal Rewards Card
Bring your David's Rewards card into one of our stores after purchasing your wedding gown.
Create a wedding registry with 15 items or more and we will send you a $25 gift card to use at
any of our 350 premier department stores nationwide,

Notes

Do Me A Favor

favors · wedding consulting · stationery

7400 SW Florence Lane
Portland, Oregon 97223
503.970.9876
By Appointment Only
www.favorflare.com   info@favorflare.com

Favors and Other Wedding Specialties

Do Me A Favor specializes in stylish, trendy and affordable bridal shower and wedding favors. We also create custom wedding gift baskets, programs and menu cards. We can also customize any favor idea that you have and create your own special, unique wedding or bridal shower favor.

Some of our wedding favors include: customized compact discs holders, scented sachets, potted plants, elegant candles, Chinese take-out boxes, decorative boxes and much more.

Do Me A Favor also carries other wedding essentials, such as unique bridesmaids gifts, individual gift cards, gift tags and rose petals. Our line of stationery includes printable invitations, thank you notes and place cards. We strive to carry products that are elegant, unique and hard to find elsewhere.

Please visit the Do Me A Favor website for more extensive information: **www.favorflare.com.** Please email or call to receive more extensive information and to schedule an appointment. In the Portland area, you can visit our office not only for your wedding favors, gifts and stationery, but to schedule your personalized **wedding consulting appointment** as well. I look forward to working with you! Happy wedding!

Lucy Palmer Boutique

460 Fifth Street • Lake Oswego, Oregon 97034
503-635-6856 • Fax 503-223-2464
E-mail: Lucyp@teleport.com

Bridal Registry, Jewelry, Gift Packages, Invitations, Favors

Make Lucy Palmer Boutique one of your first stops when planning your big day!

We invite you to set up a complimentary consultation to discuss how Lucy Palmer can help create an event to remember.

Don't forget to visit Lucy Palmer Boutique for all of your home accessories, gifts, jewelry and spa products.

Don't walk down the aisle without us!

Notes

©Polly's Cakes • See page 270

Wedding Cakes

Wedding cakes can be traced back to ancient Rome.

A simple wheat cake or biscuit was

broken during the ceremony, with the

bride and groom taking the first bites.

The remainder was then crumbled over the bride's

head to ensure a bountiful life with lots of children.

www.bravoportland.com

Cakes & Desserts

- **The wedding cake:** You'll find many flavors and styles of cakes to choose from. Visit several shops and compare quality, style and prices. Also, sample different flavors of cakes to help in selecting the flavor you want. The baker is a specialist, so ask for advice and recommendations. Remember, each tier can be a different flavor. Make sure the portfolio and samples you are viewing are work done by the current baker on staff.

- **Order your wedding cake early:** Busy wedding months are June through September; you will need to order your cake four to six months in advance if you're getting married in the summer. At ordering time, you need only an approximate number of guests. Confirm the number two to three weeks before your wedding.

- **Figuring the amount:** The baker will be helpful in advising you on the amount of cake needed based on the number of guests. The price is usually based on a per-slice amount. Be sure to ask about tier sizes and serving portions—are they pieces or slivers of cake?

- **Cake knife, server and instructions:** Don't forget to bring a knife and server to cut the wedding cake or have the caterer supply them. Make sure your baker provides the service staff with instructions for cutting and serving your wedding cake. Because of their size and elegance, wedding cakes can be tricky to serve. Appoint someone to be in charge of cutting and serving and supply that person with the instructions, or ask your caterer if their servers can be available for this task.

- **Wedding cake tops & decorations:** Most bakeries and bridal accessory stores have a large selection of cake tops: hand-blown glass, figurines, or ornaments that are permanent keepsakes. Fresh-flower arrangements are another option and can be coordinated with your baker and florist. If you have chosen colored decorations, bring some color swatches or samples when ordering.

- **Edible place cards:** Place cards made from the finest chocolates or cookies are a personalized touch for a formal wedding dinner.

- **Serve the wedding cake:** If you have waiters at your event, it is recommended to serve the cake to each guest rather than just placing cake on a table. This way guests won't take an extra piece or expect seconds.

For more assistance with staying organized during the wedding planning process, check out the Bravo! Wedding Organizer. Detailed question worksheets double as contracts. This step-by-step system will keep every detail of your wedding organized. To order, refer to the order form on page 25 in this Guide.

EXQUISITE WEDDING CAKES AND DESSERTS

Featured in The Oregonian and Grace Ormonde Wedding Style Magazine

Jane Burkholder created her business, I Dolci, according to her philosophy that a wedding cake should not only look beautiful, but should be, as well, an outstanding dessert. To this end, all of her cakes, fillings and preserves are made by hand using only the highest quality local, domestic, and imported ingredients. The result is a selection of cake flavors both traditional and innovative; always refined and sophisticated. This attention to detail extends to meticulously crafted decorations of marzipan, chocolate, and sugarpaste, or fresh floral arrangement.

A one-woman business, she has 22 years experience in pastry which includes work and study in San Fransisco and Switzerland. She draws inspiration from her skills as a calligrapher, her love of the natural world, and the textile arts. All find expression in painstaking techniques that contribute to the completion of a stunning centerpiece.

Consultations and tastings are by appointment only.

"We first began working with Jane in the spring of 1996. We had heard of her fine reputation and wanted to meet with her about a wedding cake for our daughter, Sally. When we met, she had a fabulous portfolio, resumé, and delicious cake samples. She created a beautiful cake for over 300 people and everyone was awed.

When Laurie was married in October 2001, there was no doubt that we would ask Jane to make the cake. Laurie had fallen in love with an idea incorporating ribbons of white chocolate with calligraphed words. Jane embraced the idea and created a masterpiece: five ribbons with brushed Italic calligraphy, one for each tier.

We have enjoyed working with Jane as much as we admire her artistry. She is a very lovely and gracious woman."

Anne Munro
Portland, Oregon

BAKERY &
CHOCOLATIER

4733 S.E. Hawthorne
Portland, Oregon 97215
www.jacivas.com
(503) 234-8115
Mon–Sat 7:30am–6pm

Featured on national Food Network's "Food Finds"
United States Pastry Alliance gold medal winner
Winner of the Austin Family Business Award
Recipient of Master Chocolatier Award

Types and Styles of Wedding Cakes

If you're looking for a beautiful wedding cake, exquisite looking and luscious inside...A place where you can taste a variety of flavors and then select a different flavor for each tier...A place where you can get handmade mints to match your wedding colors...A place where you can get a special first-anniversary cake, just for the two of you, free...Then JaCiva's is your answer.

You can select a rich chocolate groom's cake or an assortment of Victorian tea pastries or chocolate truffles to make your rehearsal dinner or special-occasion event truly unique.

Cost, Ordering, and Delivery

Cost varies depending on the flavor, size, and style of cake. A deposit is required upon placing the order, with the balance due two weeks before the wedding. Early ordering is suggested, especially for summer dates. JaCiva's delivers and sets up your cake free of charge in the local area. There is an additional fee for Sunday, private home and outside the metro area deliveries.

Wedding Favors and Other Gifts

JaCiva's offers a wonderful selection of wedding favors, including customized boxes with European truffles or a selection of our handmade mints, almonds, etc.

Wedding Accessories

Featuring the Beverly Clarke and Lillian Rose collection and others including; photo albums, ring pillows, pens, toasting glasses, cake and knife server, garters, etc.

"Weddings in Good Taste"

CALL FOR A CONSULTATION WITH
JACIVA'S WEDDING COORDINATOR
"THE PERFECT PLACE TO FIND
YOUR PERFECT WEDDING CAKE"

♥ *Member of Weddings of Distinction*

DESSERT
COMPANY

Portland, Oregon 97202
(503) 231-0989
E-mail: joedessert@qwest.net
www.josephsdessertco.com
Business Hours: Tues–Sat 9am–5pm
By Appointment Only

THE SCENT AND TASTE of a great cake invoke a memory, and suddenly I'm there in the warm kitchen with my grandmother. With her, I learned to bake the best way—using the finest ingredients, love and prayer. My fondest memories of childhood are in that big kitchen of hers, where we worked, ate and laughed together.

The spirit of that place and time is in our cakes today—the spirit of true quality, ingenuity, family, and love. At Joseph's, we use only the very finest ingredients: imported chocolate, Oregon unsalted butter, heavy whipping cream and the best liqueurs and natural flavors. We create cakes using old-world techniques, adding contemporary flavor combinations and design. Our work looks beautiful and tastes even better.

I've always believed that good food glows. Now I know why—it's the same reason that Grandma's kitchen was so special. Even the very best ingredients and the most beautiful designs are only the beginning—the rest is the love that goes into making it and sharing it.

Ordering, Delivery and Cost

To start the ordering process for your cake, please call us for an appointment. When we meet, we recommend that you bring any photos or color swatches you may have. We require a $50 nonrefundable deposit to hold your reception date. Two weeks prior to delivery we need the final details about numbers to be served, type of cake, delivery time and destination. We charge according to the size and complexity of the cake, and ask that you pay in full a week before delivery.

In Addition

We also make petit fours, individual desserts, celebration cakes, and sheet cakes for showers, rehearsals and other celebrations. We can coordinate any of these with your wedding cake or decorations.

You will receive a complimentary cake for your first wedding anniversary.

Patrice Chéri Wedding Cakes

503.263.8500 • www.patricecheriweddingcakes.com
E-mail: patty@patricecheriweddingcakes.com
Fax: 503.266.3560
Office: Canby, Oregon 97013
Tasting Room: Tigard, Oregon 97223
(Please call for an appointment)

Types and Styles of Wedding Cakes

Snow-white roses with frilly, hand-molded petals. Leaves painted yellow and green with a tiny paintbrush. Delicate icing webs of filigree lace. A wisp of narrow satin ribbon. Buttercream frosting made with real butter. These are the details that make a wedding cake so beautiful you can scarcely bear to cut into it. Until you taste it—then you can't bear not to. These are also the details Chef Patty Balsiger of Patrice Chéri lavishes on each wedding cake she creates. We have 17 cake flavors, 14 filling flavors and 11 icing flavors to choose from. All our cakes are made from scratch using the finest ingredients available.

Experience

Chef Patty Balsiger of Patrice Chéri bring 25 years of experience creating wedding cakes to you, assuring your wedding cake will be a truly memorable one. Chef Patty will work with you, bringing ideas to the table so you can make the choices that will make your wedding cake perfect for your very special day!

Cost, Ordering and Delivery

Patrice Chéri's cakes fall into a range of prices. A buttercream-frosted cake averages $3.50 per slice, including delivery and set up. Labor-intense fondant cakes cost about $5 per slice, plus a refundable deposit for pillars and fountains. Those also embellished with fondant flowers are $7 per slice. We suggest those on a limited budget order a small but gorgeous tier cake along with sheet cakes. A $100 nonrefundable deposit is required at time of order, with full payment due two weeks prior to the wedding. We deliver and set up your cake free of charge in the local areas.

Gift to Bride and Groom

The top tier of every wedding cake is Patrice Chéri's gift to the couple along with a special keepsake…Keepcake Box to keep alive the tradition of freezing the top tier of the wedding cake for their first anniversary.

Cake Tasting

Patrice Chéri recommends that you call for an appointment to sample the different flavors of cakes we offer. Our cake brochure is available through our Web site or by calling the office. We also have a portfolio of our work you may review at our tasting room as well as our Web site.

YUM! YUM! YUM! YUM!

PIECE OF CAKE

Established in 1979
Winner of Chocolate Safari 1991
8306 S.E. 17th • Portland, Oregon
Contact: Marilyn DeVault, food designer (503) 234-9445
Business Hours: New hours, please call
www.pieceofcakebakery.net

YUM! YUM! YUM! YUM!

AWARD WINNING! AWARD WINNING!

VOTED BEST CAKE IN PORTLAND! —*Willamette Week 2003*

We provide elegant, classical wedding cakes and fun, unique designs that are custom tailored to your wedding dreams. Ask about our lovely wedding invitations!

Gourmet Cakes from Piece of Cake

♥ **CHEESECAKE WEDDING CAKE:** decadent and beautiful. YUM! Choose from vanilla, chocolate marble, deep chocolate, Kahlua, white chocolate and more!

♥ **AWARD-WINNING FANTASY CAKE:** voted favorite of the year. Each tier consists of cheesecake, choice of filling, and cake. What a surprise. YUM!

♥ **CARROT:** a wonderfully moist, spicy carrot cake made with pineapple. YUM!

♥ **IRISH OATMEAL:** a moist oatmeal spice cake with a real homemade texture. YUM!

♥ **DOUBLE CHOCOLATE FUDGE:** the chocolate lover's choice… made with coffee and buttermilk, this cake is almost black with chocolate. YUM!

♥ **POPPYSEED:** made with sour cream and filled with marionberries. YUM!

♥ **CREAM CHEESE POUND CAKE:** a dense cake, rich with cream cheese frosting.

♥ **APPLE RUM:** packed with apples, raisins, and walnuts. YUM!

♥ **BANANA PINEAPPLE:** moist banana cake complemented with a hint of rum. YUM!

♥ **LEMON COCONUT:** a marriage of fresh squeezed lemon and coconut. YUM!

♥ **FILLINGS** range from chocolate orange brandy, Baileys, caramel, espresso and more! YUM!

TASTE!   YUM! Call (503) 234-9445 YUM!   TASTE!

LOOKING FOR SOMETHING TO ADD TO YOUR PRE-WEDDING FESTIVITIES? ORDER ONE OF OUR BACHELORETTE OR BACHELOR PARTY CAKES.

VEGAN CATERING ♥ FABULOUS HORS D'OEUVRES ♥ FULL-SERVICE CATERING

CAKE CHOICES INCLUDE: VEGAN ♥ VEGAN-WHEAT FREE GLUTEN FREE ♥ SUGAR FREE ♥ SOY FREE

Ask about our 20% discount on wedding invitations.

Marilyn and her staff are food designers, and the cakes are always a work of art.

POLLY'S CAKES

Portland (503) 230-1986; Hood River (541) 386-1221
Polly's Cakes #269
25 N.W. 23rd Avenue, Suite 6
Portland, Oregon, 97210 (mailing address only)
www.pollyscakes.com
Contact us for more information or to set up an appointment.

Couture Cakes

The magic food of cake harkens back to our childhood–part fantasy, part comfort, part taste. It can be like finding the perfect tea cup or little black dress. Certainly ceramics, china, textiles, jewelry and couture fashion inspire our cake designs. With attention to visual elements such as line, texture, color, and shape, we create stylish, award-winning cakes. These cakes range from unclutterd and classic to the avant garde and our original off kilter Whimsy Cakes.

Buttercreams, marzipan and fondant are the tools of our trade. Beneath these are the moist dessert-like interiors of our cakes with layers of tender crumbed cake and smooth mousse fillings. Each cake is designed with the individual in mind. From sketchbook to oven to table, we look forward to creating an unforgettable cake for you.

Our cake specialties include Chocolate Mousse Layer Cake, Lemon Chiffon, Caramel Espresso, Poppyseed with homemade Marion or Raspberry curds, Apricot Mocha Almond Cake, Classic White Cake with Vanilla Bean Custard, Flourless Chocolate Hazelnut Torte, Oregon Chai™ Spice Cake and many more.

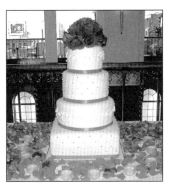

WRIGHTBERRY'S
CUSTOM WEDDING
CAKE DESIGNS

Handmade Sugar Flowers

VISIT OUR CAKE SHOW ROOM
(BY APPOINTMENT)
FOR A CONSULTATION CALL: **503-723-3930**
14796 S. THAYER ROAD • OREGON CITY, OR 97045
WEB SITE: WRIGHTBERRYWEDDINGCAKES.COM
EMAIL: WRIGHTBERY@AOL.COM

Wrightberry's combines artistry with the baking skills of our pastry chef to create the wedding cake of your dreams. Buttercream icing and fresh flowers are not your only option when designing your wedding cake. We go beyond with realistic handmade sugar flowers that will surprise and delight you and handmade fondant icing that is deliciously flavored. Our fondant icing gives the cake a beautiful smooth finish and is a wonderful medium for creating a truly special cake design.

Our philosophy regarding your wedding cake is not only to create a beautiful design, but to provide you with a moist and flavorful cake. We invite you to select a different flavor for each layer and there is no extra charge for the cake shape, such as squares, hexagons or hearts. A variety of fillings are available to compliment your cake selection.

The wedding cake will be a focal point of your reception. As such, it is important to determine how the cake will be displayed and we offer a special service in this regard. We not only deliver and set up the cake, but we will complete the finishing details such as lifting the cake, coordinating linens and fabrics, creating the cake topper and placing flowers on and around the base of the cake. We deliver to the entire Portland Metro area and to as far south as Salem and north to Woodland, Washington.

Wrightberry's provides you with a delightfully fresh cake topper on your first anniversary. In addition, when planning your wedding, don't forget about the Groom – we can provide a special Groom's Cake for him too!

"Thank you to everyone at Wrightberry's. Last year you prepared the most wonderful wedding cake for us. Your service was impeccable. You were unbelievably patient and professional when helping us choose the style and flavors of our cake. On our wedding day you set up the cake exactly when you said you would, without disturbance to anyone. When we first saw the cake set up it surpassed all of our expectations. Our many guests were astounded, many saying it was the most beautiful, unique and creative wedding cakes they had seen. This says a lot given that we looked at many of the top, high-end "boutique" cake makers in the city. Our expectations were high, and you certainly met and exceeded them. The bottom line is that you delivered a high quality, great tasting, creative and unique cake, with great service at a very, very reasonable price."

Thank you,
Carl Neidhart

Notes

photo by Woodstock Photography • See page 554

Superstitions About
Wedding Cakes

It's bad luck for the bride to

bake her own wedding cake.

The bride who samples her cake

before it is cut will forfeit her husband's love

When the bride saves a piece of her wedding cake,

she ensures her husband's fidelity for life.

www.bravoportland.com

Liquor Laws, Liability & Services

- **Liquor laws and liability:** With today's strict liquor laws, it's always advisable to check into who assumes the liability for any alcoholic beverage service. Although the event facility and/or the caterer may carry liability insurance, the host or coordinator of the function may still be considered liable. Make sure all parties involved with the event are properly insured, and consult with an insurance agent to make sure you have appropriate coverage for yourself.

- **Banquet permits:** In Oregon and Washington, functions with private hosted bars featuring hard alcohol, beer and wine are required to have a banquet permit. Many banquet sites are already registered with the states to serve alcoholic beverages, while others are not. If your banquet site requires you to purchase a liability waiver or banquet permit for the day, do it! It's for your protection. Remember that only Oregon Liquor Control Commission (OLCC) and Washington State Liquor Control Board (WSLCB) licensed food and beverage establishments can provide no-host bars. Call OLCC at (503) 872-5070 or WSLCB at (206) 464-6094 for more information. (Banquet permits can be obtained one week in advance of your function at any liquor store.)

- **Hotels and off-premise licenses:** Most hotels do not have off-premise liquor licenses, and their on-site licenses do not apply to events held on other properties. When planning an event at another site, make sure to obtain a one-time only license for any off-premise event.

- **Private hosted bars:** If you are serving hard liquor (alcohol other than beer or wine) at a hosted bar, you should consider having a state-licensed bartender. Licensed servers have a permit from the OLCC or WSLCB.

  If you have a no-host bar where money changes hands, the law requires that you have a server with a permit showing the completion of alcohol-server education.

- **Advantages of hiring professional beverage servers:** Beverage or catering service companies provide professionally trained staff who can handle complete bar services at your event. They take care of the purchasing, bar set-up and clean-up, serving, and liability. It may be worth the extra cost to ensure that the bar will be handled in a professional and legal manner. These people are trained to detect if someone should not be served more, or if someone is underage. This service also allows you to enjoy the event without worrying about your guests.

- **Beverages in bulk or case discount:** How do you get a good selection of beverages on a budget? Distributors, wine shops, and some stores offer variety and savings when you purchase in bulk. In some instances, unused beverages may be returned for a refund.

- **Area wineries:** Touring Oregon and Washington wineries can be a great place to find wines and champagnes. Spend a Saturday touring some of the wineries sampling the different varieties and select one that you and your fiancé will both enjoy.

- **Beverage-service equipment rentals:** Rental stores carry a variety of beverage-service equipment, including portable bars, kegs and taps, champagne fountains, and coffee makers.

- **Tired of punch and soda?** Try alternative beverages with a flair. Espresso bars feature a variety of drinks that you and your guests are sure to enjoy. They are also very "budget-friendly" in comparison to alcoholic beverages. Juice bars feature a wide selection of fresh-squeezed or specially mixed juices.

- **Determining the type of menu for your reception:** The time of day will help determine what you serve: for a morning wedding, you may want to serve a brunch menu; hors d'oeuvres are perfect for afternoon receptions; and a sit-down dinner or buffet is appropriate for evenings.

- **Favorite foods:** If you, your fiancé or families have favorite dishes or prefer certain types of foods, talk to your caterer about incorporating them into your menu. This extra attention to detail is always appreciated.

- **Menu selection and the weather:** Be certain that your menu selections will withstand your special day's anticipated weather. Avoid hot or heavy meals on muggy and humid days. High humidity may also wilt potato chips, cut cheeses, and similar foods. On hot days extra care should be taken to protect easily spoiled foods. Be especially careful with mayonnaise-based items, raw shellfish and the like.

- **Catering guidelines:** To avoid running out of food at your reception, it is important to plan your menu carefully. Your caterer will be able to help you determine the best style of menu, with the correct amount of food based on your budget. Be sure to ask your caterer if they prepare any extra food for unexpected guests, and if there is an additional cost for this service. Always get a written estimate for the menu you have selected from the caterers you are considering. This estimate should include all food costs, rentals, labor, gratuities and taxes. Make sure the prices quoted will be valid at the time of your event.

- **Estimating how many people:** Determine your guest count as soon as possible, as all price quotes will be based on this number. Begin by requesting prospective guest lists from both your and the groom's parents. Then put together your own list. Once all the guest lists are combined, you can use the "rule-of-thumb" that 70–75% will attend to establish final guest count. We highly recommend that you include RSVP cards with your invitations whether you serve a formal sit-down dinner or a less formal buffet.

- **What the caterer supplies:** When it comes to supplying china, flatware, glasses, cups, saucers, and table linens, every catering company is different. Some will include the cost in their catering prices, while others will not. Ask each caterer you are considering how they handle this matter and make sure you fully understand all fees before signing a contract. Some caterers will coordinate all the details of your reception, including rentals, service staff and referrals for other wedding-related businesses.

- **Serving the food:** After you have expressed your expectations for your reception, and have determined the flow of your party and time lines for the reception, your caterer will be able to suggest buffet table layouts and food start times. They may recommend that waiters serve hors d'oeuvres so that your guests can mingle, or offer you ideas about food stations which will create a more interactive reception for your guests. The important thing to remember is that you've planned well...Now it's time to leave the details of handling all the food service to the caterer so that you can enjoy your reception. The party is for you and your groom, and you should fully enjoy it without worrying about details that have already been delegated.

For more assistance with staying organized during the wedding planning process, check out the Bravo! Wedding Organizer. Detailed question worksheets double as contracts. This step-by-step system will keep every detail of your wedding organized. To order, refer to the order form on page 25 in this Guide.

503.475.6900
Portland, Oregon
dmelampy@anorthwestaffair.com
www.anorthwestaffair.com

CUSTOM MENUS FEATURING THE BOUNTY OF THE NORTHWEST
We provide culinary creativity with a Northwest flair. Executive Chef, Lindsey V. Wells, selects the freshest northwest fruits, produce, seafood, and meats to create an elegant menu for your special event.

WEDDING CAKES/ELEGANT DESSERTS
Our Chef, Lindsey, will custom design your wedding cake or dessert using the highest quality ingredients, imported chocolate, and butter creams made with real butter.

FULL-SERVICE CATERING
We provide full-service, on-location catering.

COST
Cost is based on menu selection, type of event, and on a per-person basis. A 40% deposit is required to reserve event date.

SERVERS
We supply a friendly, professional staff dedicated to making your event a memorable experience.

A NORTHWEST AFFAIR
Catering Elegance

Distinctive Catering

AN ELEGANT AFFAIR

P.O. Box 80013 • Portland, Oregon 97280
Contact: Melody
(503) 245-2802; Fax (503) 246-4309
E-mail: melody@anelegantaffaircatering.com

Brides…You are cordially invited to
An Elegant Affair…Your wedding!

Types of Menus and Specialties

Catering is our only business. An Elegant Affair catering will carefully plan, prepare, and present a tantalizing bill of fare created specifically to fit your wedding budget and needs. Whether it's a formal sit-down dinner, an intimate hors d'oeuvres reception, or a fabulous rehearsal dinner, we are committed to making your wedding an elegant one!

Services and Cost

- **Menu planning:** Our seasoned staff can prepare any type of cuisine in our fully licensed catering kitchen, and we are happy to design a menu that will suit your special occasion.
- **Estimating number of guests:** We can help you determine how many guests to expect to ensure accurate food quantities are ordered.
- **Cost:** Our prices are determined on a per-person basis and vary upon menu selection. A 35% deposit is required to reserve your event date. The balance is due before the event.
- **Beverage service:** Alcoholic and nonalcoholic beverages are available.
- **Linens and napkins:** Buffet table linen and skirting no charge; paper products no charge; white and colored linen tablecloths and napkins available.
- **Serviceware:** Silver serving trays available no charge; china, glassware, paper, plastic available.
- **Servers:** We supply experienced, professional servers and bartenders in formal black and white attire. Setup, serving, and complete cleanup of all food and beverages are always provided.

For your entertaining ease, let AN ELEGANT AFFAIR help make your special day a worry-free and memorable event.

(You'll find hosting a special occasion will never be easier or more enjoyable.)

Call today for a complimentary consultation!
(503) 245-2802

CATERING & WINE SERVICES

fresh   *creative*   *organic*

503 233-8539
www.artemisfoods.com

Exceptional cuisine with local, seasonal and organic ingredients.
Outstanding Service

Weddings, Rehearsal Dinners, Bridal Brunch

We offer as many different styles of weddings as there are brides: from a cocktail style reception of hors d'ouevres and champagne to a formal seated dinner. Let us cater at your chosen sight or Artemis Foods can direct you to one of the outstanding venues that we frequent. To name a few: The Rooftop Terrace at Ecotrust Conference Center, World Forestry Center, Portland Japanese Garden, PICA, Jenkins Estate, Contemporary Gallery of Arts, Leach Botanical Gardens, Bridal Veil Falls

"...this is the best food that I have had at a wedding..."

Roger Porter ~ Food Writer Willamette Week
Guest at a wedding catered by Artemis Foods

"Your staff was so helpful and efficient, you made everything happen just right. I am so impressed...and the food!"

—Ginny Adelsheim about a wedding catered at her wine country home

Menus:

We take advantage of seasonal and local items to create the freshest and most delicious menus that celebrate the bounty of the Northwest. Our award winning chef/owner, Grace Pae is accomplished at creating fabulous food that is elegant yet simple. Artemis Foods focuses on using organic and local ingredients, produce, meats, cheeses, wines, coffee , etc. as much as possible. While we do have sample menus to help you decide your menu, we enjoy sharing the creative process of designing a custom menu for your special day. If you do not see what you are looking for on our menus, we can probably create it for you. Themed menus are available.

Service:

Our service staff is professional and gracious. Ask for Colleen Donnelly, our catering manager, or Grace to help you with all the details. We pay attention to our client's needs and budget. We will make your event perfect. From coordinating linens and china to arranging seating, lighting, dance floor and tenting, we have the resources to provide your wedding with the best and most complete set up. We are fully licensed and insured for alcohol service.

We can coordinate all the details or can also work with your coordinator
For your special day and everyday, let us always eat good food!

BAJA CASUAL TO MODERN SOUTHWESTERN CUISINE

~ Weddings ~ Bridal Showers ~ Rehearsal Dinner ~
~ Corporate Catering ~ Cinco de Mayo ~ Holiday Parties ~

¡ PERFECT FOR YOUR SPECIAL OCCASION!

Baja Grill redefines "Mexican Food." We put the **"Love"** back into it with our new approach to traditional Mexican Food. We start with only the **freshest ingredients,** prepared in a **wholesome** and **flavorful** way. **Extra touches** going above and beyond carries through with our team's **awesome attitude, personal attention** and **flexibility.** In the rare case that we don't meet or exceed your expectations, just let us know and we'll make it right for you!

¡ BAJA BEACH CELEBRATION!

Citrus Grilled Chicken	Grilled Ahi Tuna	Grilled Veggies	Grilled Carne Asada
Casita Style Potato Salad	Southwest Slaw	Baja Shrimp Cocktail	BBQ Black Beans
Cilantro Lime Pesto Rice	Kids Quesadillas	Nachos para Ninos	Fire Roasted Salsa

Location

~ The all new Downtown **Baja Terrace**… Casual and elegant fiestas up to 225
~ Your place… "The Sky's the limit!"

RENT OUR MARGARITA MACHINE ¡HAVE CANTINA WILL TRAVEL!

~ We have ALL the Best Mexican Beers and Keg packages.
~ Servers- From setup, to serving, to clean up.
~ Rental coordination at no additional charge: Tents, tables, chairs, china, linens and much more.

Cost

We provide you with quality and value… Moderate pricing, working within your budget. Doing as much or even as little as you require. Drop off catering, full service, or come down and pick it up. Basic Catering Menu charges are based on per person and per item selection, plus 18% service charge for basic catering.

Our Mission

We strive to be the best **CATERER** and **FIESTA MAKER** possible. No matter what! Be it a party of five or 5,000. We treat our clients and their guests like old friends. Serving the best quality of food and outstanding beverages. Our staff shows the utmost attention to detail in making ALL of our fiestas a success. We make ordering for corporate and private catering accurate, simple and user friendly! We'll bring you the finest and freshest ingredients crafted with striking presentation, served with precision and care. We love what we do… We think you will too!

Ask our Friends about us

Southwest Airlines, Laura Stoecklin• **Stoel Rives,** Nancy Clark • **El Hispanic News,** Melanie Davis
Horizon Airlines, Kathie Hayatt • **Mentor Graphics,** Eve Edwards • **Allstate Insurance,** Bonnie Miller

Event Coordinator: Kawika Kahoilua
0515 SW Carolina • Portland, Oregon 97239

TEL: 503.977.2771   Web: www.bghawaiiangrille.com
FAX: 503.244.9903   E-mail: hapaguys@earthlink.net

LET US BRING PARADISE TO YOU ON YOUR SPECIAL DAY!

The Islands hold many memories for us… walking barefoot 12 months of the year, sand on the floor of the car, falling asleep to the sound of the trade winds blowing through the bamboo in the neighbor's yard and especially the magical aroma of good home-cooked island food.

ALOHA

We will add that special aloha touch to your engagement party, rehearsal dinner or wedding reception. We can accommodate up to 70 in our restaurant, which offers a relaxed Hawaiian style atmosphere, as well as being an approved caterer for most off-site event locations.

Services

- Full beverage service
- All rentals available
- Hawaiian flowers/tropical specialties
- Trained bartenders & wait staff
- OLCC licensed – on and off premises

- Hawaiian musicians
- DJ Service
- Hula dancers/lessons
- Full setup/breakdown

WESTCOAST'S PREMIER HAWAIIAN CATERER

Call us for a personal sit-down meeting and complimentary sample tasting

References Available Upon Request

53 N.W. 1st
Portland, Oregon 97209
Call: 503-750-5467
E-mail: bezinful@aol.com

be Zinful Catering delivers a menu rich in flavor, design and creativity, spiked with a healthy dose of local ingredients. Our catering staff is trained to serve events of all sizes — from small to large, from casual to sophisticated, we can make any event an unqualified success. Whether hosting a buffet breakfast, planning an afternoon reception or serving a sit-down dinner, be Zinful will creatively present your food, deliver and set-up in a timely manner and graciously assist you with any special requests.

Menu:

Our catering staff is flexible with menu development and will work within your budget. Executive Chef, Kevin Kennedy, is skilled at developing a menu to fit your needs, whether it is themed, traditional or contemporary selections. We also have several menus to help in making your selections.

Event Types:

Wedding receptions, rehearsal dinners, bridal luncheons, bridal showers and engagement parties.

Cost:

Menu is priced on per-guest count and can vary depending on menu selection, but the price per guest includes the following amenities and services free of charge:

- China
- Linen
- Flatware
- Glassware

Additional Services:

- Fully trained and professional servers and bartenders
- We offer full liquor, beer, wine and champagne selections as well as non-alcoholic beverages. We are fully licensed by OLCC and carry liability insurance.

Our catering staff is skilled in developing a memorable event and can assist with any and all steps involved in planning your event. Some of our additional services include:

- Designing, printing and mailing invitations
- Decorations
- Party favors
- Theme development

Event Facilities:

be Zinful is happy to cater at the location of your choice. We also have exclusive catering availability at the Crown Ballroom and Garden Court.

12003 N.E. Ainsworth Circle, Suite A
Portland, Oregon 97220
Contact: Christian or Annette Joly
(503) 252-1718; Fax (503) 252-0178
Business Hours: Mon–Fri 7am–7pm
Web site: www.caperscafe.com

If You're Entertaining Very Important People… We Deliver

When you want to electrify a crowd, nothing causes quite the stir like food prepared by Capers Cafe and Catering Company. Bold, imaginative food… presented with both precision and panache. You've probably got some great ideas. So do we. And together we will plan an event that's destined to be remembered and implemented precisely as planned. All foods are prepared from fresh Northwest products with emphasis on taste and appearance.

Banquet and Reception Site

Capers is able to accommodate private rehearsal dinners and receptions.

Cost

Cost is based on the food selection and type of event. All costs are itemized and on a per person basis. A 50% deposit is required upon confirmation of event. Cancellations may be made 10 days prior to the event.

Experience

With 25 years experience in the industry, Christian Joly has prepared international events for 2,000, as well as intimate dinners for two.

Services

Capers Cafe and Catering Company is a fully licensed and insured caterer, capable of providing any style of food and beverage that a customer may require. Seven days a week.

Food Preparation and Equipment

Capers Cafe and Catering Company prepares all foods with flair, putting heavy emphasis on taste and visual appearance.

Serving Attendants

To ensure a successful event, we provide all the necessary professionals to prepare, serve, and clean up. Gratuities are optional.

OUR FOODS AND SERVICES
ARE 100% GUARANTEED

Capers Cafe and Catering Company is an extremely successful business because of its employees. Our staff believes in satisfying all the needs of our customers. We never take shortcuts and guarantee our foods and services 100%, or we return your money. *We are at your service.*

Wedding Receptions, Full Service Catering
& Wedding Coordination
(503) 238-8889
Kitchen Address: 611 S.E. Grant Street, Portland, Oregon 97214
Mailing Address: PO Box 82956, Portland Oregon 97282
Web site: www.caibpdx.com ~ E-mail: rhonda@caibpdx.com or dorothy@caibpdx.com

Customized Wedding Planning

Whether you're planning a Wedding Reception, Rehearsal Dinner, Shower or Family Party ~
let our team of Professional Wedding Planners, Culinary Staff and Experienced Catering
Servers create a unique reception your guests will be sure to enjoy and remember!

Elegant Wedding Packages

Call us for our new Elegant Wedding Packages. These all-inclusive (see packages for
details) offer a wide variety of menu items for a range of budgets. From a simple, yet
Elegant Hors d'oeuvres reception to a grand Dinner Buffet, these packages let you
customize the perfect menu for your reception. Our delicious food, professional service and
elegant presentation will help make this a day you will long remember.

Services

Catering At Its Best provides complete wedding services. Our knowledge and experience will
attend to all of the requirements and details to ensure the success of your reception.
 Our services include:
• Customized wedding planning and site location

• On site service staff manager

• Experienced professional servers and OLCC licensed bartenders

• Complete rental coordination (tents, chairs, china, and glassware)

• Floral decorations and props

• Entertainment services (live music, disc jockeys, and dance floors)

Variety of Venues

From a beautiful church setting to a private home or a public park, we are adaptable to any
environment. We are approved to serve at major locations in and around the Portland area.
Portland Center For The Performing Arts, Portland Classical Chinese Garden, Historic
Portland City Hall, Forestry Discovery Center, Elk Cove Vineyards, The Sternwheeler Rose,
Norse Hall and Gray Gables are just some of the many locations.

Call now and let us show you that we truly are "CATERING AT ITS BEST!

736 S.E. Powell • Portland, Oregon 97202
(503) 222-4553; (503) 493-1960 Fax
E-mail: CDJCatering@aol.com

NO THEME TOO EXOTIC; NO CUISINE TOO ESOTERIC

Chef du Jour has been a full-service caterer for Portland-Metro and surrounding areas for the past 11 years. Each event we do can be tailored to our clients' whims.

We utilize the freshest product of the season—including growing our own herbs and edible flowers and specialty vegetables for selected use. Wild game, seasonal mushrooms, nuts and fruits are standard ingredients. In recent events, we have provided pheasant and salmon, exotic fish including whole Mahi Mahi flown in from Hawaii, kosher meats, spit roasted pig, rotisserie lamb, sushi and (fire code permitting) flaming desserts.

We have produced wedding receptions in wineries, on yachts, in outdoor venues, under tents, in conservatories and in warehouses. We have provided plated and buffet dinners for large and small groups alike, both corporate and social.

Many unique client challenges have been solved by our skill, knowledge and creativity. For every event we plan a multitude of details for the client including:

- Full Beverage Service
- Rental equipment
- Serviceware
- Floral
- Food design
- Mobile cooking equipment
- Tenting

- Floor plans
- Lighting
- Special theme props
- Music
- Mobile refrigeration
- Backdrops

Chef du Jour is a fully licensed, full-service caterer. We can provide alcohol, linens, glassware, centerpieces or anything else you need for your event. We have a professionally trained staff, attractive and healthy food and innovative food styling. We also offer decorating and florist services, pickup and delivery.

CATERING WITH A DIFFERENCE!

9037 S.W. Burnham Street • Tigard, Oregon 97223
Contact: Steve DeAngelo (503) 620-9020
Available for catering seven days a week
www.cateringbydeangelos.com

Types of Menus and Specialties

DeAngelo's offers all types of menus from self-serve buffets to full-service formal sit-down affairs. We are well-known for our Pasta Bars. On-site cooking is always a hit with attendees. All foods are prepared from scratch. Low-fat and vegetarian menus are happily accommodated. A wide range of ethnic menus are available, such as Asian, Italian, Mexican, African, and Caribbean. Give DeAngelo's Catering a call when planning your wedding reception.

Cost and Experience

Price is based on a per-person basis for full-service events; however, many other options are available. DeAngelo's Catering prides itself on quality food at an affordable price. Delivery available. Food tasting and references provided upon request. Free consultation.

Services

DeAngelo's is licensed and insured to serve alcoholic beverages. Complete event coordination and site-analysis service available. To complete your event, all full-service buffets are decorated at no charge.

Presentation and Service Staff

All foods are exquisitely presented using copper chafing dishes along with granite and marble tiles and slabs. Service staff is available for all types of events. Attire is always appropriate.

Approved Caterer for the Following Locations

- Arnegards
- Elk Cove Winery
- Canterbury Falls
- World Forestry Center
- John Palmer House
- Jenkins Estate (main house and stable)
- Marshall House
- Magnus Tree Farm

Other Sites which we are Familiar with

- Lakewood Center of the Arts
- The Laurelhurst Club
- Leach Botanical Gardens
- Metzger Park Hall
- Oaks Park
- Scouters Mountain Lodge
- Senior Centers: Oregon City, Sherwood, Tigard, Wilsonville
- Sokol Blosser Winery
- North Star Ballroom

A founding member of the Association of Caterers and Event Professionals

FLEXIBILITY TO MEET YOUR NEEDS

DeAngelo's is always willing to work with clients to find a menu that fits within their budget and menu guidelines. We offer flexibility to adapt to special needs and requests. With our wide range of menus and services, we can accommodate your requests.

Decorations provided FREE with all full-service buffets!
Visit our Web site: www.cateringbydeangelos.com

833 N.W. 16th Avenue
Portland, Oregon 97209
Contact: Linette True 503-243-3324
E-mail: Linette@DelilahsCatering.com
Web site: www.DelilahsCatering.com

Classic or Trendy

Your reception reflects your style, just as your bridal gown, flowers and music do. The food we prepare and the table we set show your guests the care you've taken to celebrate your wedding day.

Cuisine

- **Northwest:** Freshly prepared local seafood, meats, fruits and vegetables, changing with the season.
- **International:** Authentic ethnic dishes including European, Mediterranean, South American and Asian.

Menus

Buffet or formal table service? Brunch, lunch, mid-afternoon or dinner? Winter, spring, summer or autumn? Indoor or outdoor? Cuisine? With this many factors involved in a wedding, our menus are custom designed to suit the event. Delilah's encourages you to mix and match cuisines to include your favorite dishes. Tasty vegetarian options are available.

Beverages

- **Espresso:** A full service espresso bar is available to offer your guests their favorite hot or iced coffee drinks, as well as tea and Italian sodas.
- **Alcohol:** We provide a full selection of beer, wine and champagne. Cocktail service is also an option.

Services

- **Staff:** professional waiters, licensed bartenders, chefs for on-site cooking or carving, on-site coordinators
- **Table settings:** china, linen, silver and crystal
- **Outdoor:** canopies, tents, dance floors, arches, tables, umbrellas and chairs in many styles

Exquisite Presentation

Our luscious food merits a beautiful presentation. We artfully arrange and garnish our dishes to be a focal point for your reception.

DELILAH'S GIFT TO YOU

We know how exciting your wedding day will be, so we prepare a basket filled with goodies from your reception, for the two of you to enjoy when you're alone.

EAT YOUR HEART OUT
CATERING

Monica Grinnell, Proprietor since 1975
1230 S.E. Seventh
Portland, Oregon 97214
Kitchen/Voice Mail: (503) 232-4408
Fax (503) 232-0778
E-mail: eyho@europa.com
www.eatyourheartout.biz

Types of Menus and Specialties

Who better to cater your wedding reception than the co-author of *Newlywed Style: The Cookbook*, first in a series of life-style books for newly married couples. **Eat Your Heart Out Catering** was created in 1975 by two brides, who produced three brides-to-be along the way. Maybe you want to be involved in the menu, or just sit back and be dazzled by choices ranging from **Tuscan tenderloin of beef with Oregon Pinot Noir sauce and grilled baby lamb chops, to caviar eclairs with lemon cream and Gougere crab puffs with dried cherries and Martini Bites.** Recommended by **major facilities** including Oregon Historical Society, World Forestry Center, Jenkins Estate, The Marshall House, Portland Art Museum and BridalVeil Lakes among others—we specialize in all cuisines: ethnic, traditional, or more adventuresome with Northwest fresh products. At the heart of it, Monica Grinnell, the owner, was trained as an interior designer, so **food design and presentation** are as important as the **delicious flavors** we create. Most of all, we specialize in you because we know that **you** want to remember your wedding reception as a wonderful experience, from planning the look and the menu, to the moment you leave your reception with a beautiful food basket tucked under your arm.

Experience

Eat Your Heart Out Catering has had the pleasure to be hired by some of the finest corporations and private clients in the Northwest. Our experience includes 27 years of planning catering events; designing and packaging a line of herbed vinegars; cooking with such noted chefs as Julia Child, Marcella Hazan, Craig Claiborne, and Pierre Franey; teaching cooking classes; and appearing on local television demonstrating and teaching cooking techniques. We would be glad to furnish you a client list or recommendations, and we are happy to show you our beautiful **portfolio**.

Food Presentation, Equipment and Staff

Eat Your Heart Out Catering is a full-service caterer. We provide **dishes**, **linens**, disposable products if you need them, all **serving pieces** both traditional and unusual, **flowers**, **ice sculptures**, even props for **special themes**. Our staff includes **bartenders**, **servers**, even a substitute **"Auntie"** to cut the cake, so yours can enjoy the reception. Most importantly we give you the **confidence** to make your dreams become a reality.

WHAT MAKES US SPECIAL

You make us special. You're going to be whirlwinded, waited on, waited for, honeymooned, brided, groomed–kaazaam, you're married! And **Eat Your Heart Out** will be a part of it. Watch for our new book, *We're Married Let's Eat, simple cooking and entertaining for your first year together.*

Contact: Victoria Hellman
503.234.5261 Fax: 503.252.0750
Email: MYHALFMOON@hotmail.com

It's your wedding. . . Ask for the Moon!

At Half Moon Catering, we love food. Which is why only the freshest ingredients are used and everything is made from scratch. Every dish is designed to bring out the true flavors. We recommend celebrating the true flavor for all it has to offer.

They say variety is the spice of life. Half Moon Catering can prepare a wide range of beautiful food sampled from cuisine around the world. We can develop a traditional menu or design something unique for your occasion. If you're in the mood for delicious food, we can create the perfect selection for you and your event.

At Half Moon catering we believe food should be a celebration, whether it's a small intimate engagement dinner, or a grand wedding feast. We meet with you to plan out every step of the wedding reception and work closely with you through out all phases of the planning and the day of the wedding. Our attention to detail and attentive staff make your special day all it should be.

Services
- Personalized service from beginning to end
- Unique menus for your event
- Gracious and professional staff
- Full bar service
- Rental coordination — everything from china and linens to canopies and lighting
- Wedding cakes

Cost
Prices are based on the per person guest count, food selection and service requirements.

Hayden's
LAKEFRONT GRILL

8187 S.W. Tualatin-Sherwood Road
Tualatin, Oregon 97062
Contact: Jennie Bernard (503) 691-9111; Fax (503) 691-9112
E-mail: Catering@Haydensgrill.com
Business Hours: Mon–Fri 8am–5pm

Capacity: Boardroom up to 18; Small Lakefront Room: up to 40; Hayden Room: up to 65; Century Room: up to 65; Large Lakefront Room: up to 150; outdoors up to 500; **Off-premise:** unlimited

Price Range: rooms from $25-$600; pricing is negotiable with qualified food purchase; a $10 discount applies to each room booked at the Century Hotel. Breakfast starts at $5.50, lunch at $12.95 and dinner at $18.95

Catering: extensive catering services; both in-house and off-premise catering available; fun menus and decorative décor will accompany both our in-house and off-premise catering

Types of Events: perfect for rehearsal dinners and receptions

Availability and Terms

Hayden's Lakefront Grill has four rooms from 320 sq. ft. up to 1,400 sq. ft. Rooms require a deposit prior to events and we are flexible with date changes.

Description of Facility and Services

Seating: provided; all types of seating arrangements available
Servers: provided by Hayden's
Bar facilities: provided; fully licensed
Dance floor: available to rent
Linens and napkins: choose your own colors at no extra charge
Decorations: simple table decor provided at no charge; decorating may take place two hours prior to your event
China and glassware: bone china provided
Cleanup: provided by Hayden's
Parking: available
ADA: yes

Special Services

We can assist you in all of your party needs. We offer groups rates for $89 at the Century Hotel, located next to Hayden's Lakefront Grill.

Off-Premise Catering

We offer off-premise catering as well as in-house catering. We can handle any group size from 20 on up to 5,000. Not the average catering company, known locally for our great reputation, our off-premise catering will "wow" any guests that you may be trying to impress. Give us a call at (503) 691-9111.

CHARMING LAKEFRONT SETTING

Hayden's Grill and the Century Hotel are unique to Tualatin. Locally owned, we are located in the heart of Tualatin on the Lake of the Commons, right off I-5. Hayden's Grill is the place to take your date to the prom as well as the place to take your kids for our fun environment. We offer many options for meetings, receptions, weddings, rehearsal dinners and more. For more information, check us out at Haydensgrill.com and take a virtual tour!

HELVETIA VINEYARDS

Helvetia Vineyards and Winery
23269 N.W. Yungen Road
Hillsboro, Oregon 97124
503-647-5169
e-mail: info@helvetiawinery.com
website: www.helvetiawinery.com

*100 year-old Jakob Yungen Farmhouse
on the grounds of Helvetia Winery and Vineyards.*

FINE WILLAMETTE VALLEY WINES

WINE TOURS AND EVENTS: Your country farm, vineyard and winery experience just 25 minutes from downtown Portland and 10 minutes from high-tech Hillsboro. The grounds surrounding our historical farmhouse are available for events and picnics with a minimum wine purchase. A perfect rural setting for a perfect event.

WINE CATERING: Helvetia Winery offers a variety of fine vintage wines from our own and neighboring vineyards for winetasting at your event in your location. Order wines at special case prices and we will assist you and your guests in choosing the right Helvetia wine for your menu and your guests' taste.

CUSTOMIZED LABELS: A memento for a special event. Weddings, receptions and special thank you's are enhanced by a bottle of fine wine with your message on your own label. Because of federal regulations, please allow six weeks for delivery.

*"The north wind howls here every time it frosts.
However, the grapes often ripen full and wonderful."*

– Jakob Yungen writing to his
Swiss relatives in 1917

www.helvetiawinery.com

JAKE'S CATERING
A T T H E
GOVERNOR
H O T E L

611 S.W. 10th Avenue
Portland, Oregon 97205
(503) 241-2125; Fax (503) 220-1849
Web site: www.JakesCatering.com

Type of Menus and Specialty

Jake's Catering at The Governor Hotel is a part of the McCormick & Schmick Restaurant Group and "Jake's Famous Crawfish." Jake's is one of the most respected dining institutions in the Portland area, and Jake's Catering at The Governor Hotel upholds this prestigious reputation.

Known for offering extensive Pacific Northwest menu selections, including fresh seafood, pasta, poultry and prime cut steaks, Jake's Catering at The Governor Hotel has the flexibility and talent to cater to your needs.

From stand-up cocktail/appetizer receptions to fabulous buffet presentations, to complete sit-down dinners for groups and gatherings of all sizes, Jake's Catering at The Governor Hotel is always poised and ready to serve.

Enjoy delicious hors d'oeuvres and entrees, delectable desserts and specialty theme menus (upon request), all prepared by our talented chefs and served by our friendly and professional staff.

Customers are encouraged to review our catering menus and to tour the elegant banquet facilities at The Governor Hotel to fully appreciate the total scope of menu options, facilities, and full-service capabilities.

Cost

We base our cost on a per-person count and the type of menu developed. We require a 50% deposit to confirm your event and payment in full 72 hours prior to event for estimated charges. We ask for a guaranteed number of guests three business days prior to the event.

Services

Jake's Catering at The Governor Hotel is the exclusive caterer at The Governor Hotel, which features twelve exquisite banquet rooms with an Italian Renaissance decor and the capability to host groups from as small as 10 people up to 450 (seated) and 600 (stand-up reception).

Jake's Catering at The Governor Hotel provides off-premise catering services.

A REPUTATION FOR QUALITY
AND A RESPECT FOR TRADITION

You are guaranteed the finest quality of food and presentation, a friendly and professional staff, and a personalized customer service. Trust your important event to one of Portland's long-time favorites to ensure a truly memorable and successful experience.

See page 99 under Banquet & Reception Sites.

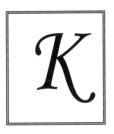

Kati's Catering

Portland, OR 97217

Web site: www.katiscatering.com

(503)283-5531

An Event of Perfection

Every bride and groom wants and deserves perfection on their wedding day. Whether a small intimate affair or a large formal event, Kati, along with her experienced and professional staff, will create a wonderful and memorable food experience for you and your guests.

Costs

The staff at Kati's Catering will work along with you to produce a customized sumptuous menu that fits your budget as well as your taste. From beautiful canapes, dips and spreads, to full course dinners, Kati's Catering is prepared to deliver that perfection for the special day.

Presentation

From the time you arrive for your first consultation at Kati's Catering, you will experience a stress-free environment where the smallest of details are worked out. You will be delighted to find that Kati and her staff can take care of your every need while you are free to enjoy the event with family and friends.

All serving tables are set with a selection of beautiful silver dishes, china, colorful linens and incredible flowers in order to enhance your particular theme or colors.

CALL NOW TO SET UP YOUR CONSULTATION...

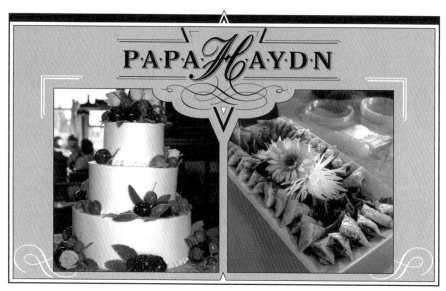

PAPA HAYDN CATERING
503-291-8350

PAPA HAYDN first opened its doors in 1978 with outstanding food, impeccable service and a pastry case full of cakes, tortes and bombes. It was only a matter of time before loyal customers realized that nothing short of Papa Haydn's quality and innovation would do when it came to choosing a caterer or wedding cake. PAPA HAYDN CATERING AND WEDDING CAKES has become a division of Papa Haydn Restaurants, continuing and extending its prestigious reputation. Our team is ready to help you create a flawless event, whether you are planning an elaborate wedding, a business gathering or an intimate dinner party.

Papa Haydn Catering will handle all phases of your event from planning to clean up. Our Catering menu is designed to accommodate your preferences: passed hors d'oeuvres, a buffet or an elegant seated dinner. We can work from our established menu or create one unique to your event.

Our Beverage service includes a full service bar as well as beer and wine selections. We have been recognized by WINE SPECTATOR MAGAZINE with an "Award of Excellence" for the past three years.

For Weddings, the cake is the centerpiece of your celebration. Whether a unique cake from our portfolio, or one designed to your specifications, we guarantee that your cake will not just meet, but exceed, your expectations. Please schedule a meeting with our pastry chef and sample our wide variety of cakes.

Papa Haydn Catering will handle all of the pesky details: from rental equipment to flowers, ice sculptures to music.

All events are based on a per-person pricing scale. Your selections and event requirements will determine the final price.

Papa Haydn Catering takes pride in making your event flawless. We will take all the hassle, headaches and stress out of the process so all you have to do is show up and have a good time.

503-291-8350

www.premierecatering.biz

Types of Menus and Specialty

Premieré Catering offers fine dining in any location, customized to fit your style of entertaining, culinary tastes, and budget. We offer location catering at its finest…on a mountain top, at the beach, or in the garden…the possibilities are endless. Let Premieré Catering make your special day a true culinary success. We specialize in on-site cooking (ask for details). Nothing compares to freshly prepared foods at your wedding. Your guests will notice the fresh flavors and quality of your menu.

Services

Premieré Catering is a full-service caterer, providing everything needed for a successful wedding.

- Event planning and site selection
- Licensed to serve alcoholic beverages
- Rental coordination (china, glassware, silverware, tables, chairs, tents)
- Props and decorations
- Entertainment (bands, disc jockeys, musicians)

Cost and Experience

Price is based on the type of services required and menu selection. Please call for price quotations for your wedding. Regardless of the type of menu or service required, you can count on the reputation Premieré Catering has earned, with over 20 years experience in the wedding business.

Serving Attendants

Premieré Catering provides all the service staff required to make your wedding successful. From setup to cleanup, you will find our staff efficient, friendly, and professional. Attendants are dressed in traditional black-and-white attire unless otherwise specified.

CALL TODAY FOR MORE INFORMATION
(503) 235-0274

Elegance in Catering

TIFFANY CENTER
1410 S.W. Morrison, Suite 600 • Portland, Oregon 97205-1930
(503) 248-9305; Fax (503) 243-7147
E-mail: rafatis@coho.net • Web site: rafatis.citysearch.com

Types of Menus and Specialty
Rafati's full-service catering staff can assist you with the selection of the perfect menu for your function. From brunches, picnics in the park, formal dinner service, elegant afternoon tea in sterling silver to the most formal or casual of wedding receptions—we've done it all. Our portfolios are filled with pictures of our work—Northwest and other American Regional cuisines to Continental and Ethnic, mirror displays of whole decorated salmon, seasonal fruits and grilled vegetables, theme buffet presentations, formal dinner services and elegant hors d'oeuvres passed on silver trays.

Cost
The cost is determined by the menu selection, level of desired service and number of guests.

Experience
Operating under the Rafati's name since 1983, our actual catering and food service experience spans more than 25 years. Experience has made flexibility our hallmark.

Food Preparation and Equipment
Rafati's specializes in delicious, freshly prepared foods set in an elegant, lavish and stylish display. From silver, copper, crystal and mirrors to baskets, china, fresh flowers and theme props—we provide all service equipment needs.

Special Services
Service attendants: trained, professionally uniformed service staff to set up, serve and clean up; OLCC licensed, professionally uniformed and equipped bartenders
Beverages: we offer full liquor, extensive wine and champagne selections, bottled and keg beer (domestic, micro and imported) and a full selection of chilled non-alcoholic beverages; OLCC licensed with liquor liability insurance
Dishes and glassware: china, glassware standard, disposables on request
Napkins and linens: linen cloths, napkins and table skirting in range of colors; paper products in selection of colors
Other: fresh flowers; table, hall and theme decorations; ice carvings—full event services.

WHEN GOOD TASTE AND EXPERIENCE COUNT ...COUNT ON RAFATI'S
Rafati's is the exclusive caterer for the Tiffany Center—a centrally located, historic building featuring event floors of traditional charm and elegance with gilded mirrors, polished woods and emerald accents. From our fully licensed commercial kitchen we also provide elegant catering services to many other facilities and venues in the Portland Metro area. Our attention to detail, safe food-handling practices, award-winning chefs, trained professional servers, bartenders and experienced event planners are all dedicated to ensuring your freedom! Freedom to enjoy one of the most momentous days of your life.

RED STAR
TAVERN AND ROAST HOUSE

503 S.W. Alder
Portland, Oregon 97204
Contact: Margie Yager, Director of Catering
(503) 417-3377
E-mail: margie.yager@redstartavern.com
Business Hours: Mon–Fri 8am–5pm

Types of Menus and Specialty

Great food, hand-crafted cocktails and fun! That is what you and your guests will experience with our friendly and knowledgeable staff at Red Star Tavern & Roast House. Let our executive Chef, Rob Pando, take you on a journey throughout America. Weather it is the Southern region, New England or Northwest Favorites, Rob's Regional American menus will surely please.

Cost

Cost is based upon menu selection (parties of 16 to 200)

Experience

Open since May 6, 1996. Portfolio and references available.

Services

Local microbrews, Northwest wines, premium bar, serviceware in house along with white and ivory linens. Catering consultants will work with you every step of the way for your event. Fully OLCC licensed service staff.

Food Preparation and Equipment

We will provide any equipment necessary.

We offer a wide variety of menu options—from wood-grilled baby back ribs with our Tavern nut brown ale barbecue glaze to Skokomish cedar-planked salmon with root vegetable puree and wild mushroom sauce—we can put together a menu that will surprise and delight you and your guests.

Serving Attendants

Servers are included in menu cost. Setup fee varies. Standard 19% gratuity on food and beverage.

EXPERIENCE OUR "CLASSIC AMERICAN CUISINE"

We feature the freshest and finest Northwest ingredients with menus to tempt and tantalize the senses. Together we create an event sure to awaken the sleepiest palate and linger in the memory.

A WORLD AWAY...FROM THE EVERYDAY!

2236 SE BELMONT ST
PORTLAND, OR 97214
(503) 297 9635 x111

WWW.SALVADORMOLLYS.COM
CATER@SALVADORMOLLYS.COM
FAX (503) 234 4051

Visit Salvador Molly's Cafes:
Westside: 1523 S.W. Sunset Blvd. in Hillsdale
Eastside: 3350 S.E. Morrison — in the Belmont Dairy

A Wedding Away from the Everyday...

Let Salvador Molly's help you create your own, unique wedding style. From elegant, formal events to tropical celebrations, Salvador Molly's understands how to make your wedding dreams come true. Our innovative chefs explore the world for new ideas and tastes to create a unique menu for your special day.

Here are just two of the scores of possible menus:

Thai basil roasted chicken with coconut curry	Wasabi marinated salmon
Poblano beef molé	Ginger roasted pork loin
Coconut jasmine rice	Yamhill Valley summer salad
Spicy black beans	Tarragon roasted carrots
Garlicky caesar salad	Herb and summer vegetable pilaf
Roasted corn bread with jalapeno lime butter	Rustica breads with roasted red pepper butter
House made tortilla chips and salsa	Fresh seasonal fruits and berries
* $14 per person	*** $19 per person**

Locations

We are on the exclusive caterers list at Portland Art Museum, Montgomery Park, Rex Hill Vineyard, Museum of the Oregon Territories, the Treasury, Lake House at Blue Lake Park, Bridal Veil Falls, Pittock Mansion, Molly's Loft on Belmont, Jenkins Estate, Marshall House in Vancouver, Pacific Northwest College of Art, Bridgeport Brewpub and other fine facilities.

Services

Our wedding coordinator can assist with site selection, décor, entertainment, menu planning, Floral, props and full rental services.

Cost

We will work within any budget parameters. Price based on a per person or per piece count, food selection, and service requirements.

West Hills Catering Company

503.228.6822

Visit our Web site:
whcc.citysearch.com
Email us at: westhillscatering@yahoo.com

Colleen Ann Schultz
Event Coordinator

Kevin D. Davin
Executive Chef

Portland's Premier Catering Service since 1994

Make your wedding reception unforgettable! West Hills Catering Company features elegant, praise-winning cuisine and first-rate service. Chef Davin, a consummate professional with a formal classic European culinary education, will create exquisite meals and hor d'oeuvres for you and your guests.

Complete Wedding Reception Planning

Let us help transform any site from ordinary to extraordinary! Beyond fine cuisine and outstanding service, West Hills Catering Company also offers a full liquor license, ice carvings, floral arrangements, tents, canopies and more! Colleen will help execute all your reception plans. Her experience and attention to detail will set your mind at ease. We are also specialists in home wedding receptions.

We Are Experts At Taking The Show on the Road

We use only state-of-the-art food preparation, handling, and transportation equipment. This ensures the safest and highest product quality. Our commissary has received a sanitation and cleanliness **Certificate of Merit** (a score of 99 or better) from the county environmental health department for every inspection.

Concerned about What to Serve? Call for Menus and Compare our Value

West Hills Catering Company offers an extensive variety of menu choices. We will create a delectable customized menu just for you. Our per-person-inclusive-menu pricing consists of all service personnel, china, flatware, glassware, beautiful silver serving pieces, linens, cake service, setup and cleanup. Elegant, full-service wedding buffets start as low as $15 per person inclusive.

Exclusive Bravo Wedding Buffet Menu

- **Raspberry Garlic Meatballs**
- **Crab Wontons with Ginger Sauce**
- **Roasted King Salmon with Hazelnut Butter**
- **Mixed Greens with Bleu Cheese and Pecans**
- **Potato or Pasta Salad with Cucumber and Dill**
- **Confetti Jasmine Rice Pilaf**
- **Fresh Seasonal Fruit Display**
- **Rosemary Ciabata Bread**
- **French Roast Coffee**
- **Cake Service**

$24 per person inclusive

**Put West Hills Catering Company to work for you.
Wedding Receptions are our specialty!**

Please let this business know that you heard about them from the Bravo! Wedding Resource Guide. **299**

Get Married in The Garden
A Fabulous Place For Your Wedding Event

1405 S.E. Tacoma Street, Portland, Oregon 97202
www.whitehatcatering.com
Email: info@whitehatcatering.com
Fax: (503-238-2143)   Phone: (503-238-6571)

Description of Facility & Services

WHITE HAT Loves To Cater!!! BIG or small. Our goal is to make your event a very memorable experience. Let WHITE HAT take care of you and your guests. We accommodate all needs from children's menus to elegant sit down dinners. We are especially creative with our presentations and food combinations. we use the finest and freshest ingredients available. Your taste buds will dance with delight and your heart will embrace the magic. You will definitely experience the difference. From picnic style to cornucopia extravaganza. From paper to china, we do it all.

During the Spring & Summer months
Our backyard garden is available with a huge fig tree surrounded by flowers blooming all spring and summer. The grass is cool and the umbrellas keep you shaded on those hot summer days. We cater to all groups in the garden: weddings, baby showers, birthdays, monthly dinner parties, etc….

During the fall & winter months
Charming inside and out built in 1922 with lots of character. The walls are painted with warm tones of reds, oranges and pinks. With a fireplace and seasonal decorations, we make every event feel special. We can provide all decorations and flowers with your request, or if you wish to bring them we can help put them up.

Catering: Full-Service Catering: Off Premise, In-House/Garden Parties, Off Site catering 1-2,000 people; All glassware, plates, napkins, tents, tables, lighting, music, flowers and balloons available

Restaurant: Tuesday—Saturday 11:00-3:00pm; Garden Seating Spring and Summer Seasons; Inside Seating Fall & Winter Seasons

Capacity: Garden Seating 30-50 /Garden Wedding 100 people, Indoor Seating 8-65

Private Room(s): Changing Rooms Available; Get Ready Here For The Big Day!!

Bar Facilities: Full-Service Bar Available Host/No Host (SPECIALTY DRINKS)

Wedding Cake Decorations: Have your favorite bakery make your cake and we can finish the final touches with fresh flowers and berries

Other Services:
Private Board Room, Party Room or Children's Room available:
Audiovisual: TV/VCR/DVD, Flip Charts, Grease Board available to rent.
Fully licensed and insured caterer, capable of providing any style of food and beverage

- Gift Certificates
- Personal Chef Service
- Valet Services
- Deliveries
- Party planning
- Private parties

Wooden Nickel Catering Company

1610 Pine Street
P.O. Box 277
Silverton, Oregon 97381
(503) 873-9979
(503) 873-6830 – fax
www.woodennickel.com

For two decades the Wooden Nickel Catering Company has been the place to go for the best dinner in the Willamette Valley. Our slow smoked authentic barbeque has won loyal fans throughout Oregon and beyond. We are now complementing our fabulous restaurant menus with full service professional catering to suit all types of events. From small, casual backyard barbeque Rehearsal Dinners, to elegant sit down Wedding Receptions. Working with only the highest quality ingredients has earned us a reputation for delicious, affordable food.

Our events staff will work with you to ensure the success of your event, providing custom menus to fit any budget. We are also happy to assist you in selecting linens and china or anything else on your big "to do" list. We love our work; you'll love the results!

Wooden Nickel Catering, our only limit is your imagination!

We frequently serve at these popular venues:

- The Oregon Garden
- Mission Mill Museum
- Landsem Wedding Gardens
- Beckenridge Vineyards
- Salem Boat and Yacht Club
- The Grand Ballroom
- Anthony Hall
- Deepwood Estate

For more information visit our web site at www.woodennickel.com or email us at catering@woodennickel.com and one of our event planners will be happy to provide you with a customized quote.

Yours Truly CATERERS

1628 S.W. Jefferson
Portland, Oregon 97201
Contact: Barbara
503-226-6266, Fax: 503-226-7616
www.yellowpagesportland.com (map, ad and email)

A PORTLAND TRADITION WITH A STANDARD OF EXCELLENCE

Menus:

At Yours Truly, we specialize in preparing menus to suit each client's needs. Yours Truly provides a variety of elegant and delectable menus ~ from simple fare to dishes that please even the most discriminating palate.

Services and Staff:

Yours Truly has been successfully catering Portland's most exciting and prestigious events for 61 years. Oregonians can rely on Yours Truly for any number of events, including but not limited to: breakfast meetings, business lunches, corporate picnics, Weddings, Anniversaries, "Open Houses" and Holiday parties.

Yours Truly is a family owned and operated business. Barbara La Valla (former hostess on Channel 6's KOIN Kitchen) and son, Scott La Valla (graduate of Portland's own Western Culinary Institute) utilize their outstanding culinary and catering skills to help prospective clients plan the "perfect" event.

Yours Truly prides itself on providing the most fully trained, efficient and professional staff. They are licensed and insured to serve wine and beer, as well as a full bar.

ANNOUNCING: Preferred Caterer for **"CAMP ONAHLEE"** of the
Camp Fire USA, Mt. Hood Council

Equipment...Included FREE of Charge:

- Linens for food, cake and bar tables
- China (paper products for picnics)
- Glassware (if we do the bar)
- Silverware
- Coffee Service

SILVER SERVING PIECES
- Candelabras
- Champagne Bucket
- Cake Knife and Server
- Nut and Mint Dishes

Come see our "SAL'S BISTRO & ESPRESSO," open Monday through Friday from 7am to 4pm and Saturday from 8:30am to 1:30pm. Sal's serves specialty coffees, pastries and lunch (including fabulous homemade soups and quiches) ~ beer and wine are also available!

SAL'S BISTRO & ESPRESSO • 1628 SW JEFFERSON • 503-227-0022

Call *Yours Truly* today!
503-226-6266

When your special event arrives you'll be able to relax and...
"Feel like a guest at your own party!"

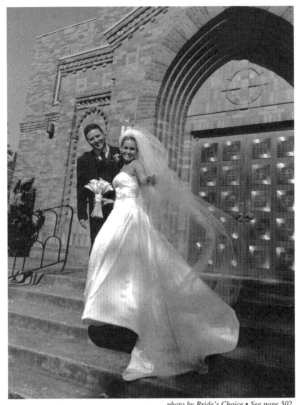

photo by Bride's Choice • See page 502

Wedding Ring Finger

In the 19th century it was believed that a main

artery ran from the fourth finger of the left hand

directly to the heart, making that finger the perfect

appendage on which to wear the wedding ring.

Ceremony Sites

- **Remember the marriage license:** Don't forget to bring the marriage-license packet to the wedding! Assign this task to a trusted friend or family member. A ceremony is not legal and complete without this

- **A handkerchief is a must:** Include a handkerchief in your wedding attire, or have your maid-of-honor carry one for unexpected tears.

- **Make your ceremony special:** The minister or priest can help to make your wedding ceremony meaningful for both of you. Ask how you can personalize the ceremony— writing your own vows, selecting special songs, etc.

- **Ring-bearer pillow:** Practice tying the rings to the pillow so that they will stay on during the walk down the aisle, but will slip off easily during the ceremony.

- **Plan how to start the music:** Prelude music is a nice touch as the guests are being escorted into the church. To start the processional music, have someone signal the musicians at the appropriate time. Setting a specific time doesn't always work because guests are still coming in, or delays get in the way of starting the ceremony on time. One way to handle this is to have your clergyman signal the musicians to start the processional music after a nod from the father of the bride. Also provide your priest, judge, or pastor and the musicians with a cue sheet. The person officiating can unknowingly cut your well-planned music.

- **Approve your music selections with clergy:** Make sure your clergyman is aware of your music selections. Ask whether there are any restrictions on music. Some ministers or priests insist on approving all the music prior to the ceremony. Your favorite love song may seem offensive to the clergyman; neither you nor your musicians will enjoy any last-minute confrontations.

- **Check all the rules:** Make sure you know all the rules and restrictions about the ceremony site. Some have strict rules about photographs or videotaping, candles and music. Sit down with the clergyman and discuss your ceremony from start to finish, so that any details can be worked out early.

- Obtaining a marriage license in Oregon: You must be at least 17 years of age or have written consent from a parent. No exams or blood tests are required.
Cost is $60 with a three-day waiting period. License is valid for 60 days.

Washington State
Clark County
Clark County Public Service Center
1300 Franklin Street • Vancouver, WA 98666
(360) 397.2243

Oregon
Clackamas County
Clackamas County Clerk Recording Division
104 11th Street • Oregon City, OR 97045
(503) 655.8551

Multnomah County
Multnomah County Taxation and Assessment
501 SE Hawthorne Suite 175 • Portland, OR 97214
(503) 988.3027

Abernethy Center

EVENTS ♦ GARDENS

606 15th Street • Oregon City, Oregon 97045
(503) 722-9400; Fax (503) 722-5377; Web site: www.abernethycenter.com
Business Hours: Mon–Fri 9am–5pm; appointments recommended

Capacity: indoors up to 300; outdoors 300+
Price Range: varies according to event; please call for information
Catering: full service, in-house catering only
Types of Events: We have complete indoor and outdoor facilities for all of your events, including but by no means limited to: weddings, receptions, corporate meetings and banquets, fundraisers, sit-down dinners, trade shows, retreats, seminars, reunions and auctions.

Availability and Terms
Every attempt will be made to accommodate your event no matter when it is booked; however, we do recommend early reservations. A deposit is required at the time of booking.

Description of Facility and Services
Seating: table and chair setup for up to 300 is included in the site rental
Servers: provided with catering service
Bar facilities: available through Abernethy Center
Dance floor: included in the site rental
Linens: available through Abernethy Center
China: provided with catering service
A/V: Bose® surround sound system, 9x12 ft. screen and projector, DVD, VCR and CD players, wireless microphones available (indoor only)
Equipment: podium and staging available
Cleanup: included in the site rental
Parking: 125 free parking spaces; additional street parking
ADA: fully accessible

INDOOR OR OUTDOOR, WE HAVE IT ALL!
Abernethy Center is the perfect location for any event. Built in 1960 as an Oregon City Post Office and completely remodeled and renovated in 2001, the Center has character and charm that are not often seen in venues of similar size. From the granite, tile and marble entry leading to over 5,000 square feet of beautifully appointed event space, to the spacious rooms with 13 to 15-foot high ceilings displaying chandeliers and wall sconces that add elegance and ambience, the Abernethy Center has everything you need to create a memorable event. The outdoor patio hosts a babbling brook, gorgeous flower baskets and a quiet escape. Adjacent to the Center, over 3.5 acres of outdoor garden area are nestled along Abernethy Creek. Its gradual slope will accommodate groups of 100 to 1,000. Clients my choose from one of two gazebo gardens for the ceremony; a full-size tent with closeable sidewalls is included for the reception.

Just three blocks from I-205 in Oregon City, the Abernethy Center is conveniently located for the Portland area. The Center offers over 125 free parking spaces, with plenty of street parking as well.

Indoors or out, we can accommodate your needs and look forward to meeting with you soon.

$\mathcal{A}$moore
Wedding Chapel

7506 N. Chicago Avenue • Portland, Oregon 97203
(503) 240-8144; www.amooreweddings.com

Newly restored chapel with bridal shop,
florist and wedding DJ service
all at one location.

Amoore Wedding Chapel

This chapel in historic St. John's was built in the early 1930s. Close to the historic St. John's Bridge and Cathedral Park and just ten minutes north of downtown Portland., the pristine chapel has been completely remodeled. Features include air conditioning, oak floors and beautiful chandeliers in a vaulted ceiling. Private bride's dressing rooms are decorated with Italian furniture, marble tabletops and floor to ceiling mirrors. Large windows allow for perfectly lighted photos. A beautifully landscaped courtyard features a gazebo, rose garden and a waterfall available to guests for photos or for enjoyment during the summer months. Amoore wedding chapel can accommodate seating for up to 125 guests.

Amoore Bridal

While viewing our chapel, visit our bridal store next door. Select your wedding gown from our selection of over 700 gowns. We also carry an extensive selection of bridal accessories including bridesmaids and flower girl dresses, bridal veils and invitations. Tuxedos, gloves, shoes, candles, cake knives and guest books are also available in our bridal store.

Amoore Florists

Looking for one of the top wedding florists in the area? Stop in the flower shop and talk to P.J. As your wedding floral specialists, great personal attention will be given to every detail. Capturing your personal style to complement your gown, the season and the wedding sight will make for a memorable day.

Amoore Wedding DJ

Your reception is too important to choose a DJ from a photo or brochure which is why at Amoore we invite you to visit our office and showroom. Hear the music on our state-of-the-art equipment and choose the quality lighting that will be most appropriate for your event.

CRYSTAL SPRINGS RHODODENDRON GARDEN

S.E. 28th North of Woodstock
Mailing Address: 7215 S.E. Hawthorne
Portland, Oregon 97215
Contact: Rita Knapp, Event Coordinator
(503) 256-2483
Web site: www.bravowedding.com/or/crystalsprings
Business Hours: please call for appointment

Capacity: approximately 125 indoor, 300 outdoor

Price Range: individually calculated; varies according to size and time use (must include setup, takedown, rehearsal time, ceremony/reception, and photography)

Catering: no kitchen; catering by family (no alcohol) or caterer; separate entrance for deliveries

Types of Events: weddings, receptions, reunions, Bar/Bat Mitzvahs, seminars, memorials; mainly on lawn; building available in rainy weather for groups up to 125 who have reserved the meadow. Cleaning fee may apply.

Availability and Terms

Events are scheduled mid-May through mid-October. In the event of inclement weather a tent may be rented. Reservations are accepted a year or more in advance. Fee is 50% of agreed terms, balance due 30 days prior to event date. For cancellation, a sliding scale for 90, 60, and 30 days ahead, if space can be re-marketed.

Description of Facility and Services

Seating: tables and chairs for 150 available to rent on-site; larger groups must use a rental company

Servers: provided by caterer

Bar facilities: champagne, wine, and beer only (no kegs) by permit only. Caterer must provide bartender. No private pay.

Dance floor: rustic floor inside; floor available through a rental company for outdoors; 70 decibel sound restriction

Linens, china, and glassware: provided by caterer

Cleanup: site to be clear of refuse–dumpster on site; refundable deposit

Decorations: no tiny metallic pieces, please; only birdseed for confetti

Parking: two parking lots on site, and across the street at Reed College

ADA: ADA entrance path, limited vehicle access via service road available with reserved events

Special Services

Building is used for dressing and to serve as your "base of operations." Sperate men's dressing room. Your reserved space is protected from non-guests.

WORLD-CLASS BOTANICAL GARDEN

This world-class botanical garden bounded by a sparkling lake filled by 13 natural springs invites a wide variety of both land and water birds. Lush greenery of mature trees and shrubs combine with winding pathways to provide unsurpassed beauty throughout spring bloom season and summer, followed by outstanding fall colors. Three waterfalls enhance the garden's natural beauty. An atmosphere of peace, seclusion, and solitude pervades the garden.

29500 S.W. Grahams Ferry Road • Wilsonville, Oregon 97070
Contact: Deanna Forseth (503) 682-5683, (800) 893-1000
Fax (503) 682-4275; Business Hours: Mon-Fri 9am–5pm
E-mail: weddings@lecworld.org; Web site: www.lecworld.org

LIVING
ENRICHMENT
CENTER

Capacity: up to 950 guests for indoor wedding, 250 outdoor wedding, 350 seated reception, 500 stand-up reception

Price Range: wedding range $350-$1,250, $500 for reception; call for details

Catering: our in-house catering provides everything from an afternoon ice cream social to an exquisite full dinner buffet

Types of Events: outdoor and indoor weddings and receptions; several locations dependent upon size and style.

Availability and Terms

A cozy wedding chapel, a beautiful gazebo garden with a meandering stream, patios and a formal indoor Sanctuary are all available for your wedding and/or reception. Event is confirmed upon receipt of signed contract and 10% non-refundable deposit. Payment in full is due two weeks prior to your event.

Description of Facility and Services

Seating: wedding: up to 950 in main Sanctuary, 250 on Gazebo lawn, 75 in Hanson room; 55 in Chapel; **reception:** round tables for up to 100, rectangular tables for up to 300

Servers: we provide all servers

Bar facilities: host or no-host service available; we serve beer, wine and champagne only

Linens: white linen and green table skirting provided

China: off-white china with burgundy colored rim provided for up to 100; plain white porcelain tableware provided for up to 250

Audiovisual: sound technician to play music and operate professional sound system with multiple microphones during wedding

Equipment: silk plants, lamps, altar and candelabras available

Cleanup requirements: we provide set up and cleanup of tables, chairs, china and linen; guests provide clean up of all extra decorations

Ministry service: a non-denominational minister is available to perform personalized ceremonies

Wedding coordination: price includes our on-site wedding coordinator who will assist you with the smallest of details, help you plan your event, run the rehearsal and be the hostess on your wedding day

ADA: we are fully complient

Parking: 800 on-site parking spaces

CREATE YOUR DREAM COME TRUE

We construct your wedding and reception to your specific detail. From where to place the cake to where to share your first dance, you make all of the decisions. Your personal wedding coordinator will lead you the entire way. Our non-denominational ministers work with you to provide a unique and personal ceremony. We have it all: beautiful surroundings, great food, helpful and friendly staff, all of the supplies and the flexibility to work within a budget to create your Dream Come True.

OLD LAURELHURST CHURCH

3212 S.E. Ankeny Street
Portland, Oregon 97214
Contact: Coordinator (503) 231-0462; Fax (503) 231-9429
www.oldlaurelhurstchurch.com

Old Laurelhurst Church is located at the corner of 32nd and Ankeny, in southeast Portland, just one block south of Burnside, half a block from the Music Millennium store, centrally and conveniently located. The church rose garden and beautiful Laurelhurst Park, just one block from the church, are favorite sites for wedding photography. Parking is available one block east around the park, and one block north on Burnside Street. Attractive wheelchair access is available through the rose garden.

Built in 1923, Old Laurelhurst Church is an outstanding example of the Spanish Colonial Revival-style of architecture. With an arcaded entrance, curvilinear gables and domed corner bell towers with round-arched openings, the church features wrought-iron balconet and 11 magnificent cathedral-quality stained glass windows. The live acoustics and warm ambiance provide an intimate feeling complementing the long and stately aisle in the sanctuary, which features the ornate original wooden beams and trim.

An independent Christian church, Old Laurelhurst Church seeks to be of service to the community. The church is available for weddings, receptions, concerts, seminars, and community events. The sanctuary acoustics have been acclaimed by musicians and speakers. The church allows couples to bring in an approved Christian minister to officiate, or will provide referrals. Brides may have their musicians perform in front or in the balcony.

For weddings, the church provides a five hour time slot on the day of the wedding, in addition to a one hour prior rehearsal time, large dressing rooms for the bride and groom, snack room, gold-leafed unity candle table, grand piano, Allen computer organ, a quality sound system with CD player holding up to five discs, cassette player, gold-leafed table in foyer, guest book stand and podium. A 50% deposit is required at the time of booking. Selected items including candelabras, candle accessories and pillars are available for an additional charge.

Couples may book the on-site reception facilities separately, or have their reception at another facility. The reception hall accommodates up to 250 guests and includes a stage and dance area, separate serving room, and a commercial grade kitchen for approved caterers from our list.

Please visit our web site at www.oldlaurelhurstchurch.com for additional information.

Appointments by phone are required to view and tour the church. Please call (503) 231-0462 for more information.

"AFFORDABLE EXCELLENCE"

SHILO INNS HOTEL & CANYON GRILL RESTAURANT

9900 Canyon Road • Portland, Oregon 97225
Contact: Catering Office 503-297-2551 ext 552
Hours: Monday–Friday 9am–5pm; Saturday by appointment

Capacity: 4,206 sq. ft. of flexible banquet space
Price Range: tailored to fit most budgets
Catering: full service at our newly remodeled location
Types of Events: ceremonies, receptions, rehearsal dinners and business meetings

Availability and Terms:
Come tour the property and discuss your special day. Be sure to reserve your dates as early as possible.

Description of Facility:
Seating: Banquet seating for up to 200 people with a dance floor
Servers: professional, full-service staff provided by us
Entertainment: DJ referral available
Dance floor: available by requested size
Linens: specially ordered to match your color scheme
China and glassware: beautiful place settings provided by us
Cleanup: all done by us with no stress to you
Decorations: newly decorated banquet rooms with chandeliers; table and buffet decorations included
Accommodations: Three-Diamond full-service hotel with 141 guest rooms, full-service restaurant, Martini Lounge and Sports Den Cigar Bar.
Amenities: heated pool and fitness center; complimentary hot breakfast, local phone calls, popcorn, fresh fruit and cookies available in the lobby. All guest rooms are equipped with a refrigerator, microwave oven, coffee maker, data port and an iron and ironing board.
Parking: free parking on site
ADA: disabled access available

Have your wedding in our beautiful courtyard complete with a picturesque gazebo and three beautiful fountains in the background.

**See page 156 under Banquet & Reception Sites,
and page 182 under Rehearsal Dinner Sites.**

ABIQUA
COUNTRY ESTATE
WEDDING AND EVENT CENTER
503.874.8341

18401 Abiqua Road NE • Silverton, OR 97381
www.abiquacountryestate.com
For tours and information, contact: Jude Strader, Event Coordinator
503.829.9280, jude@molalla.net

You're planning for that special day, and you want it to be perfect. What better location to celebrate your union than a stunning, 100-acre retreat?

Abiqua Country Estate is the ideal outdoor setting for your wedding and reception, with its towering firs, lush gardens, expansive pastures and lakes.

Imagine the bride in a horse-drawn carriage, winding her way down a country lane to a gazebo on a lake. Visualize her walking a wooded path to an expansive lawn bordered with a multitude of flowers. Or descending the staircase as the wedding march plays on an antique pump organ.

You will find charm, comfort and class at Abiqua, with spacious dressing areas and patios for the bridal party as well as the groom. A convenient 50 minutes from Portland and 30 minutes from Salem, your guests will enjoy the country drive to the foothills of the cascades.

Whether your guest list is forty or four hundred, our staff provides the warmth, hospitality and attention to detail necessary for your wedding day to be nothing less than perfection.

Michelle Koplan, Camp Director
6651 SW Capitol Highway • Portland, OR 97219
bbcamp@oregonjcc.org • www.bbcamp.org • Phone: 503.452.3444 • Fax: 503.245.4233

B'nai B'rith Camp offers a uniquely beautiful setting for your wedding and reception. Nestled on beautiful Devil's Lake, near Lincoln City, B.B. Camp is only two hours from Portland and only minutes from the untamed beauty of the Oregon coast! Various packages are available for up to 250 guests indoors, and 500+ guests outdoors. Our buildings and scenic grounds provide for the perfect spot to make your special day the most romantic and memorable day of your lives. Overnight accommodations are available in our beautiful lakefront Executive House, which is ideal for enjoying the coziness with family and friends. This elegant four bedroom, three bath home sleeps up to 10 people, with a private kitchen and dock. Also available are our many heated cabins. ***Facilities include:*** Reception Hall, Outdoor Amphitheater, Library, Indoor Stage, Meeting Rooms, Ropes Challenge Courses, Tennis Courts, Softball Field, Sand Volleyball Court, Gym, Game Room, Heated Swimming Pool & Hot-tub and Canoeing. Whatever your vision, at B'nai B'rith Camp: It's possible! We look forward to working with you to make your special day the most memorable and amazing day of your life!

CANBY PIONEER CHAPEL

N.W. Third and Elm
Canby, Oregon 97013
Contact: Darlene Key (503) 263-6126
Viewing hours by appointment

Canby Pioneer Chapel is Oregon's most beautiful pioneer church that is open to the public.

This is the chapel for the couple who wish to have their marriage memories cherished in the romance of a Victorian country church. Built in 1884, this turn-of-the-century, traditional, steepled church features ornate interior walls of pressed tin in white, with a vaulted ceiling and leaded stained-glass windows. Both the side lawn and front stairway are perfect locations for additional wedding portraits.

The garden features include rose trellis and arbor, stone terrace and benches, and English cottage-style flower beds, creating a perfect setting for your summer reception.

The chapel will seat up to 120 guests. The basic fee includes rehearsal time plus four hours on your wedding day. You may select your own minister and musicians, or we will be happy to provide you with a list of referrals.

When it comes to something as special as your wedding, the church or chapel you select will set the tone for the day. We'll work closely with you to make sure everything is just as you've always dreamed it would be.

The Carus House
23200 S Hwy 213 • Oregon City, Or 97045
503.632.2253
TheCarusHouse@aol.com
Business Hours ~ By appointment

Historic Elegance ~ This beautiful Queen Anne chapel has been restored to its original splendor where it has stood for nearly a century. The perfect site for your wedding or reception or you may choose to do both at this location.

Intimate & Romantic ~ The romantically adorned chapel seats up to 145 guests ~ the perfect location for a intimate ceremony ~ and may be set up to accommodate your reception as well. With a floral arbor, altar baskets and candelabras additional decorating is not necessary but welcomed. our many amenities include a quaint Brides room, guest book table, oak podium, hardwood floors ~ perfect for dancing, ample parking, disabled access, air-conditioning, and a sound system ~ or you may choose your own soloist or D.J. A full kitchen is available for your catering needs.

Natures Splendor ~ The beautifully landscaped private garden is a lovely setting for your wedding or reception as well as a wonderful backdrop for wedding photos.

Nondenominational ~ You may choose your own minister or we will gladly provide a referral.

Pricing ~ Packages ranging from $300 for 1&1/2 hrs to $700 for a 5 hour package. Rehearsal time available with all packages (included with 5 hour package) with additional hours available on most packages

Visit our Facility ~ Call to schedule and appointment or to receive a brochure. A registered historic landmark located just outside of Oregon City. Easy access from I -205, Park Place exit # 10, continue South on Hwy 213 for approx. 7 1/2 miles, located on the East side of the Hwy just past Carus Rd, across from the grade school @ 23200 S. Hwy 213 Oregon City, OR 97045

The Chapel
at Camp Colton

30000 S. Camp Colton Drive
Colton, Oregon 97017
Contact: Mary, Jarred or Kathy Lundstrom
(503) 824-2267; Fax (503) 824-5779
www.campcolton.com
Business Hours: Please call for an appointment

For that most memorable day, Camp Colton offers unique indoor and outdoor settings for the discriminating couple. The rustic chapel, seating up to 250 guests, sits in a handsome garden among towering firs and cedars. Its style is one that lends itself to smaller weddings without a loss of coziness.

With 80 wooded acres, we can offer one of several appealing sites for outdoor weddings. The spacious outdoor reception area is well set up to make guests feel at home, while giving them an intimate connection to the cathedral-like atmosphere among the trees and an awareness of the tumbling creeks.

Colton is a small rural community 30 miles from downtown Portland. We can offer overnight accommodations for select members of the bridal party in pleasant cottages nestled in the woods.

We feel that the serenity of our setting is a most appropriate backdrop to the exchanging of vows, while giving guests a wonderful holiday.

See page 78 under Banquet & Reception Sites.

FIRST CONGREGATIONAL CHURCH
United Church of Christ
Rev. Dr. Patricia S. Ross
Rev. John Paul Davis III

1126 S.W. Park Avenue
Portland, Oregon 97205
(503) 228-7219
pdxfirst@aol.com
Business Hours: Mon–Fri by appointment

For more than a century, couples have selected First Congregational Church, United Church of Christ, as the perfect site for their wedding ceremony. A beautiful sanctuary, filled with handcarved woodwork and magnificent stained-glass windows, provides a special setting for a wedding or commitment ceremony of any size. A First Congregational Church minister will officiate at your ceremony, and our organist and wedding coordinator will assist you with your ceremony plans.

Located in the South Park Blocks in downtown Portland on the corner of Southwest Park and Madison, First Congregational Church is a Portland Historic Landmark and is listed on the National Register of Historic Places. The church is known for its Venetian Gothic architecture and the red-roofed bell tower that can be seen from many parts of the city. And yes, the church bell, obtained in 1871, will ring before and after your ceremony. For additional information, please call 228-7219, Tuesday through Friday.

FIRST UNITARIAN CHURCH

1011 S.W. 12th Avenue
Portland, Oregon 97205
503-228-6389 ext. 23
E-mail: office@firstunitarianportland.org

First Unitarian Church has been a voice for liberal religion in Portland since 1866. We welcome inquiries for both weddings and commitment ceremonies and are happy to accommodate couples of all religious beliefs, races and sexual orientations. Both of our sanctuaries are available throughout the year for weddings. Our historic Salmon Street Sanctuary, viewed here, seats up to 300; our Main Street Sanctuary seats up to 600. Reception facilities are also available.

Fees vary depending upon membership to the church and the scope of the ceremony. To check a date for availability, find out more about our fees and policies and/or to request a copy of our wedding booklet, please contact us at 503-228-6389, ext. 23 or office@firstunitarianportland.org.

HISTORICAL CHURCH WEDDINGS

38736 Pioneer Blvd. • Sandy, Oregon • www.historicalchurch.com
Wedding Ministers: Michelle and Kurt Winner
(503) 816-1558

Looking for a beautiful, meaningful ceremony in an intimate setting? We welcome you to visit our quaint 102-year-old church located in the heart of Sandy, "gateway" to our stunning Mount Hood area. Hand-built by pioneer families, it features a vaulted ceiling, hardwood floors and soaring 8ft windows. We can even "announce" the newly married couple by ringing our church bell in the bell tower! We can seat 50 comfortably and there is a small kitchen and reception area on site. Our Bose Surround Sound System is yours to use for the ceremony or we can refer you to vocalists and musicians for hire. Florists, catering, photography and transportation are all available in our area and can be referred to you to make your day peaceful and worry free.

Our mission is to accommodate couples of all faiths and beliefs by providing a calm and nurturing setting as a backdrop to support the day's most important people: YOU. We recognize your individuality and freedom to express your love your way. To that end we welcome your inquiries and invite you to make an appointment for a casual tour of the church. Chat with us about officiating at your wedding or ask any questions that we would be happy to answer. Congratulations! You're going to be married! **See page 486 under Ministers & Officiants.**

Hostess House, Inc.

10017 N.E. Sixth Avenue
Vancouver, Washington 98685
(360) 574-3284
www.thehostesshouse.com

Featured in *Modern Bride Magazine*
as the place to have your wedding
in the Pacific Northwest!

Open seven days a week;
please call for an appointment

The Hostess House is the only facility in the Pacific Northwest that was designed and built especially for weddings. The candlelit chapel seats 200 guests and looks out onto a beautiful garden setting with a waterfall.

Although we primarily provide wedding and reception accommodations, ceremony packages are available. We offer four packages ranging in price from $150 to $500. Our packages includes our nondenominational House Minister, or your own minister is most welcome! DIRECTIONS: We are located 10 minutes North of Portland. From I-5 North or South, take the 99th Street exit (#5) and go West two blocks. Turn right onto Sixth Avenue.

See page 222 under Bridal Salons and page 109 under Banquet & Reception Sites

---

LAKECLIFF BED & BREAKFAST

3820 Westcliff Drive
Hood River, Oregon 97031
Allyson Pate (541) 386-7000
E-mail: allyson@lakecliffbnb.com

Get Married in the Gorge

Whether you would like an outdoor summer wedding for up to 150 guests on the lawn overlooking the Columbia River, or a small wedding indoors by our massive stone fireplace, Lakecliff is the romantic wedding site for you.

Lakecliff

Our four guest rooms in our 1908 summer lodge has everything you need to have the perfect wedding in the Gorge. Our freshly redecorated rooms are included in our site fee and have fireplaces and river views — all with private baths. We are located on the west end of Hood River, on three acres of terraced lawns, firs and ferns.

Everything You Need

We have the resources for everything you need to make the planning easy and your wedding day perfect. Give us a call to learn more.

Visit our web site at www.lakecliffbnb.com

Please let these businesses know that you heard about them from the Bravo! Wedding Resource Guide. **315**

MCLEAN HOUSE AND PARK

5350 River Street
West Linn, Oregon 97068
(503) 655-4268

McLean
HOUSE & PARK

The McLean House is a lovely 1920s home that borders the beautiful Willamette River in West Linn. The interior includes hand-crafted woodwork, charming fixtures, fireplace, spacious rooms, a sun-drenched conservatory, and a complete kitchen. The **2.4-acre park** surrounding the McLean House is a cornucopia of majestic evergreens, mighty deciduous trees, well-groomed gardens, large grassy expanses, winding trails, and secluded spots.

Through every season of the year, the McLean House and Park is the site of wedding and anniversary celebrations, family gatherings, class reunions, company meetings, seminars, formal and informal dinners, fund raisers, and religious services. **Guest capacity is 100.**

The McLean House and Park is owned by the City of West Linn and managed by the Friends of McLean House, a nonprofit organization dedicated to preserving the McLean House and grounds as well as making it a useful part of the surrounding communities.

For a special tour of the house, please call for an appointment Monday through Friday.

MT. HOOD BED & BREAKFAST

8885 Cooper Spur Road, Mt. Hood/Parkdale, Oregon 97041
Contact: Jackie or Mike Rice
Phone Number: (541) 352-6858, (800) 557-8885
Mid May–September 30th
Web Site: www.mthoodbnb.com

For the most perfect wedding day, Mt. Hood B & B offers the most stunning outdoor setting for you and your guests.

Nestled high in the beauty and majesty of the upper Hood River Valley, with superb views of Mt. Hood, Mt. Adams and Mt. Rainier, our ground and facility offer unique and perfect site for your wedding.

Flower and vegetable gardens, lawns, orchard, ponds, stream, gazebos, paths and fields await you, as though you were stepping back into a Norman Rockwell picture. Our grounds are carefully manicured by our staff to offer beauty and ease of use for your event.

Mt. Hood B&B is a working family ranch and is surrounded by mountains and forests. Breathtaking views, country gardens, livestock and wildlife offer many photographic opportunities for lasting memories.

See page 129 under Banquet and Reception Sites.

OAKS PIONEER CHURCH
Portland's most popular wedding chapel-museum
455 S.E. Spokane
Portland, Oregon 97202
Contact: (503) 233-1497; Fax (503) 236-8402
Web site: www.oakspioneerchurch.org

Located at the southern edge of Sellwood Park and overlooking the Willamette River, the historic chapel-museum was rescued from demolition in 1961. Originally built in 1851, the chapel served the congregation of St. Johns Episcopal Church. The chapel-museum is now managed by the Sellwood Moreland Improvement League, S.M.I.L.E, in partnership with the City of Portland Parks Bureau.

Designated a National Historic Landmark, the chapel-museum has been historically restored. Two original pews remain in use. The 1889 stained glass window, recently restored, provides a beautiful interior photo backdrop for day or evening weddings. Modern air conditioning keeps the chapel-museum comfortable year-round. The park-like location provides a beautiful setting for outdoor photography. An antique pump organ is available for the "Wedding March," or choose your own favorite music.

The historic chapel-museum accommodates 75 guests plus the wedding party. An added wing provides modern dressing rooms for the bridal party. The S.M.I.L E. Station, just 10 blocks away, is available for receptions. Both locations are ADA accessible. Wedding reservation times are flexible, starting at only $250 for two hours. Telephone, fax or visit our Web site for more information or to receive our "Bridal Packet."

THE OLD CHURCH
THE OLD CHURCH SOCIETY, INC.
1422 S.W. 11th Avenue • Portland, Oregon 97201
Contact: Trish Augustin
(503) 222-2031; Fax (503) 222-2981
Web site: www.oldchurch.org
Office Hours: Mon–Fri 11am–3pm; Sat by appointment

The Old Church, located at Southwest 11th and Clay streets, has been a Portland landmark since its completion in 1883. On the National Register of Historic Places since 1972, it no longer serves Portland as a dedicated church but as an independent historical society. As a non-religiously affiliated church building, it allows each couple the opportunity to bring in the officiator of their choice. The Old Church stands as a striking example of Carpenter Gothic architecture with its Corinthian columns supporting a cathedral ceiling. The original ornate stained-glass windows filter the afternoon light into the chapel. Hand-carved pews surround the center aisle and slope to the altar area, giving an intimacy to the chapel that belies its 300-person capacity. An historic Hook & Hastings tracker pipe organ adds a warm ambiance to your wedding. Kinsman Hall, adjacent to the chapel, holds 200 for a standing buffet. Off Kinsman Hall, the Lannie Hurst Parlor can be used for small, intimate parlor weddings. Experienced wedding coordinators will assist you during your rehearsal and ceremony. Call The Old Church to schedule an appointment to discuss your wedding plans.

Paradise Found

Outdoor Wedding and Photo Site
7480 N.W. Kaiser Road • Portland, OR 97229
503.645.6801 • Email: Lorina@gte.net
Viewing by appointment

Paradise Found is close-in and easily found: just 7 miles west of Portland, 3 miles north of Hwy 26. This setting is a beautifully landscaped waterfall without a neighbor in sight. Peaceful—serene and private. This is a site for a small, intimate wedding with guests limited to 20 (negotiable). Covered area available with ample paved parking. Restroom and dressing room also available.

As a professional florist I can fill all your floral needs. I have created a lovely wedding arch and two beautiful brides bouquets that can be rented. E-mail for photos and request a complete packet of information. Better yet—come and see for yourself.

SKYLINE CHURCH & RETREAT
11539 N.W. Skyline Boulevard • Portland, Oregon 97231
www.skylinechurch.info
Phone: 503-629-9700 • Fax: 503-848-2409

"A place to gather and grow"

Imagine a beautiful, intimate chapel, lush fields and a gorgeous view of Portland's westside horizon as the perfect setting for your wedding day at Skyline Church & Retreat. Built over 70 years ago on a hilltop in rural Portland, this pioneer church has been lovingly restored to reflect its historic roots. Rolling farmland surrounds the building and is visible from our charming sanctuary, complete with stained glass windows, original upholstered pews and a baby grand piano. An adjacent community room and bathroom provide ample space for the bridal party to dress. Couples can select from our list of wedding day packages, which start at $225 for a two-hour reservation. Our air conditioned facility provides rehearsal and wedding space for the bride and groom and up to 90 guests. By summer 2004 Skyline Church will be equipped to host small to medium-size receptions both indoors and outdoors. Our Director of Ceremonies would love to meet with you to design a wedding day dream that is uniquely yours!

ST. ANNE'S CHAPEL
Enchanting and Elegant
17600 Pacific Highway (Hwy. 43)
Marylhurst, Oregon 97036-0261
(503) 699.6249, (800) 634-9982
Fax: (503) 636-9526
visit our Web site: www.marylhurst.edu; E-mail: campusevents@marylhurst.edu

St. Anne's Chapel at Marylhurst University is a pleasant 20-minute drive from downtown Portland and a world away from urban hustle and bustle. Easy to find but tucked away, it has a peaceful yet vibrant atmosphere. St. Anne's Chapel is surrounded by open, grassy fields, large evergreen trees and attractive landscaping. On clear days, the snowy peak of Mount Hood seems an arm's length away.

The chapel is bright and spacious, with large aisles flanked by colorful stained glass windows, a high peaked ceiling and a skylight. It provides a range of resources to simplify the planning of your wedding, ministerial services, and musical accompaniment. Organist, pianist, and wedding consultation can be arranged for you. Reception space is available on campus; gourmet catering and full dining service are also available. Marylhurst can arrange for outdoor ceremonies during drier and warmer times of the year.

Terraced Gardens
At Dayl Ann's Cherry Lane
600 Carroll Road • Mosier, Oregon 97040
541.478.3743
www.dalyanns.com
Email: terracedgardens@daylanns.com

Description of Facility: Outdoors only, May through October
Capacity: 150 upper terrace, 300 lower terrace

Types of Events: Weddings, receptions, reunions, birthday parties, any occasion. Any religion or lifestyle welcome. Gazebo located on upper terrace. Power is available at both terraces for sound systems, video, etc. 30x30 tent available for nominal rental fee.
Catering: your choice. Professional caterer, or family style.
Parking: two acres of adjacent off-street parking.
ADA: accessible; sloping, grassy access between terraces with no steps.

Availability and Terms: $1000 per day. Only one event per day for the entire facility, with 100 chairs included. Make your reservation as early as possible. $200 non-refundable deposit will hold your date.

Enjoy the wonderful scenery of the Columbia River Gorge in an easy-to-access garden facility. Just an hours drive from the Portland area, only five miles from Hood River. The Terraced Gardens is ready to provide you with a GORGEous outdoor event site.

Vintage Chapel Weddings

www.vintagechapels.com
13360 S.E. Richey Road
Boring, Oregon 97009
503-669-0901

Are you dreaming of a romantic Victorian wedding? Vintage Chapels Limited offers a unique and elegant Victorian chapel and beautiful gardens for your special day! Our turn-of-the-century chapel has been newly renovated to meet today's wedding needs. Situated only blocks from historic downtown Boring, Oregon on the east side of Portland, our white chapel, built in 1907, stands proud and waits to serve you. Inside you will find stained glass windows, hardwood floors and crystal chandeliers hanging from cathedral ceilings. For your convenience we have a bridal room, grooms room, kitchen and reception hall. Outside our gardens are love inspiring. Walk the bridge to the gazebo or sit in the shade of a tree. All services can be provided including ministerial, ceremony coordination, floral, photo, bakery and full catering. We can accommodate up to 150 persons inside or outside surrounding the gazebo. Reception services can include party music with our state of the art sound system and disco lights. To book your special day call 503-669-8976 and click over to our web site at www.vintagechapels.com.

Outdoor Weddings, Events and Family Occasions

14101 N.E. 144th Street • Brush Prairie, Washington 98606
Contact: Kevin or JoLyn Cornelsen
Local Phone 360-891-2448; Toll Free Phone, Fax & Message 888-817-1496
E-mail: wisteriagardens@bigplanet.com
Business Hours: By appointment

Wisteria Gardens is close-in and easily accessible, just 1.2 miles off Hwy 503. Nestled in the heart of Clark County's farm country, it is a 20 acre oasis, a mix of wild landscape, country gardens, gently rolling meadows, groves of shady oaks and majestic evergreens. The winding drive surprises visitors with the feeling of leaving the city far behind. Choose a natural forest hideaway, a grassy meadow, or the more formal landscape with Wisteria trees, arbor, fountain and shrubs. This unique, versatile outdoor setting provides simple elegance with plenty of space for your special occasion.

- Handicap accessible restroom available
- Ample parking

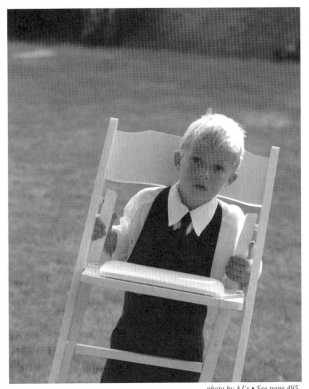

photo by AJ's • See page 495

Traditions

In Roman times a man gave his bride-to-be a coin or

gold ring as "down payment" for the bride and to

show his good intentions to wed her.

•

The bride stands to the groom's left because in

Medieval times he needed to keep his

sword hand free to fend off attacks from those

not wanting the wedding to take place and/or

to keep an unwilling bride at his side.

www.bravoportland.com

Professional childcare provided for your event

Wedding ceremonies, Receptions, Rehearsal dinners, Individual hotel guests
Contact: Michelle Davenport
Office: 503.518.CCSI (2274);
Fax: 503.518.0880
E-mail: michelle@munchkincare.com
Web site: www.munchkincare.com

Creative Childcare Solutions, Inc.

You've reserved the hall, the pastor, and the band...
Now, what are you going to do with the children?

At **Creative Childcare Solutions**, we believe children should be allowed to be children—not act like "little adults." That's why we offer on-site childcare for your special event or your out-of-town hotel guests. We go wherever you are.

We would love to assume that all children will behave appropriately when need be, but we know that is not always realistic. Parents enjoying themselves at a special occasion can get distracted from watching their children and problems can arise. That's where we come in! We provide care for individual families or a group of children so everyone can enjoy themselves. You provide the space and we will do the rest.

Prior to your wedding, we send out our Childcare "Laundry List" to your guests with children. This informs them of your wishes for their children during the ceremony and reception. It tells them where childcare will be provided, what time and what food will be served to the children, and how to contact us to discuss any allergies or special needs their child may have. If you don't mind having children at the reception, parents are free to choose when they would like to be in charge of their children and when they want to return them to us. We specify your wishes!

During the wedding, we will keep the children entertained with arts and crafts, toys, games and music. We decorate the room in our theme or we can implement your theme into our activities. We will play a movie near the end of the evening for children wanting to rest.

Creative Childcare Solutions will customize each special event to meet your unique needs. We provide safe, fun care for children of all ages and group sizes: from one child in a hotel room to one hundred children at a picnic wedding. We send you only qualified caregivers who bring with them many years of childcare expertise, CPR and First Aid Certification, and an element of fun and professionalism.

For your wedding, rehearsal dinner or reception, let the kids be kids and let the adults relax in the knowledge that their children are nearby in a safe, exciting, loving environment with **Creative Childcare Solutions, Inc**. We carry **commercial liability insurance** for your peace of mind.

COST—Custom designed to meet your specific needs. Call today to receive a more specific quote based on your unique needs. Visa, MasterCard, AmExpress accepted.

HELVETIA VINEYARDS

Helvetia Vineyards and Winery
23269 N.W. Yungen Road
Hillsboro, Oregon 97124
503-647-5169
e-mail: info@helvetiawinery.com
website: www.helvetiawinery.com

*100 year-old Jakob Yungen Farmhouse
on the grounds of Helvetia Winery and Vineyards.*

FINE WILLAMETTE VALLEY WINES

WINE TOURS AND EVENTS: Your country farm, vineyard and winery experience just 25 minutes from downtown Portland and 10 minutes from high-tech Hillsboro. The grounds surrounding our historical farmhouse are available for events and picnics with a minimum wine purchase. A perfect rural setting for a perfect event.

WINE CATERING: Helvetia Winery offers a variety of fine vintage wines from our own and neighboring vineyards for winetasting at your event in your location. Order wines at special case prices and we will assist you and your guests in choosing the right Helvetia wine for your menu and your guests' taste.

CUSTOMIZED LABELS: A memento for a special event. Weddings, receptions and special thank you's are enhanced by a bottle of fine wine with your message on your own label. Because of federal regulations, please allow six weeks for delivery.

> *"The north wind howls here every time it frosts.
> However, the grapes often ripen full and wonderful."*

– Jakob Yungen writing to his
Swiss relatives in 1917

www.helvetiawinery.com

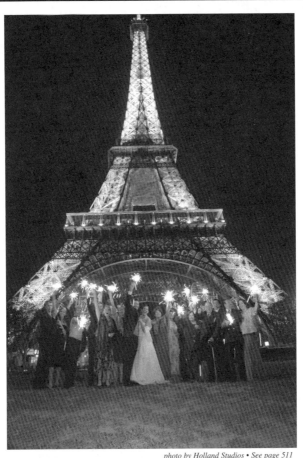

photo by Holland Studios • See page 511

"Gravity cannot be held responsible

for people falling in love."

– Albert Einstein

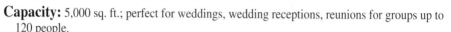

RESORT

1555 Hwy 101 • Yachats, Oregon 97498
Sales Office: 541-547-3141 or 800-522-3623
Reservations: 800-522-3623
E-mail: skeys@adoberesort.com or adobeinfo@adoberesort.com
Web site: www.adoberesort.com http://www.adoberesort.com

Capacity: 5,000 sq. ft.; perfect for weddings, wedding receptions, reunions for groups up to 120 people.

Price Range: Prices vary according to group size and menu selected, please call. Will work with your budget.

Catering: Full in house catering only

Types of Events: Weddings by the ocean, rehearsal dinners, wedding receptions, business meetings and conferences, sit down dinners, anniversaries, birthdays, holiday parties, retreats, reunions, luncheons, class reunions and corporate functions.

Availability and Terms:

Advance bookings are encouraged.

Description of Facility and Services:

Seating: Provided to accommodate group size: up to 120
Servers: Provided by the Resort
Bar facilities: Provided by the Resort
Dance Floor: Portable parquet dance floor available, various sizes
Linens: Provided by the Resort
China: China and glassware provided
Decorations: Pre-approval from Resort; early access for decorating
Clean up: Provided by the Resort
Parking: Ample complimentary parking
ADA: Yes

Special Services:

Our Award Winning Chef will make your wedding rehearsal dinner, reception or private dinner party an event to remember. Our experienced staff will work with you on every detail so you can enjoy your special event.

UNFORGETTABLE MEMORIES . . .

The Adobe Resort, a full service resort on ocean's edge has one of the most spectacular views on the Central Oregon Coast and is located on Pacific Coast Highway 101. This full service hotel offers 108 rooms. Most guest rooms have a panoramic ocean view: some have fireplaces and whirlpool tubs. The Adobe Resort features an all-new fitness center with a large indoor pool, kiddy's pool and whirlpool, sauna and exercise room at no extra charge to your guest plus an on site massage therapist by appointment only. Our full service restaurant open 7 days per week serves breakfast, lunch, dinner or a sumptuous champagne Sunday Brunch that serves the best mouth-watering fresh seafood, steak, or just about anything your taste buds have been craving. We will help you plan the wedding/wedding reception you have always wanted.

A Complete Source for ❤ Weddings in The Gorge

Columbia Gorge

Wedding Guild

visit our website at: www.gorgeweddingguild.com   866-386-6555   info@gorgeweddingguild.com

The Columbia River Gorge has become the premiere location for weddings in the Pacific Northwest. You can get married on a mountain top, in a field, in a barn, at a winery, or at a bed & breakfast overlooking the river. The choices are endless. CGWG has responded to the rising demand for high quality events in the Gorge by gathering a select group of artisans, vendors and venues, representing the best in the wedding and special events industry.

CGWG provides everything you need to plan the perfect wedding; wedding and reception sites, flowers, food, cakes, music, invitations, photography and videography. Call today and our free referral source will assist you with all or any detail. If details aren't your specialty, let a wedding consultant ensure your experience is joyous and relaxed.

CGWG offers planning, consultation, appointment scheduling, brochures, testimonials, and referrals. Call or email us today and have a wedding to remember, in a place of unforgettable beauty.

- Accommodations
- Alterations/Seamstress
- Cakes
- Caterers
- Wedding & Party Planning Consultants
- Family Events/Kids
- Flowers
- Hair/Makeup/Spa
- Custom Designed Jewelry
- Photography/Video

- DJs
- Printing/Invite Design
- Rentals
- Officiants
- Transportation
- Wedding Gifts/Registry
- Party Favors
- Party Dresses
- Venues
- Music
- and more...

Visit our web site at: www.gorgeweddingguild.com or call us
toll free at: 866-386-6555 or email: info@gorgeweddingguild.com

LINCOLN CITY
VISITOR AND CONVENTION BUREAU

801 S.W. Hwy 101, Suite #1
Lincoln City, Oregon 97367
(541) 994-1274/1-800-452-2151
Fax (541) 994-2408
www.OregonCoast.org

Ever since Jason Lee and Cyrus Shepard traveled to Lincoln City in 1837 with their new brides for a honeymoon, Lincoln City has been a destination for those making or celebrating life-long commitments to each other. A variety of beautiful sites set the stage for that memorable occasion. Some choose to celebrate their vows in tuxedos and gowns with the ocean lapping at their toes. Others choose indoor locations, like the Inn at Spanish Head banquet room, with the beautiful Pacific in the background. Still others prefer a garden setting at the Eden that is the Connie Hansen Garden. Brides will find charming chapels by the sea or glamorous ballrooms overlooking the crashing waves. Breathtaking scenery can provide a very romantic backdrop for weddings at Siletz Bay, Devils Lake or Cascade Head.

Clergy from every denomination is available to perform the ceremony. Florists, bakers, rentals, formal attire, limousines, catering and party supplies are easily located to dress the details of that wedding and reception. And a number of excellent professional photographers can be on hand to capture the moment.

Since Lincoln City boasts more lodging choices than any other coastal town from San Francisco to Seattle, there are honeymoon rooms available for any budget, from the elegant four-star surroundings of the O'dysius Hotel or the spectacular views of the Inn at Spanish Head, to the charms of a bed and breakfast. Many offer honeymoon packages to make your stay even more memorable, some including in-room Jacuzzi tubs and fireplaces.

After the honeymoon is over, the wedding need not be just a distant memory. It can be celebrated again each year with a renewal of vows at the beautiful Pacific. For your free bridal guide, contact the Lincoln City Visitor and Convention Bureau at 800-452-2151.

www.OregonCoast.org

photo by Holland Studios • See page 511

Ensure Good Luck

During the Elizabethan era, to ensure good luck,

the bride and groom were encouraged to

kiss over a stack of small sweet buns that

formed a centerpiece on a table.

It was the French who, in the 17th century,

started to frost the stack of cakes with a

white sugar frosting so that they would stay upright.

Thus was born the tiered wedding cake

that brides use today.

CELEBRATION MUSIC & EVENTS
WEDDING SERVICES

6916 S.E. 17th Avenue • Portland, Oregon 97202
Contact: Peggy or Michael Winkle
(503) 234-2492; Fax (503) 233-0835
E-mail: info@cmevents.com
Web site: www.cmevents.com

About Us
Representing the finest musicians and entertainers in the Northwest since 1980. We have the most comprehensive roster of talent in the Portland area with the experience and expertise to help you from concept to conclusion for your wedding or any event.

Free Consultation
We offer a free consultation and are available for evening appointments or weekends for our out-of-town clients who require service.

Pricing
Whether your event calls for a string duo or an 18-piece band, we can accommodate you with the highest quality at reasonable rates. Contact our office about specific prices.

Talent
We have hand-picked our roster of musicians, bands, soloists and DJs, and offer them to you with the utmost confidence stemming from long-term relationships with artists who strive to provide our clients with the quality that you would expect from exceptionally talented professionals.

Client References
We are on the preferred list for the following venues: Oswego Lake Country Club, Waverley Golf Club, Columbia Edgewater Golf Club, The University Club, Portland Golf, Edgefield McMenamins, Broken Top, Black Butte Resort, The Benson and many others.

For a complete listing of ceremony and or reception music options, please visit our Web site at cmevents.com or call us at (503) 234-2492.

Northwest Artist Management
Musicians, Concerts & Fine Events

6210 S.E. 41st Avenue
Portland, Oregon 97202
Contact: Nancy Anne Tice • Phone/Fax (503) 774-2511
Business Hours: Mon–Fri 9am–6pm
E-mail: nwartmtg@bigplanet.com; Web site: www.nwam.com

Entertainment Consultant Services

Since 1989 Northwest Artist Management has been proud to offer the finest in classical, jazz, and international music for weddings and all fine occasions. From Arias to Zydeco, soloists to elegant dance bands and hot jazz ensembles, we can accommodate just about any entertainment need or musical preference, including assistance with technical details.

Specialty

We represent only the finest Northwest artists whom you can select with complete confidence, knowing they are as dedicated to creating special memories as you are! We offer string quartets, brass ensembles, classical soloists, and vocalists of all kinds, a wide variety of dance bands, jazz ensembles, and international music such as Italian, Irish, Mediterranean, Middle Eastern, Flamenco, Mariachi, Reggae, the Blues, Latin Salsa, Caribbean, and Cajun/Zydeco to suit most budgets. **FEATURING RUPPERT BLAIZE.**

Budget and Terms

Northwest Artist Management can accommodate any budget, ranging from $250 for soloists to a large big band or orchestra. Reception bands and ensembles average between $500 and $2,000, depending on size, type, and reputation of the group.

How Much Can We Save?

Our commission is built into the artist's fee. We consult with you to determine just exactly what your preferences are, and can usually offer several choices from which to choose. We provide complete promotional materials, photos, demo tapes, references, and frequently, live performance observation possibilities so you can be assured of making an informed and confident decision.

How Far In Advance Should We Meet?

We have provided musicians as late as the day of the wedding, but usually prefer to consult with you six to nine months in advance. To engage certain groups, a one-year-in-advance reservation is advisable so you won't be disappointed, especially if your wedding is on a Saturday in August.

Experience

All of the artists on our roster are gifted, polished professionals with years of experience in helping couples "custom-design" every detail of their wedding music. We are knowledgeable about all music from the grand Baroque period to the hottest Top 40. We are available to consult with you personally to help you select the perfect repertoire that will create and enhance the romance and magic of your special day, and accommodate the needs of your guests. We offer only the best, because you deserve nothing less!

Member of:
Weddings of Distinction, Jazz Society of Oregon,
Portland Oregon Visitors Association, Washington County Visitors Association

Notes

photo by AJ's • See page 495

The First Dance

The traditional bride and groom's first dance

represents the start of their new life together. After

the first dance together, the bride dances with her

father and the groom with his mother.

www.bravoportland.com

aaaaah! The Sounds of Music

Frank Luke Director (503) 255 3507 • (e-mail) leuck29@easystreet.com

Let **"The Voice," "Marky Mason"** and **"aaaaah! The Sounds of Music"** bring back
the memories with a unique and memorable program for your special guests.

Music From Las Vegas!!!

"The Voice"	Marky Mason
A unique music experience for any occasion! John's rich baritone voice brings Sinatra's romantic ballads and dance music to life… *"Best Sinatra impression I've heard! Remember Joe Piscapo of Saturday Night Live—man, this guy's good."* —P. Schulberg	Marky's warm alto voice brings you romantic ballads and the most popular dance music of the past 50 years. *"Wonderfully warm voice …real presence on stage…fantastic performance."* —Waverly Country Club

Frank Luke and "aaaaah! The Sounds of Music"
Special Music For Your Special Day

A Northwest Favorite…Portland's Premier Musical Group. *"Your performance was great!
Our guests loved the band and the wonderful singers."*
—Frank Dilapo Multnomah Athletic Club

*"Your musical selections were just "right." Everyone felt your music was great!
They particularly liked the Singers."*
—Portland Convention Center

Enjoy musical arrangements from the great Jerry Blake Orchestra of Las Vegas, Nevada.
Seasoned, Talented Professionals
Unforgettable Music…Decades of Experience…
The Most Popular Dance Hits of the Past Five Decades

Ask About the "Half-Priced Band!"
(Live Performers and Singers with prerecorded rhythm tracks, saving half the cost.)
Surprisingly Affordable!
A unique music experience for any occasion!

Quality Service Is Our Goal

Add some magic and a crowning touch to a perfect day…
find out why past clients refer "aaaaah! The Sounds of Music."
*"Frank Luke and aaaaah! The Sounds of Music, Marky Mason and John English "The Voice"
add a touch of class!"* —Special Occasion Consulting

Call for a FREE consultation and demo tape!

A Memorable Occasion…An Elegant Affair
"It was a perfect band for the evening…many, many compliments."
—Entertainment Coordinator, Oregon State Fair
*"I've recommended "aaaaah! The Sounds of Music" for years. Real professionals!
Real Talent! Great Program!"*—Northwest Artist Management

Another Night
with

503.255.0974
www.johnnymartin.com/bravo.htm

Sinatra Swing, Inc.
From supper-club swing to dance floor romance.
"We couldn't have picked a better performer for our wedding reception! Johnny and his band sounded great and we all had a blast dancing to their music. In addition, Johnny was accommodating, entertaining and very professional. We highly recommend him!"
– Dan and Jane MacLellan 2003

"Johnny sang from his heart to ours. His repertoire, style and charisma charmed our guests to join us on the dance floor for a great celebration and many fond memories."
– Kim & Noel Juaire 2002

"Johnny Martin and his band are total class. Everyone in the room can relate to his music because it is timeless. Every generation had something to say about Johnny. Big band, jazzy, loungy. Pure cool."
– Shawna & Jason McMillen 2001

Make Your Wedding Swing!
Entertainer Johnny Martin brings 20 years of experience to the stage. He's made quite a splash at the Multnomah Athletic Club, Columbia Edgewater Country Club, Waverley Country Club, Queen of the West Cruise Line and various Oregon casinos—to name a few.
   Widely recognized as an emerging vocal talent in Portland.

Something Old, Something Borrowed, Something Blue-eyed
Sinatra swing as performed by Johnny and backed up by the finest musicians in town.
   Not a variety act. Highly specialized swing music made popular by great artists such as Nelson Riddle, Billy May, Cole Porter and Sammy Cahn. Brings all generations to the dance floor.

A Day Like This Should Be Special
Make your reservations now. Advanced booking recommended. Whenever there's a need for highly specialized music and entertainment.

SUMMER WIND • LET'S FALL IN LOVE
HELLO YOUNG LOVERS • SOUTH OF THE BORDER
COME FLY WITH ME • OLD BLACK MAGIC
NIGHT AND DAY • UNDER MY SKIN
WITCHCRAFT • LADY IS A TRAMP

Call for a free demo tape or live performance video. E-mail: singer@johnnymartin.com
Please let this business know that you heard about them from the Bravo! Wedding Resource Guide. **335**

503-286-8277 • www.bokamarimba.com

Type of Music

Boka Marimba plays exhilarating dance music from Zimbabwe and South Africa. The nine members of Boka Marimba play seven marimbas, drums and other percussion. Boka Marimba's music is a pleasing blend of lyrical interwoven melodies with a rhythm that will keep your party or event moving all night. A demo and promotional material are available upon request (no fee). You can also visit the band's web site for a sample of the music, detailed information about the band and a schedule of the band's public concerts.

Experience and Audience Response

Boka Marimba has been performing in the Northwest since 1988 for many of the area's public events such as Portland's Rose Festival, The Mayor's Ball and Portland Art Museum exhibit openings. We have performed for numerous private parties, weddings, birthdays, reunions and for groups like Kaiser Permanente, Nike and Adidas. The audience response has been overwhelming. Most people, no matter what age or disposition, are moved to dance.

Cost and Terms

Cost is comparable to other professional ensembles, is based on date, time, location and length of event, and is outlined in contract. Please call for a quote.

www.bokamarimba.com

BYLL DAVIS & FRIENDS
(503) 644-3493

WE BE A FUN BAND!
TRY US AT YOUR NEXT PARTY!

Type of Music
Byll Davis & Friends offers complete flexibility in all styles and eras of music, including ethnic, Big Band, good time rock 'n' roll and Top 40.

Instrumentation
Byll Davis can accommodate your needs with one to eight musicians. Dress is usually formal, but we'll dress to suit the occasion. Call for more details.

Experience
Byll Davis has a master's degree in music, has participated in several successful road tours and has led and performed in bands that specialize in Big Band, rock 'n' roll, Top 40 and variety and society musical styles. The Byll Davis & Friends ensemble has performed in literally thousands of engagements locally for a wide variety of events and audiences.

Musical Style and Audience Rapport
The following comments represent the kind of feedback Byll Davis & Friends receives:

"Byll, you were fabulous as always and a delight to work with."

"It was the perfect band for the evening...many, many compliments from our guests."

"Your selections for our event were based on your ability to adjust and come through with what people like."

"Your music was so good it made it difficult to keep the outsiders from crashing in."

Free Consultation
If hiring a band is new to you, or if you want to find out more about Byll Davis & Friends, make an appointment to meet with Byll. The service is free, the information invaluable.

Cost and Terms
Prices, space and electrical requirements will vary depending on the size of the band and location of engagement. Please call for additional information.

**RELIABLE
APPROPRIATE
PRICED RIGHT
FUN ! ! ! !**

(503) 644-3493

Dance Machine™ Live Hits of the 60s - 70s - 80s - 90s and 2K

503.827.7370
info@dancemachinetheband.com
www.dancemachinetheband.com

You have been waiting for this day all of your life
Leave the entertainment to us

Wedding receptions are the perfect time to celebrate life, love and happiness. Music is the single determining factor to whether your reception becomes a party or a PARTY! If they liked the music your guests will talk about your wedding reception long after the last dance.

Types of Music

Dance Machine is a six-piece variety band that performs hit music spanning over five decades. Our music includes jazz standards, rhythm and blues, Motown, disco, rock and roll, top 40 and current chart hits. Our energy and enthusiasm is contagious and guests can't help but get up and join us on the dance floor.

You can count on everyone at your special day knowing our songs. We craft our performance to fit the mood of your engagement. We can provide live easy listening music for things such as dinner and the receiving line – and when it is time to get your guests moving we are ready to provide the spark.

Instrumentation

We feature exceptional male & female lead vocals, rich vocal harmonies, tenor/soprano saxophone, keyboard/synthesizer, bass and guitar, drums and accent percussion. We bring all the elements to your reception including sound and lighting equipment, which can comfortably handle any indoor or outdoor venue.

Our Specialty

We are experienced and understand the demands of a well-planned wedding reception. We will help you transition activities including toasts, cake cutting, and the bouquet and garter ceremony. Are you planning a first dance? If so, we will perform the song live for you, or play the recorded version. It's your choice. We make sure to get the details right so the night goes according to your wishes.

Services, Costs and Terms

We gladly provide Master of Ceremonies and we welcome you to use our PA for toasts, activities or announcements. Our pricing is extremely competitive and is determined by month, day, time, location and duration. Please call or email us to discuss Dance Machine's availability for your special day.

Above all, it is your day to make all the rules.
We will do whatever it takes to make your wishes come true.
www.DanceMachineTheBand.com

Please let this business know that you heard about them from the Bravo! Wedding Resource Guide.

David Cooley Band

SWING - ROCK - BLUES - VARIETY - DANCE

503.227.1866
360.693.1707
info@davidcooley.com
www.davidcooley.com

Too cool for words. Simply, this is class entertainment. David Cooley's onstage charm and blazing talent have earned him the Oregonian's praise as "the Frank Sinatra of Portland." Together with an impressive repertoire of **swing** music, **R & B** vocals, **pop** standards and **rock & roll** classics, this charismatic performer constitutes the **perfect professional package.** Cooley knows his business, and whether providing subtle background music or taking charge to fire up the dancers, he's got the right stuff. **Special requests always welcome.**

Experience

Hired entertainment can make or break an event. David Cooley has been responsible for successful parties and receptions for 15 years. Cooley is a **champion-grade singer** and band leader with a canny sense of style and pace. His performance credits include venues in **Europe, Asia, Hawaii, Canada** and throughout the **United States**.

Instruments

From a **quartet, five, six, seven, or eight-piece group**, the David Cooley Band comes as you like it. These variations allow great flexibility in choosing the appropriate sound and price range to meet your needs.

Special Services

David Cooley is an **accomplished Emcee.** He will help coordinate announcements, toasts, first dance — all the special activities you wish to have included in your reception. David is also available to **assist in advanced planning**, offering **creative ideas**, **suggestions** and **tips** to make your reception unique.

Cost and Terms

Pricing is flexible, according to the size of the band, venue and location. **Please contact our office for an estimate: 503.227.1866 or 360.693.1707**

Credits

Oregon Symphony • OMSI • Portland Center for the Performing Arts • Multnomah Athletic Club • Museum After Hours • University Club • Salishan Lodge • Portland Hilton • Seattle Sheraton • Four Seasons Olympic • Washington Athletic Club • Seattle Tennis Club • Governor Hotel • Racquet Club • Town Club • Portland Marriott • Waverly Country Club • Portland Golf Club • Skamania Lodge • Crystal Ballroom • Westin Seattle • Hotel Vintage Plaza McMenamins Edgefield • 5th Avenue Suites • Rose Garden • Benson Hotel • Riverplace Hotel

If you're looking for a premier reception band, call now: 503.227.1866 or 360.693.1707
*The **David Cooley Band** will provide you, and your family and guests*
with an extraordinary celebration.

DENNIS COSTI DUO, TRIO & "SWING DC"
Woodwind Trio and Eight-Piece Swing Band

Call 503: 774-2511, www.nwam.com, or e-mail nwartmgt@bigplanet.com
Clarinet, Flute, Soprano and Tenor Saxophones, with Guitar & Bass

Since the beginning of his professional career, DENNIS COSTI has played in many different musical settings including Classical, Jazz and Pop genres. He has performed as a Soloist, in Duos, Small Combos, Big Bands, Show Bands and Symphony Orchestras, including in the Oregon Symphony Orchestra's Classical and Pop Series. He has a large and diverse music library, which includes Light Jazz, Latin, Beautiful Ballads, The Blues, Swing, Show Tunes, Pop and Light Classical favorites. His ensembles have played for countless weddings, concerts and private and corporate events of all kinds.

In addition to the elegant, traditional classical favorites most bridal couples want for their ceremonies, the group is also glad to incorporate your requests for other styles whenever possible. Duo's and Trio's are beautiful combinations for ceremonies. An up to, 8pc Swing/Jazz "small" Big Band, Swing DC, is available for listening and dancing at receptions. Swing DC is in their fifth consecutive season of performances, every Thursday evening, on board the sternwheeler, Queen of the West, that cruises the Columbia River between Astoria and Idaho.

Custom-design your wedding music with polished, experienced, caring professionals, who are as dedicated to making special memories as you are!

Call for free promotional info, price quote, and demo CD.

The E S S E N T I A L S

3010 S.E. 56th Avenue, Portland, Oregon 97206
Contact: Bob Thompson (503) 775-9420
E-mail: bobnancy21@msn.com
www.TheFabulousEssentials.com/

Type of Music and Demo

Nowhere in the Northwest will you find another band with the amazing versatility of the Essentials. From 40s swing to current favorites, country to pop, the Essentials have something for everyone.

The Essentials are dedicated to customizing our services to meet your needs, including emcee services, use of our sound system for presentations, specialty songs, wedding party introductions, first dance, father-daughter dance, bouquet and garter toss. Ceremony and/or dinner music is also available.

Linda Philips, Lead Vocals

Linda Philips combines stunning vocals, high fashion and engaging stage energy.

Instrumentation

The Essentials Band consists of guitar, bass, keyboards, drums, trumpet, saxes and trombone.

Experience

Each Essentials member has over 20 years experience playing with some of the Northwest's most popular acts. The Essentials have been performing at weddings since 1989.

Repeat Clients

Some of The Essentials repeat clients include: The Trail Blazers, The Assistance League of Portland, The Multnomah Athletic Club, The Willamette Yacht Club, The Rose Festival, Oregon State Fair, The Bite, The American Cancer Society

Costs and Terms

Quotes are made on an individual basis and determined by location, length of engagement, season and size of venue.

For availability, pricing and promotional information including the Essentials Wedding Music Planner, contact Bob Thompson at (503) 775-9420, or E-mail at bobnancy21@msn.com

HIGH STREET BAND

Contact: Becky Stroebel
503-590-5840
www.sterlingtalent.com

High Street is a show band that not only has aesthetic appeal but the solid musicianship to go with it. One of the Northwest's most popular and entertaining bands, their repertoire includes cover songs and originals in a mixture of swing, blues, Disco, R&B, Latin, oldies and ballads.

High Street's nine member band has been playing professionally for more than ten years and consists of Stuart Dennis, keyboard/manager; Randy McKellip, saxophone; and Bruce Wehler; drums; along with Tom Dale, trombone/vocal; Paul Harman, bass; Erik Larson, trumpet; Shane Powers, trumpet/vocal; Matt Summers, vocal/percussion; and Bruce West, guitar/vocal.

High Street's performances include headlining the 2003 Ft. Vancouver 4th of July Celebration, Walt Disney World, Boise River Festival, The American Heart Association Gala, the Idaho Governor's Inaugural Gala Concert, and many other national and regional festivals and fundraisers. Most recently they were the showcase band for the International Festivals & Events Association Convention at Bally's in Las Vegas.

High Street's beautiful costumes and high energy dance music along with their ability to interact with audiences of all ages, makes them the perfect choice for weddings, concerts, festivals and corporate events alike.

High Street's musical demos and songlist can be viewed on our website at www.sterlingtalent.com. Just click on their picture and sit back and enjoy listening to one of the finest bands in the Pacific Northwest.

A couple of comments on High Street:

"High Street is a must see. The musicians have a ball, put on a great show, and their music is infectious to crowds of all ages..."   —The Idaho Statesman

"High Street was a highlight of our IFEA International Convention in Las Vegas. It's not easy to impress an industry of special event professionals, who have 'been there and done that' when it comes to entertainment, but High Street had the place jumpin' with their special brand of high energy, high quality showmanship. We continue to hear praise for their performance from our members around the world." Steven Wood Schmader, President/CEO International Festivals & Events Association

For a free consultation as well as pricing and availability information, call today!

KIM RALPHS & COMPANY

(503) 282-3421

Sinatra & Swing, Rock & Motown!

Band leader, Kim Ralphs, has assembled an exciting group of professional musicians that play a wide variety of popular styles. Usually, they begin with tasty jazz instrumentals, and the romantic melodies of Tony Bennett, Frank Sinatra and Glenn Miller. For your dancing pleasure, they offer sophisticated swing from the 1940s big-band era, and smooth latin favorites.

Or to take the temperature up....popular rock, blues, disco, and motown hits. Recently, Kim has added a very talented singer and exciting performer, LaRhonda Steele. Her roots are in gospel, an influence you'll hear when she belts out a song. She has appeared at both The Mt. Hood Jazz Festival and The Waterfront Blues Festival.

Or, if you're after a bigger sound, Kim can add a three piece horn section (sax, trumpet, trombone). Big band sound in a smaller package, playing swing, R&B, and even disco! Pick your style, we can tailor the music to your taste. We can even bring a DJ for more variety!

Kim and his group have years of experience at the finest hotels and country clubs, and are often recommended by event planners and talent agents. Kim will make announcements for you, and help coordinate your party. Standard attire is black tuxedos.

Kim Ralphs & Company will create a warm and sparkling atmosphere at your special event!

LISTEN TO WHAT THE PROFESSIONALS SAY:
"Kim is a fine pianist...and I always enjoy seeing him here."
Dennis Yamnitsky, F&B Manager, **Oswego Lake Country Club**

"Kim plays here often, and always does a great job...highly recommended."
Susan O'Neill, **Waverley Country Club**

"All the music that I have listened to, over the years and all the conventions that I have gone to, I can truly say that this band was the best!"
Colleen Greenen, Convention Sales Mngr, **Portland Oregon Visitors Association**

"Impeccably professional and experienced...a pleasure to work with."
Nancy Tice, **Northwest Artist Management**

WHO WANTS TO HEAR... THE

MILLIONAIRE$

c/o Berkshire Snow Productions
P.O. Box 14159
Portland, Oregon 97293-0159
(503) 235-3071   (503) 637-6657
E-mail: berksnow@teleport.com

Good Time R&R, R&B, Blues,
Oldies and more, 40's thru 90's

Types of Music and Demo

The Millionaires bring a wealth of musical experience to your wedding reception or special event. With a repertoire that covers the history of rock 'n' roll, The Millionaires let the music speak for itself and the fun begin. From the days of Big Joe Turner and Howlin' Wolf, when the blues began to rock, through the hits of Elvis Presley, Roy Orbison and Chuck Berry and on to the British Invasion with the Rolling Stones and Beatles.

The Millionaires play the best of rock 'n' roll, rhythm and blues, blues, country and more—familiar songs from the '40s to the '90s. Our demo is available upon request.

Instrumentation and Personnel

We feature three male lead vocalists, accompanied by the classic four-piece format of electric guitar, Fender bass, electric piano/synthesizer/Hammond organ and drums.

Experience

Michael Kearsey, Bob Logue and Jim Stein are backed by drummer Fred Ingram. These musicians have been members of some of the best loved groups in Oregon including Nu Shooz, Upepo, Diamond Hill, Razorbacks, the Larry Mahan Band, Thin Man, Walkin' After Midnight and the Brothers of the Baladi. The Millionaires have played weddings, corporate events and club dates since 1992.

Musical Style and Audience Rapport

The Millionaires love to entertain and deliver songs that you love to hear. We will work with you to customize our sets to please the wide-range of ages that may be at your event and include styles from decades of great popular music. We are always happy to provide specialty songs that are most important to our clients. The bottom line for The Millionaires is to create the best musical memories for your needs.

Cost and Terms

Our prices will vary based on location, season, availability, length of engagement and special services you may need. We are flexible because we are The Millionaires!!

Odon Soterias

Celtic and Medieval music
for wedding ceremonies and receptions
www.OdonSoterias.com
Contact: Daniel Ryan
503-254-6281

From the incredibly eclectic land of the Pacific Northwest comes a band that has made many a wedding surreal. Odon Soterias has a wide variety of airy instruments which enable the band to set many different types of moods. From mystical Celtic and Medieval melodies that create a magical background to fast and driving Irish and Scottish dance tunes, Odon Soterias can help make your fairytale wedding a reality.

The band's instruments include:

The Medieval Bagpipes:
These pipes come from Germany and have been played at weddings and festivals for over 800 years.

The Mystical Penny Whistle:
These whistles were invented by the Irish to play at weddings and private parties when the English outlawed the bagpipes.

The Fiddle and Violin:
Yes, Odon Soterias has both, but to be quite honest, they are actually the same instrument.

The Celtic Bouzouki:
This eight stringed instrument originated in Ancient Greece but was given a unique twist by the Celts.

Percussion:
Odon Soterias' percussion section includes drums from Ireland, India, Africa and Portland, Oregon.

Testimonial
"I knew Odon Soterias would be perfect for our wedding after I talked to the band members, they were so friendly and accommodating. We wanted something unique and memorable. Our guests were so enchanted they didn't want to leave, the band could scarcely take a break."
—Stephanie & Matt Leon
July 12th, 2003

Contact: Emily Dunlap
(503) 335-0790; Fax (503) 892-0790
www.patricklamb.com
E-mail: emily@patricklamb.com

Types of Music and Demo

Imagine the sound of sweet saxophone permeating the atmosphere of your event. Patrick is versatile and plays music appropriate for the occasion including jazz, blues, motown, 70s retro, disco and original music of his own. His recent invitation to play at the White House and appearances at major festivals around the U.S. have given his career momentum. His new release, *Sunshine Alley*, is commercially available, and recently made "Top 10 in the Northwest" for Northwest bands. Patrick has a funky, versatile group which can tune itself for the needs of almost *any occasion*. From the traditional, relaxed background jazz which is needed for a dinner party, to the 70s party down retro, funk, R&B and motown, Patrick's band is a consistent crowd-pleaser. Please call for a promotional package, demo tape and/or more information.

Instrumentation and Personnel

High quality professional musicians including saxophone, male/female vocals, bass, drums, guitar, percussion, piano/organ as appropriate for the size and intimacy of the occasion.

Experience

You might be familiar with Patrick's music from his many appearances which include: The Mount Hood Festival of Jazz, The Bite, The Newport Jazz Festival, Hillsboro Concert in the Park, Lake Oswego Concert Series, Nordstrom, or the private parties he has played including one for FOX49. Or you might have heard his new "Top 10 in the Northwest" release on KINK. Patrick has also toured and recorded with recording artists Tom Grant and Grammy recipient Diane Schuur, opening at festivals for people like Kenny G., Wynton Marseilles, Branford Marseilles, B.B. King, and many others. Patrick has experience in all aspects of the music business form touring, recording, and playing for all kinds of different occasions.

Cost and Terms

Prices are competitive and computed on an individual basis depending on month, day, time, and length of engagement. Our PA and lighting systems are always available for your use. Call for quotations.

Testimonials

"Patrick Lamb's music adds so much to any event or to any venue. He is someone you want to follow and listen to wherever he plays. Any event or venue would greatly benefit from his appearance because of his reputation, his crowd appeal, and the draw that he brings in. Patrick Lamb is simply the greatest!" —Teri Joly, Concentrex, Portland, OR

"I want to thank you for your beautiful holiday performance at the White House. Your appearance helped to make our 1996 Christmas holiday program truly memorable." —Ann Stock, social secretary, White House, Washington, D.C.

photo by Jorge Vinueza

ENTERTAINMENT — BANDS

TRADITIONAL CUBAN MUSIC
THE ROBERTO GONZALEZ GROUP
Contact: Mr. Jan DeWeese (503) 236-6752

Cuban music has enjoyed unexpected popularity in the United States since the release of Ry Cooder's "Buena Vista Social Club." Over this same period Cuban political conditions have sent many exiles to this country. Amongst them are two fine musicians from Havana who have chosen to celebrate their cultures in their new Portland home. Arriving here in 2000, the young singer-songwriter Roberto Gonzalez gathered his repertoire from two Cuban styles, "Trova" (traditional guitar music blended with country poetry), and "Nueva Trova" (post-revolution music reflecting themes of protest, love and social change). His own compositions draw from this rich set of influences. The following year he met newly-arrived Roberto G. del Pino, a professional pianist with 30 years experience as a producer and educator. Together they weave remarkable sounds based on son, guajira, cha-cha-cha and other styles from their country.

Joining them on mandolin and "tres" (a three-course string instrument from the Cuban countryside) is local folklorist and music educator Jan DeWeese. Their percussionists have included African rhythm specialist Jeff Strang, Pink Martini's Derek Reith and Peruvian Fernando Casafranca. The group has played for Portland audiences at clubs and restaurants, festivals and art galleries, schools and libraries. Venues also include weddings and parties. The ensemble is available as a duo, trio or quartet with repertoires suitable for both ceremonies and receptions.

Please call for our demo CD and price quote.

Rose in the Heather

Contact: Julie Samudio (503) 892-6277
Email: julie@shamrockgold.com • Web site: www.ShamrockGold.com

Type of Music
Rose in the Heather is a group of six musicians — playing fiddle, upright bass, bodhran, guitars and percussion — who perform a mixture of happy, upbeat traditional tunes. Our tunes are mostly Irish or old-time American, but also include bluegrass and other styles — a little like "O Brother Where Art Thou" and a little like the Titanic steerage band. Our drummer, John, has a beautiful warm baritone voice which is perfect for ballads and love songs.

Special Services
We provide our own high quality sound system which can comfortably handle any indoor or outdoor venue. Special tune and song requests are always welcome. We have tune samples and more on our web site, but we'd love to talk to you in person. Call for more information and for a copy of our CD.

Experience
We have played for many weddings in a variety of locations — gardens, grange halls, ballrooms, breweries, back yards, riverboats and resort hotels. We would love to bring the joy and energy of live traditional music to your wedding.

www.ShamrockGold.com

RUPPERT BLAIZE BAND
"UNPARALLELED CELEBRATIONS"

Contact: Nancy Anne Tice
Phone/Fax (503) 774-2511
E-mail: nwartmgt@bigplanet.com
Web site: www.nwam.com

TYPES OF MUSIC and DEMO
Singer, songwriter and recording artist, RUPPERT BLAIZE, originally from St. Johns, Antigua, West Indies, moved to Portland, Oregon, in the fall of 2001, from Tampa, Florida, where he enjoyed a successful 20 year career. His exciting, sun-splashed treatments of Jazz, Calypso, Reggae, R & B, Soca and Contemporary Pop Hits made him a sought-after and much admired entertainer from Canada to the Caribbean, and at all the coolest hot-spots on the Bay. He now offers an exciting mix of elegant, romantic favorites, intoxicating rhythms and all the best dance tunes for weddings, concerts, corporate and private events. The music of RUPPERT BLAIZE issues an irresistible call to the dance floor. No one can sit still when RUPPERT BLAIZE is on the bandstand! Call for free promotional package and demo CD.

INSTRUMENTS
THE RUPPERT BLAIZE BAND includes keyboards, bass, drums, saxophone or guitar and RUPPERT on lead vocals and Master of Ceremonies. Other instruments may be added as the budget allows.

EXPERIENCE, STYLE and AUDIENCE RAPPORT
RUPPERT BLAIZE is a warm and polished entertainer who has earned many loyal and enthusiastic fans in his new home in the Northwest. His heartfelt and soulful renditions of much-loved Jazz, R&B, Calypso and Pop Standards always leaves the audience cheering for more. They love the personal attention he lavishes on them as he moves around the room with his cordless microphone. He has appeared at the Tigard Balloon Festival, headlined the Lake Oswego Arts Festival, the Roehr Park Summer Concert Series in Lake Oswego, the Cathedral Park Jazz Festival that was simulcast on KMHD FM 89.1 radio, the Oregon State Fair, The Bite and at the Chinook Winds Casino in Lincoln City. He regularly appears in the elegant lobby lounge in the Heathman Hotel. His new band includes many of the finest musicians in the area. Soon after his arrival in the Rose City, RUPPERT BLAIZE released his 15th album, Caribbean Classics to rave reviews.

SPECIAL SERVICES, COSTS and TERMS
RUPPERT welcomes your requests, including ethnic favorites, and invites you to use the PA system for announcements and toasts. He is happy to serve as Master of Ceremonies and Emcee for all of the wedding and dance traditions. Taped music is provided for band breaks. Competitive prices based on date, playing time and venue. All details are outlined in contract.

**CAPTURE THE MAGIC OF RUPPERT'S WONDERFUL MUSIC
FOR YOUR NEXT PARTY OR SPECIAL EVENT!**

photo: Owen Carey

SWINGLINE CUBS

1414 N.E. 115th Avenue • Vancouver, Washington 98684
Contact: Joe Millward (360) 254-3187; Fax (360) 604-8392
E-mail: joe@swinglinecubs.com; Web site: swinglinecubs.com

Ruppert Blaize: Antguan-born via Tampa Bay, Florida, this consummate entertainer connects the audience with the music and makes everyone feel like they are part of the performance. Ruppert covers songs from the Big Band era to Calypso to Reggae to R & B.

Tarshene Daugherty: Hailing from Vancouver, WA, this young lady has been singing professionally since her high school days. One of her first gigs was with the popular Portland R&B band Body and Soul. She can sing styles ranging from Billie Holiday standards to knock-your-socks-off R&B and Disco!

Types of Music

We play all types of swing, '60s Motown, '70s hits, rhythm & blues, awesome renditions of standards and ballads, and all varieties of rock 'n' roll as well as contemporary pop and jazz. Tarshene and Ruppert are featured in music from the '40s to '00s and then join to sing awe-inspiring duets. Ruppert brings rhythm-infused Island Music coupled with Tarshene's high energy Dance Sets, as well as Big Band Swing sets by both of these multi-talented entertainers...you will not stay in your seat! Exceptional lead female and male vocals accompanied by keyboards, trumpet, sax, guitar, bass and drums.

Quotable Quotes From Past Clients:

"We don't want to jeopardize the business of other Portland-area bands, but after experiencing the Swingline Cubs at our wedding reception, we must give the following unsolicited advice: Hurry. Call the Swingline Cubs. Talk to them. Book them. Any season. Any year. If you want to party, call the Cubs. If you want to sleep, well, still call the Cubs, Yes, they're that good."

—Aaron & Jennifer Corpus

"Thank you so much for your wonderful performance...as usual, everyone was pleased and had a great time dancing the night away to the band's music. I look forward to working with you in the future."

—Nora Totonchy, "Bridal Bliss"

..."your high energy, enthusiasm and great music was a fantastic pre-amble to the race kickoff and events. To say that Waterfront Park rocked is an understatement!!"

—Helen Williams, Race for the Cure

Musical Style and Audience Rapport: The primary goal of the Cubs is to make your reception or event as enjoyable and memorable as possible. We are especially responsive to volume considerations. We will provide you with soft music for conversation and enthusiastic, energetic music for dancing.

Special Services: Ethnic music and special requests are gladly accepted. We can MC any activity from bouquet toss to door prizes. Our PA and lighting systems are always available.

photo by Remembrance Photography • See page 542

Ancient Greek Tradition

Instead of figuring their ages from their birthdates,

ancient Greek women determined their ages from

their dates of marriage.

www.bravoportland.com

Disc Jockeys

- **Deciding on a disc jockey:** Always be sure to check professional references on the service you are interested in hiring! Ask questions such as "what styles of music they provide" and "do they have an adequate library of the music styles you are looking for?" Ask if they are familiar with your venue and if they have worked there before. Be sure to check if they will take requests at your event. A great way to check if the DJ is a good fit for you is to see them at an event. This is a good time to look and listen to their equipment, see how they dress and how the DJ handles the event.

- **Written contract:** It is advisable to get a written contract stating exactly what you have agreed upon: date, number of hours, types of equipment, who will be doing the show, the total cost, what is included, and so on.

- **Master of ceremonies:** Be sure to ask whether your disc jockey can act as master of ceremonies at your reception. This will help the flow of events like cake cutting, bouquet toss and announcing the first dance. Go over the order of these events with the disc jockey service in advance. A traditional order is: the toast, cutting of the cake, first dance, parent dance, then open the dance floor. Bouquet and garter toss takes place about 30 minutes to an hour into dancing.

- **Volume of music:** Discuss with your disc jockey the volume you wish and the selection of music. Keep the volume of music low for the first hour of your reception, allowing guests to mingle and ensuring that the level is comfortable for older guests. Then, when the dancing begins, the volume can be raised.

- **Set-up requirements:** Inquire about whether the site can accommodate dancing. Find out when your disc jockey needs access to the room and what the space and electrical requirements are. Make sure your facility contact knows about these needs and that they can be met.

- **Cut-off hours:** When you make all the final arrangements with your facility, be sure to ask if they have any specified time cut-offs for music. Some facilities require that music be stopped as early as 10pm for the comfort of neighboring homes, businesses, or other guests.

- **Special effects and requests:** Some disc jockeys offer extra services such as fog, lighting systems, strobes, mirror balls and bubbles. Before you decide on any special effects, check with your facility to see if they will allow them. For example, fog may set off smoke detectors, and both fog and bubbles may leave a slippery film on the dance floor.

For more assistance with staying organized during the wedding planning process, check out the Bravo! Wedding Organizer. Detailed question worksheets double as contracts. This step-by-step system will keep every detail of your wedding organized. To order, refer to the order form on page 25 in this Guide.

A.A. TWO'S COMPANY DJ SERVICE

P.O. Box 68211 • Portland, Oregon 97268
Contact: Chris Tjaden
(503) 786-9090
E-mail: aatwosco@comcast.net

Type of Music

We supply your event with a wide range of music. You may choose from the '40s, '50s, '60s, '70s, '80s, '90s, big band, ballroom, jazz, country and Top 40. Our collection contains over 20,000 title songs, all on compact discs and mini discs. We play to you and your guests.

Demo and Equipment

Our equipment is state-of-the-art with a clean professional look. We will give you a full, high-quality sound at a level you want. Our lighting adds a special effect to your event. Upon request, we will mail you a promotional package, including photo, that will answer all of your questions.

Experience and Attire

With over 25 years experience in the entertainment industry, A.A. Two's Company knows what it takes to make your event a success. We always dress in appropriate attire for your occasion.

Cost and Terms

We prefer to speak with each client and ask a few questions about their plans for the event. We then describe our service and quote a price. A deposit is required with the signing of the agreement. As always with any special event, it is best to book as early as possible.

Special Services

We help coordinate all the events during your wedding reception. We will make any special announcements during the event. Our cordless microphone is always available to you and your guests. Special requests are always welcome before and during the event. For the adventurous group, we are happy to get out on the dance floor and teach your guests the "Macarena", "Electric Slide" or even the "Octoberfest Chicken Dance."

QUALITY SERVICE IS OUR GOAL

A.A. Two's Company is a unique husband-and-wife team who pride themselves on providing quality service. We feel every event deserves our focused attention, so we only book one event per day. Our goal is to make your event a total musical success.

A DANCING PENGUIN MUSIC

LIVE MUSIC & DJ

LIVE PIANO WITH A DJ WILL MAKE YOUR EVENT SPECIAL!

(503) 282-3421

A Dancing Penguin Music owner, Kim Ralphs, is a professional pianist and DJ with over 15 years of experience entertaining Northwest audiences. His company is very well known and respected in Portland. This outstanding reputation was built with great customer service and attention to detail. He listens to you!

Playing the right song at the right time keeps the dance floor full and your guests happy. Swing, rock, disco, 80s, 90s, top 40, country, or jazz…It's up to you!

You'll have total control of music style and volume.

You'll hear your favorites and special requests, always.

Master of ceremonies and help coordinating your event are included.

Black tuxedo is standard attire.

Ceremony music a specialty.

Also available: electric piano, sax, flute, guitar, drums and vocalists.

LISTEN TO WHAT THE PROFESSIONALS SAY:

"Kim plays here often, and always does a great job…highly recommended."
Susan O'Neil, **Waverley Country Club**

"Kim is a fine pianist…and I always enjoy seeing him here."
Dennis Yamnitsky, F&B Manager, **Oswego Lake Country Club**

"Whenever I need a DJ, A Dancing Penguin Music is the first company I call."
Nancy Tice, **Northwest Artist Management**

"I've recommended Dancing Penguin Music for years. Real professionals."
Diane Parke, event planner, **Occasions Etc. Inc.**

"Kim's piano and DJ combination really adds a touch of class to your event."
Charlotte Seybold, event planner, **Special Occasion Consulting**

Call for a free consultation and demo tape!

Kimberly Fogg
Professional DJ/MC, Line dance instructor, vocalist
Wedding Specialist
Office: (503) 997-3357 / aplusmobilemusic@comcast.net
aplusmobilemusic.com

Here are what customers say!
"You were great at getting people up and dancing. (Not too much, not too little.) Everyone said they had a blast at the reception and we attribute these compliments to your excellent services! I would recommend you to everyone I know." – Mr. & Mrs. Peter & Genifer Grout

"You did an extraordinary job, everyone thought that you were wonderful and said we threw the 'party of the century' and it was all because of the entertainment you provided!"
– Mr. & Mrs. Jason and Kirsten Beijer

I only use quality **professional rack mounted equipment** in a clean stand-alone unit. Additional equipment is available for indoor/outdoor events any size. This system can deliver an incredible sound at background and dance levels. Backup equipment is always available at all events.

The first three special dance songs are **guaranteed** at receptions. If it isn't in my collection of a 9,450 song-list, I will purchase it at no additional cost to you! Shouldn't a DJ have the music you want? I think so. An **extensive music library and knowledge** goes beyond the "normal play list." Titles include blues, jazz, Latin, Hawaiian, Irish, German and Armenian.

My book of recommendations from past clients and other wedding professionals proves that I have held true to my personal and professional values. **No hype advertising /sales**, *only* honest, fair, detailed service with a straightforward contract.

Services:
*Ceremony Services *Coordination Services, *Master of Ceremonies, *Professional* Disc Jockey, *Karaoke (**Intelligent lighting**, fog machines, bubble machine, props, games and a quality cordless microphone is offered at **no extra cost to you!**)

Twelve years of experience Disc Jockeying private parties and in some of the largest clubs in Portland. Continual learning keeps our show fresh and on the cutting edge. This is **not** a hobby, but a full time job I take very seriously.

Vocalist services and Dance Instruction are available. Ten years of vocal training and performing around Portland and Nevada. Learn to dance the smooth Waltz or Nightclub Two-Step to your first dance and look like you've been dancing together for years.

A+ Mobile Music would be happy to meet with you for a **free no obligation consultation**. It's important to meet any DJ before you book a date. To ensure you get top-notch quality, **all meetings and performances are done by Kimberly Fogg and only one event is booked a day.**

All your hard work and planning will come down to one day... your wedding day. This day is too important to let just any DJ be in charge. As a full time Professional DJ, I guarantee you'll get just that, a Professional. As your DJ, I interact with your guests, encourage requests, and provide classy yet fun entertainment for the whole family. I understand and gladly accept the responsibility because I treat every reception as if it were my very own!

A **ound Choice** ENTERTAINMENT
Professional DJs
Digital Photo Montages

Anthony Wedin Productions, Inc.

1665 Edgewater Court • West Linn, OR 97068
Phone: (503) 557-8554
Fax: (503) 742-1302
Web sites: awpdj.com
sayIdo.com
bravowedding.com

How to Pick a Professional Disc Jockey?

Anyone can make promises on a page. To ensure you are hiring a professional DJ service ask your other wedding professionals for a DJ referral. Remember photographers, videographers and caterers work with good and bad DJs every weekend. **A Sound Choice Entertainment** professional staff will provide great service, quality entertainment and MC your special day. **Just ask your wedding professionals about the proven quality of A Sound Choice Entertainment & Anthony Wedin Productions.**

Experience

Wedding DJ experience has a lot to do with the success of your event. Wedding DJs and radio DJs are not one in the same. Just because a person has a lot of radio experience does not make them a good wedding DJ. Knowing how to read the crowd, coordinate your event and keep the attention on the bride and groom are some aspects that can only be learned from hands on experience. **ASC** staff members are experienced professionals and will always strive to go above and beyond your expectations.

Master of Ceremonies

The DJ you hire should also be the master of ceremonies for your wedding reception. The right personality is needed to keep the event professional yet comfortable enough to put people at ease. Remember playing dance music is only a quarter of the duties of the DJ. The ability of your DJ to work with others and translate information to you and your guests over the mic will leave a lasting impression on the success of your day.

Why A Sound Choice Entertainment?

• 15 years of experience
• Professionalism and attention to detail
• Ask other wedding professionals
• We enjoy what we do for a living

Photo Montage Presentations and Related Services

ASC can compose a photo montage presentation for your reception that will be the envy of all, and create a lasting and unforgettable memory. The presentation is shown live at your reception and you are given a copy on DVD to cherish through the years. All equipment is included in the price of the show. **ASC** can also supply the music for your ceremony. If you would like a consultation regarding any of the above services please feel free to call us.

Music

Any professional DJ service will provide a wide variety of musical selections for your special day. When you bring different age groups and backgrounds of people together you need to have a vast selection of music to please all tastes. **ASC** also lets you bring your special music to the event if needed. **ASC** provides a song list so you can pick out your favorite dance music months before your wedding.

Absolutely ONLY
Big Mo Productions

Contact: Mel "Big Mo" O'Brien
503-936-9469 Portland Metro
888-449-5099 National Toll Free
Web site: www.OregonDJ.com
E-mail: melobrien@harborside.com

Type of Music

Big Mo Productions offers a massive music library of DANCEABLE, FUN and ROMANTIC reception music for ALL ages and musical tastes: all eras and music types, from 1920s Jazz and Big Band (and before) to the CURRENT HITS (music with explicit words or profanity will not be played). You choose from over 100,000 titles and 30 styles of music to be played at your ceremony and reception that meet YOUR NEEDS and DESIRES. We know YOU are the STARs, not the DJ.

Equipment

Only state-of-the-art Digital Professional Equipment and Concert Quality Speakers.

Experience and Attire

Recommended by many reception facilities. Tuxedo; or as you request. Big Mo will send you more client and reception (venue) site references than you would probably ever want. If you book with *Absolutely ONLY Big Mo Productions*, "Big Mo" will be your DJ/MC/Music Host, providing wedding reception DJ/MC/Music Host services for over a decade, specializing in receptions that are romantic, fun and have a touch of panache.

Here are a few SAMPLES of what our clients have written about our services:
- "You [Big Mo] weren't the least, nor the most expensive DJ… but you are the BEST !"
- "Everybody loved your music for all tastes, EVEN my new mother-in-law. There were guests dancing who I never thought danced. It was fun watching my great-grandparents dance too."
- "Quality was EXCELLENT. Service was EXCELLENT. Fun factor was A++."
- "Thank you [Big Mo]. You were right, 'The music was the most important part of our reception.' You [Big Mo] helped make OUR DAY romantic and fun."

Cost and Terms

No travel, setup or breakdown time charges. No hidden costs, no surprises. No extra charge, or "up charge" for ceremonies at the same site other than total time. Booking deposit required to reserve your date. Credit/Debit Cards and Internet payments welcomed. Special non-Saturday, Spring, Fall and Winter minimums and rates. Ask for our complimentary CD-ROM.

Special Services

- Internet download of our promotional packet (references, special offers and music lists) is available, if your server allows downloads; or by MAIL.
- Our solid "NO WORRY" policy for our clients; assisting you with any concerns about ANY aspect of your reception. On-line wedding professional consultation, referrals, advice and suggestions to help make your day that SPECIAL DAY you will always fondly remember and WANT to recount to YOUR grand children in the DISTANT future.

Disc Jockey and Videography
(503) 408-7857
www.aamdjs.com   info@aamdjs.com

Premiere Service: All our music packages include a two-person DJ team to provide complete services one person cannot accomplish alone. Our packages come standard with four-speaker sound; our full music selection of over 7,500 songs; emcee services; audience interaction; dance instruction; a cordless hand-held microphone for guest use and props for your party.

Planning Ahead: We focus on you and your needs individually. Wedding planning can be complicated, so we are available to you for assistance **anytime**. Ask our customers, Dan and Linda Stoica, "You treated our wedding with great precision and care, as if it was your own."

Quality Events: We specialize in AP — Audience Participation — by interacting with your crowd to get them dancing. We work with vendors and guests, acting as a coordinator to make sure your event flows well and we provide emcee services so that everyone is well informed throughout the event. For more animated crowds, we also teach group dancing.

Considering filming your wedding? Our videography service is first-rate; it provides you with a beautiful and entertaining memory of your special day that you can share with family and friends. There is a total bill reduction for packages including DJ and videography services.

Before you book a DJ... Anthony and I will be at your wedding! We are available for appointments and prefer to meet with you ahead of time, to establish a relationship with you. This is **your wedding** — we will customize our services to fit your needs. A 10-minute video presentation, recommendations and pictures are available at the appointment. We can provide you with many references from recent events. Call or e-mail us for available times. In the meantime, check out our web site for a full music list.

We look forward to hearing from you soon! — A & W

ALL AROUND MUSIC DJ SERVICE

Contact: Ed and Manina Scipio
(503) 659-3113 or (503) 317-4137
E-mail: allaroundmusic@msn.com

TYPE OF MUSIC
Our music library ranges from 40s to current, big band, piano, classical, country, ethnic, jazz, movie sound tracks and much more. Because every event we play is different, as well as the guests, we will work with you in selecting the best music to make your wedding a success. Requests from your guests are always welcome.

EQUIPMENT
We have state of-the-art equipment to accommodate any size facility. Our lighting system will give your event that touch of elegance and splash of fun you seek. We welcome the opportunity to meet with our clients for a demonstration. Our attire is always appropriate to the specific event.

EXPERIENCE
With over 20 years of experience in the music industry, we have the background you need to make your wedding a success. Upon request we can teach your guests the popular line dances such as the Macarena, Electric Slide and Cha Cha Slide, as well as involving the children in dances such as the Chicken Dance and Hokey Pokey.

SPECIAL SERVICES
We will help coordinate your wedding ceremony which, when possible, includes attending your rehearsal. We can make all announcements and also offer a mobile microphone for use by you and your guests. Using your selections, we will accent all the activities of your reception, from the cake cutting to the garter belt toss, with music.

COST AND TERMS
Once we have had an opportunity to speak with our client and determine their needs, we will quote a price. A deposit is required at the time you sign our agreement. We only book one event per day and this agreement reserves your date.

As the owners of All Around Music, we take a personal interest in your wedding being a COMPLETE MUSICAL SUCCESS. Our goal is to help your plans and dreams become a reality.

P.O. Box 3282
Portland, Oregon 97208
Contact: Eric Wright
(503) 635-1115
Web site:
www.allwrightmusic.com

All Wright Music!

We love music! AWM DJs mix music from every era—Big Band to '90s top dance hits. Our collection also includes ballroom, disco, club hits, Latin and Top 40. We send out a detailed questionnaire to find YOUR wants and needs because every reception is unique. We also encourage all guests to make requests.

Sound and Lighting

Our sound and lighting systems are custom-built in Portland. The systems are compact and detail-finished for professional appearance. Lighting systems are designed for each reception and are always included in the wedding package!

Experience

All Wright Music Disc Jockeys have performed at over 3,500 events. Weddings are our favorite because they are true celebrations! We have also performed at private celebrations for celebrities, including Kevin Costner and Sylvester Stallone. AWM has been flown all over the USA to create magical, festive receptions. Our résumé speaks for itself!

Cost and Terms

We speak with each client to find out the specific wishes and needs for their event. Please call me for a free personal consultation—brochures and information will always be mailed upon request.

Our Guests Have Spoken

"It has been over two years, and people still remember our reception as the best they've ever attended!"
—Mrs. R. Roake

"For the fifth year, you've made our annual event a true success! You are our 'Mr. Music!'"
—Julie Papen/Special Events, NIKE

"Thanks for the GREAT job! My daughter's night was truly memorable. Best wishes for success!"
—Governor Neil Goldschmidt

"Thank you for a fabulous evening! Our night was pure magic! Your music was outstanding!"
—Audrey Stewart, *Bridal Magazine*

It is your day!
Let us help you turn your reception into
a party of elegance, excitement, and lots of fun!

"FOR ALL YOUR MUSICAL NEEDS"
Live Music & DJ

503-543-SONG (7664)
bart@bartpro.com • www.bartpro.com
Live piano adds that extra touch of class to your event!

"Hey, I just wanted to say a big Thank You for everything you did for us on our wedding day. You handled the pre-ceremony music w/o any issues and very little guidance from us. The piano music during the cocktail hour was fantastic!!! and you guys were wonderful during the reception. The pictures of people dancing are so great and everybody tells me they had such a good time." —Quote from a bride

Experience
Bartholomew Productions owner, Bart Hafeman, is a professional pianist and DJ with 17 years experience in northwest entertainment. His company specializes in custom music packages to make your event special. With countless songs from all eras our DJ,s are always appropriate and musical style and volume are always in your control. Our DJs are available at any time to make announcements at your event.

Types of Music
Because each event is special and unique, we listen and cater to your needs. We have songs from all eras and all styles and have a full DJ catalog for clients to view upon request.

Options
Bartholomew Productions also offer vocalists, saxophonists, classical guitarists, and full bands. We have four distinct bands available for hire for your event, Jazz combos playing classic standards, 70s disco, 80s, and Variety Bands playing songs from the 50s to current hits.

Equipment
We have many state-of-the-art sound systems for different size rooms. With Bartholomew Productions you'll always get the right system for the venue size and acoustics. Lighting and wireless mics are available upon special request.

Cost and Terms
Because each event is different and unique, each event price is quoted accordingly. Black Tux is standard attire with Bartholomew Productions. Your DJ will arrive at least one hour prior to the event for set up. All we require is a standard 6-ft. table and one electrical outlet. We have piano music demos and full DJ catalogs available to download off our web site at www.bartpro.com. We will also be happy to mail out a cd and brochure upon request. Call or email today for a free consultation on your event.

Partial Client List Includes
Abernathy Center Gardens • Adrianna Ballroom • Beckonridge Winery • David Hill Winery Willamette Gables • Bridal Veil Lakes • Settlemier Mansion • East Moreland Golf Course Timberline Lodge • Governor Hotel • Portland's White House • University Club • Hilton Hotel Benson Hotel • Mt Hood Community College • Hotel Vintage Plaza • Kell's Irish Pub Portland Convention Center • Rose Festival • Seattle Center • Celebrity Auctions The Wedding House • Seattle Sheraton • Heathman Hotel • Marriott Hotel • Alcove Vineyards

Blue Box Productions

An "Audio Entertainment Experience!"

(503) 706-8420 or (888) 587-3737
Web site: www.blueboxprod.com
Email: sales@blueboxprod.com

Type of Music

Blue Box Productions offers an extensive music library which allows us to play what you and your guests want to hear. Select as much of the music as you like, or let us select music appropriate for your event. Feel free to bring your own CDs, and of course we take requests.

Attire

We always dress appropriately for your event. Generally, this means a dress shirt and tie, but we will wear a tuxedo or theme attire if you prefer.

Equipment

Blue Box Productions uses only top quality, professional gear. Our speakers are concert grade. You can hear the difference!

Cost and Terms

Because each event is different, we provide custom quotes. Call today for your customized quote, or to schedule a no-obligation consultation. Credit cards are welcome. A contract and deposit reserve your date.

Options

Whether your event is indoors or outdoors, 50 guests or 2000, whether you need music for just the reception - or ceremony too, we have an audio system and entertainment solution for you. With our state-of-the-art projection system, guests can be treated to a digital photo slideshow, home movies, and music videos. To set the right mood, or to help motivate your guests to get on the dance floor, add one of our exciting lighting packages – starting at just $50. Dance Floor lighting packages may include sound-reactive lights, intelligent lighting, lasers, fog and more.

Why Choose Blue Box Productions?

We send two people to every event – a DJ and an assistant, which allows for a smoother show! We will act as Master of Ceremonies for your event, which means we will make announcements at the appropriate times and keep the event moving on schedule. We are happy to meet with you in advance to help make every detail of your event perfect. Choose Blue Box Productions – the quality you deserve!

CHAD DOWLING PRODUCTIONS

P.O. Box 16172 • Portland, OR 97292-0172
Contact: Chad Dowling (503) 320-0895
Email: DowlingChad@Hotmail.com
www.chaddowling.biz

"At last I found the perfect DJ!"

Type of Music
What a selection of music! You'll feel like a kid in a candy store when you feast your eyes on my song list. I maintain such a huge inventory to be sure I can give you exactly the music YOU want to hear. Yes, I play requests. Prepare yourself for a wonderful evening!

Equipment
Wait until you hear one of my sound systems in action! I use a professional digital sound system for a clearer sound at any volume. To add to that personal touch, I will utilize a wireless microphone for interacting with your guests during the best man's toast, cake cutting and on the dance floor. If you would like to add color and style to your wedding, try one of my deluxe lighting packages. My light systems are extremely compact and bring a special ambience to any size room or venue.

Experience
I have over 14 years of DJ experience on the radio and in the mobile DJ field. I have also taught professional mobile DJ/MCs throughout the Northwest, to know your target audiences and understand each event is special. You as my client, invest a lot of time and money to show your guests a great time! Cutting corners on entertainment can break an event. I focus on only the level of interaction which you, my client, requests resulting in guaranteed success.

Cost and Terms
Please call for pricing information and availability of my reception packages for your special day. I offer many options, including bubble & snow machines, party favors, confetti cannons, karaoke, exciting lighting packages, ceremony music and extra hours of dance music. A $100 deposit and a signed contract are needed to reserve your date.

Special Services
When you reserve Chad Dowling Productions for your wedding day, you are guaranteed to get me, Chad Dowling as your DJ, in a tuxedo. I specialize in personalized service. I work with you on the important musical details of your wedding. I'm not only the DJ, but I'm also the Master of Ceremonies, Event Planner and a Coordinator. I handle all your announcements, from the introduction of the bride and groom, the bridal party, the first dance and more! I make sure you and your guests are well informed of the events to come. Consultations and wedding planning worksheets are free.

Setting and Requirements
I arrive an hour and half prior to the start of the event for set up. All that is required is one standard six foot banquet table, skirting if available, one 110 electrical outlet and a 8x6-ft. space. I am committed to Excellence! I am committed to Customer Service! I am committed to you!

CLUB BEAT MUSIC MOBILE DJ SERVICE
STARRING "ROCK-ON-DON"
WWW.CLUBBEATDJS.COM
503.810.6710

TYPE OF MUSIC
50s, 60s, disco 70s, 80s, 90s pop, rock-n-roll, swing, rap, basically a little of everything….

EQUIPMENT
Digital state-of-the-art Pro DJ High Quality, whether your party is 100 or 2000 we can handle it!

ATTIRE
Standard attire is white shirt and a tie; we don't want to look like the groom. It's your special day!

COST
Our show starts at $299 for 3 hours. Additional hours are $70/hour and karaoke is only $125. Extra lights are $75 and extra speakers are $75/box.

EXPERIENCE
I have been doing weddings around the state for over 15 years.

SPECIAL SERVICES
We meet with each client before a show to go over the special day!

TESTIMONIALS

Dear Don,
Thanks for being a part of what will be one of the most memorable days of our lives together.
—Scott and Shauna

Dear Don,
Thanks for the great music selection at our reception. Thanks for your services.

Sincerely,
Rachel and Josh

Dear Don,
Thanks for providing the most imporatnt part at our teen Halloween Party.

Sincerely, Susan Labhart
Shriners Hospital

Decades Mobile Music

6312 N. Willamette Lane
Portland, Oregon 97203
Contact: Brian Darby or Loretta Korsun
(503) 283-4886 or (503) 515-2571
E-mail: decadesmobilemusic@comcast.net

Type of Music

The act of celebration has been associated with dancing since the dawn of time. When you invite Decades Mobile Music to your event, you and your guests can relax and celebrate as we play favorites for everyone— from the youngsters to the young-at-heart. We stock popular dance music and Top 40 for every decade: from the '40s, '50s, '60s, '70s, '80s, and '90s and beyond.

We will also act as Master of Ceremonies, if you request, so that every part of your special event flows smoothly.

Song List and Equipment

We provide a song list to help you select your favorite music. Our equipment is the latest professional gear, and all recordings are on compact disk. This assures the clarity that makes music enjoyable at any volume level you and your guests prefer.

Experience and Attire

Others talk… WE LISTEN! Our Event Coordinator is at each engagement to ensure smooth flow and good communication between the host, guests and DJ. We tailor our services to meet your specific needs; your agenda is ours. Our skilled people and people skills make the difference.

In addition to drawing on a great depth of knowledge for appropriate music selections, our DJs will play dedications and requests. Can't remember the name?… hum a few bars! Our Event Coordinator will make announcements, pick up requests, respond to schedule changes, and keep the party going!

Attire is normally a jacket and tie. We are happy to wear whatever is appropriate for your event.

Cost and Terms

A three-hour show starts at $350. A $100 deposit is required. Additional hours are $75. Lighting and props can be added to make your event more memorable. Special music requests, made in advance, are always free. You are given a written agreement to assure that our services will match your expectations.

Our Customers Say it Best

"…the dancing was a great part of the wedding!!"

"…our dance was a '10' rating"

"…you got them to dance!!!"

A Party in Every Package

Professional...Experienced...Recommended...

503.295.2212
WWW.DEEJAYENTERTAINMENT.COM
SPECIALIZING IN WEDDINGS

Type of Music
DeeJay Entertainment can play a wide variety of music at your special event, including Top 40, Country, 70s/80s Retro, Classic Rock and Oldies. Every crowd is different and every event is unique. DeeJay Entertainment reacts with the appropriate selections every time.

Experience
DeeJay Entertainment is fortunate to represent some of the most experienced and professional disc jockeys available in the Portland Metro area. Our dedicated and professional entertainers take pride in the success of each and every event. DeeJay Entertainment is owned and operated by radio stations: Z100, K103, 105.9 The River, 1190 KEX and 620 KTLK. Our relationship with these stations brings a higher level of credibility and professionalism to our performances. You can feel confident when you choose us to play your next event.

Demo
The most complete information is available on our web site, **www.deejayentertainment.com.** In addition to packages and rates, you will also find a sample song list and comments from customers who have used our service.

Costs and Terms
Each package is designed to give you exactly what you are looking for from your DJ. DeeJay Entertainment wedding packages include the DJ, a state-of-the-art sound system and a cordless microphone. Rates start as low as $295. We can also provide music at your wedding ceremony.

PROFESSIONAL...

EXPERIENCED...

RECOMMENDED...

Most of the events scheduled with DeeJay Entertainment are referrals, so we encourage you to check on availability as soon as you have set a date. We invite you to call with questions or schedule an appointment with one of our representatives.

DW DUO

Contact: Dawn Grishow
(503) 642-9509
Web site: www.dwduo.com

The elegance of live music…or the variety of a deejay?
Now you can have both!

Wedding ceremony to reception, DW Duo has the flexibility to make your day unique and special. Here's one example of how your reception could be set up…
The first part of the celebration would consist of LIVE MUSIC!
1. Guests arrive to classical guitar, solo piano and harp.
2. Hors D'ouerves and meal — progress to standards, smooth jazz and bossa novas.
3. First Dance — romantic lighting effects, special musical selections performed LIVE or on CD.
4. Then…smoothly merge into CD DANCE MUSIC!

Experience

Dawn started singing and playing at 14 years of age. She studied communications and has had eight years of experience in the Hollywood film industry, providing her with knowledge in lighting, sound and set decorating.

William, is an accomplished multi-instrumentalist and can perform anything from classical guitar, piano, harp, and cello to bagpipes for your special day! He has played for numerous theater productions and is a seasoned recording and performing artist who has just released a CD of 15th century classical guitar.

Dawn and William

Experienced, versatile and always professional. They are fun to dance to, listen to and to be around. The blending of talents, knowledge of songs from decades of popular music, quality compact discs, along with the latest in state-of-the-art equipment, guarantees your guests will really enjoy themselves!

Cost and Terms

Rates are very competitive and based on your personal event and structure. For booking information, Demo CD, prices, referrals and options available, please call (503) 642-9509 or visit our web site at www.dwduo.com.

"We love what we do…we do what we love."
When it's time to celebrate…DW Duo!

See page 395 under Musicians.

4306 NE Sandy Blvd. • Portland, OR 97213 • (503)249-0144

Why Go With Elite Events?

We believe that you won't find any other company around that is as excited as much we are about your special day. We can't wait to meet with you and your fiancé to make every detail of your wedding perfect. Our customer feedback says it best:

"Dear Elite Events,

Thank you very much for working our reception. The music was great and your involvement with the crowd was just right. It was great that you could do this on such short notice, too. We will pass your name on to others for their events.

Sincerely, Chris Rianda"

Cost and Terms

At Elite Events our packages start at only $450 for four hours. Want to add lights? It's only $100 more to add a full, elegant dance floor setup! Extra hours are always available to pre-book or on the day of your special event. Call today for your quote!

Type of Music

What don't we have? You'll find just about every hit past and present located in our extensive music library. Of course you can select as much of the music as you like, or let us take care of it. You won't have to be shy about bringing your own selections of music out either, we'd love to play it!

Experienced M.C.s

From your entrance into the room, to your bouquet toss, to your first dance, every Elite Events' Mobile Jockey has the ability to M.C. and coordinate your entire reception. Our team of professionals has over 20 years combined experience to help your ceremony or reception run smoothly. Remember playing the music is only part of the job — we also come dressed to your expectations!

Equipment

All of our equipment is state of the art, Pro gear. By staying abreast of the latest in technology, we are proud to state that all of our equipment is under two years old. We take great pride in the way your wedding sounds.

Portland, Oregon
(503) 255-8047
Disc Jockey • Photography • Videography

Web site: www.encore-studios.com

BOOK PHOTO & VIDEO AND RECEIVE
DISC JOCKEY SERVICES FREE!
*Certain restrictions apply.

We'll coordinate your reception for you! Music sets the mood for any occasion and is particularly important during your ceremony or wedding reception. Whether you need disc jockeys or musicians, let us assist you in providing the music you want for your wedding ceremony and/or reception.

Type of Music
For your listening pleasure and convenience, we provide music of all styles and have an extensive library of music from the 20s to the present including: Top 40, Country, Jazz, Classical, Rock 'n' Roll, Motown, Rhythm & Blues, Swing, Ballroom, Big Band, Latin, Hawaiian, Rap, Reggae, Disco, Hip Hop and Ethnic. Your favorites are always welcome!

Equipment and Demo
We have state-of-the-art mobile equipment which sets up quickly in a 6' x 6' area with a standard 110-volt outlet. You are welcome to a private or live viewing.

Experience and Attire
With over 20 years of experience, you are assured of knowledgeable service with our professional disc jockeys. We are not only disc jockeys but masters of ceremony as well, ensuring your wedding runs smoothly and successfully. We play the music you want to hear, and our packages are designed for every budget and musical preference. Casual or theme attire, tuxedos or suits and ties are available.

Cost and Terms
Wedding music packages start at $150. Please call for pricing for your specific needs. Ceremony and/or reception music. Visa, MasterCard and Discover welcome with no interest applied.

Special Services
Special lighting, strobes, spots, mirror balls, ropes, and fog available for special effects.
    Should you prefer live music for your entertainment needs, please ask one of our consultants for assistance.

**Please call for an appointment to view our DJs live
and to see our extensive music library.**

Please also see us under Photographers on page 509.

360-576-6589 • 877-2-Get-A-DJ toll free
email: eventinfo@hifidjs.com • www.hifidjs.com

Professional DJ and Entertainment Services

Type of Music

High Fidelity Music Catering offers a wide variety of music from all eras and styles, including rock, country, alternative, rap, disco, Top 40, swing, jazz, classical, Latin and ethnic. You decide what type of music you want, including specific requests, or let our professional DJ select music that will delight your guests. With over 10,000 songs to choose from, High Fidelity Music Catering has something for everyone.

Other Services

High Fidelity Music Catering offers much more than music — we provide custom-designed entertainment that will keep your guests lively and engaged throughout your event. You may choose any combination of extras to create a total entertainment package:

- Lighting
- Special Effects
- Fog Machines
- Line Dancing
- Karaoke
- Interactive Games

High Fidelity Music Catering caters to your needs, and your consultation and event planning are always complimentary.

Wedding Planning

High Fidelity Music Catering also has years of experience in planning memorable, meaningful weddings. Please call us for a complimentary wedding planning guide and to schedule a free consultation regarding our wedding and event planning services.

Experience

With over 15 years of experience providing entertainment to hundreds of wedding ceremonies, receptions, class reunions, school dances, work parties, holiday celebrations and outdoor events, you can count on High Fidelity Music Catering to provide professional, complete entertainment that is perfectly suited to your guests and your ideas for the event. References are available upon request.

Cost

Since our services are always custom-designed for each event, we need specific information to help us provide you with an accurate cost quote. Our rates are very competitive, and your consultation costs nothing.

Call High Fidelity Music Catering today for a free consultation!

Member of Vancouver Chamber of Commerce
American Disc Jockey Association

Portland 503-222-6476
Eugene 541-914-2815
Toll Free 1-866-531-5047
Fax 541-465-9528 (call first)
www.jtmproductions.com

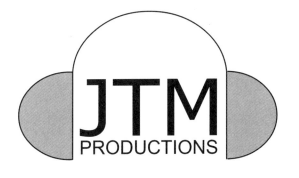

About Us
Expect only the best from JTM Productions, an innovative leader of the mobile disc jockey industry. It is our goal to provide the absolute highest quality service possible. Our-state-of-the-art sound systems deliver, and our fantastic light show will dazzle you. We have been serving your community for over 20 years. Our experienced 11 member DJ staff includes just the right DJ personality for you!

Music
Our music library is contains over 25,000 songs. We have music from the 1920s to today's top hits. Browse our selection online at www.jtmproductions.com. We unconditionally guarantee that all requests submitted online at least two weeks prior to the event will be available.

Equipment
We can accommodate parties of all sizes, indoors or outdoors. We use only rack mounted or freestanding professional JBL and Peavey sound systems. This equipment is designed to minimize visual impact. Linen tablecloths are used to hide wires at the DJ's table. Our speakers are new and without scratches, dents or dings. All wires are taped down for your safety.

Cost and Terms
Wedding packages cost $595 for the Portland/Vancouver area and $495 for Salem and other areas. Booking requires a $100 non-refundable deposit and a completed, signed contract. The package includes four hours of DJ mixed music and is designed to have everything you need. Microphone, light package and a fogger are included free of charge. Travel cost and other options may however increase the cost of your event.

Special Services
We offer free consultations and event planning. Upon request our DJs can act as your master of ceremonies. Leave the talking to the experts!

Our interactive web site is powered by a custom built DJ Intelligence engine. You can use the engine to search our online music database of over 25,000 songs, check for availability, get a quote and even book your show.

MOBILE MUSIC ENTERTAINMENT SERVICES

Since 1978

Professional DJ Services...

Contact: David Efaw
Office (503) 638-0624, Fax (503) 638-0625
Visit our Web site: www.mobilemusicentertainment.com

Now serving Salem Area and the Willamette Valley
Salem (503) 380-6319

Type of Music

Mobile Music has over 300 hours of music we bring to each event. Music selection ranges from big band, '50s, '60s, '70s, '80s, country, Top 40, rock, and jazz. We always play the music you want, and of course we play requests.

Equipment

The sound systems Mobile Music uses are custom built for mobile use. You won't find any home gear in our systems. The systems are compact and can be set up in 20 minutes. We do have larger setups for functions up to 3,000 people.

Experience

Mobile Music has been in business since 1978. We provide music and entertainment at over 1,000 events each year. We base our business on providing friendly, professional service to our clients. What you want comes first with us.

Cost and Terms

The basic package starts at $400 for three hours and $100 for each additional hour. Mobile Music also has light shows and other special effects available for rent. A 20% deposit and a signed contract hold your date for you.

Corporate Events

For corporate events, Mobile Music has a wide variety of activities, including **karaoke, casino games, contests and games**—all hosted by a professional master of ceremonies. Please call for more information and rates on packages.

Special Services

Mobile Music uses only professional mobile disc jockeys and club DJs from around the Portland area. Whether you want a life-of-the-party DJ or just music, we have the disc jockey for your event.

Setting and Requirements

The standard setup requires a 10' x 4' space. Larger systems and lights require additional space. A 110-volt AC outlet is needed for power.

MUSIC THE WAY YOU WANT IT

We at Mobile Music pride ourselves on providing quality music the way you want it played. We use only professional disc jockeys with experience, who will help make your event everything you want it to be. If you have any questions or special requirements, feel free to call.

David Efaw

$\mathcal{NOTE}$ $\mathcal{WORTHY}$ $\mathcal{MUSIC}$

3921 N.E. 135th
Portland, Oregon 97230
Contact: John Mears (503) 258-1258

Types of Music

At Note Worthy Music we offer the music you want—and at a price that is affordable. We draw from any era of music that you desire! Whether you want Big Band, jazz, country, classic rock or Top 40, we will meet your needs. Because this is your event we will do everything to make it special. Our disc jockeys will meet with you to discuss any special needs.

Equipment

Note Worthy Music uses top of the line equipment to provide you with crystal clear music from our vast CD collection. Music volume is constantly monitored for your listening pleasure.

Services

Our disc jockeys will serve as your master of ceremonies if you desire and will dress according to your theme. With 15 years in the music industry, we will help make your special day a truly wonderful experience.

To enhance your special day we usually have soft background music provided as your guests enter your reception. As the party progresses we will announce special moments such as cutting of the cake, throwing of the bridal bouquet, shooting of the garter and the couple's first dance. As the reception continues the music is constantly monitored for both volume and style that you desire. From soft jazz to rock 'n' roll, it's all for you!

Our disc jockey services are provided for either indoors or outdoors. All that is needed is a standard wall plug and one banquet table.

Satisfied Customers are Saying

"Thank you for making our 50th wedding anniversary party such a wonderful occasion. Everyone enjoyed your musical selections which made for great dancing as well."
~Jo and Slats Austin, Forestry Center

"Thank you for the great music at Bob's birthday, and for the music you have provided for our Optimist dances. Everyone always enjoys your wide selection of music."
~Adele Hemstreet, President, The Optimist Club of Lloyd Center

"Our wedding would not have been the same without your services—Thanks again!"
~Robert Heinrich

"John, not only were you easy to work with but very accommodating to all our special needs for our wedding reception."
~Shelly Vanness

BRAVO! SPECIAL **$75 off**
Three hours for $300
$50 each additional hour

Mobile Disc Jockey Services
1332 S.E. Carlton
Portland, Oregon 97202
Contact: Earl Forster, Owner
(503) 235-2743
E-mail: OmegaAudio@aol.com

"Earl really plays to the crowd, knows how to get them on the dance floor and is great about making sure everyone is having a good time. I have been to a lot of different events that had DJs doing the music and Omega Audio is by far the most impressive." – Susan Harney

Experience

Omega Audio has been providing reasonably priced, top quality mobile music and lighting services for over 22 years. Our disc jockeys are professional in both attitude and appearance. We are ready to work with you to ensure that your event is everything you want it to be.

Type of Music

Omega Audio brings a tremendous selection of the most loved songs in America to your event. From hits of the '20s right up to today's chart-busters, we play the music you want to hear. Requests from your guests are always welcome, and our disc jockeys are happy to act as master of ceremonies.

Equipment

Our disc jockeys use systems with professional grade equipment to provide a state-of-the-art experience. We have sound systems to suit whatever size room your event requires. Thinking about an outdoor event? Not a problem for Omega Audio.

Special Services

We can bring any room to life with lighting and special effects such as intelligent lighting, mirror balls, strobes, fog and much more. For added excitement, we have **Karaoke, Dance Lessons, and Casino Gaming,** as well as outdoor inflatable games for kids and adults.

Cost and Terms

Packages start at $450 for four hours of uninterrupted music; no charge for set-up time. The rate for each additional hour is $100. A minimum deposit of $100 is required upon signing the contract. Be sure to reserve your date as far in advance as possible—it's never too soon to hire the best.

Everything you choose for your wedding day is a reflection of your dreams.
We at Omega Audio would like to make those dreams come true!

Pacific NW Sound

OREGON - WASHINGTON

(503) 652-1509   (503) 709-0724

pacificnwsound@msn.com

Elegant • Memorable • Classy

Why Pacific Northwest Sound?

Music and entertainment are the most important factors in the success of any event. When you choose Pacific Northwest Sound, you get more than a DJ, you get our experience, quality and professionalism. We are actively involved before, during and after your event, which is why we stand by our reputation as "the best in the business."

Professional

When you choose Pacific Northwest Sound, you are guaranteed to get a personable and professional disc jockey who will arrive promptly with state of the art sound an lighting equipment. We take personal care of your event and work closely with you and your coordinator, making sure everything goes as planned so you can relax and enjoy your day.

Vendor Research

Pacific Northwest Sound will gladly provide information about possible vendors for your event. These include facilities, limousine services, photographers, videographers, florists and tent rental services.

Services We Offer

- Latin weddings
- Ceremony music
- Professional event coordination

Experience you can trust

503.331.9195
Toll-Free   866.530.1110
www.prodjsoregon.com

Your wedding is one day
The memory is a lifetime

What will you remember most about your wedding? *The food? The flowers?* Maybe. However, our memories are emotional. Most likely, you will remember how much fun you had, or how stressed out you were. This places more importance on the DJ. A good job is a pleasant memory. A bad job is not so pleasant, and there is no second chance.

PRO DJs is the only mobile DJ service with a Satisfaction Guarantee

What does this mean?

- References upon request

- The most experienced group of DJs in the Portland-area. You will have immediate and unlimited communication with your DJ to make you feel comfortable and confident about your wedding

- We always take requests. You will also love how easy it is to prepare for your wedding with our on-line planner

- One package – one rate. We won't charge you extra for lights, or a cordless microphone – everything is included

Visit our website today for a complete list of what we do to ensure your wedding is a success; www.prodjsoregon.com

One additional hour FREE!

Contact us today and mention you found us in the Bravo Wedding Guide or through the Bravo website and we will give you one additional hour FREE when you schedule your wedding with PRO DJs

RICH'S PORT-A-PARTY
QUALITY MOBILE DISC JOCKEY
SERVICE

Contact: Vicki and Rich (503) 621-3074
E-Mail: vrmay5355@aol.com

A wedding reception is more than just playing music. It's important to have a disc jockey who has experience performing at weddings. We will handle all of your announcement needs, and we will work with your coordinator to keep your event on schedule by coordinating the toast, cake cutting ceremony, couples first dance, bouquet toss, etc. It's our job to make this a very memorable day for you and your guests.

EXPERIENCE
Providing quality entertainment for over 10 years. Our goal is to provide you with professional equipment , attire and service for your wedding reception, rehearsal dinner, reunion, holiday parties, birthday and anniversary celebrations, company picnics, retirement dinners, corporate functions or community events. * References available upon request

MUSIC LIBRARY
We Specialize in Country and Vintage Rock & Roll. Our CD Library contains over10,000 songs from the 1950's through today's top hits. Classic Country, New Country, Big Band, Easy Listening, '50s & '60s, '70s & '80s , etc. We can format your own personal requests. If we don't have your song we will get it.

RATES
$300 minimum (up to 3 hours) includes set up time and travel. Each additional hour is $75. *additional mileage and travel fee for events more than 20 miles from downtown Portland. Custom packages for special events.

If you're looking for entertainment and the opportunity for socializing during your event, Country Dance Lessons are just the ticket.

RATES—$100 minimum (up to 1 hour) includes set up time and travel within 20-mile radius of downtown Portland. Each additional hour is $50 *additional fee for events more than 20 miles from downtown Portland.

CONTACT: Connie Jo Collins, CJ's Country Dance Instruction (360) 892-1406 or (503) 320-3545

Professional Shows for All Occasion

Extensive Musical Selections

SAILING ON PRODUCTIONS

5531 N.E. 66th Ave. • Vancouver, Washington 98662

Tel/Fax 360-694-1120 /Cell 360-608-0677

E-mail: rocky@rockyrhodes.com; Web site: www.sailingonproductions.com

Type of Music

With over 2,000 CDs and 25,000-plus karaoke songs, (over 11,000 in English and 14,000 in other languages), Rocky & Associates can provide music from all eras as well as ethnic music (i.e. Hispanic, Japanese, Hawaiian, Italian, Jewish, Greek, many other Asian languages, German, Irish, etc.). Theme shows are Rocky's specialty.

Equipment

With a state-of-the-art system, which includes special effects, sound and lighting, Rocky can cater your look and sound to be intimate or Vegas-style. Designed to fit in all settings with a look of class, professionalism is the word.

Experience

A Pacific Northwest tradition since 1983 and having performed nationally since the 1960s, Rocky brings years of experience to every event. Rocky has a resume and portfolio to prove why he can be versatile enough for birthdays, anniversaries, weddings, divorce parties (yes! I have played them), bar mitzvahs, bat mitzvahs, family gatherings, quinceaneras and corporate events.

Cost and Terms

A basic charge of $500 will give you up to five hours of entertainment with no extra charge for setup or travel, unless the event is outside the Portland/ Vancouver area. The distance will determine the travel fee. Any show for less than three hours can be negotiated. Overtime is $50 an hour. A 50% nonrefundable deposit is required in advance to hold the date and the cost includes all sound, lighting and karaoke.

Settings and Requirements

There is no setting too demanding for this show. The only needs are one electrical outlet (two would be beneficial), and a space of at least 8x10 ft.

Versatility

The uniqueness to Rocky's show is his versatility and one-on-one service to each client. No two shows are exactly alike, and the ability to adapt to each client's need has made him marketable worldwide. No request is too difficult, and if we don't have it, you can bring it to be played. Only the client's satisfaction is the main concern of Sailing On Productions.

For further details and/or booking arrangements, please contact
ROCKY RHODES at the above listed address and/or telephone numbers.
Online information also available.

STEELES MUSIC

503-830-5806
steelesmusic@teleport.com
www.steelesmusic.com

Steeles Music

Not all DJ's are the same! Wonderful memories are created when you match talent with experience. With over 9 years of experience we at Steeles Music create elegant, fun and unique wedding receptions regardless of your budget. We're not "Game Show Hosts" with cheesy personalities—we're professional entertainers.

Type of Music

Steeles Music has an extensive music library from every era. If we don't have it, we'll get it. Feel free to bring your own music and we'll play it.

Special Services

Steeles Music will act as master of ceremonies and help coordinate the entire reception from start to finish (unless you hired a wedding coordinator). We plan the itinerary with you and then provide the information to your photographer, videographer, catering manager and other event professionals that need to know the time schedule in advance. This allows you and your families the opportunity to truly enjoy your day without worrying about the minute details. We're there for you.

Cost and Terms

Steeles Music offers many different wedding packages. Rates start at $450.00 for a four-hour package. A $100 down payment is required at contract signing. Steeles Music will arrive at least an hour early to setup before your wedding. There are no charges for the setup and tear down of equipment.

We are here for you
www.steelesmusic.com

SUNRISE ENTERTAINMENT SERVICES
Music • Lighting • Karaoke • Video Projection Services

(503) 357-6699, (877) 710-1600
Fax (503) 357-2899, (877) 710-1800
1226 Emily Street
Forest Grove, OR 97116
E-mail: joe@sunrisedjs.com

Web site: www.sunrisedjs.com

Joe

Jeromy

About Sunrise Entertainment Services
Jeromy Reinhardt (longtime family friend), Nicole Burruss (my wife and office manager) and myself, Joe Burruss, are the owners. We have been in business for 7 years. We guarantee that you will get to meet Jeromy or myself and know in advance which one of us will be your DJ. Because we as DJs are also owners we have the highest level of passion and concern for your satisfaction. Jeromy and I have never been late, missed an event, or cancelled on one of our clients. Our client list includes movie stars, politicians, large corporations and many other satisfied clients. We gladly provide references upon request.

Consultation and Planning
We offer free consultations and would love to meet with you in person. We can meet with you at our office or at a location of your convenience. We listen to your needs then help you plan our level of interaction and attire. We can act as day coordinators and make any announcements that you would like. We also offer comprehensive online planning for your ceremony, reception and music selections.

Types of Music
We offer both ceremony and reception music, and virtually every hit from past to present. In addition to all of the hits you would normally expect we also offer underground favorites and cultural music, including Jewish, Hawaiian, Jawaiian (Hawaiian reggae) and almost every type of Latin music imaginable.

Equipment
We offer sound, lighting, video projection, karaoke, wireless microphones, bubble machines and fog machines. We use the best professional equipment available. Our systems are compact and elegant. You can choose from one our packages or customize one to fit your needs.

Video Montages
We create DVD / VHS video montages, using your pictures / video footage. We then project your montage onto our 10-foot screen, during your reception, for your guests to enjoy.

Thank You Videos
Using the pictures / video footage from your wedding we create DVD / VHS videos that you can send to your guests, to replace or accompany thank you cards.

National Association of Mobile Entertainers

N.A.M.E.

Fully Insured for Your Protection

Clara's Own
ULTIMATE ENTERTAINMENT
Portland's Premier
Full Service DJ Company
916 S.E. 29th Avenue
Portland, Oregon 97214
(503) 234-3055, (888) 332-6246
E-mail: Claraswe@Sprynet.com

Find Us On The Web: ultimatedjs.com

Type of Music
We feel strongly about giving you the right music. Songs that are proven to get your guests up and dancing. That's why we provide you with a catalog of the biggest party songs of all time. Choose from any era… Big Band, Country, '50s & '60s, '70s & '80s, R&B, Top 40, Classic Rock and more! All music is on compact disc to provide clear digital sound. Special requests are always welcome.

Equipment
What's great music without great sound? At Ultimate Entertainment, we use sound systems that contain the finest audio components available. Sound checks are made before guests arrive to ensure excellent sound at every location, both indoors and out. We have a wireless microphone at every event for your convenience. For nighttime functions, a dazzling array of lighting is an option you may choose to enhance your celebration. From the smallest backyard to the largest banquet hall, Ultimate Entertainment has the equipment to handle any situation effectively and efficiently.

Experience
Ultimately, it's our people that make the difference. When you choose Ultimate Entertainment, you get more than a DJ, you get our 15 years of experience, quality, and professionalism. We entertain and energize your guests. We play your style of music and take care of all your wedding day announcements and events.

Cost and Terms
Our price is based on a four hour event. This includes cocktail/dinner music, dance music, along with a free dazzling light show and free event planning sheets. Dance floor lighting is available for an additional charge. We accept Visa, MasterCard, and Discover. Only a $100 nonrefundable deposit holds your date. Please call us to learn more about availability and price information.

Special Services
Our disc jockeys are trained event coordinators and will handle your special activities during your reception. Whether you are looking for an "interactive DJ" or a "low key DJ," our DJs can help you with your event. Ultimate Entertainment also has: karaoke, special effect lighting, fog machines, snow machines, and party kits (novelty items...leis, sunglasses, inflatable guitars, saxophones, and beach balls). We also can provide music for your ceremony. Please call for a price quote.

See page 226 under Full Service Bridal Salons, 571 under Transportation, and 81 under Banquet & Reception Sites.

Notes

MIND-BOGGLING

MAGIC

Tim Alexander
(503) 331-8542

E-mail: tim@parlorofwonders.co
Web site:
www.parlorofwonders.com

Create an atmosphere of astonishment and wonder...
Bring the **award-winning MAGIC** of **Tim Alexander** to your event!

Your audience will laugh with amazement as I perform **classics of magic** and **original tricks** manipulating balls, bills, coins, cards, rope, rings, and every day objects close-up or on stage. **Things will appear, multiply, transform, and vanish at my fingertips,** *and in your guests hands!*

Strolling: Close-up or table-to-table Magic is perfect for:
• **Receptions** • **Cocktails** • **Fairs** • **Buffets**

Parlor Show: Stand-up Magic is the ideal entertainment for:
• **Meetings** • **Banquets** • **Parties** • **Holiday Gatherings**

Stage Show: Marvelous for family audiences:
• **Sleight-of-Hand** • **Live Bunny!** • **Levitation** • **Music**

Your guests will be delighted by my visual artistry, tasteful music and 19th century styling. Mystery, humor and sleight-of-hand combine to create a uniquely entertaining and **unforgettable magical experience!**

"Your tricks were original and unique...Truly top notch!"
–Kenny Ruffo, CoMotion Venture Capital

"Judging from the looks of awe and puzzlement, and the gasps of surprise, everyone who crossed paths with you enjoyed your amazing art."
–Nancy Buley, J. Frank Schmidt & Son Co.

"Thank you very much for providing such great entertainment...a pleasant delightful evening...As the organizer of the party, it was great to hear so many positive comments!"
–Kazuko Arai Mahoney, James Gray Co.

"...top local entertainer..."
–Portland Family Magazine

Please let this business know that you heard about them from the Bravo! Wedding Resource Guide.

WW KARAOKE EXPRESS

With Wayne Weatherbee

Providing Pizazz to your Gathering

503-774-7464

E-mail: wwkexp@nwlink.com

Web site: www.wwkaraokeexpress.com

Experience

Introducing Wayne Weatherbee of WW Karaoke Express, who was the pivotal person running the *Portland Goes Hollywood Star Search* in Spring of 2002. This Star Search involved 10 establishments throughout the Portland area.

Wayne has been associated with music for over 30 years, singing with his brother's band in the east. He has performed karaoke for 11 years. He sings like a lark and appreciates all kinds of music. Wayne's sociability and reliability provide a welcome oasis in services, whether working with individuals or groups at weddings, parties, and small or large gatherings. We provide quality at reasonable prices.

State-of-the-Art Equipment

Wayne has his own karaoke business, providing state-of-the–art sound equipment and approximately 6,000 songs in his growing collection. Our music taps many styles and tastes. We also have Pioneer video karaoke CDs available as well as CDGs. We have a variety of speakers, powered and hand-held microphones, as well as TV monitors to view your song text and videos. Our attire can be formal, theme or casual. We can provide lights, strobes and fog. Whatever your wish, we will discuss and provide when feasible. Budget conscious to "Champagne" tastes, we aim to please!

Wayne can record for you. We are able to record on location or in our home recording studio.

We have had experience setting up our sound systems in establishments.

**Soon offering CDs, burners, mixers, recorders
and all types of karaoke equipment for sale.**

Notes

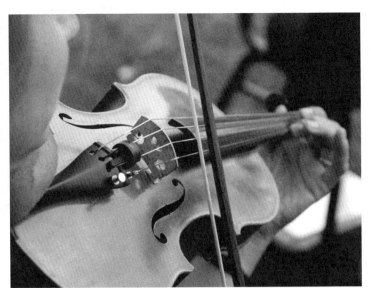

"Those who love deeply never grow old;

they may die of old age, but they die young."

– Sir Arthur Wing Pinero

Entertainment – Musicians

www.bravoportland.com

Elaine Hesselman

· Harpist ·

(503) 636-0349; E-mail: elaineharp@comcast.net
Web site: www.bravowedding.com/or/elainehesselman

Types of Music

No musical instrument compares to the harp when it comes to bringing style and beauty to complement your special occasion. Elaine Hesselman has played for many types of events and locations including:

- Weddings and Receptions
- Open Houses
- Corporate Events
- Restaurants and Hotels
- Banquets
- Private Parties

Ms. Hesselman's varied and extensive solo repertoire includes classical music, rhythmical arrangements, and popular show tunes. She also plays celtic and sacred music upon request. Also available are duo combinations—harp and flute, harp and violin, and harp and voice.

Experience

Ms. Hesselman is a harp instructor at Lewis & Clark College and Marylhurst University, and former music specialist at Oregon Episcopal School. Her professional background is impressive. Her affiliations include the following orchestras:

- Portland Opera
- Oregon Symphony
- Vancouver Symphony
- The Musical Theater Company
- Ballet West
- Chamber Music Northwest
- Sunriver Music Festival
- Rose City Chamber Orchestra

Education

Ms. Hesselman acquired her B.A. degree in music education at the University of Southern California. She has an M.F.A. in harp performance from California Institute of the Arts.

Cost

For a personal quotation and consultation regarding music for your event, please call Elaine Hesselman at (503) 636-0349.

AN ELEGANT ACCOMPANIMENT
TO YOUR EVENT

Harpist
Ellen Lindquist

(503) 626-4277
E-mail: harpmuse@aol.com
Web site: www.bravowedding.com/or/ellenlindquist

DISCOVER THE AMBIANCE AND ELEGANCE OF HARP MUSIC AT YOUR WEDDING AND RECEPTION

Types of Music
Harp music adds elegance and magic to any wedding and reception. Ellen's repertoire spans many decades to include Classical, Love Songs, Movie Themes, Show Tunes, Oldies and New Age. Her repertoire ensures each wedding and reception is personal and unique.

Harp Music is Perfect for
- Ceremonies
- Receptions
- Rehearsal Dinners
- Engagement Parties
- Bridal Showers
- Bridal Luncheons

Experience
With over 20 years of professional experience, Ellen knows what her clients want and expect. She has played at hundreds of weddings and receptions. She has played at most of the bridal sites in Portland/Vancouver and can make suggestions to the bride/groom to enhance their wedding day. She has played with the Columbia Symphony, Portland Chamber Orchestra, Eugene Symphony, Oregon Festival of American Music, Ernest Bloch Music Fest and Peter Britt. Her experience includes working on cruise ships, hotels in Japan and she has played with celebrities from Kenny Rogers to the Moody Blues. She was trained at the Music Academy of the West, Julliard School of Music in New York and California State University Northridge.

All wedding packages include a one hour consultation.

LET HARP MUSIC CREATE
THAT EVERLASTING MEMORY

Call for a free brochure, references and prices. Harp/flute also available.

STRING QUARTET

For that perfect wedding...

The Stradivari String Quartet

Winchester Enterprises
(503) 232-3684
Fax (503) 236-2920
Hugh Ewart, Assoc.
Concertmaster Emeritus
Oregon Symphon

Types of Music

For that perfect wedding or event...perfect music by The Stradivari String Quartet for ceremonies and receptions in your church, synagogue, private club, residence, or garden. The style is elegant, distinctive, and affordable. Information packet including music list available upon request.

Experience

Distinguished wedding music since 1961. Our clientele has included prominent Northwest social and business leaders. In 1980 Stradivari String Quartet appeared in the Paramount motion picture "First Love" filmed on location in Portland.

Additional Options Available

A trumpeter and vocalist are also available.

Cost

Call for current prices and availability.

CHARMING AMBIANCE

"The Stradivari String Quartet added a charming ambiance to the event."
Barbara Jordan
The Oregonian

Call for your FREE demo CD or cassette.

CLASSICAL GUITARIST, ALFREDO MURO

Contact: Nancy Anne Tice,
Phone/Fax (503) 774-2511
E-mail: nwartmtg@bigplanet.com;
Web site: www.nwam.com

Type of Music

Originally from Lima, Peru, Alfredo Muro's elegant, sensitive and polished style has been honed by many years on concert stages around the world. He has studied with masters such as Carlos Hayre and Manuel Lobez Ramos, and performed in all mediums from television to small intimate gatherings. While on tour in Italy in 1986, he played for Pope John Paul II at a Vatican "Special Audience." His repertoire includes European Classical composers such as Bach, Handel and Albeniz, Latin American Traditional Folklore, Latin Jazz, Caribbean, Bosa Nova and Samba, Andian, and Latin American Classical composers such as Villa-Lobos, Barios, Laureo and a touch of new flamenco. Ask about Alfredo's six-piece Latin Dance Band for hot, exciting times on the dance floor—perfect for receptions!

Experience and Cost

A celebrated soloist, Alfredo Muro also leads small ensembles for weddings, corporate events, private parties, concerts, dances and festive celebrations of all kinds. His recent CD, "Journey Through the Strings," which includes solo as well as arrangements with violins, cello, bass, flute and percussion, was praised by Jose Feliciano as "elevating the guitar to a higher plane…moody and melodic, and richly eloquent." Call for free promotional materials, demo and quote.

American Federation of Musicians

Local 99

325 N.E. 20th Avenue
Portland, Oregon   97232
(503) 235-8791; (503) 296-5775 Fax
local99@afm99.org; www.afm99.org

Experience

Founded in 1899, the A.F. of M., Local 99 is a nonprofit organization established by professional musicians for musicians. We represent the finest musicians from Portland, Salem, northwest Oregon and southwest Washington. With a membership of about 700 musicians, we are able to offer a wide variety of musical styles:

- Chamber groups of all sizes, from a solo musician to a string quartet to a full blown symphony orchestra
- Pianists, organists, harpsichordists, classical guitar, flute and harp
- Jazz, Big Band and Dixieland groups of all sizes
- Rock and Blues bands, Country, Folk and everything in between

No Agency Fees . . . . Free Referral Service

Most of our artists will provide you with tools to facilitate your entertainment selection process. CDs, tapes, video, photos and website addresses are available for the asking.

We put you in touch with experienced, professional musicians; you make the choice. Call now to find the perfect group for your event.

Live music is best!

The Ariel Consort

Contact: Jen Bernard (503)231-1423
arielconsort@lazybullmusic.com

www.lazybullmusic.com

Type of Music

The Ariel Consort is a multi-instrumental chamber ensemble featuring an enchanting blend of musical voices. Our versatile instrumentalists fuse their unique talents and textures to create a hauntingly evocative musical tapestry.

A "consort" is, by definition, a highly experienced troupe of rotating musicians, allowing you to create any ensemble you choose. Instrumentation and ensemble size changes to meet your preferences and budget. We appear as solo performers, duos, trios and quartets. Instruments available are flute, voice, harp, violin, cello, classical guitar and piano.

We pride ourselves on our musical eclecticism. Repertoire selections feature an ethereal blend of Classical, Baroque, Celtic, European Folk, Wedding Traditional, Romantic, Renaissance/Medieval, Slow Airs & Ballads and even Jazz. We can adapt our repertoire to suit your taste. Amplification is available upon request.

Experience

With the combined experience of over 1,200 weddings and special event engagements, the Ariel Consort's musicians approach your event with the highest level of professionalism, customer service and sensitivity. Consultation and planning are included in our prices.

Please call to receive a complimentary demo CD and brochure.

Aurora Strings

Quartets, Trios, Duos and Soloists
Contact: Kiersten Oquist (503) 491-1802
E-mail: kierstenoquist@aol.com

Portland's premier wedding ensemble, The Aurora Strings (formerly The Mezzanotte Strings), specializes in major event and wedding performance, and combines musical excellence, a wealth of experience and personalized attention to create an elegant ambiance for your celebration.

Type of Music

While the group specializes in classical and baroque music, our extensive repertoire also includes romantic favorites, jazz ballads, popular love songs, waltzes, holiday music and Broadway hits. If we don't already have your favorite piece, we can arrange it for you.

Experience

The members of The Aurora Strings perform with Portland's finest orchestras and ensembles, and have played countless special event engagements together in the area's most prestigious locales, including the wedding of Miss America 2002, Katie Harman. They bring a commitment to personalize service and the experience from playing hundreds of weddings together, and will be responsive to your suggestions.

Quotes given include musicians in formal attire, length of engagement, travel allowance if applicable, and consultations for your music planning. Amplification is available upon request. Call for your free promotional packet, demo CD and repertoire list.

CELTIC WEDDING MUSIC BY INNISFREE

Contact: Brenda or Jim 503-282-3265
E-mail: musicbyinnisfree@aol.com
Web site: www.musicbyinnisfree.com

We are a husband-and-wife duo with a tremendous love of Irish music, which we have found to be perfectly adaptable for ceremonies and receptions. It's full of haunting slow airs, lilting marches, spirited dance music, lovely waltzes, and songs of deep longing. We take great pleasure in adapting the most moving pieces we know from this tradition, fitting them to specific spots in the ceremony.

Our instruments are various pennywhistles, guitar, button accordion, concertina and mandolin. We also sing. Please inquire about additional musicians; we have strong friendships among the Irish musical community and can make arrangements for other musicians to join us. We've played at most wedding sites in Portland and make sure we check out the venue beforehand if we have questions. Also, our top-quality PA system is yours to use. Our goal is to make sure that you, the bride and groom, are not stressed about the music details, because we can easily help you arrange them so that they feel just right for you. Our experience (400 weddings and counting!) guarantees that we can give you wise guidance if you need it.

UNFORGETTABLE MUSIC

We've found that couples are thrilled to use the Irish music they love, tailored to fit their own wedding, played by two musicians who give of their own deep love of the music, to make their wedding day shine.

Flute, Violin & Cello

www.collagetrio.com
Contact: Susan Nelsen 503.653.6138

Music that Reflects Your Style

You've chosen the perfect dress, the most luscious flowers, an exquisite cake and a truly magical site. Now let us collaborate with you to design a musical accompaniment that perfectly coordinates with your personal style.

Skillful Orchestration, Perfectly Timed

Listen for a moment to the sweet melody of an enchanting serenade over the murmur of your guests as they mingle in anticipation. Imagine heads turning to a magnificent, regal overture that marks your procession. Celebrate with a joyous finale - a classical allegro, or maybe a provocative, zesty tango! Our delicious blend of instruments will create a rich, full sound for every piece, and you can count on our impeccable sense of timing.

Beyond Classical

Our collage of flute and strings will make ancient music sound fresh and modern tunes sound timeless. We are specialists in the classical repertoire, but we love swing, Latin and klezmer, to name a few of our favorite styles. We'd love to arrange your favorite song for you!
Call us for a complimentary demo CD and brochure. We offer a no-cost, no-obligation consultation. We look forward to meeting with you!

PIANO
DARLENE HARKINS
(503) 357-9037

Types of Music
Darlene has an easy-listening style enjoyed by all ages. She performs your requests for music from all eras, including contemporary love songs, country, sacred and light classics, Broadway show tunes, New Age, and current favorites.

Experience
Darlene has studied piano from age five. She received a music scholarship to and graduated from Pacific University. An accomplished pianist, she can hear a tune and adapt it to the piano to fulfill special requests. Her personality is reflected in the warmth and charm of her playing, setting whatever mood you desire for your event. Her music will indeed calm the nerves and make the ceremony flow smoothly.

Free Consultation and Planning
Call Darlene to play for you over the phone–"a neat idea and real time saver," say many brides and grooms. She will play your choices and, if you wish, offer suggestions based on her extensive experience. In addition, a suggested list of music will be sent to you.

For your ceremony, she carefully correlates music to the proceedings, timing your selections to the entrances of candlelighters, parents, and the wedding party.

For your reception, her ability to play requests from your guests can contribute greatly to creating the happy, upbeat atmosphere for a festive celebration.

PIANO • DAVE LEE
(503) 648-1796 or (503) 317-9270 • dave@daveleemusic.com

Electronic Garage
Productions

Your Wedding Is Special
Your wedding should be unique and special. The heartfelt music of **Dave Lee** can help make it that way. Hear Dave at Washington Square Nordstrom, Portland City Grill, on his six CD's or online at **www.daveleemusic.com.**

Experience
Dave Lee has played keyboards for 38 years...28 professionally. Dave has played for Nordstrom for 14 years.

FREE Stuff
Dave offers a **FREE** consultation to discuss your entertainment requirements AND a FREE CD of your ceremony music recorded at his studio...**Electronic Garage Productions.**

Recordings
Dave has recorded six CD's… Together We Stand, Piano ,Christmas Morning, After the Storm,When Your Eyes Met Mine and Jukebox. Dave's music has been heard on over 130 radio stations across the USA.

More Than Piano
Dave's music can be on piano or electronic keyboards. Dave Lee & Friends is available from 2-6 members. Dave can arrange for vocalists for your ceremony. Dave can also be your emcee drawing upon 16 years experience in radio broadcasting.

VIOLIN & CELLO DUO/STRING TRIO & QUARTET

Duo con Brio

7455 SW Alpine Drive Beaverton, Oregon 97008
Corey Averill (503) 526-3908; Cell Phone (503) 887-4448
Web site: www.duoconbrio.com; E-mail: singandbow@attbi.com

Types of Music
Duo con Brio is a professional ensemble founded by cellist Corey Averill. The duo may be augmented to a string trio or quartet; flute, harp and trumpet are also available. We have a large repertoire, from Baroque to Contemporary, and we pride ourselves on fulfilling most special song requests at no additional fee.

Experience and Cost
Formed in 1989, the Duo has performed more than 1,000 weddings and other special occasions. Over the years we have performed both locally and abroad in Europe and Asia. Duo con Brio has played a number of memorable events, including performances on Tri-Met's MAX, the opening for NW Portland's Fred Meyer, a Nike International Croquet Tournament, the University of Phoenix graduation ceremonies, OHSU conventions, marriage proposals at Blue Lake Park, and weddings in Oxbow Park (with a deer wandering through the service). We offer a wide range of services, including free consultations and a demo CD. We look forward to assisting you with your special event.

$150 – Solo Cello/1st hour ($75 each add. hr) $275 – Duo/1st hour ($135 each add. hr.)
$375 – Trio/1st hour ($170 each add. hr) $475 – Quartet/1st hour ($195 each add. hr.)

DW Duo

Contact: Dawn Grishow (503) 642-9509 • Web site: www.dwduo.com
The elegance of live music…or the variety of a deejay?
Now you can have both!
Wedding ceremony to reception, DW Duo has the flexibility to make your day unique and special. Here's one example of how your reception could be set up…

The first part of the celebration would consist of LIVE MUSIC!
1. **Guests arrive to classical guitar, solo piano and harp.**
2. **Hors D'ouerves and meal — progress to standards, smooth jazz and bossa novas.**
3. **First Dance — romantic lighting effects, special musical selections performed LIVE or on CD.**
4. **Then…smoothly merge into CD DANCE MUSIC!**

Dawn started singing at 14 years of age. She studied communications and has had eight years of experience in the Hollywood film industry, providing her with knowledge in lighting, sound and set decorating.

William is an accomplished multi-instrumentalist, and can perform anything from classical guitar, piano, harp, cello to even bagpipes, for your special day. He has played for numerous theater productions and is a seasoned recording and performing artist who has just released a CD of 15th century classical guitar.

Rates are very competitive and based on your personal event and structure. For booking information, Demo CD, prices, referrals and options available, please call (503) 642-9509 or visit our web site at www.dwduo.com

395

Please let these businesses know that you heard about them from the Bravo! Wedding Resource Guide.

Fiona Sanders © 2002

ăt-mōs-phēre: your style, your music.

www.effesenden.com
503.860.7688

Effesenden Music will work with you to select and craft the music that best fits and distinguishes your style for your wedding.

Select from Classical works to create a formal, elegant, and traditional style or, alternatively, make selections from Jazz and other Acoustic arrangements to fit your unique style and create the unique atmosphere of your wedding and reception. Available solo and with ensemble.

Elizabeth Nicholson

Harpist

4922 N.E. 7th Avenue
Portland, Oregon, 97211
(503) 287-7780

E-mail:
elizabeth_nicholson@hotmail.com
Web site: www.harpmagic.net

Types of Music

The bright, ethereal sound of the Celtic harp is the perfect complement to any special occasion. Elizabeth Nicholson is a national award-winning Celtic harp player whose specialty is performing highly expressive Celtic, medieval, renaissance and American folk music, as well as traditional wedding material. Also an accomplished soprano, Elizabeth is able to accompany herself on a wide range of vocal music. She may appear as a soloist or with other instruments such as violin, flute, keyboards or Irish whistle. Elizabeth is also available for hire as part of an ensemble, which performs rousing traditional dance music – perfect for any wedding reception.

Experience

A life-long musician, Elizabeth studied harp and voice at Northwestern University and Reed College. An active member of Portland's traditional music community, Elizabeth performs frequently at numerous venues around town, both under her own name and as a member of the band "ElizaBob," which she fronts with fiddler Bob Soper. She has also played at hundreds of weddings, corporate events, festivals and other special occasions. Costs depend upon the season, location and duration of the event.

Demo recordings are available upon request.

Emerald String Quartet

Contact: Kim Lorati (503) 244-5208
Email: emeraldstrings@aol.com

◆ Specializing in weddings and receptions

◆ We cater to your needs

◆ Performing as a string quartet for over 15 years

◆ Members perform with Oregon Symphony,
Baroque Orchestra, Portland Opera
and Ballet

◆ Highest standards of excellence

◆ **Call for complimentary CD, price quote and availability**

ERIC SKYE

Acoustic jazz guitar soloist

503.675.6268   www.ericskye.com

Standard Jazz Recording Artist

"One of the best new rising stars of the American acoustic jazz scene."
                                    – 20th Century Guitar Magazine.

"A musician you must go see live."

                                    —KMHD Radio

"Taste, tone and technique!"

                                    —JAZZIZ Magazine

Classical repertoire as well.

FLUTE/SAX AND GUITAR DUO

GARY HARRIS AND MATT SCHIFF

Contact: Nancy Anne Tice, Phone/Fax (503) 774-2511
E-mail: nwartmtg@bigplanet.com; www.nwam.com

Types of Music

Gary Harris and Matt Schiff blend a vast knowledge of
musical styles ranging from classical to jazz and the
popular music of the 20th century into a polished, versatile
ensemble perfect for weddings, receptions and elegant
celebrations of all kinds. For weddings they play all the most beloved and requested
traditional pieces. For receptions, they offer lighter, more upbeat jazz and contemporary
favorites played on flute as well as tenor and soprano saxophone with guitar. Call for free
promotional packages, demo tape, play list, references and price quote.

Experience

Their many years of national and international touring and performing experiences enable
them to create a perfect mood and sparkling atmosphere for your next special occasion. Either
as a duo or with added rhythm selection, their music is appropriate for listening and dancing.
They are always happy to play your requests.

Cost

Highly cost-effective, professional ensemble. All details in contract. Tuxedo, semi-formal or
casual attire.

VIOLINIST GEORGE SHIOLAS
AND THE LYDON ENSEMBLE

George Shiolas (503) 657-3476
String Music and More

History

Founded in 1986 by violinist George Shiolas, The Lydon Ensemble has performed to public
and critical acclaim in North America, Europe and Asia. George Shiolas has been a soloist on
numerous occasions with the Oregon Symphony, as well as the Columbia and Vancouver
Symphonies. Mr. Shiolas lead the Mt. Hood Chamber Orchestra on a Canadian tour in which
he was both soloist and conductor in Vivaldi's "The Four Season," and has sailed throughout
the Pacific as violinist aboard the Queen Elizabeth II.

Types of Music

George Shiolas and The Lydon Ensemble have performed at hundreds of weddings and other
special events. You may request solo violin, string duo, trio or quartet; flute, harp and trumpet
are also available. Besides classical music, The Lydon Ensemble's repertoire includes popular
songs, holiday and ethnic music, and we will make every attempt to accommodate your
special requests.

Call today to enquire about availability and to receive your free demo cassette or CD.

𝓛ove𝓝otes

Cheryl Alex & Jerry Hahn
Flute, Guitar & Vocal Duo
Cheryl Alex (503) 772-4539; (503) 544-7076 (cell)
Email: alexflute2@yahoo.com

Types of Music
For ceremonies, we provide classical, jazz, contemporary, ballads, pop songs and more. For receptions, we provide jazz standards, latin, swing and more. (Rhythm section available.)

Experience
Cheryl Alex is a gifted and versatile flutist, vocalist, keyboardist and educator. Jerry Hahn is a highly respected, world-class guitarist and educator. Together they will help to create a beautiful and romantic ambience, perfect for your wedding day.

Credits
Cheryl Alex, winner of KMHD's "Best New Talent" award, the Jazz Society of Oregon's "Musician of the Month" award and a Berklee scholarship, has recorded with Rebecca Kilgore, Tall Jazz, Nancy King, Brad Merserau and others. Jerry Hahn, Director of Jazz Guitar Program at P.S.U., has toured and recorded with artists such as Paul Simon, Gary Burton, John Handy, Mose Allison, Ginger Baker and David Friesen, and has performed at jazz festivals including Montreux, Newport, Copenhagen, Wichita, and Portland.

Call for free demo CD, promo package, references and price quotes.

Peterson Entertainment
P.O. Box 86066 ¥ Portland, OR 97286
503-703-9516
noah@noahpeterson.com
www.noahpeterson.com

The Noah Peterson Quartet plays jazz, a swinging troupe of hep cats, these guys play like lions on the prowl; bold and fiery one passage, sweet and tender the next. The excitement they create when they play is tangible, it passes through their audience; completing the circuit. The electric moment; where fact, fiction and fancy fall away. Celebration of the now; Jazz, real jazz, good jazz.

The repertoire embraces the best in jazz and popular music. Songs that touch and delights their audience come dancing from the horn of Noah Peterson. Romantic indigo moods to funky festivals of sound; the band makes every performance come alive with an inner fire their audiences never forget.

True professionals in every sense, this group reflects a clear vision at center of their improvisation. Turning pop tunes into jazz classics; polishing jazz standards into bright new gems. Like the best high-wire act these gentlemen perform without a net as they groove to the mystic depths of Noah's untamed saxophone.

If you need a fun, affordable, professional act to enliven your upcoming event or celebration contact the Noah Peterson Quartet today. Please remember that dates are confirmed with a first called, first served policy, so to make sure your dates are booked, don't delay. Call Noah Peterson for the finest in entertainment value.

PORTLAND BRASS QUINTET

503 224-2048 • john@jwnet.com

If glorious, elegant, beautiful and spirited music will make your wedding ceremony memorable, then you should consider the Portland Brass Quintet. The PBQ was founded in 1991 and is one of finest ensembles of brass musicians in the Northwest. All musicians are currently members of and regularly perform with regional symphonies, as well as other chamber and jazz ensembles. PBQ provides music for weddings and a variety of other events each year. We would like to help you create the ceremony of a lifetime.

Choices in musical offerings are available from renaissance, classical, and romantic selections, as well as traditional wedding music. We can include unique selections to convey the desired feeling of your special wedding ceremony. We also gladly offer recommendations based on your ideas to welcome your guests, provide ceremonial music, and even music for your reception. Let the PBQ help proclaim the glory of your wedding day!

For more information please visit our web site: www.weddingtrumpet.com/pbq

Contact: Nancy Anne Tice (503) 774-2511
nwartmgt@bigplanet.com; www.nwam.com

EXPERIENCE

Collectively, the ensemble members are seasoned, polished professionals that have played in numerous symphony orchestras, including the Oregon Symphony, Portland Opera and Ballet Orchestras, as well as in others in the Northwest, throughout the United States, in Europe, the Mediterranean and South Pacific. The Ruslan Strings have also performed recitals in the Portland metropolitan area, as well as providing lovely background music for corporate parties, weddings, anniversaries and conventions.

TYPE OF MUSIC

The Ruslan String's repertoire includes all of the elegant, classical pieces most often requested for weddings and parties, as well as traditional concert music. They also play many lighter, romantic favorites from the Celtic and Scottish traditions and the Renaissance. They are pleased to play requests, and are happy to assist their clients with selecting the perfect accompaniment for their special event.

COST

Rates are highly competitive and based on date, location, and length of playing time. Quartets and Trios are available. Please call for complimentary demo CD, promotional information, repertoire list and references. Formal or semi-formal attire. All details in contract.

MUSIC FOR OCCASIONS

Weddings • Receptions • Events… Bach to Beatles
Carol M. Hawes (503) 254-3740

Piano, Organ, Portable Keyboard *and the…*

Satin Strings Quartet
Since 1984

Types of Music

The sweet harmonies of **Satin Strings Quartet, Trio or Duet** will greet your guests and create an elegant and memorable ambiance for your wedding, reception and dinner. This versatile group features **violins**, **viola** and **cello** for the traditional string quartet. They specialize in light classical but in keeping with their motto "Bach to Beatles" they play music from the timeless strains of Pachelbel's "Canon in D" to current love ballads, hymns, sing-a-longs, Broadway tunes, waltzes, tangos and ragtime. Replace one violin with a **flute**, add **organ** or **trumpet** for a majestic processional, or simply have a **piano** soloist.

Experience

Satin Strings Quartet was formed in 1984 by four professional musicians who were performing together throughout the Northwest. They were featured at the Greater Portland Bridal Faire for 1984 and several successive years. They have a huge repertoire of music and will help you select music to reflect your dream and personal taste.

Cost

Call or E-mail **satinstr@quik.com** for a demo CD, price and music list. Contract always provided. **Visit www.satinstringsmusic.com**

Member American Guild of Organists and American Federation of Musicians

PIANO • KEYBOARDS • VOCALS

SUSY WOLFSON

(503) 662-5420 • Web site: www.havemusicwilltravel.net

Solo Background

Susy Wolfson is a musician of uncommon versatility. She is equally comfortable as a solo pianist or accompanying her own vocals, moving smoothly from contemporary styles, jazz standards, rock 'n' roll or rhythm & blues to classical music. Her background includes a magna cum laude performance degree from the prestigious Indiana University School of Music and performances at numerous festivals and engagements including the Spoleto Festival in Italy as well as many years as a freelance musician.

Trio/Quartet/Quintet

Using the classic format of the piano trio plus guitar (with vocals or instrumental only), these musicians are in constant demand for receptions, corporate events, country clubs and winery festivals. From black tie and smooth jazz one night to a kick-off-your shoes rock 'n' roll dance the next, this group will keep 'em dancing! Their song list ranges from Duke Ellington to Sheryl Crow to Stevie Ray Vaughn… and all points in between!

Performance Combinations

- **Solo Piano or Keyboard**
- **Trio/Quartet/Quintet** (vocals, keyboard, guitar, bass, drums—optional saxophone or flute)
- **Vocals and Piano/Keyboard**
- **Flute and Piano Duo** (vocals optional)
- **Klezmer Band**

Demos, song lists and references for all musical combinations are available upon request.

Trio Trachée

A Unique Ensemble
For your Special Event
Contact: Denise Westby, 503-246-7279
triowest@juno.com

Styles of Music

Trio Trachée is a one-of-a-kind ensemble featuring flute, clarinet and bassoon. Fun to watch, even more entertaining to listen to. From Mozart to Joplin, classical to jazz, all styles are covered for your special event. Traditional to the tunes of today--your personal request is always honored. Trio Trachée is the original choice for your rehearsal dinner, wedding and reception.

Experience the Difference

The highest professional quality of performance is experienced with Trio Trachée. As members of the Portland Opera, Oregon Ballet Theatre and Sinfonia Concertante Orchestras, as well as the top-name Broadway shows, Trio Trachée brings years of experience to your occasion. Additionally, as members of the American Federation of Musicians, Local #99, you're protected by contract. If you're looking for the best possible professional musicians with a blend that is different from the rest, Trio Trachée is the group for you. Contact us for a free demo c.d., photo and quote today!

Tom Grant

(503) 297-6304 • tom@tomgrant.com

Tom Grant is an internationally known pianist/recording artist with 18 albums to his credit and a career stretching back 30 years. His music is a delightfully stylish blend of jazz and pop that has made fans in far corners of the globe. Tom has played numerous European music festivals, as well as headlining in major venues in nearly every American city. In 1992 he appeared on the Jay Leno show. His music is a staple of smooth jazz radio all over the world. Tom plays private events, either as a solo pianist or with a larger group appropriate to that event. He will tailor the presentation to the needs of the client and can provide a demo, press photos and bio upon request. Also, go to **www.tomgrant.com** for more information.

William Jenks
Classical Guitarist
503-654-0082 • www.williamjenks.com • info@williamjenks.com

Type of Music
The music of William Jenks will brighten up your wedding day, giving you and your guests a truly peaceful and joyful experience. His repertoire includes beautiful solo classical guitar from the Renaissance through Romantic eras.

Experience and Cost
William Jenks has performed at many weddings and corporate events across the Northwest. His musical talent was discovered at a young age, which later led to his performance at Carnegie Hall in New York. He graduated with honors from Colorado Christian University and later was selected to perform for world-renowned guitarist Christopher Parkening. For more information, call for a free live demo at his studio located at the Island Station Wedding Emporium, or log onto www.williamjenks.com to hear music samples and see a current performance price list.

Notes

Notes

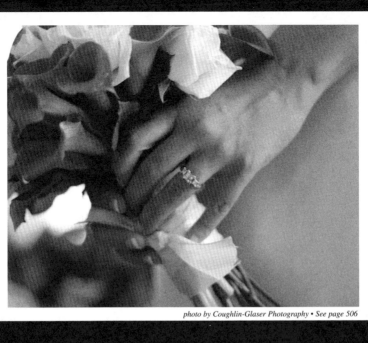

The Bride's Bouquet

The first flowers carried by brides were a

combination of fragrant herbs whose strong aromas

were purported to keep evil spirits at bay.

As time passed, flowers were added

and came to represent the bride's

virginity, femininity, and fragility.

Florists & Flower Preservation

www.bravoportland.com

Florists

- **Selecting a florist:** Most florists have a portfolio of their work. Choose a florist who will spend time getting to know your style and desires for your wedding and who respects your ideas while offering their expertise. If you plan to arrange your own flowers, it is a good idea to consult a floral designer who can offer advice and help get the flowers you need.

- **Setting a budget:** As with everything else, it is important to set a budget for your flowers. Your florist can inform you about what flowers will be in season and styles that will appropriately fit your theme and budget. Be honest about your budget so the florist can cater their services to fit your needs. One of the best ways to stay within a budget is to select a color scheme rather than specific flowers. For example, if you go to your florist saying you only want a certain type of orchid, you are subject to whatever the market price is at the time. Be open to a variety of flowers that will match your colors and theme.

- **Develop a plan:** Think about your floral design and decorations and write it down. Determine what you will need for the various people involved, arrangements for the church, and decorations for the reception.

- **Meeting with the florist:** You should meet with your florist as soon as possible. A florist can only commit to a limited number of weddings or events, especially during the busy summer months. If it is not possible for them to see the wedding and reception sites ahead of time, it is a good idea to provide photos of the locations so the arrangements can best fit the surroundings.

- **Being prepared for your florist:** It is good to bring ideas to the first meeting with your florist. Although the florist may have photos of arrangements and bouquets or books of ideas, it is important to give a sense of what you are looking for. Take advantage of the florist's expertise. Be sure to tell the floral designer if there are flower types that you absolutely do not like; also let them know what you love!

- **Flower shades and colors:** Colors and shades can be challenging when selecting flowers. Always use a fabric swatch or ribbon sample to show your florist the exact color you are thinking of.

- **Bouquet toss:** Consider having a separate, smaller bouquet for the bouquet toss. Many brides wish to have their bridal bouquet preserved.

- **Beyond the bridal bouquet:** Corsages and boutonnieres should be ordered for the wedding party and the mothers of the bride and groom. Also decide what type of arrangements you would like at the ceremony and the reception. If flowers will be near the food, be sure to choose mildly scented ones so as to not overwhelm the scent or taste of the food.

- **Delivery and setup of flowers:** It is very important that your flowers be delivered at the right time. Always put the location and date on your contract, as well as the desired time of delivery so to prevent questions or last-minute problems. They should arrive before the photographs are taken and kept out of direct heat or sunlight. Check to see if delivery and set-up are included in the contract. Be sure to read the entire contract before signing a final agreement with any florist.

For more assistance with staying organized during the wedding planning process, check out the Bravo! Wedding Organizer. Detailed question worksheets double as contracts. This step-by-step system will keep every detail of your wedding organized. To order, refer to the order form on page 25 in this Guide.

A Blooming Bouquet

A Unique and Romantic Florist

Westside	Eastside
Kelly Cruickshank	Linda Negus
(503) 626-4333	(503) 254-3281
BLOOMINGBOUQUETS@juno.com	BlmnBokays@aol.com

"Award-Winning Florist"
Elegant Wedding and Special Occasion Florist!

For bouquets that are controlled, but not contrived, softly sophisticated, traditional or contemporary, with a European flair, limited only by your imagination and personal style.

❀ **Bridal Party Flowers:** bridal bouquets that are unique and one of a kind. Bridesmaids, flower girl bouquets, hair flowers, corsages and boutonniere

❀ **Ceremony Flowers:** altar bouquets, pew decorations, candelabras, gazebos, unity candles, garlands, arbor arches, topiaries, chuppas and pagalla decorations

❀ **Reception Flowers:** fresh floral cake decorations, cake table, buffet, serving and guest table bouquets

Costs and Terms

We are very conscientious about working with a budget and are able to give you more flowers at a more comfortable price. Every stem we purchase is used for your wedding only, giving you full and gorgeous bouquets. We never skimp. A nonrefundable deposit of $150 holds the date of your wedding and is applied to your total balance.

Consultations

We have an extensive portfolio for you to look at during a free consultation. We have many creative, fresh and original ideas to make your wedding and reception one of a kind. We invite you to bring any pictures, fabric swatches and your own special ideas so that we can create your "Special Day."

WEDDINGS ARE OUR AREA OF EXPERTISE

A Blooming Bouquet has more than 15 years of design experience with an unique and romantic style. We can create any design you want, from romantic to contemporary wildflowers to orchids. We offer very personal attention in a comfortable atmosphere with attention to every detail. We take extra time to listen to your needs and fit your flowers to your style. We have done flowers for many satisfied brides, Portland's Rose Festival and have appeared on *AM Northwest* and *Good Day Oregon!*

Voted "Most Outstanding Florist" at the 2002 Portland Bridal Show
Winners of the "Best Booth Award" at the 2002 Portland Bridal Show
Please call for a free consultation, anytime Monday through Saturday

*"for Wedding Bouquets that are as beautiful and
timeless as the love that you have for each other."*
Mention this ad and receive a free toss bouquet with order!

Visit our Web site at ABloomingBouquet.com

FLOWERS & GIFTS

901 N.W. Sixth Ave ¥ Camas, WA 98607
Phone: 360.834.5571
Fax: 360.834.5591
Toll Free: 1.877.777.5571
Contact: Shelly Crespi
or Rebekah Crawford
www. afleuraffaire.com

Flowers • Invitations • Accessories • Fine Chocolates

Cutting Edge and Far From Ordinary

Extraordinary Weddings
Allow our wedding detail and design staff to sit with you and create a breathtaking wedding that is yours alone. With over 20 years of wedding experience, Shelly and Rebekah will suggest ideas suited to your specific location and venue. Our expertise and creativity will surround you with astonishing arrangements that will fulfill your most cherished dreams.

Services and Specialties
We provide exceptional detailed service and complimentary consultations at your convenience. We have designed weddings in some of the most prestige locations of Southern California and Arizona and have relocated to the Northwest. Shelly and Rebekah will meet with you in the beginning and will be present the day of your special event to ensure that you receive the personalized service you deserve. The past 2 years in the Northwest, we have appeared at The Benson, The Crown Ballroom, The Fairgate Inn, The Governor's Hotel and The Portland Art Museum. We also design for churches, cathedrals, parks, restaurants and homes. Displayed in our studio are just some of the unique prop and fixture rentals that we offer. We provide delivery, setup and transfer from ceremony to reception locations.

Fees and Terms
We reserve your special day with a 25% deposit. Balance owing is paid 2 weeks prior to your wedding day. Flower prices vary as your event is individual and unique. Delivery and set-up is priced according to distance traveled and complexity of your event.

Complimentary Toss Bouquet is Our Gift to You

A Floral Motif

Exclusively
Wedding Floral Design

By appointment only
503.772.3324
www.afloralmotif.com

Specialist in Wedding Design

Exclusive to wedding floral design, A Floral Motif will exceed your expectations of your wedding day flowers. From simplistic elegance to exquisite and grand, our skills go beyond the ordinary.

Whether your taste is lush peonies embellished with lily of the valley, the simplistic elegance of a hand-tied bouquet of calla lilies, or maybe your passion is the delicate composition of an English garden or the vibrant colors of fall — A Floral Motif has the expertise you should expect for your wedding.

As floral designer and owner of A Floral Motif, Tammy has over 10 years design experience with a forte that allows her to remain on the terrace of today's emerging trends. Tammy has built a reputation of going beyond the call of just a florist; personable and accommodating, you will feel at ease in preparation of your wedding day flowers. Tammy really listens to her future brides and their grooms as they explain the vision they have of their special day, taking note of every last detail, thus unique floral design and atmosphere emerge.

Personalized Services

Complimentary consultation

Second consultation on-site, ceremony/reception

Customized floral designs unique to each wedding

Evening and weekend appointments available

Delivery and set-up at no charge locally with minimum order

Re-delivery from ceremony to reception is available with your order

If we don't have a particular prop for your wedding design/décor we will find it for you

No minimum order required

Terms

We require a 25% deposit to secure your wedding date with balance due two-weeks prior to the event.

Please visit our web site for more information and view a sample of our designs.

www.afloralmotif.com

1121 North Loring Street
Portland, Oregon 97227
503.223.9267 Office
1.888.838.8444
503.223.4746 Facsimile
www.anaffairtoremember.com

Fantasy Flowers

About Us

Designing spectacular weddings is what we are all about!

With over 10 years experience in wedding design and production, we combine gorgeous flowers with the most extensive collection of wedding props in the Portland area and creative artistic skill to produce events of uncompromising elegance and style.

Color, Texture, Scent, and Scale

Attention to detail is what makes the ordinary wedding an extraordinary experience!

Color: What bride could resist falling madly in love with the classic color combinations: gorgeous hotel silver candelabras dripping with tones of white, cream and butter roses, lilacs, peonies and tulips on a table draped with pewter organza chiffon; rusted Italian iron urns and compotes crammed with lush fall dahlias, hypericum berries, orchids and vine maple over rich mocha damask linens and gilded chairs; sparkling estate cut crystal ware with jewel-tone gloriosa lilies, hot pink cockscomb, chartreuse viburnam, and coral sweetpeas on a table draped in crystal beaded champagne moiré.

These are just but a sampling of the myriad of color combinations a bride could choose. The fun will come in finding the right palate to suit your wedding.

Texture: Utilizing materials other then standard flowers gives your wedding flowers a feeling of depth and texture. We love to let our imagination run wild in combining non-traditional elements into our work: moss covered cake urns, birch trees full of hanging votives; fresh berries, citrus, kumquats, grapes, artichokes and pomegranates gracing magnificent wedding cakes; tables covered in the most exquisite linens, damasks and organza, stone water fountains, urns, pillars and garden ornamenture, wrought iron pergolas, arches and gazebos.

Scent: The freshest flowers provide the most exquisite scents. David Austen garden roses, lilacs, peonies, lily of the valley and freesia to name a few. Our flowers excite the senses!

Scale: Understanding scale is of vital importance in wedding design. Your décor and flowers should fit the formality of the event, the size, scale and look of the event space, the time of day and the time of the year.

Contact Us

Please call for your no cost - no obligation wedding consultation

See page 241 under Bridal Consultants.

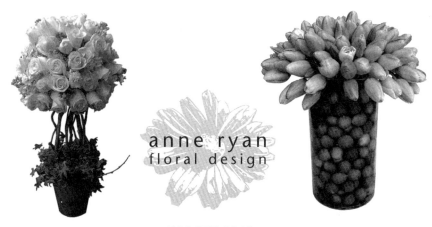

503.722.9949

Anne Ryan Floral Design

Flowers as art. Over the top. Out of the box. Stunningly beautiful. Visionary and magic. Glorious color and style...And that's just the flowers. Anne Ryan herself is flexible, creative, wise and enthusiastic, PLUS fun and easy to work with! All this according to her clients.

Anne Ryan is a freelance floral artist who specializes in exceeding wild dreams and creating exquisite ambience with flowers. Anne Ryan Floral Design has brought world class work to our doorstep. Take time to tour the web site: www.anneryan.com

"Anne is truly an artist. Her flowers are the canvas in which her creations come to life. She puts her heart and soul into each arrangement. The flowers she did for our wedding somehow captured the whole essence of us, and they were so stunningly beautiful they made Monica cry when she saw them."

—Lane Powell & Monica Mayer-Powell, owners of Divine Designs

Starting price for weddings: $1500 (see web site for more details)

Consultation fee: $50 for 2 hours (credited in full toward your wedding if you use Anne Ryan Floral Design)

Complete decor planning is available: rental items such as chairs, lighting, tents, etc.

www.anneryan.com

Balendas' Flowers

1924 S.E. Tanager Circle — Hillsboro, Oregon 97123

Contact: Balenda Weisskirchen

503.693.6086

Business Hours: Please call for an appointment (days or evenings available)

Checkout our website at **www.balendasflowers.com**

View our wedding packages, portfolio and testimonials online

A WEDDING TO REMEMBER

No matter what the look or feel, from the simplest idea to the most extravagant, Balenda's Flowers will be able to transform your wedding fantasy into a beautiful and enchanting reality. With over 19 years of wedding floral design experience, we provide the personal and professional service required so your wedding day is a flawless event.

WEDDING FLOWERS

From the brides bouquet to the reception flowers, look over our many design books or bring your own customized ideas, Balenda's Flowers will realize your vision and make your special day a memory for a lifetime.

OUR SERVICES INCLUDE

Free consultation
Set-up and delivery by an experienced designer
Delivery is free within 50 miles for weddings over $1,000
Transporting flowers from wedding to reception site is extra
Pinning of corsages and boutonnieres
Candelabras and alter stands provided with purchase of floral bouquets

COST AND TERMS

Costs vary with types of flowers and size of bouquets. Packages or individual pricing are available. A 20% deposit is required with the balance due three weeks prior to the wedding.

TESTIMONIALS FROM A FEW SATISFIED CUSTOMERS

"I cannot thank you enough for the amazing flowers you put together. Honestly they were my favorite part of the wedding. My bouquet, the bridesmaids and cake were so much more than what I had expected. I was so impressed with how well the roses matched with the bridesmaids dresses. I am so happy I used your services compared to some of the stuffy flower shops I visited. Every time I see my pictures I remember how happy I was that day. I promise to recommend you to all my friends." – Sara D.

"Thank you so much for the beautiful flowers you prepared for our wedding. From the bridal bouquet to the centerpieces everything was perfect and exactly what I had asked for. All of our guests were overwhelmed with the beauty of the ceremony and your flowers truly set the mood for the entire evening. I can't thank you enough for your exquisite work." – Alison

See more testimonials and accompanying wedding photos at www.balendasflowers.com

4201 N.E. Fremont • Portland, Oregon 97213
Contact: Pattie Scarpelli, Amy Walling, or Doug Lotz
(503) 281-5501
Business Hours: Mon–Fri 8am–5:30 pm; Sat 8am–3pm

Wedding Flowers

At Beaumont Florist we can do any wedding size from one simple bouquet to an extravagant affair.

Services Offered

- **Rehearsal dinner flowers:** centerpieces
- **Wedding-party flowers:** bridal and bridesmaid bouquets, flower-girl basket, headpieces, toss bouquet, boutonnieres, corsages
- **Ceremony flowers:** altar bouquets, pew decorations, garlands, and candelabra arrangements
- **Reception flowers:** buffet, serving and cake-table arrangements, guest book flowers, fresh flower decorations for the cake

Cost and Terms

We require a 25% deposit to book your wedding date with the balance due two weeks before the wedding. Delivery and setup are complimentary in the Portland metro area. Please call to make an appointment for consultation, so we can give you our undivided attention.

WE MAKE WEDDING DREAMS COME TRUE

Our design staff has a combined total of 55 years experience. We take great pride in meeting our customer's complete satisfaction. Feel free to bring in your fabric swatches, pictures, and dreams, and we will design a wedding to match your color scheme and budget.

Beautiful Blossoms Of Lake Oswego
Lake Oswego's Most Prestigious Floral Shop
544 N. State Street • Lake Oswego, Oregon 97034
503-636-0777 or toll free 888-636-0777
Consultations by appointment only

Come in to Beautiful Blossoms for your complimentary bridal consultation and experience comfort and confidence. Our creative suggestions and artistry will inspire you. We will work with you to meet all your floral needs. We will exceed your expectations.

• We have a unique garland maker with which we create the most extraordinary garlands

• We have created weddings from ballrooms to vineyards

• References provided upon request

• 20% down to hold your special day

• Complimentary "toss" bouquet

• Over 25 years of experience

www.beautifulblossoms.com

Becky's Country Garden

13700 S. Mueller Road
Oregon City, Oregon 97045
632-7303

Freeze-Dried Bouquets
We can preserve your wedding flowers in a stunning display.

A Floral Package for Your Wedding Beginning at $349

Green fields hug the land like a familiar quilt, an orchard appears with tree after tree in perfect symmetry, towering pines line the horizon. Your worries fall away as you drive along the hinterland road toward Becky's Country Garden. This peaceful setting is the perfect place for you to choose the flowers for your wedding day.

Just 10 minutes from I-205 south of Oregon City and you have arrived for your appointment. Owned by mother and daughter team Kathy Cook and Becky McEahern, the business is located on an acre of lovingly-tended land where dahlias, gladiolas, sweet peas, snapdragons, lilies, roses, herbs and greenery grow—all to be used in the floral designs. A white lattice gazebo, swing, arbor and archway grace the pastoral setting, adorned by a brook tumbling into a pond.

The shop is filled with cut flowers and floral designs—the perfect place to choose the flowers for your wedding. Becky's Country Garden's floral packages begin at just $349 and includes bouquets for the bride and maid of honor, two mothers' corsages, four boutonnieres, and two large altar arrangements. *"Brides are amazed at our prices,"* says Becky. *"Most say they've been quoted $300 for the bridal bouquet alone."*

If you need more bouquets, corsages and boutonnieres, Becky and Kathy will adjust the package to meet your needs. The duo easily design flowers for large, elaborate weddings, or for smaller, intimate celebrations. No matter the size of the wedding, they put their hearts into creating exactly what each bride wants.

Once you leave the shop at Becky's Country Garden, you'll put all the worries about flowers for your wedding day behind you. You'll know you will have the flowers of your dreams, at a price you can afford. Call Becky at (503) 632-7303 to schedule your free consultation.

Terms
Becky and Kathy recommend that you bring pictures, swatches or any ideas that you may have to the complimentary consultation so that they can best meet your needs. The terms are a $50 nonrefundable deposit to reserve your wedding day (which is applied to your order) and the balance is due two weeks before the wedding.

Rental Items, Decorations and Accessories
For your convenience, we have wedding accessories available such as Unity candles, frames, cake tops, pens, glasses, knive sets, etc. We have the following items available for rent: aisle runner, candelabra (in brass or white), wedding arch, lattice pillars, Roman pillars (three sizes), tall white wicker baskets, lanterns, brass baskets and free standing style altar holders. All $25 each pair, one arch or one aisle runner.

Visit our Web site: www.bctonline.com/users/flowers; E-mail: weddings@BCTonline.com

Please let this business know that you heard about them from the Bravo! Wedding Resource Guide. **415**

Blooming Buds
Wedding flowers extraordinaire

Tracy Grimstad 503-538-7943

Web site: www.bloomingbudsflorist.com

Your Flowers

Our focus is solely on weddings. Achieving designs that you would want for your ceremony and reception is our priority. We want you to have dream flowers to carry down the aisle. Flowers are naturally exciting. My job is to put them together so they radiate your personal style! When the focus is on you, your groom and the spirit of the day, and that photo is snapped, you are framed by bowers of floral bouquets, garlands and altar arrangements. After the ceremony is over these same items can ignite the atmosphere of your reception.

Just about everyone has a love for flowers. The fragrances cause emotions. The color combinations, textures and forms catch the eye, create beauty and memories. Let us fashion something glorious for your wedding day!

Consultations

I want to make sure my clients know they are being well taken care of and getting the flowers they hoped for. After discussing what the Bride's expectations are and bouncing around ideas, I watch people react to different flowers, colors and designs. This is a sure way of knowing what they like!

Terms

A nonrefundable deposit of $100 is required to reserve my services for your wedding. The balance is due two weeks before the wedding date. Everything we design for you is delivered and set up—down to every beautiful detail.

For a personal consultation, please contact Tracy.

www.bloomingbudsflorist.com

Bouquets & Balloons

6650 N.W. Kaiser Rd • Portland, Oregon 97229
Contact: Cheryl Skoric, CBA 503.629.5827; Fax 503.645.9404
Oregon's First Certified Balloon Artist
Business Hours: to suit your schedule, day or evening by appointment
www.bouquetsandballoons.com

Complete Wedding Decor: Flowers and Balloons

Quality, service, competitive prices, and one-on-one personalization are the character of this business. I have 16 years experience as a florist and 13 years experience in balloon design, a staff member of International Balloon Arts Conventions, and I continue to educate myself by attending conventions nationwide. Come in for a *free* consultation and review samples and portfolios of my work.

Services Offered

Bouquets & Balloons provides complete, individualized service for any occasion.

- **Free consultation:** at your business, your home, my home, or the job site
- **Wedding, ceremony and reception flowers:** bouquets, headpieces, corsages, boutonnieres, altar arrangements, candelabra arrangements, kneeling bench decorations, unity candle, pew bows, garlands, topiaries, table arrangements, garden baskets, buffet table arrangements, and cake flowers
- **Balloons: (Centerpieces)** choose from an original assortment of balloon bouquets for your dining, buffet, and head tables
  (Sculptures) spiraled balloon hearts, pearl or spiral arches and swags will enhance rooms of any size; consult us about the variety of balloon designs available.
- **Special effects:** add excitement during the first dance with our exploding balloons filled with confetti, balloons or both and explode them over the bride and groom.
- **Theme parties and events:** a special theme can be created for your wedding with custom balloon decorations and flowers

Color and fabric swatches are recommended so that the arrangements designed will complement, blend, and accent your wedding setting as well as your attendants' attire.

Cost and Terms

Upon confirmation, a 25% deposit is required, with the balance due two weeks before your event. Make your initial appointment at least three months before your event. This consultation allows me to offer ideas and suggestions while fully discussing all your plans and needs. However, you can reserve service just a few weeks prior to the wedding.

Mention this ad and receive a free toss bouquet with order!

Burkhardt's
Flower Shoppe Ltd.

2155 NW 185th • Hillsboro, Oregon 97124
Phone: 503.645.6492 • Fax: 503.645.3559
Toll Free: 1.800.376.6492
www.burkhardtsflower.com

Established in 1882, Burkhardt's European Flower Shoppe has helped generations of brides create original and innovative floral designs to make their wedding day beautiful and unique.

Your Wedding Flowers

Every girl dreams of her wedding day. It is her day to be the princess in the fabulous dress, complete with tiara, who is rescued by Prince Charming and carried away to his castle, emblazoned with sparkling jewels, gorgeous flowers and even a glass slipper. Try as we might, at Burkhardt's we have had a little trouble finding Prince Charming and the castle, but we can provide the flowers of your dreams. Whether it is an elaborate extravaganza or a simple elegant wedding at your home, our designers will help you select flowers, colors and designs that meet your needs, your budget and your heart's desire.

Complimentary Consultation

We ask our brides to schedule an appointment for a comprehensive consultation to discuss her floral needs. We feel you deserve our full attention without interruptions to plan your special day. We schedule daytime and evening appointments. It is helpful but not necessary to bring pictures, fabric swatches and any ideas you may have to the consultation. Follow-up consultations are welcomed and available as needed.

Design

Our experienced staff will create the designs you have selected with the freshest and most beautiful flowers available.

Setup and Delivery

An experienced designer will deliver and setup all floral displays at the ceremony and reception sites. We pin on all corsages and boutonnieres. We will also transport your flowers from the ceremony site to the reception site.

Rental Items

We have a generous selection of vases, urns, pillars, candelabras, etc., available for rental with your wedding flower order.

Terms

Burkhardt's requires a 25% deposit when placing the wedding order with the balance due 30 days prior to the wedding date.

Our Gift to You

Each bride receives a complimentary toss bouquet with her wedding order.

BURLINGAME *Flower Shop*
246-1311
FLOWERS TO SUIT THE OCCASION

8605 S.W. Terwilliger Boulevard
Portland, Oregon 97219
Contact: Jan Patella (503) 246-1311
Business Hours: Mon–Fri 8am–6:15pm; Sat 8am–5:30pm

Wedding Flowers

Our wedding flowers are created to fit the individual and her unique personality. Selected staff will work personally with each bride, designing everything to fit her and her needs. For over 40 years, we've worked with all kinds of budgets from small to large, and we'll be happy to show you how to get the most from your wedding or event flower budget. Come in for a consultation and to review samples and portfolios of our work.

Services Offered

- **Rehearsal-party flowers:** table arrangements, garden baskets, and more
- **Wedding-party flowers:** bridal and bridesmaid bouquets and headpieces, flower-girl bouquets and baskets, men's boutonnieres, corsages
- **Ceremony flowers:** altar bouquets, candelabra arrangements, pew bows, etc.
- **Reception flowers:** buffet, serving, and cake-table arrangements; guest-table arrangements; fresh cake flowers

We recommend you provide us with color and fabric swatches so that the floral arrangements we design for you will complement, blend, and accent your wedding and reception settings as well as you and your attendants' attire.

Cost and Terms

Burlingame Flower Shop requires a 25% deposit when placing the wedding order, with the balance due one week prior to the wedding date. We ask our brides to schedule an appointment for a comprehensive consultation to discuss her floral needs. We feel you deserve our full attention without interruptions. Our services should be reserved as soon as possible.

Specialties, Rental Items and Decorations

Burlingame Flower Shop carries a large selection of unique flowers for you to choose from for your event. Trained, experienced personnel are available to work with you personally to provide you with the European to traditional styles you prefer. We pay special attention to flowers, plants, and natural materials to enhance your worship settings. For the finishing touches at your ceremony and reception sites, Burlingame Flower Shop has candelabra and other wedding props available for rent. We work with each bride to make sure she has just what she'll need.

WE DESIGN FLOWERS TO FIT YOU AND YOUR NEEDS

Burlingame Flower Shop has been serving the needs of bridal couples in the Portland metropolitan area for over 49 years. Because each customer is unique and special to us, we work hard to ensure they always get the kind of service and craftsmanship they deserve. Your flowers for this very special day should reflect your style and personality. We'll take the time and care to make sure they do!

Pearl District

124 NW 9ᵗʰ Avenue
Portland, Oregon 97209
503-228-4700

City Flowers in the Pearl District

Your wedding day should feel like your dream come true, and for the past 15 years City Flowers has been making dreams come true all over the Portland-Vancouver area. Whether you want your flowers to be dramatic and contemporary or formal and elegant, you can trust City Flowers to surpass your expectations.

It's All About You!

Please call or email us for a complimentary consultation. Within a few days after the consultation, we will mail or email you a formal proposal. From that point, City Flowers will keep in regular contact with you to answer any questions or make any last-minute changes you may have.

Terms

A 25 percent deposit is required to reserve your wedding date with the balance in full due 10 days prior to the ceremony.

"Ooos!" and "Ahhs!" Guaranteed

"You are miles ahead of the other florists we dealt with in Portland before coming to you. The whole experience was great!" — May 2003 Bride

"We gave her our budget and she listened to what we really wanted!" — July 2003 Bride

"Everything was right on time and looked great! You were on top of everything and quick to respond. Thank you!" — July 2003 Bride

"We loved the creativity – had so many compliments!" — August 2003 Bride

"We're recommending you to all out friends!" — August 2003 Bride

See samples of our designs online!

www.cityflowerspdx.com

CRYSTAL LILIES
exquisite flowers

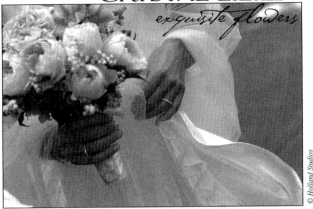

© Holland Studios

134 S.E. Taylor Street • Portland, Oregon 97214
503.221.7701
By appointment only • www.crystallilies.com

Crystal Lilies creates weddings with style, elegance and timeless beauty. We suggest unique concepts and unexpected elements that reflect each bride's unique personality and taste. In our studio you will meet with Kimberley to privately review our extensive portfolios of our previous weddings. As a floral artist, Kimberley has the experience and expertise to make your wedding a fabulous success. Crystal Lilies continues to stay in the fore of emerging floral trends and innovations and continually receives accolades for the stunning originality of our work.

> *"Flowers help define a mood, establish a sense of style and create texture. Whether you find yourself in a ballroom overflowing with luscious roses, or the sent of the bride's gardenia bouquet as she walks down the aisle, flowers invite our senses to depart from our everyday lives and transport us to a magical environment."*

We feature a wide range of styles from European to contemporary, understated elegance to baroque opulanence. Handtied bouquets, alter arrangements flowing from urns, creative cake decors, English countryside garlands, fabric draped ceilings, centerpieces elaborate and romantic or clean and simple, candle lined aisles and more, the possibilities are endless. We have an amazing selection of custom and unique props; columns, aisle runners, iron arches, urns, unique silver containers, topiaries, candelabras, etc. which are unequaled by any other florist in Portland.

Crystal Lilies specializes in using only the most beautiful of flowers, seasonal botanicals, fruits, berries, and interesting and unique elements whether local or from around the world.

We are wedding specialists, starting with the concept and design to the finishing touches on your special day. Whether grand or intimate, Crystal Lilies is there for every detail to make your wedding an affair to remember.

See page 237 in Bridal Concept & Theme Design.

Terms: 20% deposit is required to reserve your special day, with the balance due two weeks prior to your wedding. Consultations are complimentary and by appointment.

Phone: 503.232.7977 • www.daisychainflora.com

Flower Power with a Twist

Flowers are more than mere decorations. They add zest, color, texture, and natural perfume to your wedding day. We enjoy working with each bride to create extraordinary wedding flowers that both showcase her individual style and convey the couple's personality.

Brides want their flowers to be beautiful yet distinctive. Consider a surprising touch, such as a purse composed of leaves and blossoms. Add a bit of nostalgia by incorporating vintage fabric flowers, beading, love knots, or an antique button collar to create an exceptional bridal bouquet. Indulge the fanciful with bejeweled nosegays, a tussie-mussie, herb-laced boutonnieres, or blossom circlets to grace an attendant's hair or a flower girl's wrist.

Combining diverse elements such as citrus, vegetables, branches, seed pods, herbs, and sugared fruit, we create vibrant tablescapes, lush *pots-et-fleurs*, festive garlands, aromatic pomanders, and kissing balls that celebrate the essence of your day—be it classic, traditional, whimsical, or contemporary.

There are no rules about what a wedding should look or feel like. *Flora with a twist* is our motto and it exemplifies the creativity we bring to our design approach.

The Daisy is in the Details

Because your flowers are a custom design project, we purposefully limit the number of weddings we book. We are a design studio, rather than a retail establishment, so we are able to focus primarily on weddings—our passion.

During our initial consultation, in addition to reviewing our portfolio and idea books, we will collaborate with you to realize your vision for your wedding day. We will also visit both the ceremony and reception sites with you, to exchange ideas firsthand that may further enhance the locations' existing beauty. From the ideas we generate, we will create a proposal for your consideration. You will receive a contract that outlines all the details, eliminating any worries that your flowers won't be absolutely perfect. Our commitment to service carries through to your wedding day, when we are available to deliver, set up, and distribute flowers as well as manage any last-minute necessities.

Our Business Is Blooming

Because every ceremony is unique, we price each event on an individual basis after the comprehensive initial consultation, which is followed by a detailed written proposal. All consultations are complimentary. We are happy to meet with you at your convenience— weekend and evening appointments are easily arranged. A 25% deposit will reserve your wedding date, with the balance due three weeks prior to the event.

> "Flowers...are a proud assertion that a ray of beauty outvalues
> all the utilities of the world."
> —Ralph Waldo Emerson

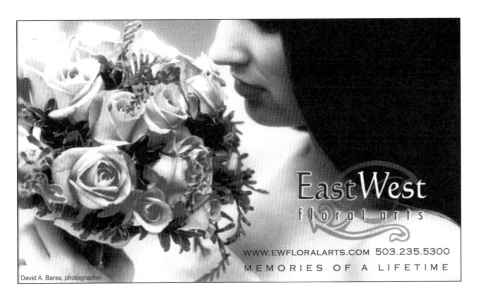

David A. Barss, photographer

East West
f l o r a l   a r t s

WWW.EWFLORALARTS.COM 503.235.5300
MEMORIES OF A LIFETIME

"The flowers, cake, lights and trees and EVERYTHING was absolutely magnificent and wonderful beyond description! Everyone RAVED about the flowers!!! I mean RAVED!! The feeling was exactly what we wanted, and we can't thank you enough!!"

—Dixie Lee Samuels

"I want to express how much your creativity made our wedding perfect. The flowers were fabulous, I could not have ever imagined them being so beautiful! I have had so many comments about how great they were. I have already referred you to another couple who just got engaged two weeks ago."

—Maria Jerome

"I was just blown away by how beautiful everything was! My bridesmaids and I wanted to have our bouquets preserved. I just don't know how you did it. It was unbelievable! It was stunning! I just don't have enough good things to say about it. I will recommend you to anyone and everyone I can. It was a pleasure working with you."

—Sandy Humpfrey

"Thank you so much for the wonderful flowers you did for my wedding! I absolutely loved them. I had dreams about wanting to bathe in their beauty. I didn't want the night to end so I could spend more time with the flowers. They really added a wonderful emotional element for me that I can't describe."

—Anne Scott

"You did a fabulous job!!! You truly turned the tent into a magnificent rose garden. Words cannot describe the transformation. It was beautiful and everyone commented on how lovely it looked. From the beginning, the honeysuckle arbor with the lovely white roses at the top, the bouquets on the aisle chairs, the plants around the stage, the islands of flowers and plants, and the table arrangements, and all the lights, the flowers on the cake and cake table, the bride, attendants and the flower girls' bouquets and head pieces were all spectacular. I took it all in and know how much you and your crew worked to make it so magical. We thank you so much…. You were a dear to work with and I value the time we spent over coffee discussing all the details. I would be happy to recommend you to anyone!"

—Barbara Preston

EUROPEAN FLORAL DESIGN

FRANÇOISE WEEKS

503.236.5829

WWW.FRANCOISEWEEKS.COM

What is European Floral Design?

In recent years European Floral Design has received a warm reception in the Pacific Northwest. The style is characterized by simple and harmonious floral compositions using a wide variety of flowers and foliage. The look is natural, yet vivid and exciting.

Françoise Weeks Florist

Françoise Weeks was born and raised in Belgium, where flowers are a part of everyday life. Her passion and enthusiasm for flowers were nurtured from an early age - Françoise has over 20 years of training and experience as a European floral designer. Since she opened her business here in Portland in 1996, her elegant and pleasing designs have attracted attention from wedding consultants, caterers, and photographers. And brides appreciate her personalized and artistic attention to detail.

Inspired by Flowers

I visited Françoise in her studio early one morning in April. She was in the middle of preparing for a wedding and the delicate fragrance of sweet peas and lily of the valley, combined with the intoxicating scent of lilacs and oriental lilies filled the room. Vases with soft colored spring blooms brightened the workbench, while vases of tall stems of cherry blossoms and stunning delphiniums lined the floor. As she lead me around tables brimming with hand-tied bouquets, altar arrangements, garlands and centerpieces she explained, "Every wedding is unique. And working with a bride to choose the right arrangements for her wedding is really exciting!"

As I left, we stepped out into a colorful spring garden, which seemed like an extension of her studio. A worn brick path meandered through the flower beds. "The garden is a constant source of inspiration," *said Françoise.* "I love the process of arranging interesting shapes, different textures and complementary colors to satisfy every bride's dream."

~ Shannon Spence

Terms

Consultations are by appointment only. A 20% deposit is requested to reserve your wedding day, with the balance due two weeks prior to the wedding date.

"MAKING YOUR EVENT A REALITY"

503.241.2225
Email: eventfloral@aol.com
www.eventfloral.biz
www.premierweddingflorists.com
(as seen in Martha Stewart's Weddings Magazine)

Custom Floral Designers
Specializing in Weddings and Large Events

- Weddings and receptions
- Private functions
- Floral, decor and party favors
- Holiday decorating
- Budget and planning
- Site and rental selections
- Post event arrangements/setup/take down
- Event management

CREATIVE DESIGNS TO IMPACT YOUR WEDDING

Event Floral was created in 2000 to meet the special needs of the catering and event industry. Cheri Baber and Sheila Bozikovich bring 20 years of design experience to the floral and party market. Both have worked design shows in Portland, Oregon and Vancouver, Canada, designing with and being trained by some of the top floral designers in the country.

We create wedding dreams come true, as well as corporate parties, private celebrations, foundation and fundraising functions. We have outstanding design ideas and pride ourselves in thinking "outside of the vase," to create a greater impact at your event.

www.eventfloral.biz

"In some ways, it is almost too bad you only get married once, because the way you completely took care of my wedding, it would be easy to have you do it again. Everything was so wonderful, I can't even begin to tell you how perfectly you captured what I talked about."
~ Kali

FABULOUS WEDDING FLOWERS LTD.

6010 S.W. Corbett • Portland, Oregon 97201
Contact: Cydne Pidgeon, AIFD • Phone/Fax: (503) 246-6522
Web site: www.Fabulousweddingflowers.com
By appointment; days or evenings

Your Flowers

If you feel you are too individual to be put into a package, we need to talk. As a member of the prestigious American Institute of Floral Design, I believe every bride deserves an *original* creation, and over a cup of tea in our elegant studio, you can pore over our extensive portfolios of photos and references while we plan all the special details that will make your wedding unique. As Portland's premiere wedding florist, our creativity and exceptional flair for color and proportion will surround you with outstandingly photogenic arrangements that will complement your gown, the season, and the wedding and reception sites. From custom veils with fresh flowers to gazebos that drip with fresh wisteria, accomplishing your dreams is our mission. Even Valentine's and Mother's Day weddings are available if you book early.

Services and Specialties

Presentation is everything and we have Portland's largest collection of exclusive props and rentals, from coordinating suites of ornate or classic pillars, urns, and cherubs in old garden cement, antique ivory, verdigris, silver and gold-leaf finishes, custom-designed aisle and altar candelabra, lighted topiaries, garden arbors, huppahs, fountains, French-wired aisle ribbons, and tapestry and brocade aisle runners.

Unforgettable cakes, adorned with fresh flowers, are presented on special tables draped in antique French lace, silk, moiré, brocades, even galax leaves for a garden setting, or under our wrought-iron cake arbors.

Our two extensive cutting gardens are overflowing with fragrant antique and English roses, English and French lavender, rare and beautiful perennials, hydrangea, and foliages grown especially for your wedding. It's a joy to work with such lovely flowers.

Terms

A 25% deposit is required with the balance due two weeks before the wedding. We recommend securing our services as soon as possible as we will not overbook a weekend. Delivery and setup charges vary with the complexity of the setup and distance travelled and always include a designer—your guarantee of perfection!

THE WEDDING OF YOUR DREAMS

Your wedding is the culmination of all your hopes and dreams and probably the biggest party you will ever throw. We would love to enhance the passion and perfection of your day by surrounding you in the magic of Fabulous Wedding Flowers.

Flowers & Stuff

Milwaukie, Oregon
Contact: Craig or Stacey McCollam
(503) 786-7231
Business Hours: Please call for an appointment

© Photography By Craig

About Us

As Husband and Wife, we work together to create a wedding day to remember. Filled with the soft, fresh beauty of flowers, we capture those treasured moments forever with photographs that reflect your personality. We bring an artistic elegance to your custom flowers and photography. We love working together and truly enjoy helping you create a spectacular day.

What We Do

In a relaxed and quiet atmosphere, both Craig and Stacey will meet with you at a time convenient for you. Weekend and evening consultations are available for your busy schedules.

Stacey will spend time getting to know what you envision for your wedding flowers. From that vision, she will help you choose the flowers that fulfill your dreams and create a wedding day filled with the romance of flowers. Everything from a tulle draped aisle, to your custom bridal bouquet, to a handmade head piece for the littlest of flower girls, is created with artistic and loving attention to the smallest of details.

Craig will also take the time to help you choose a photography package that is right for you. Your wedding portraits will reflect the love and warmth of your special day. Whether you are planning a formal affair or a casual garden wedding, Craig's relaxed, casual style will capture your personality in portraits that you and your family will cherish for a lifetime.

About You

It is a wonderful time for you...filled with the excitement and anticipation of your wedding day. Let us help you create a day to cherish forever. Consultations are complimentary. To make an appointment to meet with us and view our portfolio of work, give us a call at (503) 786-7231.

As Husband and Wife we love working together and
look forward to being a part of your Wedding Day!

Flowers by

"The Northwest's Family-owned
Wedding Specialist for Over 25 Years"

435 N.W. Sixth Avenue
Portland, Oregon 97209
(503) 464-1234, (800) 343-1235
Fax (503) 464-1218
E-mail: info@jacobsens.com
Web site: www.jacobsens.com

◆ Flowers ◆ Photography ◆ Videography ◆
◆ Music ◆ Event Rentals ◆ Open 7 Days a Week ◆

Wedding Flowers
Exquisite bridal bouquets, attendant and flower-girl designs, candelabra designs, pew decorations, boutonnieres, corsages, and specialty pieces. We are well known for our international flowers and designers, including European, Oriental, Hawaiian, and contemporary.

Reception Flowers
Centerpieces, garlands, arches, topiaries, buffet and table designs.

Rental Services
We offer a complete line of wedding and reception accessories such as Roman pillars, candelabra, and arches.

Costs
We will tailor our services to fit your needs. Call and make an appointment with one of our consultants. We provide exceptional references.

Some Extra Services We Provide
- Open 7 days a week with real people on weekends
- Fabulous gourmet baskets
- We have a liquor license
- Daily Portland and Vancouver metro area delivery

Please visit our Web site:
www.jacobsens.com

Geranium Lake Flowers

Gorgeous Flowers

red door studios ©

U.S. Bancorp Tower • 555 SW Oak • Portland, OR 97204
Phone 503.228.1920 • 800.228.1920 • Fax 503.228.5567 • *www.geraniumlake.com*

HIP • FRESH • AMAZINGLY WONDERFUL

They Love Flowers!

Geranium Lake Flowers is in love with flowers. Their work is fabulous, creative, amazing, wonderful and overwhelmingly beautiful. They are inspired by unusual flowers, especially those timeless ones like lilac, peonies, lily of the valley, old fashioned roses, tulips and lavender to name a few. They love herbs, rocks, fruit, lichen, sticks, exotic greens, or whatever strikes their imagination.

Bursting With Talent and Creativity!

Owner Kim Foren was trained as a fine art painter and until recently was showing her whimsical oil paintings for 16 years at Quartersaw Gallery in Portland, OR. In 1993, bursting with creativity and entrepreneurship, she started selling flowers out of her VW Van. Ten years later after moving her business in the US Bancorp tower, she has attracted the most impressive clients that range from Nike to the Benson and Governor hotels. The Willamette Week in July 2003 voted Geranium Lake Flowers as the best flower shop in the city. She has a long standing relationship with Fox12 "Good Day Oregon" appearing frequently and is often described as "Martha Stewart with an edge". She is dynamic and has been featured by the Oregonian, City Search.com, Vancouver Columbian and the Portland Business Journal.

They Love Weddings!

Geranium Lake Flowers loves weddings. Their wedding work is incredible, fresh and the best in the city. They do over a 100 weddings per year and are recommended constantly by sites, hotels, other vendors and brides. They have access to the best sourcing for flowers and have yearly trips to Holland that account for their incredible selection and year around flowers like lily of the valley. Kim loves her work with brides, loves hearing their stories before they even talk flowers. Be sure to visit their award winning website or visit their store. Kim personally offers complimentary consultations.

There is no minimum, complimentary consultations, fresh hip ideas and a wealth of experience.

Innerscapes
floral vision / artistry & design

Dena Hastings
Proprietor
3735 S.E. Hawthorne Blvd.
Portland, OR 97214
503.407.9928
myinnerscape@yahoo.com
Sunday noon-6, Monday-Thursday 11-7, Friday-Saturday 10-7

FRESH   VIVID   DISTINCTIVE

YOUR WEDDING FLOWERS
From simple to elaborate,
casual to elegant,
traditional to modern…
It is your day and your dream; we are here to bring it to life.

WHEN WE MEET
On our initial visit together, we will establish a creative foundation through a discussion of ideas, taste, style and themes, with as many follow-up visits as it takes to ensure your comfort, confidence and satisfaction. This includes meeting you on location at your chosen wedding and reception site(s) to accommodate every detail of the vision we have conceived for your amazing day.

ABOUT US
~ Specializing in smaller intimate affairs
~ Emphasis on using local resources
~ Ability to work within your budget
~ Available to travel if necessary

Jitterblooms
WEDDING & FLORAL ❀ DESIGN

www.jitterblooms.com

Please contact us for
a free consultation.

www.shumakerphotography.com

(503) 452-2327 ~ Located In SW Portland

"We Take Care Of Your Wedding Flower Jitters"

Who We Are
Jitterblooms Floral Design concentrates exclusively on weddings and large events to better serve your needs. You can expect that on your special day, your wedding is Jitterblooms' highest priority. Being our highest priority means better quality of work and attention to details that are an important part of your wedding.

Our Goal
We know planning your wedding can be stressful. Jitterblooms strives to take the stress out of your floral decisions, to make your special day hassle free!
• Visit wedding location & reception site before the wedding.
• A designer is always on site the day of your wedding.
• Arrange a walk through of site locations with you to ensure your wedding floral vision.
• Contact you the week of the wedding to ensure delivery time and/or last minute needs.

Consultation
We bring the consultation to you. This is a good way to include family and/or friends into your decision making process without the hassle of directions or crowding into a floral shop. We bring ribbon samples, books and magazines for you to view, bettering our sense of what you desire.

Terms
A 25% deposit is required at the time of booking to secure your date. The remaining balance is due two weeks prior to your wedding day.

For more information please don't hesitate to call or e-mail. Plus, checkout our website for monthly Internet specials!

Lillypilly

Floral Artistry
Specializing in Wedding and Event
Flowers

503-626-7410
www.lillypilly.net

"Two creative gals with a bucket load of flowers"

We are full of fun and creative ideas that we would love to share. Even if you know nothing about flowers, we will help you personalize an extraordinary floral package that will compliment your own unique sense of style and imagination. Our goal is to be an important part of helping you plan the wedding of your dreams - you know, the dreams that you've had since you were a little girl with the pillow case wedding veil - and we will strive to provide you with an upbeat and positive experience from the initial beginnings all the way through your spectacular wedding day. Let's talk about all the details from season to site, from theme to budget, and get to know each other in the process!

Your Custom Designed Floral Package can be as low as $250!

Services include

- Complimentary consultations
- Evening and weekend appointments available to fit your busy schedule
- A detailed written proposal including cost breakdown
- Flowers and decorating for your engagement, bridal shower and rehearsal parties
- Customized design service
- We visit ceremony and reception sites before your wedding so that there will be no surprises
- Your designer will personally deliver and set up your order
- Ceremony and reception site decorating; including floral arrangements that can be displayed for both ceremony and reception
- Rental item services available
- Free toss bouquet with your wedding order!

Terms

A $50 non-refundable deposit reserves your wedding date and will be applied toward your wedding order. 20% of your final balance will be due upon order approval and contract signing. Remaining balance will be due two weeks prior to your event.

Please contact us for your free personalized consultation.
www.lillypilly.net

Metropolitan Floral

weddings@metrofloral.com
503.231.7762
www.metrofloral.com

Creating designs of interest, to complement your life.

Your Personal Floral Resource: The studio of Metropolitan Floral excels in creating breath-taking floral artistry. Fun, formal, casual or elegant, we design vibrant, distinctive arrangements and accents that complement your personal style and wedding choices. From simple elegance to lavish extravagance, and anywhere in between. By providing the personal touch every step of the way, our attention to detail guarantees you a successful and stress-free event.

Inspiration: We begin the planning process with a free personal consultation in the privacy of your own home, or anywhere that's convenient for you. Weekend or evening appointments are easily arranged. An additional consultation on-site at your ceremony/reception location is also provided, allowing us to exchange ideas and ensure no detail is overlooked. We custom-design all of our arrangements to match your colors, location and personal style, making your wedding flowers truly unique. From current magazine pictures to Grandma's silk scarf, we encourage you to bring anything to your initial consultation that will help paint a picture of your wedding vision. Your wedding is an expression of who you are; our goal is to work with you using all of our knowledge and creativity to create the beautiful flowers you dream of.

Complete: Our commitment to service extends beyond the planning process, up to and including the day of your special event. Some of our services include:
* Reliable delivery
* Comprehensive set-up
* On-site boutonniere and corsage pinning
* Seamlessly transferring arrangements between ceremony and reception sites

Flexible: Our well-rounded knowledge of available seasonal flowers, innovative use of materials, and individually customized designs allow us to work within any budget. We understand the importance of developing creative solutions that provide our clients with the greatest value for their dollar. Metropolitan Floral is a design studio, without the overhead and distraction of an expensive retail location. This allows us to dedicate all of our attention and design resources to your event. Our ultimate goal is to help you create the wedding of your dreams, and to bring that dream to life.

Terms: A $50 non-refundable deposit reserves your exclusive wedding date; 25% payable upon signing contract, with the balance due two weeks prior to the event.

In celebration of this special occasion, floral shoe accents or a complimentary throwing bouquet is offered as a personal gift to each bride.

Discover the Extraordinary!

Pettigrew's
FLOWERS & MORE
503.317.1061
Aloha, Oregon
www.pettigrewsflowers.com

Gorgeous Flowers at Great Prices

Pettigrew's Flowers & More is a home-based business with a passion for weddings. Our focus is on quality floral designs, attention to detail and uncompromised customer service. By being a home-based business, Pettigrew's is able to give you the absolute best price due to lower over-head without compromising quality. To ensure each bride gets our undivided attention, Pettigrew's only books one wedding per day. Your wedding day is all about you, and we will be available only to you ensuring the success of your wedding day.

All wedding flowers are a design collaboration between the bride's unique ideas and those of our floral designers. At Pettigrew's we only buy the freshest flowers. Being located in Aloha, Pettigrew's has access to all the wonderful locally grown roses as well as other regional flowers. This insures maximum performance and freshness from each bloom. We also work closely with premiere importers so that we have access to most flowers on a year round basis.

We offer free Consultations by appointment only. We accommodate any schedule by offering day, evening and weekend appointments. We will even come to you if that is more convenient. Call us at 503.317.1061 to schedule a free consultation.

Cost and Terms
- A 50% deposit is due at the time the wedding is booked.
- The remaining balance is due 4 weeks before the wedding date.
- Delivery in the Portland Metropolitan area is free. A small fee will be charged to those outside the area.

FLOWER &
GARDEN, LTD

Murray Scholls Town Center
14845 S.W. Murray Scholls Drive, Suite 106
Beaverton, Oregon 97007
503.524.8878; Toll Free: 866.524.8878
E-mail: flowers.plog@verizon.net

Dreams Become Reality

If you are like most women, you have been imagining your wedding since you were young. We are here to make your dream wedding a reality. Our experienced designers will help you select flowers that set the mood, style, and season of your wedding.

We Love What We Do

At Plog Flower and Garden, we have designers who are enthusiastic and enjoy working on your wedding from the initial consultation to an exquisite masterpiece. We have worked with all types of wedding sizes and budgets from small to large.

Getting To Know You

During your consultation we take the time to listen and understand each couple's special requests. We encourage you to bring pictures, color swatches, and any other items or ideas you may have that will help us create your special day. Call today to schedule your free consultation.

Terms

To reserve your special day, a 25% deposit is required with the balance due two weeks prior to your wedding date.

Free Toss Bouquet
(With your wedding order)

P O S I E S

CHELSEA FUSS
P:503.697.9330
F:503.697.9370
269 A AVENUE
LAKE OSWEGO, OR 97034

POSIESBYCHELSEA@AOL.COM

Photos by Patrick Prothe

Our Style
Designed with their settings in mind, our fresh flower arrangements are full of impact and inspiration. Combinations of the freshest, most beautiful, seasonal flowers are paired with unexpected containers and lush ribbons for a simple and stylish result. Never cluttered or contrived, flowers from Posies reflect a natural beauty and a pure style. From fragrant violets to dramatic peonies, our flowers always demand a reaction. Even as we continually search out new materials and ideas, our look remains both sweet and modern, fresh and exciting.

Weddings
Working with Posies will ensure satisfaction and delight with your wedding flowers. From bridal party flowers to site decorations, our wedding designs reflect the personality of the couple, always taking into consideration the season and the venue. Our particular attention to detail enables us to tie the flowers into various other elements of the wedding to make certain the look is cohesive. Experience our personable service. Contact Chelsea by phone or e-mail to schedule a complementary consultation in which you will be able to view our full portfolio.

Visit our Studio
Stop by the Posies flower studio to see our work firsthand. The studio is located at 269 A Ave, Lake Oswego. Winter hours: Tues-Sat 10-5. Also by appointment. Please call for summer hours.

Pressed For Time

Specializing in pressed and framed wedding bouquets
Contact: Gail Ringo
(503) 892-9334
E-mail: pressedfortime@qwest.net
www.pressedfortimeflowers.com

Just as an original masterpiece is treasured, your wedding bouquet can become the most important and unique piece of artwork in your home…a happy remembrance of your special day in its most versatile form, to enhance any room in the years ahead.

The color is captured by pressing each petal and leaf with a variety of padded boards, and drying under controlled temperatures. Each flower is then rebuilt. The design work is placed on the fabric of your choice. A large variety of the highest quality frames is available in several sizes. Conservation glass which blocks harmful UV rays ensures vibrant color and bright whites that last a lifetime.

THE PLAN
- Feel free to visit our studio where you will see many samples and photos.
- Ask your florist for fresh flowers.
- Make an appointment to have someone bring us your bouquet (boutonniere, or other flowers to be included) QUICKLY, the same evening or next day if possible.
- If shipping your flowers is necessary, contact us for information.
- Please keep the STEMS WET but the petals DRY.
- Do NOT cover or refrigerate them.
- A $50 deposit and phone number is required at time of delivery.
- We will contact you in approximately three weeks to arrange a convenient time for a layout using your dried flowers, various possible backgrounds and frames.
- You may want to incorporate an invitation, photo, special fabric, or order extra pieces.

Visa, MasterCard, Payment Plans, and Gift Certificates are available.

Pressed For Time Studio
1385 SW Taylors Ferry Road, Portland, OR 97219

"Came but for friendship, and took away love."

—*Thomas Moore*

Formal Wear & Tuxedos

www.bravoportland.com

Formal Wear & Tuxedos

- **Selecting formal wear:** There are a variety of formal wear styles available. The formal wear shop you decide to work with can offer suggestions for styles and colors that will appropriately fit the time of day. Accessories to match the bridesmaid dresses are available for rent or purchase, or can be special ordered. Although the bride may help in deciding what the groom will wear, make sure that he is comfortable with the style selected.

- **Questions to ask:** Is the formal wear stocked locally? Are the locations convenient for the groomsmen? What is the price, and what does that include?

- **She keeps the gown, why shouldn't he keep his tux?:** A wonderful surprise for your groom is to purchase the tuxedo for his wedding present. This will make your groom feel as special as you do on the wedding day, with a tuxedo tailored to fit only him. There will be occasions to wear this tuxedo following the wedding day. Check into the purchase prices at your formal wear shop. If a tuxedo is worn four or more times per year for special occasions, it may be more cost-effective to own it.

- **Final fitting and pickup date:** You must instruct each member of the wedding party to pick up his own tuxedo. Make sure they try on the entire outfit at the store. This will avoid the most common problem with formal wear—proper fit. If adjustments or replacements need to be made, they can usually be done right on the spot, or arrangements for substitutions can be made.

- **Out-of-town groomsmen and ushers:** If some of the groomsmen and ushers live out of town, the formal wear shop can supply you with measurement cards to mail back to them. Any clothing or alterations shop in the groomsman's home town should be able to do a complimentary fitting. It is imperative that these gentlemen take the time to try on their entire tuxedos when they pick them up!

- **Bring extra socks:** Have the groom buy a couple of extra pairs of socks to match the formal wear. Be sure these extra socks are on hand where the groomsmen plan to dress. It never fails that someone will show up with only white athletic socks. This may seem minor, but they stick out like a sore thumb in photographs.

- **Group rates and discounts:** Many formal wear shops offer special group rates, discounts or rebates for black-tie or black-tie-optional events. Ask about setting up a special rate for all the guests who will attend.

For more assistance with staying organized during the wedding planning process, check out the Bravo! Wedding Organizer. Detailed question worksheets double as contracts. This step-by-step system will keep every detail of your wedding organized. To order, refer to the order form on page 25 in this Guide.

Frocks -n- Britches

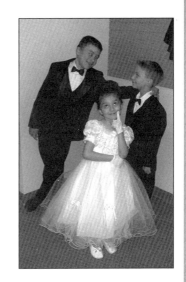

13815 SW Pacific Hwy, Suite 10
Tigard, Oregon 97223
(503) 624-7782
Hours: Mon 10am–8pm,
Tues-Sat 10am-6pm,
Sun Noon–5pm

Children's Formal Wear

Frocks -n- Britches would like to say congratulations on your wedding. We know that you want everything to be just right, and we are here to help you with the little ones in your wedding party. Stop in, or give us a call, and let us help you with all your children's formal wear needs.

Dresses: We offer a wide range of formal wear and dressy dresses in sizes NB-14. We also have just the right accessories to complete the look you are hoping for. Along with our great selection of white dresses, we have a nice variety of colored dresses to complement your wedding colors.

Tuxedos: We have new tuxedos in sizes 2-14; along with other boys' dress wear items. Did you know that you can purchase a new tuxedo for about the same cost as renting one? Stop in and we'll help fit all your special little men.

Specialty Items: We take pride in being able to offer some items that are sometimes difficult to find. We would love to help make other special events even more wonderful with dressy items and beautiful christening gowns and outfits.

Look to us for your future needs: We are here to help with your wedding and beyond. We are a complete children's store offering fantastic new and resale clothing, toys, accessories and furniture. We carry sizes preemie through ten and always offer special baby gift items. We also carry stylish resale maternity clothing and accessories.

Owner: Sally Pauly
Manager: Katie Pauly
Specialists: Lisa, Shannon, Cameron, Ana and Sara.

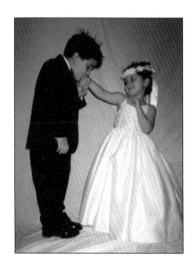

325 N. Main Avenue
Gresham, Oregon 97030
(503) 492-9378
Hours Mon–Sat 10am-6pm

Looking for Children's Wedding Attire, at an affordable price?

Come see us at Lil' Britches. Our wide selection and professional staff are here to make your wedding dreams reality.

For Your Flowergirls

• Large selection of in stock dresses
• Special orders available
• Price range $42.95 - $99.95
• Size range 3 months through 16
• Affordable alterations

For Your Ring Bearers

• Large selection of in stock tuxes, vest sets and suits
• Special orders available
• Price range $36.95 - $73.95
• Size range 3 months through 16

Head To Toe Accessories

• Custom Hair Accessories & Tiaras
• Slips, Gloves & Jewelry
• Flowergirl Baskets & Ring Pillows
• Shoes & Hosiery
• Guest Book Sets & Much More

Other Services

We have a unique collection of Wedding Invitations, Napkins and Specialty Engraved Accessories.

Ask us how to save 10% on your total wedding purchase.

Please let this business know that you heard about them from the Bravo! Wedding Resource Guide. **443**

Notes

Gown Pressing, Cleaning & Preservation

Valls Photography • See page 550

The Wedding Torch

In ancient times the wedding torch

— a symbol of life and love —

was carried ahead of the bridal procession.

www.bravoportland.com

Gown Pressing & Preservation

- **Preparing your gown for the wedding day:** After alterations are performed on a new gown, have it pressed, and padded with tissue so it is perfect and ready to go on your wedding day. Make an appointment for cleaning or pressing a new gown at least one week before the wedding. When you pick up your wedding gown, bring a clean sheet to wrap around the dress in the car. It is best to lie it flat as possible in the back; do not fold the skirt as it will create a crease.

- **Preserving your precious gown:** Your wedding dress is a sentimental and costly investment. Saving this investment means special handling, packaging, and dry cleaning by experts. You should not only clean the gown, but preserve and save its beauty as an heirloom for future generations as soon as possbile after the wedding. Many brides today have the pleasure of wearing their mother's or grandmother's dress on their wedding day because it was properly cleaned and preserved.

- **Dealing with stains:** When you bring your gown to your dry cleaner, it is important to point out any stains. Different stains require different treatments. Champagne stains in particular can be very difficult to discover, because they do not show up right away, but darken with age.

- **Choosing a wedding gown specialist:** Today's wedding gowns feature beading, sequins and pearls that require delicate care and special handling. Be sure to select a cleaner that specializes in gown cleaning and preservation.

- **Avoiding common mistakes:** Avoid hanging your wedding gown over a prolonged time. This may cause the gown to stretch and sag. Fragile gowns should not be put in plastic bags, because moisture can form inside and promote mildew and fabric rot. Strong light, heat, or open air are other factors that will cause deterioration. Have your gown professionally preserved in a box.

For more assistance with staying organized during the wedding planning process, check out the Bravo! Wedding Organizer. Detailed question worksheets double as contracts. This step-by-step system will keep every detail of your wedding organized. To order, refer to the order form on page 25 in this Guide.

TAILORS & CLEANERS SINCE 1951

939 S.W. 10th
Downtown at the corner of 10th & Salmon
Portland, Oregon 97205
(503) 227-1144
Business Hours: Mon–Fri 6:30am–6pm; Sat 7:30am–12:30pm

Highest Quality Unique Cleaning Solvent

Our unique, environmentally safe solvent is guaranteed to be gentle to delicate wedding dresses. **It is proven not to harm beading, lace and handwork, or melt sequins on wedding gowns, formals, or special occasion dresses.** This solvent, as clear as water and odor free, is the safest method for properly cleaning your dress.

We clean all wedding dresses separate from any other clothes to ensure the best results. We produce the whitest, cleanest dress available because it is our policy not to compromise, and to go the extra step for our customers.

Professional Pressing

We pride ourselves on having the finest silk pressers in the city. With over 18 years of experience, you can be assured that your gown will be perfectly pressed for your special day.

Simply call to schedule, or bring in the dress a few days before the wedding, and we will have it pressed, delicately filled with tissue, and enclosed in plastic ready for your wedding day. Delivery to the church is available in certain areas. Fees begin at $55.

Expert in Preservation

We feel strongly that your special day should be remembered far into the future. After expertly cleaning your gown, we pack it in the highest quality box available with an acid-free liner and a mailing box, so that it may be easily shipped if necessary.

Between each fold we use museum approved, acid-free tissue and a bodice form, so that many years from now, when the time comes to pass it to the next generation, your gown will be as fresh as the day it was worn. Preservation fees begin at $125.

A Long History of Service

We have been in business for over 50 years with the same ownership. Because of this, we are well into our third generation of brides and wedding parties. We have perfected gown cleaning and preservation like no other cleaner in the area. Come see for yourself!

> **Bee Tailors & Cleaners was voted by a Downtown newspaper as "Best Dry Cleaner" in Portland for four years in a row.**

Cascade Summit CLEANERS

(Cleaners *Westlake* Laundry)

Cleaning and Preservation by Westlake and Cascade Summit Cleaners

14547 Westlake Drive • Lake Oswego, Oregon
-and-
2110 Salamo Road • West Linn, Oregon
(503) 639-2444 or (503) 655-3217
Store Hours: Mon–Fri 7am–6pm, Sat 9am–5pm, closed Sundays
Owned and operated by Steve Arena

Located in Lake Oswego and West Linn, Westlake and Cascade Summit professional dry cleaners specialize in the cleaning, pressing and preservation of your valuable wedding dress.

Why Should You Go to Westlake and Cascade Summit Cleaners?

- **State-of-the-art equipment:** Westlake and Cascade Summit Cleaners use state-of-the-art equipment to guarantee the best results for a lifetime.

- **Locally owned and operated:** We pride ourselves in giving each of our customers our undivided attention.

- **Quality care and customer service:** Our professional staff realizes how special your wedding day is and is willing to serve you with ultimate professional care.

Our Services:
- Pre-wedding alterations
- Pre-wedding cleaning and pressing
- Post-wedding cleaning
- Preservation

Simply call to make an appointment to discuss the delicate care of your wedding dress. We are here to help and provide the finest wedding dress care to ensure your memories are preserved forever.

Press only prices begin at $75.
Cleaning, pressing and preservation begin at $150.

photo by Holland Studios • See page 511

Flinging The Stocking

A custom passed down by the British started

when guests would invade the bridal chamber and

vie for the bride's and groom's stockings.

They then took turns flinging the stockings at

the newlyweds, with the belief that whoever landed

the stocking on the bride or groom's nose

would be the next person to marry.

www.bravoportland.com

Guest Accommodations

- **Accommodations for wedding attendants and guests:** Attendants and guests arriving from out-of-town often stay with relatives or friends, but this may not always be possible. Hotel accommodations may be more comfortable for everyone. Don't try to have attendants or relatives stay with you before the wedding...things will be hectic enough without worries about house guests.

- **Who pays for accommodations?** The bride and groom usually pay for the wedding attendants' accommodations. Out-of-town guests, both relatives and friends, pay for their own accommodations. As a courtesy to these guests, facilities and costs should be researched by the bride and groom to ensure comfort, convenient location and reasonable price.

- **Special group rates:** Most hotels offer a special group rate for your guests. Many have information and special cards that you can send to your guests in the invitations, or separately.

- **Transportation:** Inquire about transportation from the airport to the hotel. Some hotels provide complimentary service for your guests' convenience.

- **Bed-and-breakfast hospitality:** Most bed-and-breakfasts are private homes offering overnight accommodations. Traditionally, guests receive a homemade breakfast each morning. Unlike hotels, bed-and-breakfast rooms are individually unique, with furnishings that give a guest an "at-home" feeling. Generally the bed-and-breakfast owner will take your reservation, check you in and out, prepare and serve your breakfast, clean your room, and act as concierge and host. A minimum stay may be required, depending on the size of your group and days of the week involved. A deposit is generally required to guarantee your room at the time of reservation. Most bed-and-breakfasts are non-smoking.

- **Honeymoon getaways:** Wonderful honeymoon getaways or special accommodations for your wedding night are listed on the following pages. Many newlyweds are too exhausted and tired from the day's festivities to leave for the honeymoon on the night of the wedding. Look into some of the great local places available for your wedding night. These hotels, resorts and bed-and-breakfast establishments offer special honeymoon packages, and some offer free transportation to the airport the next day. If your budget doesn't allow for an exotic honeymoon this year, try a luxury resort at the beach, a relaxing ranch, or a remote cottage in the mountains. Whatever you plan, the two of you will be together, enjoying each other's company.

For more assistance with staying organized during the wedding planning process, check out the Bravo! Wedding Organizer. Detailed question worksheets double as contracts. This step-by-step system will keep every detail of your wedding organized. To order, refer to the order form on page 25 in this Guide.

611 S.W. Tenth at Alder
Portland, Oregon 97205
(503) 224-3400 or (800) 554-3456; Fax (503) 224-9426
E-mail: sales@govhotel.com; Web site: www.govhotel.com

Romantic, Boutique Hotel In The Heart Of It All

Discreet luxury awaits the newly married and their families in the elegant, turn-of-the-century Governor Hotel. Featuring 100 rooms, including 24 suites, this centrally located hotel offers lodging options that may include jet spa baths, terraces with city-scape views, or fireplaces. Combining services such as 24-hour room service, concierge services, wireless Internet, twice-daily maid service with evening turndown, laundry and dry cleaning services, shoe shine, morning newspaper and coffee in the lobby, The Governor offers a place of charm and style in which to prepare for and unwind from the event of a lifetime.

Special Packages and Pricing

The Governor Hotel's Romance Package is available for honeymoon or anniversary guests. Package prices vary depending on room selection and number of nights. Call (503) 224-3400 for pricing and details.

The Hotel also offers group rates for wedding parties. Families and friends will enjoy the downtown location, close to shopping, city attractions, dining, the arts, and entertainment. Group rates vary. Call (503) 241-2106 for details.

Banquets and Catering

The Governor's West Wing is the former historic Elk's Lodge building. Here guests may create banquets and catering events that complement the love and magic of the wedding day. Superbly hand-crafted rooms serve from 6 to 600 for elegant seated meals or energizing standing receptions. Jake's Catering at The Governor will assist in all phases of planning and preparation, and will also accommodate off-site catering plans. Call (503) 241-2125 for information and details.

Hotel Ambiance and Services

Built in 1909, and fully restored to its original grandeur, The Governor Hotel is listed on the National Register of Historic Places. The striking exterior of terra cotta and white brick is an architectural beauty. A wood-burning fireplace, hand-painted, sepia-colored murals, and traditional furnishings create a warm Northwest impression in the lobby. The restaurant and bar, Jake's Grill, is located off the main lobby. Offering traditional American cuisine, the restaurant has been named "one of the city's best" by *Condé Nast Traveler* magazine.

Historically tailored guest rooms and suites create a residential feel where guests may refresh from private bars and relax with movies or cable TV. For a small fee, fitness-minded guests may enjoy privileges at the hotel's on-site, full-service, adult-only athletic club.

The Mark Spencer Hotel

409 S.W. 11th Avenue at Stark
Portland, OR 97205
503-224-3293 or 1-800-548-3934
www.markspencer.com
hospitality@markspencer.com

A Warm Welcome:

We invite you to experience the hospitality and exceptional value of The Mark Spencer Hotel, a one-of-a-kind treasure in downtown Portland. Built in 1907, The Mark Spencer retains a bit of old-world warmth with its intimate European-style lobby, comfortable guest rooms and friendly, attentive service.

Each of our 101 guest rooms and suites offers a *fully-equipped kitchen, wireless high speed internet, voice mail, air conditioning* and *windows that open.*

Daily *continental breakfast* and *afternoon tea* are featured in our Library. A visit to our *roof top garden deck* is a relaxing way to enjoy wonderful city and mountain views.

Location, Location, Location:

Just outside our doors, your guests will discover everything downtown Portland has to offer. Oregon's tax-free shopping; restaurants to satisfy every palate, performing and visual arts venues, and plenty of outdoor adventure start the list. Our staff is happy to assist your guests in enjoying the city to its fullest.

Special Rates for Family and Friends:

The Hotel offers wedding discounts with no minimum room block required. In addition, our *complimentary room night program* makes it easy for you to earn free room nights – to be enjoyed by you or others in your party.

Event Space:

Flexible catering options are sure to meet your needs. Our meeting areas are perfect for small bridal luncheons or informal receptions. The roof top garden deck can also accommodate small groups for casual gatherings.

452

Please let this business know that you heard about them from the Bravo! Wedding Resource Guide.

THE PARAMOUNT HOTEL

A WESTCOAST HOTEL

808 S.W. Taylor Street
Portland, Oregon 97205
Contact: Kristine Thayer (503) 276-1763
Web site: www.paramounthotel.net

Downtown's Newest Boutique Hotel

Description of Hotel
European-style, 15-story boutique hotel boasts 154 oversized guestrooms including 46 Executive Kings with whirlpool baths, 20 Deluxe Balcony rooms, and two one-bedroom Grand Suites with whirlpool baths and fireplaces.

Location
Located in the heart of downtown Portland's business, retail and cultural districts, Nordstrom, Pioneer Square Park, Portland Center for the Performing Arts, Arlene Schnitzer Concert Hall, Portland Art Museum and Portland State University are all within a short stroll.

Accommodations
Deluxe guestrooms feature King or two Queen beds, two telephones with dataport and voicemail, hair dryers, iron and ironing board, refrigerated mini-bar, 25" televisions, Nintendo, TazoTeas, pay movies and in-room coffee from Cafe Appasionato, the Northwest coffee experts. Executive rooms have oversized jetted bathtubs and a separate glass standing shower. Paramount rooms also have a private patio.

Guest Amenities
- Signature restaurant and lounge, Dragon Fish Asian Café
- Includes complimentary morning newspaper Monday through Friday
- Fully equipped fitness room open 24 hours
- Business Services
- Valet Parking
- Valet Laundry and Dry Cleaning Services
- Room Service
- Accessible Guestrooms

Meeting Space
- Two intimate 750-square-foot function rooms, accommodating up to 70 people

RIVERSIDE ESTATE

10323 Schuler Road • Aurora, Oregon 97002
Contact: Laurel and Scott Cookman
(503) 678-2195
E-mail: w.gables@juno.com
www.willamettegables.com

Wedding receptions and special events in an intimate country setting on the banks of the Willamette River

If you love crisp sheets, cozy robes, gourmet breakfasts, chocolate truffles, bouquets of fresh flowers and gorgeous views, then you will love it at Willamette Gables Riverside Estate.

Willamette Gables is a five-acre country estate on the banks of the Willamette River, 30 minutes south of Portland and 30 minutes north of Salem. This beautiful southern plantation-style home provides the perfect backdrop for your wedding and reception.

The adjacent gardens overlook the meandering Willamette River, offering gorgeous views and solitude. Willamette Gables specializes in quality customer service and attention to detail.

Willamette Gables is shown by appointment only from 11am to 5pm. The property will not be shown if guests are present.

Rooms: five uniquely decorated rooms with private baths.

Catering: choose your own caterer (we reserve the right to approve your selection) or choose from our list

Types of Events: weddings, receptions, picnics, garden parties, teas, anniversaries, private parties, meetings, seminars and retreats

Availability and Terms

Available year round; all reservations must be accompanied by a 50% deposit; the balance is due 45 days prior to your arrival.

Description of Facility and Services

Seating: indoor: tables and chairs provided
Servers: provided by caterer
Bar facilities: caterer provides licensed bartender and liability insurance; beer, wine and champagne only
Linens and table service: provided by caterer; linens must be ground length
Setup and tear down: provided; caterers are expected to provide their own cleanup and trash removal
Decorations: many items are provided; little decoration needed; no rice, birdseed or confetti
Sound system: responsibility of client
Parking: ample parking; parking attendants included in the fee

Special Services

* **Covered Area:** 40′ x 40′ canopy (upon request) for an additional charge
* **Wedding and Event coordination:** experienced assistance is available

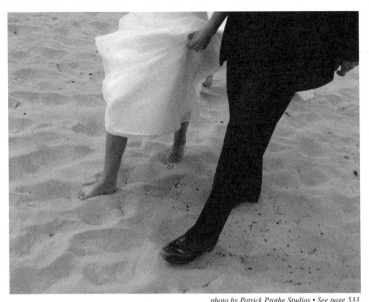

photo by Patrick Prothe Studios • See page 533

"Keep your eyes wide open before marriage,

and half-shut afterwards."

– Benjamin Framklin

Honeymoon & Travel Specialists

www.bravoportland.com

An Unforgettable HONEYMOON ®

Romantic Travel for Couples

www.unforgettablehoneymoon.com

134 S.E. Taylor, Portland, OR 97214
Contact: Reneé Duane
(503) 249-8444, Toll-free (888) 343-6413

Hundreds of Honeymoon and Destination Wedding Packages… to fit every budget!

Local to worldwide. We offer the widest range of honeymoon travel packages available. Our clients have honeymooned in quaint Northwest inns to exclusive private island hideaways in the South Pacific.

Our Service…a step beyond the ordinary

Informative Consultations—Honeymoon Consultant Renee Duane works closely with each couple, personally meeting and consulting with them several times before plans are finalized. She offers a lifetime of travel experience and first-hand knowledge of many of the destinations that couples most often choose for their honeymoon. Renee provides each couple with tips and suggestions on what to see, where to dine and what to pack.

Free Honeymoon—bridal registry

Your dream honeymoon becomes reality with our fabulous new registry program. We provide elegantly designed cards to be distributed to your wedding guests. Well-wishers can contribute to your honeymoon by ordering travel gift certificates.

Couples Only—All-inclusive Resorts…everything is included!

Honeymoon couples love the all-inclusive resorts that allow them to completely relax in a beautiful resort that includes all meals, drinks, activities and even tips!

Exotic South Pacific…authentic island-style weddings and honeymoons

Imagine being whisked away on a glass bottom boat to a deserted motu (tiny private island) to enjoy an unforgettable, traditional island-style wedding! Afterwards…relax in your own beachfront villa with private pool overlooking pure paradise. Accommodations: private island hideaways, luxury resorts, rustic bungalows (cheap!), intimate cruises and yacht charters.

Complimentary weddings…with your honeymoon

We represent many luxury resorts and hotels that include a beautiful wedding ceremony, flowers, cake, and much more at no additional charge.

www.unforgettablehoneymoon.com

**Call us today to schedule your
free Honeymoon Consultation.
(503) 249-8444**

Honeymoons
By
Focus on Travel, Inc.
"Friendly Oregon Service Since 1986"

www.focusontravel.com • email: honeymoons@focusontravel.com

14335 SW Allen Blvd., Suite 100 • Beaverton, OR 97705
Phone: 503-646-3700 • Toll Free: 888-233-9890

It's your Honeymoon – Ask us. Someone has been there!!
We work with 30 local travel planners waiting to make your dreams come true.

Getting Started

Order our free honeymoon planner. You have so many details preparing for your wedding. This will help you organize your Honeymoon Dreams—place, price, time, and what if we? Dare to Dream. We work with you designing your Honeymoon, fitting your budget, style, and imagination: Private Island in Fiji, Chateau in France, Condo in Maui, Ski Slopes of Sun Valley, Paris in Las Vegas, or a Chartered Yacht Sailing the Virgin Islands.

Pictures Worth a Thousand Words

• Video and CD Library
• Destination, resort, cruise, rail, tour brochures
• Websites – Our favorites
• Travel Books – Recommendations from customers and us

What Kind of Honeymoon

Cruises – 3 nights or more – Seattle, Los Angeles, Honolulu, Miami, New Orleans, Athens…
All Inclusive Resorts – Caribbean & Mexican Favorites – does it include everything?
I Want Something Different – Dive in Bahamas, trek in Nepal, sail in Tonga, bike Provence
How About Local Places – Houseboats, spas, bed & breakfasts, park lodges, city stays
Plus: Include a Free Wedding, Upgrade to a Concierge Suite for free china and crystal!!

Making It Reality

Use the research tools or let us plan it all – your choice. We work closely with couples in person, by phone, or through email. Focus on Travel, Inc. has been planning honeymoons for more than 18 years for all budgets and ages. We love travel and it shows.

All our Honeymooners get extras including local area coupons for luggage, clothes, travel books, and a suggested itinerary with restaurant and activity suggestions.

Moms, Aunts, Grandmas—Relive the Romance—Renew your vows on a second honeymoon!

Honeymoon Registry * Wedding Planning * Specialists * Rail Passes * Foreign Currency

Associated with Lisa Hetzler at a Taste for Adventure; see Honeymoon Registry, page 255

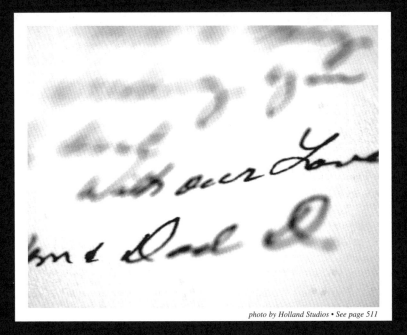

Becoming Engaged

The act of engagement has been

symbolized in many different ways.

During the Middle Ages, an engagement

was assumed if a woman drank wine or

another alcoholic beverage with

a member of the opposite sex.

In American colonial times, a couple who shared

food in a kitchen were thought to be engaged.

www.bravoportland.com

Invitations & Announcements

- **Where do you draw the line with the guest list:** The bride's family, groom's family and bride and groom generally each develop a "wish list". Then the list is narrowed down closer to the attendance you have budgeted for. Usually the attendance will be between 60-75% based on if family and friends live in town or not. A good rule of thumb to narrow down the list—if you haven't made contact with the person in the last year, leave them off.

- **Single Friends and Guests:** If friends are single and you encourage them to bring a guest, you can write "and Guest" on the invitation. If a couple is living together, you can send one invitation with both their names listed alphabetically.

- **Don't forget to include the wedding party:** Remember, even though special people are playing a role in your wedding you *do* need to send invitations to them: parents, grandparents, clergy, attendants and immediate family. A good idea is to even send an invitation to yourself to track the date guests will receive the invitation.

- **Number of invitations needed:** When figuring the number of invitations to order, combine the lists from the bride's parents, the groom's parents, the bride, and the groom. The mother of the bride or the bride should discuss with the groom's mother the number of invitations available to the groom's family. When the lists are compiled, any additions, deletions, and corrections can be made by everyone. Be sure you are counting families or couples not individual guests for the number of invitations needed.

- **Invitation styles:** Thousands of invitation styles are available: traditional, contemporary, custom designs, some with double envelopes or a folding invitation sealed with a sticker. When it comes time to select your invitations, pick the one that best suits your tastes, personal style and budget. This is the first presentation of your wedding to both your family and guests.

- **Ordering your invitations:** Ideally, you should order your invitations three to four months before the wedding to allow enough time for delivery. Some shops offer quick-print service in one day to one week. Invitations should be sent six to eight weeks before the wedding.

- **Engagement announcements or Save the Date cards:** It is nice to let out-of-town guests know as far as a year in advance of your wedding. A simple card with your names, the date and city and state of the wedding are all that is needed. Hotel information may also be included.

- **Wording the invitation:** When you order, be sure to work with a shop that specializes in invitations. These experts can help you fill out the complicated order forms, and will help you with correct wording for the invitation.

- **Correct spelling of names:** Etiquette books cover proper addressing of both inner and outer envelopes. Before addressing your envelopes, make sure you double check on your master list for the CORRECT spelling of names.

- **Calligraphy and addressing:** Invitations can be hand calligraphed or by machine. This adds a very personal touch to your invitations.

- **Custom hand-crafted and graphic designed invitations:** Invitations can tie in with the decor.

For more assistance with staying organized during the wedding planning process, check out the Bravo! Wedding Organizer. Detailed question worksheets double as contracts. This step-by-step system will keep every detail of your wedding organized. To order, refer to the order form on page 25 in this Guide.

Specializing in...

Custom Invitations, Thermographed

& Traditional Invitations

Selections and Styles

The theme of your wedding can be introduced to your guests through your wedding invitation. From simple to elegant, traditional to custom. Anders Printing invites you to come in, sit down and browse through our wide selection of catalogs, as well as our samples of custom wedding invitations, announcements, save the date and programs.

Special Services

Our friendly staff will gladly answer your questions from wording etiquette to saving money on your order. Let us help you get the invitations you'll be proud of at a price you can afford. Got your own ideas? Want something a bit more original? We can help you come up with that perfect invitation. And remember, just because its "custom" doesn't mean it costs more! In fact, our custom prices are quite comparable to catalog invitations!

Ordering

We recommend that you order your invitations at least three months prior to your wedding day, but we also can accommodate those last minute weddings (depending on the quantity and complexity of your order) in as little as two days to two weeks.

A 60% deposit is required to start your order, with the balance due upon receipt.

Other

Don't forget, we also do thank you notes, table cards, napkins and personalized gifts.

Please check our web site for a free gift.

Annie Occasion

Elegant. Vibrant. Fresh. Funky. Beautiful. Romantic.

Hand-crafted event invitations, announcements, and favors.

To schedule your personal consultation, please contact:
Annie Burn, owner/designer
(503) 407-8847 annieoccasion@yahoo.com
See what we've created at www.annieoccasion.com

Innovative Style Unites with Bold Materials

Your wedding invitation is the first impression of the special day to come. It creates the theme, atmosphere and personal style of your event. You're invited to experience the most unique and vibrant invitations, all of which are tailored to reflect your individuality and personal chic. Annie Occasion specializes in creating an original and innovative design that will set you and your event apart from the ordinary.

The Process

We first meet with you one on one to discuss all the elements that make up your special day. Consultations are complimentary and can be scheduled weekdays, evenings or weekends. You can browse through the huge selection of sample invitations to get ideas and inspiration. Once the style, colors and materials for the invitation are determined, a price quote will be given to you within 24 hours. If the quote is accepted, a 50% deposit is required to begin production and you will soon receive a proof of your invitation. The remaining 50% is due prior to delivery.

Pricing

Because each invitation is unique and tailored specifically for each individual, price will vary depending on design, complexity, type of print and availability of materials.

Stun Your Guests

Before you say "I Do," entice your guests with a glimpse into your special day with a distinctive, one-of-a-kind invitation.

What Annie Occasion can do for you:

• Design and produce a unique and personalized invitation
• Create coordinating pieces such as save-the-date cards, menus, programs, maps, Thank You cards and much more
• Share ideas on invitation wording and etiquette
• Offer flat printing, thermography, foil stamping and embossing
• Create correspondence to fit most budgets

CHÉRIE RONNING
& ASSOCIATES

Calligraphy
and
Addressing Service
Local: 360.573.5461
Toll Free 800.676.3030
Web site: www.weaddressforyou.com; By Appointment Only

ADD STYLE TO YOUR INVITATIONS!

The arrival of your wedding invitation gives your guests insight to the style of your special day! Give an extra special look to your carefully chosen invitations with calligraphic addressing of the envelopes.

We have purchased a special calligraphic plotter that actually holds a calligraphic pen and "hand-writes" the names and addresses on the envelopes. It is the same machine used at The White House for the addressing of all social stationary, place cards, menus and other items required for important dinners and special events. We also have a commercial printer capable of printing in any font or color.

The service is very affordable. Pricing begins at $1 per outer envelope. For an additional $.50 per name we will coordinate and stuff the envelopes, affix your provided postage and drop them in the mail. This is the perfect service for very busy brides!

Place cards are available in many styles. The price for a single line is $.75 per card, with an additional $.25 for each line inside the card. Use them at the rehearsal dinner, bridesmaid's luncheon, wedding reception, wedding brunch and any number of other special occasion events.

Table names or numbers begin at $1, depending on the size required. Special frames are available in silver or gold tones for table signs. We can also create menus, programs, favor tags and other printed items.

See sample book at:
The Wedding Cottage
4775 S.W. Watson Avenue
Beaverton, OR
or
421 SW 4th Avenue
Portland, OR.

We offer free pickup and return in the Portland area, with a one week turn-around.

Complete Wedding Printing, Inc.

Portland
2236 N.E. 82nd Avenue
(503) 252-6222

Beaverton
117th and S.W. Canyon Road, Suite E
(503) 646-0821

Open Mon–Fri and Sun; Evenings by appointment
Web site: www.completeweddingprinting.com

For **Stress Free** ordering and **Quick** turnaround come to
Complete Wedding Printing.

"Old Fashioned Service with New Ideas"

All Major Books • Custom Designs • Your Design

The Personal Touch

Complete Wedding Printing is a locally-owned, specialty print shop. We are proud to offer an in-house printing facility along with one of the largest selections of wedding invitations from associated suppliers. The hallmark of our business is the "personal touch." If a bride wants a unique invitation with her artwork or calligraphy, we are glad to create the invitation she wants.

Competitive Prices

Shop and compare Complete Wedding Printing's personally printed invitations, prices and services, or choose from all the major books. We will work within your budget!

Personalized Printing

It's your wedding and we encourage you to do it your way, by creating the perfect wedding invitation. Our professional consultants are able to work with you to create your own special invitation. Using your design, ideas, artwork or photo our skilled printers can produce that unique image that is you. Whether printed personally or printed from a supplier, invitations with a rich appearance, raised lettering and a wide selection of designs are available. We also feature the popular layered look, using handmade paper.

Accessories

Many different accessories are available to personalize your wedding. These range from custom printed wedding programs, matches, napkins, ribbons, thank-you's, photo tissues to toasting glasses or unity candles. We are glad to provide that special accessory you need.

**When placing your order, please mention that you saw
this listing to receive 20% off on your invitations,
and 50 FREE Thank-you's.**

1385 McVey Avenue • Lake Oswego, Oregon 97034
Tel: 503-697-4424 • Fax: 503-697-4428 • www.grandpapery.com
Open 7 Days A Week! Mon-Sat: 10 am - 6 pm & Sun: 12 - 5 pm

You're engaged...Congratulations!
Let us help you create your perfect wedding invitation,
wedding program, placecards, menus...

Passionate Creativity and Outstanding Service.
We have over 20 years of custom invitation design and event planning experience to help you set
the scene for the wedding of your dreams! One-on-one personalized service with experienced
staff can help with wording etiquette, design options and all phases of your wedding.

Big Budget, Little Budget and Everything in Between.
Select from one of the major books: Crane's, William Arthur, Checkerboard, Sweet Pea, etc...
or we can help customize an invitation that is best suits you.

In-house Typesetting & Printing w/Same-Day Service Available.
HUGE selection of printer-ready "imprintable" invitations.
Bulk order discounts and Calligraphy addressing services available.

The Grand Papery is your one-stop location for invitations and gifts.
Engagement Parties • Save the Date Announcements
Bridal Showers • the Rehearsal Dinner • Wedding Invitations
Baby Announcements • Anniversary Parties

We are passionate about invitations and we are great at what we do.
Let us help you set the scene for the wedding of your dreams!

Invitation Station
Personalizing Life's Moments
Save **20% Off** Retail Prices
- Wedding Invitations
- Party Invitations
- Personal Stationary
- Baby Announcements
- Graduation Announcements
- Business Stationary

We carry top manufacturers such as:
- Carlson Craft
- Birchcraft
- Regency
- Stylart
- Embossed Graphics

Locally Owned, Personal Service
For an Appointment Call Tia Newcomer
503.234.1092

invitationstation@comcast.net
www.invitationstation.cceasy.com
http://invitationstation.regency.ac
http://www.yourinvitationplace.com/invitationstation

hand maiden cards
making first impressions
making lasting memories

503-408-1208
vanessa@handmaidencards.com
www.handmaidencards.com

distinctive, hand-made wedding invitations

Till it has loved, no man or woman can become itself.
— Emily Dickinson

The invitation is the beginning of your wedding event; delivering a unique presence and setting the stage. Start with an exclusive, personalized invitation from **hand maiden cards** illustrating your vow to excellence and individuality.

Two roads diverged in a woods, and I ~I took the one less traveled by,
And that has made all the difference.
— Robert Frost

Conservation is a priority for **hand maiden cards.** We use recycled papers, eco-friendly components and buy from responsible suppliers. Our philosophy is to create an exquisite product our clients are proud to send.

To schedule an initial consultation please email vanessa@handmaidencards.com or call 503-408-1208. A 50% deposit is required when placing your order, with balance due upon delivery. We can also assist you with a coordinating ensemble of:

- shower invitations
- rehearsal dinner announcements
- programs
- menus
- place cards
- thank you cards
- personalized notes

There is no end. There is no beginning. There is only the infinite passion of life.
— Federico Fellini

503.515.4814 • meyshaprice@msn.com • www.madronahill.com

Welcome to Madrona Hill Collective. Sit back and relax while we take care of your wedding and special event invitations. With over six years of experience as a designer, Meysha Price creates classic, unique and ultra modern invites. She continues to provide new packages that take a step beyond your typical invitation.

We believe that every invitation should arrive as an informative presentation. Opening the package should be an anticipated event; the first in a series of wedding celebrations. The theme of your wedding should begin with the invitation, as the invitation and announcements reflect you and the mood of your event.

We can help you select a theme or a style and assist you with coordinating colors and concepts. Choose from many unique designs and graphics, or share your vision with us and we will create a custom package just for you. Coordinating maps, programs, save-the-date-cards, place cards, menus, favor tags, rehearsal dinner invites, announcements, thank-you cards and guest books can also be ordered.

Ideally, invitations should be ordered three to four months before your wedding day and be in the mail three to six weeks before your event. We recommend sending save-the-date cards one year to six months prior to your date. Our process usually takes between four and six weeks, however we will do everything possible to accommodate your timeline. We understand the life of a bride is full of "little" details and we will take care of tracking your invitation timeline and mail dates.

Any size order is possible and we offer a wide range of prices due to the variety of combinations and choices. Prices are determined by quantity and design complexity. Generally, our fees range from $3-$8 per invitation. Please call to schedule your personal consultation, to make an appointment to look at our portfolio, or to request a specific price quote.

516 N.W. 12th Avenue • Portland, Oregon 97209
Between Glisan and Hoyt in the Pearl District
Tel. 503.223.1093 • Fax 503.295.7144
Web site: www.oblationpapers.com

HANDCRAFTED PROCLAMATIONS OF JUBILANT LIFE EVENTS

A Place for Paper Lovers in the Pearl District
- Fine Papers, Pens and Photo Albums
- Custom Wedding Invitation Gallery
- Hand-Papermaking Studios
- Letterpress Printing

We Love New Ideas!
Our experienced staff is poised to help you propel your great ideas into an artful expression of the couple you're about to become.

Along with our gallery of uniquely designed social announcements, we also offer a select handful of books filled with the most beautiful invitations imaginable:

Oblation Papers & Press • Anna Griffin • Claudia Calhoun

Take Notice • Twinrocker • Enid Wilson • Elum

Crane's • William Arthur • Envelopements • Studio Z

Wax seals, Italian photo albums, fountain pens from Paris, hand-bound guest books, and hand-dyed silk ribbons can add a richness to your personal story.

Visit our Studios
Come visit our studios, where exquisite papers are made each day. Choose the fresh flower petal inclusions we place into your invitations, or compare the textures of olive green mango paper with creamy white Italian Amalfi and sheer gold-flecked unryu from Japan.

Letterpress
This fine method of printing is more sought after than ever, with its debossed, dimensional quality that offers an integrity not found in the world of quick print. Come view our century-old cast iron presses in action, and begin to make your own impressions.

PAPER
gourmet
distinctive
cards &
invitations

503.869.5597 • rsvp@papergourmet.net • www.papergourmet.net

Tying the knot. Joining in holy matrimony. Getting hitched. Taking the plunge. Saying "I do."

However you characterize your impending nuptials, *Paper Gourmet* has the perfect invitation to capture individual tastes and unique personalities. With as many paper and design options as there are ways to say "We're getting married," *Paper Gourmet* specializes in giving your guests a first glimpse into your big day—and your life together—that reflects your style and tells your story.

Getting married on the beach or having a Mardi Gras-style reception? Maybe you share a passion for poetry, enjoy golfing or love to travel. Perhaps you're weaving a theme or color through your wedding. *Paper Gourmet* meets one-on-one with you to determine the elements that set you apart, then reflects those elements by blending colors, textures and images in glorious combinations. The result is one-of-a-kind handmade invitations, reception cards, RSVP cards, programs and thank you notes that will dazzle and delight.

Paper Gourmet offers:
• Initial no-cost consultation
• Personal, flexible attention
• A unique signature on your special event

Wedding packages vary in price depending on design, materials and complexity.

Keep *Paper Gourmet* in mind for other event necessities. *Paper Gourmet* also provides:
• Programs
• Thank you cards
• Shower/rehearsal dinner invitations
• Personalized stationery for the newlyweds
• Bridal party gifts

Visit the gallery at www.papergourmet.net for a delicious taste of what *Paper Gourmet* can do for you.

Exceptional Paper and Matching Envelopes
Custom-Printed Announcements
Hundreds of Unique Rubber Stamps
Thousands of Embellishments
Beautiful Scrapbook Papers and Album
Elegant Gift Wrappings

For our store locations or online shopping, visit:
www.paperzone.com

Vancouver	**Portland**	**Beaverton**	**Salem**
6718-A NE Fourth Plain Blvd.	1136 SE Grand Ave.	10029 SW Nimbus	1880 Commercial NE
(corner of Grand & Salmon)	(corner of Scholls Ferry Rd.)	(corner of River & Commercial)	(in Silver Star Plaza)
360.906.1644	503.233.2933	503.641.8112	503.364.9826

Huge Selection of Exceptional Paper and Matching Envelopes

Create your own unique wedding announcements from our huge selection of beautiful papers and cards, including gorgeous translucent vellum, and rich iridescent and metallic papers. You'll also find hundreds of different envelopes: from classic creamy white to deep black linen, including uncommon sizes like square envelopes and 6" X 9"s. We stock a wide variety of envelopes and cards that match our papers, many manufactured for us and not available anywhere else. Remember to get coordinated colored papers to make your programs, bridal shower invitations, favors and menus.

Custom-Printed Announcements

The Paper Zone stocks a wide variety of announcements, panel cards, and decorative wedding invitations for custom printing with our help or at home. You can special order hundreds of blank wedding invitations and announcements within a few days. Hand-make your own invitations with the help of our experienced staff and our free project sheets and guides. Complement your wedding announcements with place cards, thank-you notes, reply and accessory cards, and even guest books.

Hundreds of Unique Rubber Stamps and Thousands of Embellishments

Choose accents for your handmade invitations from hundreds of different rubber stamps, dozens of punches and literally thousands of other embellishments. Add color and dimension to pre-made announcements using embossing powders and soft metallic inks. Find the perfect look to decorate place cards, compliment programs and favors.

Beautiful Scrapbook Albums and Papers

Remember this special day with a hand-made scrapbook. We have hundreds of different 12" X 12" scrapbook papers, and beautiful albums from vibrant reds to soft butter in the latest fabrics. Embellish your pages with all the hot new items from Making Memories such as: brads, eyelets, snaps, charms, tools and much more!

Elegant Gift Wrappings

Decorate favor boxes and cover guest books with our amazing selection of specialty gift wrap and handmade papers. Design wedding invitations using background papers full of festive florals or rustic threads. Accent favors with ribbons, bows, and ties. Bag up cards and package presents, or create your own centerpieces. Let our staff assist you in finding or creating the perfect announcement and accessory that fits your style, wedding size and budget.

Recent Customer Comments

"Paper Zone has the best selection of paper in town." "It's a paper lover's heaven." "The most creatively encouraging place."

Main Store
4775 S.W. Watson Avenue
Beaverton, Oregon 97005
(503) 643-9730

Downtown
421 S.W. Fourth Avenue
Portland, Oregon 97204
(503) 827-4578

www.weddingcottageoregon.com

The most enormous selection of elegant invitations and accessories from economical to extravagant.

The Wedding Cottage is known for having the most beautiful as well as the largest selection of invitations in the Portland area. With over 17 years of experience, The Wedding Cottage is able to help brides with tough etiquette questions, as well as wording for traditional and contemporary invitations, announcements, receptions, programs and save the date cards.

Selections and Styles

The selection of paper is enormous, with over 60 books containing hundreds of invitations from which to choose. Handmade papers, vellum overlays, tea length, and of course 100% cotton papers are just some of the choices. All can be printed in a variety of fonts and ink colors. We stock beautiful ribbons, wax seals, foil seals, pressed flowers, and die cut embellishments that can be used on invitations, envelopes, favors or place cards. We carry invitations from the following companies:

Alden Grace	Elite	Nu Art
Anna Griffin	Embossed Graphics	Oblation
Birchcraft	Encore	Pulp Paper
Carlson Craft	Fred Hoskings	Regency
Chase	Gala	Sonnell
Checkerboard	Koza	Stylart
Classic	Krepe Kraft	Take Notice
Crane's	McPherson	William Arthur
Des Amie	Mission	& more!

Save the date, rehearsal dinner, shower and bridal luncheon invitations, as well as, thank you notes, place cards and table cards.

Imprintables

A variety of blank papers that you can print yourself or we can print for you is available. Envelope addressing is offered also, a beautiful touch to any invitation and such a time saver for any busy bride.

Ordering

Our knowledgeable staff provides excellent customer service and individual help in writing your invitations. Printed orders are generally back within two to three weeks, depending on the invitation. However, some can be received within two to three days, if needed. Of course allowing plenty of time is always best—four to six months prior to the wedding is recommended. Invitations are mailed out four to eight weeks before the wedding, depending on the situation. Free freight on all orders.

See page 206 under Bridal Accessories.

photo by Vall's Photographic • See page 550

Origins of the Engagement Ring

The giving of an engagement ring was considered to

show commitment on the groom's part to purchase

the bride. The use of rings within the wedding

ceremony can be traced back to the ancient

Egyptians and Romans.

www.bravoportland.com

JUDITH ARNELL JEWELERS

717 N.W. 11th • Portland, Oregon 97209
Located in the Pearl District
(503) 227-3437; Fax (503) 227-3438; E-mail: jla@spiritone.com
Web site: www.juditharnelljewelers.com
Business Hours: 10am–5:30pm Tues–Sat;
other hours reserved for private appointments

Specialty

Judith Arnell Jewelers specializes in **platinum** wedding bands and engagement rings, from antique-estate diamond jewelry to modern, custom-designed platinum wedding sets ranging in price from $250 and up. We are proud to have one of Portland's largest and most unique collections of antique platinum engagement rings.

Types of Jewelry Sold

Engagement rings, wedding bands, precious and semi-precious stone jewelry, earrings, bracelets, pendants and necklaces, custom designed and handmade fine jewelry, pearls, cufflinks and studs.

Shapes and Kinds of Stones Available

We specialize in GIA certified ideal cut diamonds in all shapes, sizes and qualities at wholesale prices, with an extensive selection of Asscher cut diamonds. We also carry a wide variety of Sapphires, Rubies, Emeralds and other precious and semi-precious stones.

Custom Design

Designer Judith Arnell has been in the wholesale jewelry business for more than 30 years as a designer and manufacturer of fine jewelry. She will personally work with you to design the perfect, one one-of-a-kind piece of jewelry…at a reasonable price! Please stop by our studio to view our work and discuss your jewelry needs in a comfortable atmosphere.

Our Mission

Our mission is to make sure our customers get the best product at the lowest possible price. Making you a satisfied customer is always our priority…and we are confident that we cannot be undersold.

Notes

photo by AJ's • See page 495

My most brilliant achievement was my ability to be

able to persuade my wife to marry me.

– Winston Churchill

A Bonding of Love
REV. ROBERT BONDS
(503) 781-9482
Web site: www.anytimeweddings.com

© Woodstock Photography

Your moment in time. Your personal sacred ceremony in your own special way. Traditional or creative in a setting of your choice or we will be happy to assist. There is no charge for our initial meeting.

Family Blending Ceremony
I offer a special ceremony for those who have children from a previous marriage. Short notice is accepted. I provide an informal get-acquainted session to go over details. I am a nondenominational minister licensed to perform ceremonies in Oregon and Washington.

A Perfect Ceremony
by Rev. Robert Griffen
(503) 289-5115; r.griffen@attbi.com

Rev. Griffen knows more about great weddings than anyone! He has been in "the business" for over 30 years; renting tuxedos while a seminary student and 25 years as a wedding photographer and Presbyterian Minister (*yes, he photographs the same couples he marries!*). He is very creative and will accommodate a broad range of liturgical styles and traditions, including those of non-traditional and alternative life-style couples. Call or e-mail for an appointment today!

"We couldn't have been happier! He was so sincere and has a warm sense of humor; I was very nervous, and he got me to relax. Our wedding was perfect!"   John & Julie R.

"He helped us plan our whole day, not just the ceremony. We avoided some big problems thanks to him, and the day was trouble-free."   Mary & Drew J.

"Griff was great! Helped us write our vows and made our ceremony simply wonderful. He had us stand so the photos were great too!"   Keith & Cindy W.

Amoore Wedding Chapel
Pastor Art Moore, Wedding Officiant
Traditional and Non-Traditional, including non-Religious, Interfaith and Reaffirmation of Vows!
(503) 240-8144

Pastor Moore is known for his warmth and professionalism. You should have no surprises at you wedding ceremony. You should know what is going to be said. Your ceremony is about you: the bride and groom.

There is no charge for our initial meeting. Pastor Moore can perform your ceremony anytime, at our wedding chapel or anywhere, including beach sites. The most important event of your life will be beautiful, inspirational and elegant. Planned weddings or last minute ceremonies are all accepted. Please call us at (503) 240-8144 for an appointment to discuss your wedding needs.

REV. SCOTT AWBREY
Non-Denominational Minister
503-582-0432

rev.scottawbrey@verizon.net • www.revscottawbrey.com
Congratulations on your upcoming marriage! I am an ordained minister, serving a local church, and have served hundreds of couples in creating ceremonies that reflect their own beliefs, wishes and hearts' desire. I perform a wide variety of ceremonies, such as non-denominational, Christian, interfaith, civil or other unique ceremonies. I can also provide such special elements as the Unity Candle, the Rose ceremony or Uniting the New Family.

It would be my privilege to assist you with your wedding. Blessings.

Dear Rev. Awbrey,
We can't thank you enough for our wedding ceremony. It was absolutely perfect, and we appreciate the special touch you gave our service. All of our guests couldn't stop talking about the beautiful and touching ceremony!   *Sincerely,*
Barbara and Charles Kaylor

REV. SHARON K. BIEHL
(503) 653-2013

Creative, personalized wedding ceremonies. It's your day, so it should be your way! I specialize in traditional, nontraditional, religious, or nonreligious ceremonies tailored to fit your wishes and beliefs. As a nondenominational minister, I can be flexible to the situation, and I'll be glad to perform the ceremony at a site of your choice. There is no charge for an initial meeting to discuss your plans for the ceremony. At that time we'll be able to determine exactly what you want and discuss the costs. Call for an appointment anytime between 8am and 8pm. **Licensed to perform weddings in Oregon and Washington.**

REV. CATHERINE CONKEY
Heart-Centered Ceremonies
(503) 234-6851

Lovingly personalized wedding ceremonies. I work together with you to create a wedding ceremony that will reflect and celebrate your uniqueness as a couple. The more your wedding ceremony reflects you, the more joyful, meaningful and memorable experience it is for you and your guests who celebrate with you.

As a nondenominational minister, I am open to, and enjoy, performing a variety of ceremony styles and can share a variety of creative touches and ideas to make your day extra special. I am licensed to perform weddings in Oregon and Washington at the location of your choice. My fee is $125 and includes a planning session and officiating your wedding. Rehearsal time and long distance travel would be additional.

CUSTOM CEREMONIES
by Marky Kelly — and You
(503) 282-2108 ext. 3   www.customceremonies.com

The coming together of loving individuals is a creative dynamic process — and the expression of their commitment to one another is an ideal opportunity to mirror that joyful enthusiasm. As you have been reading through this resource guide, no doubt you've been fueled with many exciting ideas for the visual setting of your wedding…but what words do you want your family and friends to hear that day? How do you want your wedding to be? Solemn? Playful? Sacred? Serene?

Let me help you say just the right thing. I am a licensed non-denominational minister who enjoys taking time to find out about you. Together we can collaborate in designing your ideal ceremony, one which gives you and those who celebrate with you a true sense of your decision to share life's journey.

Because my spiritual "un-focus" embraces many religious traditions, I can help you blend elements of different faiths, as well as shape the ceremony content from non-traditional and/or secular sources. Our first meeting will be no-cost, no obligation and will allow us to see whether or not we are a good fit. Check out the web site and give me a call!

REV. DIANA EVANS-BAXTER
Journeys of the Heart & Spirit
503-259-8782

Your wedding ceremony is a rite of the heart where you as a couple come before your family and friends to celebrate this very special time in your life. Let me assist you in creating a traditional or non-traditional ceremony that will make your wedding day a beautiful and memorable occasion.

- Wedding ceremonies performed throughout Oregon and Washington at a location of your choice.
- Optional pre-marital preparation is available
- Call for a complimentary "get acquainted" visit between the hours of 8am and 10pm.

Exquisite Weddings
A Subsidiary of Leadership for a Pure Heart, LLC
Jaqueline Mandell, Wedding Officiant
P.O. Box 2085 • Portland, Oregon 97208-2085
(503) 790-1064; Fax (503) 790-0602
info@pureheartsangha.com; www.pureheartsangha.com

Jacqueline Mandell would be honored to preside over your ceremony.

- Honoring the traditions of your faith
- Specializing in World Faiths and Buddhist Ceremonies
- Licensed in Oregon and Washington
- Also available for pre-wedding conversations and preparation
- Over 25 years experience
- Tailored to meet your dreams

"Love is the strength woven into the fabric of life."

REV. VICTORIA ELIZABETH FIELD

As an ordained non-denominational minister, I am committed to providing assistance in creating a personalized and creative ceremony that reflects your unique personalities. Together we will create your vision of a celebration that fully expresses the essence of who you are, individually and as a couple, the values and qualities that are the foundation of your successful and fulfilling union.

I am honored and blessed to participate in this most sacred of ceremonies.

Blessings of Light, Love and Laughter,
Rev. Victoria Elizabeth Field

For further information, please call or email
(503) 646-5566 or vefield@msn.com

REV. ROB FIGLEY

Weddings and More
(360) 693-8562
Website: www.redraccoon1.com E-mail; mail@redraccoon1.com

I am well aware that your wedding is a special and unique expression of your love for each other. It's a very busy time for you, with many things to plan and coordinate. If you are not currently a member of an area church, it can be tough to find an officiant to express your point of view. That is what I specialize in, bringing YOUR point of view, to YOUR wedding. I am a non-denominational Christian minister. I am ordained to perform weddings in Oregon and Washington and am willing to travel to where you want your ceremony to be. Your wedding is YOUR special day and I can tailor a ceremony that is very special and meaningful for the two of you, as well as help you write your own, if that is your wish. A meeting prior to the wedding is helpful, but is not a requirement. There is no charge for our initial consultation. Please call to schedule an appointment.

FRESH WEDDINGS

Rachel Foxman
Non-denominational Minister
Contact: Rachel Foxman (503) 230-9811
E-mail: foxling@teleport.com
Please call for an appointment

Beginning in 1982, Rachel has been licensed to marry couples in Oregon and Washington. Since that time she has performed hundreds of weddings. Rachel's voice is particularly suited for a warm, thoughtful presentation at either large or small gatherings. Her ceremonies (wedding, renewal and commitment) are spiritual in nature and tone. Couples are invited to choose from prepared ceremonies or design their own with Rachel's help.

Ceremonies take place at your location of choice. Prices vary according to location and services rendered. There is no charge for an initial consultation. Please call for an appointment.

Photo by Erin Berk

Rev. Rhiannon Griffiths, M.Div.
Kindred Spirit Ceremonials
(503) 631-4300

Rhiannon Griffiths weaves your beliefs, values and story with ancient and modern traditions, tailoring your unique wedding. Her generously praised experiential ceremonies, involve family and guests warmly connecting all gathered. She delights in interfaith, blended family ceremonies and Celtic handfastings, passed to her by a High Priestess in Ireland. Rhiannon's wisdom, humor and insight supports your journey to the altar through Conscious Commitment, a series of homeplay, deeply preparing the groundwork for a rich and rewarding union. *"We really enjoyed our sessions... (they) reminded us why we were marrying, confirmed we were making a good decision, and helped ground us during hectic wedding plans."*

—Duncan and Jen

Rhiannon, co-owner of Kindred Spirit House Bed & Blessing, is a spiritual mentor, counselor, educator, writer, gardener, and High Tea Priestess, who loves her two cats and dog, Emerson. Call for a get-acquainted session over a cup of tea.

HeartSong Weddings

Phone/Fax (503) 981-5242
Rev. Linda Condon, Ordained Non-denominational Minister
heartsongweddings@yahoo.com

Let me help you create the…

"Wedding Ceremony of Your Dreams"

I am a minister who genuinely cares about each and every couple. The ceremonies and personalized service I provide reflect how much I truly enjoy helping couples and families create a day that will be cherished and memorable for years to come! Choose from the many traditional or contemporary ceremonies, readings or prayers available, or I can create a unique and beautiful ceremony written especially for you, available at the location of your choice.

REV. LISA KRISTEN-SCOTT
503-460-9894
kristenscott@earthlink.net

Weddings * Unions * Commitment Ceremonies

In our close relationships we experience life's depth and richness, and discover who we really are. Committing oneself to another forms a living symbol of union and wholeness.

Together, we can create a ceremony that honors and celebrates your love and commitment. I am an artist who brings the mysteries and joy of the creative spirit as well as 20 years of ritual practice to my work—creating the perfect ceremony for you.

I respect all traditions and welcome all couples.

REV. DR. ASHLEY L. MCCORMACK

Ordained Nondenominational Minister
(503) 880-6507
E-mail: gatheredhere@comcast.net
Web site: home.comcast.net/~gatheredhere

Ashley's ministry is focused on the ancient spiritual practice of relationship. She facilitates workshops and writes about relationship as a spiritual art form, where she uniquely combines eastern and western philosophy and practices.

Ashley has been referred to as a calm presence, who is both insightful and organized.

Ashley is available to perform marriage and vow renewal ceremonies and ceremonies of union. Ceremonies may be traditional, eclectic, or interfaith and are created to reflect each couple's lifestyle. Premarriage counseling is also available. Call for an appointment.

BRIDE & GROOM™

Portland: 503.246.7799 • Salem: 503.363.8569

The Northwest's première ceremony service for Portland, Vancouver, the Greater Willamette Valley and Oregon Coast. Nondenominational ministers and civil wedding officiates are available 7 days a week including evenings and holidays. Ministers and civil officiates are dressed in black judicial or pulpit style robe, giving your ceremony that special look and style. Our attention to your needs and desires makes your ceremony truly unique.

Our fee includes the initial meeting, local travel, rehearsal, ceremony coordination, our collection of vows and readings on floppy disk or CD, our exclusive marriage certificate and our written guarantee. We accept visa and master card at www.NWBrideAndGroom.com.

Civil • Nondenominational • No Classes • No Counseling
www.NWBrideAndGroom.com • Email: Info@NWBrideAndGroom.com

REV. ROBERT RENGGLI

(Married Catholic Priest)
2115 Cunningham Lane S • Salem OR 97302
(503) 363-3156
E-mail: brenggli@comcast.com
Web site: www. rentapriest.com/brenggli

Helping couples create a **warm** and **memorable** wedding has been a great joy of my priesthood for over 30 years. Couples of all denominations are most welcome. When and where the couple feels comfortable to celebrate their wedding is always respected. Generally two planning sessions are sufficient for me to learn exactly the uniqueness of each couple and to assist them in designing their "perfect wedding." Finding a special **FOCUS** and breathing a creative **CONFIDENCE** into your unique wedding celebration is my goal for you. Please call today for a free consultation.

Sincerely, Bob Renggli • **(503) 363-3156**

483

PASTOR REBECCA SANDERS

(503) 698-1199 • rebeccasanders@earthlink.net

Rebecca is a minister, licensed to officiate weddings in both Oregon and Washington. She will work with you to create the personalized wedding ceremony that you want, and one you are happy with. Her fee is reasonable and includes all of the following:

- ♦ License information
- ♦ Phone availability/support
- ♦ At least one planning session
- ♦ Vow preparation/options
- ♦ Attending your rehearsal
- ♦ Copy of ceremony prior to wedding, if requested
- ♦ Personalized copy of your vows
- ♦ References provided upon request

Please write or call to request an informational flyer detailing more of her services, or to schedule an appointment.

REV. ROBERT H. THOMAS
UNITED METHODIST CHURCH
12820 N.W. 33rd Avenue • Vancouver, Washington 98685
(360) 573-7725

Licensed to perform weddings in Oregon and Washington, I will be happy to perform your wedding at the location of your choice. At our initial meeting, we will discuss whether you want a traditional Christian service or if you would prefer to create your own. Each wedding is personalized to suit the couple. Premarriage counseling is available but not required. My fee for planning, rehearsal and officiating at your wedding ceremony is $125.

Rev. Robin Tudor
Ceremonies Celebrating & Honoring Life's Events
Weddings ❖ Blessings ❖ Rites of Passage ❖ Christenings
Nondenominational Minister
503-524-4165; E-mail: rtudor@yahoo.com

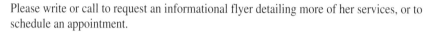

Robin is a warm, spiritual presence who will lead your ceremony with confidence and grace. An accomplished writer and event leader, she will work with you to design and create the wedding of your dreams. Robin is known for the twinkle in her eye and her powerful, soothing voice which resonates in any setting.

"Thank you for the special presence you brought to our wedding. The words spoken were so loving and moving and perfectly captured the spirit of the day. Thank you for your contribution to our beautiful day."

– Deena and Ben

Call to get acquainted and set up an appointment.

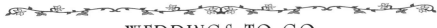

Weddings From the Heart
Rev. Dr. Sally Rutis
503-246-8993 • revrutis@bigfoot.com • www.cnwr.net/revrutis

Weddings ♥ Wedding Renewals ♥ Commitment Ceremonies

A meaningful wedding ceremony can make your special day come alive. Rev. Sally will help you create the service that everyone at your celebration will be touched by.

You can expect:

- A ceremony created specifically for you
- In-person planning session
- Phone consultations at your convenience
- Customized additions to your ceremony including family blending, Unity Candle and much more.
- Rehearsal direction
- Professional, reliable service

Feel free to call for additional details.
I look forward to supporting you in a Wedding From the Heart!

Weddings On Church Street

E-mail: info@WeddingsOnChurchStreet.com
503.540.0610 • Toll free from 503.884.3669

We have six licensed ministers available seven days a week, including evenings and holidays for the mid-Willamette Valley and Oregon Coast areas. All ministers wear black judicial style robs unless requested otherwise.

Our fee includes the initial meeting, travel, rehearsal, rehearsal guide, collection of vows and readings as well as our exclusive decorative marriage certificate. For intimate ceremonies you may choose our Salem Church House location where elopements are always welcome. We accept Visa and MasterCard at WeddingsOnChurchStreet.com

Nondenominational • No Classes • No Counseling • Bilingual Available

WEDDINGS TO GO
(Your place or mine)
Religious or Contemporary; Alternative and Commitment Ceremonies
(360) 573-4868 or (360) 608-1483; Fax (360) 546-5633

Hello there, my name is Joyce Haines and I am a marriage Commissioner licensed to perform ceremonies in Washington and Oregon. We live on a small organic farm with a peek-a-boo look at the Columbia River and enjoy having small outside weddings here which can be arranged on short notice, if necessary.

Our initial meeting is complimentary and will allow us time to share ideas to create a ceremony that is *"JUST WHAT YOU'VE ALWAYS DREAMED OF."*
If you are planning a wedding at the Rose Garden, the mountains, or dipping your feet in the ocean, we can be there.

We want to help make *YOUR DAY* a very *SPECIAL DAY.*
Joyce Haines (360) 573-4868 • (360) 608-1483 • E-mail nwgarlic@pcez.com
Counseling not required.

Please let these businesses know that you heard about them from the Bravo! Wedding Resource Guide.   **485**

KURT WINNER & MICHELLE WINNER
Wedding Ministers
www.historicalchurch.com
Inquiries: (503) 668-0107
(503) 816-1558

Your wedding ceremony should be an expression of your love, your way. Speaking from your hearts and sharing what commitment means between the two of you; your ceremony is an outward expression of your feelings. Each of us can assist you in creating your personal vows or perform a highly traditional ceremony if you so choose. What does that mean to you? Both of you can relax and enjoy your special day, your way.

Knowing that sometimes couples do not have a formal church affiliation, our quaint "Historical Church" is available for your wedding use (see page 314 under Ceremony Sites) or we will go to your location. We want your wedding to be a joyous celebration. Please call for a complimentary consultation or go to **www.historicalchurch.com** and click on "About Us" for bios. Kurt and Michelle are non-denominational ordained ministers with the All Faiths Church of the Pacific Northwest.

Your Personal Ceremony
Alan Yehudah Winter, RN, MS
(503) 287-8737
www.yourpersonalceremony.com

Together, we will create an original ceremony borrowing from the world's great spiritual and religious traditions. With over 25 years of experience, I am familiar and comfortable drawing from rituals both ancient and modern as well as spiritual and secular sources of poetry.

The ceremony will be both memorable and meaningful for you and your families and friends, because it will be a statement of who you two are. Whether it is celebrated formally or casually; indoors or out; in the shadow of Mt. Hood; in the grand ballroom of an elegant hotel or in your own backyard, the most important part is that it represents what you most value both in each other and in your lives.

I have a counseling background and use it to help couples feel comfortable and confident throughout the entire wedding experience.

Notes

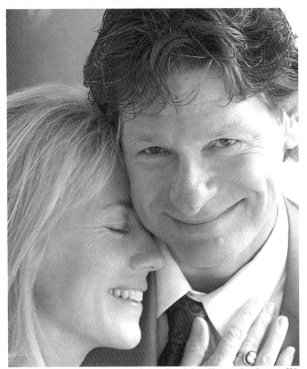

photo by Joni Shimabukuro Photography • See page 520

Traditions

Gifts to the bride's parents:

The groom would indicate how much he thought

the bride was worth by giving farm animals,

weapons or crops to the bride's family.

The more gifts, the more valuable the bride.

- **Why are photographs important?** After the cake's been eaten, the tuxes returned, the flowers wilted, and you've shaken the last grains of sand off from the honeymoon, what's left of the wedding? Those treasured glimpses captured in photographs can in a moment rekindle the joy for both of you, bring back the friends, and show the love within families.

- **Selecting a photographer:** Find a photographer whose style you feel comfortable with. Look closely at his or her sample albums, and don't be afraid to ask for references. A contract is important to reserve the date and should confirm that the estimate given will be the total cost excluding extra prints or specialty photographs ordered. Within this section you will find pages of photographers; compare the information listed and make sure they meet your needs. The prices vary from one photographer to another; make sure you understand what the "package price" is and what the extras are.

- **Consulting with your photographer:** When you finally select your photographer, sit down together so you can communicate what you imagine your photographs to be. Get specific about formal and candid photographs. Be sure you let the photographer know what you are expecting. Some provide a checklist for you to fill out.

- **Assigning a photographer's helper:** You should submit a list of photographic requests to both the photographer and helper so that your helper can guide the photographer to the right people.

- **Have formal portraits taken before the ceremony:** More brides and grooms are deciding to have formal portraits taken before the ceremony to maximize time with their guests. If you do choose to have formals done before the ceremony, make sure everyone is dressed and ready for pictures at the time designated.

- **Black and white photos:** The traditional formal wedding photos are taking on some new and exciting looks, such as the photojournalist style, which is a more candid documentation of the day. Black and whites are timeless and classic, and handpainting will make the photos an original piece of artwork.

- **Find out how you get to view your wedding photos:** There are different ways that photographers have you view your wedding photos. Some give you the proofs to take home with you, some allow you to view them on the computer and some build your album without showing you the pictures first. You should know and feel comfortable about how this process will work before booking your photographer.

- **Store your wedding photos on CD:** Ask your photographer if he or she can help you store your photos on CD for safe-keeping.

- **Storing your photos:** Store your wedding photos in a safe place; it is recommended to keep them in the box provided with the wedding album. If you just ordered the photos and no album, make sure to put them in an album soon after receiving them. Keep them out of a damp area.

- **Engagement photo guest book:** A fun idea is to use your engagement photo with a large mat area around it for your guest book. This way family and friends can sign around your photo with well wishes. This is a wonderful keepsake to frame and display on your wall. Rarely do you pull out your guest book and think about all who were there to celebrate your wedding day with you.

A Careful Budget Photography

by Rob Powell   AnselRob@aol.com
503-646-4710   www.p-usa.com/robpowell
Beaverton, Oregon

The Best Quality at Low Prices:
Prices can be sent by mail, email and fax. Photos and prices can be seen on my web site. Packages can be custom-designed just for your wedding. Some wedding dates may qualify for a complimentary studio portrait.

For $695
I will photograph your wedding for three hours using mostly medium format cameras. I will process the film and make prints. You will receive 150 original proof prints plus the complete set of negatives.

For $435
I will photograph your wedding for four hours with 35mm auto-focus Nikon cameras, and make 250 exposures. You will receive the exposed film when I leave the reception. Or, I can process the film and make prints for an additional fee. Either way, the negatives will be yours to keep.

Your Choice of Styles
Most brides prefer a mix of elegant formal photos and lively candids. Let me know if you wish an emphasis on a particular style.

Black & White, Photo CD Available
Would you like some of your photos in black & white? Would you like images delivered on CD? It's your choice. Call for details.

Commitment
I have been photographing weddings professionally since 1975. In that time I have never failed to arrive as scheduled. I have never ruined or lost anyone's film. I have never sent out a substitute photographer in my place.

I believe in the sacredness and permanence of marriage vows! My wife and I will celebrate our 24th anniversary on April 12th, 2004. We wish the same joy for you.

– Rob Powell, PPA Master Photographer

a Studio C
Portland llc

(503) 358-9504 or (503) 319-1702
Web site: studiocportland.com
(for complete details, pricing and photo gallery)

ALL NEGATIVES INCLUDED
PROOFS INCLUDED
proof albums • custom wedding albums • parent albums
artistic • candid • photojournalism • black and white
Packages from $400-1,995.

WE ALSO OFFER ELEGANT WEDDING FLOWERS
and a

Free
bride's bouquet
(call for details)
With over 20 years of wedding experience
A Studio C has formed a way to keep your big day affordable, stylish and best of all fun!

See large-scale portraits at Melody Ballroom
615 S.E. Alder, 11am-3pm Tuesday-Friday

Stephen Jones
photographer

Patrice Lampton
photographer

(503) 236 - 1871
www.aaronstadt.com

Relationship **One day… One opportunity…** We respect the importance of what *your* wedding day means to you. We place *no limits* on the number of shots. We will discuss your vision, compare it with our experience, make suggestions, then you decide how much coverage is right. *The most important detail of the day is our relationship with the bride and groom and it shows in every image that we shoot.*

Quality & Experience We present you with **25 years of experience** using a blend of **photojournalistic, fine-art and traditional styles.** We will temper this with an unobtrusive behind-the-scenes presence that creates reality from your dreams. We will provide as much or as little direction as you desire in order to make your day flow as smooth as silk. With **two photographers** at every shoot, it is possible to provide extraordinary documentation of your day.

Memories Visit our web site at *aaronstadt.com.* We have a comprehensive source of information including **sample albums, references, "package" and pricing options and just a bit of advice. You will receive all of your images on a private preview web site as well as on a CD** in viewable .jpg files and reproduction quality high-res files.

Comments

You were so willing to listen to our concerns and fears and suggest helpful ways to put them to rest. You not only made our day more special but also captured it impressively in images that we can enjoy for years. **— Becky & Dave Martin**

You kept things running smoothly and throughout the day helped us keep in mind what "the day" was about. Our pictures turned out great, every comment we receive begins with "WOW!" **— Amy & Hank Sandall**

We could not have been more pleased with your professionalism, guidance and friendliness — and the pictures turned out AWESOME! **— Sonya & Rick Snedeker**

Next call (503) 236-1871, or visit us online at **www.aaronstadt.com.** Ask to speak to Stephen or Patrice, we would love to meet you.

Adams & Faith Photography

935 S.E. Hawthorne Blvd.
Portland Oregon 97214
Contact: Tony or Lori
(503) 227-7850;
Fax (503) 227-1863

Adams & Faith Photography is undoubtedly the Northwest's premier photography studio…

Located on the corner of SE Hawthorne Boulevard and 10th Avenue, Adams & Faith has made creativity and superb-professional service the studio's hallmark since 1976.
Bride after bride acknowledges that Adams & Faith sets the standard for unique wedding images in the Northwest. In fact, most have noticed that other photographers seem to follow suit, trying to duplicate the Adams & Faith originals. These originals have brought national attention and awards, accolades from a state senator and recognition from business leaders throughout the community. During a feature on ABC's *AM Northwest*, Paul Linnman, after viewing Adams & Faith's wedding photographs, exclaimed, "These are truly works of art!"

Clients also notice the celebrity weddings that are included in Adam & Faith's collection. The photos of Everclear's Art Alexakis' wedding particularly impresses brides. "Here's a guy who could have had anyone in the world photograph his wedding," says one recent Adams & Faith bride, "and he chose this studio."

All brides and grooms receive Adams & Faith's world-class service. The attention to detail begins the second a client walks through the door and continues until the final photo is framed and the last page of the album is completed.

As owners Tony and Lori Secker and their staff go about the daily business of operating the studio, they are humbled again and again as their work gains an ever-expanding audience…a photo in *Bride's Magazine*, an image in Beverly Clark's book, *Weddings: A Celebration*, one prize-winning photograph after another. What pleases them the most, however, is the praise they receive from brides and grooms who delight in the extraordinary way Adams & Faith captured their individual personalities and relationship.

Adams & Faith, the most sought-after photography studio in the entire Northwest, is known for telling each unique story of love through compelling and artistic photos. Their spectacular photography will capture the essence of your day and create your own Adams & Faith trademark image.

Please visit us at our Web site: www.adamsandfaith.com

Aden
PHOTOGRAPHY & VIDEO PRODUCTIONS

1613 S.E. Seventh Avenue • Portland, Oregon 97214

503-230-0325

Toll Free: 877 230-0325
Web Address: www.adenphoto.com
E-Mail: kaphoto@internetcds.com

Wedding Packages

Packages are designed to suit weddings of all sizes. Wedding coverages from one hour to unlimited time, as needed. Brochures listing services and prices can be sent to you upon request. Call for an appointment at the studio to see samples of photography and video.

Services and Equipment

Only the finest camera equipment is used, Hasselblad *medium-format* cameras with backup Hasselblads, and high-end digital cameras.

- We can shoot in available light or will provide light as needed
- Formals may be done either before or after the ceremony; it's your choice
- Photo requests gladly accepted—after all, it's your wedding
- Video Coverage (3-Chip S-VHS Cameras and a state of the art Digital Editing Suite)
- Wedding Invitations, Photo Christmas/Thank-You Cards, Gift Albums
- DVD versions available for both photo and video

Original Prints and Reprints

Original prints are available in approximately three to four weeks after the wedding. Reprint sizes are 5x5 to 40x60, and start at $10. Original photographs are included in the package price. Art Leather albums are included in all plans. No minimum order required.

Terms and Payment

Reserve our services as soon as possible or six months or more in advance of your wedding. A $100 deposit is required, with the balance due 10 days before the wedding. A full refund is given for cancellations if the date and time can be filled. Travel outside the metro area may require an additional charge. Discover, Visa or Mastercard accepted.

SENSITIVE, CREATIVE AND EXPERIENCED PHOTOGRAPHY!

It's your special wedding day, a day to be remembered for the rest of your life. Through the years, your memories will become even more special, as will your wedding album and videotape. Your choice of a photographer is an important one. Since 1968, Keith Aden has been specializing in wedding and commercial advertising photography, including video production. His 37 years of experience and knowledge of the very special art of wedding photography make him sensitive to your needs and requests. Keith is a photographer who actually cares about you and your wedding.

aisha harley photography

503.233.2616

As an artist, I find that no other subject holds greater opportunities for compelling images than a wedding.

"Aisha did an amazing job as our wedding photographer and was very pleasant to work with. She has an incredible ability to capture unique moments in time in an unforgettable fashion, bringing her artistic sense fully into her wedding photography. As a result, we, our families, and friends have photos to treasure that are truly works of art. It's tempting to get married again just to have some more beautiful photos!"

– Heather and Benjy

"The best thing about having Aisha photograph our wedding was that we were able to relax, knowing she understood what we were after."

– Michele and Mike

"Thank you so much for encouraging me to budget for professional wedding photos. Of all the things we spent money on for our wedding, the photographs will be with us for the rest of our lives and they are already some of our greatest treasures. You captured the day better than we imagined possible. I know someday our children and grandchildren will treasure them. Your personable manner makes you so easy to work with and you really put me at ease. I am usually uncomfortable getting my picture taken, but I felt totally relaxed and it shows in the pictures. The photos you took of our wedding are fabulous!"

– Elizabeth and John

aisha harley photography
503.233.2616
www.aishaharley.com

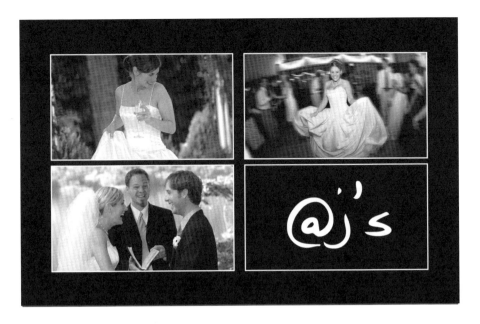

- Distinctive, unique style

- Professional husband and wife team

- Amy specializes in aussie-style black &white photography

- JP creates relaxed, contemporary color images

- Custom designed storybook wedding albums

- All inclusive coverage, no restrictive packages

- Your own wedding website

- Sepia tones, colorizations, hand painted black and whites

- DVD and CD ROM slide shows

- We love weddings!

Visit our gallery on the world wide web!

@j 's
360-694-6684
www.WeLoveWeddings.com

Mike and Carol Stein • 360-241-6585 or 503-351-4133 • www.allndigitalphotography.com

"We cater to you." We treat every wedding as if it were our own, so you get professional photographers who truly care about getting beautiful pictures of your wedding. We will help guide the way, but how and when things happen is totally up to you.

Providing two photographers allows us to get different perspectives of your wedding. For example, during the ceremony, Mike is taking close-ups of the couple, catching their loving expressions, while Carol is capturing the overview of the ceremony. Nothing is missed.

We DO NOT LIMIT the number of pictures we take at weddings. We typically take between 400 – 900 pictures, depending on the length of time of your event. Your most difficult choice will be in deciding which pictures you want to keep. You will absolutely LOVE the pictures you choose!

We offer quality pictures at affordable prices! Our packages range in price from $699 to $1999, and include much more than you would expect. We are also very flexible with our packages, so if you prefer 5"x7" prints to wallets, we will accommodate your wishes. We even have a package that includes just the time and negatives! (And that's a LOT of pictures!!) Our prices for extra prints are also incredibly reasonable: 4"x6" for $7 each; 5"x7" for $15 each; 8"x10" for $25 each.

We are more than just photographers! In addition to taking awesome photographs of your special day, we also assist in any way we can to help your wedding day go smoothly. Remember – we cater to you!

*Professional Nikon and Canon Digital Cameras
*Black & White/Color/Sepia Prints – YOUR CHOICE
*Album included in every package
*Both Posed and Candid Shots
*Minor touch ups included (blemishes, stains etc)
*Our prints are custom
*No travel fees in the Portland/Vancouver Metro area

Angelica Photography
Simply beautiful photographs

Package Prices from $899 to $2999

All packages include:
- Pre-ceremony candids
- Portraits, both casual and formal
- Photos of the ceremony
- Photos at the reception
- Folios, albums by Art Leather

Options Available:
- CD's
- Duplicate sets of photos
- Parents albums
- Hand Tinting
- Choice of Color, B&W or Sepia
- Custom packages available

503.525.2287
www.angelicaphotography.com

Mention this ad and receive a complimentary engagement portrait

Angelica Photography
Simply beautiful photographs

YOUR IMAGES FOR A LIFETIME
SMART...ELEGANT...JOYFUL PHOTOGRAPHY

Shelley and Michael Leyland are photographers who *get it* about capturing the magic of your wedding.

After all...it's a one-day dress, a brief ceremony, a meal and a party. Once the food is eaten and everyone goes home, the real essence of the event must be preserved in the photographs.

Perhaps because we are, ourselves, a romantically married couple, we take great delight in the weddings we shoot. Whether working individually or as a team, we get all the fun, tears, and frolic of your day as a photojournalistic narrative for you. This means loads of candid images, including all those important "little moments"—the small intimacies of a brief shared smile, or the way your arms entwine as you dance—as well as the day's traditional elements.

No awkward posing, here! No contrived scenes. Just fascinating takes, in rich color and dramatic B&W, on you, your loved ones and your wedding's events as The Day unfolds.

We have an array of packages for you, including our immensely popular **Storybook**—a collection of select images printed on art paper, then hand sewn and bound into a distinctive table book. Plus...there are commissioned art pieces, color tinting and cool image borders available as well—everything you could want to make your wedding memories unique.

ASPEN PHOTOGRAPHY & VIDEO STUDIO

14120 S.W. Stallion Drive
Beaverton, Oregon 97008
Contact Gregg & Lee Ann Childs
(503) 524-8230
www.aspenphotovideo.com
Business hours: by appointment

Digital Wedding Photography

Today, many brides and grooms are requesting that our professional photography services and products be provided in digital format. So, to continue to be the "best wedding photographer in the Portland metro area" (to quote Michael and Tracie), we have put together Aspen Photography's **Digital Wedding Package.**

Unlimited time: Aspen Photography will still provide the same "unlimited time" feature. The digital camera fee is $195. And, of course, there is no limitation on how many pictures will be taken.

Digital Package: The basic Digital Print Package is 40 color prints, 4X6 in size. The prints can be selected from the "proof sheet" by the bride and groom. The cost is $400. Additional prints can be ordered at the following prices: 4X6... $12; 5X7... $16; 8X10... $20; 11X14...$30.

All prints will be on Photo Quality paper, using the newest and best color printer and printed with archival ink.

CDs, DVDs, and other items: In addition to the basic Digital Print Package, other digital items are available. For example, many brides & grooms are requesting a CD or DVD that contains each and every digital image that was taken and recorded. This CD or DVD can be purchased for only $400.

Another popular item is a computerized album. Provided on a CD or DVD, the computerized album is full-screen, and the pages are turned at the click of the mouse or can be automated. Music and text can be included. Cost depends on the number of photos and other custom features. These make excellent gifts for families and friends.

Another Pop-and-Play CD or DVD that is very popular is a display of your wedding photos in a 3-dimensional format. There are a number of beautiful and different display styles. Music and/or voiceover and text narration can also be added. These make fantastic screensavers!

Equipment: We use professional cameras and lighting equipment. The digital images on the CD will be unaltered. Professional image editing is available.

Photo Journalism: Many brides and grooms are requesting additional coverage in the Photo Journalism style. Another Aspen Photography professional photographer can cover the complete wedding and reception at the cost of $195. This is a beautiful and unique way of seeing your wedding, and the digital black and white photos are stunning! Ask us about this special coverage. It has become a favorite with today's bride and groom.

Digital Video also? Are you interested in complementing your wedding photographs with a beautiful video? Look at our Aspen Photography & Video page in the Videographer's section. Also, visit our website. You'll love it. **See page 586 under Videographers.**

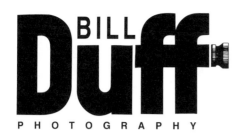

4206 S.E. 72nd Avenue • Portland, Oregon 97206-3448
(503) 775-8589
Web site: billduff.com; E-mail: bill@billduff.com
Business Hours: Mon–Fri 9am–5pm; please call first

— Your Photographer —

Wedding Packages and Prices $695–$1,995

Various packages are available for you to choose from, depending on the services you request. Packages include photographer's time, completed photographs, and your choice of two styles of albums. The number of photographs taken will depend on the package you select. Albums, folios, and wedding portraits are available for your review. Firm bids in writing are given from a price list provided upon request. Special packages include flexible combinations and photographs for the parents. May through September weddings should be booked one year in advance. I have 30 years experience in photographing people and events. Please call for additional information on convention, corporate identity, awards, and advertising photography.

Services and Equipment

Photo-session planning, portraits and news releases, studio sessions, and album planning are all part of the services available to each bride.
- Medium-format 2 1/4″ cameras and professional lighting are used.
- A new studio and an outdoor garden setting are available for portrait shots.
- Bridal announcement pictures for the newspaper are $25 per session.
- The bride chooses when to take pictures, before or after the wedding ceremony.
- The bride's input and photo requests are greatly appreciated.

Proofs and Reprints

Single or multiple proof sets can be purchased at a discounted rate. There is no minimum order. An example of costs of reprints is an 8x10 for $20. All sizes of prints and reprints are available. Proofs are available two weeks after the wedding.

Terms and Payment

A deposit of $350 is required on booking. Visa, MasterCard and American Express are accepted, and 90-day payment plans are available. Credit is given for cancellations made 60 days in advance of the event. Within the Portland area, all travel charges are included in the package price.

Additional Services

Black and white images with color added, thank-you cards, gift albums for relatives, digital retouching services and more. For an evening appointment call (503) 775-8589.

Web site: billduff.com

BRIAN FOULKES PHOTOGRAPHY

5711 S.W. Boundary Street
Portland, Oregon 97221
Contact: Brian Foulkes (503) 245-2697
Business Hours: by appointment

Wedding Packages and Prices

Brian Foulkes Photography specializes in candid photographs of weddings and wedding-related parties like your wedding rehearsal and dinner. We focus on all the fun, candid photos of family and friends. There are no packages as such, because we just charge a flat rate for time plus film costs, then hand the film over to you so you can handle the processing and place the print order yourself. Call for an appointment to see samples of our work.

Services and Equipment

- Use medium format and 35 mm cameras
- Can shoot in available light or use studio lighting as needed
- Will work with you or a person of your choice to make sure you get the photographs you want of family and friends
- You keep the negatives

Proofs and Reprints

For most couples, after the wedding we drop off their film at the lab we recommend, in the couple's name. Those who wish can also keep the film to take to a lab of their choice. All prints and reprints are thus purchased at cost with no mark-up. Those who wish to go digital can easily have their negatives scanned onto a photo CD.

Terms and Payment

Fees are based on a flat rate of $500 to $700 and include up to six hours of on-site photography. A $150 deposit is required to hold the date, with the balance due on delivery of the film. Travel time is included in the flat rate unless the site is more than 25 miles away. Overtime is negotiable.

WONDERFUL, NATURAL PHOTOS

This service is for people who want candid photographs of their wedding and party. All of the traditional portraits are taken; however, the idea is to include pictures of the preparations, the setting, your friends, and the party. For those who are getting married at a private home or outdoors, perhaps in a small ceremony followed by a reception, here is a way of getting wonderful, natural photos that record the day. Brian Foulkes is sensitive to your wishes and will fit in comfortably with your family and guests. Charges are based on a reasonable flat rate plus the cost of film used. The exposed film then is either left with you, or we will arrange processing. Either way, you keep the negatives.

Contact: Kirby & Pam Harris
(800) 362-8796 or (360) 574-7195

Brides' Choice

Business Hours: appointments available; days and evenings
Web site: www.BridesChoice.net

You've walked down the aisle and married your best friend. You've cut your cake, tossed your bouquet and partied with your family and friends. How much will you *really* remember? Your wedding photographs are among the most precious reminders of the day and are too important to entrust to anyone other than a full-time professional. Kirby has over 25 years experience photographing weddings as well as five years teaching at the college level. As a husband and wife team, we are committed to giving you superior quality photographs that capture the mood, joy and romance of your special day.

This Day Belongs To You

We welcome and encourage your participation in planning the kind of photographic service that most completely meets your needs. A pre-wedding consultation is scheduled a month prior to your wedding date covering such items as when family portraits will be taken (before or after the ceremony), scheduling of portraits and events, and reviewing the photography checklist. We work to tailor our shooting style to reflect your personal taste be it creative, romantic, traditional, candid, environmental, journalistic style, or fine art black & white.

By maintaining a low profile, remaining flexible, and flowing with events as they occur, we do our part to make your day memorable and stress-free. Brides, grooms and their families consistently thank us for helping them feel relaxed and at ease; they especially appreciate our patience; and they love their wedding photographs!

Our Brides Tell It Like It Is

"Thank you for having such a calming effect on me—it was exactly what I needed." ~ Kim H.

"I must tell you that your pictures exceeded all our hopes and expectations for our memories of our wedding day." ~ Heidi and John

"You took the meaning of 'photographer' to new heights, as I began to think of you as 'family'. You were both so wonderful, friendly, patient, and professional." ~ Sharon, bride's mother

Pricing Information

- Although pre-selected packages are available from $895 to $3,495, we will be glad to custom tailor photographic coverage to meet your specific needs.
- Color originals (proofs), presented in a preview album, are always included. They are arranged in a storybook format ***and they are yours to keep.***
- You are not required to make your package or album selections at the time you receive your preview album. Take your "storybook" home, curl up on your sofa, and leisurely select your favorites

CAMERA ART

5285 N.W. 253rd • Hillsboro, Oregon 97124
(503) 648-0851
www.cameraartphoto.com

Weddings are supposed to be one of the highlights of a couple's life, but all too often the planning—choosing a dress, selecting a florist, a bakery, or even the invitations—can become a blur.

Have you reached the frustration stage in trying to choose your photographer? Are you having trouble comparing the Gold Edition package from one photographer to the Prestige Album set from another? Or maybe three 8x10s and 40 4x5s just don't meet your needs. Well, Camera Art has a better way.

Our goal is to take all the confusion out of pricing a wedding, and at the same time, allow the bride and groom to control their own budget and what they order.

Here is How it Works

We charge a $295 camera fee to shoot your wedding. That covers the photographer's time to cover your wedding from start to finish. We'll follow you from dressing shots until your reception has wound down. The camera fee also covers all travel fees and location changes.

After you receive your proofs, you simply order what **you** want. You order what meets your needs and budget. If your order consists of three 8x10s and 40 4x5s, that's fine, but if your order is one 8x10, nine 5x7s, and 17 4x5s, that's fine, too. The cost of your "package" is simply the cost of your individual prints.

No extra fees, no hidden costs. Simple–YES. Confusing–NO, and we like it that way. So do our customers—8x10s are $29, 5x7s are $23, 4x5s are $14, and eight wallets for $25.

Services and Equipment

• Portable studio backdrop and lighting are available
• Internet proofing available
• Available-light photographs are a specialty
• Special discounts available for early return of proofs
• Contemporary photojournalistic coverage is also available

Terms and Payment

The $295 camera fee reserves your day. That is your only commitment until you order your photos.

NATIONAL AWARD-WINNING PHOTOGRAPHY
AT SENSIBLE PRICES

by Michael Bickler, Robert Kuhn, Matt Furcron, and Robert Griffin

carol yarrow photography

www.carolyarrow.com • cy@carolyarrow.com
(503) 227-5951

Weddings are glorious occasions with family and friends. Our special talent is to blend in with the joy of the celebration and capture the formal, the casual and the serendipitous moments for posterity. Also, our warmth and openness bring an element of joy that enhances photographs on your wedding day. We give special attention to personal moments that add to the poetry of the occasion.

Different wedding packages are crafted to fit your desires. Quotes are available over the phone. Prices begin at $995.

Carol has won numerous awards including first place for the Sante Fe For Visual Arts Assignment Earth 2001 competition, black and white professional category; and an Oregon Artist Fellowship Grant.

She exhibits at Mark Woolley Gallery in Portland, Oregon.

**Have a look at Carol's portfolio at www.carolyarrow.com
Call to meet and see more of her work.
(503) 227-5951**

CLASSIC PORTRAITS

in Salem
Contact: Neal White
(503) 399-1994, (800) 290-1994
Business Hours: Mon–Fri 4–9pm
E-mail: NealWhite@worldnet.att.net

Classic wedding photography for over 25 years. Your wedding memories will be preserved for a lifetime for only $780

Wedding Packages

Your wedding photography coverage starts three hours prior to the ceremony. The wedding coverage begins with candid photographs in the dressing room before the formal photography. The formals will include: portraits of the bride, the groom and the entire wedding party. This very special day also includes photographs of the immediate families of the bride and groom. We will also photograph extended family members and friends.

Formal portraits may include studio-style lighting and outdoor portraiture, candlelight and natural window light portraits. We carefully blend formal portraits with special candids of the wedding and the reception to create a love story about your wedding day.

We will photograph the ceremony using ambient light. This light enhances the warmth of your wedding ceremony. These photographs include: the processional, significant parts of the ceremony, such as the vows the ring exchange, the unity candle, the first kiss and the recessional.

After the ceremony, we will travel with you to the reception site. We will capture all the festive activities of cutting the cake, toasting, bouquet and garter toss, first dance and wedding party dance.

After the wedding, you will receive approximately 110 finished 5x7 enlargements. YOU also *keep* the negatives. This gives you the flexibility for album selection and control of the negatives.

Terms and Payment

You will receive an agreement of complete wedding coverage.
A $100 deposit is required to reserve your wedding date.

Please call (503) 399-1994 for a free consultation.

Coughlin–Glaser Photography
503.230.1181
www.portlandphotographer.com

Black & White and Color

Timeless black and white for candids and artistry.
Stunning color for details and portraits.

Real Life Documentaries

Our emphasis is on candid un-posed photography.
Unobtrusive photojournalistic approach.
Artful images of moments as they happen.
Relaxed fun formals and portraits.

Full Event Coverage and Simple Packages

Custom printed and library bound albums.
One or two photographers to fully cover your day.

We Promise To Listen To Your Needs

Communication is the key to getting the most out of your photography.
We share your images with friends and family on the web.

Visit Our Portfolio: WWW.PORTLANDPHOTOGRAPHER.COM

Call or e-mail Soren to set up an appointment to learn more.
Soren Coughlin-Glaser: Photographer

Coughlin-Glaser Photography
(503) 230-1181
www.portlandphotographer.com
soren@portlandphotographer.com
Travel Inquiries Welcome. Visa, MasterCard, American Express

David A. Barss
Photographer

503.282.1269

www.davidbarssphotographer.com

Your Wedding Day is a celebration that has been dreamed of and planned with meticulous detail to embody your beliefs, personalities and your love for one another.

My goal as a photographer is to combine my artistry and vision to reflect the beauty of your exquisite story, keeping in mind your desires and wishes, to cater to your ultimate wedding day.

Products and Services
- Quality equipment with equal back-up systems
- Engagement sessions
- Customized and pre-designed wedding packages
- Pre-wedding planning meeting
- Photography assistant/second photographer
- Variety of film used (color, black and white, and other processes)
- Digital coverage available
- Unlimited film and/or images
- Unlimited time coverage
- No multiple location fees
- Original prints of every image to take home, view and order from
- Custom designed layout and professional printing in exquisite albums

Before booking a photographer, it is important to meet with them and view recent work, discuss your ideas and see what kinds of products and services they offer. I believe it is also important to see if your personalities complement one another. You need to feel relaxed and comfortable with your photographer on your wedding day.

Remember your wedding is a grand occasion filled with family, friends, laughter and joy with the splendor of decorations, floral arrangements, food presentation, the wedding cake, a band and more. All of these like your wedding day will pass but great photographs can capture and keep the day alive forever.

**Please give me a call if you have any questions or
if you would like to schedule an appointment to view my portfolio.**

EDMUND KEENE
photographers

920 S.W. 13th Avenue
Portland, Oregon 97205
(503) 224-4410
Fax (503) 224-4429
Web site: ecomphotos.com

Business Hours: Mon–Fri 9:30am–5:30pm; other hours by appointment

Photographing Portland's important events since 1968.

Q. Why should I hire a professional photographer?

A. Photography is the only way to remember all the details of the most exciting times in your life. After nearly every wedding, we are told, "The day seemed to go by in a blur–I don't remember this. I'm so glad you got the picture." Only a trained, experienced photographer knows the difference between a "snapshot" and an image that becomes a lasting MEMORY of your most valued moments.

Q. But isn't good photography expensive?

A. Our prices are as varied as the individuals we serve. This is why we have so many options on the number of photographs and the amount of time for photography coverage. The old saying "you get what you pay for" is especially true in this instance. Our prices have always represented exceptional value. You cannot buy equivalent quality for less money anywhere.

Q. Why choose Edmund Keene Photographers?

A. Because your photographs mean as much to us as they do to you. Our aim is to make you so happy with your photographs that you'll be able to relive the day over and over again five, ten, or fifty years from now as you look through the memories kept in your wedding album.

If you're planning a **corporate event such as a holiday party, awards banquet, or seminar** that needs the careful attention and unobtrusive approach of an experienced professional ... WE CAN HANDLE THE ASSIGNMENT.

SO GIVE US A CALL. WE WOULD LOVE TO MEET YOU.
(503) 224-4410

Please visit our Web site at ecomphotos.com
for additional examples of our photography.

ENCORE STUDIOS

Portland, Oregon
(503) 255-8047

Web site: www. encore-studios.com
Photography • Videography • Disc Jockey

BOOK PHOTO & VIDEO AND RECEIVE DISC JOCKEY SERVICES FREE!
*Certain restrictions apply.

With over 20 years of experience, Encore Studios offers the widest selection of wedding packages, designed with your preferences and budget in mind. On your wedding day, we take special pride in being as unobtrusive as possible, capturing photo-journalistic, traditional, as well as those one-of-a-kind photographs and videos that are most cherished!

Equipment and Services

The finest and most current cameras are utilized, including medium format, 35mm and digital cameras. Your photographs may be printed and received usually within four weeks of your wedding. Most packages include a complimentary engagement portrait session in the settings of your choice, with prints you choose to keep and treasure. We also offer CD/DVD storage of your wedding photographs and videos.

Services

Photography:
- Black & white
- Newspaper photographs
- Wallets to 40"x60" sizes

- Sepia & hand painted portraits
- Invitation photographs
- Folios & frames

- Portraits in new studio
- Leather parent & family albums
- Canvas & poster prints

Videography:
- Pictures & keepsakes to music
- Multiple locations
- Special effects

- Engagement party video
- Cordless microphones
- Leather video cases

- Rehearsal dinner video
- DVD & duplication services
- Multiple cameras/angles

Packages and Prices

With the most comprehensive package selection in the Northwest, you are welcome to choose from our many selections or customize your own package with your budget and preferences in mind. Individual reprints are one of the lowest, and start as low as $12 for 4x5 prints. Photo packages begin at $995. Videography begins at $595, with several options from which to choose. Visa, MasterCard and Discover welcome with no interest applied.

Consultants are available day or evenings for appointments.
*Please also see us in the **Disc Jockeys** section on page 369!*

Five Gables Photography

503-550-7385
www.fivegablesphotography.com
fivegables@verizon.net

Flexibility is one of the many advantages that we can offer you when capturing your special wedding moments. Whether your personal taste is for contemporary photojournalism, more traditional poses, or a unique combination of both, Five Gables Photography is ready to serve you with creative, experienced professionals that are dedicated to making your wedding photographs a beautiful reflection of your personal style.

Affordable pricing is another aspect to consider when choosing a photographer. We offer many different options in our packages that start as low as $750. This package includes 3 hours of continuous photography time, one 8" x 10" enlargement, sixty 4" x 6" preview prints in a preview album and a complete record of your day in digital format on your very own, one-of-a-kind CD. Other packages include an engagement portrait session and prints, wedding albums and enlargements, lengthened photography time and more preview prints. Black and white photos are available in all packages at no extra charge.

More than 20 years of technical experience behind the camera and in the studio yield memorable images that you will treasure for a lifetime! Five Gables Photography is a member of Portland Metropolitan Photographers Association and you can be assured of the highest quality work.

Ron's friendly, easy-going personality draws genuine smiles from couples, their family, and friends. He has a special gift for putting everyone at ease on a day that has so many details to be considered. His desire to custom-design his work to your specific needs is evident in pre- and post wedding consultations as well as during your ceremony and reception. He is passionate about his work and it shows!

Please call for available dates as soon as possible—our calendar fills in quickly! We invite you to visit our web site to view samples of our work or call to schedule an appointment for a free consultation and to view our portfolios. Five Gables Photography looks forward to serving you with top-quality work and affordable pricing for your very special wedding day!

HOLLAND STUDIOS

SPECIAL OCCASION PHOTOGRAPHY

Professional • Relaxed • Creative

www.hollandstudios.com   503.238.5957

Located in Portland's warehouse district, Holland Studios is more than formals and cake shots — it is a working relationship between our staff and each couple. We don't limit our roll count, the types of film we use, length of coverage or style (an eclectic mix of photo-documentary, fine art and traditional). Our engagement session could be on the top of Mount Hood, on a loading dock or at the beach. We view each wedding as an exercise in improvisation where we tailor our service to our clients' distinct needs.

View our extensive website at hollandstudios.com, shop around, and then arrange a consultation with Eric, Scott, Jill or Chuck, photographers whose creativity and technical abilities are rivaled only by their charm. We have an assortment of styles, packages and presentation materials to choose from. We want to make sure you find what you're looking for, whether it's photo-documentary or traditional. Nothing is rigid; as Tami Holen says, "we're easy." It may be hard for you to distinguish our photographers from the other guests in terms of the fun they have (although that gear they lug around and the sweat on their brow could be a give away). It is with a rare mixture of elegance and ease that Holland Studios has become the Northwest's most referred wedding studio.

So how often do you get to imagine your perfect day and make that vision a reality? As most grooms and even more brides would agree this takes a lot of work. The last thing you want to worry about during the wedding is how it will look ten years from now. Go ahead. Celebrate. Forget about us. This is your day. We are your honored guests, and when the smoke clears and those wedding rings have become as familiar to your fingers as your spouses are now to your hearts, be assured, Holland Studios captured the personality and essence of your perfect day.

www.hollandstudios.com

(in Multnomah Village)
7843 S.W. Capitol Highway
Portland, Oregon 97219
(503) 245-3676 • www.imagesbyfloom.com

• Beautiful Formals
• Spectacular Candids
• Reprints starting as low as $7
• Superior customer service second to none

These are just a few of the fantastic features *Images by Floom* has to offer. You've probably already heard our name. It is commonly becoming a "buzz" word among brides, wedding and church coordinators who all want the perfect photographer to capture those treasured moments, without being pushy or controlling the event. Our job is to make your special day go as smoothly as possible, without any glitches. Our highly professional and trained staff are committed to this. Our packages start as low as $495 and go up to $2,195. Reprints at $7 per 4x6 photograph are almost unheard of in the wedding business. This is fantastic for parents, friends and relatives who want extra pictures—which we all know are usually too expensive to buy.

When we photograph your wedding it does not stop there; we will photograph your first anniversary, children's pictures, and so on. In our full-service studio, conveniently located in the heart of SW Portland, we know you'll be so pleased with the quality and customer service you'll receive at your wedding that we really will be your photographers for life!

- **$250 deposit books us for your day**–make no other package decisions until one month prior to the wedding.
- **There are no hidden costs**–at our initial meeting we will go over everything so you know exactly what you are paying.
- **We have packages for every budget.**

LOOK FOR US AT EVERY BRIDAL SHOW
OR
CALL TODAY FOR AN APPOINTMENT
(503) 245-3676

MAKE SURE YOU VISIT OUR WEB SITE AT
IMAGESBYFLOOM.COM

"They photographed three of my children's weddings beautifully. Don't bother going anywhere else." Mrs. Pat Reser, Reser's Fine Foods

J a k   T a n e n b a u m
PHOTOGRAPHY ASSOCIATES

P. O. Box 82758
Portland, Oregon 97282
Contact: Jak or Lynden Tanenbaum
Phone/Fax: (503) 232-1455

Available by Appointment

E-mail: info@photographyassociates.com
Web site:www.photographyassociates.com

Unique Wedding Documentaries

Our wedding documentaries are tailored to meet the needs of all sizes and styles of weddings. Our focus is on family, fun and friends and we work each wedding as a two-person team allowing us the creative freedom to style photographs in which you look and feel good. Select from traditional paper preview photographs, or from digital proofs which can be viewed by you and your families on your own password-protected wedding web page. We have color and black & white packages for every budget and can customize our services to meet your specific needs, from designing quality hand-crafted wedding albums to providing only the photographs. We can also create a digital wedding story on CD-ROM, which is a great way to share your memories with friends, family and co-workers. We tailor each job to your desires and we listen. We offer sensitive, informed advice gained from years of experience and provide a variety of unique photographic services. You will appreciate our personalized service and our attention to detail.

Black and White Portraits

Our fine art black and white wedding portraits capture your wedding celebration with a classic, timeless feeling. We specialize in producing archival black and white images of the highest quality. Select from a variety of styles and techniques to enhance your B&W images including hand-coloring, selective toning and professional matting.

Services and Equipment

We use medium-format Hasselblad cameras, 35mm Nikon equipment, the best studio-style lighting available and we never go on location without carrying backup equipment.

Terms and Payment

In order to guarantee our availability for your wedding date we require a $300 deposit upon receipt of our Contract for Photography. We accept all major credit cards.

FINE ARTISTS! PROFESSIONAL TRAINING! EXPERIENCE!

Jak Tanenbaum received a BFA in Photography and Design from the University of North Carolina and an MFA in Photography from the Academy of Art College in San Francisco. He has been an active exhibiting artist for over 25 years and currently is an Instructor of Photography at Clark College in Vancouver, WA. His wife and partner, Lynden Tanenbaum, received her BFA in Photography from Humboldt State University and is also actively involved in exploring photography as a tool for creative expression.

Please let this business know that you heard about them from the Bravo! Wedding Resource Guide. **513**

James Loomis Photography

A Wedding Day is Filled with Moments…

I want to capture these moments so you can relive the love, the laughter and the romance of your wedding day. By taking a documentary approach in a style that is said to be formal and casual, serious and silly. The people who didn't make it to the wedding will feel as if they were there while viewing the images. Remember the joy, relive the day and forever savor the many moments…

James,
Thank you for the incredible pictures…But more than that…Thank you for sharing with us "you" and making this day for us…
                    ~ Love, Kelly and Paul Eiden

Wedding and Event Photographer
(503) 254-1401
www.jamesloomisphotography.com

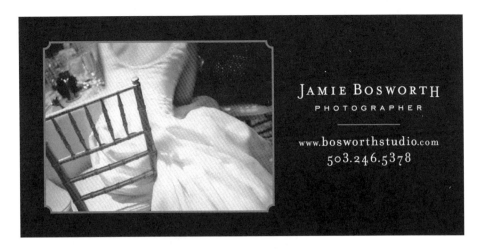

JAMIE BOSWORTH
PHOTOGRAPHER

www.bosworthstudio.com
503.246.5378

Weddings are a great gathering of moments...I find myself, camera in hand, swept along with the crowd...laughing and crying as two people stand in front of their friends and families... brave enough to face each other in public and say the words that will make them man and wife.

On film, a wedding should be just that – a series of joyous moments and private glimpses. These images will have the power of narrative, rather than the contrived dreamscapes of more traditional wedding photography.

I come to the wedding with my eyes and mind open, a certain willingness to participate in the unfolding of the day. I want to make pictures that invite you to visit that day again and again.

Seventeen years and many celebrations later, I feel I can bring a lot of heart and experience to your wedding.

Jamie Bosworth Photographer
www.bosworthstudio.com
503.246.5378

Jason E. Kaplan
photographer

www.jekphoto.com

503-285-2298

the essence of the moment.

photography as unique as your wedding.

Documenting Your Wedding... Telling Your Story.

Jason is an experienced editorial and documentary photographer whose greatest skill is to be able to unobtrusively capture moments as they happen. The best compliment he gets is, "I'm so glad you got a picture of that, I didn't even know you were there."

Beauty Preserved.

There is beauty in every instance of life, and documenting those transient moments to create a comprehensive narrative is Jason's passion.

Specializing in Non-Traditional Weddings.

Is your wedding a creative event? Will it be a vehicle of self expression or a unique celebration? If you are working hard to make your wedding a work of art consider hiring a photographer you can trust to accurately document the moments of your day as they happen. Jason creates complete photo essays of all life's most important events.

To view a portfolio see www.jekphoto.com or call 503-285-2298

Jeffrey Simon
PHOTOGRAPHY

Specializing in Wedding Photography

3656 NE 141st Ave., Portland, OR 97230

(503) 287-9835

simonphotography.tripod.com
www.jeffreysimon.com
E-mail: jsimon199@comcast.net

*Short Notice Appointments **Gladly** Accepted*

FREE CD-MP3 Player in packages!

Congratulations! I am thrilled to hear of the announcement of your wedding. You have made a big decision and I sincerely wish you and your fiancé a long, prosperous and happy life together ordained by God. As you know, selecting a wedding photographer can be a difficult task. Let me assure you that I understand your concerns and the importance of this day. By choosing Jeffrey Simon Photography, you will be assured and guaranteed that your special moments will be captured without any pressure and I will assist you in any way I can to make your day and your new start together perfect.

Why Jeffrey Simon Photography?

We offer excellent wedding coverage, the best service, quality products, affordable prices, medium and digital formats combined with 13 year of wedding of experience.

With all of our packages you receive:

♥ A one-hour pre-wedding interview that includes: Viewing wedding portfolios, discussing your wedding plans and budget, mastering and understanding the style and what you desire. But most importantly, establishing a comfortable and trustworthy relationship between the client and photographer.

♥ A Custom package which offers you four hours of coverage, 125-4x5 (you select from 200+), 1-4x5 album & pages for originals and 100 **Negatives or CD's** starting at **$600**. We offer packages with five hour and more starting as low as $800 including 150 negatives or CD's. We offer **PAYMENT PLANS** and options that allow you to choose the package that meets your needs or you can **create** one that fits your budget.

♥ Pre-bridal sitting: Allows you to take studio or outdoor engagement photos to include in your wedding announcements or an 8x10 for your guest book table. This allows you to be creative. The sitting fee is $75 including 10 proofs and 1- 8x10.

♥ Rehearsal attendance: This is an opportunity for us to meet your wedding party, family, minister and coordinator to ensure that we are all working together to make your day perfect. At this time, I'll review the wedding plans and discuss any restrictions or concerns. This service is provided **at no charge**, schedule permitting (photos optional).

♥ Your wedding day coverage: I will provide you with the BEST professional photographic coverage, while I assist you at any time during the wedding and reception. For example, with cutting the cake, toast, garter and bouquet toss, first dance, candid and formal photographs and your special requests. I help coordinate to keep your day flowing in a timely manner with no pressure on the bride and groom.

♥ After the wedding: Quickly and efficiently present you with quality photos that have been carefully processed, individually inspected and numbered.

If you want your memories to last a lifetime and a **QUALITY PHOTOGRAPHER** you can TRUST AND DEPEND ON, then call us to support and photograph you on your Wedding day.

Sincerely, Jeffrey L. Simon, Owner/Photographer

Winter & Fall Specials available NOW!!

Present the Bravo! Bridal Resource Guide when you book and receive a **FREE** 11x14 Print.

jimiller
p h o t o g r a p h y

503.273.9608
jimmillerphotography.com

Natural. Joyful. Spontaneous.

Some moments happen, some have to be planned to happen. These fleeting moments of time will become your cherished memories.

Options

The "Soho Book"-for those couples wanting a sophisticated and uniquely designed book, telling the story of their wedding day. One all inclusive price. Hourly coverages are available with many options; pictures on the web, B&W, two photographers, images on CD and engagement sessions. The choice is yours.

Your Day

Over 12 years of experience in collaborating with couples to create a relaxed and joyful day. Humor, laughter, excitement, delight, ease—your wedding day and the moments preserved. I look forward to photographing your special day.

—Jim Miller

jmmil2@comcast.net
jimmillerphotography.com
503.273.9608

Jim's PHOTOGRAPHY

Congratulations on your upcoming wedding!

Jim's Photography appreciates that you are considering us to be a part of your once-in-a-lifetime memory. We are a husband and wife team, and love what we do. Our artistic skills and professionalism will create and capture those special moments as they happen. While Jim is working with the groom and his family, Carolyn is getting those candid shots of the bride getting ready. Whether you chose to have traditional coverage or photos before your wedding, it's Your Day! We work with the bride and groom to ease those stressful moments from the time we arrive, to the time we leave.

Services

- ENGAGEMENT SESSIONS INCLUDES SIGNATURE MAT AND FRAME, OR A SIGNATURE BOOK.
- TRADITIONAL COVERAGE FOR YOUR FORMALS
- PHOTOJOURNALISTIC OR CANDID FOR NONTRADITIONAL COVERAGE
- BLACK AND WHITE COVERAGE
- HAND-COLORED BLACK AND WHITE PHOTOS
- LARGE VARIETY OF ALBUMS, FRAMES AND FOLIOS
- CD SLIDESHOW OF WEDDING AND OR ENGAGEMENT
- WEBSITE FOR EASY VIEWING AND ORDERING
- SEPIA TONE AND COLORIZATION

Terms and Payments

A retainer of $200 is required to secure your wedding date. The balance is due two weeks prior to wedding date. There is no travel charge within the Portland-Vancouver metropolitan area and we travel outside the area for a reasonable fee. We accept major credit cards. Ask about our no-interest payment plans.

Pricing

All of our Deluxe Packages come with a custom album and print credit. You choose the amount and sizes of photos you want in your album. Call for a brochure, come in for a personal interview or visit our web site for complete pricing information.

www.jimsphotography.com

View an entire wedding or just look at the highlights. Our 22 years of combined experience are sure to meet your expectations. We look forward to your visit.

Jim & Carolyn Tuchtenhagen 360.253.2412
9500 N.E. 21st Street • Vancouver, Washington 98664 • Business Hours: By Appointment

Please let this business know that you heard about them from the Bravo! Wedding Resource Guide. **519**

Joni Shimabukuro
Photography

503.282.1756 • joni@joniphoto.com • www.joniphoto.com

Joni has an eye for capturing unguarded moments. Her easygoing, professional and good natured style will place you, your wedding party, your family and guests at ease while she works unobtrusively. Joni delivers a balance of candid shots and expressive images designed to represent the unique spirit of your wedding. Because she provides personal attention and focuses exclusively on your special day, Joni chooses to work a limited number of weddings each year.

Complete Wedding Package: $2,500

- Eight hours of event coverage
- Wedding web site for online proofing and ordering
- CD containing your web site for off line viewing
- DVD containing your wedding slide show

And your choice of a keepsake wedding album:
- 8" square hand-sewn Jones Books wedding book containing approximately 200 images. *OR*
- 12" square custom designed Jones Books wedding book with your choice of fabric material for book cover and 46 custom designed pages.

Digital images are also available for reprints and sharing with family and friends for $70/image.

Client Comments:

We can't even begin to thank Joni for all the effort she put into making our wedding day special! Joni went above and beyond. She is such a positive, enthusiastic person—it's been a pleasure getting to know her. THANKS, THANKS, THANKS Joni for sharing your talent with us.
—Maryanne Fitzmaurice-Cleary
NYC, NY

Just wanted to say THANK YOU! Joni was a pleasure to work with and everybody loved her. Also she kept me on track with all the little "events" during the reception. I would have missed them all ;-).
—Amy Bennett
Portland, OR

We received MANY compliments about Joni. A few guests asked my mom if Joni was part of the family because she fit in so well (This is a compliment, but fitting in with our families might scare her!!).
—Trista Cornelius & Steve Powers
Portland, OR

Joseph Milton

PHOTOGRAPHY

josephmilton.com • 503.317.2215

Style

- I offer honest, natural, and dignified documentary-style photography that tells the true-to-life story of your wedding, capturing all the real emotions and pure joy of the day.

- My hands-off approach allows you to truly enjoy your wedding without having to endure fake posing or heavy-handed direction.

Services

- One simple fee covers your entire day up to ten consecutive hours.

- There are no constraints on the number of images. Typical weddings receive 600-800 images.

- You can receive your images as either 4x6 prints or in a convenient image catalog.

- You receive all of your images on CD, giving you the option to make your own prints and enlargements.

- All images are available for viewing and ordering on a secure web site.

- A variety of the highest quality wedding albums are available.

Details

- To view a large sample of wedding galleries, complete pricing details and more information please visit josephmilton.com.

Real. Beautiful.

josephmilton.com
503.317.2215

Kathryn Elsesser
photography

www.kephotog.com
503.335.9057

Artistic and Creative Wedding Photography
Including
Photojournalistic and Traditional Classic Images

Your wedding day is as unique as you are and your photographs should reflect your personality and individual style. I will record the memories of your day with a combination of both timeless, classic as well as photojournalistic-style images that capture the spontaneous moments of this one-of-a-kind event.

It is important to me that we meet individually at least once and communicate often before your wedding to ensure that your wedding images reflect your day, not one preconceived by a photographer. Whether you want an all black and white photo essay or the addition of color portraits, I approach each wedding as a unique event and offer more than the standard formula of traditional wedding photography

I take the utmost care to have your images developed with the highest quality processing available. Equal care is taken with presentation. Proof images are presented to you in a rich leather archival album, yours to keep. In some instances, you may prefer to have the option of processing the film yourself. In this case you then own the negatives.

Please phone or e-mail to schedule your free consultation
503.335.9057
kathryn@kephotog.com

Kloppenburg Photography

(503) 295-6728

www. lightdancestudio.com

email: charliek@spiritone.com

With the eye of a photojournalist and the heart of an artist I work passionately to portray the essence of the wedding day.

I capture on film the emotions, romance and subtle drama as they unfold. I look for the unrehearsed and unposed moments to create an artwork that reflects the memories you will cherish forever.

The final images I print will narrate a story from an artist's perspective that will give the viewer a unique insight into this most wondrous day. My style is both cooperative and , for obvious reasons, unobtrusive.

I will work to find a price point that fits your budget.

I want to shoot great photographs at your event...You want a great photographer at your wedding working for you. I think we are made for each other.

~ *Wedding Dreams Captured* ~

by

Krista Blythe Photography

4120 S.E. International Way, A111 Milwaukee, Oregon 97222
(503) 786-8206
Email: weddingdreams@mail.com
www.kristablythephotography.com

With more than 20 years experience in wedding photography, Krista will give you the personal attention with great service in a timely fashion that you are looking for. Her knowledge of wedding planning and creative images will certainly capture your wedding dreams.

Krista specializes in combining fine art wedding photography with a classical romantic style, and her flair for capturing those wonderful and fun unforeseen moments is hard to beat.

After you spend one hour with Krista, it is not hard to see that she is personable, creative, and has a true love for weddings. You will have no doubt that she will work hard to capture the images that will tell your wedding story uniquely just for you. That is her trademark, to personalize every wedding she photographs.

- Wedding packages include:
  Brides album, Two parent albums, Wedding portrait, Black & White photography, full wedding and reception coverage, and more.
- Complete wedding planning and referral service
- Affordable packages and payment plans
- Engagement session / Studio or Location

Wedding plans are designed to meet any size or style of wedding.
Packages begin at $1495

Contact Krista for your wedding consultation at (503) 768-8206

Kristie Coia Photography
weddings and portraits

"The most important thing about photographing people is not clicking the shutter...it is clicking with the subject."
~Alfred Eisenstaedt

Photography with a Fresh Perspective

- documentary-style coverage
- artistic portraits
- b&w and color images
- handcrafted leather albums
- DVD slideshows
- online proofs
- on-location engagement sessions
- packages from $2500

view online portfolio
www.KristieCoiaPhotography.com
503.890.5051

Lake Oswego Photographers

www.lophotos.com

503-624-1515

1-888-269-4000   email– info@lophotos.com   fax—503-624-5046

Making The Right Choice...
We know it is a difficult task for you to select your wedding photographer. To convince you to meet us and see our work is equally difficult, but once you do, you will understand why we have a real advantage.

It's A Gift
This husband and wife team combine photographic talent and years of photojournalism experience, with a special gift for working with couples and their families. We offer a variety of styles and packages and are committed to photographic excellence while creating a relaxed atmosphere.

Everything You've Always Wanted
Our service is intended to be simple. You select the package you desire, and we do the rest. Many packages include our time, the selected color enlargements, and a beautiful album of your choice.

The Finest Quality
Our beautiful wedding prints are produced by the finest color lab in the Pacific Northwest. This allows our studio to "guarantee your photographs for a lifetime." So, give us a call. Our showroom is a relaxed place to view sample albums and wall prints.

Invest In Friends
Once you meet us, you will see why so many of our couples consider us friends, long after the wedding photographs are delivered.

DELIVERING A LIFETIME OF PROFESSIONAL PHOTOGRAPHY

Call early for an appointment.
Dan & Teresa Poush
(503) 624-1515 or toll free (888) 269-4000

We can also handle any celebration, party, or corporate event with ease.

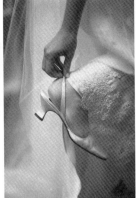

Lászl

PHOTOGRAPHING LIFE'S CELEBRATIONS   800-632-9794   *www.laszlophoto.com*

If you've seen any Miller beer commercials, you're familiar with the work of Jack Thorwegen, CEO emeritus and creative force behind the Zipatoni ad agency in St. Louis. I photographed his daugther's wedding. His letter tells my story better than I could.

Dear László:

It's rare that I take the time to commit to writing accolades to a photographer I've retained for any project. In my capacity as CEO of Zipatoni, I have overseen a photography budget exceeding $15,000,000 for many years. As you know I've worked with all the greats as well as the up and coming.

I have however never worked with a shooter who specializes in weddings. After a very painful eye-opening self-education on this field, I must say that you are indeed a gem among stones. Your history and experiences in the commercial field over the years have served you well. You bring the maturity, dedication and eye of a seasoned professional to a field filled with the opposite. You also bring a work ethic that is lacking to a trade filled with self-delusional egos that overcharge for "Blurs" and call them journalistic "art."

I looked at over 20 portfolios of wedding shooters all over the country and interviewed seven over the phone. Yours was the only call that didn't make me pour a couple of fingers of Scotch out of frustration and the only call to give me a proud relief in hiring you on the spot.

If I had another daughter I would look forward to working with you again. Not only did your work exceed our expectations but it also made me a hero to my wife and daughter. Do not hesitate to use my name or family's photos as future recommendations.

Best,
Jack Thorwegen
CEO Emeritus, The Zipatone Company, St. Louis, Missouri, www.zipatoni.com

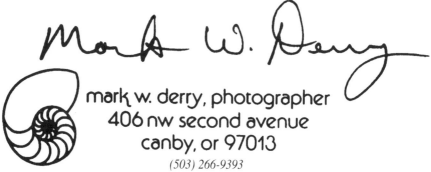

mark w. derry, photographer
406 nw second avenue
canby, or 97013
(503) 266-9393
Business Hours: Tues–Fri 9am–5:30pm; Sat by appointment

YOUR WEDDING DAY
What every bride dreams of and deserves...

Mark W. Derry, Photographer

With over 25 years of wedding photography experience, Mark is one of only 20 Certified Professional Photographers in Oregon. A Past President of Professional Photographers of Oregon, Mark has also received the National Award for "Meritorious Contribution to Professional Photography" from the Professional Photographers of America. At the 2001 Western States Regional Competition one of Mark's wedding portraits received the prestigious "Masterpiece Award" from Fuji Film Corporation. The portrait was selected for the "Loan Collection" display at the July 2001 PPA National Convention.

Wedding Consultation

Call to see if Mark is available for your wedding date. Meet with Mark for a free consultation to discuss your plans and requests. Mark has photographed weddings in Oregon, Washington, California, Idaho and Montana as well as several on the East Coast.

Engagement Session

Most couples take advantage of our complimentary "Engagement Portrait Session." This provides Mark with an opportunity to work with you before the wedding. Choose an intimate portrait at home, at the beach or on a snow-covered slope.

Wedding

Mark will create a unique and personal story of your Wedding Day using traditional formal wedding portraiture, a photojournalistic approach, black and white images or a blend of your choice. He will rely on skilled expertise, while carefully considering your requests.
We recommend formal portraits be taken before the ceremony, but scheduling is completely your choice.

Wedding Show

Later Mark will share with you the wonderful memories of your wedding day with an innovative "Wedding Memories" Show. At this time you will be able to select your portraits from 40 inch projected images. You will be able to see every detail. That isn't possible on a small monitor or paper proofs. You will be able to choose a variety of portrait sizes to create your album and capture all the moments and people important to you. Mark will work with you to design your final album. An "In Studio" wedding special is available for only $149.

M

Michael's Weddings, Etc.
Photographic Artistry
503.760.8979
www.michaelsweddingsetc.com

Uncommon Wedding and Ceremony Coverage
Including Artistic and Fun Candid Photography

WHAT PICTURES are most important to YOU!?

Wedding photography should come from the heart. When you, as the bride and groom, are looking at photographs in your hunt for the perfect photographer for your wedding, please keep a few things in mind. What is most important to YOU as far as the pictures go. What do YOU want to end up with. Are candids more important than formal photographs or the other way around. Are ceremony pictures important – the rings going on each of your fingers, your best friend singing, the unity candle being lit, roses being handed by the two of you to your parents, etc, etc. Or are pictures of the two of you – pictures that show you glowing with excitement (I have found this only happens AFTER the ceremony!) and eager to share your excitement with everyone at the reception party! How about the party pictures at the reception – the cake of course (in Black & White and color); dance pictures; toasting with the Maid of Honor, Best Man and your parents; pictures of your friends lovingly making eye contact with you and tearing up as you hug them.

Weddings are emotional — the pictures you end up with should show you have had the most elegant and fun ceremony and party that any of your friends and family have ever been to! I have photographed hundreds of weddings – they are all unique and different. Weddings are my artistic and creative outlet for photography and I am at my best around and photographing people. It is fantastic fun to capture on film the fun things people do at weddings — in other words: weddings are just a blast to photograph! What a job, if you will, for anyone to have! Few people get to do what they like — I get to do what I absolutely love: PHOTOGRAPH WEDDINGS!

WHAT PICTURES are most important to YOU!?
Let me know — I would love to make that happen for you!

Thank You!
Michael Wood

Make-up & Hair Included for Entire Bridal Party!
On-line proofing & ordering
Option to own your negatives
Dual photographers
Custom Packages
Unlimited time
Engagement photo sessions
Color, Black & White, Sepia
CD available
Payment plans

Capture your special moments to preserve for a lifetime
with our nine creative professionals.

*call for a **FREE** consultation*
503-810-8035

Please visit our web site at
www.gypsyana.com

Uncontrived Wedding Photography

As a photographer, my goal is to record the spirit of your wedding day by capturing the energy and spontaneity of everyone there. To accomplish this, I devote an entire day to your wedding alone so that I am able to document the events that play such an integral part in making your wedding day special.

Years of professional experience enables me to capture these fleeting moments in an artful, yet unobtrusive manner. It also enables me to thoughtfully compose each image, whether candid or formals, so that your wedding photos have a timeless feel with a strong sense of design, making them more than just snapshots.

These photographs are what will tell the story of your wedding day, proving to be the most important and memorable images in the years to come.

Many packages are available, each one tailored to each clients specific needs. Please call for more information or to schedule an appointment to discuss your specific wedding.

Mount Burns Photography
503.289.4234
mbphoto@comcast.net
www.mountburnsweddings.com

Major credit cards accepted

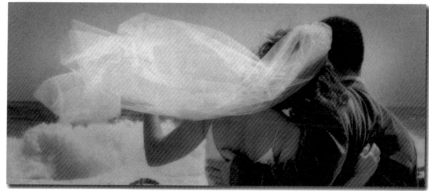

Jason & Andrea

Newby's Photography
503.640.6046

She catches his eye... He steals her heart... Love is born.

There is no better way to know us than through the people we serve.

Dear Joe & Candy,

"The images you captured of our wedding in Mexico are incredible. Never could we have imagined that our love could be so visible for all to see, but there it is! And now, as Jason serves our country in Iraq; the priceless DVDs that you created for us are one of our connections to each other. I know that when he watches his on his computer in Baghdad, and when I watch mine at home, we are together again on the sandy white beaches of Cancun and our spirits touch. Our hope is that when Jason returns home you will join us again in Mexico and create for us an "Anniversary Edition."

Much love, Andrea

"Joe and Candy Newby captured the laughter, the joy and the love which encompassed our wedding ceremony and reception. Their use of ingenuity, creativity and spontaneity created for us an extraordinarily professional and timeless product which we will treasure always. We highly recommend Newby's Photography to anyone who is seeking quality, experienced photographers who care about capturing your special moments, have passion for their work and have a flair for 'priceless' perfection."

—Deb & Earl

- Black & white and color photography
- Traditional and photojournalistic coverage
- Local & destination weddings
- Customized packages for various needs

www.newbysphoto.com

503.799.2972
protheweddings.com

PATRICK**PROTHE**
studio

Capture the spirit of your big day

Your wedding day is one of the most significant events in your life. Patrick Prothe captures the joy, emotion, spontaneity, preparation and celebration in a collection of creative images that tell your story. This will become a family heirloom that can be passed on to future generations.

Patrick spends most of the time discretely photographing in a creative documentary style, while incorporating a few fine portraits. He's there to pay attention to every emotion, from the time you arrive until the reception winds down and you depart. You receive complete coverage of your day in black and white and color with no additional costs to travel between locations. In addition to a personal online portfolio, your finished images are carefully printed and packaged in one of several custom designer albums, books or portfolios—the choice is yours.

The images speak for themselves—experience our style, service and attention to detail. Visit **protheweddings.com** for a preview of what you can expect. You will love the experience. There is a difference.

VISA AND MASTERCARD WARMLY WELCOME.

PAUL QUACKENBUSH PHOTOGRAPHY
the last word in wedding photojournalism
360.896.2117 • 800.200.5090 • E-mail: pqphotography@aol.com

It's Your Wedding
You have a vision—personal and real. Real joy. Real laughter. Real people. You imagine the planned and spontaneous moments that make your wedding day unique. You see the real story—a celebration that reflects who you are—one you'll share with some of the most important people in your life. Now you need a photographer who will capture your wedding as it unfolds.

An Accomplished Photojournalist
Paul Quackenbush is a photojournalist who specializes in weddings. After earning a degree in commercial and fashion photography from New York's renowned Fashion Institute of Technology, he worked in both New York and San Francisco before settling in the Pacific Northwest. Among his many professional accomplishments, he has photographed hundreds of weddings across the country, including destination weddings, and understands that no other wedding is exactly like yours.

Your wedding is more than a ceremony and reception. Paul offers complete coverage of every important event from engagement to rehearsal dinner to the last memorable moment at your wedding party. His services always include an engagement portrait, a framed signature print and a CD of proofs for you to keep. Paul's experience makes him an invaluable resource when it comes to planning your wedding—he can help you with referrals to other industry specialists including florists, caterers and more.

Fine Art—Black-and-White and Color
Paul specializes in superbly detailed black-and-white photography, and to ensure fine-art quality results, he prints the photographs you choose by hand. Paul also excels in vivid color photography and works to portray your wedding the way you imagine. In the end, he creates a book of exceptional images that illustrate your story, evoking all the genuine warmth and joy of your wedding day. Custom-designed and bound in a beautiful, rich ArtLeather album, it's a story you'll return to again and again. It's your wedding.

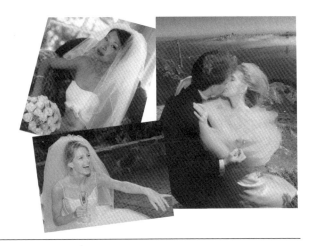

503.293.0467
Visit us at:
www.peterpaulrubens.com

If you pride yourself on well-made choices, consider Peter Paul Rubens.
Discover:
- A depth of repertoire—comprised of a seasoned mix of:
    Fresh, edgy images,
    Live-action, **Journalistic** takes,
    Traditional with Style,
    Believable **Art**
    "Language of the **Heart**" looks,
    And yes, let's mix it up with **Black and White** and **TrikClix**™ Special Effects.
- Discover why couples he works with say: *"…he puts people at ease...Peter's personality is a plus...sweetspirited."*
- He's a hard worker, known for his hustle.
- A pro, he's advanced in his craft. During the past 19 years Rubens has been accorded the Highest Award for Wedding Photography in Oregon as well as received the Kodak Gallery and Fuji Masterpiece awards. He holds a Masters Degree, Professional Photographers of America. The Chairman of Kodak wrote: *"I thought the photographs were absolutely outstanding. You obviously are an accomplished artist."*

Count on a responsive approach...
to the look you like—whether it's fun and happenin', simple and elegant, or stunningly grand.
The most frequently chosen coverages range between $1,495 and $2,695.
- He cares—enough to learn the names of everyone in your wedding party and family.
- Appropriate. Peter adapts his attire from tux to jacket/tie to professionally casual.
- Way Fun. *"…such a character. Your sense of humor is priceless."* ~ D. Nicolik
- Not a one-man show. Responsive office staff. Fast results.
- HiRes professional digital systems. Film on tap. Mix of natural and dimensional lighting.
- Digitally imaginative. Intensive training with recognized industry maestros.
- 'Coffee Table look' bound-book albums made up of magazine style, composited-images.
- Internet: Your photographs posted online if you wish.
- Skilled assistants provide technical support, enabling Peter to devote full attention to you.
The craftsmen that print your photographs do so to true photographic paper. No ink jets. Each
photograph is both machine optimized and operator fine-tuned as well as guaranteed by this
lab for a lifetime. Said Angela Hart, *"I'm embarrassed you made me look so beautiful."*

That's Photography by Peter Paul Rubens—
Unmistakably Unforgettable

Professional Photographers of America

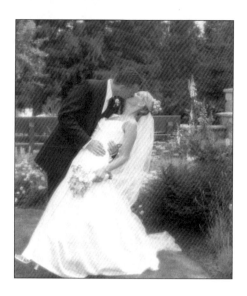

10823 Parkview Drive
Wilsonville, Oregon 97070
Contact: Danny or Linda Abrego
(503) 682-0811; Fax (503) 682-4567
Web site: www.portlandreign.com
E-mail: info@portlandreign.com
By appointment only

Besides those beautiful memories of your wedding date, your wedding photographs and portraits are two of the few things that will stay with you for the rest of your lives. The importance of choosing the right photographer cannot be overstated.

Professionalism

Danny started Portland Reign Photography in 1990 and has slowly built a full-service studio, specializing in "people photography." Attention to detail and superior customer service are trademarks of our studio. Using medium format equipment, professional lighting and services ensures superior results. Additionally, Linda can assist you as your wedding consultant to make your planning less stressful. We are proud, active members of Professional Photographers of America, Wedding & Portrait Photographers International, and Portland Metropolitan Photographers Association.

Creative, Artistic, Distinctive

We offer a pleasant mixture of varying styles, from traditional to photojournalistic and offering black and white for a unique touch in your display portraits. Creative posing and lighting ensures that your photographic experience will result in portraits you will treasure.

Simplified Yet Dynamic

Our goal is to avoid confusing packages to choose from. Instead, we offer a simplified wedding session of five hours but we'll work with you to tailor this session to meet your exacting needs. Your wedding session includes a beautiful leather album and a photographic credit to be used to order the exact number and size of portraits you need—all at competitive prices.

Building a Relationship

Call Danny or Linda for an appointment to meet with us and view our work. This is the first step in building confidence and a relationship that will make your wedding day easier for you and your families.

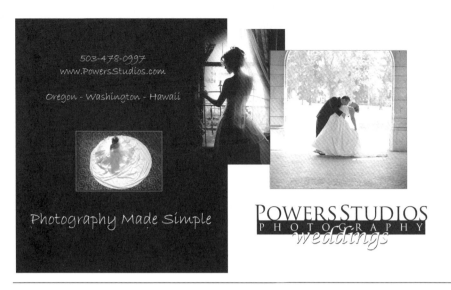

Serving Oregon, Washington & Hawaii

Powers Photography Studios of Oregon is exciting, creative and progressive. Our mix of unique photography styles and innovative products and services sets us apart within our industry. Powers Studios is quickly becoming Portland's most popular wedding photography company.

TWO PHOTOGRAPHER PACKAGE

ALL PROOFS AND NEGATIVES INCLUDED

ONLINE REPRINT VIEWING & ORDERING

MEDIUM FORMAT FILM AND EQUIPMENT

FLEXIBLE NO INTEREST PAYMENT PLANS

HONEYMOON PHOTO SESSIONS

ANYTIME MEETINGS AT YOUR HOME OR WORK

FREE TRAVEL TO NEARLY ANYWHERE IN THE UNITED STATES

503.478.0997

••••

www.powersstudios.com

••••

312 NW 10th Ave. • Portland, Oregon • 97209

PROFILE PHOTO

Location Photography by Eric Cable

888.355.4454
www.profilephoto.com

My approach to wedding photography is simple: stay out of the way and capture the day as it happens. I do not believe that couples wish to be directed about on their wedding day, and I avoid the stiff wedding poses and cheesy grins. I also believe that a wedding day should be photographed from beginning to end, starting the photography whenever and wherever the bride is starting her day, and ending when the bride and groom leave the reception. When I am photographing a wedding, I am quiet, unobtrusive and observant. It is my goal that you notice me as little as possible.

My standard coverage is simple: no time limit, no film limit, no travel fee. Wherever and whenever you are, I am covering it. Please view my web site, www.profilephoto.com. Call or email, I always have time to chat!

888.355.4454

www.profilephoto.com

YOUR WEDDING DAY
~ with a unique style and elegance

Romance the Day...

For years the most beautiful and elegant wedding stories have been illustrated by Raleigh and Lois. Your love for each other, the special time spent with family and friends, the traditional, creative, and spontaneous moments of your wedding day will all be captured with a unique style and elegance. The romance of your wedding day will always be remembered with pride when you choose Raleigh Studios.

Capture the Magic...

Every couple has a love story to tell. Raleigh will capture and create images you will treasure for a lifetime in a style that is relaxed and comfortable. The magic that started with the first kiss and grew into the love you share today will be saved in natural images that reflect this very special time in your lives and the feelings that are a part of it.

Who to Trust?

Raleigh and Lois Bennett, owners of Raleigh Studios, have specialized in beautiful story telling weddings for more than 26 years. They are committed to photographic excellence and superior client service. Their years of experience, careful planning, and attention to detail are a few of the many differences that separate Raleigh Studios from the others. If you are looking for beautiful images, color or black and white, created in an environment without stress, and that you will treasure for a lifetime, call Raleigh Studios for a free consultation.

Raleigh Bennett, Master Photographer
Lois Bennett, Consultant and Photographer
Call 503.646.4624 for additional information
www.photographyasanart.com

Ray Bidegain Studio

www.rbstudio.com

6635 N. Baltimore Street • Portland, Oregon 97203
Ray Bidegain (503) 289-5998 • ray@rbstudio.com

I love street photography. Those candid, moving images of everyday people that take us back in time and remind us of people and events in our own lives. I approach wedding photography with the same aesthetic. My photographs will trigger your memories of this time in your life and speak of this day to future generations. I will come to your wedding full of excitement and energy, and will use my talent plus a little serendipity to create my art work for you, your friends and family.

This year I am offering a different, and I think unique service. Rather than having traditional packages with proofs and albums, I am charging a flat rate to come and photograph your wedding. At the end of the evening you will receive the exposed film along with a list of vendors and labs I recommend. After the wedding you may take the film to have it processed and proofed. You will then be able to choose the prints you want to have enlarged and have as few or as many made as you wish. This will represent a substantial savings to you as well as allowing you creative control over the final album. I will help you buy traditional wedding albums if that is what you like or I can give you a list of suppliers for unique and artful books. Your proofs and enlargements will take much less time than the traditional way of having the studio handle the processing, and you will own the negatives. The flat fee for a full day is $1,200 and 1/2 day (Fridays and Sundays only) for $800.

www.rbstudio.com

The real moment.

The real emotion.

The real you.

503.558.0627

www.rebeccawidner.com

Your wedding photography should reflect the truest nature of the relationship that's brought you both to this very special point in your lives together.

With well over a decade of experience in weddings, Rebecca Widner fully understands this.

She provides the individual attention needed to define an overall vision for your photography, then works to capture all the character, personality, and emotion of the day — a day that's as unique as the bride and groom whose commitment it celebrates.

Presented in timeless custom-designed albums, her artistic blend of heirloom portraiture and spontaneous moments will retell the unfolding story of your wedding in a way that's sure to preserve your cherished memories for all time.

*Please visit **www.rebeccawidner.com** to view an extensive selection of traditional and journalistic online portfolios.*

*To make an appointment for your individual wedding consultation with Rebecca, please call **503.558.0627.***

remembrance *Photography*

ARTISTIC
Unique creative imagery: medium format Black & White and Color.

PHOTOJOURNALISTIC
Candid, natural images: the real emotions, expressions and events of your day.

PROFESSIONAL
Highly experienced and dependable, photographing weddings since 1990.

FRIENDLY
We photograph in a low-key friendly manner, allowing you to relax and have fun.

VALUE
Packages start at $1,095 and include albums and negatives purchase option.
Engagement photo sessions by Ilana Baker are $100

To see our photographs, visit our web site at:
www.remembrancephoto.com

503-957-7758
Stephen b. Hamilton, photographer
Masonia Wallin, photographer

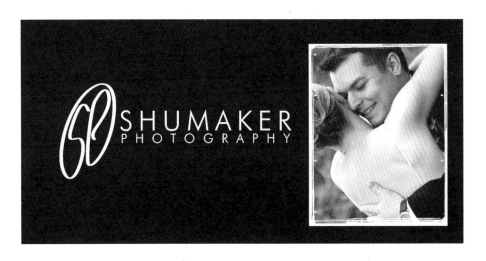

The Art of the Moment

- Each emotion, event, and intimate detail will be captured with amazing timing and artistry.

- Your entire day will be reserved. Unlimited images. No packages.

- Finest photojournalism. Fun, charismatic portraiture.

- Unparalleled, timeless style.

Visit our website, or call to schedule your free consultation.

shumakerphotography.com

360-891-8001

Truly Capturing Your Day

S.J. Harmon's photojournalistic style documents the events of your wedding day as they occur. Long sessions of posed shots result in images that look contrived and posed. Your images will reflect the joyful "moments" of your wedding experience — not bad memories of being ordered around for hours under hot lights. Your images will capture your day the way you planned it!

Full Service

S. J. Harmon is your full service Photography, Videography and Motion Picture business. All of our products and mediums work seamlessly together to provide you with all of your imaging needs in one location. From the "photo montage" at your rehearsal dinner, to a fully interactive DVD containing a masterfully edited "wedding movie," we help you all along the way. Any of our products and services can be purchased separately or together to fit any need! Our products are cutting edge and range from on-line web proofing, to DVD and even the timeless feel of 8mm motion picture film.

Style

Our product and service integrate both technical proficiency and artistic innovation — capturing the true spontaneity and emotion of your day. S.J. Harmon is not trying to fit a rigid idea of what capturing a wedding is all about. Our images are personally crafted to your style and creativity — and will reflect contemporary fashion, art and multimedia. We also love nostalgic images that capture the essence of timeless memories.

"We have had countless comments from friends and family who are truly amazed at the work that you did... thank you for making such a stressful day less stress-filled. I so appreciate how you made pictures fun and captured so much while I wasn't even looking... You were there during those priceless moments getting all of it on film..."

If you are looking for Photography, Video or Motion Picture Film, please call us for Demo or Appointment.

S.J. Harmon Imaging
2861 N.E. Martin Luther King Blvd. • Portland, Oregon 97212
503.417.1130 • 1.866.339.0405 • www.sjharmon.com
See page 602 under Videographers

Strong
photography

strongphotography.com
(503) 351-8010
917 S.W. Oak, Suite 208 • Portland

Don't say "Cheese."

There's no reason to spend your wedding day doing things you "have to do" instead of celebrating with those you love. Unfortunately, many brides and grooms (and photographers) miss out on some of the best moments of a wedding day because of an expectation that they will pose for (or shoot) long lists of pre-planned photos. Thankfully, there is an extraordinary alternative: journalistic-style wedding photography that stresses honest and genuine (not cheesy, frozen-grin) photographs. Emphasizing dramatic black-and-white images while using color to convey nuances of mood, photojournalist Craig Strong captures not only unforgettable moments, but—most importantly—the greater, sweeping story of your day.

Creative. Artistic. Honest. Different.

There is no one else like you, and your wedding will be unlike any other. If you want non-formulaic, artistic photography that beautifully records the unique details of your day while freeing you up to experience, savor, and celebrate, entrust your memories to an award-winning photojournalist with a passion for documenting life.

"We didn't want any stiffly posed or phony pictures..."

"We were looking for a photographer who could capture the mood and spirit of our wedding...we wanted real emotion and spontaneity. That's what was appealing about Craig's photojournalistic style. We never felt nervous or on the spot, as people often do around professional photographers, because Craig blended into the background. The result: he captured some wonderful private moments and emotions that I don't think would have been possible otherwise." —Leslie Constans

Telling Your Story.

Craig Strong is dedicated to chronicling the stories of couples that share a vision for spontaneity, honesty, art, and beauty. Popular Strong Photography packages include a stunning clothbound or leather book, an 8.5 x 11" spiral bound proof booklet, a password-protected website, and a DVD slide show set to the music you love best, all featuring more than 200 images from your wedding.

Experience wedding photographs that tell a story at **www.strongphotography.com**.

Visa, MasterCard, American Express, and Discover welcome.

Portland, Oregon • 800.736.9646
By appointment, for individual service
Web site: www.studio6now.com

Great wedding photography doesn't have to cost a fortune.
With every package, you keep all the negatives and the preview prints.

Standard Coverage: A more traditional approach to your wedding photographs...
Group 1: 3 hours, approx. 75 color previews, all negatives.........................$895
Group 2: 5 hours, approx. 125 color previews, 3 8x10's, all negatives.......$1195
Group 3: 7 hours, approx. 200 color previews, 6 8x10's, all negatives.......$1495

Upgrade available for Groups 1, 2 and 3:
6-month Website Posting & 10x13 Preview Book.............................$295

Elite Coverage

Elite coverage includes color and black & white film, Preview Book, 6-month Internet Posting on password-protected site, On-line Album Builder and Designer Albums.

Our unique style blends contemporary portraits with modern photojournalism, giving each wedding we photograph a truly personalized look.

Group A: 5 hours, ~175 images in 8x10 Preview Book, 24 pg. small Renaissance Album, all negatives..$1695
Group B: 7 hours, ~200 images in 8x10 Preview Book, 24 pg. Large Renaissance Album, all negatives..$1995
Group C: 8 hours, ~250 images in 10x13 Preview Book, 24 pg. Large Flush-Mount Album, all negatives (our most popular coverage!)...$2295
Group D: 9 hours, ~325 images in 10x13 Preview Book, 30 pg. Large Flush-Mount Album, Engagement Session ($299 value), all negatives...............................$2895
Group E: 10 hours, ~375 images in 10x13 Preview Book, Engagement Session ($299 value), 40 pg. Large Flush-Mount Album, 2 8x8 Flush-Mount parent albums with 24 pgs. ea., 1—16x20 wall portrait, all negatives...$3995

Free 6-month internet posting of your wedding previews included with all Elite Coverages.

Beautiful portraits, affordable pricing. It's about time.
800.736.9646

See samples from complete weddings at
www.studio6now.com

TERESA KOHL PHOTOGRAPHY

Located close to downtown Portland in the Sunset Corridor

503.296.1093

www.TFKPhotography.com

Simple yet elegant

Often posed but with style

you can trust this professional...

It's my promise

Catherine Chaney Briggs, wed May 10, 2003

Dear brides, grooms and family helpers,

I think about you every day and I have so much to share with you. You see, weddings are a huge part of my life. I've photographed over one thousand ceremonies. It's what I do because I absolutely love this profession.

Since I work from my home gallery I can save you money and still offer you the very latest in style and quality. Come and visit me in a comfortable setting with no pressure. It's a sweet little cottage filled with antiques and surrounded by gardens and meadows for awesome engagement sessions. An entire large room is filled with wedding albums, images from locations all around Oregon, letters from moms and brides, oh, and Ashes, the cat.

Come and visit us. We do things a bit differently here and you'll enjoy the adventure.

Hugs from Teresa and Ashes

P.S.

I have coverage for smaller weddings and special dates as reasonable as $495. I also offer many choices of designer style coverage with custom features to fit your needs. Prices range from $895. to $5,895. You decide how you want things done and I, along with some wonderful people who work for me, will help design your day with your desires in our focus. We can combine digital with medium format, edgy with traditional. All of our coverage is personalized, professional and fun!

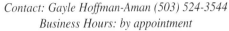

Contact: Gayle Hoffman-Aman (503) 524-3544
Business Hours: by appointment

…for photography that does much more than simply document your wedding; it helps you experience each unique moment.

In order to remember your wedding with the warmth and spontaneity of that special day, you should have the creative touch of THROUGH A LOOKING GLASS…to remember the proud look on a father's face as he escorts his daughter down the aisle, or the gleeful smile of a child being asked to dance.

Whether your desire is the timeless photojournalistic look of black and white images or the vibrancy look of color or a combination of both, THROUGH A LOOKING GLASS provides a one-of-a-kind photographic memento of the entire wedding experience—literally from rehearsal to reception—or anything in-between.

We work with the bride and groom ahead of time to make sure nothing is overlooked—neither traditional elements nor the creative, unique features you've added just for your wedding. Using a more classical, formal portraiture approach or a contemporary, relaxed, candid look or a combination of portraits and candids, with more than 20 years experience photographing weddings and people, THROUGH A LOOKING GLASS will capture everything that is special about your day.

"The pictures are fantastic! Not only is the quality superb, the photographs are fresh, fun and real. You managed to capture the joy of the celebration. Thank you for your patience and professionalism. We are thrilled with your work."

– Jim and Kristin D.

"Tonight I was looking through the wedding photos for the 100th time! The clarity, color, poses, naturalness, the great candids. These are the absolutely best photos of us ever taken. It's a miracle!"

– Nancy L.

"You did an incredible job keeping us relaxed for all the family photos prior to the ceremony. We don't have any stiff family photos thanks to you. You were very effective without being pushy. You also have an incredible eye for all the details. We really appreciate the great job you did."

– Susan and David D.

Wedding Packages and Prices

Packages are flexible and tailored to fit your individual needs. **You own all the negatives and all the proofs!** All packages include consultation, photographer's time, processing, all the original proofs and all the negatives. You can choose whether you want all black and white, all color or a combination. And when you're ready, you can do your own reprints and enlargements or we will gladly handle it for you. Complete packages begin at $850. Travel time within the Portland/Vancouver area is included. A price list for enlargements, albums and gift folios is available upon request.

Terms and Payment

A $400 deposit is required, with the balance due upon receipt of the proofs and negatives. Your deposit or booking fee is subtracted from the invoice and, in the case of cancellation, is fully refundable if the date can be rebooked.

valls photographic
fine art wedding images

Contemporary and refined. Gracious and quiet. Unposed and natural.

It all looks so easy. We arrange the details invisibly, so the work is unobtrusive. We find the magic as it happens, capturing the emotion and spirit of the day. And we choreograph our every action to blend into your wedding, rather than interrupt it. Unposed shots and informal portraits allow special moments to unfold naturally. Our editorial style makes for beautifully spontaneous images. And that is why fine photographs are just part of the reason nearly all of our business comes from referrals.

John Valls is an award-winning photographer whose images have appeared in Gourmet, Travel + Leisure and Wine Spectator.

*"Each of John's photographs is genuinely a work of art;
the images themselves as well as their presentation."*
—Nichola and Michael Voss

View the portfolio online
www.vallsphotographic.com

then call John or Theresa Valls
to schedule an appointment

503.234.7033

V I C K I   G R A Y L A N D

PHOTOGRAPHER

503. 872. 9700

Experience

I have worked in photojournalism for 30 years and have shown my work in galleries for 10 years. I bring my passion for photographing real people and real events to wedding photography. My approach is that of fine art documentary work.

Specializing in Black & White

I specialize in black & white work that I process and print myself. Fiber based paper is used, and each print is toned in selenium, giving rich, archival prints in the fine art tradition. Many clients choose a combination of color and black & white photos, from a selection of packages.

I prefer to meet with couples several times: to show them my work, to finalize details a few weeks before the wedding, and to attend the rehearsal. On the day of the wedding, all parties are prepared and comfortable with each other. I like to arrive early to start photographing the preparations, then continue through the ceremony, celebration and send-off. My working process is to be unobtrusive, to capture moments as they happen.

Please visit my web site, or phone for an appointment.

www.vickigrayland.com/weddings

503. 872. 9700

Wedding Presence Photography

Simply Unforgettable

503.201.2650

www.WeddingPresence.com

Your Day

You have spent countless hours planning, scheduling, meticulously crafting and choreographing the activities that will begin to unfold on your beautiful wedding day.
The emotions of that day will tend to blur and add a hazy aftereffect to your remembrances of all your careful planning.
When the time comes to relive your wedding day, how reassuring it is to you that you have selected among the finest and most professional of wedding photographers… you have selected *Wedding Presence.*

Our Day

We have spent countless hours planning, scheduling, meticulously crafting and choreographing our photography to capture your day as it occurs.
We move quietly and thoughtfully through your day looking to preserve those special moments that will bring a smile to your face and satisfaction to your heart.
As you relive your wedding day, how reassuring it is to you and your grandchildren that you selected among the finest and most professional of wedding photographers… you selected *Wedding Presence.*

Thank You!

Services

- Film and Digital Packages
- Custom Packages
- Beautiful Digital Retouching
- Custom Sepia Tinting and Hand Coloring
- Custom Leather Albums
- Custom Bound Coffee Table Books
- Custom CD Based Digital Albums
- Web Based Proofs and Ordering
- Engagement Portraits
- Pre Wedding Planning Web Site
- State of the Art Equipment and Backup Systems

503.452.2760   503.201.2650
www.WeddingPresence.com

White Glove Photography

Sandee Stewart
503.244.5367

Your photography is more than just picture of a wedding.
We specialize in telling the romantic story of your engagement and wedding day.
Preserving your memories for a lifetime.

We offer:

Sepia, color, tinted, crossprocessing, handpainting or black and white. Photojournalism, traditional or contemporary. With a wide range of packages tailored to almost any budget. Engagement sessions and planning sessions.

Trust your wedding story to a professional.
Call for a no-obligation appointment; after you meet the photographer and see the photographs, your decision will be an easy one.

www.whiteglovephotography.com

*W*oodstock
PHOTOGRAPHY

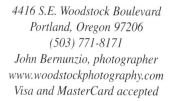

4416 S.E. Woodstock Boulevard
Portland, Oregon 97206
(503) 771-8171
John Bernunzio, photographer
www.woodstockphotography.com
Visa and MasterCard accepted

Many brides have told me that in the anxiety and rush of the day, their pictures were their first real look at the day's events. My goal in serving my clients is to provide them with a visually and emotionally pleasing record of their wedding day experiences. By providing color and black & white images in a collection of artistic, traditional, and photojournalistic styles, I strive to make sure the expectations of the bride and groom are exceeded—not just met.

To prepare for the event, I spend time with my clients, pre-planning and developing a relationship to ensure we feel comfortable working together. Whether relieving stress means taking formal photographs before the ceremony to save time, or waiting until afterward to preserve the "walking down the aisle" moment, I am flexible toward my clients' desires. My clients remember me because I am able to meet their desires without interfering upon their day. The couple may see me taking pictures, but they aren't distracted by my presence.

Whether in the church, during the reception, or behind-the-scenes, I am constantly watching for those special moments the bride and groom might be too preoccupied to notice. The most cherished photos are usually those with the least amount of planning or posing behind them. Family and friends are a very important part of your day. Images of them should be captured in addition to formal group photos.

I encourage you to invest some time with me at the studio, where you can review some of my work, and we can talk about your wedding photography needs. Please contact the studio and schedule an appointment time that is convenient for your schedule.

Yuen Lui

Beaverton (503) 644-1076
Clackamas (503) 654-7708
Portland (503) 288-9404

www.yuenluistudio.com

Who We Are

Yuen Lui photography has been family owned and operated in the Northwest for over 50 years. Our objective has always been to provide exceptional photography, excellent customer service and a final product we can all be proud of. We have an excellent staff of photographers who specialize in wedding photography. As every wedding is different, every one of our photographers' styles is unique. We have sample portfolios representing each photographer available for you to view in the comfort of our studios. You can always set up an appointment to meet with a specific photographer if desired.

Wedding Photographs

Whether you are interested in Formal Portraiture or Journalistic-Storybook Style, Black and White or Color, we can accommodate all of your needs. New this year is our state-of-the-art digital department. We are so excited about this medium because it allows for so much flexibility and the quality of the final product is incredible! Our photographers love using these cameras because they can capture images never before possible with medium format cameras. The Hasselblad cameras have always been the proven work horses for our photographers, and still are to some degree; however, the digital format allows us to offer our clients more creative options for final products. Not only do we still offer the Artleather brand albums, we can now create book bound style albums, with multiple images on a page, for the bride and groom who want something different. As always, we have helpful wedding consultants to aid you in making those tough decisions and to answer any questions you may have.

With packages ranging in price from $995 to $3000+, we have something to offer everyone. Give us a call to find out about current specials, we always have at least one.

Peace of Mind

A wedding is a new experience for a bride and groom, it shouldn't be a new experience for the photographer. The images captured at your wedding will be looked upon for years and years. You want to choose someone you can trust, with a great reputation for quality and service and who will be around long after your wedding is over. Years spent photographing families, family events and weddings, means that we always provide you with an experienced photographer that knows the profession and understands the emotions of the day. Our reputation for excellent quality and service will give you the much needed peace of mind to relax and enjoy this special event.

Notes

photo by Kristie Coia Photography • See page 525

Aisle Runner

The red carpet and white aisle runner are

vestiges of the many fanciful ways that

brides were kept "walking on air."

- Rental stores carry almost everything, from candelabras to coffee makers. They feature specialty wedding items for your ceremony and reception. You'll find such things as serviceware, portable bars, arches, tents, chairs, tables and all the tableware, dishes, glassware, flatware, and much more. Many shops also carry disposable paper products, decorations and a selection of bridal accessories.

- **Visit a rental shop while planning:** It's smart to visit a showroom for ideas and to see the types and styles of merchandise and equipment in stock. Brochures describe all the different items available for rent: style, colors, sizes and prices. Rental shops are also a terrific place to obtain decorating ideas. Meet with one of the shop's consultants and go through your wedding plans step-by-step. You'll find they will help you select just the right wedding items to suit your style and taste, as well as help you determine quantities needed.

- **Decide on formality and budget:** Keep in mind the colors and decor of the site. Pick linens or paper products and tableware that will complement the room. Prices vary depending on the formality you choose; cloth linens will be more expensive than disposable tablecloths.

- **Rental items for all occasions:** Don't forget the rental store for all your wedding-related party needs—rehearsal dinner, showers, bachelor and bachelorette parties, birthdays, anniversaries and theme parties.

- **Deposits, delivery, and setup:** Reserve your items as far in advance as possible, especially during the summer months when outdoor weddings are popular. A deposit will secure the order for your date. There is a charge on most items for delivery, setup and pickup. Make sure you ask in advance how much those charges are so you can include them in your budget. You can also make arrangements to pick up and return the items yourself.

- **Tent rental:** A tent often serves as an ideal back up location for an outdoor event, in case of unsuitable weather conditions. many tents feature transparent vinyl siding that can be raised and lowered as needed. A tent supplier can recommend sources for any portable heating or air conditioning that you might need.
     Important note: Never use canvas tents treated with mineral oil for waterproofing, they are extremely flammable.

- **Tent capacities:** The following are estimated capacities for tents of typical sizes under normal conditions:

| | | *Accommodates* | |
Tent Size	*Reception*	*Buffet w/ seating*	*Sit-down Dinner*
15' x 15'	45	32	24
20' x 20'	65	56	40
20' x 30'	100	86	60
30' x 30'	180	124	100
40' x 40'	350	280	240

- **Choosing a tent site:** When arranging tents with a single transparent vinyl side, consider the position of the sun during your event; if the clear portion faces due west through an evening reception, the sunset may be blinding. Also, be certain that you do not pitch your tent over low or uneven ground that might accumulate water runoff.
     Returning items: If you don't arrange delivery and pickup services with the rental company, you will want to put someone in charge of picking up and returning the rented items for you. You will be responsible and may forfeit any deposit for items that are damaged, broken, lost, or late.

BARBUR BLVD. RENTALS, INC.

• 246·4268 •

8205 S.W. Barbur Boulevard • Portland, Oregon 97219
Fax (503) 246-9375
www.barburrentals.com
Business Hours: Mon–Sat 7:30am–6pm; Sun 8am–4pm

Rental Items Available

- **Wedding accessories:** brass or white candelabras in various sizes, tables candelabra, flower stands, arches, arbors, new natural wood arch, kneeling benches, gazebo, balloons and helium tanks. New! Luminaries—special occasion designs candleabra 2'–3' centerpieces in a variety of styles and colors—this is a must see!
- **Serviceware:** silverplate: trays, punch bowls, coffee and tea service, bowls, candy dishes, serving utensils, chafers, cake and knife servers, goblets, champagne buckets. Glassware: punchbowls with ladle, large trays, serving bowls, chafers
- **Tables and chairs:** round, half-round, rectangle and square tables, umbrella tables, white wood and brown folding chairs; stacking chairs; Chiavari chairs; white bistro; white samsonite, poker tables, folding picnic tables
- **Glassware:** large assortment; champagne, wine and cocktail, and crystal
- **China:** white, black and clear; ivory with gold trim
- **Flatware:** stainless and silverplate
- **Linens:** over 20 colors; table covers, napkins, lace overlays, skirting
- **Beverage service:** bar, beer taps, beverage fountains, champagne/wine cooler, coffee makers (30-100 cup); new portable bar, power taps, and margarita machines
- **Decorations:** balloons, streamers, and special luminaries

Speciality Rental Items

Champagne fountains, water display, cake fountain, gold accessories, various glass and candle centerpieces, brass wedding canopy, white pillars, two and three-tiered trays. Pipe and drape in various colors; lattice panels.

Retail Party Goods

Plastic tablecloths; large assortment of colors in round and banquet sizes; matching silverware and cups; napkins: dinner, lunch and beverage in all colors; napkin imprinting available. Balloons, streamers, and luminaries; special designs for birthdays, showers and anniversaries.

Tents and Canopies

All white canopies; all sizes (10'x10' to 60'x180'). Legcovers in white, sleeves in various colors.

Professional Assistance for 40 Years

Family-owned and operated, Barbur Blvd. Rentals takes pride in providing quality merchandise, equipment and service. Our experienced personnel are available to answer your questions, will special order upon request and share their knowledge and ideas. Let Barbur Blvd. Rentals help make your event extra special.

Barclay Event Rentals
503.667.7735
www.barclayevents.com

Quality Rentals at Discount Prices

- Tents & Canopies

- Tables & Chairs

- Linens & Serviceware

- China, Glassware & Flatware

- Wedding Rental Accessories: Columns, Arbors & More

- Centerpieces: Tower Vases, Floating Flower Bowls & More

- Wedding Merchandise & Invitations

- Specialty Items such as Margarita Machines, Champagne Fountains

- Coffee Urns, Portable Bar Packages

Hundreds of items to make your event
one that you'll never forget!

Call us for a free estimate and/or catalog.

INTERSTATE *Special Events*

5420 N. Interstate Avenue
Portland, Oregon 97217-4597
(503) 285-6685; www.ISEvents.com

Tents and Canopies

Whether rain or shine is predicted for your wedding day, our white canopies will dress up your wedding and reception. Sizes begin at 10'x10'. We have many accessories to help create an elegant and finished look for your special day. These include fabric pole sleeves, dance floor, white liner, cathedral window siding, lighting and much more.

Tables and Chairs

We offer banquet, round, half-round, umbrella, bistro, and even stylish serpentine tables. One of our experts will help you determine your size and quantity needs. Classic white wood and black wood chairs are available, as well as folding Samsonites, Gold Chivari's, Silver Chivari's, white patio, Bistro, and black padded stacking chairs. And don't forget—we have one-of-a-kind wedding table linens!

Wedding Accessories

Select from different styles of floor brass candelabras, silver candelabras, brass and white wood arches, white Grecian pillars, and white lattice panels. Some of our centerpieces include 14" hurricane lamps, glass floral bowls, and 29" five-branch candelabra. Dance floors available in oak or classic black and white.

Tableware

We offer linen tablecloths, napkins, and skirting in a wide variety of colors and sizes as well as ivory and white lace. China styles include classic white, elegant ivory with gold band, white with silver trim, elegant white bone china with gold trim, and clear glass. Glassware includes styles for any reception need. Stainless and silver plate flatware and serving accessories are available.

Serviceware

We have many silver plate items such as tea services, trays, punch bowls, chafing dishes, as well as vases and bowls in glass, stainless, acrylic, and silver.

Beverage Service

We offer porta bars, beermeisters, beverage fountains, kegtainers, coffeemakers and carafes, pitchers, and insulated dispensers.

Retail and Disposables

Over 20 solid colors to choose from in paper plates, napkins, table covers, table rolls, cups, and balloons.

Ordering and Delivery

Reservations are most definitely recommended to ensure availability and assist us in meeting your needs. A deposit and rental fee are due upon receipt of the equipment. Affordable and convenient delivery, as well as setup services, are available. Please call for a price quote.

❤ Member of Weddings of Distinction, ACEP, and POVA

Please let this business know that you heard about them from the Bravo! Wedding Resource Guide.   **561**

The Party Place

A DIVISION OF PORTLAND RENT ALL

1211 North Loring, Portland, Oregon (503) 292-8875
10101 S.E. Stark, Portland, Oregon (503) 252-3466

Web site: www.portlandrentall.com

TENTS AND CANOPIES

Sizes range from 10'x10' to our 60'x160' New Century Tent. Also available: sidewall, liners, pole covers, lighting, heating, air conditioning and generators. Larger tent sizes available.

STAGING AND DANCE FLOOR

* Staging, stage skirting, and carpet
* Dance floor available in wood parquet or black and white check.

TABLES AND CHAIRS

* 6' and 8' Banquet Tables
* Conference Tables
* 30", 36", 48", 60", 72" Round Tables
* Card and Serpentine Tables
* Childrens Tables

* White, Black and Natural Wood Folding Chairs
* Resin Black and White Bistro Chairs
* Brown, White or Ivory Samsonite Folding Chairs
* Black Stack Chairs (padded)
* Elegant Chivari Chairs in Gold, Silver or Natural
* Childrens Chairs

LINENS AND SERVICEWARE

* Solid color and prints available
* Banquet Cloths (60"x120")
* 90", 108", 120" Rounds
* Card Table Cloths
* Elegant Gathered Skirting or Box Skirts (prints also available)

* Chafers in Plain Stainless, Brass Trim or Silver
* Stainless, Silver or Copper Trays (variety of sizes)
* Serving Bowls in Plastic, Glass or Silver
* Other Silver Pieces and Gold Holloware
* Coffee Makers and Insulated Dispensers

CHINA, GLASSWARE AND FLATWARE

Our china styles include Clear Glass, White, Ivory with a Gold Band, White with a Silver Band, Black Octagonal and Fiestaware. We also offer a wide variety of glassware options, such as Crystal, Cutglass or Black Stem and our standard glass barware. From Margaritas to Martinis, you'll find the glassware you're looking for. Flatware styles available are plain stainless, hammered stainless, baguette stainless, silver plate or gold.

WEDDING ACCESSORIES

* Columns and Flower Stands
* Pew Candelabras
* Flower Bowls and Mirrors
* White Wishing Well

* Gazebo
* Aisle Runners
* Candle Holders
* Kneeling Benches

* Table and Floor Candelabras in Gold and Silver
* Brass and White Wood Arbors
* Guest Book Stands

WEDDING MERCHANDISE

* Balloons
* Centerpieces
* Trays and Bowls

* Wedding Organizers
* Invitations
* Doilies

* Wedding and Guest Books
* Paper Plates and Napkins
* Paper and Plastic Table Covers
* Plastic Flatware, Cups, Plates

THE PARTY PRO'S

Visit us at...

2460 N.E. Griffin Oaks Street Suite 1500 • Hillsboro, Oregon 97124

(503) 844-9798; Fax (503) 844-2902

FOR DELIVERY OR PICKUP SERVICE TO...

Portland, Beaverton, Hillsboro, Tualatin, Tigard, Clackamas,
Oregon City, West Linn, Wilsonville and Outlying Areas
Business Hours: *Mon–Sat 9am–5:30pm*
E-mail: PARTYPRO1@juno.com ♥ *Web site: www.THEPARTYPROS.com*

Rental Items Available

♥ **Wedding accessories:** gazebo, arbors, arches, lattice screens, guestbook stands, Grecian pillars, urns, wicker flower stands, fountains, candelabra, several styles in silver and brass, candlelighters, silver tabletop candelabra, a wide selection of centerpiece bowls and decorations for floating flowers or candles.

♥ **Tents and canopies:** many sizes to fit your needs and elegant tent liners.

♥ **Tables and chairs:** banquet and round tables, umbrella tables, folding chairs, white wood and white wedding chairs.

♥ **Linens:** fine-quality linens available in a variety of colors, banquet for 6' or 8' tables, 90″ round, 120″ round, napkins and skirting.

♥ **China:** sophisticated ivory with gold trim and simple clear glass.

♥ **Glassware:** champagne, punch, coffee, rocks, wine, water, or specialty.

♥ **Serving pieces:** punch bowls, chafing dishes, acrylic, stainless and silver bowls, trays, tongs, spoons and servers, silver tea service; stainless flatware.

♥ **Beverage service:** champagne fountains, coffee makers, insulated beverage dispensers, carafes, pitchers, keg coolers and beer taps.

VISIT OUR STORE FOR ALL YOUR WEDDING NEEDS!

Specialty Wedding Items

Custom silk flower bouquets, wishing wells, decorations, centerpieces and ideas galore. Wedding invitations, imprinted napkins, mylar and latex balloons in many colors as well as curling ribbons and helium tanks. Beautiful pew flowers and bows.

Tableware Retail Items

Paper tableware: floral and solid plates, cups and napkins. Plastic cups, cutlery, glasses, table covers, skirting, bowls and trays. Balloon designs and bouquets. Floating or dripless taper candles available in many colors. Cake tops, pens, guest books, unity candles and ring bearer pillows.

Full On-site Decorating Service; Ordering and Delivery

Were you wondering how to decorate your reception site, church, house or backyard to complete that special feeling for your wedding? We will meet you at your location to design a decorating plan to best fit the site with the ambiance you would like to create. On your wedding day we will take care of everything from setup to cleanup.

Reservations are highly recommended so that we can guarantee item availability for your special wedding. Delivery and pickup service is available. Call our ***PARTY PRO'S*** today for an estimate or to set up a free consultation.

QUALITY & SERVICE IS OUR GOAL!

Our ultimate goal is total customer satisfaction during and after the hustle and bustle of your wedding planning. Large or small, we can make it happen for you!

Please let this business know that you heard about them from the Bravo! Wedding Resource Guide. **563**

★ ★ ★

Peter Corvallis Productions

SINCE 1959

2204 N. Clark Avenue • Portland, Oregon 97227
(503) 222-1664; Fax: (503) 222-1047
E-mail: athena@petercorvallis.com
Business Hours: Mon–Sat 8am–6pm

Tents and Canopies
- Canopies from sizes 10'x10' up to 100'x100'
- Chiffon canopy liners & pole sleeves
- Clear canopy tops
- Sidewall: clear, white & windows
- Lighting & generators
- Flooring
- Heating & air conditioning

Dance Floor/Staging
- Wood parquet dance floor
- Black & white checkered dance floor
- Stage risers
- Stage carpet & skirting

Tables and Chairs
- 4', 6' & 8' banquet tables
- 24", 30", 36", 48", 60", & 72" round tables
- Umbrella tables with umbrellas
- Black padded stack chairs
- Bistro resin chairs: white or black
- Folding chairs: white, black or brown
- White, black & natural wood folding chairs
- Gold, silver & black Chivari chairs

Linen
- Various colors & sizes
- Banquet & round linens
- Cloth table skirting
- Table runners
- Napkins: solid & damask
- Custom designed linens
- Lace & gold lame cloths
- Chair covers, wide range of color & style
- Aisle runners

China, Glassware and Flatware
- China: ivory with gold rim, white white lace, glass, white with platinum, black and white square
- Flatware: silver, stainless & gold
- Glassware & stemware: many styles

Serviceware
- Silver five-piece coffee service
- Champagne fountains & punch bowls
- Barware, blenders & bar accessories
- Silver serving trays & bowls
- Portable bars & beermeisters
- Coffee makers
- Silver or gold plate chargers
- Chafers: silver & stainless

Wedding Specialty Items
- Gazebos: lattice & wrought iron
- Arches: lattice & wrought iron
- Picket fencing & lattice panels
- Guest book stands
- Candelabras: floor, table, pew
- Water fountains
- Audio visual, lighting, & sound systems
- Grecian columns
- Chiffon draping
- Centerpieces & vases
- Ficus trees, floral garlands
- Market umbrellas
- Candle lighters & unity candles
- *and much, much more!*

Special Events Co. offers a spectacular variety of rental items. Our company is dedicated to quality service at affordable prices. We have 40 years of industry expertise and event planning to ensure a successful event. Our staff can assist you in design and implementation of your wedding needs. Delivery, pickup and decorating services are also available.

141st & Tualatin Valley Highway
Beaverton, Oregon 97005
(503) 641-6778
E-mail: sneadspartytime@aol.com
Mon–Sat 7:30am–6pm; Sun 8am–4:30pm

Rental Items Available *(call for free brochure)*

- **Wedding accessories:** Arches, arbors, gazebos, flower stands, pillars, pedestals, and columns. Candelabra: brass in 12 styles, pew, spiral, and heart shapes (some styles in white, silver, and pewter), silver and brass table candelabra. Centerpieces: rose bowls, brandy snifters, champagne glasses for floating candles or flowers, marbles and mirrors, socialite votive holders with pastel candle rings.
- **Tableware:** Tables: banquet, round, heart, serpentine, card, and cocktail. Chairs: white folding, bistro and samsonite. China: ivory, white, and black. Flatware: stainless or silver plate. Glassware: stemware, lead crystal, black stem, and barware. Linens: 22 colors, banquet, round or cardtable. Napkins. Skirting: four styles.
- **Serviceware:** Trays, bowls, candy and nut dishes, and food servers. Chafers, food warmers, and prep. equipment, champagne or wine coolers. Cake knife and servers.
- **Beverage service:** Silver, gold, glass punch bowls, fountains, goblets, coffee and tea service. Coffee makers and servers. Bars, beer dispensers and taps.

Specialty Rental Items

- **For the wedding:** White heart-shaped arbor. Chuppa canopy. White and gray carpet aisle runners. Bride's full-length mirror. Guest-book stands. Kneeling benches. Ornate white bird cage. Silk flower church bouquets. Lighted ficus trees, ivy and floral garlands. Sound systems. Camcorders.
- **For the reception:** *Antique* silver table items. Deluxe white canopies in many sizes and white, silky, linen canopy liners and leg drapes. 16′ white market umbrella. Dance floors: outdoor and indoor, oak, white or black. Staging, lighting, and fountains. Umbrella tables and umbrellas, barbecues, and helium tanks.

Wedding Accessories, Invitations, Disposables, and Balloons

- Huge selection of **Paper Tableware**: 22 colors. **Balloons**: 45 colors in 2 sizes. We rent heart and column frames with lights. **Helium**: we rent 8 sizes. We teach you how to decorate with balloons. **Invitations**: large selection. *See invitations in this book*. **Imprinting is our specialty!** Quality imprinting in our store of your napkins, matches, etc. Assorted type styles and colors, wedding symbols, emblems. Fast service!

FOR A PERFECT WEDDING, VISIT SNEAD'S

Advance reservations and delivery available. Serving West Portland for 39 years. Our staff will make your event ours...by providing service and quality products at reasonable prices. Receive a 10% discount on *wedding rental items* with this book!

Uniquely Yours

Chair & Table Styling Linens

Louena Denny, Owner
360.885.3169
E-mail: UniquelySew@aol.com
Web site: www.uniquely-yours.biz

Congratulations! You're getting married and ready to start planning the most exciting celebration of your life – your wedding! As you consider all the possibilities of color themes and design for your wedding, you'll want to incorporate them with the place you'll be greeting your guests – your reception!

The Reception

Uniquely Yours believes that your reception should be as elegant as your wedding and the Bride's table should be the focus of the reception. We specialize in the 'unique' requests and cater to the individual style of each bride, so that your wedding and reception is 'Uniquely Yours.'

Therefore, we pay close attention to every design detail so we can continue to reflect your personal style. Whether it is traditional, contemporary, vintage, garden party theme, or paradise party, we can help create the mood.

Chair Covers

Uniquely Yours specializes in chair cover styling. Chair covers make a stunning appearance to your table setting the way a veil compliments the wedding gown. They can make a polite, distinguishing statement between the bride's table and the guest table when decorated with different colored sashes or overlays. Often chair covers are used to bring elegance to a bridal tea, engagement party, wedding brunch or any special event. Chair covers can transform any hotel chair into a thing of beauty to enhance your room decor.

Table Linens

Uniquely Yours has a wide selection of table styling linens to choose from. We offer table cloths, skirting, overlays, table runners and napkins.

Table Decorations

We have a wonderful selection of table decorations. From lead crystal hurricane candle lamps to unique floating candle arrangements, we can help you.

Uniquely Yours want to provide personal service and attention to detail, so we offer delivery and set up of rental items. Ask for details.

Uniquely Yours looks forward to helping you plan that extraordinary time when you get the chance to let all your guests know just how much they mean to you both as they join you in sharing this special day.

"Uniquely Yours is well worth the effort to pursue. Lou is a breath of fresh air amongst a sea of fast-paced planning. The product she provides is high quality with comparable pricing, service is prompt, reliable and flexibility comes easy. I thoroughly enjoyed working with Lou and would not hesitate recommending her services for any social event!"

– Chris Patterson

West Coast Event Productions, Inc.

1400 N.W. 15th Avenue
Portland, Oregon 97209
(503) 294-0412; Fax (503) 294-0616
Business Hours: Mon–Sat 8:30am–6pm
Appointments available any hour

Services

West Coast Event Productions is the Northwest's premier idea center for all events and special occasions. We specialize in the custom planning and design of your wedding decorations to mirror your vision. Our many divisions offer you everything you might need: centerpieces, tents and custom canopies, glassware, china, catering supplies, tables and chairs, dance floors, stages, audio visual equipment, lighting, candleabras in a variety of finishes, carpeting and aisle runners, the Northwest's largest selection of linens, and the list goes on. Our wedding specialists will help you make all of your important planning decisions. Come in to visit our showroom and to tour our warehouses.

Rental Items Available

Tents and canopies: Sizes range from 10' x 10' to 100' x 200'+ and vary in color from solid white to striped red, green, blue or yellow. Custom tent decorating includes elegant fabric liner, fabric tent pole covers in any color, floral garlands, ambient tent lighting and twinkle lights. French and Cathedral window sidewalls, heaters, air conditioning and flooring are also available.

Wedding accessories: Select from several styles of candelabras, brass and silver table candelabras, brass and contemporary full standing candelabras; wedding aisle and carpet runners; custom chuppah; gazebos and arches; wood, ceramic, marble finish and Grecian columns; table accessories include urns, vases, hurricanes, votives, cherubs and table lamps.

Tables and chairs: Choose from our complete selection of tables and chairs in a variety of sizes and styles: White wood garden chairs, black wood chairs, gold ballroom chairs, folding and stacking chairs. *Ask about our new specialty chair covers.*

Linens and skirting: The largest selection of linens in numerous patterns, solid colors and types of material. Various skirting colors and sizes are also available for any type of event or theme.

China, flatware, glassware and serviceware: Impressive selection of china in 14 different patterns: ivory with gold, white, black octagon and clear octagon. Solid colors in red, yellow, blue and green, formal bone china, contemporary patterns. Stainless, silver plate and goldplate flatware. Glassware for every occasion. Catering items for food service and many other items available.

Sound system, lighting and audio visual: Complete array of sound equipment from amplifiers, microphone and mixing counsels to high-end data projectors. We offer a variety of unique lighting fixtures and special effects for outdoor receptions.

Stage and dance floor: An assortment of floors from elegant oak parquet to black and white or colored checks. Elevated foundations for ceremony, head table riser and entertainment—all attractively carpeted and skirted.

Notes

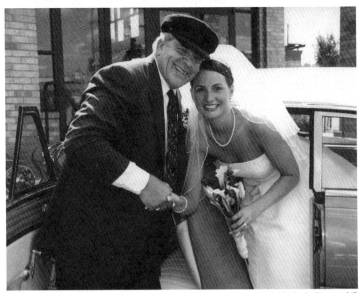

photo by Studio 6 • See page 547

When Traveling

Newlyweds were thought to be particularly

vulnerable while traveling, so tin cans,

horns and other noisemakers were tied to

the carriage or wagon to create such a racket

that evil spirits would be scared away.

www.bravoportland.com

Transportation

- **Renting special transportation:** Everyone enjoys the experience of riding in a luxury limousine at least once in a lifetime. It can be the final touch that makes your wedding day or event complete, so be sure to include some kind of transportation category in your budget.

  You may want to include transportation for your guests to and from the wedding. If you have a lot of out of town guests and your wedding location is hard to get to, you may want to rent a bus for your guests. Renting guest transportation is also nice so that they can enjoy the wedding and don't have to worry about having to drive back to their hotel. This may be something else you want to include in your wedding budget.

- **Don't reserve a limousine over the phone:** Go to the limousine service and personally inspect the vehicle you are considering renting. Be sure you're dealing with an established, reputable company. These businesses will display or readily have available important information like a business license and liability insurance certificate. If you have any concerns or questions about the service, ask for references and check them out.

- **Be sure to get what you paid for:** Make sure the limousine will be cleaned and presentable when it arrives on your wedding day. Read the contract carefully before paying a deposit. Make sure the date, times, locations (addresses), and the specific limousine you want are spelled out in writing on your contract. Remember that gratuities are usually additional. If the vehicle is not presentable and the chauffeur isn't professional, you are under no obligation to pay a tip.

For more assistance with staying organized during the wedding planning process, check out the Bravo! Wedding Organizer. Detailed question worksheets double as contracts. This step-by-step system will keep every detail of your wedding organized. To order, refer to the order form on page 25 in this Guide.

Clara's Limousine Service

2900 S.E. Belmont
Portland, Oregon 97214
(503) 234-3484; Fax (503) 234-0404
E-mail: claraswe@sprynet.com
Web site: www.claraswedding.com

Every Bride Deserves The Best!
We Are Portland's Wedding Limousine Specialists.

Clara's Limousine Service is a division of Clara's Wedding Establishment Ltd. We specialize in providing the best service possible for your wedding day. Our limousines are white stretch Lincoln limousines. We cater to your every need for that special day with:
• Immaculate stretch limousines
• Professional, formally attired drivers
• Complimentary soft drinks
• All of the amenities necessary

Our Customers Say
• "The end to a perfect wedding!"
• "The service was outstanding… we will recommend you to everyone."
• "The driver went out of her way to give us special treatment."
• "Just perfect."

ASK US ABOUT OUR CLASSIC CARS!

Make an appointment today
to see one of our limousines!

Call **(503) 234-3484** to reserve a
limousine for your wedding day.

LET CLARA'S LIMOUSINE SERVICE PROVIDE YOUR CHARIOT FOR YOUR DREAM WEDDING!

Visit our web site at: www.claraswedding.com

See page 226 under Full Service Bridal Salons, 381 under Disc Jockeys, and 81 under Banquet Sites.

ENGLISH CLASSIC LIMOUSINES

Office: 503-736-1182; Fax 503-736-0907

1215 S.E. Gideon Street • Portland, Oregon 97202

www.englishclassiclimos.com

Your Every Wish Is Our Command. Let Us Spoil You

*Featuring a 1955 Bentley, 1957 Bentley S1,
1959 Bentley, 1961 Bentley S2*

Gift Certificates	Elegant Golf Packages
Hotel and Airport Service	Sightseeing Adventures
Romantic Cruises	Luxurious Spa Arrangements
Memorable Photo Packages	Bachelor/Bachelorette Parties
Wedding Shuttles	Dinner Packages
	Wedding Packages

1 HOUR SERVICE AVAILABLE

(503) 736-1182

GOLDEN TIMES CARRIAGE SERVICE

Contact: Duane or Roberta Ogle
(503) 666-4647

Types of Horse-drawn Carriages
- **Vis-à-vis carriage:** single horse; driver; midnight blue; holds four people
- **Enclosed Cinderella coach:** white; team of horses; driver and doorman; holds up to six people; completely upholstered inside the coach.

Service Fee
Fees are based on time. Carriage: $250 for up to one and a half hours, $125 for each additional hour. Coach: $400 for up to one and a half hours, $200 for each extra hour. There is an additional charge for transporting carriage/coach if location is outside of Portland area. Gratuities are extra and much appreciated.

Reservations
The carriage or coach should be reserved as soon as possible, especially during the summer months. A deposit is required on both the carriage and coach; $75 and $100 respectively. The deposit is applied to the total charge for the carriage or coach. In case of cancellation the *deposit is nonrefundable*. Prices are subject to change without notice.

Decorations
The carriage and coach may be decorated, but please, nothing that will damage the finish.

Portland's Oldest Carriage Service
Golden Times Carriage Service has been providing brides and grooms with the most professional and courteous service available for more than 20 years.

AN AFFORDABLE REMEMBRANCE
Golden Times Carriage Service—carriage for hire. This is a special form of transportation on a day you will always cherish, an affordable remembrance for any occasion: weddings, birthdays, anniversaries, proms, and special events to make a grand entrance or departure.

HORSEPOWER RANCH CARRIAGES
"The Hoofbeat of America"™
Gaston, Oregon
(503) 985-0459
Web site: www.horsepower-ranch.com

Add special memories to a very special day by using our horse drawn carriage as your mode of transportation.

Types of Carriages and Capacity
Several white Vis a Vis wedding carriages are available. All new, with beautiful green velour interior and a convertible top, which can be partially or fully closed. Seats up to four adults comfortably. Pulled by our gentle draft horse giants.

We also have several people movers that hold up to 25 adults each to transport your wedding party.

Cost, Terms and Experience
We have various package pricing available. Please call with your specific requirements. A nonrefundable deposit is required upon booking.
Special requests such as "Champagne for two" can be added upon request.

Your experienced carriage driver will dress according to your wedding theme, informal or formal (i.e. Romantic, Victorian or Western).

Decorations
We will supply a "Just Married" sign for the back of the carriage. All other decorations must be approved by Horsepower Ranch.

ADD SPECIAL MEMORIES...
We are a family owned and operated business that is centrally located in Northwest Oregon. We travel from Hood to Coast — Longview, Washington to Salem, Oregon.

Let us add special memories to your very special occasion!

Parke Avenue Limousine

(503) 750-3891 • (503) 544-8490 • www.parkeavenuelimousine.com

Welcome to Parke Avenue Limousine
Portland's Wedding Specialists

When intimate elegance and luxury are required, Parke Avenue Limousine is your choice. We offer first class service and attention to details. Let us escort you in our stately Rolls Royce Silver Cloud. Our goal is to make your wedding a very special day with lasting memories.

- 1958 Rolls Royce Silver Cloud
- 1972 Presidential Lincoln Continental
- Eight person Tuxedo Stretch Lincoln
- Professional Vintage & Contemporary attired chauffeurs
- Complimentary red carpet

Make an appointment to see our vintage limousines or see them on our web site
www.parkeavenuelimousine.com

Parke Avenue Limousine
(503) 750-3891

Specializing in Vintage Rolls Royce

LLC

"Parking with a Personal Touch"

(503) 244-7758; Fax (503) 244-6558
www.premierevalet.com

Have You Thought About Parking?

Let us do the thinking for you…When planning for your next big event, selecting the right valet service will add a great first impression, as well as smooth, convenient parking accommodations.

Consider the unparalleled level of personalized service and professionalism that Premiere Valet Service has been providing Portland residents and restaurants for ten years. Superior guest service and responsiveness to our clients' needs are our preeminent themes. From the relaxed, comfortable initial consultation to the graciously assisted departure of your last guest, Premiere Valet Service, LLC will make the impression that you and your guests will notice and appreciate.

With our experience and knowledge, we have the ability to solve any parking problem. Insurance, claim checks, and signs are provided. All valets are trained, screened and field tested to ensure that you will receive only the finest service available.

Services

- Shuttle vans
- Lot attendants
- Parking consulting services
- Fully insured and licensed

Cost and Terms

Charges vary according to parking circumstances and time duration. Please reserve your event date as far in advance as possible to ensure availability. A deposit of 50% of the total bill is required upon booking. Balance is due the day of the event.

LET PREMIERE VALET SERVICE, LLC
ENHANCE YOUR WEDDING OR EVENT

(503) 244-7758 • Fax (503) 244-6558

www.premierevalet.com

"Valet parking is a welcome trend these days and no one does it better than Premiere Valet." – The Oregonian

Presidential Limousine

(503) 252-4449
(360) 883-5880
www.president-limo.com

Let us provide you with Presidential service on your wedding day.

At Presidential Limousine, we are committed to making sure your wedding day goes smoothly and beautifully. We want to provide you with the comfort to know that we will ensure excellent service and make your day even more special than it already is.

Packages include Red Carpet treatment so you can walk in and out of your chauffeured limousine in high style. Your wedding day is special, and you will feel as though you are as pampered and revered as the President. Let us provide you with a wedding day you will never forget. Please give us a call or go to our web site at www.president-limo.com and reserve your car online.

Presidential Limousine would like to introduce our newest addition:
a 1955 Rolls Royce

24 hour service available
call us today for all of your transportation needs!

Phone: (503) 252-4449
or (360) 883-5880
Web Site: www.president-limo.com
E-Mail: Info@president-limo.com

Leading the Way.
NLA
NATIONAL LIMOUSINE ASSOCIATION

Nationally Recognized for Outstanding Safety and Service

Certified Professional Chauffeur

Notes

photo by Aisha Harley Photography • See page 494

The Marriage Sacrament

In many parts of Sicily, Italy, the bride and groom

did not take the marriage sacrament until the death

of one of them. The reason for this is that until they

had lived a life together they were not spiritually

bound by the marriage tie.

www.bravoportland.com

Video Services

- **Why hire a professional videographer?** Once their wedding is over, many brides say they regret not having hired a professional videographer. Your wedding day will be filled with thousands of emotional nuances, moments you'll savor forever, moments you'll undoubtedly forget. A professional has the skills and equipment to capture those moments that would otherwise be lost.

- Don't rely on a friend or family member to record your wedding day with their home camcorder. While it might save you some money, it will also leave you with a video that's either too dark, too shaky, totally inaudible, or all of the above.

- **Videography has changed.** Gone are the days of big cameras, bright lights and long cables that would normally overpower a wedding. Rapid advances in video production technology have allowed videographers to become as discreet and unobtrusive as any photographer. Additionally, videographers have begun reaping the benefits of new computer-based editing systems which have allowed for more stylish and entertaining videos unlike those from the past.

- **Costs.** Shop quality, then price. There's no reason to spend less money on a video that you won't be happy with. A well-produced video takes many hours to piece together, therefore you should expect to pay at least as much for a good video as you would for a good photographer. If your budget is tight, eliminate love stories or photo montages. Top priority should be filming the day's essential events, including the nervous anticipation before the ceremony, the ceremony itself, and, of course, as much of your reception as possible.

- **Finding the right videographer.** Much like photography, videography ranges far and wide in both quality and price. In general, the higher the price, the more polished your finished video will be. Start by requesting demo tapes or visiting the studios of candidates who make a good impression. Once you've narrowed the field, concentrate on those candidates you feel most comfortable with. Don't base your final decision on a slick demo video—ask to see full-length videos from a variety of weddings. When you feel confident with a particular videographer's work, ask for references. You'll want to make absolutely sure their presence will complement the atmosphere of your wedding day. More importantly, you'll want to be 100% certain your videographer will make your guests feel comfortable.

- **Clarify your expectations.** Be sure to discuss your ideal video with your videographer. Do you want something with a romantic edge or something slanted more toward the humorous side? Do you want a lot of black and white or do you want mostly color? Do you want a lot of guest interviews or would you prefer the videographer concentrate on other areas? Clearly, there are many options to consider. Your videographer should be flexible enough to accommodate your special requests and honest enough to tell you whether or not he'll be able to meet your expectations. A true professional should take time to collaborate with you beforehand so that he fully understands what elements you consider most important in telling your unique story.

- **DVD.** Many videographers offer the option of putting your finished video on DVD. You should definitely consider this option since the expected lifespan of DVD, as well as the picture and sound quality, are significantly better than the VHS standard.

- **Photo Montages.** The past few years have seen a growing trend toward projecting a photo montage or "love story" segment at either your rehearsal dinner or reception. Again, these options vary quite a bit in both price and quality. Be sure to investigate your options.

A HYBRID MOON
2580 N.W. Upshur
Portland, Oregon 97210
(503) 295-1991
E-mail: eric@hybridmoon.com
Web site: www.hybridmoon.com

The Ultimate in Wedding Video

At A Hybrid Moon Video our work speaks for itself, and so do our clients. Here is what a few of them had to say when asked what advice they would give to brides in selecting a videographer:

"Spend the money to get it done right...A Hybrid Moon Video did an excellent job of capturing the magic and beauty of the wedding. Others have seen my video and wished that they had used A Hybrid Moon also." **—Dave & Melina, August 24, 2001**

"Find someone that fits your style...Find someone with a good reputation and ask for recommendations from others who have used them and/or worked with them in the industry. We would definitely recommend A Hybrid Moon because of the quality of their work and amazing editing and style was exactly what we were looking for." **—David & Leah, October 27, 2001**

"Choose a videographer that will cater to your needs. Eric never said no...even when we had changes or special requests he just did it happily. I know he put in many, many hours for our wedding coverage, all with a great attitude and the quality and artistry of the final product was definitely better than any other work we've seen!" **—Jake & Jessica, July 14, 2001**

"Our wedding video is very important to us...A Hybrid Moon was very professional and has a great eye for capturing great moments. Watching our video makes us feel so excited about all the hard work we put into planning. It was well worth the expense. Choose A Hybrid Moon!! There is no other comparison out there." **—Peter & Genifer, April 13, 2002**

"(When planning my wedding) I received advice to spend money on a professional video. I am so glad took the advice...Talk on the streets is "you are the best out there" and I could tell you really love what you do. You created a sense of excitement at our wedding and our guests couldn't wait to see the video...it's so true that you get what you pay for." **—Steve & Shari, August 18, 2001**

"Our wedding video is just as valuable to us as our wedding pictures. A Hybrid Moon could not have done a better job, they were never obtrusive, yet captured all of the important moments." **—Nathan & Tiffany, November 25, 2000**

At A Hybrid Moon we are raising the standards of true quality film-style wedding productions.

Our work reflects the unique and personal style of each of our clients in an entertaining and moving documentary. Because you won't get a second chance to record the important moments that will take place on your wedding day, you will want a professional behind the camera that shares your personal vision and excitement. A Hybrid Moon Video Productions has the expertise and skill to capture the feelings, expressions and moments of your day.

Call today for a free demo!

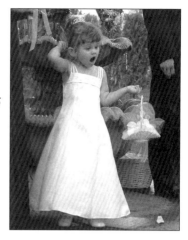

A Pierce Video Production

(503) 504-2075 or (360) 695-6800 or (877) 504-2075
Contact: Steve Pierce, Owner
E-mail: spierce@piercevideo.com
Web site: www.piercevideo.com

RELIVE THE DREAM OF YOUR WEDDING DAY!

Why A Pierce Video Production?

A Pierce Video Production is Portland & Vancouver's premier male/female videography team. Our reputation is built on ten years of experience spanning over 275 weddings as well as professional experience directing "live" broadcast television. We own all of our equipment outright, so there is no overhead or other costs associated. These savings are then passed on to you. We know how wonderful this day is and you can rest assured that the same pride and care you put into planning this memorable occasion is captured in a video memory that will allow you to "Relive the Dream" again and again. Trust your day with an educated video professional, not a hobbyist.

What About Cost?

We offer one and two camera packages, from one to eight hours of competitively priced video coverage from **$350 – $1,750. We also include a free DVD copy of your wedding video in most of our packages (at your request).** We offer several different payment plans. We accept cash, check, money order, Visa, MasterCard and AMEX. **Clients who pay "in full" at the time of booking will receive 10% off their package price.**

Equipment

We use all the latest digital equipment including, discreet wireless diversity microphones, digital three chip cameras, non-linear digital editing, lighting (if needed), etc.

Additional Features

We have several additional features that can be added to most of our packages at no additional charge. These include: "best wishes" interviews with guests at reception, video coverage of your rehearsal, childhood photo montage with music, short "how we met" interview with bride and groom, up to five additional VHS copies of your video, additional DVD's and "candid" digital still pictures shot and posted on the web for those who can't attend (this is very popular)! Please see our web site for full package details and samples of our work.

**Call or e-mail us seven days a week, day or evening, for your
no obligation demo video and complete pricing information!**

A. Shields
Artistic Wedding Cinematography
www.shieldsfilms.com   503.516.8576

Your wedding video should be more than just a document of your day, it should be a work of art. When produced from start to finish by A. Shields, your video becomes a cinematic wedding story that moves and entertains. A personal movie that you will want to show off to all the important people in your life. Digitally captured, edited, and mastered to DVD, your wedding movie will be cherished and preserved for generations.

To book your day, call or visit **www.shieldsfilms.com.**

Video. 8mm Film. Cinematography.

Portland. Seattle. International.

A VIDEO REFLECTION
503-631-7054

Contact: John or Kris Gardner
Web site: www.avideoreflection.com
E-mail: avideoreflection@hotmail.com

John and Kris Gardner

Call Now for a Free Wedding Demo and Information

When you call A Video Reflection, you will not listen to a big sales pitch or be told you have to come in to see samples of our work. The only thing we will ask for is your name, date of your wedding,and address so we can send out a free wedding demo on DVD or VHS. We want you to view our 3-chip digital camera quality in the comfort of your own home. Isn't the sight, sound, and most of all the person shooting the event's camera work what you're really shopping for, not just sales talk? Did we mention we are a husband and wife team?

Being in the business 10 years, and shooting over 800 weddings will enable us to create the most memorable day of your life. Call now so we can send you our demo on your choice of DVD or VHS. You will view over an hour of weddings with lots of wonderful ideas you may use for your own wedding day.

All Packages Include:

• Three DVDs with firewire technology
• 3 chip digital Sony cameras
• Always two to three camera ceremony coverage (Never only one!)
• Pro-diversity lapel microphone on groom and other microphones as needed.
• Post production digital editing in our studio using slow motion, computer graphics and special effects to polish off your wedding DVD.
• Our dress code, always Professional.

Five Wedding Packages And Prices to Choose From

Corsage Package I : Twenty baby to engagement pictures, two camera ceremony coverage, plus your reception. Four hours, one videographer, three DVDs. $1,299

Bouquet Package II : Twenty-five baby to engagement pictures, pre- wedding activities, dressing, the moment, two camera ceremony coverage, plus your reception. Six hours, one videographer, three DVDs. $1,499

Bridal Gown Package III : Thirty baby to engagement pictures, pre-activities, dressing, the moment in slow motion, two videographers covering ceremony for close-ups and different angles, plus reception. Six hours, plus three DVDs. $1,699

Black Tie Package IV : Thirty five baby to engagement pictures, all package III, plus three cameras at ceremony, wedding day montage set to your own music. Seven hours, three DVD's. $1,999

The Ultimate Wedding Day Package V : All of package IV plus rehearsal dinner, taping your photo shoot, showing your baby to engagement pictures at your reception. Eight huge hours, master digitally edited tape, six DVDs and a brand new DVD player! $2,999

Aden
PHOTOGRAPHY & VIDEO PRODUCTIONS

1613 S.E. Seventh Avenue • Portland, Oregon 97214

503 230-0325

Toll Free: 877 230-0325
Web Address: www.adenphoto.com
E-Mail: kaphoto@internetcds.com

Since 1968, Keith Aden Photography has been specializing in wedding photography. Our professional and unobtrusive style bends perfectly with even the most elegant of weddings. We feel that you are the most important part of the wedding and therefore we listen very carefully to your wants and needs. Every wedding is unique and must be recorded in a way that reflects your personality, not ours!

Equipment
We use professional 3-chip SVHS stereo Hi-Fi cameras with 700 lines of resolution for quality that surpasses most home video playback equipment, at 240 lines of resolution, even after editing and duplication. Also, we use broadcast quality wireless remote microphones for superb sound. In some plans we offer two-camera coverage of the ceremony and digital non-linear studio editing with special effects. In the edited versions we can, depending on the plan chosen, include childhood, engagement, wedding and honeymoon photographs, titles, music and interviews with family and friends.

Personalized Wedding Coverage
Many plans designed for different needs are available to choose from. Basic Coverage starts at $500 for a four hour coverage. Ask about our extra bonus gift to you for also booking Photography Coverage.

Reservations and Overtime
You should make your reservation right away. Six months or more in advance would be wise during the peak summer season. A deposit of $100 will hold your date and the balance is due 10 days before the wedding. Duplicate VHS tapes are $25, DVDs are $100. Additional coverage time is $75 per hour. Corporate events, conventions, industrial, business, educational, and other special events by quotation, based on your specific needs. Discover, Visa or Mastercard accepted.

SOMEONE WHO CARES
It's your special wedding day, a day to be remembered for the rest of your life. Through the years, your memories will become even more special, as will your wedding album and videotape. Your choice of a photo or video professional is an important one. Since 1968, Keith Aden has been specializing in wedding and commercial advertising photography, including video production. His 37 years of experience and knowledge of the very special art of wedding photography and video make him sensitive to your needs and requests. Keith is a photographer who actually cares about you and your wedding.
See page 493 under Photographers.

ASPEN PHOTOGRAPHY & VIDEO STUDIO

14120 S.W. Stallion Drive
Beaverton, Oregon 97008
Contact: Gregg and Lee Ann Childs
(503) 524-8230
www.aspenphotovideo.com
Business Hours: by appointment

Selecting a Professional Wedding Videographer

Selecting a professional videographer for your wedding is a very difficult adventure. There are several factors to consider: 1) you want a professional that is an artist and enjoys what he/she is doing; 2) you want someone who is very personable, someone that can blend in with you and your guests; 3) yet you want someone who will be discreet and not attract attention; 4) you want a studio that uses top-of-the-line equipment; and 5) you want an editor that is sensitive and artistic.

Exceeding Your Expectations

Many brides and grooms, their families, and their friends have told us that Aspen Video & Photography meets and exceeds all these factors. We are professional videographers by trade and by training. And we go one big step further than all other video studios: we are also professional photographers. We have been professional wedding photographers and videographers in the Portland area for over 20 years. In fact, we are the only professional photographers who are also professional videographers in the metro area. The artistic lighting and composition talents we have developed as photographers transfer very well to the medium of video.

Experience

We are experienced with the needs and desires of brides and grooms, of families, and of friends. The experiences gained at over 600 weddings make us one of the best wedding service providers in the area.

Coverage

• 2 Videographers, 2 digital cameras;
• No time limit!

Wedding Package

Our wedding package is awesome: edited highlights of wedding/reception, growing-up pictures with music, two-camera coverage at wedding and reception, honeymoon pictures, all with sensitive and artistic editing. Three copies on VHS or DVD are included. Price: $895

Please come and meet us, see our portfolios, and ask for references. We love working weddings, and our results show it.

"Awesome! The video was much better than I ever expected!" P.G. — 1999

"We've seen all of our friends' wedding videos, and we were left with the "blahs." However, your video of our wedding exceeded our expectations: great footage, thorough coverage, and sensitive editing! And, you and your assistant were great." Todd L — 2001

See page 499 under Photographers.

AS TIME GOES BY

503-669-6418
walkervideo@netscape.net

VIDEO PHOTOGRAPHY

It's the moment you have always dreamed of. It's the time of your life you never want to forget.

AS TIME GOES BY would love the privilege of creating the perfect wedding video for you and your loved ones.

AN ULTIMATE TREASURE...
• all weddings are shot with 3CCD digital cameras

• slow motion and photo montage,nonlinear editing,

• wireless mics, lighting, FX, ect. Ask about DVD.

"I had no idea that our video could be this beautiful."
~ Scott & Tanya M.

"The most beautiful wedding video we've seen"
~ Brian & Terri C.

"Thank you so much, you did a fantastic job on our wedding"
~ Bert & Jaime W.

Call us for your free demo
503-669-6418
AS TIME GOES BY

www.bluedogcreative.com
503.544.9744

2861 NE MLK Boulevard
Portland, OR 97212

Complete Details Online

DVD with All Packages

Exceptional Service

blue dog creative

Captivating. Sincere. Video.

Professional. Unobtrusive. Creative.

Before the cameras roll, we'll meet with you informally to get acquainted, learn your likes and dislikes, and come away with a shared vision for the look and feel of your unique wedding day story. From the ceremony to final dance, **we'll capture the faces, emotions and details that hold the most meaning for you.** Our finished productions are as original as you are and enjoyable to watch. We work hard to tell the story of your wedding day.

"I just got the video today and I love it! Tell Brian that he did a wonderful job. I just want to watch it over and over again. Thank you so much for everything, I have been very happy with the results." ~ Kelly & Joseph, April 2001

"You have been a such a pleasure to work with — thank you for joining us in the gorge and on the mountain capturing our wedding celebration. We look forward to recommending you for years to come!" ~ Kimberly & Lee, October 2002

"Just wanted to add my thanks for your efforts at our wedding, your professionalism was well noted. I think the best compliment you probably received from most of our guests was 'wow, we didn't even know you hired a videographer.'" ~ Rennie & Sara, November 2002

"I came home this afternoon and watched your CD-ROM with my fiancée, and you are just what we are looking for! We love the format of your videos, and how creative and personal they are! We would love to work with you. We were thinking about asking a relative or friend to do our video, but we have realized what an awesome keepsake a video is, and really is something that we will watch frequently." ~ Amber & Donny, July 2003

Visit us online at **www.bluedogcreative.com** to view demo clips, packages, and a complete list of services. Request a free demo online in DVD, VHS or CD-Rom format or call us at (503) 544-9744 for more details.

We welcome you to pay us a visit at 2861 NE MLK Boulevard. Make your appointment now for a complimentary, no-obligation consultation.

Visa, MasterCard accepted. Member of WEVA.

CVP Multimedia Studio

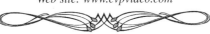

8375 S.W. Beaverton-Hillsdale Hwy. Suite C
Portland, Oregon 97225
Owner: Randy Stumman (503) 524-1780
Web site: www.cvpvideo.com

Premiere Video Production Company

CVP Multimedia Studio is a premiere video production company. With more than ten years of experience and hundreds of weddings produced, we will produce for you a grand and elegant wedding DVD/video that will amaze and astound you and your family. Our wedding productions rival the high standards and extreme perfection of broadcast television. We will bring our television commercial expertise and broadcast level equipment to your ceremony and reception, thus bringing to you the very finest in wedding picture quality and romantic effects. We do all this in a way that our clients find incredibly unobtrusive. Then back in the studio, we meticulously review and edit all the footage gathered at the wedding to build you a marvelous and luxurious movie documenting your wedding event.

Production Tools

Ceremony: CVP Multimedia Studio will use only television broadcast true digital 3-Chip Sony 300AL DVCAM cameras producing over 800 lines of sharp resolution with the best low light capabilities, multiple UHF tru-diversity wireless microphones for capturing all the audio. We use only human manned cameras with professional tripods for stability and composed videotaping for truly professional results.

Studio: CVP Multimedia Studio can utilize five state-of-the-art unique non-linear/linear "hybrid" computer editing systems, computer graphic programs, computer 3D animation, television graphic composers, photo montages, frame accurate editing, slow motion effects, picture-in-picture effects, dissolve-on-dissolve effects, morphing, split screen effects, music composition capabilities, Betacam SP mastering, digital transitions and other Hollywood-type special effects. All of our broadcast commercial capabilities are at your disposal and everything is edited in our studio, not on location and you can come in to view this process.

Production Prices

CVP Multimedia Studio has a tremendous amount of production capabilities in which to produce for you a truly unique and elegant wedding DVD/video. We have taken these capabilities and built ten different productions with prices starting at $495 up to $4,995. You can also customize a production using one of our packages as a starting point. This allows you the best in customized features and creative development. We offer one to three camera coverage, two hours to all day taping, and a vast array of editing features all designed to bring to you the finest in loving and creative wedding videography.

Final Thoughts

CVP Multimedia Studio will help guide you through the video production process to insure you receive the highest quality wedding DVD/video on the market today. We have a price for all budgets but only one high level of quality. Call today for an appointment and then stop by our new studio for your free award winning demo copy and a "no-hassle" consultation to see how *CVP Multimedia Studio* can turn the most important day of your life into a loving and lasting memory. Please visit our web site at www.cvpvideo.com

CVP Multimedia Studio offers DVD, Video, CD-ROM and Web Streaming distribution!
VISA - MASTERCARD

Da Video

www.DaVideoProductions.com

(503) 375-7363

Hi! I'm David and my company's name is DaVideo Productions, which is a combination of my name, David, and the word, Video. That's my way of saying that I put all of my creative energies into every wedding video my company creates. Each wedding video is individual and unique, just like you. We work hard at telling your story. And while I do have package prices, I will also work with you on an hourly rate and come up with the perfect video that tells your story at a price you can afford! I hope I have the opportunity to tell your wedding day story.

—David McGinnis, Owner
  DaVideo Productions

YOUR IMAGINATION ON VIDEO

Call for an appointment or free demo video: 503-375-7363

EMA VIDEO PRODUCTIONS

1306 NW Hoyt, Suite 101
Portland, OR 97209
Phone: 503-241-8663
Fax: 503-224-6967

Visit us online at:
www.emavideo.com/weddings.html

Capture The Moment

EMA Video Productions, Inc. is a full service award winning video production company with over 25 years of experience in all aspects of video production.

Why should you hire EMA for your wedding?

- No wedding is too small or large for EMA, and we use high quality digital 3-chip cameras to give you crisp pictures and sound.

- Whether it be one camera or three cameras, or just the ceremony, we offer wedding packages to fit every budget.

- We are discreet and maintain a professional appearance at all times. We also make it a priority to be as unseen and as quiet as humanly possible.

- We take pride in our work. Bringing you beautiful, artistically composed video footage and digitally mastered sound.

- We offer a professional un-compressed non-linear editing facility with the ability to create custom graphics and quality digital transitions. This also allows us to maintain perfect image quality all the way through to the final product.

We also give you the option of transferring your wedding to DVD. Even if you don't yet have a DVD player, this is an ideal way to digitally preserve your memories in pristine quality for generations to come.

It is our ultimate goal to help make your wedding day the special experience that it should be. With our help this momentous occasion will be beautifully recorded forever.

image**Wise** productions

**unobtrusive & sensitive
to style
romance
& family**

image**Wise**productions

18150 N.W. Clarno Court Portland, Oregon 97229
voice & fax: 503.439.8282
weddings@imageswiseproductions.com
www.imagewiseproductions.com

WITH A SENSITIVITY FOR STYLE & ROMANCE, our professional production team works alongside your photographer to capture your day as it unfolds through the eyes of your guests. We put our heart into every project and our creative team thoughtfully edits and preserves the planned, and maybe not so planned, events of your day.

OUR UNOBTRUSIVE STYLE lets us blend with your guests. We record the special moments that should not be missed and find those that sometimes are! We gather greetings and messages from your willing guests and establish shots of your chosen location.

WITH PACKAGES STARTING AT $500, planning your very special video production with imageWise Productions is "a piece of cake!"

Here is a sample of what we offer, you can call or go to the website for more details.
• **A Taste of the Icing.** *On a budget? Try our unedited digital coverage, transferred to VHS*

OR COOK UP YOUR OWN CUSTOM CREATION. Using dual cameras for full coverage provides multiple angles, which enhances the editing process; we capture all our images using Cannon's XL1 and GL1 cameras. The image quality of these cameras is unparalleled and the same technology used in professional broadcasting. Then, with the latest in computer technology we edit, add special effects, along with your own music, and present it to you usually within two weeks (Special requests and additional options may take longer).

TASTE THESE SAMPLES. Then go to our website for the full menu, or give us a call and we'll send you the recipe.

• **1st Tier – Basic Package – $1,495** Our most popular. Providing eight hours coverage, creatively edited to a memorable video with your choice of music

• **2nd Tier – add the DVD Package – $1,895** For those who prefer to view on DVD with chapters and menus for easy searching, plus extra ingredients

• **3rd Tier – stir in the Web Package – $ 2,295** We sprinkle in some extra treats to share with out-of-town family and friends and post it on the web. Your site or ours

• **The Icing on the Cake – $2,995** For those who want their cake and eat it too! Add other pre-ceremony events such as the engagement party, shower, bachelor party, special dates or proposals etc. (call for more info)

EXTRA LAYERS. We have many extra ingredients you can add or substitute to personally cook up your own creation. With imageWise productions you can just take a taste of the icing or have your cake and eat it too!

Please let this business know that you heard about them from the Bravo! Wedding Resource Guide. **593**

ron@masterpiece-video.com

Masterpiece
Video
Productions

Ron W. Miller (503) 254-7149
10250 N.E. Morris Court • Portland, Oregon 97220
E-mail: ron@masterpiece-video.com

- Over 1,100 Weddings in the Portland Area
- 14 Years Experience
- Most Unobtrusive Style in Portland
- Fantastic Relationship with Best Wedding Vendors
- Creative Excellence at its Best! (Call for References)

Options and Techniques

- **DVD** (All packages)
- **Wireless microphones:** to hear the vows
- **Studio editing special effects:** slow motion, titling audio dub. Montage video available incorporating childhood, couple, and honeymoon shots.
- **Summary tape:** 15 minute tape capturing emotional highlights of your wedding day
- **Multiple cameras:** fading between different angles for that smooth professional touch

Call for Package Prices

"The Ultimate Way to Remember Your Wedding Day"

Grand Prize Winner of the 1995 Wedding Video Competition at the MBA National Wedding Videographers Convention, held at the MGM Grand Hotel in Las Vegas.

The Finest in Wedding Videography

503.559.6290   Mtage.com

Grant Your Wishes

Whether it be fanciful, elegant, classic or fun,
let Meritage blend imagination and skill
to create your perfect wedding story.
Choose from standard wedding packages
or create an ala carte video customized
with your personal tastes in mind.
Call one of our wedding consultants today
or visit us on the web at Mtage.com

Your Package Includes:

Complimentary videos for you and your wedding party,
Coverage free of time and travel constraints,
Rehearsal attendance and coordination,
a Hollywood style DVD with scene selections and
a Silver plated video keepsake case engraved
with your names and wedding date.

Visa and Mastercard accepted for your convenience.

Do you really need a wedding video?.....YES!!!!!!!

Working in the wedding industry, the regret I hear expressed most my couples is that they didn't hire a videographer. This is your opportunity to ensure that you will be able to relive one of the best days of your life!

Monkus Studios is a creative production company specializing in digital filmmaking. When you hire me for your wedding, you can be sure that I will capture every important, beautiful and funny moment, capturing these memories forever. I shoot each project artistically with state-of-the-art broadcast digital cameras. Footage is then creatively edited on the latest in digital equipment, ensuring no loss in image or sound quality.

I'm sure you will love your video and will want to watch it over and over. Your video will reflect your style, personalities and will be the most invaluable keepsake you'll have after it's all over!

Call me to receive a free demo or visit my web site at www.monkus.net.
I look forward to working with you.

Cinematically,
Collin

Toll Free
866-642-1004

Visit Us on The World Wide Web:

PORTLAND WEDDINGVIDEO .COM

PAX VIDEO SERVICES

DVD

An Incredible Wedding DVD Isn't Expensive...It's Priceless

Excellent video service on your wedding day needn't be expensive nor complex. Because your wedding day will be different and unique from all others, every Pax video and DVD is custom designed and pre-planned. Enjoy non-intrusive documentary-style digital video production with state-of-the-art technology: fully digital, multi-camera service, stereo wireless microphones, personalized music selections and more. Select one of our coverage plans which best fits your needs:

2 Hours	**$499**
4 Hours	**$799**
6 Hours	**$999**
8 Hours	**$1,299**
Unlimited Hours	**$1,999**

Your Wedding On DVD

Pax Video Services is pleased to offer your wedding video on DVD. DVD technology offers many advantages over regular VHS tape: permanence far exceeding tape, superior image quality and Dolby Digital Audio, interactive menus (no need to rewind or fast-forward to locate specific moments, simply click on the menu button and play). Unlike other wedding videographers, every Pax DVD disc is digitally mastered and produced in-house to ensure optimal quality.

Our Wedding Gift To You...A Free DVD Player

Mention you saw this ad in the *Bravo! Resource Guide* and receive a free DVD player when you schedule your wedding video and DVD package and we'll give you a free DVD player.

Free Demo DVD or Tape

Call 866-642-1004 today for more information or to receive your complimentary five minute demo tape, or visit us online at www.portlandweddingvideo.com.

ROYAL VIDEO AND ELECTRONICS
Specializing in Special Event Videography
Web site: http://home.comcast.net/~royalvideo; E-mail: royalvideo@comcast.net
(503) 390-4220 or (877) 402-5107 Toll Free; Fax (503) 390-3125
224 Northridge Court, N. • Keizer, Oregon 97303
Contact: Wes Jensen; Business Hours: by appointment

Description of Video Service
Video for all special occasions; specializing in wedding photography, photo montages, multi-camera live video event coverage, editing and copying service.
Providing video services for weddings, seminars, and more since 1987.

Options and Techniques
• **Digital** format for best picture quality.
• **Non-Linear Editing** with dazzling **3-D Transitions** and **Digital Effects**
• True Diversity **Wireless Mic** is used when direct connect to sound system is not possible.
• Studio editing providing **Special Effects** (as appropriate) such as 3-D transitions, mosaics, slow motion, dissolves, paint, titles, and inclusion of still photographs.
• Studio audio mixing to add **Music** for viewing pleasure
• Tape copies on VHS, or available on Hi-8, 8mm, or S-VHS. DVD option now available (see DVD option below).

Packages and Prices for 2004 Full Coverage! No travel fees or extra charges.
• **"Basic" Package $648: One camera;** includes titles (scrolling names of everyone in wedding party), pre-ceremony family group pictures, ceremony, and reception. Still pictures such as engagement or baby pictures can be incorporated into your final video. Music added in the studio for your viewing pleasure. Price includes three copies. Additional copies may be purchased for $15 each. A video "highlights" (5-10 minute short of entire video) as part of the finished video is standard.
• **"Basic+" Package $798:** All the features of our "Basic" package, including one cameraman, plus a second camera for the ceremony. The second camera is remote controlled.
• **"Royal" Package $948:** All the features of our "Basic" package, but with two cameras and two camera operators, providing two angles for better coverage. We are a husband/wife team.
• DVD Option $100: Includes one copy. Additional copies $15 each. Video quality is equal to the source. It is more permanent than tape. DVDs may be substituted for tape copies.
Typical coverage begins around 2 hours before the ceremony, while the photographer is taking the formal pictures, and continues through the reception—often around 2 hours into the reception, allowing for the cake cutting, toast, dance, bouquet and garter toss. Up to 6 hours coverage—no extra charges. Over 6 hours negotiable fee. No travel fee within the Salem/Portland general areas, otherwise negotiable.

Reservations
Most weddings are booked months in advance. Book early to reserve your date.

Deposit
A 50% deposit is required at the time of booking, with the balance due on your wedding day.

Relive the Sights and Sounds of Your Wedding Day!
Sit back and relax with friends and relatives, and watch the beauty and excitement of your wedding unfold. See pictures and hear comments from your friends and relatives wishing you a life of happiness together.

RYDER
Video
Productions

10607 S.E. Main Street
Milwaukie, Oregon 97222
(503) 652-2650
www.ryder.org

Professional Wedding Videography

Special Sale Packages Available!

Special $895 Includes 1,2,3
Regular $ 1195 Includes 1,2,3,5,6
Deluxe $ 1495 Includes 1,2,3,4,5,6

Build Your own Wedding Video

1. **Ceremony:** The I do's, groom has a wireless mic, opening and ending graphics, single camera 3-chip DV. Only $600.
2. **Reception:** Cake cut, bouquet and garter toss, first dance, talk with family and friends. Only $250
3. **Perfect Ending:** Video highlights of the day with a song. Only $100
4. **Reflections:** Bride and groom share first date and courtship. Only $300
5. **Highlights:** Coverage before ceremony. Only $150
6. **Montage:** 20 still photos of precious moments. Only $150
7. **Two Cameras:** Two people, two DV 3-chip cameras. Only $300.

Call for appointment

Imagine...
...reliving your wedding day for years and years to come

Imagine...
...sharing this experience with family, friends, children and grandchildren

Imagine...
...this documentation being **artistic, unique** and **captivating**

Imagine...
...no further!

experience the difference
www.shaka-brah.com

telephone: 503.913.7611
email: shaka@shaka-brah.com

503-699-1017
Fax 503-699-5050; Cell 503-997-3703

We capture **your** day the way **you** want it.

Whether it's done documentary style or at a fast-paced MTV style, we shoot and edit your video the way **you** want it to be done.

Package #1 $585
Four hours coverage; you determine what is covered.

Package #2 $885
Six hours coverage; pre-ceremony moments, formal pictures, ceremony and reception covered.

Package #3 $1,100
Eight hours coverage; all of above plus photo montage.

Each package includes 2 VHS or DVD copies. Additional VHS or DVD copies may be purchased for $15 each.

Custom packages can be created to meet your special needs. (Such as rehearsal and rehearsal dinner, etc.)

We use CD quality cordless microphones and high-end professional equipment to shoot and edit your video to ensure the best quality finished product. Years of filmmaking experience make it easy for us to create a video that you will love to watch again and again.

Visa and Mastercard accepted

photography - video - 8mm film
503.417.1130   www.sjharmon.com

Truly Capturing Your Day

S.J. Harmon's photojournalistic style documents the events of your wedding day as they occur. Long sessions of posed shots result in images that look contrived and posed. Your images will reflect the joyful "moments" of your wedding experience — not bad memories of being ordered around for hours under hot lights. Your images will capture your day the way you planned it!

Full Service

S. J. Harmon is your full service Photography, Videography and Motion Picture business. All of our products and mediums work seamlessly together to provide you with all of your imaging needs in one location. From the "photo montage" at your rehearsal dinner, to a fully interactive DVD containing a masterfully edited "wedding movie," we help you all along the way. Any of our products and services can be purchased separately or together to fit any need! Our products are cutting edge and range from on-line web proofing, to DVD and even the timeless feel of 8mm motion picture film.

Style

Our product and service integrate both technical proficiency and artistic innovation — capturing the true spontaneity and emotion of your day. S.J. Harmon is not trying to fit a rigid idea of what capturing a wedding is all about. Our images are personally crafted to your style and creativity — and will reflect contemporary fashion, art and multimedia. We also love nostalgic images that capture the essence of timeless memories.

"We have had countless comments from friends and family who are truly amazed at the work that you did... thank you for making such a stressful day less stress-filled. I so appreciate how you made pictures fun and captured so much while I wasn't even looking... You were there during those priceless moments getting all of it on film..."

**If you are looking for Photography, Video or Motion Picture Film,
please call us for Demo or Appointment.**

S.J. Harmon Imaging
2861 N.E. Martin Luther King Blvd. • Portland, Oregon 97212
503.417.1130 • 1.866.339.0405 • www.sjharmon.com

photo by Rebecca Widner Photography • See page 541

Tradition

To symbolize family unity, three candles are lit: first the

bride's parents light the candle on the right, then the

groom's parents light the candle on the left, and finally,

the bride and groom light the third candle, called the

unity candle, from the flames of the other two candles.

PORTLAND AREA CEREMONY SITES_____

Abernethy Center — 606 15th Street, Oregon City, OR 97045
Capacity: up to 300 — W/R/B/S/M/
Contact: Event Coordinator (503) 722-9400 *See page 305*

Amoore Wedding Chapel — 7506 N. Chicago, Portland, OR 97203
Sit-down: up to 125
Contact: Art Moore (503) 240-8144 — W/R/B/ *See page 306*

Canby Pioneer Chapel — N.W. Third and Elm, Canby, OR 97013
Capacity: up to 120 — W/
Contact: Darlene Key (503) 263-6126 *See page 312*

The Carus House — 23200 S. Highway 213, Oregon City, OR 97045
Sit-down: up to 145 — W/R/B/
Contact:(503) 632-2253 *See page 312*

Crystal Springs Rhododendron
Garden — S.E. 28th/North of Woodstock, Portland, OR 97215
Indoor: up to 125; Outdoor: up to 300 — W/R/
Contact: Rita Knapp (503) 256-2483 *See page 307*

First Congregational Church — 1126 S.W. Park Ave., Portland, OR 97205
Ceremony: 40 to 850 — W/
Contact: Church Office (503) 228-7219 *See page 313*

First Unitarian Church — 1011 S.W. 12th Ave., Portland, OR 97205
Capacity: up to 600 — W/R
Contact: (503) 228-6389 ext.23 *See page 314*

The Grotto Catholic Church —
N.E. 85th at Sandy, P.O. Box 20008, Portland, OR 97294
Indoor: up to 450; Outdoor: up to 700 — W/
*bride or groom must be a practicing Catholic and registered in a parish
Contact: Sr. Ruth Arnott (503) 254-7371

Living Enrichment Center — 29500 S.W. Grahams Ferry Rd., Wilsonville, OR 97070
Indoor: up to 950; Outdoor: up to 250 — R/B/S/M/W
Contact: DeannaForseth (503) 682-568. 800-893-1000 *See page 308*

McLean House — 5350 River St., West Linn, Oregon 97068
Indoor/Outdoor: up to 100 — W/R/B/S/M/P/
Contact: (503) 655-4268 *See page 316*

Oaks Pioneer Church — 455 S.E. Spokane St., Portland, OR 97202
Capacity: up to 75 — W/
Contact: Lorrain Fyre (503) 233-1497 *See page 317*

The Old Church — 1422 S.W. 11th Ave., Portland, OR 97201
Ceremony: 300; Reception: 200 — W/R/
Contact: Trish Augustin (503) 222-2031 *See page 317*

Old Laurelhurst Church — 3212 S.E. Ankeny, Portland, OR 97214
Ceremony: up to 250 — W/R/M/
Contact: Event Coordinator (503) 231-0462 *See page 309*

St.Anne's Chapel — 17600 Hwy. 43, Marylhurst, OR 97036
W/R/B/S/M
Contact: (800) 699-6249 *See page 319*

Shilo Inn — Canyon — 9900 S.W. Canyon Rd., Portland, OR 97225
Capacity: up to 200 — W/R/B/
Contact: Catering Office (503) 297-2551 ext.552 *See page 310*

W=Wedding Ceremony   R=Reception   B=Banquet   S=Seminar   M=Meeting   P=Picnic

Please let these businesses know that you heard about them from the Bravo! Wedding Resource Guide.

ALOHA/AURORA

Heritage House Farm & Gardens — Aurora, OR 97002
Outdoor: up to 250 — W/R/B/S/M/P
Derolyn Johnson (503) 678-5704, (888) 479-3500 *See page 106*
Langdon Farms — 24377 N.E. Airport Rd. Aurora, OR 97002
Capacity: up to 250 — W/R/B/S/M/P
Contact: (503) 678-GOLF (4653) *See page 119*

BEAVERTON

The Greenwood Inn — 10700 S.W. Allen Blvd., Beaverton, OR 97005
Capacity: up to 500; Guest Rooms: 250 — W/R/B/S/M/
Contact: Private Dining (503) 626-4558
Kingstad Center for Meeting & Events— 15450 S.W. Milikan Way., Beaverton, OR
Capacity: up to 300 — W/R/B/S/M/
Contact: (503) 626-6338 *See page 115*
Stockpot Restaurant and Catering Co. —
8200 S.W. Scholls Ferry Rd., Beaverton, OR 97005
Capacity: up to 350 — W/R/B/S/M/P/
Contact: Murray Miller (503) 643-5451 *See page 158*

BRIDAL VEIL

Bridal Veil Lakes — P.O. Box 5, Bridal Veil, OR 97010
Capacity: up to 400 — W/R/B/M/S/
Contact: Jennifer Miller (503) 981-3695 *See page 75*

COLUMBIA GORGE/HOOD RIVER

Cherry Hill Bed & Breakfast — 1550 Carroll Rd., Mosier, OR 97040
Indoor: up to 150; Garden: up to 200; Guest Rooms: 3 — W/R/B/
Contact: Elizabeth Toscano (541) 478-4455 *See page 80*
The Dalles Ranch — 6289 Upper Five Mile Rd., The Dalles, OR 97058
Capacity: 50 indoor, 100 outdoor — W/R/B/
Contact: (360) 892-7352, (541) 298-9942 *See page 163*
Mt. Hood Bed & Breakfast — 8885 Cooper Spur Rd., Parkdale, OR 97041
Indoor/Outdoor: up to 200+; Guest Rooms: 4 — W/R/B/P/
Contact: Jackie Rice (541) 352-6885 *See page 129*
Skamania Lodge — 1131 Skamania Lodge Way, Stevenson, WA 98648
Capacity: up to 500; Guest Rooms: 195 — W/R/B/S/M/
Contact: Janet Nelson (509) 427-2503
Stonehedge Gardens — 3405 Cascade Avenue, Hood River, OR 97031
Indoor: Up to 100; Outdoor: up to 250 — R/W/M
Contact: Leilani Caldwell (541) 386-3940 *See page 159*

COLTON

Camp Colton, The Chapel at — Colton, OR 97017
Chapel seating: up to 250 — W/R/B/S
Contact: Jarred, Mary or Kathy Lundstrom (503) 824-2267 *See pages 78*

W=Wedding Ceremony   R=Reception   B=Banquet   S=Seminar   M=Meeting   P=Picnic

Please let these businesses know that you heard about them from the Bravo! Wedding Resource Guide.

CORNELIUS

Pumpkin Ridge Golf Course — 12930 Old Pumpkin Ridge Rd., North Plains, OR 97133
Capacity: up to 500 — W/R/B/S/M/
Catering Director (503) 647-4747   *See page 143*

FAIRVIEW

The Lake House at Blue Lake Park — 21160 N.E. Blue Lake Rd., Fairview, OR 97024
Capacity: up to 150, outdoor 250 — W/R/B/M/S/
Contact: (503) 667-3483   *See page 116*

FOREST GROVE

Elk Cove Vineyards — 27751 N.W. Olson Rd., Gaston, OR 97119
Capacity: up to 150 — W/R/B/S/M/
Hospitality Coordinator (503) 985-7760
McMenamins — Grand Lodge — 3505 Pacific Ave., Forest Grove, OR 97116
Capacity: up to 150 indoor, 1,000 outdoor; Guest Rooms: 77 — W/R/B/S/M/
Contact: Group Sales (503) 992-9530   *See page 101*

GRESHAM

East Fork Country Estate — 9957 S.E. 222nd, Gresham, OR 97080
Indoor/Outdoor: up to 250 — W/R/B/S/M/P/
Contact: Tami Kay Galvin (503) 667-7069   *See page 93*
Persimmon Country Club — 500 S.E. Butler Rd., Gresham, OR 97080
Sit-down: up to 300; Reception: up to 500 — W/R/B/S/M/
Contact: Catering (503) 674-3259   *See page 141*

HELVETIA

Garden Vineyards — Helvetia, Oregon
Capacity up to 500+ — R/B/S/M/
Contact: Melinda (503) 647-5192   *See page 98*

HILLSBORO

McMenamins —
   Cornelius Pass Roadhouse — 4045 N.W. Cornelius Pass Rd., Hillsboro, OR 97124
Capacity: up to 600 — R/B/S/M/P/W/
Contact: Group Sales (503) 693-8452   *See page 84*
Sweet Oregon Grill — 6393 N.W. Cornelius Pass Rd., Hillsboro, OR 97124
Indoors: up to 200; Outdoors: up to 300 — W/R/B/S/M/
Contact: (503) 614-8747   *See page 161*
Tuality Health
   Education Center — 334 S.E. Eighth Ave., Hillsboro, OR 97123
Sit-down: up to 250; Reception: up to 400 — R/B/S/M/
Contact: (503) 681-1700   *See page 167*

LAKE OSWEGO

Clarke's — 455 Second St., Lake Oswego, OR 97034
Capacity: up to 90 — /R/B/S/M/
Contact: Laurie or Jonathan Clarke (503) 636-2667   *See page 176*

W=Wedding Ceremony   R=Reception   B=Banquet   S=Seminar   M=Meeting   P=Picnic

   Please let these businesses know that you heard about them from the Bravo! Wedding Resource Guide.

Crowne Plaza — 14811 Kruse Oaks Dr.., Lake Oswego, OR 97035
Capacity: up to 300; Guest Rooms: 161 — W/R/B/S/M/
Contact: Director of Catering (503) 624-8400 ext.6253 *See page 87*
Lakewood Center for the Arts —
368 S. State St., Lake Oswego, OR 97034
Sit-down: up to 150; Reception: up to 225; Theater: 200 — W/R/B/S/M/
Contact: Executive Director (503) 635-6338 *See page 118*

MCMINNVILLE / NEWBERG / DAYTON

McMenamins Hotel Oregon — 310 N.E. Evans St., McMinnville, OR 97128 *See page 111*
Capacity: up to 120; Guest Rooms: 42 — R/B/S/M/
Contact: (503) 472-8427 or (888) 472-8427
Willamette Farms of Oregon — 8000 N.E. Parrish Rd., Newberg, OR 97132
Capacity: up to 250 — W/R/B/S/M/
Contact: Jeffrey Leal Silva, Farm Manager (503) 538-9895, Cell (503) 569-6745 *See page 168*

MILWAUKIE

Amadeus at the Fernwood — 2122 S.E. Sparrow, Milwaukie, OR 97222
Capacity: up to 300 — W/R/B/S/M/
Contact: Kristina Poppmeier (503) 659-1735 or (503) 636-6154 *See page 174*
Historic Broetje House — 3101 S.E. Courtney, Milwaukie, OR 97222
Indoor/Outdoor: up to 150; Guest Rooms: 3 — W/R/B/S/M/P/
Contact: Lorraine or Lois (503) 659-8860 *See page 77*
Gray Gables Estate — 3009 S.E. Chestnut, Milwaukie, OR 97267
Indoor/Outdoor: up to 290; Guest Rooms: 7 — W/R/B/S/M/P/
Contact: (503) 654-0470 *See page 102*
Milwaukie Center
(in North Clackamas Park) — 5440 S.E. Kellogg Creek Dr., Milwaukie, OR 97222
Sit-down: up to 400; Reception: up to 600 — W/R/B/S/M/P/
Contact: Facility Use Coordinator (503) 653-8100 *See page 126*

MOLALLA

Camp Onahlee — 15706 S. Hwy 211, Molalla, OR
Capacity: 300 outdoor/daytime; 100 indoor/overnight — W/R/B/
Contact: Kevin Kelley (503) 656-2530 ext. 29

MOUNT HOOD/SANDY

Cedar Springs Country Estate — 12353 S.E. Lusted Rd., Sandy, OR 97055
Capacity: up to 250 — W/R/B/
Contact: Event Coordinator (503) 663-0772 *See page 79*
Cooper Spur Mountain Resort —
10755 Cooper Spur Rd., Mt. Hood, OR 97041
Capacity: up to 70 indoors, or outdoors Guest Rooms: 41 — W/R/B/S/M/
Contact: (541) 352-6692, (800) ski-hood *See page 83*
Mt. Hood Bed and Breakfast — 8885 Cooper Spur Rd., Parkdale, OR 97041
Indoor/Outdoor: up to 200+; Guest Rooms: 4 — W/R/B/P/
Contact: Jackie Rice (541) 352-6885 *See page 129*
Mt. Hood Meadows Ski Resort — 1975 S.W. First Ave., Suite M, Portland, OR 97201
Capacity: up to 400 — W/R/B/S/M/P/
Contact: Portland Sales Office (503) 287-5438

W=Wedding Ceremony   R=Reception   B=Banquet   S=Seminar   M=Meeting   P=Picnic

Please let these businesses know that you heard about them from the Bravo! Wedding Resource Guide.

The Resort at the Mountain — 68010 East Fairway Ave., Welches, OR 97067
Capacity: up to 450— W/R/B/S/M/
Contact: (503) 622-2220, (800) 733-0800   *See page 148*
Timberline Lodge — Timberline, OR 97028
Capacity: up to 200; Guest Rooms: 70 — W/R/B/S/M/P/
Contact: Catering (503) 622-0722   *See page 165*

OREGON CITY

Abernethy Center — 606 15th Street, Oregon City, OR 97045
Capacity: up to 300 — W/R/B/S/M/
Contact: Event Coordinator (503) 722-9400   *See page 59*
Clara's Own Grand Oregon Lodge — 604 Seventh St., Oregon City, OR 97045
Capacity: up to 299 — W/R/B/S/M/
Contact: (503) 232-9904   *See page 81*
Museum of the Oregon Territory — 211 Tumwater Dr., Oregon City, OR 97045
Capacity: up to 299 — W/R/B/S/M/
Contact: Judi Isbell (503) 655-5574   *See page 130*
Oregon City Golf Club at Lone Oak —
20124 S. Beavercreek Rd., Oregon City, OR 97045
Sit-down: up to 125; Reception: up to 160, 300 outdoor — W/R/B/M/S/
Contact: Rose Holden (503) 518-1038   *See page 134*
Red Tail Canyon Event Center— Oregon City, OR
Capacity: up to 200 — W/R/B/M/S/
Contact: (503) 656-6428   *See page 147*

PORTLAND DOWNTOWN

The Adrianna Hill
Grand Ballroom — 918 S.W. Yamhill, 2nd Floor, Portland, OR 97205
Capacity: up to 300 — W/R/B/S/M/
Contact: (503) 227-6285, (503) 227-4061   *See page 62*
The Atrium — 100 S.W. Market St., Portland, OR 97201
Reception: up to 300 — W/R/B/S/M/
Contact: Catering Director (503) 220-3929   *See page 69*
The Benson Hotel — 309 S.W. Broadway at Oak, Portland, OR 97205
Sit-down: up to 400; Reception: up to 600; Guest Rooms: 286 — W/R/B/S/M/
Contact: Sales (503) 295-4140   *See page 73*
Cassidy's Restaurant — 1331 S.W. Washington, Portland, OR 97205
Capacity: up to 120 — W/R/B/S/M/
Christine, Bob or Mercedes (503) 223-0054   *See page 175*
The Crown Ballroom
and Garden Court — 918 S.W. Yamhill, 5th Floor, Portland, OR 97205
Sit-down: up to 200; Reception: up to 300 — W/R/M/S/B/
Contact: Raven David (503) 227-8440   *See page 86*
Crystal Ballroom — 1332 W. Burnside, Portland, OR 97209
Sit-down: up to 300; Reception: up to 1,000 — W/R/B/S/M/
Contact: Events Coordinator (503) 288-3286   *See page 88*
Days Inn City Center — 1414 S.W. Sixth Ave., Portland, OR 97201
Capacity: up to 200; outdoor up to 400 Guest Rooms: 173 — W/R/B/S/M/
Contact: Catering Sales Manager (503) 221-1611, (800) 899-0248   *See page 89*

W=Wedding Ceremony   R=Reception   B=Banquet   S=Seminar   M=Meeting   P=Picnic

DoubleTree Hotel Downtown — 310 S.W. Lincoln, Portland, OR 97201
Capacity: up to 250; Guest Rooms: 235 — W/R/B/S/M/
Contact: Sales Office (503) 221-0450   *See page 90*

Dragonfish Cafe — 808 S.W. Taylor, Portland, OR 97205
Capacity: up to 70 — W/R/B/S/M/
Contact: (503) 243-5991 x.1668   *See page 177*

Embassy Suites — Portland Downtown — 319 S.W. Pine St., Portland, OR 97204
Sit-down: up to 180; Reception: up to 300; Guest Rooms: 276 — R/B/S/M/
Contact: Catering (503) 279-9000   *See page 95*

Greek Cusina — 404 S.W. Washington, Portland, OR 97204
Capacity up to 200 — R/B/S/M/
Contact: Ted (503) 224-2288   *See page 103*

Jake's Catering at The Governor Hotel — 611 S.W. 10th St., Portland, OR 97205
Sit-down: up to 450; Reception: up to 600; Guest Rooms: 100 — W/R/B/S/M/
Contact: Catering Sales (503) 241-2125   *See page 99*

The Heathman Restaurant — 1001 S.W. Broadway at Salmon St., Portland, OR 97205
Sit-down: up to 200; Reception: up to 300; Guest Rooms: 75 — W/R/B/S/M/
Contact: Catering Manager (503) 790-7126   *See page 105*

Kells—Portland's Irish
Restaurant and Pub — 112 S.W. Second Ave., Portland, OR 97204
Sit-down: up to 150; Reception: up to 300 — W/R/B/S/M/
Contact: Banquet Manager (503) 227-4057   *See page 113*

The Mallory Hotel — 729 S.W. 15th Ave., Portland, OR 97205
Capacity: up to 120; Guest Rooms: 150 — W/R/B/S/M/
Contact: (503) 223-631, (800) 228-8657   *See page 121*

Marriott Hotel—Portland — 1401 S.W. Naito Parkway, Portland, OR 97201
Capacity: up to 1,000; Guest Rooms: 503 — W/R/B/S/M/
Contact: Sales & Catering (503) 499-6360   *See page 122*

Pazzo Ristorante Hotel Vintage Plaza — 627 S.W. Washington, Portland, OR 97205
Sit-down: up to 300; Guest Rooms: 107 — W/R/B/S/M/
Contact: Catering (503) 412-6316   *See page 179*

RiverPlace Hotel — 1510 S.W. Harbor Way
Capacity: up to 200; Guest Rooms: 84 — W/R/B/S/M/
Contact: Sales & Catering (503) 423-3112   *See page 150*

Tiffany Center — 1410 S.W. Morrison, Portland, OR 97205
Capacity: up to 1,200; Theatre: up to 975 — W/R/B/S/M/
Contact: Events Manager (503) 222-0703 or (503) 248-9305   *See page 164*

The Treasury — 326 S.W. Broadway St., Portland, OR 97204
Capacity: up to 300 — R/B/C/M/W
Contact: (503) 226-1240   *See page 166*

World Trade Center — Two World Trade Center, 25 S.W. Salmon St., Portland, OR 97204
Sit-down: up to 300; Reception: up to 400;
Outdoor: Sit-down: up to 500; Reception: up to 800 — W/R/B/S/M/
Contact: Reservations (503) 464-8688   *See page 171*

NORTH PORTLAND

Courtyard Marriott —
Portland North Harbour — 1231 N. Anchor Way, Portland, OR 97217
Indoor: up to 100; Outdoor: up to 500; Guest Rooms: 132 — R/B/S/M/
Contact: (503) 735-1818   *See page 85*

W=Wedding Ceremony   R=Reception   B=Banquet   S=Seminar   M=Meeting   P=Picnic

Please let these businesses know that you heard about them from the Bravo! Wedding Resource Guide.

NORTH PORTLAND

DoubleTree Hotel — Hayden Island Complex
Columbia River — 1401 N. Hayden Island Dr., Portland, OR 97217
Capacity: up to 1,400; Guest Rooms: 351 — W/R/B/S/M/
Contact: Sales Office (503) 283-2111   *See page 91*
DoubleTree Hotel — Hayden Island Complex
Jantzen Beach — 909 N. Hayden Island Dr., Portland, OR 97217
Capacity: up to 1,400; Guest Rooms: 320 — W/R/B/S/M/
Contact: Sales Office (503) 283-4466   *See page 91*
Historic Kenton Firehouse
Community Center — 8105 N. Brandon, Portland, OR 97217
Upstairs: up to 50; Downstairs: up to 100 — P/R/M/S/B/W/
Contact: Coordinator (503) 823-4524; Fax (503) 285-7843; www.historickenton.com
John Palmer House— 4314 N. Mississippi Ave., Portland, OR 97217
Capacity: up to 49 indoor, 100 outdoor; — W/R/B/S/M/
Contact: Roger Goldingay (503) 493-1903   *See page 112*
The Overlook House — 3839 N. Melrose Dr., Portland, OR 97227
Indoor: up to 75; Outdoor: up to 150 — W/R/S/M/P/
Contact: Building Coordinator (503) 823-4524   *See page 138*
Queen Anne Victorian Mansion — 1441 N. McClellan, Portland, OR 97217
Capacity up to 300 — W/R/B/S/M/
Contact: Bridal Coordinator (503) 283-3224   *See page 144*
River City Promotions — 251 St.Helens Street, St. Helens, OR 97051
Capacity up to 260— W/R/B/S/M/
Contact: (503) 366-1664   *See page 149*
Widmer Gasthaus — 955 N. Russel, Portland, OR 97227
Capacity: up to 75 — B/P/M/S/
Contact: Manager (503) 281-3333   *See page 184*

NORTHEAST PORTLAND

The Acadian Ballroom — 1829 N.E. Alberta, Portland, OR 97211
Capacity: up to 600 (open floor) — W/R/B/M/
Contact: (503) 546-6800, (360) 258-7533   *See page 61*
Albertina's Restaurant at
The Old Kerr Nursery — 424 N.E. 22nd Ave., Portland, OR 97232
Capacity: up to 200 — W/R/B/
Contact: Event Coordinator (503) 231-3909   *See page 64*
Ballroom Parkrose — 4848 N.E. 105th Ave., Portland, OR
Capacity: up to 150 — W/R/B/M/
Contact: (503) 254-1920   *See page 71*
Columbia Edgewater Country Club — 2220 N.E. Marine Drive, Portland, OR 97211
Capacity: up to 300 — R/B/M/S/M/
Contact: Stephanie Akin (503) 285-3676   *See page 82*
Courtyard by Marriot — Lloyd Center — 435 N.E. Wasco St., Portland, OR 97232
Capacity: up to 40; Guest Rooms: 202 — S/M/
Contact: Sales (503) 234-3200
Courtyard by Marriott — Portland Airport — 11550 N.E. Airport Way, Portland, OR 97220
Capacity: up to 125; Guest Rooms: 150 — R/B/S/M/
Contact: Catering (503) 252-3200; Fax (503) 252-8921
Portland Conference Center (Ambridge) —
300 N.E. Multnomah St., Portland, OR 97232
Capacity: up to 1,000 — W/R/B/S/M/
Event Coordinator (503) 239-9921   *See page 66*

Please let these businesses know that you heard about them from the Bravo! Wedding Resource Guide.

DoubleTree Lloyd Center — 1000 N.E. Multnomah, Portland, OR 97232   *See page 92*
     Capacity: up to 1,100;— R/B/S/M/
     Contact: Catering (503) 249-3121

The Grotto Conference Center —
     N.E. 85th Ave. at Sandy Blvd., P.O. Box 20008, Portland, OR 97294-0008
     Capacity: up to 225 — R/B/S/M/
     Contact: Conference Center Coordinator (503) 254-7371

Holiday Inn — Airport — 8439 N.E. Columbia Blvd., Portland, OR 97220
     Capacity: up to 1,000; Guest Rooms: 286 — W/R/B/S/M/
     Contact: Sales & Catering (503) 256-5000   *See page 107*

Holiday Inn — Portland — 1441 N.E. Second Ave., Portland, OR 97232
     Capacity: up to 200; Guest Rooms: 238 — R/B/S/M/
     Contact: Sales Department (503) 233-2401   *See page 108*

McMenamins Kennedy School — 5736 N.E. 33rd Ave., Portland, OR 97211
     Reception: up to 112 — R/B/S/M/; Guest Rooms: 35
     Contact: (503) 288-3286   *See page 114*

North Star Ballroom — 635 N. Killingsworth Court, Portland, OR 97217
     Capacity up to 300; — W/R/B/S/M/
     Contact: Claire (503) 240-6088   *See page 131*

Portland Conference Center (Ambridge) —
     300 N.E. Multnomah St., Portland, OR 97232
     Capacity: up to 1,000 — W/R/B/S/M/
     Event Coordinator (503) 239-9921   *See page 66*

Ramada Inn — 6221 N.E. 82nd Ave., Portland, OR 97220
     Capacity: up to 300; Guest Rooms: 202 — W/R/B/S/M/
     Contact: Ann Conger (503) 255-6511   *See page 145*

Red Lion — 1021 N.E. Grand Ave., Portland, OR 97232
     Capacity: up to 300; Guest Rooms: 174 — W/R/B/S/M/
     Contact: Sales & Catering (503) 235-2100   *See page 146*

Riverside Golf & Country Club — 8105 N.E. 33rd Dr., Portland, OR 97211
     Capacity: up to 300 — W/R/B/S/M/
     Contact: Bill Price or Richard Ransome, (503) 288-6468   *See page 152*

Salty's on the Columbia — 3839 N.E. Marine Dr., Portland, OR 97211
     Contact: up to 200 — W/R/B/S/M/
     Contact: Sales (503) 288-4444   *See page 180*

Sheraton Portland
     Airport Hotel — 8235 N.E. Airport Way, Portland, OR 97220-1398
     Sit-down: up to 420; Reception: up to 750; Guest Rooms: 215 — W/R/B/S/M/
     Contact: Catering Department (503) 249-7606   *See page 154*

Shilo Inn Suites Hotel and Convention Center —
     Portland Airport/I-205 — 11707 N.E. Airport Way, Portland, OR 97220-1075
     Capacity: up to 400; Guest Rooms: 200 — W/R/B/S/M/
     Contact: Catering Office (503) 252-7500 ext. 270   *See page 155*

NORTHWEST PORTLAND

Bluehour — 1250 N.W. 13th Ave. at Everett, Portland, OR 97209
     Capacity: up to 160, 200 cocktail — W/R/B/
     Contact: (503) 226-3394   *See page 74*

BridgePort Brewery — 1313 N.W. Marshall, Portland, OR 97209
     Sit-down: up to 220 *Non-smoking — R/B/S/M/
     Contact: Manager of Special Events (503) 241-7179 ext. 210   *See page 76*

     W=Wedding Ceremony   R=Reception   B=Banquet   S=Seminar   M=Meeting   P=Picnic

Please let these businesses know that you heard about them from the Bravo! Wedding Resource Guide.

Il Fornaio — 115 N.W. 22nd Ave., Portland, OR 97210
Capacity: up to 230 — R/B/S/M/
Contact: Catering (503) 248-9400 *See page 178*
l'heure bleue — 1220 N.W. Everett, Portland, OR 97209
Capacity: up to 60, 100 cocktailil — W/R/B/
Contact: (503) 226-3394 *See page 74*
Montgomery Park — 2701 N.W. Vaughn St., Portland, OR 97210
Sit-down: up to 400; Reception: up to 800 — W/R/B/S/M/
Contact: Event Coordinator (503) 224-6958 *See page 128*
Paragon Restaurant and Bar — 1309 N.W. Hoyt, Portland, OR 97209
Capacity: up to 150 — R/B/S/M/
Contact: Sales (503) 833-5060 *See page 140*
Rock Creek, The Clubhouse at — 5100 N.W. Neakahnie Ave., Portland, OR 97229
Capacity: up to 500 — R/B/S/M/
Contact: Michelle Edwards (503) 645-8843 *See page 153*
Urban Wineworks — 407 N.W. 16th Ave., Portland, OR 97209
Sit-down: up to 80; Reception: up to 150, 250 with tented parking lot — R/B/M/S
Contact: (503) 226-9797, (866) GO-PINOT

SOUTHEAST PORTLAND

Arnegards — 1510 S.E. Ninth, Portland, OR 97214
Capacity: up to 450 — R/B/S/M/
Contact: (503) 236-2759 *See page 68*
Eastmoreland Grill at the
Eastmoreland Golf Course — 2425 S.E. Bybee Blvd., Portland, OR 97202
Capacity: up to 250 including outdoor area — R/B/S/M/
Contact: Jerilyn Walker (503) 775-5910 *See page 94*
Lakeside Gardens — 16211 S.E. Foster Rd., Portland, OR 97236
Indoor: up to 180; Indoor/Outdoor: up to 300 — W/R/B/S/M/P/
Contact: Consultant (503) 760-6044 *See page 117*
The Melody Ballroom — 615 S.E. Alder St., Portland, OR 97214
Capacity: up to 1,100 — W/R/B/S/M/
Contact: Kathleen Kaad (503) 232-2759 *See page 124*
Molly's Loft — 2236 S.E. Belmont, Portland, OR 97214
Capacity: up to 80 sit-down, 120 reception — R/B/S/
Contact: 503) 297-9635 ext.111 *See page 127*
Oaks Park Historic Dance Pavilion
At Oaks Park (Sellwood) — Portland, OR 97202
Capacity: up to 700— W/R/B/S/M/P/
Contact: Volanne Stephens (503) 238-6622 *See page 133*
NCP Pantheon Banquet Hall — 5942 S.E. 92nd Ave., Portland, OR 97266
Capacity: up to 450— W/R/B/S/M/
Contact: (503) 775-7431 *See page 139*
Persimmon Country Club — 500 S.E. Butler Rd., Gresham, OR 97080
Sit-down: up to 300; Reception: 300+ — W/R/B/S/M/
Contact: Sales (503) 674-3259 *See page 141*

SOUTHWEST PORTLAND

Oregon Zoo — 4001 S.W. Canyon Rd., Portland, OR 97221
Capacity: up to 400 — W/R/B/S/M/P/
Contact: Catering (503) 220-2789 *See page 137*

Please let these businesses know that you heard about them from the Bravo! Wedding Resource Guide.

Rivers Restaurant at Avalon Hotel — 0470 SW Hamilton Court, Portland, OR 97239
Capacity: up to 180— W/R/B/S/M/
Contact: Catering (503) 802-5814 *See page 151*
Shilo Inn — Canyon — 9900 S.W. Canyon Rd., Portland, OR 97225
Capacity: up to 200 — W/R/B/
Contact: Catering Office (503) 297-2551 ext.552 *See page 156*
World Forestry Center — 4033 S.W. Canyon Rd., Portland, OR 97221
Sit-down: up to 250; Reception: up to 300; Outdoor: up to 1,000 — W/R/B/S/M/P/
Contact: Facilities Coordinator (503) 488-2101 ext.101 *See page 170*

SHERIDAN

Mill Creek Gardens — 4430 Mill Creek Rd. Sheridan, OR 97378
Capacity: up to 200 — W/R/B/S/M/
Contact: (503) 843-4218, (877) 792-4737 *See page 125*

SHERWOOD

Nottinghams — 198 N. Pine St., Sherwood, OR 97140
Indoor: up to 200 — R/B/S/M/
Contact: Lorrie or Carrie (503) 925-8779 *See page 132*

TIGARD/TUALATIN

Embassy Suites Hotel —
Washington Square — 9000 S.W. Washington Sq. Rd., Tigard, OR 97223
Capacity: Up to 800; Guest Rooms: 354 — W/R/B/S/M/
Contact: Catering Sales (503) 644-4000 *See page 96*
Hayden's Lakefront Grill — 8187 S.W. Tualatin-Sherwd Rd., Tualatin, OR 97062
Sit-down: up to 150; Reception: up to 500
Contact: Jennie Bernard (503) 691-9111 *See page 104*
Sweetbrier Inn — 7125 S.W. Nyberg Rd., Tualatin, OR 97062
Capacity: up to 400; Guest Rooms: 132 — R/B/S/M/
Contact: Catering Office (503) 692-5800, (800) 551-9167 *See page 162*

TROUTDALE

McMenamins Edgefield — 2126 S.W. Halsey, Troutdale, OR 97060
Sit-down: up to 200; Reception: up to 250; Theater: up to 125;
Guest Rooms: 103 — W/R/B/S/M/P/
Contact: Sales Office (503) 492-2777 *See page 123*

WEST LINN

The Oregon Golf Club— 25700 S.W. Pete's Mountain Rd., West Linn, OR 97068
Capacity: up to 500 — W/R/B/S/M/P
Contact: Sales & Catering Office (503) 650-6900 *See page 136*

WILSONVILLE/CANBY

Willamette Valley Country Club — 900 Country Club Place, Canby, OR 97013
Capacity: up to 250 — R/B/S/M/W
Contact: Catering Department (503) 266-4066 *See page 169*

Notes

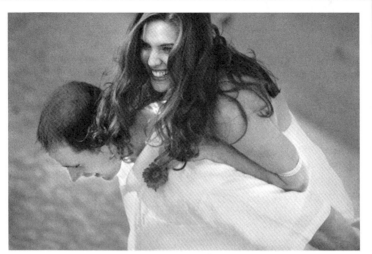

photo by Strong Photography • See page 546

Boat & Park Listings

"Now join your hands, and with

your hands your hearts."

— William Shakespeare

BOATS & YACHTS

Crystal Dolphin — 110 S.E. Caruthers, Portland, OR 97214
Reception: up to 120 — W/R/B/S/M/
Contact: Sales Office (503) 224-3900, (800) 224-3901   *See page 54*

Sternwheeler "Columbia Gorge" — P.O. Box 307, Cascade Locks, OR 97014
Sit-down: up to 200; Reception: up to 350 — W/R/B/S/M/P/
Contact: (541) 374-8427, (800) 643-1354   *See page 55*

Portland Spirit — 110 S.E. Caruthers, Portland, OR 97214
Sit-down: up to 350; Reception: up to 540 — W/R/B/S/M
Contact: Sales Office (503) 224-3900, (800) 224-3901   *See page 54*

The Sternwheeler Rose — 6412 S.W. Vermont St. Portland, OR 97219
Capacity: up to 130 — W/R/B/S/M/P/
Contact: (503) 286-ROSE (7673)   *See page 56*

Willamette Star — 110 S.E. Caruthers, Portland, OR 97214
Sit-down: up to 80; Reception: up to 120 — W/R/B/S/M/
Contact: Sales Office (503) 224-3900, (800) 224-3901

    See page 54

CASCADE LOCKS

Marine Park and
Thunder Island — Port of Cascade Locks, Cascade Locks, OR 97014
Outdoor: up to 4,000; Covered: up to 175 — W/R/B/P/
Contact: Columbia Gorge Sternwheeler (541) 374-8427, (800) 643-1354   *See page 55*

MILWAUKIE

The Milwaukie Center (in North Clackamas Park) —
5440 S.E. Kellogg Creek, Milwaukie, OR 97222
Indoor: up to 600; Outdoor (shelter): up to1,200 — W/R/S/M/P/
Contact: Lynn (503) 653-8100   *See page 126*

PORTLAND

Crystal Springs
Rhododendron Garden — S.E. 28th/North of Woodstock, Portland, OR 97215
Indoor: up to 125; Outdoor: up to 300 — W/R/
Contact: Rita Knapp (503) 256-2483   *See page 307*

Hoyt Arboretum — 4000 S.W. Fairview Blvd., Portland, OR 97221
Outdoor (shelter): up to 140 — W/R/P/
Contact: Parks Permit Center (503) 823-2514

Hoyt Wedding Meadow — 4000 S.W. Fairview Blvd., Portland, OR 97221
Outdoor (no shelter): up to 100 — W/R/P/
Contact: Parks Permit Center (503) 823-2525

Oaks Park — S.E. Portland (Sellwood area), Portland, OR 97202
Capacity: up to 700 — W/P/R/B/S/
(503) 238-6622   *See page 133*

W=Wedding Ceremony   R=Reception   B=Banquet   S=Seminar   M=Meeting   P=Picnic

616   *Please let these businesses know that you heard about them from the Bravo! Wedding Resource Guide.*

WASHINGTON COUNTY

Jenkins Estate — Grabhorn Rd. at S.W. 209th & Farmington, Aloha, OR 97006
Indoor: up to 110; Outdoor: up to 175; Stable: up to 225 — W/R/B/S/M/P/
Contact: Bobbie White, Program Coordinator (503) 642-3855; Fax (503) 591-1028;
E-mail: bwhite@thprd.com

WEST LINN

McLean House — 5350 River St., West Linn, Oregon 97068
Indoor/Outdoor: up to 100 — W/R/B/S/M/P/
Contact: (503) 655-4268   *See page 316*

Notes

"Being deeply loved by someone gives you strength;

loving someone deeply gives you courage."

— Lao Tzu

www.bravoportland.com

AMBOY

Anderson Lodge — 18410 N.E. 399th St., Amboy, WA 98601
Indoor: up to 100; Outdoor: up to 200 — R/B/P/
Contact: (360) 247-6660   *See page 67*

CAMAS

The Fairgate Inn Bed and Breakfast — 2213 N.W. 23rd Ave., Camas, WA 98607
Capacity: up to 150 indoor, 400 outdoor— W/R/B/S/M/
Contact: (360) 834-0861   *See page 97*

VANCOUVER

The Academy Chapel
and Ballroom — 400 E. Evergreen Blvd., Vancouver, WA 98660
Ceremony: 225; Sit-down: up to 225; Reception: up to 300 — W/R/B/S/M/
Contact: Windsor Consultants (360) 696-4884   *See page 60*
Aero Club — 9901 N.E. Seventh Ave., Vancouver, WA 98685
Capacity: up to 100 — W/R/B/S/M/
Contact: Cheryl Taylor (360) 574-7124   *See page 63*
Hostess House Chapel and
Reception Center — 10017 N.E. Sixth Ave., Vancouver, WA 98685
Ceremony: up to 200; Reception: up to 300 — W/R/B/S/M/
Contact: (360) 574-3284   *See page 109*

WOODLAND

Lewis River Golf Club — 3209 Lewis River Rd., Woodland, WA 98674
Capacity: up to 400 — W/R/B/S/M/
Contact: (360) 225-8254, (800) 341-9426   *See page 120*

W=Wedding Ceremony   R=Reception   B=Banquet   S=Seminar   M=Meeting   P=Picnic

620   *Please let these businesses know that you heard about them from the Bravo! Wedding Resource Guide.*

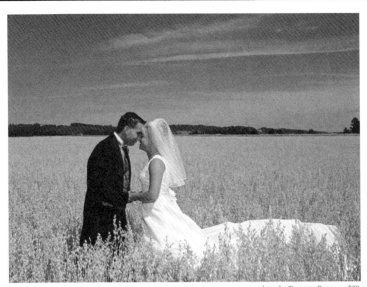

photo by Encore • See page 509

The Wedding Slip

A law was passed in 1547 stating that if

a woman wore only a slip at her wedding,

it would be considered a public announcement that any

debts she or a previous husband may have incurred

were not her new husband's responsibility.

www.bravoportland.com

DALLAS

BeckenRidge Vineyard — 300 Reuben-Boise Rd., Dallas, OR 97338
Indoor: up to 150; Outdoor: up to 250 — W/R/B/S/M
Contact: Becky (503) 831-3652   *See page 72*

NORTH SALEM/KEIZER

Weddings On Church Street — 1080 Church Street N.E., Salem, OR 97301
Capacity: up to 30 — W/
Contact: (503) 540-0610   *See page 485*

SHERIDAN

Mill Creek Gardens — 4430 Mill Creek Rd. Sheridan, OR 97378
Capacity: up to 200 — W/R/B/S/M/
Contact: (503) 843-4218, (877) 792-4737   *See page 125*

SALEM DOWNTOWN

The Grand Ballroom — 187 High Street N.E., Salem, OR 97301
Capacity: up to 270; W/R/B/S/M/
Contact: (503) 362-9185   *See page 100*

SUBLIMITY

Silver Falls Vineyards — 4972 Cascade Hwy., S.E., Sublimity, OR 97385
Indoor/Outdoor: up to 300 — W/R/M/B/
Contact: (503) 769-5056   *See page 157*

WOODBURN

Settlemier House — 355 N. Settlemier Ave., Woodburn, OR 97071
Indoor: up to 85; Oudoor: 300+ — W/R/B/M/
Contact: (503) 982-1897   *See page 181*

W=Wedding Ceremony   R=Reception   B=Banquet   S=Seminar   M=Meeting   P=Picnic

622   *Please let these businesses know that you heard about them from the Bravo! Wedding Resource Guide.*

photo by James Loomis • See page 514

"There is no more lovely, friendly

and charming relationship, communion

or company than a good marriage."

— Martin Luther

www.bravoportland.com

OREGON WINERY SITES

BeckenRidge Vineyard — 300 Reuben-Boise Rd., Dallas, OR 97338
Indoor: up to 150; Outdoor: up to 250 — W/R/B/S/M
Contact: Becky (503) 831-3652   *See page 72*

Elk Cove Vineyards — 27751 N.W. Olson Rd., Gaston, OR 97119
Indoor/Outdoor: up to 150 — W/R/B/S/M/P/
Contact: Hospitality Director (503) 985-7760

Eola Hills Wine Cellars — 501 S. Pacific Hwy., W., Rickreall, OR 97371
Indoors: up to 250; Outdoors: up to 250+ — W/R/B/S/M/P/
Contact: Carrine Burrow (503) 623-2405; Fax (503) 623-0350

Helvetia Vineyards — 23269 N. Yungen Rd., Hood River, OR 97301
Indoor/Outdoor: Call for details — W/R/B/P/
Contact: John Platt (503) 647-5169   *See page 291*

Marquam Hill Vineyards — 35803 S. Hwy. 213, Molalla, OR 97038
Outdoor: up to 500 — W/R/M/P/
Contact: Jude Strader (503) 829-9280

Rex Hill Vineyard — 30835 N. Hwy. 99W, Newberg, OR 97132
Indoor: up to 64-100; Outdoor: up to 200
Contact: Katie Quinn (800) REX-HILL; Fax: (503) 538-1409

Silver Falls Vineyards — 4972 Cascade Hwy. S.E., Sublimity, OR 97385   *See page 157*
Indoor/Outdoor: up to 300
Contact: (503) 769-5056

Urban Wineworks — 407 N.W. 16th Ave., Portland, OR 97209
Sit-down: up to 80; Reception: up to 150, 250 with tented parking lot — R/B/M/S
Contact: (503) 226-9797, (866) GO-PINOT

Willamette Valley Vineyards— 8800 Enchanted Way S.E., Turner, OR 97392
Indoor/Outdoor: up to 600 — W/R/B/S/M/P/
Contact: Hospitality Coordinator (503) 588-4024, (800) 344-9463

W=Wedding Ceremony   R=Reception   B=Banquet   S=Seminar   M=Meeting   P=Picnic

624   *Please let these businesses know that you heard about them from the Bravo! Wedding Resource Guide.*

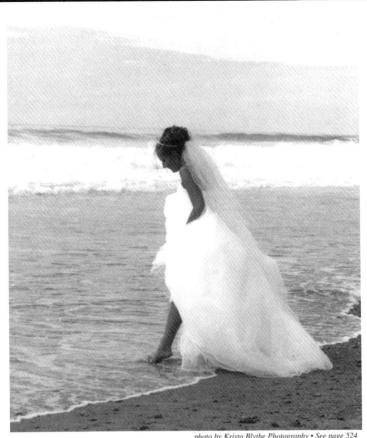

photo by Krista Blythe Photography • See page 524

"There is nothing nobler or more admirable

than when two people who see eye to eye

keep house as husband and wife, confounding

their enemies and delighting their friends."

– Homer

www.bravoportland.com

COASTAL OREGON SITES_____

B'Nai B'Rith Camp — 6651 S.W. Capitol Highwy, Portland, OR 97219
Located in Lincolon City, Oregon
Capacity: 250 indoors, up to 500+ outdoors — W/R/B/S/M/
Contact: (503) 452-3444   *See page 70*

Hotel Elliott — 357 12th St., Astoria, OR 97103
Capacity: up 75 — W/R/B/S/M/
Contact: (503) 325-2222   *See page 110*

Inn at Spanish Head — 4009 S.W. Hwy. 101, Lincoln City, OR 97367
Reception: Up to 150 Sit-down: Up to 150 — W/R/B/S/M/
Contact: Tonya Weaver (800) 452-8127, (541) 996-2161

Oregon Coast Aquarium — 2820 S.E. Ferry Slip Rd., Newport, OR 97365
Sit-down: Up to 120, Reception: Up to 1,000 — R/B/S/M/
Contact: Events Office: (541) 867-3474 ext. 5224   *See page 135*

Surfsand Resort — P.O. Box 219, Cannon Beach, OR 97110
Capacity: up to 300— W/R/B/S/M/
Contact: 1 (800) 797-4666   *See page 160*

W=Wedding Ceremony   R=Reception   B=Banquet   S=Seminar   M=Meeting   P=Picnic

Notes

Notes

A

B

C

F

G

H

I

J

K

633

L

M

N

R

S

T

Notes